# WEBSTER'S NEW WORLD™

# POCKET GEOGRAPHICAL DICTIONARY

Based on
**Webster's New World Dictionary**®
of American English
Third College Edition

**Donald Stewart, Project Editor**
**Laura Borovac, Geography Editor**

W9-CPB-669

Prentice Hall
New York • London • Toronto
Sydney • Tokyo • Singapore

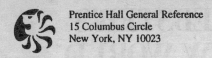

Prentice Hall General Reference
15 Columbus Circle
New York, NY 10023

This book is based on and includes material from
Webster's New World Dictionary®, Third College Edition,
copyright © 1994

A Webster's New World™ Book

Dictionary Editorial Offices:
New World Dictionaries
850 Euclid Avenue
Cleveland, Ohio 44114

**Library of Congress Cataloging-in-Publication Data**

Webster's New World pocket geographical dictionary/
    Donald Stewart, project editor, Laura Borovac,
    geography editor.
        p.   cm.
        "Based on Webster's New World dictionary of
    American English, third college edition."
        ISBN 0-671-88348-8
        1. Gazetteers. I. Stewart, Donald, 1955-.
    II. Borovac, Laura. III. Webster's New World
    dictionary of American English.
    G103.5. W43 1994              93-27567
    910' .3--dc20                 CIP

Database service and principal typesetting by
Lexi-Comp, Inc., Hudson, Ohio.
The typefaces used are Century Schoolbook and Athena.

Manufactured in the United States of America

1  2  3  4  5  6  7  8  9  10        94 95 96 97 98

# Guide to Use of the Dictionary

The geographical entries in this book are drawn from the computer database of *Webster's New World Dictionary,* Third College Edition. The extraction of entries has not, however, been a purely mechanical one: all entries have been carefully scrutinized, reevaluated, and, where necessary, updated.

Unlike many competing works, this geographical dictionary includes entries from various categories outside the strictly geographical. Here you will find place names from the world's religions, mythologies, and folklore; places from the Bible, world literature, and popular culture; and nicknames. In addition, etymologies are included for more than 1,400 entries.

The typical geographical entry consists of the place name, pronunciation, and definition. Boldface entry names are divided into syllables by centered dots; if at all possible, however, written or printed proper names should not be divided at line ends.

Pinyin transcriptions are given for all Chinese entries; alternate transcriptions of longstanding convention are also shown.

Entries follow strict alphabetical order. Thus,

> **Mackenzie**
> **Mackinac**
> **Mayo**
> **McKinley, Mount**

When two or more places with the same name are entered, they are numbered and placed in a single entry block. Place names with the word "Saint" or the abbreviation "St." are alphabetized accordingly:

> **Saint John**
> **Stafford**
> **St. Albans**

Cross-references are printed in small capitals, for example,

> **Dacca** *old sp. of* DHAKA

# PRONUNCIATION

Pronunciations are provided in parentheses immediately after the entry word. The complete pronunciation key for English sounds is printed on the inside back cover. A key for foreign sounds is given below. The pronunciations use many of the letters of the alphabet to represent their usual sounds (e.g., (b) for the *b* in *bed* or *rob*, (d) for the *d* in *dog* or *bad*, etc.). A few additional special symbols are used to cover other native sounds of English and foreign sounds. The *key words* that accompany each symbol in the key have been chosen to assist the user in identifying the correct sound associated with that symbol.

Heavy (′) and light (′) stress marks are used to indicate primary and secondary stress, respectively. The stress mark is placed *after* the stressed syllable.

Variant pronunciations are often truncated, as in the following example:

Col-o-rad-o (käl′ə rad′ō, -rä′dō)

## Foreign Sounds

The following special symbols are used to represent non-English sounds in various foreign languages:

à     pronounced as intermediate between (a) and (ä).

ë     approximated by rounding the lips as for (ō) and pronouncing (e).

ö     approximated by rounding the lips as for (ō) and pronouncing (ä).

ô     any of a range of sounds between (ô) and (u).

ü     approximated by rounding the lips as for (ō) and pronouncing (ē).

| kh | approximated by placing the tongue as for (k) but allowing breath to escape in a stream, as in pronouncing (h). |
|---|---|
| H | formed by placing the tongue as for (sh) but with the tip pointing downward to produce air friction against the forward part of the palate. |
| *n* | indicates that the preceding vowel sound is nasalized; that is, the vowel is pronounced with breath passing through both the mouth and the nose; the letter *n* is not pronounced. |
| *r* | any of various trilled (r) sounds, produced with rapid vibration of the tongue or uvula. |
| ' | in French, indicates that the preceding consonant, normally voiced, is voiceless;<br>in Russian, used with *y* to indicate an unvoiced (y) sound. |

## Staff of
## Webster's New World Dictionaries

*Executive Editor*
Michael Agnes

*Editor and*
*Database Administrator*
Donald Stewart

*Biography and*
*Geography Editor*
Laura J. Borovac

*Citation Readers*
Joan Felice
Batya Jundef
Patricia Nash

*Senior Editors*
Andrew N. Sparks
Jonathan L. Goldman

*Editors*
Andra I. Kalnins
James E. Naso
Katherine Goidich Soltis
Stephen P. Teresi

*Data Processing and*
*Administrative Staff*
Alisa Murray Davis
Cynthia M. Sadonick
Betty Dziedzic Thompson

# Abbreviations and Symbols
# Used in This Book

| | | | |
|---|---|---|---|
| abbrev. | abbreviation, abbreviated | Ch. | Church |
| | | Chin | Chinese |
| abl. | ablative | Chron. | Chronicles |
| acc. | accusative | Class. | Classical |
| adj. | adjective | Col. | Colossians |
| adv. | adverb | Colloq. | Colloquial |
| Afr | African | comb. | combination, combining |
| Afrik | Afrikaans | | |
| Alb | Albanian | comp. | compound |
| alt. | alternative | compar. | comparative (grammar) |
| Am | American | | |
| AmFr | American French | conj. | conjunction |
| AmInd | Amerindian | contr. | contraction (grammar) |
| AmSp | American Spanish | | |
| | | Cor. | Corinthians |
| Anglo-Fr | Anglo-French | cu. | cubic |
| Anglo-Ind | Anglo-Indian | Dan | Danish |
| Anglo-Ir | Anglo-Irish | Dan. | Daniel (Bible) |
| Anglo-L | Anglo-Latin | dat. | dative |
| Anglo-Norm | Anglo-Norman | deriv. | derived, derivative |
| Ar | Arabic | | |
| Aram | Aramaic | Deut. | Deuteronomy |
| Arm | Armenian | dial. | dialect, dialectal |
| art. | article (grammar) | dim. | diminutive |
| assoc. | associated, association | Du | Dutch |
| | | dupl. | duplicated, duplication |
| Assyr | Assyrian | | |
| Astrol. | Astrology | E | eastern; English (in etyms) |
| aug. | augmentative | | |
| Austral | Australian | EC | east central |
| Bab | Babylonian | Eccl. | Ecclesiastes |
| back-form. | back-formation | Eccles. | Ecclesiastical |
| Beng | Bengali | EFris | East Frisian |
| BrazPort | Brazilian Portuguese | e.g. | for example |
| | | Egypt | Egyptian |
| Bret | Breton | Eng. | English |
| Brit | British | Eph. | Ephesians |
| Bulg | Bulgarian | equiv. | equivalent |
| c. | circa; century (in etyms) | Esk | Eskimo |
| | | esp. | especially |
| cap. | capital city | est. | estimated |
| caus. | causative | etc. | and/or the like |
| Cdn | Canadian | Etr | Etruscan |
| CdnFr | Canadian French | etym | etymology |
| Celt | Celtic | Ex. | example; Exodus |
| cent. | century, centuries | exc. | except |
| cf. | compare | Ezek. | Ezekiel |

| | | | |
|---|---|---|---|
| fem. | feminine | interj. | interjection |
| fig. | figurative, figuratively | Ir | Irish |
| Finn | Finnish | Iran | Iranian |
| Fl | Flemish | irreg. | irregular |
| fl. | flourished; lived (of people) | Isa. | Isaiah |
| fol. | following entry | It | Italian |
| Fr | French | Jer. | Jeremiah |
| Frank | Frankish | Josh. | Joshua |
| freq. | frequentative | Jpn | Japanese |
| Fris | Frisian | Judg. | Judges |
| ft. | foot, feet | KJV | King James Version |
| fut. | future | km | kilometer(s) |
| Gael | Gaelic | Kor | Korean |
| Gal. | Galatians | L | classical Latin |
| Gaul | Gaulish | Lam. | Lamentations |
| Gen. | Genesis | L(Ec) | Ecclesiastical Latin |
| gen. | genitive | Lev. | Leviticus |
| Geog. | Geography | LGr | Late Greek |
| Ger | German | LGr(Ec) | Ecclesiastical Late Greek |
| ger. | gerund, gerundive | Linguis. | Linguistics |
| Gmc | Germanic | lit. | literally |
| Goth | Gothic | Lith | Lithuanian |
| gov. | governor | LL | Late Latin |
| gov. gen. | governor general | LL(Ec) | Ecclesiastical Late Latin |
| Gr | classical Greek | LME | Late Middle English |
| Gr(Ec) | Ecclesiastical Greek | LowG | Low German |
| Hab. | Habakkuk | LWS | Late West Saxon |
| Hag. | Haggai | LXX | Septuagint |
| Haw | Hawaiian | m | meter(s) |
| Heb | classical Hebrew (language) | Macc. | Maccabees |
| Heb. | Hebrews | Mal. | Malachi |
| Heb-Aram | Hebrew-Aramaic | masc. | masculine |
| Hos. | Hosea | Matt. | Matthew |
| Hung | Hungarian | MDu | Middle Dutch |
| Ice | Icelandic | ME | Middle English |
| IE | Indo-European | met. | metropolitan |
| i.e. | that is | Mex | Mexican |
| imper. | imperative | MexSp | Mexican Spanish |
| imperf. | imperfect | MFl | Middle Flemish |
| incl. | including | MFr | Middle French |
| Ind | Indian; Indic (in etyms) | MGr | Medieval Greek |
| indic. | indicative | MHeb | Medieval Hebrew |
| inf. | infinitive | MHG | Middle High German |
| infl. | influenced, influence | mi. | mile(s) |
| intens. | intensive | Mic. | Micah |

| | | | |
|---|---|---|---|
| MIr | Middle Irish | OIt | Old Italian |
| mistransl. | mistranslation | OL | Old Latin |
| ML | Medieval Latin | OLowFranc | Old Low Franconian |
| ML(Ec) | Ecclesiastical Medieval Latin | OLowG | Old Low German |
| MLowG | Middle Low German | ON | Old Norse |
| ModE | Modern English | OPers | Old Persian |
| ModGr | Modern Greek | OProv | Old Provençal |
| ModHeb | Modern Hebrew | OPrus | Old Prussian |
| ModL | Modern Latin | orig. | origin, originally |
| MScot | Middle Scottish | OS | Old Saxon |
| Myth. | Mythology | Osco-Umb | Osco-Umbrian |
| N | northern | OSlav | Old Church Slavonic |
| NAmFr | North American French | OSp | Old Spanish |
| | | OSw | Old Swedish |
| n. | noun | O.T. | Old Testament |
| Nah. | Nahum | OWelsh | Old Welsh |
| NC | north central | oz. | ounce(s) |
| NE | northeast, northeastern | PaGer | Pennsylvania German |
| Neh. | Nehemiah | part. | participle, participial |
| Netherl | Netherlandic | | |
| neut. | neuter | pass. | passive voice |
| n.fem. | feminine noun | perf. | perfect tense |
| NGmc | North Germanic | pers. | person; personal (grammar) |
| n.masc. | masculine noun | | |
| nom. | nominative | Pers | Persian |
| Norm | Norman | Pet. | Peter (Bible) |
| NormFr | Norman French | PGmc | Proto-Germanic |
| Norw | Norwegian | Phil. | Philippians |
| n.pl. | plural noun | Philem. | Philemon |
| n.sing. | singular noun | Phoen | Phoenician |
| N.T. | New Testament | phr. | phrase |
| Num. | Numbers | PidE | Pidgin English |
| NW | northwest, northwestern | PIE | Proto-Indo-European |
| obj. | object, objective | pl. | plural |
| OAr | Old Arabic | Poet. | Poetic |
| Ob. | Obadiah | Pol | Polish |
| Obs., obs. | obsolete | pop. | popular; population |
| occas. | occasionally | | |
| OCelt | Old Celtic | Port | Portuguese |
| ODan | Old Danish | poss. | possessive |
| ODu | Old Dutch | pp. | past participle |
| OE | Old English | prec. | preceding entry |
| OFr | Old French | prep. | preposition |
| OFris | Old Frisian | pres. | present tense |
| OHG | Old High German | Pres., pres. | President |
| OIce | Old Icelandic | pret. | preterit |
| OInd | Old Indic | prin. pts. | principal parts |
| OIr | Old Irish | priv. | privative |

| | | | |
|---|---|---|---|
| prob. | probably | transl. | translated, |
| pron. | pronoun | | translation |
| pronun. | pronunciation | Turk | Turkish |
| Prov | Provençal | ult. | ultimately |
| Prov. | Proverbs | UN | United Nations |
| prp. | present participle | uncert. | uncertain |
| Prus | Prussian | U.S. | United States |
| Ps. | Psalms | U.S.S.R. | Union of Soviet |
| pseud. | pseudonym | | Socialist |
| pt. | past tense | | Republics |
| redupl. | reduplicated, | v. | verb |
| | reduplication | var. | variant; variety |
| ref. | reference, refer | v.aux. | auxiliary verb |
| refl. | reflexive | vi. | intransitive verb |
| Rev. | Revelation | VL | Vulgar Latin |
| Rom. | Roman | voc. | vocative |
| Russ | Russian | vt. | transitive verb |
| S | southern | Vulg. | Vulgate |
| Sam. | Samuel (Bible) | W | western |
| SAmSp | South American | WAfr | West African |
| | Spanish | WC | west central |
| Sans | Sanskrit | WFris | West Frisian |
| SC | south central | WGmc | West Germanic |
| Scand | Scandinavian | WInd | West Indian |
| Scot | Scottish | WS | West Saxon |
| SE | southeast, | Yidd | Yiddish |
| | southeastern | Zech. | Zechariah |
| Sem | Semitic | Zeph. | Zephaniah |
| Serb | Serbian | | |
| sing. | singular | Note that in etymologies, |
| Sino-Jpn | Sino-Japanese | periods are not used with these |
| Slav | Slavonic, Slavic | abbreviations. |
| S. of Sol. | Song of Solomon | |
| Sp | Spanish | |
| sp. | spelling, spelled | |
| specif. | specifically | |
| sq. | square | |
| S.S.R. | Soviet Socialist | |
| | Republic | **Symbols** |
| subj. | subject, subjective | * | not attested |
| | | | (in etyms) |
| subjunc. | subjunctive | | |
| superl. | superlative | + | plus |
| SW | southwest, | ° | degree |
| | southwestern | < | derived from |
| Swed | Swedish | | (in etyms) |
| TalmudHeb | Talmudic Hebrew | > | from which |
| Theol. | Theology | | is derived (in etyms) |
| Thess. | Thessalonians | ? | uncertain |
| Tim. | Timothy (Bible) | | or unknown; perhaps |
| Tit. | Titus (Bible) | & | and |

ix

# Pronunciation Key

## English Sounds

| Symbol | Key Words | Symbol | Key Words |
|--------|-----------|--------|-----------|
| a | cat | b | bed, dub |
| ā | ape | d | dip, had |
| ä | cot | f | fall |
| | | g | get, dog |
| e | ten | h | help |
| ē | me | j | joy |
| | | k | kick, quit |
| i | fit | l | leg, bottle |
| ī | bite | m | meat |
| | | n | nose, kitten |
| ō | go | p | put |
| ô | all, or | r | red |
| oo | look, pull | s | see |
| ōō | tool, rule | t | top, cattle |
| oi | oil, toy | v | vat |
| ou | out, plow | w | wish, quick |
| | | y | yard |
| u | cup | z | zebra |
| ʉr | turn | | |
| | | ŋ | ring, drink |
| ə | ago, agent, pencil, atom, focus | | |
| | | ch | chin, arch |
| ər | perhaps, mother | hw | where |
| | | sh | she, motion |
| | | th | thin, truth |
| ' | cattle (kat''l), cotton (kät''n) | *th* | then, father |
| | | zh | measure |

The key for foreign sounds can be found
on page iv in the front of the book.

# A

**Aa·chen** (ä′kən; *Ger* ä′khən) city in North Rhine-Westphalia, W Germany, on the Belgian border: pop.
241,000: Fr. name, Aix-la-Chapelle

**Aal·borg** (ôl′bôrg′, -bôr′) *alt. sp. of* Ålborg

**Aalst** (älst) city in WC Belgium, near Brussels: pop.
78,000

**Aar** (är) *alt. sp. of* Aare

**Aa·re** (ä′rə) river in central and N Switzerland, flowing
into the Rhine: *c.* 180 mi. (290 km)

**Aar·gau** (är′gou′) canton of N Switzerland: 542 sq. mi.
(1,405 sq. km); pop. 465,000

**Aar·hus** (ôr′hoos′) *alt. sp. of* Århus

**AB** *abbrev. for* Alberta

**A·ba·dán** (ä′bə dän′, ab′ə dan′) **1** island in the Shatt al
Arab, SW Iran: 40 mi. (64 km) long **2** city on this
island: an oil-refining center: pop. 302,000

**A·bad·don** (ə bad′'n) ⟦Heb, destruction, abyss⟧ *Bible*
the place of the dead; nether world: Job 26:6

**Ab·bots·ford** (ab′əts fərd) estate (1812-32) of Sir Walter Scott, on the Tweed River in SE Scotland

**Ab·er·deen** (ab′ər dēn′; *for 3,* ab′ər dēn′) **1** former
county of E Scotland, now in the region of Grampian:
also **Ab′er·deen′shire′** (-shir′) **2** fishing port in E Scotland, on the North Sea: pop. 190,000 **3** town in NW
Md.: pop. 13,000: site of Aberdeen Proving Ground of
the U.S. Army

**Ab·i·djan** (ab′ə jän′) seaport in the Ivory Coast, on the
Gulf of Guinea: former capital (until 1983): pop.
1,850,000

**Ab·i·lene** (ab′ə lēn′) ⟦ult. < Luke 3:1 < ?⟧ city in central Tex.: pop. 107,000

**Ab·ing·ton** (ab′iŋ tən) ⟦prob. after *Abington* parish,
Cambridgeshire, England⟧ urban township in SE Pa.,
near Philadelphia: pop. 56,000

**Ab·kha·zi·a** (äb käz′ē ə) region in NW Georgia, on the
Black Sea: cap. Sukhumi

**Å·bo** (ō′boo) *Swed. name of* Turku

**A·bra·ham** (ā′brə ham′), **Plains of** plateau in the city of
Quebec, on the St. Lawrence: site of a battle (1759) in
which the British under Wolfe defeated the French
under Montcalm, leading to British control of Canada

**A·bruz·zi** (ä brōō′tsē) region of central Italy, on the Adriatic: 4,168 sq. mi. (10,794 sq. km); pop. 1,244,000

**A·bu Dha·bi** (ä′bōō dä′bē) 1 largest emirate of the United Arab Emirates: *c.* 26,000 sq. mi. (67,300 sq. km); pop. 537,000 2 its chief city, on the Persian Gulf: capital of United Arab Emirates: pop. 243,000

**A·bu·ja** (ä bōō′jä) capital of Nigeria, in the central part: pop. 379,000

**A·bu·kir** (ä′bōō kir′) bay at the mouth of the Nile, near Alexandria, Egypt: site of the British victory (1798) under Nelson over the French: also sp. **A·bu Qir**

**A·bu Sim·bel** (ä′bōō sim′bəl) village in S Egypt, on the Nile: site of two temples, built (13th cent. B.C.) for Ramses II

**A·bu Za·by** (or **Za·bi**) (ä′bōō zä′bē) *Ar. name of* ABU DHABI

**A·by·dos** (ə bī′däs′) 1 ancient city in Asia Minor, on the Hellespont 2 ancient city in central Egypt, near the Nile, north of Thebes

**Ab·y·la** (ab′ə lə) *ancient name of* a mountain at Ceuta, N Africa: see PILLARS OF HERCULES

**Ab·ys·sin·i·a** (ab′ə sin′ē ə) *old name of* ETHIOPIA

**Ac·a·deme** (ak′ə dēm′, ak′ə dēm′) ⟦ < Gr *akadēmeia*, the grove of *Akadēmos*, figure in ancient Greek legend ⟧ the ACADEMY

**A·cad·e·my** (ə kad′ə mē), the the public park near Athens where Plato taught and founded a school for the study of philosophy

**A·ca·di·a** (ə kā′dē ə) ⟦Fr *Acadia*, prob. < *Archadia*, name given by It explorer Giovanni da Verrazano (1524), after *Arcadia*, place of rural peace⟧ region & former French colony (1604-1713) on the NE coast of North America, including what are now the Canadian provinces of Nova Scotia, New Brunswick, and Prince Edward Island, plus parts of Quebec and parts of Maine

**Acadia National Park** national park in SE Maine, mostly on Mount Desert Island: 62 sq. mi. (160 sq. km)

**A·ca·pul·co** (ä′kə pool′kō, ak′ə-) city in S Mexico, on the Pacific: a winter resort: pop. 409,000: in full **A′ca·pul′co de Juá·rez** (-dä hwär′ez′, -wär′-; -əs)

**A·ca·ri·gua** (ä′kə rig′wə) city in NW Venezuela: pop. 126,000

**Ac·ar·na·ni·a** (ak'ər nā'nē ə) region on the W coast of ancient Greece

**Ac·cad** (ak'ad', äk'äd') *alt. sp. of* AKKAD

**Ac·cra** (ə krä') capital of Ghana: seaport on the Gulf of Guinea: pop. 954,000

**A·cel·da·ma** (ə sel'də mə) ⟦L < Gr *Akeldama* < Aram *chakal-dema*, field of blood⟧ *Bible* the field near Jerusalem bought with the money given Judas for betraying Jesus: Acts 1:19; Matt. 27:8

**A·chae·a** (ə kē'ə) ancient region in the N Peloponnesus: also **A·chai·a** (ə kā'ə, -kī'-)

**A·cher·nar** (ā'kər när') ⟦Ar ʔakhir nahr < ʔakhir, the end, final + nahr, river: the Ar name of the constellation itself is nahr ʔurdunn, lit., river Jordan⟧ the brightest star in the constellation Eridanus, with a magnitude of 0.6

**Ach·er·on** (ak'ər än') ⟦L < Gr; assoc. with *achos*, pain, hence "river of woe"⟧ **1** *Gr. & Rom. Myth.* a river in Hades: often identified as the river across which Charon ferries the dead: cf. STYX **2** Hades; infernal regions

**A·con·ca·gua** (ä kôn kä'gwə) mountain of the Andes in W Argentina: 22,835 ft. (6,960 m): highest peak in the Western Hemisphere

**A·cre¹** (ä'kər, ā'-) AKKO

**A·cre²** (ä'krə) state of westernmost Brazil: 58,915 sq. mi. (152,589 sq. km); pop. 358,000; cap. Rio Branco

**A·crop·o·lis** (ə kräp'ə lis) the fortified upper part of Athens, on which the Parthenon was built

**Ac·ti·um** (ak'tē əm, -shē əm) cape on the NW coast of Acarnania (in ancient Greece): the forces of Mark Antony and Cleopatra were defeated by those of Octavian in a naval battle near Actium (31 B.C.)

**Ad·ams** (ad'əmz) **1 Mount** ⟦after John *Adams* (1735-1826), U.S. president⟧ mountain of the Cascade range, S Wash.: 12,307 ft. (3,751 m) **2 Mount** ⟦after Pres. John *Adams*⟧ peak of the White Mountains, N.H.: 5,798 ft. (1,767 m)

**A·da·na** (ä'də nä') city in S Turkey: pop. 575,000

**A·da·pa·za·ri** (äd'ə pä'zə rē') city in NW Turkey: pop. 131,000

**Ad·dis A·ba·ba** (ad'is ab'ə bə) capital of Ethiopia, in the central part: pop. 1,413,000

**Ad·e·laide** (ad''l ād') capital of South Australia: port on the SE coast of the state: pop. 969,000

**A·dé·lie Coast** (ad″l ē′; *Fr* à dā lē′) region in Antarctica, south of Australia, claimed by France: *c.* 150,000 sq. mi. (388,500 sq. km): also **Adélie Land**, Fr. name **Terre A·dé·lie** (ter à dā lē′)

**A·den** (äd″n, ād″n) **1** former British colony & protectorate in SW Arabia, on the Gulf of Aden: now part of the Republic of Yemen **2** seaport in this region: capital of the former People's Democratic Republic of Yemen: pop. 264,000 **3 Gulf of** gulf of the Arabian Sea, between the S coast of Arabia and Somalia in E Africa

**A·di·ge** (ä′dē jä′) river in N Italy, flowing south & east into the Gulf of Venice: *c.* 250 mi. (400 km)

**Ad·i·ron·dack Mountains** (ad′ə rän′dak′) mountain range in NE New York: highest peak, Mt. Marcy: also **Adirondacks**

**Ad·mi·ral·ty Islands** (ad′mə rəl tē) group of small islands in the Bismarck Archipelago, in Papua New Guinea: *c.* 800 sq. mi. (2,070 sq. km): also **Admiralties**

**A·do·wa** (äd′ə wə, ad′-) *var. of* ADWA

**A·dri·an·o·ple** (ā′drē ə nō′pəl) *old name of* EDIRNE

**A·dri·an·op·o·lis** (-näp′ə lis) *ancient name of* EDIRNE

**A·dri·at·ic (Sea)** (ā′drē at′ik) arm of the Mediterranean, between Italy and the Balkan Peninsula

**A·du·wa** (äd′ə wə, ad′-) *var. of* ADWA

**Ad·wa** (äd′wə) town in N Ethiopia: site of Menelik II's defeat of the Italians (1896), which led to recognition of Ethiopian independence: pop. 27,000

**Ae·ge·an Islands** (ē jē′ən, i-) the islands in the Aegean Sea; specif., Lesbos, Samos, Chios, the Cyclades, and the Dodecanese

**Aegean (Sea)** arm of the Mediterranean, between Greece and Turkey

**Ae·gi·na** (ē jī′nə) island off the SE coast of Greece; 32 sq. mi. (83 sq. km)

**Ae·gos·pot·a·mi** (ē′gäs′pät′ə mī′) small river in ancient Thrace, flowing into the Hellespont: at its mouth, the Spartan fleet under Lysander defeated the Athenian fleet (405 B.C.), ending the Peloponnesian War: also **Ae′gos′pot′a·mos** (-məs)

**Ae·o·li·a** (ē ō′lē ə) *var. of* AEOLIS

**Ae·o·lis** (ē′ə lis′) ancient region on the NW coast of Asia Minor, consisting of a group of cities settled by the

Aeolians

**Aet·na** (et′nə) *alt. sp. of* ETNA

**Ae·to·li·a** (ē tō′lē ə) region of ancient Greece, on the Gulf of Corinth

**Af·ghan·i·stan** (af gan′i stan′) country in SC Asia, between Iran and Pakistan: 250,000 sq. mi. (647,497 sq. km); pop. 15,425,000; cap. Kabul

**Af·ri·ca** (af′ri kə) ⟦L < *Africa* (*terra*), African (land), fem. of *Africus* < *Afer*, an African⟧ second largest continent, situated in the Eastern Hemisphere, south of Europe: *c.* 11,677,000 sq. mi. (30,243,000 sq. km); pop. *c.* 484,000,000

**A·ga·dir** (ä′gə dir′, ag′ə-) seaport in SW Morocco, on the Atlantic: pop. 246,000

**A·ga·na** (ä gän′yə) capital of Guam: pop. 1,100: also sp. **A·ga′ña**

**A·gin·court** (aj′in kôrt′; *Fr* à zhan kōōr′) village in N France, near Calais: site of a battle (1415) won by England in the Hundred Years' War with France

**A·gra** (ä′grə) **1** city on the Jumna River, in Uttar Pradesh, India: site of the Taj Mahal: pop. 770,000 **2** former province of India: now part of Uttar Pradesh

**Ag·ri·gen·to** (ä′grē jen′tō) city in S Sicily: site of ancient Greek and Roman ruins: pop. 49,000: ancient Latin name **Ag·ri·gen·tum** (ag′rə jen′təm)

**A·guas·ca·lien·tes** (ä′gwäs kä lyen′tās) **1** small, inland state of central Mexico: 2,112 sq. mi. (5,471 sq. km); pop. 556,000 **2** its capital: pop. 181,000

**A·gu·lhas** (ə gul′əs; *Port* ə gōō′lyəsh), **Cape** southernmost point of Africa, in Cape Province, South Africa

**Agulhas current** a fast, warm ocean current flowing southwest along the SE coast of Africa

**Ah·med·a·bad, Ah·mad·a·bad** (ä′məd ə bäd′) city in W India, in Gujarat state: pop. 2,515,000

**Ah·vaz** (ä väz′) city in SW Iran: pop. 471,000: also **Ah·waz′** (ä wäz′)

**Ah·ve·nan·maa** (ä′ve nän mä′) group of Finn. islands at the entrance to the Gulf of Bothnia: 590 sq. mi. (1,527 sq. km); pop. 24,000

**Ain·tab** (in täb′) *old name of* GAZIANTEP

**A·ïr** (ä′ir′, ä ir′) mountainous region of the S Sahara, in NC Niger: *c.* 30,000 sq. mi. (77,700 sq. km)

**Aisne** (en) river in N France, flowing into the Oise: 175 mi. (282 km)

**Aix-en-Pro·vence** (eks än prô väns′) city in SE France, near Marseille: pop. 125,000: also called **Aix** (eks)

**Aix-la-Cha·pelle** (eks lȧ shȧ pel′) *Fr. name of* AACHEN

**Ai·yi·na** (a′yi nä′) *modern Gr. name of* AEGINA

**A·jac·cio** (ä yät′chō) chief city of Corsica, a seaport on the W coast: birthplace of Napoleon: pop. 47,000

**Aj·mer** (uj mir′) city in NW India, in Rajasthan state: pop. 374,000

**AK** *abbrev. for* Alaska

**A·kha·ï·a** (ä′kä ē′ä; ə kä′ə, -kī′ə) region of modern Greece, corresponding approximately to ancient Achaea

**A·ki·ta** (ə kēt′ə, ä-) city in N Honshu, Japan, on the Sea of Japan: pop. 288,000

**Ak·kad** (ak′ad′, äk′äd′) **1** ancient region in N Babylonia (fl. *c.* 2300-2100 B.C.) **2** its chief city, for a time the capital of Babylonia

**Ak·ko** (ä kō′) city in NW Israel, on the Mediterranean: pop. 34,000

**Ak·ron** (ak′rən) ‖ < Gr *akron*, highest point: because of the city's location between two rivers ‖ city in N Ohio: pop. 223,000 (met. area 658,000): see CLEVELAND

**Ak·sum** (äk′soom′) town in N Ethiopia: capital of an ancient kingdom that controlled the surrounding region: pop. 13,000

**Ak·tyu·binsk** (äk tyoo′binsk) city in W Kazakhstan: pop. 231,000

**AL** *abbrev. for* Alabama

**Ala** *abbrev. for* Alabama

**Al·a·bam·a** (al′ə bam′ə) ‖ < Fr *Alibamon* < name of a Muskogean tribe < ? ‖ **1** Southern State of SE U.S., on the Gulf of Mexico: admitted, 1819; 51,609 sq. mi. (133,667 sq. km); pop. 4,041,000; cap. Montgomery: abbrev. *AL* or *Ala* **2** river flowing through central and SW Ala., joining the Tombigbee to form the Mobile River: 315 mi. (607 km)

**A·la Dag, A·la·dagh** (ä′lä dä′, -däk′) mountain of the Taurus range, S Turkey: *c.* 12,000 ft. (3,658 m)

**A·la·gez** (u′lə gyôs′) ARAGATS

**A·la·go·as** (ä lə gō′əs) state of NE Brazil, on the Atlantic: 10,706 sq. mi. (27,731 sq. km); pop. 2,245,000; cap. Maceió

**A·lai Mountains** (ä lī′) mountain range in S Kyrgyzstan: highest peak, *c.* 19,500 ft. (5,944 m)

**Al·a·me·da** (al'ə mē'də, -mä'-) ⟦Sp < *alameda*, tree-lined walk < *álamo*, poplar tree⟧ city on an island in San Francisco Bay, Calif.: pop. 76,000

**Al·a·mo** (al'ə mō') ⟦Sp: see prec.⟧ Franciscan mission at San Antonio, Tex: scene of a siege and massacre of Texans by Mexican troops (1836)

**A·la·mo·gor·do** (al'ə mə gôr'dō) ⟦Sp < *álamo*, poplar tree + *gordo*, big⟧ city in S N.Mex.: pop. 28,000: site of testing range where first atomic bomb was exploded (June, 1945)

**Å·land** (ō'lənd, ä'-) *Swed. name of* AHVENANMAA

**Alas** *abbrev. for* Alaska

**A·las·ka** (ə las'kə) ⟦prob. via Russ *Aliaska* < Aleut *Alax̂sxax̂*, name of the Alaska Peninsula⟧ 1 State of the U.S. in NW North America, separated from Asia by the Bering Strait: land bought from Russia in 1867: admitted, 1959; 586,400 sq. mi. (1,518,770 sq. km); pop. 550,000; cap. Juneau: abbrev. *AK* or *Alas* 2 **Gulf of** inlet of the Pacific in the S coast of Alaska between the Alaska Peninsula and the Alexander Archipelago

**Alaska Highway** highway between Dawson Creek, Brit. Columbia and Fairbanks, Alas.: 1,523 mi. (2,451 km)

**Alaska Peninsula** peninsula extending SW from the mainland of Alas.

**Alaska Range** mountain range in SC Alas.: highest peak, Mount McKinley

**Al·ba·ce·te** (äl'bä sä'tä) city in Murcia, SE Spain: pop. 117,000

**Al·ba Lon·ga** (al'bə lôn'gə) city in ancient Latium, near where Rome is today: legendary birthplace of Romulus and Remus

**Al·ba·ni·a** (al bā'nē ə, -bän'yə) country in the W Balkan Peninsula, on the Adriatic: 11,099 sq. mi. (28,746 sq. km); pop. 3,020,000; cap. Tirana

**Al·ba·ny** (ôl'bə nē) ⟦after the Duke of York and *Albany*, later James II (1633-1701), king of England and Scotland⟧ 1 capital of N.Y., on the Hudson: pop. 101,000: see SCHENECTADY 2 city in SW Ga.: pop. 78,000

**Al·be·marle Sound** (al'bə märl') ⟦after Wm. Keppel, 2d Earl of *Albemarle*, gov. of colony of Virginia (1737-54)⟧ arm of the Atlantic extending into NE N.C.: *c.* 60 mi. (97 km) long

**Al·bert** (al'bərt), **Lake** lake in EC Africa, on the Uganda-

Zaire border: 2,064 sq. mi. (5,346 sq. km): renamed (1973) *Lake Mobutu Sese Seko*

**Al·ber·ta** (al bʉrt′ə) ⟦after Princess Louise *Alberta*, daughter of Queen Victoria & wife of the Marquess of Lorne, Cdn gov. gen. (1878-83) ⟧ province of SW Canada: 255,285 sq. mi. (661,186 sq. km); pop. 2,366,000; cap. Edmonton: abbrev. *AB* or *Alta*

**Albert Canal** ship canal in Belgium, from Liège to Antwerp: 81 mi. (130 km)

**Albert Memorial** monument to Prince Albert of England in Kensington Gardens, London: 175 ft. (53 m) high

**Albert Ny·an·za** (nī an′zə, nē-) Lake ALBERT

**Al·ber·ton** (al′bər tən) city in the Transvaal, South Africa, in the Witwatersrand: pop. 231,000

**Al·bi·on** (al′bē ən) ⟦L < Celt *Albio*, gen. *Albionus* (> Ir *Alba*, gen. *Albann*, name for Scotland); understood as if < L *albus*, white, because the cliffs of S England are white, but thought by some scholars to be of non-IE orig. ⟧ *an old poet. name for* ENGLAND

**Ål·borg** (ôl′bôr′) seaport in N Jutland, Denmark: pop. 155,000

**Al·bu·quer·que** (al′bə kʉr′kē, -byə-) ⟦after the Duke of *Alburquerque*, viceroy (1702-11) of New Spain: altered prob. by confusion with Affonso de *Albuquerque* (1453-1515), Port navigator ⟧ city in central N.Mex.: pop. 385,000

**Al·ca·lá de He·na·res** (äl′kä lä′ de e nä′res) city in central Spain, near Madrid: pop. 143,000

**Al·can Highway** (al′kan) ⟦AL(ASKA) + CAN(ADA)⟧ ALASKA HIGHWAY

**Al·ca·traz** (al′kə traz′) ⟦after Sp *Isla de Alcatraces*, Island of Pelicans ⟧ small island in San Francisco Bay: site of a Federal prison (1934-63)

**Al·cor·cón** (äl′kôr kôn′) city in central Spain, near Madrid: pop. 141,000

**Al·cy·o·ne** (al sī′ə nē′) ⟦L < Gr *Alkyonē*, daughter of Aeolus ⟧ the brightest star in the Pleiades in the constellation Taurus, with a magnitude of 2.96

**Al·dan** (äl dän′) river in EC Russia, flowing north and east into the Lena River: *c.* 1,700 mi. (2,735 km)

**Al·deb·a·ran** (al deb′ə rən) ⟦Ar *al-dabarān* < *al*, the + *dabarān*, following < *dubara*, to follow: so called because it follows the Pleiades ⟧ an orange, giant binary star, the brightest star in the constellation Taurus, with a magnitude of 0.86

**Al·der·ney** (ôl′dər nē) northernmost of the Channel Islands: 3 sq. mi. (8 sq. km); pop. 2,000

**A·lep·po** (ə lep′ō) city in NW Syria: pop. 977,000: also **A·lep** (ä lep′)

**A·les·san·dri·a** (ä′lə sän′drē ə) city in NW Italy, in Piedmont region: pop. 101,000

**A·leu·tian Islands** (ə lōō′shən) chain of islands extending *c.* 1,200 mi. (1,900 km) southwest from the tip of the Alaska Peninsula: constituting, with the W half of the Alaska Peninsula, a district of Alas.: 15,501 sq. mi. (40,147 sq. km); pop. 12,000: also **Aleutians**

**Al·ex·an·der** (al′ig zan′dər) island of Antarctica, just west of the base of the Antarctic Peninsula, in the British Antarctic Territory: *c.* 235 mi. (378 km) long

**Alexander Archipelago** ⟦after *Alexander* II, Russian czar at the time Alas. was sold to the U.S. (1867)⟧ group of *c.* 1,100 islands in Alas., off the SE coast

**Al·ex·an·dret·ta** (al′ig zan dret′ə) *old name of* ISKENDE-RUN

**Al·ex·an·dri·a** (al′ig zan′drē ə) **1** seaport in Egypt, on the Mediterranean at the W end of the Nile delta: pop. 2,318,000: founded by Alexander the Great and, later, a center of Hellenistic culture **2** ⟦after the seaport, but with allusion to the *Alexander* family, owners of the town site⟧ city in NE Va., on the Potomac, near Washington, D.C.: pop. 111,000 **3** ⟦after ALEXANDRIA, Egypt⟧ city in central La.: pop. 49,000

**A·lex·an·drou·po·lis** (ä′leks än drōō′pə lis) seaport in NE Greece, on the Aegean, near the border of Turkey: pop. 35,000

**Al·ge·cir·as** (al′ji sir′əs, -sī rəs; *Sp* äl′he thē′räs′) seaport in S Spain, on the Strait of Gibraltar: pop. 86,000

**Al·ge·ri·a** (al jir′ē ə) country in N Africa, on the Mediterranean: *c.* 919,000 sq. mi. (2,380,000 sq. km); pop. 22,817,000; cap. Algiers

**Al·giers** (al jirz′) capital of Algeria; seaport on the Mediterranean; pop. 2,400,000: a base of Barbary pirates until its capture by the French in 1830

**Al·gol** (al′gäl′) ⟦Ar *al ghūl*, lit., the ghoul⟧ an eclipsing binary star in the constellation Perseus: its overall brightness regularly changes from the second to the third magnitude as the fainter star blocks its brighter companion

**Al·gon·quin Park** (al gäŋ′kin, -kwin) provincial park & game preserve in SE Ontario, Canada: 2,910 sq. mi. (7,537 sq. km)

**Al·ham·bra** (al ham′brə) **1** ⟦ Sp < Ar *al ḥamrā'*, lit., the red (house): fem. form of adj. *aḥmar*, red ⟧ citadel of the Moorish kings near Granada, Spain, built during the 13th and 14th cent. **2** ⟦ after the citadel, popularized through Washington Irving's *The Alhambra* ⟧ city in SW Calif.: suburb of Los Angeles: pop. 82,000

**A·li·can·te** (ä′lē kän′te; *E* al′ə kan′tē) seaport in SE Spain, on the Mediterranean: pop. 251,000

**A·li·garh** (al′i gär′, ä′li gʉr′) city in N India, in Uttar Pradesh: pop. 320,000

**Al·i·oth** (al′ē äth′) ⟦ Ar *alya(t)*, lit., fat of the tail of a sheep ⟧ a binary star in the constellation Ursa Major with a magnitude of 1.8: the brightest star in the handle of the Big Dipper

**Al Is·kan·da·ri·yah** (äl′ is kän′də rē′yä′) *Ar. name of* ALEXANDRIA (Egypt)

**Alk·maar** (älk′mär′) city in NW Netherlands: pop. 85,000

**Al·la·ha·bad** (al′ə hä bäd′) city in NC India, in Uttar Pradesh, at the juncture of the Jumna and Ganges rivers: pop. 642,000

**Al·le·ghe·ny** (al′ə gā′nē) ⟦ prob. < an Algonquian (? Delaware) name ⟧ river in W Pennsylvania, joining the Monongahela at Pittsburgh to form the Ohio: 325 mi. (523 km)

**Allegheny Mountains** mountain range of the Appalachian system, in Pa., Md., W. Va., and Va.: highest peaks, over 4,800 ft. (1,463 m): also **Alleghenies**

**Al·len·town** (al′ən toun′) ⟦ after Wm. *Allen*, the founder ⟧ city in E Pa., on the Lehigh River: pop. 105,000 (met. area, incl. Bethlehem & Easton, 687,000)

**Al·lier** (ȧl yā′) river in central France, flowing northward into the Loire: *c.* 250 mi. (402 km)

**Al·ma-A·ta** (äl′mə ä′tə) capital of Kazakhstan, in the SE part: pop. 1,068,000

**Al·me·lo** (äl′mə lō′) city in E Netherlands: pop. 63,000

**Al·me·ri·a** (äl′mə rē′ə) seaport in SE Spain, on the Mediterranean: pop. 141,000

**Al-O·beid, al-O·beid** (al′ō bād′) *var. of* EL OBEID

**A·lost** (à lôst′) *Fr. name of* AALST

**Al·pha Cen·tau·ri** (al′fə sen tô′rī′) the brightest star in the constellation Centaurus, with a magnitude of -0.27: it is the nearest of the stars that are visible to the naked eye, except for the Sun

**Alps** (alps) mountain system in SC Europe extending from S France through Switzerland, Italy, SW Germany, Austria, Slovenia, Croatia, and Bosnia and Herzegovina into Yugoslavia: highest peak, Mont Blanc

**Al·sace** (al sās′, -sas′; al′sas′; *Fr* ál zàs′) 1 historical region of NE France 2 metropolitan region of NE France; 3,196 sq. mi. (8,280 sq. km); pop. 1,585,000; chief city, Strasbourg

**Al·sace-Lor·raine** (-lô rän′, -lə-; *Fr*, -lô ren′) region in NE France consisting of the former provinces of Alsace and Lorraine: under German control, 1871-1919 and 1940-1944: restored to France, 1945

**Alta** *abbrev. for* Alberta

**Al·ta·de·na** (al′tə dē′nə) [ < L *alta*, fem. of *altus*, high + (PASA)DENA, which is at a lower elevation ] suburb of Los Angeles, adjacent to Pasadena: pop. 41,000

**Al·tai** (or **Al·tay**) **Mountains** (al′tī, al tī′) mountain system of central Asia, extending from E Kazakhstan & SC Russia into NW China and W Mongolian People's Republic: highest peak, *c.* 15,000 ft. (4,572 m)

**Al·ta·ir** (al tä′ir) [Ar *al-tā′ir*, the bird < *tara*, to fly ] the brightest star in the constellation Aquila, with a magnitude of 0.77: see SUMMER TRIANGLE

**Al·ta·mi·ra** (äl′tä mē′rä) complex of caves in N Spain, near Santander, containing paleolithic drawings

**Alt·dorf** (ält′dôrf′) town in Switzerland near Lake Lucerne: pop. 8,000: scene of legendary exploits of William Tell

**Al·too·na** (al tōō′nə) [prob. < *Allatoona*, Cherokee name of unknown meaning: ? infl. by *Altona*, Ger seaport ] city in central Pa.: pop. 52,000

**Al-U·bay·yid** (al′ōō bā′yid, -bā′id) *var. of* EL OBEID

**A·ma·ga·sa·ki** (ä′mə gə sä′kē) city on the S coast of Honshu, Japan, near Osaka: pop. 506,000

**A·ma·pá** (ä′mə pä′) state of N Brazil, on the Atlantic: *c.* 53,000 sq. mi. (137,300 sq. km); pop. 214,000

**Am·a·ril·lo** (am′ə ril′ō) [Sp, yellow: prob. from color of banks of a nearby stream ] city in NW Tex.: pop. 158,000

**Am·a·zon** (am′ə zän′, -zən) ⟦so named by Spaniards, who believed its shores inhabited by female warriors, in reference to a race of female warriors in Greek mythology⟧ river in South America, flowing from the Andes in Peru across N Brazil into the Atlantic: *c.* 4,000 mi. (6,400 km)

**A·ma·zo·nas** (ä′mə zō′nəs) state of NW Brazil: 604,035 sq. mi. (1,564,445 sq. km); pop. 1,728,000; cap. Manaus

**Am·ba·to** (äm bät′ō) city in central Ecuador: pop. 221,000

**Am·boi·na** (am boi′nə) AMBON

**Am·boise** (än bwȧz′) town in WC France, on the Loire, near Tours: pop. 10,000: site of a royal residence (1483-1560)

**Am·bon** (am′bän′) **1** one of the Molucca Islands, southwest of Ceram, in Indonesia: 314 sq. mi. (813 sq. km) **2** seaport on this island: pop. 209,000

**A·mer·i·ca** (ə mer′i kə) ⟦ModL, name assoc. (1507) by Martin Waldseemüller (*c.* 1470-*c.* 1522), Ger cosmographer, with *Americus* Vespucius, Latinized form of *Amerigo* Vespucci (1454-1512), It explorer; but < ? Sp *Amerrique*, name of a mountain range in Nicaragua, used by early explorers for the newly discovered lands < ? AmInd⟧ **1** North America, South America, and the West Indies, considered together: also **the Americas 2** North America **3** the United States of America

**American Samoa** island group consisting of seven islands in the S Pacific, north of Tonga: an unincorporated territory of the U.S.: 76 sq. mi. (197 sq. km); pop. 47,000; cap. Pago Pago on Tutuila Island: abbrev. *AS*

**A·mer·i·ka** (ə mer′i kə) ⟦Ger, America⟧ AMERICA (the country): spelling used to suggest that U.S. society is variously fascist, repressive, racist, etc.

**A·mers·foort** (ä′mərs fôrt′) city in central Netherlands: pop. 88,000

**Ames** (āmz) ⟦after Oakes *Ames*, railroad official⟧ city in central Iowa, near Des Moines: pop. 47,000

**Am·ha·ra** (äm hä′rə) former province of NW Ethiopia

**Am·i·ens** (ȧ myan′; *E* am′ē ənz) city in N France, on the Somme River: pop. 136,000

**A·min·di·vi Islands** (ä′min dē′vē) group of islands in the N Laccadives, off the west coast of Kerala, India

**Am·man** (ä′män′, ä män′) capital of Jordan, in the NW part: pop. 778,000: it is the Biblical city *Rabbah*

**Am·mon** (am′ən) *Bible* an ancient kingdom east of the Dead Sea

**A·moy** (ä moi′) *old name of* XIAMEN

**Am·ra·va·ti** (äm räv′ə tē′, um-) city in Maharashtra state, central India: pop. 261,000

**Am·rit·sar** (äm rit′sər, um-) city in Punjab state, N India: pop. 589,000

**Am·stel·veen** (äm′stəl vān′) city in W Netherlands: suburb of Amsterdam: pop. 68,000

**Am·ster·dam** (am′stər dam′) constitutional capital of the Netherlands: seaport on an inlet of the IJsselmeer & a ship canal to the North Sea: pop. 676,000: see also HAGUE, The

**A·mu Dar·ya** (ä moo′ där′yä) river in central Asia rising in the Pamir Mountains & flowing west & northwest into the Aral Sea; *c.* 1,600 mi. (2,575 km)

**A·mund·sen Sea** (ä′moon sən) part of the Pacific Ocean bordering on Antarctica, east of the Ross Sea

**A·mur** (ä moor′) river in NE Asia, flowing along the Russia-China border across E Siberia into Tatar Strait: *c.* 1,800 mi. (2,900 km), with principal head-streams, 2,700 mi. (4,345 km)

**A·na·dyr, A·na·dir** (ä′nä dir′) river in NE Siberia, flowing south & east into the Bering Sea: *c.* 700 mi. (1,125 km)

**Anadyr Range** *old name of* CHUKOT RANGE

**An·a·heim** (an′ə hīm′) ⟦after the Santa *Ana* River (after Saint *Anne*, mother of the Virgin Mary) + Ger *heim*, home⟧ city in SW Calif.: pop. 266,000 (met. area, with Santa Ana, 2,411,000)

**A·na·pur·na** (an′ə poor′nə, ä′nə-; -pʉr′-) *alt. sp. of* ANNA-PURNA

**An·a·to·li·a** (an′ə tō′lē ə) 1 [Obs.] Asia Minor 2 the part of modern Turkey that is in Asia

**An·chor·age** (aŋ′kər ij) ⟦from the anchoring there of early supply ships⟧ seaport in S Alas., on Cook Inlet: pop. 226,000

**An·co·na** (än kō′nə) seaport in central Italy, on the Adriatic: pop. 105,000

**An·da·lu·si·a** (an′də loo′zhə, -shə; -zhē ə, -shē ə) region of S Spain on the Mediterranean & the Atlantic: 33,739 sq. mi. (87,268 sq. km); pop. 6,442,000; cap. Seville: Sp. name **An·da·lu·ci′a** (än′dä loo thē′ä)

**An·da·man Islands** (an′də mən) group of islands in the

Bay of Bengal, west of the Malay Peninsula: with the Nicobar Islands, constituting a territory of India (**Andaman and Nicobar Islands**): 3,202 sq. mi. (8,293 sq. km); pop. 188,000

**Andaman Sea** part of the Indian Ocean, west of the Malay Peninsula and east of the Andaman and Nicobar Islands

**An·der·son** (an'dər sən) ⟦after Chief *Anderson*, Delaware Indian leader⟧ city in EC Ind.: pop. 59,000: see INDIANAPOLIS

**An·der·son·ville** (-vil') ⟦after Major Robt. *Anderson* (1805-71), U.S. Army⟧ town in SW central Ga.: site of a Confederate prison in the Civil War

**An·des (Mountains)** (an'dēz') mountain system extending the length of W South America: highest peak, Aconcagua

**An·dhra Pra·desh** (än'drə prə desh') state of S India, on the Bay of Bengal: 106,878 sq. mi. (276,814 sq. km); pop. 53,404,000; cap. Hyderabad

**An·di·zhan** (än'di zhän', an'di zhan') city in E Uzbekistan, on the upper Syr Darya: pop. 275,000

**An·dor·ra** (an dôr'ə) 1 country in the E Pyrenees, between Spain and France: 180 sq. mi. (466 sq. km); pop. 49,000 2 its capital: pop. 30,000: in full **Andorra la Vel·la** (lä väl'yə)

**An·drom·e·da** (an dräm'ə də) ⟦L < Gr *Andromedē*⟧ a N constellation between Cassiopeia and Pisces containing the nearest spiral galaxy, Andromeda galaxy M31, which is just visible to the naked eye

**An·dro·pov** (än drō'pôf') *old name of* RYBINSK (the city)

**A·ne·to** (ä nā'tō), **Pi·co de** (pē'kō dā') highest mountain in the Pyrenees, in Spain: 11,168 ft. (3,404 m)

**An·ga·ra** (än'gə rä') river in SC Siberia, flowing from Lake Baikal north & west to the Yenisei River: 1,150 mi. (1,850 km)

**An·garsk** (än gärsk') city in S Asian Russia, near Irkutsk: pop. 256,000

**An·ge·les** (än'hə läs') city in WC Luzon, the Philippines: pop. 189,000

**An·gel Falls** (or **Fall**) (ān'jəl) waterfall in SE Venezuela: over 3,200 ft. (975 m)

**An·gers** (än zhā') city in NW France: pop. 141,000

**Ang·kor** (aŋ'kôr') an accumulation of Khmer ruins in NW Cambodia, consisting mainly of **Angkor Thom**

(tôm), the capital of the ancient Khmer civilization, and including **Angkor Vat** (vät) or **Angkor Wat** (wät), an ancient Khmer temple

**An·gle·sey, An·gle·sea** (aŋ′gəl sē′) 1 former county of NW Wales, now part of Gwynedd county 2 large island in the Irish Sea off the NW coast of Wales: part of Gwynedd county: 276 sq. mi. (715 sq. km)

**An·gli·a** (aŋ′glē ə) *Latin name of* ENGLAND

**An·glo-E·gyp·tian Sudan** (aŋ′glō ē jip′shən) territory jointly administered by Egypt & Great Britain (1899-1956): see SUDAN

**An·go·la** (aŋ gō′lə, an-) country on the SW coast of Africa: formerly a Portuguese territory, it became independent (1975): 481,351 sq. mi. (1,246,700 sq. km); pop. 8,164,000; cap. Luanda

**An·gou·lême** (än gōō lem′) city in SW France: pop. 104,000

**An·guil·la** (aŋ gwil′ə) island of the Leeward group in the West Indies: with nearby islands, it constitutes a dependency of the United Kingdom; 60 sq. mi. (155 sq. km); pop. 7,000

**An·gus** (aŋ′gəs) former county of E Scotland, on the North Sea: now in the region of Tayside

**An·halt** (än′hält′) region of central Germany, formerly a German state and now part of the state of Saxony-Anhalt

**An·hui** (än′hwē′) province of E China: c. 54,000 sq. mi. (140,000 sq. km); pop. 49,666,000; cap. Hefei: also *old form* **An′hwei′** (-hwā′)

**An·jou** (an′jōō′; *Fr* än zhōō′) historical region of W France: the ruling family of Anjou gave rise to the Plantagenet house of England through Henry II, son of Geoffrey (IV) Plantagenet, Count of Anjou

**An·ka·ra** (aŋ′kər ə, äŋ′-) capital of Turkey, in the central part: pop. 2,800,000

**An·na·ba** (an nä′bə) seaport in NE Algeria, on the Mediterranean: pop. 348,000

**An·nam** (a nam′, an′am′) historic region and former French protectorate in EC Indochina: the central part of Vietnam

**An·nan·dale** (an′ən dāl′) ⟦prob. after Queen *Anne* of Great Britain (1665-1714) + *dale*⟧ suburb of Washington, D.C., in NE Va.: pop. 51,000

**An·nap·o·lis** (ə nap′ə lis) ⟦after *Anna*, Princess, later

Queen *Anne* of Great Britain (1665-1714) + Gr *polis*, city ] capital of Md., on Chesapeake Bay: pop. 33,000: site of U.S. Naval Academy

**An·na·pur·na** (än'ə poor'nə, ä'nə-; -pʉr'-) mountain mass of the Himalayas, in central Nepal: highest peak c. 26,500 ft. (8,075 m)

**Ann Ar·bor** (an är'bər) [prob. after *Ann* Allen, early settler, and the woody site ] city in SE Mich.: pop. 110,000

**An·ne·cy** (àn sē') city in SE France, in the N Alps: pop. 113,000

**An·shan** (än'shän') city in NE China, in central Liaoning province: pop. 1,500,000

**An·ta·kya** (än'tə kyä') *Turk. name of* ANTIOCH (Syria)

**An·tal·ya** (än'təl yä') seaport in SW Turkey, on the Mediterranean: pop. 174,000

**An·ta·na·na·ri·vo** (an'tə nan'ə rĕ'vō') capital of Madagascar, in the central part: pop. 600,000

**Ant·arc·tic** (ant ärk'tik; -är'-), **the** ANTARCTICA

**Ant·arc·ti·ca** (ant ärk'ti kə, -är'-) land area about the South Pole, completely covered by an ice shelf: c. 5,500,000 sq. mi. (14,245,000 sq. km): sometimes called a continent

**Antarctic Circle** [*also* a- c-] an imaginary circle parallel to the equator, c. 66°34′ south of it

**Antarctic Ocean** popularly, the S parts of the Atlantic, Pacific, and Indian oceans surrounding Antarctica

**Antarctic Peninsula** peninsula in Antarctica, extending toward South America: c. 800 mi. (1,300 km) long

**An·tar·es** (an ter'ēz') [ [Gr *Antarēs* < *anti-*, like + *Arēs*, Gr god of war: so named because of its color ] a supergiant, red binary star, the brightest star in the constellation Scorpio, with a magnitude of 0.98

**An·ti·cos·ti** (an'ti käs'tē) [ < ? AmInd *natiscotec*, lit., where bears are hunted ] island at the mouth of the St. Lawrence River, in Quebec, Canada: c. 3,000 sq. mi. (7,700 sq. km); pop. 500

**An·tie·tam** (an tēt'əm) [AmInd < ? ] creek in W Md.: its juncture with the Potomac is the site of a bloody, but indecisive, Civil War battle (1862)

**An·ti·gua** (an tē'gwə, -gə; -tig'wə, -tig'ə) island of the Leeward group in the West Indies: 108 sq. mi. (280 sq. km): see ANTIGUA AND BARBUDA

**Antigua and Barbuda** country in the E West Indies,

consisting of three islands, including Antigua and Barbuda: formerly a British colony, it became independent (1981) & a member of the Commonwealth: 171 sq. mi. (442 sq. km); pop. 82,000; cap. St. John's (on Antigua)

**An·ti-Leb·a·non** (an′ti leb′ə nän′, -nən) mountain range in W Syria, east of and parallel to the Lebanon Mountains: highest peak, Mt. Hermon

**An·til·les** (an til′ēz′) main island group of the West Indies, including all but the Bahamas: see GREATER ANTILLES, LESSER ANTILLES

**An·ti·och** (an′tē äk′) 1 capital of ancient Syria (until 64 B.C.), an early center of Christianity: now, a city in S Turkey: pop. 91,000: Turk name ANTAKYA 2 city in ancient Pisidia, Asia Minor 3 ⟦after ANTIOCH, Turkey⟧ city in W Calif., on the San Joaquin River: pop. 62,000

**An·ti·sa·na** (an′ti sä′nə, än′-) volcanic mountain of the Andes, in NC Ecuador: *c.* 18,700 ft. (5,700 m)

**Ant·li·a** (ant′lē ə) ⟦ModL *Antlia* (*Pneumatica*), lit., (air) pump < L *antlia*, water pump < Gr, bilge water < *antlos*, hold (of a ship)⟧ a S constellation between Hydra and Centaurus

**An·to·fa·gas·ta** (än′tô fə gäs′tə) seaport in N Chile: pop. 170,000

**An·trim** (an′trim′) district in NE Northern Ireland, in the S part of a former, much larger county (also called **Antrim**) of which Belfast was the chief city

**An·tung** (än′dooŋ′; *E* an tooŋ′) *old form of* DANDONG

**Ant·werp** (an′twurp′) 1 province of N Belgium: 1,104 sq. mi. (2,493 sq. km); pop. 1,583,000 2 its capital, on the Scheldt River: pop. 487,000 Fl. name **Ant·wer·pen** (änt′ver′pən)

**An·zi·o** (an′zē ō′; *It* än′tsyô) port on the W coast of Italy, south of Rome: pop. 27,000: site of Allied beachhead (Jan., 1944) in the invasion of Italy, World War II

**Ao·mo·ri** (ou′mə rē′) seaport in northernmost Honshu, Japan, on an inlet of the Sea of Japan: pop. 291,000

**A·o·ran·gi** (ou räŋ′ē) *old name of* Mount COOK

**Aosta, Valle d'** *see* VALLE D'AOSTA

**Ap·a·lach·ee Bay** (ap′ə lach′ē) ⟦< AmInd (? Choctaw) tribal name⟧ inlet of the Gulf of Mexico, on the NW coast of Florida

**Ap·a·lach·i·co·la** (ap′ə lach′i kō′lə) ⟦ < AmInd, ? a tribal name ⟧ river in NW Fla., flowing from the Fla.-Ga. border southward into the Gulf of Mexico: 90 mi. (145 km)

**A·pel·doorn** (ä′pəl dōrn′) city in EC Netherlands: pop. 145,000

**Ap·en·nines** (ap′ə nīnz′) mountain range of central Italy, extending the full length of the peninsula: highest peak, 9,560 ft. (2,914 m)

**A·pi·a** (ä pē′ə) seaport and the capital of Western Samoa, on Upolu island: pop. 35,000

**Ap·pa·la·chi·a** (ap′ə lā′chə, -chē ə; -lach′ə) the highland region of the E U.S. including the central and S Appalachian Mountains and the Piedmont plateau

**Appalachian Mountains** ⟦ < ? *Apalachee* Indians < ? AmInd (Choctaw) ⟧ mountain system in E North America, extending from S Quebec to N Ala.: *c.* 1,600 mi. (2,575 m); highest peak, Mount Mitchell: also **Appalachians**

**Ap·pen·zell** (ap′ən zel′; *Ger* ä′pən tsel′) canton of NE Switzerland: 161 sq. mi. (417 sq. km); pop. 62,000: divided into two politically independent half cantons

**Ap·pi·an Way** (ap′ē ən) ⟦ after the Roman censor *Appius* Claudius Caecus, by whom it was begun in 312 B.C. ⟧ ancient Roman paved highway from Rome to Capua to Brundisium (Brindisi): *c.* 350 mi. (563 km)

**Ap·ple** (ap′əl), **the** the BIG APPLE

**Ap·ple·ton** (ap′əl tən) ⟦ after S. *Appleton* (died 1853), Boston philanthropist & father-in-law of founder of a local university ⟧ city in E Wis.: pop. 66,000

**Ap·po·mat·tox** (ap′ə mat′əks) ⟦ < Algonquian tribal name ⟧ town in central Va., near Lynchburg: pop. 1,700: at a former nearby village (**Appomattox Court House**) Lee surrendered to Grant (April 9, 1865), ending the Civil War: now a national historical park

**A·pu·li·a** (ə pyōōl′yə, -ē ə) region on the SE coast of Italy, on the Adriatic Sea & the Gulf of Taranto: 7,469 sq. mi. (19,345 sq. km); pop. 3,978,000; cap. Bari: It. name *Puglia*

**A·pu·re** (ä pōō′re) river in WC Venezuela, flowing from the Andes into the Orinoco: *c.* 500 mi. (800 km)

**A·pus** (ā′pəs) ⟦ ModL, the Old World swift (genus name) < Gr *apous*, lit., footless < *a*-, without + *pous*, foot, ult. < IE *ₚēd-, foot, to go ⟧ a S constellation near the celestial pole

**A·qa·ba** (ä′kə bä′), **Gulf of** arm of the Red Sea between the Sinai Peninsula and NW Saudi Arabia

**A·quar·i·us** (ə kwer′ē əs) 〚L, the water carrier < *aquarius*, of water < *aqua*, water 〛 **1** a large S constellation, near the celestial equator between Cetus and Capricornus; Water Bearer **2** the eleventh sign of the zodiac, entered by the sun about January 21

**Aq·ui·la** (ak′wi lə) 〚L, eagle 〛 a N constellation in the Milky Way, nearly centered on the celestial equator

**Aq·ui·taine** (ak′wə tān′) **1** historical region of SW France: orig., a division of Gaul; later, a duchy under the French crown, passed to English control when Eleanor of Aquitaine married Henry II; returned to France after Hundred Years' War **2** metropolitan region of modern France of much smaller size, 15,949 sq. mi. (41,308 sq. km); pop. 2,688,000; chief city, Bordeaux: Latin name **Aq′ui·ta′ni·a** (-tā′nē ə)

**AR** *abbrev. for* Arkansas

**A·ra** (ä′rə) 〚L, altar 〛 a S constellation between Scorpio and Pavo

**A·ra·bi·a** (ə rā′bē ə) peninsula in SW Asia, between the Red Sea and the Persian Gulf, largely an arid desert plateau: *c.* 1,000,000 sq. mi. (2,590,000 sq. km): also **Arabian Peninsula**

**A·ra·bi·an Desert** (-ən) **1** desert in E Egypt, between the Nile valley and the Red Sea **2** popularly, the desert area of Arabia

**Arabian Sea** part of the Indian Ocean, between India and Arabia

**Ar·a·by** (ar′ə bē, er′-) *archaic and old poet. name for* ARABIA

**A·ra·ca·ju** (ar′ə kə zhoo′) seaport in NE Brazil, capital of Sergipe: pop. 293,000

**A·rad** (ä räd′) city in W Romania, on the Mureş River: pop. 171,000

**A·ra·fu·ra Sea** (ä′rə foo′rə) part of the South Pacific Ocean, between Australia and New Guinea

**A·ra·gats** (ä′rä gäts′) extinct volcano in NW Armenia: 13,435 ft. (4,095 m)

**Ar·a·gon** (ar′ə gän′, er′-) region in NE Spain: from the 11th to the 15th cent., a kingdom which at various times included the Balearic Islands, Sardinia, Sicily, & several other Mediterranean areas; united with Cas-

tile, 1479: 18,405 sq. mi. (47,669 sq. km); pop.
1,213,000: cap. Saragossa

**A·ra·gua·ia** (ä′rə gwä′yə) river in central Brazil, flowing
north into the Tocantins: *c.* 1,300 mi. (2,090 km)

**A·rak** (ə räk′) city in WC Iran: pop. 210,000

**A·ra·kan Yo·ma** (ar′ə kan′ yō′mə) mountain range in W
Myanmar, along the Indian border: highest peak, over
10,000 ft. (3,050 m)

**A·raks** (ä räks′) river flowing from E Turkey along the S
border of Armenia & Azerbaijan, into the Kura River
and the Caspian Sea: *c.* 600 mi. (965 m)

**Ar·al Sea** (ar′əl) inland body of salt water in SW Asia,
east of the Caspian Sea: slowly decreasing in area,
partly from overuse for irrigation: *c.* 15,500 sq. mi.
(40,145 sq. km): formerly also called **Lake Aral**

**Ar·am** (er′əm) ⟦Heb⟧ ancient country in SW Asia, generally identified as Syria

**Ar·a·rat** (ar′ə rat′, er′-) mountain in E Turkey, near the
Armenian and Iranian borders: supposed landing place
of Noah's Ark (Gen. 8:4): higher of its two peaks, *c.*
17,000 ft. (5,182 m)

**A·ras** (ä räs′) *Turk. name of* ARAKS

**A·rax·es** (ə rak′sēs′) *ancient name of* ARAKS

**Ar·be·la** (är bē′lə) ancient city in Assyria, often erro-
neously identified as the site of a battle (331 B.C.) in
which Alexander the Great defeated Darius III of Persia: see also IRBIL

**Ar·ca·di·a** (är kā′dē ə) **1** ancient, relatively isolated
pastoral region in the central Peloponnesus **2** region
of modern Greece occupying the same general area **3**
⟦after the ancient region, in allusion to its rural sim-
plicity⟧ city in SW Calif.: suburb of Los Angeles: pop.
48,000

**Ar·ca·dy** (är′kə dē) *old poet. name for* ARCADIA (the
ancient region)

**Arch·an·gel** (ärk′ān′jəl) *var. of* ARKHANGELSK

**Arch·er** (är′chər) Sagittarius, the constellation and
ninth sign of the zodiac

**Arch·es National Park** (är′chiz) national park in E
Utah, on the Colorado River, with extensive natural
rock formations: 115 sq. mi. (298 sq. km)

**Arc·tic** (ärk′tik, är′-), **the** the region around the North
Pole, including the Arctic Ocean and the lands in it
north of the 70° latitude

**Arctic Archipelago** group of mostly large islands in the Arctic Ocean off the N coast of Canada, in the Northwest Territories

**Arctic Circle** [*also* **a- c-**] an imaginary circle parallel to the equator, *c.* 66°34′ north of it

**Arctic Ocean** ocean surrounding the North Pole, north of the Arctic Circle: *c.* 5,500,000 sq. mi. (14,245,000 sq. km)

**Arc·tu·rus** (ärk toor′əs, -tyoor′-) ⟦L < Gr *Arktouros* < *arktos,* a bear + *ouros,* a guard < IE \**woros,* heedful < base \**wer*-, to heed⟧ a giant orange star in the constellation Boötes, the brightest star in the N celestial sphere, with a magnitude of -0.1

**Ar·da·bil** (ard′ə bēl′) city in NW Iran, near the Caspian Sea: pop. 222,000: also sp. **Ar′de·bil′**

**Ar·den** (ärd′'n) wooded area in Warwickshire, Eng.: the "Forest of Arden" of Shakespeare's *As You Like It*

**Ar·den–Ar·cade** (-är käd′) ⟦? after prec. & ARCADIA, place of rural peace⟧ suburb of Sacramento, in central Calif.: pop. 92,000

**Ar·dennes** (är den′) wooded plateau in NE France, S Belgium, and Luxembourg: scene of heavy fighting in World War I &, esp., at the "Battle of the Bulge" (Dec. 1944-Jan. 1945) in World War II

**A·re·ci·bo** (ä′re sē′bō) ⟦after *Arasibo,* local Indian chief⟧ seaport in N Puerto Rico: pop. 93,000

**Ar·e·op·a·gus** (ar′ē äp′ə gəs, er′-) ⟦L < Gr *Areiopagos* < *Areios,* of Ares + *pagos,* hill⟧ rocky hill northwest of the Acropolis, Athens

**A·re·qui·pa** (ä′rə kē′pə) city in S Peru: pop. 447,000

**A·rez·zo** (ä *ret*′tsō) city in Tuscany, central Italy: pop. 87,000

**Ar·gen·teuil** (*ár* zhän të′y′) city in N France, on the Seine near Paris: pop. 96,000

**Ar·gen·ti·na** (är′jən tē′nə) country in S South America: 1,070,000 sq. mi. (2,771,300 sq. km); pop. 31,186,000; cap. Buenos Aires

**Ar·gen·tine** (är′jən tēn′, -tīn′), **the** [Now Chiefly Brit.] Argentina

**Ar·go** (är′gō) ⟦L < Gr *Argō*⟧ *old name for* a large S constellation between Canis Major and Crux; Ship: now subdivided into the constellations Carina, Puppis, Pyxis, and Vela

**Ar·go·lis** (är′gə lis) region on the NE coast of the Pelo-

ponnesus, Greece: in ancient times, a region dominated by the city-state of Argos

**Ar·gonne** (är′gän′) wooded region in NE France, near
the Belgian border

**Ar·gos** (är′gäs′, -gəs) ancient city-state in the NE Peloponnesus: it dominated the Peloponnesus from the 7th
cent. B.C. until the rise of Sparta

**Ar·go·vie** (ȧr gô vē′) *Fr. name of* AARGAU

**Ar·gyll** (är′gil) former county of W Scotland, now combined with Bute as a district (**Argyll and Bute**) in the
region of Strathclyde: also **Ar′gyll·shire′** (-shir′)

**År·hus** (ôr′hōōs′) seaport in E Jutland, Denmark, on the
Kattegat: pop. 252,000

**A·ri·ca** (ə rē′kə) seaport in N Chile, just south of the
Peru border: pop. 123,000: see also TACNA

**Ar·i·el** (er′ē əl, ar′-) ‖ < Gr(Ec) *ariēl* < Heb *ariel*, lion of
God: a name applied to Jerusalem in the Bible ‖ a
satellite of the planet Uranus

**Ar·i·es** (er′ēz′, ar′-; -ē ēz′) ‖ L, the Ram ‖ **1** a N constellation between Pisces and Taurus **2** the first sign of
the zodiac, entered by the sun about March 21

**Ar·i·ma·the·a, Ar·i·ma·thae·a** (ar′ə mə thē′ə) town in
ancient Palestine, possibly in Samaria

**A·rim·i·num** (ə rim′ə nəm) *ancient name of* RIMINI

**Ariz** *abbrev. for* Arizona

**Ar·i·zo·na** (ar′ə zō′nə, er′-) ‖ AmSp < Papago *Arizonac*,
lit., little springs ‖ State of the SW U.S., on the Mexican border: admitted, 1912; 113,909 sq. mi. (295,023
sq. km); pop. 3,665,000; cap. Phoenix: abbrev. *AZ* or
*Ariz*

**Ark** *abbrev. for* Arkansas

**Ar·kan·sas** (är′kən sô′) ‖ < Fr (*la rivière des*) *Arkansas*
< Illinois *Akansea, Akansa,* Quapaw (a Siouan people
of this river valley) ‖ **1** State of the SC U.S.: admitted,
1836; 53,104 sq. mi. (137,539 sq. km); pop. 2,351,000;
cap. Little Rock: abbrev. *AR* or *Ark* **2** river flowing
from Colorado southeast into the Mississippi: 1,450
mi. (2,333 km)

**Ar·khan·gelsk** (är khän′gelsk′) seaport in NW Russia,
at the mouth of the Northern Dvina river: pop.
408,000

**Arles** (ärlz; *Fr* ȧrl) city in SE France, on the Rhone: pop.
42,000

**Ar·ling·ton** (är′liŋ tən) ‖ orig. after an Eng place name ‖

**1** urban county in NE Va., across the Potomac from Washington, D.C.: pop. 171,000: site of a national cemetery (**Arlington National Cemetery**) **2** suburb of Boston, in E Mass.: pop. 45,000 **3** city in NE Tex.: suburb of Fort Worth: pop. 262,000

**Arlington Heights** ⟦after ARLINGTON, Va.⟧ village in NE Ill.: suburb of Chicago: pop. 75,000

**Ar·magh** (är mä′) district in S Northern Ireland, in the N part of a former, much larger county also called **Armagh**

**Ar·ma·vir** (är′mə vir′) city in SW Russia, in the Caucasus, on the Kuban River: pop. 168,000

**Ar·me·ni·a¹** (är mēn′yə, -mē′nē ə) **1** region & former kingdom of W Asia, south of the Caucasus Mts.: now divided between Turkey, Iran, and present-day Armenia **2** ARMENIAN SOVIET SOCIALIST REPUBLIC **3** country in W Asia: became independent upon the breakup of the U.S.S.R. (1991): 11,500 sq. mi. (29,800 sq. km); pop. 3,320,000; cap. Yerevan: formerly, *Armenian Soviet Socialist Republic*

**Ar·me·ni·a²** (är mä′nē ə, -män′yə) city in WC Colombia: pop. 187,000

**Armenian Soviet Socialist Republic** a republic of the U.S.S.R.: now ARMENIA¹

**Ar·men·tières** (är′mən tirz′; *Fr* àr män tyer′) town in N France, near the Belgian border: pop. 25,000

**Ar·mor·i·ca** (är môr′i kə) region of ancient Gaul, between the mouths of the Loire and Seine rivers: invaded by Britons in the 5th cent. & thereafter known as *Brittany*

**Arn·hem** (ärn′hem′, är′nəm) city on the Rhine, in E Netherlands: pop. 128,000

**Ar·no** (är′nō) river in Tuscany, central Italy, flowing west into the Ligurian Sea; *c.* 150 mi. (240 km)

**A·roos·took** (ə rōōs′tək) ⟦< an Eastern Algonquian language: meaning unknown⟧ river in N Me., flowing into the St. John River in New Brunswick, Canada: *c.* 140 mi. (225 km)

**Ar·ran** (ar′ən) island in the Firth of Clyde, SW Scotland: 165 sq. mi. (427 sq. km)

**Ar·tois** (är twä′) historical region of N France, on the Strait of Dover

**A·ru·ba** (ə rōō′bə) self-governing island in the Caribbean, off the NW coast of Venezuela, under the protection of the Netherlands: formerly (until 1986) part of the Netherlands Antilles: 74 sq. mi. (193 sq. km); pop. 67,000

**A·ru Islands** (ä'roō) group of islands of Indonesia, part of the Moluccas, in the Arafura Sea southwest of New Guinea: *c.* 3,300 sq. mi. (8,547 sq. km)

**Ar·u·na·chal Pra·desh** (är'ə näch'əl prə desh') territory of NE India, on the borders of Tibet & Myanmar: 32,270 sq. mi. (83,578 sq. km); pop. 628,000

**Ar·vad·a** (är vad'ə) ⟦after Hiram *Arvada* Haskins, a member of the founding family⟧ city in NC Colo.: suburb of Denver: pop. 89,000

**AS** *abbrev. for* American Samoa

**A·sa·hi·ka·wa** (ä sä'hē kä'wə) city in central Hokkaido, Japan: pop. 361,000

**A·san·sol** (äs'ən sōl) city in NE India, in the state of West Bengal: pop. 365,000

**As·bur·y Park** (az'ber'ē, -bər-) ⟦after Francis *Asbury* (1745-1816), 1st Methodist bishop in U.S.⟧ city in EC N.J., on the Atlantic: an ocean resort: pop. 17,000

**As·cen·sion** (ə sen'shən) ⟦so named because discovered on *Ascension Day* (1501)⟧ small island in the S Atlantic: part of the British territory of St. Helena: 34 sq. mi. (88 sq. km); pop. 1,700

**As·gard** (äs'gärd') ⟦ON *Āsgarthr* < *āss*, a god + *garthr*, yard < IE *\*gherdh-*, to enclose, surround < base *\*ǵher-*, to grasp, contain⟧ *Norse Myth.* the home of the gods and slain heroes: also **As·garth** (äs'gärth')

**A·shan·ti** (ə shän'tē, -shan'-) region in central Ghana: orig. a native kingdom, it was a protectorate in the Gold Coast from 1901 to 1957: 9,417 sq. mi. (24,390 sq. km); pop. 2,090,000; cap. Kumasi

**Ashe·ville** (ash'vil') ⟦after Samuel *Ashe* (1725-1813), gov. of N.C.⟧ city in W N.C.: pop. 62,000

**Ash·ke·lon** (ash'kə län') *alt. sp. of* ASHQELON

**Ash·kha·bad** (äsh'khä bäd') capital of Turkmenistan, in the SC part, near the Iranian border: pop. 356,000

**Ash·qe·lon** (ash'kə län') city in SW Israel, on the Mediterranean: pop. 43,000: nearby is the site of an ancient city-state (often sp. *Ashkelon*) of the Philistines, 12th cent. B.C. (cf. 1 Sam. 6:17; Jer. 25:20)

**Ash·ton–un·der–Lyne** (ash'tən un'dər lin') city in NW England, near Manchester: pop. 50,000

**A·shur** (ä'shoor') ⟦Akkadian⟧ **1** ancient Sumerian city

on the upper Tigris River in what is now N Iraq: the
orig. capital of Assyria **2** *orig. name of* ASSYRIA

**A·sia** (ā′zhə; *chiefly Brit*, -shə) ⟦L < Gᴦ < ? Akkadian
*āṣū*, to rise (of the sun), go out⟧ largest continent,
situated in the Eastern Hemisphere, bounded by the
Arctic, Pacific, and Indian oceans, and separated from
N Europe by the Ural Mountains: it includes, in addition to the nations on the land mass, Japan, the Philippines, Taiwan, Malaysia, & Indonesia: *c.* 17,140,000
sq. mi. (44,390,000 sq. km); pop. *c.* 2,633,000,000

**Asia Minor** large peninsula in W Asia, between the
Black Sea and the Mediterranean, including Asiatic
Turkey west of an undefined line from the Gulf of
Iskenderun to the Black Sea: cf. ANATOLIA

**A·sir** (ä sir′) region of SW Saudi Arabia, on the Red Sea,
now constituting the Southern Province

**As·ke·lon, As·ka·lon** (äs′kə län′) ASHQELON

**As·ma·ra** (äs mä′rä) capital of Eritrea, in the W part:
pop. 275,000

**As·niè·res–sur–Seine** (à nyeʀ süʀ sen′) city in N
France, on the Seine: suburb of Paris: pop. 75,000

**A·so** (ä′sō) a large volcanic crater in central Kyushu,
Japan, with five cones: highest cone, 5,223 ft. (1,592
m); crater, *c.* 15 mi. (24 km) wide: also **A′so–san′**
(-sän′)

**As·pen Hill** (as′pən) ⟦in allusion to the aspens which
grow there in abundance⟧ suburb of Washington,
D.C., in central Md.: pop. 45,000

**As·sam** (a sam′, as′am) state of NE India, south of Bhutan, west of Myanmar, & almost completely separated
from the rest of India by Bangladesh: 30,318 sq. mi.
(78,523 sq. km); pop. 19,903,000

**As·shur** (ä′shoor′) *alt. sp. of* ASHUR

**As·sin·i·boine** (ə sin′ə boin′) ⟦< Fr < Ojibwa *asinii-
bwaan*, lit., stone Sioux⟧ river in SC Canada flowing
from E Saskatchewan through S Manitoba into the
Red River at Winnipeg: *c.* 600 mi. (966 km)

**As·si·si** (ə sē′zē, -sē′sē; *It* äs sē′zē) town in Umbria, central Italy: birthplace of St. Francis: pop. 25,000

**As·siut** (ä syoot′) *alt. sp. of* ASYUT

**As·suan** (ä swän′) *alt. sp. of* ASWAN

**As·sur** (ä′soor) *var. of* Ashur

**As·syr·i·a** (ə sir′ē ə) ancient empire in SW Asia in the
region of the upper Tigris River: at its height (7th

cent. B.C.), it extended from the head of the Persian
Gulf to Egypt and Asia Minor: original cap. Ashur;
later cap. Nineveh

**As·ti** (äs′tē) city in Piedmont, NW Italy: center of a
winegrowing region: pop. 77,000

**As·tor·i·a** (as tôr′ē ə) ⟦after John Jacob *Astor* (1763-
1848), who founded a trading post on the site (1811)⟧
seaport in NW Oreg., on the Columbia River: pop.
10,000

**As·tra·khan** (as′trə kan′; *Russ* äs′trə khän′y′) city &
port in SW Russia, on the Volga River delta near the
Caspian Sea: pop. 493,000

**As·tu·ri·as** (as toor′ē əs; *Sp* äs tōōr′yäs) region of NW
Spain, on the Bay of Biscay: formerly (8th-9th cent.),
a kingdom: 4,079 sq. mi. (10,565 sq. km); pop.
1,127,000; cap. Oviedo

**A·sun·ción** (ä soon syôn′) capital of Paraguay, a port on
the Paraguay River: pop. (of met. area) 708,000

**As·wan** (äs wän′, as-; as′wän′) city in S Egypt, on the
Nile: pop. 144,000: three miles (4.5 km) south is a dam
(completed 1902) providing irrigation for the surrounding region: a larger dam (**Aswan High Dam**, completed 1970) is four miles (6.5 km) farther south

**As·yut** (ä syōōt′) city in central Egypt, on the Nile: pop.
214,000

**A·ta·ca·ma Desert** (ä′tä kä′mä) desert area in N Chile:
its nitrate deposits were once a chief source of the
world's supply: 30,000 sq. mi. (77,000 sq. km)

**At·ba·ra** (ät′bä *r*ä) river flowing from N Ethiopia into
the Nile in NE Sudan: 500 mi. (800 km)

**Ath·a·bas·ca** (ath′ə bas′kə) ⟦Cree dial. *ahthapaskaaw*,
name of lake, lit., there are reeds here and there <
*ahthap-*, net(like) + *-ask-*, vegetation + formative suf-
fixes⟧ **1** river rising in the Rocky Mountains of SW
Alberta, Canada, and flowing northeast into Lake Athabasca: 765 mi. (1,231 km) **2 Lake** lake extending
across the N Alberta-Saskatchewan border: 3,100 sq.
mi. (8,000 sq. km)

**Ath·e·nae·um, Ath·e·ne·um** (ath′ə nē′əm) ⟦LL *Ath-
enaeum* < Gr *Athēnaion*⟧ the temple of Athena at
Athens, where writers and scholars met

**Ath·ens** (ath′ənz) **1** capital of Greece, in the SE part:
pop. 886,000: Athens became established as the center
of Greek culture in the 5th cent. B.C., when it was the

capital of ancient Attica **2** 〖after the Greek capital; in allusion to its learning and culture, because of the University of Georgia〗 city in NE Ga.: pop. 46,000

**A·thi·nai** (ä thē′ne) *modern Gr. name of* ATHENS

**Ath·os** (ath′äs, ā′thäs) **1 Mount** autonomous monastic district occupying the tip of the easternmost prong of the Chalcidice peninsula, NE Greece: 130 sq. mi. (336 sq. km); pop. 1,470 **2 Mount** mountain, in this district: 6,670 ft. (2,030 m)

**At·lan·ta** (at lan′tə) 〖after Western & *Atlantic* Railroad, of which it was the terminus〗 capital of Ga., in the NC part: pop. 394,000 (met. area 2,834,000)

**At·lan·tic** (at lan′tik) 〖L *Atlanticum* (mare), Atlantic (ocean) < *Atlanticus*, of the Atlas Mountains < *Atlas*, the Titan in Greek mythology who supported the heavens on his shoulders〗 ocean touching the American continents to the west and Europe and Africa to the east: *c.* 31,800,000 sq. mi. (82,362,000 sq. km); greatest known depth, *c.* 28,000 ft. (8,500 m)

**Atlantic City** city in SE N.J., on the Atlantic: an ocean resort: pop. 38,000

**At·lan·tis** (at lan′tis) 〖L < Gr〗 legendary island or continent supposed to have existed in the Atlantic west of Gibraltar and to have sunk into the ocean

**At·las Mountains** (at′ləs) mountain system in NW Africa, extending *c.* 1,500 mi. (2,400 km) across Morocco, Algeria, and Tunisia: highest peak (in Morocco), *c.* 13,600 ft. (4,150 m)

**At·ti·ca** (at′i kə) 〖Gr *Attikē*〗 **1** state of ancient Greece, occupying a peninsula in the SE part &, after the 5th cent. B.C., a region dominated by Athens **2** region of modern Greece, in the same general area

**At·tu** (at′o͞o) westernmost island of the Aleutians: 338 sq. mi. (875 sq. km)

**Au·ber·vil·liers** (ō ber vē lyä′) city in France: NE suburb of Paris: pop. 73,000

**Auck·land** (ôk′lənd) seaport of N North Island, New Zealand: pop. of urban area 894,000

**Augs·burg** (ôgz′bərg; *Ger* ouks′bo͞ork) city in S Germany, in the state of Bavaria: pop. 246,000

**Au·gus·ta** (ô gus′tə, ə-) **1** 〖after *Augusta* (*c.* 1719-72), Princess of Wales & mother of George III〗 city in E Ga., on the Savannah River: pop. 45,000 (met. area with nearby South Carolina, 397,000) **2** 〖prob. after

Pamela *Augusta* Dearborn, daughter of a general in the Am Revolution ‖ capital of Me., on the Kennebec River: pop. 21,000

**Au·rang·a·bad** (ou ruŋ′ə bäd′) city in WC India, in Maharashtra state: pop. 316,000

**Au·ri·ga** (ô rī′gə) ‖ME < L, lit., charioteer < *aurea*, bridle + *agere*, to drive < IE base *ag̃-‖ a N constellation between Perseus and Gemini

**Au·ro·ra** (ô rôr′ə, ə-) ‖after the Gr goddess of dawn, prob. because of pleasant connotations ‖ 1 city in NC Colo., near Denver: pop. 222,000 2 ‖after the goddess‖ city in NE Ill., near Chicago: pop. 100,000

**Ausch·witz** (oush′vits′) city in S Poland: pop. 45,000: in World War II, site of a Nazi concentration camp notorious as an extermination center: Pol. name Oświęcim

**Aus·ter·litz** (ôs′tər lits′; *Ger* ou′stər lits) town in SE Czech Republic, near Brno: scene of Napoleon's victory (1805) over the combined Russian and Austrian armies: Czech name Slavkov

**Aus·tin** (ôs′tən) ‖after Stephen *Austin*, founder of first Am colony in Tex. in early 1820's ‖ capital of Tex., on the Colorado River: pop. 466,000 (met. area 782,000)

**Aus·tral·a·sia** (ôs′trə lā′zhə) 1 generally, the islands of the SW Pacific 2 Australia, New Zealand, New Guinea, the Malay Archipelago, and all islands south of the equator and between E longitudes 100 and 180 3 Oceania

**Aus·tral·ia** (ô strāl′yə) ‖ModL < L (*terra*) *australis*, southern (land) ‖ 1 island continent in the Southern Hemisphere between the S Pacific and Indian oceans 2 country comprising this continent and Tasmania: a member of the Commonwealth: 2,967,907 sq. mi. (7,686,848 sq. km); pop. 15,793,000; cap. Canberra: official name **Commonwealth of Australia**

**Australian Alps** mountain range in SE Austtalia, in the states of Victoria and New South Wales: S end of the Great Dividing Range: highest peak, Mt. Kosciusko

**Australian Antarctic Territory** region in Antarctica, claimed by Australia, between E longitudes 45 and 160, exclusive of the Adélie Coast

**Australian Capital Territory** federal territory in the SE part of New South Wales: site of Canberra, Australian capital: 939 sq. mi. (2,432 sq. km); pop. 245,000

**Aus·tra·sia** (ôs trā′zhə) ‖ML < OHG *ostarrih*: see fol.‖

easternmost part of the kingdom of the Merovingian Franks from the 6th to the 8th cent., composed of what is now NE France, Belgium, and W Germany

**Aus·tri·a** (ôs′trē ə) ⟦ML < OHG *ostarrih* < *ostan*, east + *rihhi*, realm⟧ country in central Europe: 32,369 sq. mi. (83,835 sq. km); pop. 7,546,000; cap. Vienna

**Aus·tri·a–Hun·ga·ry** (-huŋ′gə rē) former monarchy in central Europe (1867-1918) consisting of territory that became Austria, Hungary, and Czechoslovakia, as well as parts of Poland, Romania, Yugoslavia, and Italy

**Aus·tro·ne·sia** (ôs′trō nē′zhə) ⟦< ModE *austro-*, southern < L *auster*, the south + Gr *nēsos*, island + suffix *-ia*⟧ the islands of the central and S Pacific

**Au·vergne** (ō vʉrn′; Fr ō ver′ny′) 1 historical region of SC France 2 metropolitan region in SC France: 10,044 sq. mi. (26,013 sq. km); pop. 1,335,000; chief city, Clermont-Ferrand 3 mountain range running north to south through this region: highest peak, 6,188 ft. (1,886 m): in full **Auvergne Mountains**

**Av·a·lon, Av·al·lon** (av′ə län′) ⟦Fr < ML *Avallonis* (*insula*) < Welsh (*ynys yr*) *Afallon*, (island of) apples⟧ *Celt. Legend* the isle of the dead, an island paradise in the west where King Arthur and other heroes are taken after death

**Avalon Peninsula** peninsula forming the SE corner of Newfoundland, Canada

**A·vel·la·ne·da** (ä ve′yä ne′*th*ä; *locally, also* ä ve′zhä-) city in E Argentina, on the Río de la Plata: suburb of Buenos Aires: pop. 330,000

**Av·en·tine** (av′en tīn′, -tēn′) *see* SEVEN HILLS OF ROME

**A·vi·gnon** (á vē nyō*n*′) city in SE France, on the Rhone River: seat of the papacy (1309-77): pop. 91,000

**Áv·i·la** (äv′i lə) city of central Spain, WNW of Madrid: pop. 86,000

**A·von** (ā′vən, -vän′; av′ən) 1 county of SW England, on the Severn estuary & Bristol Channel: 517 sq. mi. (1,338 sq. km); pop. 940,000; county seat, Bristol 2 any of three rivers in S & SW England, esp. the one flowing from Northamptonshire into the Severn, on which lies Stratford, Shakespeare's birthplace: 96 mi. (155 km)

**Ax·um** (äk′sŏŏm) *alt. sp. of* AKSUM

**A·ya·cu·cho** (ä′yä kŏŏ′chô) city in SC Peru: site of a battle (1824) which marked the end of Spanish rule in

South America: pop. 69,000

**Ayr** (er, ar) **1** former county of SW Scotland, now in the region of Strathclyde **2** seaport in SW Scotland, on the Firth of Clyde: pop. 49,000

**Ayr·shire** (-shir) Ayr (the county)

**A·yut·tha·ya** (ä yōō′tä yä) city in central Thailand, on the Chao Phraya River: capital (1350-1767) of a former Thai kingdom: pop. 47,000: in full **Phra Na·khon Si Ayutthaya** (prä′nä kôn′sē)

**AZ** *abbrev. for* Arizona

**Az·er·bai·jan** (äz′ər bī jän′, az′-) **1** region of NW Iran **2** Azerbaijan Soviet Socialist Republic **3** country in W Asia, south of the Caucasus Mountains: became independent upon the breakup of the U.S.S.R. (1991): 33,430 sq. mi. (86,580 sq. km); pop. 6,614,000; cap. Baku: formerly, *Azerbaijan Soviet Socialist Republic*

**Azerbaijan Soviet Socialist Republic** a republic of the U.S.S.R.: now Azerbaijan

**A·zores** (ā′zôrz′, ə zôrz′) group of islands in the N Atlantic, *c.* 800 mi. (1,200 km) west of Portugal and constituting an autonomous region of that country: 905 sq. mi. (2,344 sq. km); pop. 251,000; chief city, Ponta Delgada

**A·zov** (ā′zôf; *Russ* ä′zôf), **Sea of** northern arm of the Black Sea, in SE Europe: *c.* 14,000 sq. mi. (36,260 sq. km)

# B

**Baal·bek** (bäl′bek′) town in NE Lebanon: pop. 16,000: site of ruins of Heliopolis

**Ba·bel** (bā′bəl, bab′əl) ⟦Heb *bavel* < Akkadian *bābilu*, altered (by folk-etym. assoc. with *bāb*, gate & *ili* god) < pre-Akkadian city name *babila*, Babylon⟧ *Bible* a city in Shinar in which Noah's descendants tried to build a very high tower to reach heaven and were prevented by God from doing so by a confusion of tongues: Gen. 11:1-9

**Bab el Man·deb** (bab′ el man′deb′) strait joining the Red Sea and the Gulf of Aden: 20 mi. (32 km) wide

**Bab·y·lon** (bab′ə lən, -län′) ⟦L < Gr *Babylōn* < Heb *bavel*: see Babel⟧ ancient city on the lower Euphrates River (in what is now central Iraq), the capital of Babylonia: noted for wealth, luxury, and wickedness

**Bab·y·lo·ni·a** (bab′ə lō′nē ə) ⟦ L < Gr *Babylōnia* < *Babylōn*: see prec. ⟧ ancient empire in SW Asia, in the lower valley of the Tigris & Euphrates rivers: it flourished *c.* 2100-689 B.C. and again, as Chaldea or "New Babylonia," *c.* 625-538 B.C.

**Ba·cău** (bə kou′) city in Moldavia, E Romania: pop. 157,000

**Back** (bak) ⟦ after George *Back* (1796-1878), Arctic navigator ⟧ river in central Northwest Territories, Canada, flowing NE into the Arctic Ocean: *c.* 600 mi. (965 km)

**Ba·co·lod** (bä kō′lôd) seaport on Negros island, the Philippines: pop. 262,000

**Bac·tri·a** (bak′trē ə) ancient country between the Hindu Kush & the Oxus River in what is now NE Afghanistan (fl. 250-130 B.C.)

**Ba·da·joz** (bä′*th*ä hôth′) city in SW Spain, on the Guadiana at the border of Portugal: pop. 114,000

**Ba·da·lo·na** (bä′*th*ä lō′nä) seaport in NE Spain, on the Mediterranean: suburb of Barcelona: pop. 228,000

**Ba·den** (bäd′′n) **1** region of SW Germany that, since the 12th cent., has taken the form of several political units, including duchy, electorate, state of West Germany, etc.: now mostly in the state of Baden-Württemberg **2** BADEN-BADEN

**Baden–Baden** city in SW Germany, in the state of Baden-Württemberg: a health resort: pop. 50,000

**Baden–Würt·tem·berg** (-wurt′əm burg′; *Ger*, vür′təm berk′) state of SW Germany: 13,800 sq. mi. (35,750 sq. km); pop. 9,243,000; cap. Stuttgart

**Badg·er State** (baj′ər) *name for* WISCONSIN

**Bad·lands** (bad′landz′) barren plateau in SW South Dakota east of the Black Hills; marked by dramatically eroded hills and containing many fossil deposits: part has been reserved as the **Badlands National Monument**

**Baf·fin** (baf′in) **1** island off the NE coast of Canada, north of Hudson Strait: largest in Canadian Arctic: *c.* 183,800 sq. mi. (476,000 sq. km) **2** Region of Northwest Territories, Canada, in the N & E part: 393,009 sq. mi. (1,017,889 sq. km)

**Baffin Bay** ⟦ after William *Baffin* (1584-1622), its Eng discoverer ⟧ arm of the N Atlantic, between Greenland & Baffin Island

**Bagh·dad** (bag′dad, bäg däd′) capital of Iraq, on the

Tigris River: pop. 2,184,000: as the capital of a caliphate, it flourished (8th-9th cent.) as a commercial & cultural center and the chief city of Islam: also sp. **Bag′dad**

**Ba·gui·o** (bä′gē ō′; *Sp* bä′gyồ) city in NW Luzon: summer capital of the Philippines: pop. 119,000

**Ba·ha·mas** (bə hä′məz, -hä′-) country on a group of islands (**Bahama Islands**) in the West Indies, southeast of Fla. & north of Cuba: formerly a British possession, it became independent (1973) & a member of the Commonwealth: 5,380 sq. mi. (13,934 sq. km); pop. 235,000; cap. Nassau: official name **Commonwealth of the Bahamas**

**Ba·hi·a** (bə hē′ə; *Port* bä ē′ə) state on the EC coast of Brazil: 216,613 sq. mi. (561,026 sq. km); pop. 10,731,000; cap. Salvador

**Ba·hí·a Blan·ca** (bä ē′ə bläŋ′kä) seaport on the E coast of central Argentina: pop. 233,000

**Bah·rain** (bä rān′) country on a group of islands in the Persian Gulf, between Qatar & the E coast of Saudi Arabia: formerly a British protectorate, it became an independent state (1971) & a member of the Commonwealth: 260 sq. mi. (676 sq. km); pop. 422,000; cap. Manama: also sp. **Bah·rein**

**Ba·ia–Ma·re** (bä′yə mär′ə) city in NW Romania: pop. 124,000

**Bai·kal** (bī käl′), **Lake** large lake in SE Siberia: deepest lake in the world, *c.* 5,700 ft. (1,737 m): *c.* 12,000 sq. mi. (31,080 sq. km)

**Baile Atha Cliath** (blä′klē′ə) *Gael. name of* DUBLIN

**Ba·ja Ca·li·for·nia** (bä′hä kä′lē fôr′nyä) 〚*Sp*, lit., lower California〛 peninsula in Mexico, between the Pacific & the Gulf of California: divided into a northern state (**Baja California**): 26,997 sq. mi. (69,921 sq. km); pop. 1,321,000; cap. Mexicali; and a southern state (**Baja California Sur**): 28,369 sq. mi. (73,475 sq. km); pop. 249,000; cap. La Paz: also [Colloq.] **the Baja**

**Bak·ers·field** (bä′kərz fēld′) 〚after Col. T. *Baker,* early landowner〛 city in SC Calif.: pop. 175,000

**Bakh·ta·ran** (bak′tə rän′) city in W Iran: pop. 531,000

**Ba·ku** (bä kōō′) capital of Azerbaijan: port on the Caspian Sea: pop. 1,693,000

**Ba·la·kla·va** (bäl′ə klä′və) seaport in the Crimea, now part of Sevastopol: site of the incident (1854) in the

Crimean War celebrated in Alfred, Lord Tennyson's "Charge of the Light Brigade"

**Bal·ance** (bal′əns) Libra, the constellation and seventh sign of the zodiac

**Ba·la·ton** (bä′lä tôn), **Lake** lake in W Hungary: largest lake in central Europe: *c.* 230 sq. mi. (595 sq. km)

**Bal·bo·a** (bal bō′ə) seaport in Panama, at the Pacific entrance to the Panama Canal: pop. 2,000

**Bald·win Park** (bôld′win) 〖after E. J. *Baldwin,* local rancher〗 city in SW Calif.: suburb of Los Angeles: pop. 69,000

**Bâle** (bäl) *Fr. name of* BASEL

**Ba·le·a·res** (bä′le ä′res) region of Spain comprising the Balearic Islands: 1,935 sq. mi. (5,014 sq. km); pop. 685,000; cap. Palma

**Bal·e·ar·ic Islands** (bal′ē er′ik) group of islands in the W Mediterranean, off the E coast of Spain: see BALEARES

**Ba·li** (bä′lē, bal′ē) island of Indonesia, east of Java: 2,173 sq. mi. (5,623 sq. km); pop. 2,470,000

**Ba·li·ke·sir** (bäl′i ke sir′) city in NW Asiatic Turkey: pop. 124,000

**Bal·kan Mountains** (bôl′ken) mountain range extending across central Bulgaria, from the W border to the Black Sea: highest peak, *c.* 7,800 ft. (2,377 m)

**Balkan Peninsula** peninsula in SE Europe, between the Adriatic & Ionian seas on the west & the Black & Aegean seas on the east

**Balkans** countries of the Balkan Peninsula (Yugoslavia, Slovenia, Croatia, Bosnia and Herzegovina, Macedonia, Bulgaria, Albania, Greece, & the European part of Turkey) & Romania: also **Balkan States**

**Balkh** (bälkh) town in N Afghanistan: site of an ancient city that flourished as the capital of Bactria &, later (7th-13th cent.), as a center of Islam

**Bal·khash** (bäl khäsh′), **Lake** large lake in SE Kazakhstan, half saline & half freshwater, the halves separated by a sandbar: *c.* 6,500 sq. mi. (16,835 sq. km)

**Bal·la·rat** (bal′ə rat′) city in SC Victoria, Australia: pop. 63,000

**Bal·sas** (bäl′säs) river in SC Mexico, flowing into the Pacific: *c.* 450 mi. (725 km): in full **Río (de las) Balsas**

**Bal·tic Sea** (bôl′tik) sea in N Europe, south & east of the Scandinavian Peninsula, west of the Baltic States, & north of Poland, connecting with the North Sea through the Kattegat & Skaggerak: *c.* 160,000 sq. mi. (414,400 sq. km)

**Baltic States** countries on the Baltic Sea (Latvia, Lithuania, & Estonia)

**Bal·ti·more** (bôl′tə môr; *locally*, -mər) [after Lord *Baltimore* (*c.* 1580-1632), Eng statesman, founder of Maryland] seaport in N Md., on an arm of Chesapeake Bay: pop. 736,000 (met. area 2,382,000)

**Ba·lu·chi·stan** (bə lōō′chə stan′, -stän′) region in SW Pakistan and SE Iran, on the Arabian Sea

**Ba·ma·ko** (bä mä kō′) capital of Mali, in the SW part: port on the upper Niger River: pop. 404,000

**Ba·nat** (bä nät′) agricultural region in the Danube River basin in NE Yugoslavia & W Romania: formerly, a part of Hungary (1779-1919)

**Ban·da Sea** (bän′də) part of the S Pacific Ocean, within E Indonesia, between Celebes & New Guinea, south of most of the Molucca group

**Ban·djar·ma·sin** (bän′jər mä′sin) *alt. sp. of* Banjarmasin

**Ban·dung** (bän′dooŋ′, ban′-) city in W Java, Indonesia: pop. 1,463,000

**Banff** (bamf) **1** former county in NE Scotland, now in the region of Grampian: also **Banff′shire** (-shir) **2** [after the county, birthplace of an early pres. of the Canadian Pacific Railway] town in Banff National Park: summer & winter resort: pop. 4,000

**Banff National Park** Canadian national park on the E slopes of the Rockies, SW Alberta: 2,564 sq. mi. (6,640 sq. km)

**Ban·ga·lore** (baŋ′gə lôr′) city in S India, the capital of Karnataka state: pop. 2,914,000

**Bang·ka** (bäŋ′kä) island of Indonesia, off the SE coast of Sumatra: tin-mining center: 4,600 sq. mi. (11,910 sq. km)

**Bang·kok** (baŋ′käk′) capital of Thailand, a seaport on the Chao Phraya River, near its mouth on the Gulf of Thailand: pop. (met. area) 5,175,000

**Ban·gla·desh** (bäŋ′glə desh′, baŋ′-) country in S Asia, at the head of the Bay of Bengal: formerly (1955-71) the province of East Pakistan, it became independent (1971) & a member of the Commonwealth: 55,598 sq. mi. (143,998 sq. km); pop. 104,205,000; cap. Dhaka

**Ban·gor** (baŋ′gôr′) [prob. after a borough in Wales or

Northern Ireland, or ? after an old hymn title ] city in S Me., on the Penobscot River: pop. 33,000

**Ban·gui** (bän gē′) capital of the Central African Republic, on the Ubangi River: pop. 388,000

**Bang·we·u·lu** (baŋ′wē o͞o′lo͞o) shallow lake in N Zambia: including swamps, 3,800 sq. mi. (9,840 sq. km)

**Ba·nja Lu·ka** (bän′yə loo′kə) city in N Bosnia and Herzegovina: pop. 184,000

**Ban·jar·ma·sin** (bän′jər mä′sin) seaport in S Borneo, Indonesia, near the Java Sea: pop. 381,000

**Ban·jul** (bän′jo͞ol′) capital of Gambia, a seaport on an island at the mouth of the Gambia River: pop. 45,000

**Ban·ka** (bäŋ′kä) *alt. sp. of* BANGKA

**Banks Island** (baŋks) ⟦after Sir Joseph *Banks* (1743-1820), Eng botanist & explorer⟧ westernmost island of the Canadian Arctic: *c.* 26,000 sq. mi. (67,340 sq. km)

**Ban·nock·burn** (ban′ək bʉrn′) town in central Scotland: site of a battle (1314) in which the Scots under Robert Bruce defeated a much larger English force led by Edward II, thereby securing Scottish independence

**Bao·tou** (bou′dō′) city in the SW Inner Mongolian Autonomous Region: pop. 1,050,000

**Ba·ra·cal·do** (bar′ə käl′dō, bär′-) city in the Basque country, N Spain: pop. 117,000

**Bar·a·nof** (bar′ə nôf′) ⟦after A. A. *Baranof*, 1st gov. of the Russ colonies in America⟧ island in Alexander Archipelago, Alas.: *c.* 1,600 sq. mi. (4,144 sq. km): largest city, Sitka

**Bar·ba·dos** (bär bā′dōs, -dōz) country on the easternmost island of the West Indies: formerly (1663-1966) a British dependency, it became independent & a member of the Commonwealth (1966): 166 sq. mi. (430 sq. km); pop. 253,000; cap. Bridgetown

**Bar·ba·ry Coast** (bär′bər ē) ⟦< L *Barbaria*, lit., a foreign country < *barbarus*, barbarous < Gr *barbaros*, foreign, strange, ignorant < IE echoic base *\*barbar-*, used for unintelligible speech of foreigners⟧ **1** coastal region of N Africa, extending from Egypt to the Atlantic, inhabited chiefly by Berbers and once (until early 19th cent.) dominated by pirates: also called **Barbary** **2** ⟦after the BARBARY COAST of Africa⟧ the waterfront district in San Francisco from the gold rush of 1849 to the earthquake of 1906, known for its saloons, gambling places, & brothels

**Barbary States** semi-independent Turkish provinces along the coast of N Africa (16th-19th cent.); Tripolitania, Tunisia, Algeria, & Morocco

**Bar·bu·da** (bär bōō'də) island of the Leeward group in the West Indies: 62 sq. mi. (161 sq. km): see ANTIGUA AND BARBUDA

**Bar·ce·lo·na** (bär'sə lō'nə) **1** seaport in NE Spain, on the Mediterranean: pop. 1,757,000 **2** city in N Venezuela: pop. 284,000

**Ba·reil·ly, Ba·re·li** (bə rā'lē) city in Uttar Pradesh, N India: pop. 438,000

**Bar·ents Sea** (bar'ənts, bär'-) part of the Arctic Ocean, north of Norway & W Russia, between Svalbard & Novaya Zemlya

**Bar Harbor** ⟦ after a sand bar connecting Mount Desert I. with a nearby island ⟧ resort town on Mount Desert Island, Me.: pop. 4,400

**Ba·ri** (bä'rē) seaport in SE Italy, on the Adriatic: pop. 368,000

**Ba·ri·sal** (bar'ə sôl') river port in S Bangladesh, in the Ganges delta: pop. 142,000

**Bar·king** (bär'kiŋ) former municipal borough of SE England: now, with Dagenham, constituting a borough (**Barking and Dagenham**) of Greater London: pop. 149,000

**Bar·na·ul** (bär'nä ōōl') city in SC Russia, on the Ob River: pop. 578,000

**Bar·net** (bär'nət) borough of Greater London, England: pop. 298,000

**Barns·ley** (bärnz'lē) city in NC England: pop. 226,000

**Ba·ro·da** (bə rō'də) *old name of* VADODARA

**Bar·qui·si·me·to** (bär kē'sē mä'tô) city in NW Venezuela: pop. 504,000

**Bar·ran·quil·la** (bä'rän kē'yä) seaport in NW Colombia, on the Magdalena River: pop. 1,121,000

**Bar·rie** (bar'ē) city in SE Ontario, Canada: pop. 48,000

**Bar·row** (bar'ō, ber'-), **Point** ⟦ after Sir John *Barrow* (1764-1848), Eng geographer: he promoted Arctic exploration ⟧ northernmost point of Alas.: cape on the Arctic Ocean

**Bar·row-in-Fur·ness** (bar'ō in fur'nəs, ber'-) seaport in SW Cumbria, England, on the Irish Sea: pop. 65,000

**Ba·sel** (bä'zəl) **1** city in NW Switzerland, on the Rhine: pop. 176,000 **2** canton of NW Switzerland: 179 sq. mi.

(465 sq. km); pop. 421,000: divided into two politically independent half-cantons

**Ba·shan** (bā′shan) *Bible* fertile region east & northeast of the Sea of Galilee, in ancient Palestine

**Ba·si·lan** (bä sē′län) largest island of the Sulu Archipelago, the Philippines, Southwest of Mindanao: 495 sq. mi. (1,282 sq. km)

**Bas·il·don** (baz′əl dən) city in SE England, in Essex; pop. 160,000

**Ba·sil·i·ca·ta** (bä sē′lē kä′tä) region in S Italy, on the Gulf of Taranto: 3,858 sq. mi. (9,992 sq. km); pop. 617,000

**Basle** (bäl) *old name of* BASEL

**Basque Country** (bask, bäsk), **The** region comprising three provinces in N Spain, on the Bay of Biscay, inhabited by Basques: 2,803 sq. mi. (7,261 sq. km): pop. 2,135,000: also called **Basque Provinces**

**Bas·ra** (bus′rə, buz′-) port in SE Iraq, at the head of the Shatt al Arab: pop. 334,000: Arabic name **Al′-Bas′rah** (al′-)

**Bas·sein** (bə sān′) river port in S Myanmar, on the Irrawaddy delta: pop. 356,000

**Basse-Nor·man·die** (bås nôr män dē′) metropolitan region of NW France, on the English Channel, including the historic region of Normandy: 6,791 sq. mi. (17,589 sq. km); pop. 1,361,000; chief city, Caen

**Basse·terre** (bäs ter′) seaport on St. Kitts island in the Leeward Islands, West Indies: capital of St. Kitts and Nevis: pop. 15,000

**Basse-Terre** (bäs ter′) **1** W island of the two major islands of Guadeloupe, West Indies: 327 sq. mi. (848 sq. km) **2** seaport on this island: capital of Guadeloupe: pop. 16,000

**Bass Strait** (bas) strait separating Victoria, SE Australia from Tasmania: 80-150 mi. (130-240 km) wide

**Bas·tille** (bas tēl′), **the** a state prison in Paris that was stormed and destroyed (1789) in the French Revolution: its destruction is commemorated on Bastille Day, July 14

**Bas·togne** (bas tōn′; *Fr* bå stôn′y′) town in SE Belgium: besieged by the German Army (Dec. 1944-Jan. 1945) during a counteroffensive in World War II, but relieved after fierce fighting (Battle of the Bulge)

**Ba·su·to·land** (bə sōōt′ō land′) *old name of* LESOTHO

**Ba·taan** (bə tan′, -tän′) peninsula on SW Luzon, the Philippines: in World War II (1942), scene of a Japanese victory over American-Philippine forces, marking the completion of the Japanese conquest of the Philippines

**Ba·tan·gas** (bə taŋ′gəs, -täŋ′-) city on the S coast of Luzon, the Philippines: pop. 144,000

**Ba·ta·vi·a** (bə tä′vē ə) *old name of* JAKARTA

**Bath** (bath, bäth) city in SW England: pop. 83,000: health resort known for its hot springs

**Bath·urst** (bath′ərst, bäth′-) *old name of* BANJUL

**Bat·na** (bat′nə) city in NE Algeria: pop. 123,000

**Bat·on Rouge** (bat″n ro͞ozh′) ‖ Fr transl. of Choctaw *ítuúma*, red pole, a boundary mark, prob. between the hunting grounds of two tribes ‖ capital of La., on the Mississippi: pop. 220,000

**Bat·ter·sea** (bat′ər sē) former district of London, on the south bank of the Thames, now part of Wandsworth

**Bat·ter·y** (bat′ər ē) **the** a park in New York City, at the S tip of Manhattan: 21 acres: also called **Battery Park**

**Ba·tu·mi** (bä to͞o′mē) seaport in Georgia, on the Black Sea, near the Turkish border: pop. 123,000: formerly called **Ba·tum′** (-to͞om′)

**Bat–Yam** (bät′yäm′) city in W Israel, on the Mediterranean, near Tel Aviv: pop. 129,000

**Ba·var·i·a** (bə ver′ē ə) state of SW Germany: formerly (1918-33) a republic and, before that, a duchy, an electorate, & a kingdom with varying boundaries: 27,241 sq. mi. (70,553 sq. km); pop. 10,966,000; cap. Munich

**Ba·ya·món** (bä′yä mōn′) city in NE Puerto Rico, near San Juan: pop. 220,000

**Bay City** ‖ from its location at the head of Saginaw *Bay* ‖ city in E Mich.: pop. 39,000

**Bay·ern** (bī′ərn) *Ger. name of* BAVARIA

**Bay·kal** (bī käl′), **Lake** *var. of* Lake BAIKAL

**Ba·yonne** (bä yōn′) **1** city in SW France: pop. 43,000 **2** ‖ after city in France, ? infl. by its location on a bay ‖ city in NE N.J., on Newark Bay: pop. 61,000

**Bay·reuth** (bī roit′, bī′roit) city in SE Germany, in the state of Bavaria: known for its annual Wagnerian music festivals, begun in 1876: pop. 71,000

**Bay State** *name for* MASSACHUSETTS

**Bay·town** (bā′toun′) city in SE Tex., on Galveston Bay, near Houston: pop. 64,000

**BC, B.C.** *abbrev. for* British Columbia

**Bear** ⟦ for the grizzly bears once abundant in the region ⟧ river flowing from the Uinta Mountains through Utah, Wyo., & Ida. into Great Salt Lake: *c.* 350 mi. (560 km)

**Bé·arn** (bā àrn', -àr') historical region in SW France, in the Pyrenees

**Beau·fort Sea** (bō'fərt) ⟦ named in honor of Sir Francis *Beaufort* (1774-1857), Brit naval officer ⟧ part of the Arctic Ocean, north of Alaska & northwest of Canada

**Beau·mont** (bō'mänt') ⟦ after J. *Beaumont*: so named by his brother-in-law, Henry Millard, who purchased land for a town site (1835) ⟧ city in SE Tex., on the Neches River: pop. 114,000

**Beau·port** (bō pōr') city in S Quebec, Canada: suburb of Quebec: pop. 63,000

**Bech·u·a·na·land** (bech'oo än'ə land') former British territory (1884-1966) in S Africa: now the country of Botswana

**Bed·ford** (bed'fərd) **1** county seat of Bedfordshire: pop. 89,000 **2** Bedfordshire

**Bed·ford·shire** (-shir', -shər) county in SC England: 477 sq. mi. (1,235 sq. km); pop. 516,000

**Bed·lam** (bed'ləm) ⟦ ME *Bedlam, Bethlem,* var. of Beth-lehem ⟧ an old insane asylum (in full, *St. Mary of Bethlehem*), later a hospital for the mentally ill, in London

**Bed·loe's** (bed'lōz) ⟦ after Isaac *Bedloe,* first owner ⟧ *old name of* Liberty Island

**Beer·she·ba** (bir shē'bə, ber-) city in S Israel, the principal city of the Negev: pop. 111,000: in ancient times, marking the southernmost extremity of Israelite territory: cf. Dan

**Bei·jing** (bā'jiŋ', bā zhiŋ') capital of the People's Republic of China, in the NE part; pop. 9,500,000

**Bei·ra** (bā'rə) seaport on the SE coast of Mozambique: pop. 114,000

**Bei·rut** (bā rōōt'; bā'rōōt') capital of Lebanon: seaport on the Mediterranean: pop. *c.* 702,000

**Be·jai·a** (bə ji'ə) seaport in NE Algeria, on the Mediterranean: pop. 124,000

**Bel·a·rus** (bel'ə rōōs') country in central Europe: became independent upon the breakup of the U.S.S.R. (1991): 80,300 sq. mi. (208,000 sq. km); pop. 9,900,000; cap. Minsk: formerly, *Belorussian Soviet Socialist Republic*

**Be·lau** (bə lou′) group of islands in the W Pacific, east of Mindanao, with (since 1981) an autonomous government, but legally within the Trust Territory of the Pacific Islands: 180 sq. mi. (465 sq. km): pop. 15,000: abbrev. *PW*

**Be·la·ya Tser·kov** (bel′ə yə ser′kôf) city in WC Ukraine: pop. 181,000

**Be·lém** (bə len′) seaport in NE Brazil, in the Amazon delta, on the Pará River: capital of Pará state: pop. 756,000

**Bel·fast** (bel′fast; bel fast′) seaport & capital of Northern Ireland, on the North Channel: pop. 319,000

**Bel·fort** (bel fôr′) city in Alsace, E France: pop. 53,000

**Bel·gaum** (bel goum′) city in Karnataka state, SW India: pop. 300,000

**Bel·gian Con·go** (bel′jən kä\ŋ′gō) former Belgian colony (1908-60) in central Africa: now the country of ZAIRE

**Bel·gium** (bel′jəm) kingdom in W Europe, on the North Sea: independence established in 1831: 11,792 sq. mi. (30,540 sq. km); pop. 9,868,000; cap. Brussels: Fr. name **Bel·gique** (bel zhēk′); Fl. name **Bel·gi·ë** (bel′gē ə)

**Bel·go·rod** (bel′gə räd′, byel′gə rät′) city in W European Russia, on the Donets River: pop. 280,000

**Bel·grade** (bel′grād, -gräd′; bel grād′, -gräd′) capital of Yugoslavia, on the Danube: pop. 1,470,000

**Bel·gra·vi·a** (bel grā′vē ə) a fashionable residential area surrounding Belgrave Square in Westminster, London

**Be·li·tung** (bə lē′toon) island of Indonesia, in the Java Sea, between Borneo & Sumatra: 1,866 sq. mi. (4,833 sq. km)

**Be·lize** (bə lēz′) 1 country in Central America, on the Caribbean: formerly a British colony & territory, it became independent (1981): 8,862 sq. mi. (22,963 sq. km); pop. 160,000; cap. Belmopan 2 seaport on the coast of this country: pop. 52,000: also called **Belize City**

**Bel·leau Wood** (be lō′) small forest in N France: site of a battle (1918) in World War I in which U.S. forces stopped a German advance on Paris

**Belle Isle** (bel), **Strait of** ‖ after the small island, *Belle Isle* (Fr, beautiful island), at its Atlantic entrance, the first land seen by incoming ships ‖ strait between Labrador & Newfoundland: 10-15 mi. (16-24 km) wide

**Belle·ville** (bel'vil) 〚Fr, lit., beautiful town〛 city in SW Ill., near St. Louis, Mo.: pop. 43,000

**Belle·vue** (bel'vyōō') 〚Fr, lit., beautiful view〛 city in NW Wash.: suburb of Seattle: pop. 87,000

**Bell·flow·er** (bel'flou'ər) 〚so named (1909) as the site of an orchard of *bellflower* apples〛 city in SW Calif.: suburb of Los Angeles: pop. 62,000

**Bel·ling·ham** (bel'iŋ ham') 〚after *Bellingham* Bay, so named (1793) by Capt. Vancouver (see VANCOUVER) after his associate, Sir William *Bellingham*〛 seaport in NW Wash., at the N end of Puget Sound: pop. 52,000

**Bel·lings·hau·sen Sea** (bel'iŋz hou'zən) part of the S Pacific Ocean, west of the Antarctic Peninsula

**Bel·mo·pan** (bel'mō pan') capital of Belize, in the central part: pop. 4,000

**Be·lo Ho·ri·zon·te** (bā'lō hôr'ə zän'tē; *Port* be'lô̄ rē zôn'te) city in SE Brazil: capital of Minas Gerais state: pop. 1,442,000

**Bel·o·rus·sia** (bel'ō rush'ə, bye'lō-) 1 historical region in central Europe corresponding to present-day Belarus 2 BELORUSSIAN SOVIET SOCIALIST REPUBLIC 3 BELARUS

**Belorussian Soviet Socialist Republic** a republic of the U.S.S.R.: now BELARUS

**Bel·sen** (bel'zən) village in W Germany, near Hanover: with the nearby village of Bergen, the site of a Nazi concentration camp and extermination center (called **Ber'gen–Bel'sen**)

**Bel·ve·dere** (bel'və dir', bel'və dir') a court in the Vatican, housing a collection of classical art

**Be·na·res** (bə nä'rēz') *old name of* VARANASI

**Ben·di·go** (ben'di gō') city in central Victoria, Australia: pop. 62,000

**Be·ne·lux** (ben'ə luks') 〚< BE(LGIUM), NE(THERLANDS), LUX(EMBOURG)〛 economic union of Belgium, Netherlands, & Luxembourg, established by treaty in 1948: in full **Benelux Economic Union**

**Ben·gal** (ben gôl', beŋ'gəl) 1 region in the NE part of the Indian peninsula, divided between the Indian state of West Bengal & Bangladesh 2 **Bay of** part of the Indian Ocean, east of India & west of Myanmar & the Malay Peninsula

**Ben·gha·zi, Ben·ga·si** (ben gä'zē, beŋ-) seaport in NE Libya, on the Gulf of Sidra: formerly (1951-72) one of the country's two capitals: pop. 650,000

**Ben·gue·la Current** (ben gā′lə) 〚after *Benguela,* city in W Angola〛 a strong ocean current in the South Atlantic, flowing northward along the SW coast of Africa

**Be·ni** (bā′nē) river in NW Bolivia, rising in the Andes, flowing northward to join the Mamoré and form the Madeira: *c.* 1,000 mi. (1,600 km)

**Be·nin** (be nēn′) **1** former native kingdom (fl. 14th-17th cent.) in W Africa, including what came to be known as the Slave Coast **2** country in WC Africa, on the Bight of Benin: formerly a French territory, it became independent (1960): 43,484 sq. mi. (112,622 sq. km); pop. 4,141,000; cap. Porto Novo **3 Bight of** N part of the Gulf of Guinea, just west of the Niger delta

**Ben·i Su·ef** (ben′ē ssoo āf′) city in NE Egypt, on the Nile: pop. 118,000

**Ben Ne·vis** (ben nē′vis, -nev′əs) mountain in the Grampian Mountains, WC Scotland: highest peak in the British Isles: 4,406 ft. (1,342 m)

**Ben·ning·ton** (ben′iŋ tən) 〚after *Benning* Wentworth (1696-1770), 1st gov. of New Hampshire〛 town in SW Vt.: in a Revolutionary battle (1777) fought nearby, Hessians sent by Burgoyne were defeated by colonial forces: pop. 16,000

**Be·no·ni** (bə nō′nī) city in the Transvaal, South Africa, on the Witwatersrand: gold-mining center: pop. 207,000

**Ben·sa·lem** (ben sā′ləm) 〚orig., *Salem*; renamed (*c.* 1700) < ? *Ben,* son of + *Salem*〛 urban township in SE Pa., near Philadelphia: pop. 57,000

**Be·nue** (bā′nwā) river in W Africa, a tributary of the Niger, flowing through Cameroon and Nigeria: *c.* 900 mi. (1,450 km)

**Ben·xi** (bun′shē′) city in Liaoning province, NE China, near Shenyang: pop. 750,000

**Be·o·grad** (be′ō gräd′) *Serbo-Croatian name of* BEL-GRADE

**Ber·ber·a** (bʉr′bər ə) seaport in NE Somalia, on the Gulf of Aden: pop. 65,000

**Be·re·zi·na** (ber′ə zē′nə; *Russ* bə rez′i nä′) river in Belarus, flowing into the Dnepr: *c.* 365 mi. (590 km): site of a battle (1812) in which Napoleon's army suffered severe losses while making its retreat from Moscow

**Be·rez·ni·ki** (bər yôz′nə kē) city in E European Russia, at the foot of the Urals, on the Kama River: pop. 195,000

**Ber·ga·ma** (ber′gə mä′) town in W Turkey, on the site of ancient Pergamum: pop. 24,000

**Ber·ga·mo** (ber′gä mō′) commune in Lombardy, N Italy: pop. 120,000

**Ber·gen** (ber′gən; *E* bur-) 1 seaport in SW Norway, on an inlet of the North Sea: pop. 207,000 2 village in NW Germany: see BELSEN

**Ber·gisch Glad·bach** (ber′gish glät′bäk′) city in W Germany, in the state of North Rhine-Westphalia: pop. 101,000

**Ber·ing Sea** (ber′iŋ, bir′-) [after Vitus *Bering* (c. 1680-1741), Dan explorer] part of the N Pacific Ocean, between NE Siberia & Alas.: c. 878,000 sq. mi. (2,274,000 sq. km)

**Bering Strait** [after Vitus *Bering* (c. 1680-1741), Dan explorer] strait between Siberia & Alas., joining the Pacific & Arctic oceans: c. 55 mi. (90 km) wide

**Berke·ley** (burk′lē) [after George *Berkeley* (1685-1753), Ir philosopher & bishop] city in W Calif., on San Francisco Bay, just north of Oakland: pop. 103,000

**Berk·shire** (burk′shir, -shər; *Brit* bärk′-) county in SC England: 485 sq. mi. (1,256 sq. km); pop. 715,000; county seat, Reading: also called **Berks** (bärks)

**Berkshire Hills** [after *Berkshire*, England] region of wooded hills in W Mass.: resort area: also called **Berkshires**

**Ber·lin** (bər lin′; *Ger* ber lēn′) city and state of E Germany: capital of Germany (1871-1945; 1990- ): after World War II and before reunification of Germany in 1990, it was divided into four sectors of occupation (U.S., British, French, and Soviet); the eastern (Soviet) sector (**East Berlin**) was the capital of East Germany; the three western sectors (**West Berlin**) constituted an exclave state of West Germany: 341 sq. mi. (883 sq. km); pop. 3,063,000

**Ber·me·jo** (ber me′hô) river flowing southeastward across N Argentina into the Paraguay River: c. 650 mi. (1,050 km)

**Ber·mu·da** (bər myōō′də) [after Juan de *Bermúdez*, Sp explorer who discovered it (c. 1515)] group of islands in the W Atlantic, c. 570 miles (920 km) southeast of

N.C.: a self-governing colony under British control since 1684: 20.5 sq. mi. (53 sq. km); pop. 55,000; cap. Hamilton

**Bermuda Triangle** a triangular region in the Atlantic Ocean, bounded by Bermuda, Puerto Rico, and Florida: in this area, many ships and aircraft have been reputed to have disappeared mysteriously, esp. since the 1940's

**Bern, Berne** (bʉrn; *Fr* bern) **1** capital of Switzerland & of Bern canton, on the Aare River: pop. 141,000 **2** canton of WC Switzerland: 2,336 sq. mi. (6,049 sq. km); pop. 912,000

**Bern·ese Alps** (bɚn ēz′) range of the Alps, in SW Switzerland: highest peak, Finsteraarhorn

**Ber·ry, Ber·ri** (be rē′) historical region in central France: chief city, Bourges

**Ber·wick** (ber′ik) former county in SE Scotland, on the North Sea, now in the region of the Borders: also called **Ber′wick·shire** (-shir, -shər)

**Ber·wyn** (bʉr′win) ⟦after *Berwyn* Mts., Wales⟧ city in NE Ill.: suburb of Chicago: pop. 45,000

**Be·san·çon** (bə zän sōn′) city in E France, on the Doubs River: pop. 120,000

**Bes·sa·ra·bi·a** (bes′ə rā′bē ə) region in SE Europe, between the Dnestr & Prut rivers: historically associated with Moldavia since the 14th cent.; ceded by Romania to the U.S.S.R. in 1940 & incorporated into the Moldavian S.S.R. (now Moldova)

**Be·tel·geuse, Be·tel·geux** (bet′'l jōōz′, bēt′'l-) ⟦Fr *Bételgeuse* < Ar *baytal-jauzā*ʔ, lit., house of the middle (of the sky)⟧ a reddish supergiant star, sometimes the brightest star in the constellation Orion, having a variable magnitude of 0.1 to 0.4 and an average diameter larger than the earth's orbit

**Beth·a·ny** (beth′ə nē) ⟦LL (Vulg.) *Bethania* < Gr *Bēthania* < Heb *betanya* < *bet*, house + ? *hayan*, late-season green figs⟧ ancient town in Palestine, near Jerusalem, at the foot of the Mount of Olives (Luke 19:29; John 11:1): now a village in Israeli-occupied Jordan

**Beth·el** (beth′əl) ancient city in Palestine, just north of Jerusalem (Gen. 35:1-15; Judg. 20:26): now a village in Israeli-occupied Jordan

**Be·thes·da** (bə thez′də) ⟦after the Biblical *Bethesda* (in

RSV, *Bethzatha*): John 5:2 ] suburb of Washington, D.C., in central Md.: pop. 63,000

**Beth·le·hem** (beth'lə hem′) 〚LL (Vulg.) < Gr *Bēthleem* < Heb *bet-lechem*, lit., house of bread〛 **1** ancient town in Judea: traditionally regarded as the birthplace of Jesus (Matt. 2:1): now a town in Israeli-occupied Jordan: pop. 16,000: Ar. name *Bayt Lahm* or *Beit Lahm* **2** 〚after *Bethlehem*, Judea〛 city in E Pa.: steel-producing center: pop. 71,000: see ALLENTOWN

**Beu·lah** (byoo'lə) 〚name for Israel (Isa. 62:4) < Heb *beula*, married〛 in Bunyan's *Pilgrim's Progress*, a country of peace near the end of life's journey: in full **Land of Beulah**

**Bev·er·ly Hills** (bev'ər lē) 〚after *Beverly* Farms, in Mass.〛 city in Calif., surrounded by Los Angeles: pop. 32,000

**Bex·ley** (beks'lē) borough of Greater London, England, on the Thames: pop. 218,000

**Bé·ziers** (bā zyā′) city in S France: pop. 78,000

**Bha·rat** (bu'rut) *Sans. name of* INDIA (the republic)

**Bhav·na·gar** (bou nug'ər) seaport in Gujarat state, W India, on the Arabian Sea: pop. 308,000: sometimes sp. **Bhau·na'gar**

**Bho·pal** (bō päl′) city in central India; capital of Madhya Pradesh: pop. 672,000

**Bhu·ba·nes·war** (boo'bə nesh'wər) city in E India, noted for its Hindu shrines: capital of Orissa: pop. 219,000

**Bhu·tan** (boo tän′) independent kingdom in the Himalayas, north of the Indian state of Assam: monarchy established in 1907: *c.* 18,000 sq. mi. (46,620 sq. km); pop. 1,446,000; cap. Thimphu

**Bi·a·fra** (bē äf'rə), **Bight of** eastern part of the Gulf of Guinea, on the W coast of Africa

**Bia·lys·tok** (byä'lis tôk′) city in NE Poland: pop. 240,000

**Bi·ar·ritz** (bē'ə rits′; *Fr* byà rēts′) resort town in SW France, on the Bay of Biscay: pop. 27,000

**Bible Belt** 〚coined (*c.* 1925) by H. L. Mencken (1880-1956), U.S. writer〛 those regions of the U.S., particularly areas in the South, where fundamentalist beliefs prevail and Christian clergy are especially influential

**Biel** (bēl) city in NW Switzerland: pop. 53,000

**Bie·le·feld** (bē'lə felt′) city in NW Germany, in North Rhine-Westphalia: pop. 304,000

**Bi·el·sko-Bi·a·ła** (bē el'skô bē äl'ə) city in S Poland, at the foot of the Carpathian Mountains: pop. 172,000

**Bienne** (byen) *Fr. name of* BIEL

**Bif·rost** (bēf'räst') ⟦ON *bifrǫst,* lit., the tremulous way: *bif-* < *bifask,* to tremble + *rǫst,* a distance⟧ *Norse Myth.* the rainbow bridge of the gods from Asgard, their home, to Midgard, the earth

**Big Apple, the** ⟦orig., jazzmen's slang for "the big time" (top-ranking vaudeville)⟧ *name for* NEW YORK (City)

**Big Ben 1** the great bell in the Parliament clock tower in London **2** the clock in this tower **3** the tower itself

**Big Bend National Park** triangular-shaped national park in W Tex., in a bend formed by the Rio Grande: 1,158 sq. mi. (3,000 sq. km)

**Big D** *slang name for* DALLAS

**Big Dipper** a dipper-shaped group of stars in the constellation Ursa Major

**Big·horn** (big'hôrn') ⟦after the *bighorn* sheep⟧ river in WC Wyo. flowing northward into the Yellowstone River in S Mont.: *c.* 450 mi. (725 km)

**Bighorn Mountains** range of the Rocky Mountains in N Wyo. and S Mont.: highest peak, 13,165 ft. (4,013 m)

**Bi·har** (bi här') state of NE India: 67,144 sq. mi. (173,876 sq. km); pop. 69,823,000; cap. Patna

**Biisk** (bisk, bēsk) *alt. sp. of* BIYSK

**Bi·kan·er** (bē kə nir', bik'ə ner') city in NW India, in the Thar Desert, Rajasthan state: pop. 280,000

**Bil·ba·o** (bil bä'ō, bil bou') port in the Basque country, N Spain, near the Bay of Biscay: pop. 433,000

**Bil·lings** (bil'iŋz) ⟦after F. *Billings* (1823-90), pres. of Northern Pacific railroad, which founded the town⟧ city in S Mont., on the Yellowstone River; pop. 81,000

**Bil·li·ton** (bi lē'tän') *old name of* BELITUNG

**Bi·lox·i** (bə luk'sē, -läk'sē) ⟦after the Indian people⟧ city in SE Miss., on the Gulf of Mexico: pop. 46,000

**Bing·ham·ton** (biŋ'əm tən) ⟦after Wm. *Bingham* (1752-1804), land donor⟧ city in SC N.Y., on the Susquehanna River: pop. 53,000

**Bi·o·ko** (bē ō'kō) island in the Bight of Benin, off the coast of Cameroon, part of Equatorial Guinea: 779 sq. mi. (2,017 sq. km); pop. 70,000

**Bir·ken·head** (bur'kən hed') seaport in W England, at the mouth of the Mersey River: pop. 144,000

**Bir·ming·ham** (bur'miŋ əm; *for 2,* -ham') **1** industrial city in central England: pop. 1,116,000 **2** ⟦after the English city⟧ city in NC Ala.: iron and steel center: pop. 266,000 (met. area 908,000)

**Bir·o·bi·dzhan, Bir·o·bi·djan** (bir'ō bi jän') autonomous region in Khabarovsk territory, E Siberia, set aside for Jewish settlement in 1934 (current pop. is 5.5% Jewish): 13,895 sq. mi. (36,000 sq. km); pop. 204,000: officially called *Jewish Autonomous Region*

**Bis·cay** (bis'kā, -kē), **Bay of** part of the Atlantic, on the N coast of Spain & the W coast of France

**Bish·kek** (bish kek') capital of Kyrgyzstan, in the NC part: pop. 617,000

**Bisk** (bisk, bēsk) *alt. sp. of* Biysk

**Bis·marck** (biz'märk') ⟦after Otto von *Bismarck* (1815-98), Prus chancellor of the German Empire, in recognition of financial aid to the local railroad by Ger investors⟧ capital of N.Dak., on the Missouri River: pop. 49,000

**Bismarck Archipelago** group of islands north and east of New Guinea; part of Papua New Guinea: 19,200 sq. mi. (49,730 sq. km)

**Bis·sau** (bi sou') seaport & chief city of Guinea-Bissau, on the W coast of Africa: pop. 109,000

**Bi·thyn·i·a** (bə thin'ē ə) ancient country in NW Asia Minor, in what is now Turkey: fl. 3d cent. B.C.-1st cent. A.D.

**Bi·tolj** (bē'tōl'yə) city in S Macedonia: pop. 138,000: also **Bi·to·la** (bē'tō'lə)

**Bit·ter·root Range** (bit'ər rōōt') ⟦after ModE *bitterroot*, an edible plant, found esp. in the foothills⟧ range of the Rocky Mountains, along the Ida.-Mont. border: highest peak, *c.* 11,000 ft. (3,350 m)

**Biysk** (bisk, bēsk) city in SC Siberia, in the Kuznetsk Basin: pop. 226,000

**Bi·zer·te** (bi zʉr'tə, -tē; *Fr* bē zert') seaport in northernmost Tunisia, on the Mediterranean: pop. 95,000: also **Bi·zer'ta** (-zʉr'tə)

**Black·burn** (blak'bərn) **1** city in NW England, in Lancashire: textile center: pop. 140,000 **2 Mount** mountain in the Wrangell Mountains, SE Alas.: 16,523 ft. (5,036 m)

**Black Forest** wooded mountain region in SW Germany

**Black Hills** ⟦from their dark appearance, because heavily forested⟧ mountainous region in SW S.Dak. &

NE Wyo.: highest peak, 7,242 ft. (2,207 m)

**Black Hole** a small dungeon at Calcutta: it was once believed that over 100 Europeans were confined there one night in 1756 by their Indian captors and died from heat and lack of air

**Black Mountains** [prob. < AmInd descriptive name] highest range of the Appalachians, in W N.C.: branch of the Blue Ridge Mountains: highest peak, Mount MITCHELL

**Black·pool** (blak′pōōl′) city in NW England, on the Irish Sea: resort: pop. 151,000

**Black Sea** sea between SE Europe & Asia, north of Turkey: *c.* 160,000 sq. mi. (414,400 sq. km)

**Black Volta** *see* VOLTA

**Bla·go·vesh·chensk** (bläg′ə vesh′chensk′) city in SE Siberian Russia, on the Amur River, at the border of China: pop. 195,000

**Blanc** (blän), **Mont** (mōn) mountain in E France, on the Italian border: highest peak in the Alps: 15,781 ft. (4,810 m)

**Blan·ca Peak** (blaŋ′kə) [Sp *blanca,* white (with snow)] highest peak of the Sangre de Cristo range, S Colo.: 14,317 ft. (4,364 m)

**Blar·ney stone** (blär′nē) a stone in Blarney Castle in the county of Cork, Ireland, said to impart skill in blarney to those who kiss it

**Blen·heim** (blen′əm) village in S Germany, in the state of Bavaria: site of a battle (1704) in the War of the Spanish Succession in which the English-Austrian army under Marlborough & Prince Eugene defeated the Franco-Bavarian forces

**Bli·da** (blē′dä′) city in NC Algeria: pop. 191,000

**Blind·heim** (blint′hīm′) *Ger. name of* BLENHEIM

**Block** (bläk) [after Adriaen *Block,* 17th-c. Du navigator who explored it] island in S R.I., at the entrance to Long Island Sound

**Bloem·fon·tein** (blōōm′fän tān′) city in central South Africa; capital of Orange Free State: pop. 231,000

**Blois** (blwà) city in central France, on the Loire River: pop. 49,000

**Bloom·field** (blōōm′fēld′) **1** [prob. descriptive] township in SE Mich.: suburb of Detroit: pop. 42,000 **2** [after Gen. J. *Bloomfield* of the Am Revolutionary army] town in NE N.J.: suburb of Newark: pop.

45,000

**Bloom·ing·ton** (bloom′iŋ tən) ⟦prob. in allusion to abundance of wildflowers⟧ **1** city in central Ill.: pop. 52,000 **2** city in SC Ind.: pop. 61,000 **3** ⟦? after *Bloomington,* Ind.⟧ city in E Minn., near Minneapolis: pop. 86,000

**Blooms·bur·y** (bloomz′bə rē, -brē; -ber′ē) a district in central London, formerly an artistic and literary center

**Blue·grass Country (or Region)** (bloo′gras′) region in central Ky. where there is much bluegrass: also called the Bluegrass

**Blue Mountains** ⟦from their bluish appearance at a distance⟧ heavily forested mountain range of NE Oreg. & SE Wash.: highest peak, 9,105 ft. (2,775 m)

**Blue Nile** *see* NILE

**Blue Ridge Mountains** ⟦from their bluish appearance at a distance⟧ easternmost range of the Appalachians, extending from S Pa. to N Ga.: see BLACK MOUNTAINS

**Bo·bru·isk** (bə broo′isk) city in central Belarus: pop. 223,000: also sp. **Bo·bru′ysk**

**Bo·ca Ra·ton** (bō′kə rə tōn′) ⟦after nearby Lake *Boca Raton* < Sp < *boca,* mouth, inlet + *ratón,* mouse, hidden rock that frays ships' cables: with ref. to the lake's outlet to the sea⟧ city in SE Fla., near Fort Lauderdale: pop. 61,000

**Bo·chum** (bō′kəm, -khoom) city in W Germany, in the Ruhr valley, in the state of North Rhine-Westphalia: pop. 387,000

**Bo·den·see** (bōd′'n zā′) *Ger. name of* Lake (of) CONSTANCE

**Boe·o·ti·a** (bē ō′shə, bē ō′shē ə) **1** in ancient times, a region dominated by the city of Thebes (Greece): fl. from *c.* 600 B.C. until the destruction of Thebes in 336 B.C. **2** region of EC Greece, northwest of Attica

**Bo·gor** (bō′gôr′) city in W Java, Indonesia: pop. 247,000

**Bo·go·tá** (bō′gə tä′) capital of Colombia, in the central part of the country, on an Andean plateau: pop. 3,968,000

**Bo Hai** (bō′hī′) arm of the Yellow Sea, north of Shandong peninsula in NE China: *c.* 300 mi. (483 km) long

**Bo·he·mi·a** (bō hē′mē ə, -hēm′yə) former independent kingdom in central Europe (13th-15th cent.): thereafter under Hapsburg rule until 1918, when it became the nucleus of the new country of Czechoslovakia

**Bo·hol** (bə hôl′) island in the SC Philippines, between Cebu & Leyte: one of the Visayan group: 1,492 sq. mi. (3,864 sq. km)

**Boi·se** (boi′zē, -sē) [[ < Fr *boisé*, wooded ]] capital of Ida., in the SW part: pop. 126,000: also **Boise City**

**Bo·kha·ra** (bō khä′rä; bō kär′ə) *var. of* BUKHARA

**Boks·burg** (bäks′bərg) city in S Transvaal, South Africa, on the Witwatersrand: pop. 150,000

**Bo·liv·i·a** (bə liv′ē ə) [[ after Simón Bolívar (1783-1830), South American general ]] inland country in WC South America: secured independence from Spain, 1825: 424,164 sq. mi. (1,098,581 sq. km); pop. 6,350,000; caps., La Paz & Sucre

**Bo·lo·gna** (bə lōn′yə) commune in Emilia-Romagna, NC Italy, at the foot of the Apennines: pop. 459,000

**Bol·ton** (bōl′tən) city in Greater Manchester, NW England: pop. 261,000

**Bol·za·no** (bōlt sä′nō, bōl zä′-) city in the S Tirol, N Italy: pop. 105,000

**Bom·bay** (bäm′bā′) seaport in W India, on the Arabian Sea: capital of Maharashtra state: pop. 8,227,000

**Bo·mu** (bō′mōō′) river in central Africa, flowing westward along the border of the Central African Republic and Zaire, joining the Uele to form the Ubangi: *c.* 500 mi. (800 km)

**Bône** (bōn) *old name of* ANNABA

**Bonn** (bän) city in W Germany, in North Rhine-Westphalia: capital of the Federal Republic of Germany (West Germany), 1949-90: pop. 292,000

**Boom·er State** (bōōm′ər) *name for* OKLAHOMA

**Bo·ö·tes** (bō ō′tēz′) [[ L < Gr *boōtēs*, lit., plowman < *bous*, ox < IE base *$gu ou$-, cow, ox ]] a N constellation between Virgo and Draco including the bright star Arcturus; Herdsman

**Boo·thi·a** (bōō′thē ə), **Gulf of** inlet of the Arctic Ocean between Boothia Peninsula & Baffin Island

**Boothia Peninsula** [[ after Sir Felix *Booth* (1775-1850), London distiller & promoter of Arctic expeditions ]] peninsula in the Northwest Territories, Canada: its N tip is the northernmost point of the North American mainland

**Boo·tle** (bōōt′'l) seaport in Merseyside, NW England, adjoining Liverpool: pop. 62,000

**Bo·phu·that·swa·na** (bō'pŏŏ tät swän'ə) group of non-contiguous black homelands in N South Africa, on the Botswana border: granted independence in 1977: 17,000 sq. mi. (44,000 sq. km): pop. 1,660,000

**Bor·deaux** (bôr dō') 1 seaport in SW France, on the Garonne River: pop. 211,000 2 region around this seaport, noted as a winegrowing area

**Bor·der** (bôr'dər), **the** the district on and near the boundary between Scotland and England

**Bor·ders** (bôr'dərz) region of S Scotland, on the border of England: 1,800 sq. mi. (4,662 sq. km); pop. 101,000

**Border States** Slave States bordering on the Free States before the Civil War: Mo., Ky., Va., Md., & Del.

**Bor·ne·o** (bôr'nē ō') large island in the Malay Archipelago, southwest of the Philippines: the S portion (KALIMANTAN) is a part of Indonesia; the N portion is composed of the Malaysian states of Sabah & Sarawak, and of BRUNEI: total area, *c.* 288,000 sq. mi. (746,000 sq. km)

**Born·holm** (bôrn'hōlm') Danish island in the Baltic Sea, south of Sweden: 227 sq. mi. (588 sq. km); pop. 47,000

**Bo·ro·di·no** (bôr'ə dē'nō) Russian village just west of Moscow: site of a battle (1812) in which the Russian army retreated before Napoleon's army

**Bo·ru·jerd** (bôr'ə jerd') city in WC Iran: pop. 178,000

**Bos·ni·a and Herzegovina** (bäz'nē ə) country in SE Europe: 19,741 sq. mi. (51,129 sq. km); pop. 4,124,000; cap. Sarajevo: it came under Turkish rule in the 15th cent. and under Austro-Hungarian control in 1878: it was part of Yugoslavia (1918-92): also **Bos'ni·a–Her'ze·go·vi'na**

**Bos·po·rus** (bäs'pə rəs) strait between the Black Sea and the Sea of Marmara: *c.* 20 mi. (32 km) long: also **Bos'pho·rus** (-fə rəs)

**Bos·sier City** (bō'zhər) ⟦after Pierre E. J. B. *Bossier,* 19th-c. general⟧ city in NW La., on the Red River opposite Shreveport: pop. 53,000

**Bos·ton** (bôs'tən, bäs'-) ⟦after *Boston,* port in NE England⟧ cap. of Mass.; seaport on an arm (**Boston Bay**) of Massachusetts Bay: pop. 574,000 (met. area 2,871,000; urban area with Lawrence & Salem 4,172,000)

**Bos·worth Field** (bäz'wərth) field in Leicestershire, England: scene of the final battle (1485) in the Wars of the Roses, in which Richard III was killed; the crown passed to the victor, the Earl of Richmond (Henry VII)

**Bot·a·ny Bay** (bat′'n ē) bay on the SE coast of Australia, near Sydney: site of Captain Cook's original landing in Australia

**Both·ni·a** (bäth′nē ə), **Gulf of** arm of the Baltic Sea, between Finland & Sweden

**Bot·swa·na** (bät swä′nə) country in S Africa, north of South Africa: formerly the British territory of Bechuanaland, it became independent (1966) & a member of the Commonwealth: 231,805 sq. mi. (600,372 sq. km); pop. 1,104,000; cap. Gaborone

**bottomless pit, the** the underworld; hell

**Bot·trop** (bä′träp) city in W Germany, in the Ruhr valley, in the state of North Rhine-Westphalia: pop. 113,000

**Boua·ké** (bwäk′ä) city in central Ivory Coast: pop. 175,000

**Bou·gain·ville** (bōo′gən vil′) largest of the Solomon Islands, in Papua New Guinea: 3,880 sq. mi. (10,050 sq. km)

**Boul·der** (bōl′dər) ⟦from the abundance of large rocks there⟧ city in NC Colo.: pop. 83,000: see DENVER

**Boulder Dam** *old name of* HOOVER DAM

**Bou·logne** (bōo lōn′; *Fr* bōo lôn′y′) port in N France, on the English Channel: pop. 48,000: also **Bou·logne′-sur-Mer′** (-sür mer′)

**Bou·logne-Bil·lan·court** (-bē yän kōor′) city in France, on the Seine: SW suburb of Paris: pop. 103,000

**Bourges** (boorzh) city in central France: pop. 79,000

**Bour·gogne** (bōor gôn′y′) *Fr. name of* BURGUNDY

**Bourne·mouth** (bôrn′məth, boorn′-) resort city in S England, on the English Channel: pop. 151,000

**Bow·er·y** (bou′ər ē, bou′rē), **the** a street in New York City, or the surrounding district: center of cheap hotels, bars, etc.

**Bowl·ing Green** (bōl′iŋ) ⟦after the local popularity of the game of lawn bowling⟧ city in S Ky.: pop. 41,000

**Boyne** (boin) river in E Ireland: site of a battle (1690) in which the forces of William III of England defeated the Jacobites of James II, resulting in his flight to France

**Boz·caa·da** (bōz′jä dä′) Turkish island in the Aegean, near the Dardanelles: 15 sq. mi. (39 sq. km): in Greek legend, as *Tenedos*, the base of the Greek fleet in the Trojan War

**Bra·bant** (brə bant', -bänt') 1 former duchy of W Europe, originating in the late 12th cent.: since 1830, divided between the Netherlands (*North Brabant* province) & Belgium (provinces *Antwerp* & *Brabant*) 2 province of central Belgium: 1,297 sq. mi. (3,359 sq. km); pop. 2,217,000; cap. Brussels

**Brad·ford** (brad'fərd) city in N England, in West Yorkshire: pop. 467,000

**Brah·ma·pu·tra** (brä'mə pōō'trə) river flowing from the Himalayas of SW Tibet through Assam (India) & Bangladesh, where it joins the Ganges to form a vast delta at the head of the Bay of Bengal: *c.* 1,800 mi. (2,900 km)

**Brǎ·i·la** (brə ē'lä) city in E Romania, on the Danube: pop. 215,000

**Bramp·ton** (bramp'tən, bram'-) 〖after *Brampton*, town in NW England〗 city in SE Ontario, Canada, near Toronto: pop. 189,000

**Bran·den·burg** (bran'dən burg'; *Ger* brän'dən boork) 1 former province of Prussia: the region was divided between Poland & East Germany in 1947 2 state of NE Germany: 10,039 sq. mi. (26,000 sq. km); pop. 2,700,000; cap. Potsdam 3 city in E Germany, west of Berlin, in Brandenburg: pop. 94,000

**Bran·don** (bran'dən) 〖prob. after a local family name〗 village in WC Fla.: suburb of Tampa: pop. 58,000

**Bran·dy·wine** (bran'dē wīn') 〖< ?〗 creek in SE Pa. & N Del.: site of a battle (1777) of the Revolutionary War, in which Washington's army failed to check the British advance on Philadelphia

**Brant·ford** (brant'fərd) 〖after Joseph *Brant* (1742-1807), Mohawk Indian chief〗 city in SE Ontario, Canada: pop. 83,000

**Bra·sil** (brä zēl') *Port. name of* BRAZIL

**Bra·sí·lia** (brä zē'lyä; *E* brə zil'yə) capital of Brazil, in the EC part: pop. 411,000: constituting, with surrounding area, a federal district, 2,245 sq. mi. (5,814 sq. km); pop. 1,579,000

**Bra·şov** (brä shôv') city in central Romania: pop. 291,000

**Bra·ti·sla·va** (brä'ti slä'və) capital of Slovakia, on the Danube: pop. 401,000

**Bratsk** (brätsk) city in SC Siberian Russia, on the Angara River: pop. 240,000

**Braun·schweig** (broun'shvīk') *Ger. name of* BRUNSWICK

**Bra·zil** (brə zil') ⟦Port, short for *terra de brasil,* land of brazilwood⟧ country in central & NE South America, on the Atlantic: declared independence from Portugal (1822): 3,286,540 sq. mi. (8,512,100 sq. km); pop. 143,277,000; cap. Brasília

**Bra·zos** (brä'zəs, braz'əs) ⟦Sp, lit., arms, branches (of a river)⟧ river in central & SE Tex., flowing southeastward into the Gulf of Mexico: 870 mi. (1,400 km)

**Braz·za·ville** (brä'zə vil'; *Fr* brà zä vēl') capital of Congo, on the Congo River: pop. 422,000

**Brec·on·shire** (brek'ən shir, -shər) former county of SE Wales, now part of Powys county: also called **Breck' nock·shire** (brek'näk-, -nək-) or **Breck'nock**

**Bre·da** (brā dä') city in S Netherlands: pop. 119,000

**Bre·men** (brem'ən; *Ger* brā'mən) **1** state of NW Germany, consisting of the cities of Bremen & Bremerhaven: 156 sq. mi. (404 sq. km); pop. 672,000 **2** capital of this state: port on the Weser River: pop. 536,000

**Bre·mer·ha·ven** (brem'ər hä'vən; *Ger* brā'mər häf'ən) seaport at the mouth of the Weser River, in N Germany, forming an exclave of Bremen state: pop. 136,000

**Bren·ner Pass** (bren'ər) mountain pass across the Alps at the border between Italy & Austria: 4,495 ft. (1,370 m) high

**Brent** (brent) borough of Greater London, England: pop. 255,000

**Brent·wood** (brent'wood) ⟦prob. after *Brentwood,* town in SE England, home of early settlers⟧ town in central Long Island, N.Y.: pop. 45,000

**Bre·scia** (bre'shä) commune in Lombardy, N Italy, at the foot of the Alps: pop. 202,000

**Bres·lau** (bres'lou) *Ger. name of* WROCŁAW

**Brest** (brest) **1** seaport in W France, on the Atlantic: pop. 160,000 **2** city in SW Belarus, on the Bug River: pop. 222,000: site of the signing of a separate peace treaty (March, 1918) between Russia & the Central Powers: formerly called **Brest–Li·tovsk** (brest'li tôfsk')

**Bre·tagne** (brə tàn'y') *Fr. name of* BRITTANY

**Bret·ton Woods** (bret''n) ⟦after *Bretton* Hall, Eng countryseat of one of the founders⟧ resort in the

White Mountains, N.H.: site of a UN monetary conference (1944) at which the International Monetary
Fund was established

**Brezh·nev** (brezh′nef, -nev) *old name of* NABEREZHNIYE
CHELNY

**Brick** (brik) 〖orig. a place where bricks were made〗
urban township in E N.J.: pop. 66,000

**Bridge·port** (brij′pôrt′) 〖for the bridge across the
Pequonnock River there〗 seaport in SW Conn., on
Long Island Sound: pop. 142,000

**Bridge·town** (brij′toun′) capital & seaport of Barbados:
pop. 7,500

**Brigh·ton** (brīt″n) city in S England, on the English
Channel: seaside resort: pop. 163,000

**Brin·di·si** (brin′də zē; *It* brēn′dē zē) seaport in Apulia,
SE Italy, on the Adriatic: pop. 90,000

**Bris·bane** (briz′bān′, -bən) capital of Queensland, Australia: seaport on the eastern coast: pop. 942,000

**Bris·tol** (bris′təl) **1** seaport in SW England: pop. 434,000
**2** 〖after seaport in England〗 city in central Conn.:
pop. 61,000 **3** 〖after the seaport〗 urban township in
SE Pa., on the Delaware River, near Philadelphia:
pop. 57,000

**Bristol Bay** 〖after Admiral A. J. Hervey (1724-79), 3d
Earl of *Bristol*〗 arm of the Bering Sea between the
SW Alas. mainland & the Alaska Peninsula

**Bristol Channel** arm of the Atlantic, between S Wales &
SW England: *c.* 85 mi. (135 km) long

**Brit·ain** (brit″n) GREAT BRITAIN

**Bri·tan·ni·a** (bri tan′ē ə, -tan′yə) 〖L〗 **1** [Old Poet.] a
female figure symbolizing Great Britain or the British
Empire **2** *Rom. name for* GREAT BRITAIN (the island),
esp. the southern part **3** BRITISH EMPIRE

**British Antarctic Territory** British territory (est. 1962)
including that part of Antarctica between 20° and 80°
west longitude, the South Orkney Islands, & the South
Shetland Islands

**British Columbia** 〖after the COLUMBIA River〗 province
of SW Canada, on the Pacific: 366,255 sq. mi. (948,597
sq. km); pop. 2,884,000; cap. Victoria: abbrev. *BC* or
*B.C.*

**British Commonwealth (of Nations)** *old name of* the
COMMONWEALTH

**British Empire** [Brit. Historical] the United Kingdom

and the British dominions, colonies, etc.

**British Guiana** *see* GUYANA

**British Honduras** *see* BELIZE

**British India** the part of India formerly under direct British rule

**British Indian Ocean Territory** British territory (est. 1965) in the Indian Ocean, between Sri Lanka & Mauritius, consisting of the Chagos Archipelago: 23 sq. mi. (60 sq. km)

**British Isles** group of islands consisting of Great Britain, Ireland, & adjacent islands

**British Museum** national museum in London, containing antiquities, one of the largest libraries in the world, a department of natural history, etc.

**British Somaliland** former British protectorate (est. 1887) in E Africa: merged with Italian Somaliland (1960) to form Somalia

**British West Indies** former British possessions in the West Indies, including Jamaica, Barbados, the Bahamas, Trinidad & Tobago, etc.

**Brit·ta·ny** (brit′n ē) metropolitan region of NW France, occupying a peninsula between the English Channel & the Bay of Biscay: 10,505 sq. mi. (27,208 sq. km); pop. 2,738,000; chief city, Rennes

**Br·no** (bʉr′nô) city in SE Czech Republic: pop. 381,000

**Broad·way** (brôd′wā′) [transl. of Du *Breed Wegh*] street running north and south through New York City, known as the center of the city's main theater and entertainment section

**Brob·ding·nag** (bräb′diŋ nag′) in Jonathan Swift's *Gulliver's Travels*, a land inhabited by giants about 60 feet tall

**Brock·en** (bräk′ən) mountain in the Harz Mountains, central Germany: 3,747 ft. (1,142 m): in German folklore, the meeting place of witches on Walpurgis Night

**Brock·ton** (bräk′tən) [after Sir Isaac *Brock* (1769-1812), Lt. Gov. of Canada] city in E Mass., near Boston: pop. 93,000

**Brom·ley** (bräm′lē) borough of Greater London, England: pop. 298,000

**Bronx** (bräŋks) [after Jonas *Bronck*, early N.Y. settler] northernmost borough of New York City, between the Harlem River & Long Island Sound: pop. 1,204,000: commonly called **the Bronx**

**Brook Farm** ⟦descriptive name⟧ a farm near West Roxbury (now part of Boston), Mass., where a group of U.S. writers & scholars set up an experimental community (1841-47) based on cooperative living

**Brook·line** (brook′lin′) ⟦after the estate of Judge Samuel Sewall (1652-1730), which was bounded by two brooks⟧ suburb of Boston, in E Mass.: pop. 55,000

**Brook·lyn** (brook′lən) ⟦after *Breukelen*, village in the Netherlands⟧ borough of New York City, on W Long Island: pop. 2,301,000

**Brooklyn Park** ⟦after *Brooklyn*, village in S Mich., orig. home of first settlers⟧ city in SE Minn.: suburb of Minneapolis: pop. 56,000

**Brooks Range** (brooks) ⟦after A. H. *Brooks* (1871-1924), U.S. geologist⟧ mountain range extending across N Alas.: highest peak, 9,239 ft. (2,816 m)

**Bros·sard** (brô sär′, -särd′) ⟦after the several *Brossard* families who settled there⟧ city in SW Quebec, Canada: suburb of Montreal: pop. 57,000

**Brother Jon·a·than** (jän′ə thən) ⟦apparently first applied to New England militia besieging Boston by Brit soldiers evacuating the city (March, 1776)⟧ [Historical] the United States or its people: predecessor of Uncle Sam

**Browns·ville** (brounz′vil) ⟦after Fort *Brown*, named for Major J. *Brown*, killed in defending it (1846)⟧ city & port in S Tex., on the Rio Grande: pop. 99,000

**Brug·ge** (broog′ə) city in NW Belgium: pop. 118,000: Fr. name **Bruges** (brüzh)

**Brun·dis·i·um** (brən diz′ē əm) *ancient Rom. name of* BRINDISI

**Bru·nei** (broo nī′) independent sultanate on the N coast of Borneo, consisting of two enclaves in the Malaysian state of Sarawak: under British protection, 1888-1983: 2,226 sq. mi. (5,765 sq. km); pop. 240,000; cap. Bandar Seri Begawan: official name **Brunei Da·rus·sa·lam** (där′ əs ə läm′)

**Bruns·wick** (brunz′wik) **1** former duchy (13th-19th cent.) in NC Europe: now part of the German state of Lower Saxony **2** city in NC Germany, in the state of Lower Saxony: pop. 255,000

**Brus·sels** (brus′əlz) capital of Belgium, in the central part: pop. (with suburbs) 980,000: Fl. name **Brus·sel** (brö′səl); Fr. name **Bru·xelles** (brü sel′)

**Bry·an** (brī'ən) ⟦after W. J. *Bryan,* orig. owner of the town site⟧ city in EC Tex.: pop. 55,000

**Bry·ansk** (brē änsk'; *Russ* bryänsk) city in W European Russia: pop. 430,000

**Bryce Canyon National Park** (brīs) ⟦after E. *Bryce,* early settler⟧ national park in SW Utah, with colorful & unusual eroded rock formations: 56 sq. mi. (145 sq. km)

**Bu·ca** (bo͞o'kə) city in W Asiatic Turkey, near Izmir: pop. 103,000

**Bu·ca·ra·man·ga** (bo͞o'kä *r*ä mäŋ'gä) city in NC Colombia: pop. 440,000

**Bu·cha·rest** (bo͞o'kə rest', byo͞o'-) capital of Romania, in the S part: pop. 1,834,000 (urban area, 2,228,000)

**Buch·en·wald** (bo͞o'kən wôld'; *Ger* bo͞okh'ən vält') village in central Germany, near Weimar, in the state of Thuringia: site of a Nazi concentration camp and extermination center

**Buck·eye State** (buk'ī') *name for* OHIO

**Buck·ing·ham Palace** (buk'iŋ əm) the official residence in London of British sovereigns

**Buck·ing·ham·shire** (-shir', -shər) county in SC England: 727 sq. mi. (1,883 sq. km); pop. 595,000: also called **Buckingham**

**Bu·co·vi·na** (bo͞o'kə vē'nə) *alt. sp. of* BUKOVINA

**Bu·cu·reşti** (bo͞o ko͞o resht') *Romanian name of* BUCHAREST

**Bu·da·pest** (bo͞o'də pest') capital of Hungary, in the NC part, on the Danube: pop. 2,072,000

**Bud·weis** (bo͞ot'vīs) *Ger. name of* ČESKÉ BUDĚJOVICE

**Bue·na Park** (bwā'nə pärk') ⟦Sp *buena,* good + *park*⟧ city in SW Calif.: suburb of Los Angeles: pop. 69,000

**Bue·na·ven·tu·ra** (bwe'nä ven to͞o'rä) seaport in W Colombia, on an island in a Pacific inlet: pop. 123,000

**Bue·na Vis·ta** (bwā'nə vis'tə, byo͞o'nə) site of a battle (1847) of the Mexican War, near Saltillo, Mexico, in which Santa Ana's army withdrew after a stalemated engagement with U.S. forces under Zachary Taylor, giving Taylor control of N Mexico

**Bue·nos Ai·res** (bwā'nəs er'ēz, -i'rēz; bō'nəs; *Sp* bwe'nôs ī'res) **1** capital of Argentina, seaport on the Río de la Plata within a federal district: 77 sq. mi. (200 sq. km); pop. 2,923,000 (urban area 9,677,000) **2** province of E Argentina, on the Atlantic: 118,844 sq. mi. (307,804 sq.

km); pop. 10,865,000; cap. La Plata **3 Lake** lake in the
S Andes, on the Chile-Argentina border: 865 sq. mi.
(2,240 sq. km)

**Buf·fa·lo** (buf′ə lō′) 〚transl. of the name of a Seneca
Indian who lived there〛 city in W N.Y., on Lake Erie
& the Niagara River: pop. 328,000 (met. area
1,189,000)

**Bug** (bo͞og) **1** river in S Ukraine, flowing southeastward
into the Black Sea: 530 mi. (853 km): also called
**Southern Bug 2** river in W Ukraine, flowing northwestward into the Vistula near Warsaw and forming
part of the border with Poland: 500 mi. (805 km): also
called **Western Bug**

**Bu·jum·bu·ra** (bo͞o′jo͞om bo͞or′ə) capital of Burundi: port
at the N end of Lake Tanganyika: pop. 141,000

**Bu·ka·vu** (bo͞o käv′o͞o) city in E Zaire, on Lake Kivu:
pop. 209,000

**Bu·kha·ra** (bo͞o kär′ə) region of Uzbekistan: *c.* 55,000 sq.
mi. (142,500 sq. km)

**Bu·ko·vi·na** (bo͞o′kə vē′nə) region in central Europe,
partly in N Romania & partly in SW Ukraine: an
Austrian crown land from 1775 to 1918

**Bu·la·wa·yo** (bo͞o′lə wä′yō) city in SW Zimbabwe: pop.
of urban area 386,000

**Bul·gar·i·a** (bəl ger′ē ə, bo͞ol-) country in SE Europe, on
the Black Sea: founded in the 7th cent. & under Turkish control from late 14th cent. until independence in
1908: 42,823 sq. mi. (110,912 sq. km); pop. 8,990,000;
cap. Sofia

**Bull** (bo͞ol) Taurus, the constellation and second sign of
the zodiac

**Bull Run** 〚< ?〛 small stream in NE Va.: site of two Civil
War battles (1861 & 1862) in which Union forces were
defeated

**Bun·ker Hill** (buŋ′kər) 〚prob. after G. *Bunker,* early
resident of Charlestown〛 hill in Boston, Mass.: in a
battle (1775) of the American Revolution, colonial
forces besieging Boston were dislodged by British
troops, but the victory failed to break the siege

**Bur·bank** (bʉr′baŋk) 〚after Dr. D. *Burbank,* one of the
city planners〛 city in SW Calif.: suburb of Los Angeles: pop. 94,000

**Bur·gas** (bo͞or gäs′) seaport in SE Bulgaria, on the Black
Sea: pop. 183,000

**Bur·gos** (boo͞r′gôs) city in NC Spain: pop. 363,000

**Bur·gun·dy** (bur′gən dē) **1** historical region in SE France of varying extent **2** metropolitan region in SE France: 12,194 sq. mi. (31,582 sq. km); pop. 1,596,000; chief city, Dijon

**Bur·ki·na Fa·so** (boor kē′nə fä′sō) country in W Africa, north of Ghana: under French control from 1895, it became independent (as *Upper Volta*) in 1960: 105,870 sq. mi. (274,200 sq. km); pop. 7,094,000; cap. Ouagadougou

**Bur·ling·ton** (bur′liŋ tən) 〖after local pronun. of *Bridlington*, port in NE England〗 town in SE Ontario, Canada, on Lake Ontario: pop. 115,000

**Bur·ma** (bur′mə) *old name of* MYANMAR

**Bur·na·by** (bur′nə bē) city in British Columbia, Canada; suburb of E Vancouver; pop. 137,000

**Bur·sa** (boor sä′) city in NW Turkey: capital of the Ottoman Empire in 14th cent.: pop. 445,000

**Bu·ru** (boo͞o′roo͞) island of Indonesia, in the Molucca group: *c.* 3,500 sq. mi. (9,000 sq. km)

**Bu·run·di** (boo roon′dē, -run′-) country in EC Africa, east of Zaire: 10,747 sq. mi. (27,834 sq. km); pop. 4,807,000; cap. Bujumbura: see RUANDA-URUNDI

**Bur·y** (ber′ē) borough in NW England, part of Greater Manchester: pop. 68,000

**Bute** (byoot) **1** island in the Firth of Clyde: 46 sq. mi. (119 sq. km) **2** former county of SW Scotland, including this island, now combined with Argyll as a district (**Argyll and Bute**) in the region of Strathclyde: also **Bute′shire** (-shir)

**Bu·tu·an** (bə too′än) city on the NE coast of Mindanao, the Philippines: pop. 172,000

**Bu·tung** (boo͞o′too͞oŋ) island of Indonesia, SE of Celebes: *c.* 2,000 sq. mi. (5,200 sq. km)

**Bu·zău** (bə zou′) city in Walachia, SE Romania: pop. 120,000

**Buz·zards Bay** (buz′ərdz) arm of the Atlantic, on the SE coast of Mass., at the base of Cape Cod peninsula

**Byd·goszcz** (bid′gôshch) city in NC Poland: pop. 358,000

**Bye·lo·rus·sian Soviet Socialist Republic** (bye′lō rush′ən) BELORUSSIAN SOVIET SOCIALIST REPUBLIC: also **Bye′lo·rus′sia**

**By·tom** (bi′tôm) city in SW Poland: pop. 230,000

**Byz·an·tine Empire** (biz'ən tēn', -tīn'; bi zan'tin) empire (A.D. 395-1453) in SE Europe & SW Asia, formed by the division of the Roman Empire: cap. Constantinople: see also EASTERN ROMAN EMPIRE

**By·zan·ti·um** (bi zan'shē əm, -tē əm) ancient city (founded *c.* 600 B.C.) on the site of modern ISTANBUL: name changed to CONSTANTINOPLE, A.D. 330

# C

**CA** *abbrev. for* California

**Caa·ba** (kä'bə) *alt. sp. of* KAABA

**Ca·ba·na·tuan** (kä'bə nə twän') city in SC Luzon, in the Philippines: pop. 139,000

**Ca·bin·da** (kə bin'də) exclave of Angola, on the W coast of Africa, separated from the rest of Angola by 18.5 mi. (30 km) of Zaire: 2,807 sq. mi. (7,270 sq. km)

**Ca·diz** (kə diz', kä'diz) 1 seaport in SW Spain, on the Atlantic: pop. 158,000: Sp. name **Cá·diz** (kä'*th*ēth') 2 city in N Negros, in the Philippines: pop. 130,000

**Cae·li·an** (sē'lē ən, sēl'yən) 〚after L *Caelius Mons*, Caelian hill, named after the Tuscan *Caeles Vibenna*〛 *see* SEVEN HILLS OF ROME

**Cae·lum** (sē'ləm) a small S constellation between Columba and Eridanus

**Caen** (kän) chief city of Basse-Normandie, NW France: pop. 117,000

**Caer·nar·von·shire** (kär när'vən shir', -shər) former county of NW Wales, now part of Gwynedd: also **Caer·nar'von**

**Caes·a·re·a** (ses'ə rē'ə, sez'-, sē'zə-) 1 seaport in ancient Palestine, on the Mediterranean, S of Haifa, Israel: Roman capital of Palestine 2 city in ancient Palestine, near Mt. Hermon: also **Caesarea Phi·lip·pi** (fi lip' ī) 3 *ancient name of* KAYSERI

**Ca·ga·yan de O·ro** (kä'gə yän' dā ôr'ō) city in E Mindanao, in the Philippines; pop. 227,000

**Ca·glia·ri** (käl'yä rē') capital of Sardinia; seaport on the S coast: pop. 224,000

**Ca·guas** (kä'gwäs') city in EC Puerto Rico: pop. 133,000

**Cai·cos Islands** (kāk'əs) *see* TURKS AND CAICOS ISLANDS

**Cai·ro** (kī'rō; *for* 2 ker'ō) 1 capital of Egypt, at the head of the Nile delta: pop. 5,074,000 2 〚after the capital of Egypt〛 city in S Ill., at the confluence of the Ohio &

Mississippi rivers: pop. 4,800

**Caith·ness** (kāth′nes′, kāth nes′) former county of NE Scotland, now in the region of Highland: also **Caith′ness·shire′** (-shir′, -shər)

**Cal** *abbrev. for* California

**Cal·a·bar** (kal′ə bär′, kal′ə bär′) seaport in SE Nigeria: pop. 103,000

**Ca·la·bri·a** (kə lā′brē ə; *It* kä lä′bryä) **1** region occupying the southernmost part of the peninsula of Italy, opposite Sicily: 5,822 sq. mi. (15,080 sq. km); pop. 2,117,000 **2** former region (until 11th cent.) constituting what is now S Apulia, in SE Italy

**Ca·lais** (ka lā′, kal′ā′; *Brit also* kal′i; *Fr* ka le′) **1** seaport in N France, on the Strait of Dover: pop. 77,000 **2 Pas de Ca·lais** (pät kä le′) *Fr. name of* Strait of DOVER

**Cal·cut·ta** (kal kut′ə) seaport in NE India, on the Hooghly River: capital of West Bengal state: pop. 9,166,000

**Cal·e·do·ni·a** (kal′ə dōn′yə, -dō′nē ə) *old poet. name for* SCOTLAND

**Caledonian Canal** canal in N Scotland, extending northeastward from the Atlantic to Moray Firth: *c.* 60 mi. (100 km)

**Cal·ga·ry** (kal′gə rē) 〚after a location on the Isle of Mull, Scotland〛 city in S Alberta, Canada: pop. 636,000

**Ca·li** (kä′lē) city in SW Colombia: pop. 1,398,000

**Cal·i·cut** (kal′ə kut′) seaport in SW India, on the Arabian Sea, in Kerala state: pop. 546,000

**Calif** *abbrev. for* California

**Cal·i·for·ni·a** (kal′ə fôr′nyə, -nē ə) 〚Sp, orig. name of a fabled island〛 **1** State of the SW U.S., on the Pacific coast: admitted, 1850; 158,693 sq. mi. (411,013 sq. km); pop. 29,760,000; cap. Sacramento: abbrev. *CA, Cal,* or *Calif* **2 Gulf of** arm of the Pacific, between Baja California and the Mexican mainland

**Cal·la·o** (kə yä′ō) seaport in W Peru: pop. 479,000

**Cal·lis·to** (kə lis′tō) 〚L < Gr *Kallistō*〛 the second largest satellite of Jupiter: discovered in 1610 by Galileo

**Cal·pe** (kal′pā) *ancient name of* Rock of Gibraltar: see also PILLARS OF HERCULES

**Cal·u·met City** (kal′yə met′) city in NE Illinois, south of Chicago: pop. 38,000

**Cal·va·ry** (kal′və rē) 〚LL(Ec) *Calvaria* < L, skull: used to translate Gr *kranion*, skull & by the Evangelists to transl. Aram *gŭlgŭlthā*, GOLGOTHA ] *Bible* the place near Jerusalem where the crucifixion of Jesus took place: Luke 23:33, Matt. 27:33

**Cal·y·don** (kal'ə dän') ancient city in S Aetolia, central Greece

**Ca·ma·güey** (kä'mä gwā') city in EC Cuba: pop. 262,000

**Cam·bo·di·a** (kam bō'dē ə) country in the S Indochinese Peninsula: a French protectorate from 1863 until independence, 1954: 69,898 sq. mi. (181,035 sq. km); pop. 6,388,000; cap. Phnom Penh: also, formerly, sometimes known as *Kampuchea*

**Cam·bri·a** (kam'brē ə) [ML, var. of *Cumbria* < base of OCelt *Combroges*, lit., co-landers > Celt *Cymry*, Welshmen ] *old poet. name for* WALES

**Cambrian Mountains** mountain system of central Wales: highest point, 2,970 ft. (905 m)

**Cam·bridge** (kām'brij') [ME *Caumbrigge* < OE *Grantanbrycge*, lit., bridge over the Granta (now called the Cam) River ] **1** city in EC England, in Cambridgeshire: pop. 100,000: site of Cambridge University **2** CAMBRIDGESHIRE **3** [after the English city ] city in E Mass., across the Charles River from Boston: pop. 96,000 **4** [after the English city ] city in SE Ontario, Canada: pop. 77,000

**Cam·bridge·shire** (-brij shir') county in EC England: 1,316 sq. mi. (3,409 sq. km); pop. 609,000; county seat, Cambridge

**Cam·den** (kam'dən) **1** [after Charles Pratt, Earl of *Camden* (1714-94) ] city in SW N.J., on the Delaware River, opposite Philadelphia: pop. 87,000 **2** borough of N Greater London: pop. 177,000

**Ca·mel·o·pard** (kə mel'ə pärd') the constellation Camelopardus

**Ca·mel·o·par·dus** (kə mel'ə pär'dəs) [see prec. ] a N constellation between Ursa Major and Cassiopeia; Giraffe; Camelopard: also **Ca·mel'o·par'da·lis** (-pär'də lis)

**Cam·e·lot** (kam'ə lät') *Arthurian Legend* the English town where King Arthur has his court and Round Table

**Cam·e·roon** (kam'ə rōōn') **1** country in WC Africa, on the Gulf of Guinea: formerly a German protectorate (est. 1884), most of area was under French administration from 1919 until independence was proclaimed in 1960: 183,568 sq. mi. (475,439 sq. km); pop. 10,009,000; cap. Yaoundé: cf. CAMEROONS **2 Mount** mountain in W Cameroon: 13,350 ft. (4,070 m)

**Cam·e·roons** (-rōōnz′) former region in W Africa consisting of two trust territories, **French Cameroons** (in 1960 forming the republic of CAMEROON) and **British Cameroons** (in 1961 divided between Cameroon and Nigeria)

**Ca·me·roun** (kam′ə rōōn′; *Fr* kåm *rōōn′*) *Fr. name of* CAMEROON

**Cam·pa·gna di Ro·ma** (käm pä′nyä dē *rô′*mä) low-lying plain in central Italy, around Rome: *c.* 800 sq. mi. (2,070 sq. km)

**Cam·pa·ni·a** (kam pä′nē ə; *It* käm pä′nyä) 〚L, lit., plain < *campus*, a field < IE *\*kampos*, a corner, cove < base *\*kamp-*, to bend〛 region in S Italy, on the Tyrrhenian Sea: 5,249 sq. mi. (13,595 sq. km); pop. 5,608,000; chief city, Naples

**Cam·pe·che** (kam pē′chē; *Sp* käm pe′che) **1** state of SE Mexico, in the W Yucatán peninsula: 19,619 sq. mi. (50,812 sq. km); pop. 408,000 **2** capital of this state, a port on the Gulf of Campeche: pop. 152,000 **3 Gulf** (or **Bay**) **of** arm of the Gulf of Mexico, west of the Yucatán peninsula

**Cam·pi·na Gran·de** (käm pē′nə grän′də) city in NE Brazil, in E Paraiba state: pop. 248,000

**Cam·pi·nas** (käm pē′nəs) city in SE Brazil, near São Paulo: pop. 567,000

**Cam·po·bel·lo** (kam′pō bel′ō) island of New Brunswick, Canada, in the Bay of Fundy

**Cam·po Gran·de** (käm′pō grän′də) city in SW Brazil: capital of Mato Grosso do Sul: pop. 292,000

**Cam·pos** (käm′pəs) city in SE Brazil, in Rio de Janeiro state: pop. 349,000

**Ca·na** (kā′nə) village in Galilee, N Israel: scene of Jesus' first two miracles: John 2:1-9; 4:46-54

**Ca·naan** (kā′nən) 〚LL (Vulg, Gen. 10) *Chanaan* < Gr *Chanan* < Heb *kena'an*〛 ancient region at the SE end of the Mediterranean, extending eastward to the Jordan River; the Biblical Promised Land: Gen. 17:8

**Can·a·da** (kan′ə də) 〚Fr < L, a word for village in an extinct (before 1600) Iroquoian language of the lower St. Lawrence River valley〛 country in N North America: complete British control achieved, 1763; dominion established, 1867; complete autonomy, 1931: a member of the Commonwealth: 3,849,672 sq. mi. (9,970,610 sq. km); pop. 25,310,000; cap. Ottawa

**Ca·na·di·an** (kə nā′dē ən) river flowing eastward from N N.Mex., across NW Tex., to the Arkansas River in E Okla.: 906 mi. (1,458 km)

**Canadian Shield** an area of about 2,000,000 square miles (5,000,000 sq. km) of Precambrian strata, consisting largely of granite, gneiss, marble, and other igneous and metamorphic rocks that occupy most of eastern and central Canada & part of NE U.S.

**Canal Zone** strip of land in Panama that extends five miles on either side of the Panama Canal, excluding the cities of Panama and Colón: formerly under lease to the United States, which governed it (1904-79); now under control of the United States (through 1999) for the administration and defense of the canal

**Ca·nar·y Islands** (kə ner′ē) group of islands in the Atlantic, off NW Africa, forming a region of Spain: 2,808 sq. mi. (7,273 sq. km); pop. 1,445,000: Sp. name **Is·las Ca·na·ri·as** (ēz′läs kä nä′rē äs)

**Ca·na·ver·al** (kə nav′ər əl), **Cape** ⟦Sp *cañaveral*, canebrake⟧ cape on the E coast of Fla.: U.S. proving ground for missiles and spacecraft: temporarily renamed *Cape Kennedy* (1963-73)

**Can·ber·ra** (kan′bər ə, -ber′ə) capital of Australia, in the Australian Capital Territory: pop. 256,000

**Can·cer** (kan′sər) ⟦ME & OE < L, a crab; later, malignant tumor; by dissimilation (? already in IE) < IE *\*karkar-*, redupl. of base *\*kar-*, hard⟧ **1** a N constellation between Gemini and Leo **2** the fourth sign of the zodiac, entered by the sun about June 21 **3** *see* TROPIC

**Can·di·a** (kan′dē ə) **1** *old name of* CRETE **2** *old name of* IRAKLION

**Ca·ne·a** (kə nē′ə) capital of Crete: pop. 133,000

**Ca·nes Ve·nat·i·ci** (kā′nēz′ və nat′ə sī′) a N constellation between Ursa Major and Boötes

**Ca·nic·u·la** (kə nik′yōō lə) ⟦L, dim. of *canis*, dog <IE base *\*kwon-*, dog⟧ [Rare] Sirius, the Dog Star

**Ca·nis Major** (kā′nis) ⟦L, the Greater Dog⟧ a S constellation between Monoceros and Columba, containing the Dog Star, Sirius

**Canis Minor** ⟦L, the Lesser Dog⟧ a N constellation

near Gemini and Cancer, containing the bright star Procyon

**Can·nae** (kan′ē) ancient town in SE Italy: site of a battle (216 B.C.) in which the Carthaginians under Hannibal defeated the Romans

**Cannes** (kan, kanz; *Fr* kȧn) city in SE France, on the Riviera: pop. 73,000

**Ca·no·pus** (kə nō′pəs) 〚L < Gr *Kanōpos*〛 **1** a supergiant binary star in the constellation Carina, the second brightest star, with a magnitude of -0.86 **2** seaport in ancient Egypt, near the mouth of the Nile

**Can·ta·bri·a** (kan tā′brē ə) region of N Spain, on the Bay of Biscay: 2,042 sq. mi. (5,289 sq. km); pop. 511,000; cap. Santander

**Cantabrian Mountains** mountain range in N & NW Spain, parallel to the Bay of Biscay: highest peak, 8,687 ft. (2,648 m)

**Can·ter·bur·y** (kan′tər ber′ē, -bər ē) **1** city in Kent, SE England: seat of a primate of the Church of England: pop. 31,000 **2** city in New South Wales, SE Australia: suburb of Sydney: pop. 127,000

**Can·ton** (kan tän′; *for 2* kan′tən) **1** *old form of* GUANG-ZHOU **2** 〚after *Canton*, suburb of Boston, named for the Chinese city〛 city in EC Ohio: pop. 84,000 (met. area 394,000)

**Can·yon·lands National Park** (kan′yən landz′) national park along the Green & Colorado rivers, in SE Utah, with deep canyons & unusual rock formations: 527 sq. mi. (1,365 sq. km)

**Cape, the 1** Cape of Good Hope **2** Cape of Good Hope Province **3** Cape Cod

**Cape Breton Island** 〚prob. after *Canbreton*, coastal town in France〛 island constituting the NE part of Nova Scotia, Canada: 3,970 sq. mi. (10,282 sq. km)

**Cape Colony** *old name of* CAPE PROVINCE

**Cape Coral** 〚< ?〛 city in SW Fla.: pop. 75,000

**Ca·pel·la** (kə pel′ə) 〚L, dim. of *capra*, she-goat〛 a yellow, giant multiple star, the brightest star in the constellation Auriga, with a magnitude of 0.13

**Cape Prov·ince** (präv′ins) southernmost and largest province in Republic of South Africa: 249,331 sq. mi. (646,767 sq. km); pop. 5,091,000: in full **Cape of Good Hope Province**

**Ca·per·na·um** (kə pʉr′nē əm) city in ancient Palestine,

on the Sea of Galilee: cf. Matt. 4:12-13; John 2:12

**Cape Town** seaport & capital of Cape Province: seat of the legislature of South Africa: pop. 214,000

**Cape Verde** (vʉrd) country on a group of islands in the Atlantic, *c.* 300 mi. (480 km) west of Cape VERDE: the islands were under Portuguese control from 1587 until the granting of independence, 1975: 1,560 sq. mi. (4,040 sq. km); pop. 318,000; cap. Praia

**Cape York Peninsula** (yôrk) large peninsula in NE Australia, part of Queensland, between the Gulf of Carpentaria & the Coral Sea

**Cap Hai·ti·en** (kap′ hät′ē en′, -hä′sē-; -hä′shən) seaport on the N coast of Haiti: pop. 64,000: Fr. name **Cap–Ha·ï·ti·en** (kȧ pȧ ē tyan′, -syan′)

**Cap·i·tol** (kap′ət ′l) ⟦ME & OFr *capitolie* < L *Capitolium*, temple of Jupiter in Rome; < ? (but possibly related to *caput*, head⟧ **1** the temple of Jupiter on the Capitoline Hill in ancient Rome **2** the building in which the U.S. Congress meets in Washington, D.C. **3** CAPITOLINE

**Capitol Hill** the hill in Washington, D.C. on which stands the Capitol building

**Cap·i·to·line** (kap′ət ′l īn′, -ēn′) one of the SEVEN HILLS OF ROME

**Capitol Reef National Park** ⟦for a white, dome-shaped rock resembling the CAPITOL in Washington⟧ national park in S Utah, characterized by sandstone cliffs & deep gorges: 378 sq. mi. (980 sq. km)

**Cap·o·ret·to** (kap′ə ret′ō) Italian village (now in Slovenia): scene of a battle of World War I in which the Italian army was defeated by Austro-German forces (1917): Slovene name KOBARID

**Cap·pa·do·cia** (kap′ə dō′shē ə, -shə) ancient kingdom, later a Roman province, in E Asia Minor: fl. 3d cent. B.C.-1st cent. A.D.

**Ca·pri** (kä prē′, kə-; kä′prē′) island near the entrance to the Bay of Naples: 4 sq. mi. (10.5 sq. km)

**Cap·ri·corn** (kap′ri kôrn′) ⟦ME < OFr < L *capricornus* < *caper*, he-goat (< IE *kapro-) + *cornu*, horn⟧ **1** Capricornus **2** the tenth sign of the zodiac, entered by the sun about Dec. 22 **3** *see* TROPIC

**Cap·ri·cor·nus** (kap′ri kôr′nəs) a S constellation between Aquarius and Sagittarius

**Ca·pri·vi Strip** (kə prē′vē) narrow strip of land, *c.* 50 mi.,

(80 km) wide, of NE Namibia, extending eastward to the Zambezi River: *c.* 300 mi. (480 km) long

**Cap·u·a** (kap′yoo ə) town in S Italy, near Naples: pop. 18,000: ancient city of Capua (destroyed A.D. 841) was on a nearby site

**Ca·ra·cas** (kə räk′əs, -rak′-; *Sp* kä rä′käs) capital of Venezuela, in the NC part: pop. 1,163,000: within a federal district 745 sq. mi. (1,930 sq. km), pop. 2,071,000

**Car·cas·sonne** (kär′kə sän′; *Fr* kȧr kȧ sôn′) city in S France: site of a restored medieval walled city: pop. 42,000

**Car·diff** (kär′dif) seaport in SE Wales, on the Bristol Channel: capital of Wales & county seat of South Glamorgan: pop. 281,000

**Car·di·gan Bay** (kär′di gən) inlet of St. George's Channel, on the W coast of Wales

**Car·di·gan·shire** (-shir′, -shər) former county of W Wales, now part of Dyfed; also **Car′di·gan**

**Car·i·a** (ker′ē ə) ancient region in SW Asia Minor: fl. 4th-2d cent. B.C.

**Car·ib·be·an** (kar′ə bē′ən, kə rib′ē ən) CARIBBEAN SEA

**Caribbean Sea** part of the Atlantic, bounded by the West Indies, Central America, and the N coast of South America: *c.* 750,000 sq. mi. (1,942,500 sq. km)

**Ca·ri·na** (kə rī′nə, -rē′-) a S constellation between Vela and Pictor containing the bright star Canopus: see ARGO

**Ca·rin·thi·a** (kə rin′thē ə) region of central Europe, bordering Italy and Slovenia: divided between Austria and Yugoslavia (1918)

**Car·lisle** (kär lil′, kär′lil′) city in NW England; county seat of Cumbria: pop. 71,000

**Carls·bad Caverns National Park** (kärlz′bad′) [from the resemblance of the springs in the park to those at Karlovy Vary (Ger *Carlsbad*), Czechoslovakia] national park in SE N.Mex., containing large limestone caverns with stalactites and stalagmites: 73 sq. mi. (189 sq. km)

**Car·mar·then·shire** (kär mär′thən shir′, -shər) former county of SW Wales, now part of Dyfed

**Car·mel** (kär′məl), **Mount** mountain ridge in NW Israel, extending as a promontory into the Mediterranean: highest point, *c.* 1,800 ft. (550 m)

**Car·mi·chael** (kär'mĭ'kəl) ⟦after D. *Carmichael*, early developer⟧ urban community in NC Calif., northeast of Sacramento: pop. 49,000

**Car·nat·ic** (kär nat'ĭk) region in SE India, between the Coromandel Coast and the E Ghats

**Car·o·li·na¹** (kar'ə lĭ'nə) ⟦ModL, fem. of *Carolus*, a given name (Charles): in honor of Charles I (1600-1649), king of England, Scotland & Ireland, who issued a grant (1663) for lands south of Virginia⟧ English colony (1663-1729) including what is now N.C., S.C., Ga., and N Fla.

**Ca·ro·li·na²** (kär'ə lē'nə) ⟦after Doña *Carolina* Andino, donor of the town site⟧ city in NE Puerto Rico, near San Juan: pop. 178,000

**Carolinas**, the North Carolina and South Carolina

**Car·o·line Islands** (kar'ə lĭn', -lin) archipelago in the W Pacific: pop. 87,000: in 1979 four of its five districts gained internal self-government as the *Federated States of Micronesia*, but remained a part of the Trust Territory of the PACIFIC ISLANDS

**Car·pa·thi·an Mountains** (kär pā'thē ən) mountain system in central Europe, extending southeast from S Poland through Czech Republic and Ukraine into NE Romania: highest peak, 8,737 ft. (2,663 m): also **Carpathians**

**Car·pen·tar·i·a** (kär'pən ter'ē ə), **Gulf of** arm of the Arafura Sea, indenting the N coast of Australia: *c.* 480 mi. (770 km) long; 400 mi. (640 km) wide

**Car·ra·ra** (kə rär'ə) commune in Tuscany, NW Italy: a fine white marble is quarried nearby: pop. 68,000

**Car·roll·ton** (kar'əl tən) ⟦after *Carrollton*, Ill. (the home of the founders), named for Charles *Carroll* (1737-1832), Am Revolutionary leader⟧ city in NE Tex.: suburb of Dallas: pop. 82,000

**Car·son** (kär'sən) ⟦after G. H. *Carson* (1829-1901), local landowner⟧ city in SW Calif.: suburb of Los Angeles: pop. 84,000

**Carson City** ⟦after Kit *Carson* (1809-68), U.S. frontiersman⟧ capital of Nev., near Lake Tahoe: pop. 40,000

**Car·stensz** (kär'stənz), **Mount** old name of DJAJA PEAK

**Car·ta·ge·na** (kär'tə hā'nə, -tə jē'-) 1 seaport in NW Colombia, on the Caribbean: pop. 530,000 2 seaport in Murcia, SE Spain, on the Mediterranean: pop. 173,000

**Car·thage** (kär'thĭj) ancient city-state in N Africa,

founded (9th cent. B.C.) by Phoenicians near the site of
modern Tunis and destroyed by the Romans in 146
B.C.: rebuilt by Romans (44 B.C.) & destroyed by Arabs
(A.D. 698)

**Ca·sa·blan·ca** (kas'ə blaŋ'kə, kä'sə bläŋ'kə) seaport in
NW Morocco, on the Atlantic: pop. 2,158,000

**Ca·sa Gran·de** (kas'ə gran'dē, kä'sə grän'dä) [Sp, large
house] the massive, prehistoric structure within
Indian ruins in S Ariz., now constituting a national
monument

**Cas·bah** (käz'bä', kaz'-) the crowded quarter of Algiers

**Cas·cade Range** (kas kād') [for the cascades on the
Columbia River] mountain range extending from N
Calif., through W Oreg. and Wash., into S British
Columbia: highest peak, Mt. Rainier

**Cas·co Bay** (kas'kō) [< Algonquian, muddy: for the
mud flats in the bay] bay on the SW coast of Maine,
on which Portland is located

**Cas·per** (kas'pər) [earlier Fort *Caspar*, after Lt. *Caspar*
Collins, killed there] city in central Wyo.: pop. 47,000

**Cas·pi·an Sea** (kas'pē ən) inland salt sea between Asia
and extreme SE Europe, north of Iran: *c.* 144,000 sq.
mi. (373,000 sq. km)

**Cas·si·o·pe·ia** (kas'ē ō pē'ə, -pē'yə) [L < Gr *Kassi-
opeia*] a N constellation between Andromeda and
Cepheus

**Cassiopeia's Chair** the five brightest stars in the constellation Cassiopeia

**Cas·ta·li·a** (kas tā'lē ə) [L < Gr *Kastalia*] spring on
Mount Parnassus, Greece: in ancient times it was
sacred to the Muses and was considered a source of
poetic inspiration for those who bathed in it

**Cas·te·llón** (käs'təl yōn') seaport in E Spain, on the
Mediterranean: pop. 127,000: in full **Castellón de la
Pla·na** (-dä' lä plä'nä')

**Cas·tile** (kas tēl') region & former kingdom in N and
central Spain: gained autonomy in 10th cent. & united
with León, & later with Aragon (15th cent.), & became
the nucleus of the Spanish monarchy: traditionally
divided between Old Castile, to the north (now the
region of **Castilla-Leon**, 36,350 sq. mi. or 94,147 sq.
km, pop. 2,577,000; cap. Burgos) and New Castile, to
the south (now the region of **Castilla-La Mancha**,
30,590 sq. mi. or 79,226 sq. km, pop. 1,628,000; cap.

Toledo): Sp. name **Cas·ti·lla** (käs tēl′yä)

**Cas·tor** (kas′tər) ⟦L < Gr *Kastōr*⟧ a multiple star, actually the second brightest star in the constellation Gemini although it is considered the twin of Pollux, with a magnitude of 1.5

**Cas·tries** (kas trēz′, kas′trēz) capital of St. Lucia, a seaport on the NW coast: pop. 45,000

**Cas·tro Valley** (kas′trō) ⟦after G. *Castro*, local rancher⟧ suburb of Oakland, in W Calif., near San Francisco Bay: pop. 49,000

**Cat·a·li·na (Island)** (kat′ə lē′nə) ⟦Sp, in honor of St. Catherine of Alexandria⟧ SANTA CATALINA (Island)

**Cat·a·lo·ni·a** (kat′ə lō′nē ə) region in NE Spain, on the Mediterranean: 12,328 sq. mi. (31,930 sq. km); pop. 5,958,000; cap. Barcelona: Sp. name **Ca·ta·lu·ña** (kä′tä lōō′nyä′)

**Ca·ta·nia** (kə tän′yə, -tän′-) seaport on the E coast of Sicily, at the foot of Mt. Etna: pop. 380,000

**Ca·tan·za·ro** (kä′tän zä′rō) city in S Italy, southeast of Naples: cap. of Calabria: pop. 102,000

**Ca·thay** (ka thā′, kə-) ⟦ML *Cataya* < Uighur *Khitay*, a Mongol people who ruled in Beijing (936-1122)⟧ *old name of* CHINA

**Cats·kill Mountains** (kats′kil′) ⟦Du, cat′s stream; reason for name unknown⟧ mountain range of the Appalachian system, in SE N.Y.: resort area: highest peak, *c.* 4,200 ft. (1,280 m): also **Catskills**

**Cat·te·gat** (kat′i gat′) *alt. sp. of* KATTEGAT

**Cau·ca** (kou′kä) river in W Colombia, flowing from the Andes northward into the Magdalena River: *c.* 600 mi. (1,300 km)

**Cau·ca·sia** (kô kā′zhə, -shə) the Caucasus region

**Cau·ca·sus** (kô′kə səs) **1** border region between SE Europe and W Asia, between the Black and Caspian seas: often called **the Caucasus 2** mountain range in the Caucasus, running northwest to southeast between the Black and Caspian seas: highest peak, Mt. Elbrus: in full **Caucasus Mountains**

**Cau·ver·y** (kô′vər ē) river in S India, flowing from the W Ghats southeastward into the Bay of Bengal: *c.* 475 mi. (765 km)

**Ca·vi·te** (kä vē′te) seaport on Manila Bay, SW Luzon, the Philippines: pop. 88,000

**Cay·enne** (kī en′, kā-) capital & chief town of French

Guiana, on the Atlantic: pop. 38,000

**Cay·man Islands** (kā'mən, kī män') British Crown Colony in the Caribbean, consisting of a group of three islands 150 mi. (240 km) northwest of Jamaica: 100 sq. mi. (260 sq. km); pop. 22,000

**Ca·yu·ga Lake** (kā yōō'gə, kī-) ⟦< *Cayuga* < *kayó·kwe*ⁿ, name of a 17th-c. village of the Cayuga people⟧ lake in WC N.Y., one of the Finger Lakes: 38 mi. (61 km) long

**Ce·a·rá** (se'ä rä') state on the NE coast of Brazil: 58,159 sq. mi. (150,630 sq. km); pop. 5,893,000; cap. Fortaleza

**Ce·bu** (sā bōō') 1 island in the SC Philippines, between Negros & Leyte: 1,703 sq. mi. (4,411 sq. km) 2 seaport & chief city on this island: pop. 490,000

**Čech·y** (chekh'ē) *Czech name of* Bohemia

**Cedar Rapids** ⟦for the rapids of the nearby Cedar River⟧ city in EC Iowa: pop. 109,000

**Ce·la·ya** (sə li'ə) city in Guanajuato state, central Mexico: pop. 220,000

**Cel·e·bes** (sel'ə bēz', sə lē'bēz') island of Indonesia, in the Malay Archipelago, east of Borneo: with small nearby islands, 88,459 sq. mi. (229,108 sq. km); pop. 10,410,000; chief city, Makassar: Indonesian name Sulawesi

**Celebes Sea** part of the South Pacific Ocean, north of Celebes and south of the Philippines

**Celestial Empire** ⟦transl. of a former Chin name for China⟧ Chinese Empire

**Ce·nis** (sə nē') 1 Mont (mōn) mountain pass between France and Italy in Graian Alps: 6,830 ft. (2,082 m) high 2 Mont (mōn) nearby railroad tunnel (8.5 mi., 13.5 km long) that runs between Italy and France

**Cen·taur** (sen'tôr') the constellation Centaurus

**Cen·tau·rus** (sen tô'rəs) ⟦L < Gr *Kentauros*, Centaur⟧ a S constellation between Hydra and Crux, containing Alpha Centauri

**Cen·tral** (sen'trəl) region of SC Scotland, including the former county of Stirling & parts of Dunbarton & Perth: 1,000 sq. mi. (2,590 sq. km); pop. 273,000

**Central African Republic** country in central Africa, north of Zaire and the Congo: a French territory, it became independent (1960): 240,535 sq. mi. (622,984 sq. km); pop. 2,744,000; cap. Bangui

**Central America** part of North America between Mexico and South America; often considered to extend from the Isthmus of Tehuantepec to the Isthmus of Panama

**Central Province** province of Saudi Arabia: *c.* 450,000 sq. mi. (1,165,500 sq. km); pop. 4,000,000; chief city, Riyadh

**Cen·tre** (sän'tr′) region of central France, southwest of Paris: 15,390 sq. mi. (39,062 sq. km); pop. 2,264,000; chief city, Orleans

**Ceph·a·lo·ni·a** (sef′ə lō'nē ə) largest of the Ionian Islands, off the W coast of Greece: *c.* 300 sq. mi. (775 sq. km): Gr. name KEFALLINIA

**Ce·phe·us** (sē'fē əs, -fyo͞os′) ⟦L < Gr *Kēpheus*⟧ a N constellation near the celestial pole

**Ce·ram** (si ram′) one of the Molucca Islands, in Indonesia, west of New Guinea: 6,622 sq. mi. (17,150 sq. km)

**Ce·res** (sir'ēz′) ⟦L, after *Ceres*, the Roman goddess of agriculture⟧ the first asteroid discovered (1801), and the largest (*c.* 1,000 km or 621 mi. in diameter)

**Cer·ri·tos** (se rē'tōs) ⟦Sp, little hills⟧ city in SW Calif.: suburb of Los Angeles: pop. 53,000

**Cer·ro de Pas·co** (ser'ō dä päs'kō) mining town in the mountains of WC Peru: alt. *c.* 14,000 ft. (4,250 m): pop. 72,000

**Cer·vin** (ser van′), **Mont** (mōn) *Fr. name of* the MATTERHORN

**Čes·ké Bu·dě·jo·vi·ce** (ches'ke bo͞o'de yô'vit sə) city in SW Czech Republic, on the Vltava River: pop. 93,000

**Čes·ko·slo·ven·sko** (ches'kô slô ven'skô) *Czech name of* CZECHOSLOVAKIA

**Ce·tus** (sēt'əs) ⟦L, whale⟧ an equatorial constellation near Pisces

**Ceu·ta** (syo͞ot'ə; *Sp* thä'o͞o tä′) Spanish seaport in NW Africa, opposite Gibraltar: an enclave in Morocco: pop. 71,000

**Cé·vennes** (sā ven′) mountain range in S France, west of the Rhone: highest peak, 5,755 ft. (1,754 m)

**Cey·lon** (sə län′, sā-, sē-) *old name of* SRI LANKA

**Cha·co** (chä'kô) extensive lowland plain in central South America, stretching across parts of Argentina, Paraguay, and Bolivia: *c.* 300,000 sq. mi. (770,000 sq. km)

**Chad** (chad) 1 country in NC Africa, south of Libya: formerly a French territory, it became independent

(1960): 496,000 sq. mi. (1,284,634 sq. km); pop.
5,231,000; cap. N'Djamena **2 Lake** lake mostly in
Chad, at the juncture of the Chad, Niger, Cameroon,
and Nigeria borders: 4,000-10,000 sq. mi. (10,000-
26,000 sq. km), reflecting seasonal fluctuation

**Chaer·o·ne·a** (ker'ə nē'ə) ancient Greek town in
Boeotia: site of a battle (338 B.C.) in which the
Macedonians under Philip II established supremacy
over the Greeks

**Cha·gos Archipelago** (chä'gəs) group of islands in the
Indian Ocean 1,180 mi. (1,899 km) northeast of Mauritius, comprising the British Indian Ocean Territory:
chief island, Diego Garcia

**Cha·gres** (chä'gres) river in Panama, dammed to form
Gatun Lake, flowing into the Caribbean

**Chal·ce·don** (kal'sə dän') ancient Greek city on the
Bosporus, opposite Byzantium: site of the 4th ecu-
menical council, A.D. 451

**Chal·ci·di·ce** (kal sid'ə sē') peninsula in NE Greece,
extending into the Aegean, & terminating in three
prongs

**Chal·cis** (kal'sis) seaport in E Greece, on WC Evvoia
island: pop. 45,000

**Chal·de·a, Chal·dae·a** (kal dē'ə) **1** ancient region along
the lower courses of the Tigris and Euphrates rivers: S
part of Babylonia **2** Babylonia: so called during Chal-
dean supremacy, c. 6th cent. B.C.

**Châ·lons–sur–Marne** (shä lōn sür marn') city in NE
France, on the Marne River: scene of defeat (A.D. 451)
of Attila by the Romans: pop. 54,000: also **Chalons**

**Cha·mae·le·on** (kə mē'lē ən) 〚L < *chamaeleon* (the lizard) < Gr *chamaileōn* 〛 a S constellation near the
celestial pole

**Cha·mo·nix** (shȧ mô nē') valley in E France, north of
Mont Blanc: a resort area of the French Alps

**Cham·pagne** (sham pān'; *Fr* shän pȧn'y') agricultural
and historical region of NE France: now mostly in the
region of **Champagne–Ardennes**, which also includes
part of the Ardennes plateau: 9,887 sq. mi. (25,606 sq.
km); pop. 1,349,000; chief city, Reims

**Cham·paign** (sham pān') 〚after *Champaign* county, in
which located: so called for its flat land (champaign) 〛
city in EC Ill.: pop. 64,000

**Cham·plain** (sham plān'), **Lake** 〚after Samuel de

*Champlain* (1567-1635), Fr explorer who discovered it ‖ lake on the N section of the border between N.Y. and Vt.: *c.* 125 mi. (200 km) long

**Chan·cel·lors·ville** (chan'sə lərz vil') ‖after a local family name ‖ hamlet in NE Va. (now called *Chancellor*): site of a Civil War battle (May, 1863) won by Confederate forces

**Chan·der·na·gor, Chan·der·na·gore** (chun'dər nə gôr') port in NE India, near Calcutta: former French dependency, it became part of Republic of India (1950): pop. 102,000

**Chan·di·garh** (chun'dē gər) **1** city in N India; joint capital of the states of Punjab and Haryana: pop. 421,000 **2** territory of India, constituted of this city & the surrounding area: 44 sq. mi. (114 sq. km); pop. 450,000

**Chan·dler** (chand'lər) ‖after A. J. *Chandler* (1859-1950), its founder ‖ city in SC Ariz.: pop. 91,000

**Chang** (chäŋ) largest river and chief commercial highway of China, flowing from Tibet into East China Sea near Shanghai: *c.* 3,400 mi. (5,440 km): old name YANGTZE

**Chang·chia·kou** (chäŋ'jyä'kō') *old form of* ZHANGJIAKOU

**Chang·chou** (chäŋ'chou'; *Chin* jäŋ'jō') *old form of* CHANGZHOU

**Chang·chun** (chäŋ'choon') city in NE China; capital of Jilin province: pop. 1,740,000

**Chang·de** (chäŋ'də) city in N Hunan, in SE central China: pop. 120,000

**Chang·hua** (chäŋ'hwä') city in W Taiwan: pop. 199,000

**Chang·sha** (chäŋ'shä') city in SE China; capital of Hunan province: pop. 850,000

**Chang·teh** (chäŋ'də) *old form of* CHANGDE

**Chang·zhou** (jäŋ'jō') city in Jiangsu province, E China, on the Grand Canal: pop. 300,000

**Channel Islands 1** group of islands in the English Channel, off the coast of Normandy: British crown dependencies with internal self-government: 75 sq. mi. (194 sq. km); pop. 133,000 **2** SANTA BARBARA ISLANDS

**Chan·til·ly** (shan til'ē; *Fr* shän tē yē') town in N France, near Paris: noted for a kind of lace first made there: pop. 11,000

**Chao Phra·ya** (chou' prä yä', -prī'ə) principal river of Thailand, in the W part, flowing past Bangkok into the Gulf of Thailand: *c.* 160 mi. (260 km)

**Cha·pul·te·pec** (chə pool'tə pek', -pul'-) 〚Nahuatl, lit., grasshopper hill〛 fortress on a rocky hill near Mexico City: captured (Sept., 1847) in an American assault led by Gen. Winfield Scott in the Mexican War

**Cha·ri** (shä'rē) *alt. sp. of* SHARI

**Char·i·ot·eer** (char'ē ə tir') the constellation Auriga

**Char·le·roi** (shär'lə roi'; *Fr* shàr lə rwä') city in SW Belgium, in Hainaut: pop. 211,000

**Charles** (chärlz) 〚after *Charles* I (1600-49) of England〛 1 river in E Mass., flowing into Boston Bay: *c.* 60 mi. (95 km) 2 **Cape** cape in SE Va., at the mouth of Chesapeake Bay, forming the tip of Delmarva Peninsula

**Charles·bourg** (shärl'boorg; *Fr* shàrl boor') city in S Quebec, Canada: pop. 69,000

**Charles's Wain** [Brit.] BIG DIPPER

**Charles·ton** (chärls'tən) 1 〚after *Charles* II (1630-85) of England〛 seaport in S.C.: pop. 80,000 2 〚after the founder's father, *Charles*〛 capital of W.Va., in the W part: pop. 57,000

**Charles·town** (chärlz'toun') 〚after *Charles* I (1600-49) of England〛 oldest part of Boston, at the mouth of the Charles River: site of the battle of Bunker Hill

**Char·lotte** (shär'lət) 〚after Queen *Charlotte*, wife of George III〛 city in S N.C.: pop. 396,000 (met. area, with Gastonia and Rock Hill, 1,162,000)

**Charlotte A·ma·lie** (ə mäl'yə, ə mäl'ē) 〚after Queen *Charlotte Amalie*, wife of Christian V of Denmark, to which the islands formerly belonged〛 capital of the Virgin Islands of the U.S., on St. Thomas: pop. 12,000

**Char·lottes·ville** (shär'ləts vil') 〚after Queen *Charlotte*, wife of George III〛 city in central Va.: pop. 40,000

**Char·lotte·town** (shär'lət toun') 〚after Queen *Charlotte*, wife of George III〛 capital of Prince Edward Island, Can.: pop. 16,000

**Cha·ron** (ker'ən) 〚L < Gr *Charōn*〛 the satellite of Pluto: discovered in 1978, it has an orbital period equal to Pluto's rotational period

**Char·ter·house** (chärt'ər hous') a boys' school in Surrey, England, moved from its orig. location in London that was on the site of a Carthusian monastery

**Char·tres** (shär'tr'; *E* shär'trə, shärt) city in NC France, near Paris: site of a 13th-cent. Gothic cathedral: pop.

39,000

**Cha·ryb·dis** (kə rib′dis) ⟦ L < Gr ⟧ *old name of* a whirlpool off the NE coast of Sicily, in the Strait of Messina (now called *Galofalo*): see SCYLLA

**Châ·teau–Thier·ry** (sha′tō′tē er′ē; *Fr* shȧ tō tye rē′) town in N France, on the Marne: battle site in World War I: pop. 13,000

**Chat·ham** (chat′əm) **1** seaport in Kent, SE England: pop. 62,000 **2** city in SW Ontario, Canada: pop. 42,000

**Chatham Islands** group of islands of New Zealand, *c.* 400 mi. (640 km) east of North Island: 372 sq. mi. (963 sq. km)

**Chat·ta·hoo·chee** (chat′ə hōō′chē) ⟦ < AmInd (Creek), lit., pictured rocks (found in the river) ⟧ river flowing from N Ga. southward along the Ga.-Ala. border into the Apalachicola: 436 mi. (702 km)

**Chat·ta·noo·ga** (chat′ə nōō′gə) ⟦ < AmInd (Creek or Cherokee); meaning uncert. ⟧ city in SE Tenn., on the Tennessee River at the Ga. border: pop. 152,000

**Chau·tau·qua** (shə tô′kwə) ⟦ < Seneca name; prob., lit., "one has taken out fish there" ⟧ **1** lake in SW N.Y.; 18 mi. (29 km) long **2** town on this lake: pop. 5,000

**Che·bok·sa·ry** (cheb′äk′sär′ē) city in WC Russia, on the Volga W of Kazan: pop. 389,000

**Che·ju** (chä′jōō′) island in the East China Sea, southwest of the Korean peninsula: 705 sq. mi. (1,825 sq. km); pop. 482,000

**Che·kiang** (che′kyaŋ′; *Chin* jū′jyäŋ′) *old form of* ZHEJIANG

**Chel·sea** (chel′sē) former borough of London, now part of the borough of Kensington and Chelsea

**Chel·ten·ham** (chelt′′n ham′; *Brit* chelt′nəm, -′n əm) city in Gloucestershire, SW England: pop. 74,000

**Chel·ya·binsk** (chel yä′binsk) city in SW Russia, in the S Urals: pop. 1,096,000

**Chel·yus·kin** (chel yoos′kin), **Cape** northernmost point of Asia, on the Taimyr Peninsula, Siberia

**Chem·nitz** (kem′nits′) city in E Germany, in the state of Saxony: pop. 317,000

**Che·nab** (chi näb′) river rising in N India, flowing through Jammu and Kashmir and then SW into the Sutlej River in Pakistan: *c.* 675 mi. (1,085 km)

**Chen·chi·ang** (jen′jē äŋ′) *old form of* ZHENJIANG

**Cheng·chow, Cheng·chou** (jen′jou′) *old form of*

Zhengzhou

**Cheng·de** (chuŋ'du') city in NE Hebei province, in NE China, NE of Beijing: the former summer residence of the Manchu emperors of China: pop. 120,000

**Cheng·du** (chuŋ'dōō') city in SC China; capital of Sichuan province: pop. 2,470,000

**Cheng·teh** (chuŋ'du') *old form of* Chengde

**Cheng·tu** (chuŋ'dōō') *old form of* Chengdu

**Cher** (sher) river in central France, flowing northwest into the Loire near Tours: *c.* 200 mi. (320 km)

**Cher·bourg** (sher'boorg'; *Fr* sher bōōr') seaport in NW France, on the English Channel: pop. 30,000

**Che·re·po·vetz** (cher'ə pə vets') city in NE Russia, on the Rybinsk Reservoir: pop. 299,000

**Cher·kas·sy** (chər kas'ē, -käs-) city & port in central Ukraine, on the Dnepr River: pop. 273,000

**Cher·ni·gov** (cher nē'gəf) city in NC Ukraine: pop. 278,000

**Cher·no·byl** (cher nō'bəl) city in NC Ukraine: site of a nuclear power plant where a serious accident occurred in 1986

**Cher·nov·tsy** (cher nuf tsē') city in W Ukraine, on the Prut River: pop. 244,000

**Cherry Hill** ⟦after an old farm on a hill, named for its cherry trees⟧ city in SW N.J., east of Camden: pop. 69,000

**Ches·a·peake** (ches'ə pēk') ⟦after fol.⟧ city in SE Va., at the base of Chesapeake Bay: pop. 152,000

**Chesapeake Bay** ⟦< Algonquian, lit., place on a big river⟧ arm of the Atlantic, extending north into Va. and Md.: *c.* 200 mi. (320 km) long

**Chesh·ire** (chesh'ir, -ər) county of W England: 897 sq. mi. (2,322 sq. km); pop. 937,000

**Ches·ter** (ches'tər) **1** city in NW England, south of Liverpool: pop. 59,000 **2** *old name of* Cheshire **3** ⟦after *Chester* (now Cheshire) county, England⟧ seaport in SE Pa., on the Delaware River, near Philadelphia: pop. 42,000

**Chev·i·ot Hills** (chē'vē ət, chev'ē ət) range of hills along the border between England & Scotland: highest point, 2,676 ft. (816 m)

**Chey·enne** (shī an', -en') ⟦after *Cheyenne* (the Indian people) < Fr < Dakota *šahíyena*: meaning unknown⟧ **1** capital of Wyo., in the SE part: pop. 50,000 **2** river

in E Wyo. and W S.Dak., flowing northeast into the
Missouri: 527 mi. (848 km)

**Chiang Mai, Chiang·mai** (jyäŋ′mī′) city in NW Thailand, on a headstream of the Chao Phraya: pop.
102,000

**Chi·a·pas** (chē ä′pəs) state of SE Mexico, on the Guate-
malan border & the Gulf of Tehuantepec: 28,653 sq.
mi. (74,211 sq. km); pop. 2,252,000; cap. Tuxtla
Gutiérrez

**Chi·ba** (chē′bä) city on the E coast of Honshu, Japan, on
Tokyo Bay, opposite Tokyo

**Chi·ca·go** (shə kä′gō, -kô′-) ⟦< Fr < Algonquian, lit.,
place of the onion: from the wild onions growing
there⟧ city and port in NE Ill., on Lake Michigan:
pop. 2,784,000 (met. area 6,070,000; urban area, with
Gary and Hammond, Ind. & Kenosha, Wis., 6,803,000)

**Chi·chén It·zá** (chē chen′ ēt sä′) ruined Mayan city in
Yucatan, SE Mexico: fl. 10th-12th cent.

**Chi·chi·haerh** (chē′chē′här′) *old form of* QIQIHAR

**Chick·a·mau·ga** (chik′ə mô′gə) ⟦AmInd: meaning
uncert.⟧ creek in NW Ga.: site of a Civil War battle
(Sept., 1863) in which Confederate forces routed the
Union army

**Chi·cla·yo** (chē klä′yō) city in NW Peru: pop. 280,000

**Chic·o·pee** (chik′ə pē) ⟦< AmInd, lit., swift river⟧ city
in SW Mass., on the Connecticut River: pop. 57,000

**Chi·cou·ti·mi** (shi kōō′ti mē′) ⟦< Algonquian *shkou-
timeou*, end of the deep water⟧ city in SC Quebec,
Canada, on the Saguenay River: pop. 61,000

**Chi·hua·hua** (chi wä′wä) 1 state of N Mexico, on the
U.S. border: 94,571 sq. mi. (244,938 sq. km); pop.
2,035,000 2 capital of this state: pop. 407,000

**Chi·le** (chil′ē; *Sp* chē′le) country on the SW coast of
South America, between the Andes and the Pacific:
gained independence, 1818: 292,258 sq. mi. (756,945
sq. km); pop. 12,261,000; cap. Santiago

**Chil·koot Pass** (chil′kōōt′) ⟦after the *Chilkoot* Indians
who inhabited the region⟧ mountain pass in the N
Rockies, on the Alas.-British Columbia border, leading
to the Klondike: *c.* 3,500 ft. (1,065 m) high

**Chi·llán** (chē yän′) city in SC Chile: pop. 124,000

**Chil·li·wack** (chil′i wak′) city in S British Columbia:
pop. 41,000

**Chi·lo·é** (chē′lō ä′) island off SC Chile: 3,241 sq. mi.

(8,394 sq. km); pop. 116,000

**Chi·lung** (jē′lōōŋ′) seaport in N Taiwan: pop. 351,000

**Chim·bo·ra·zo** (chim′bə rä′zō) peak of the Andes, in central Ecuador: *c.* 20,500 ft. (6,250 m)

**Chim·bo·te** (chim bō′tā) city in central Peru, on the Pacific coast: pop. 216,000

**Chim·kent** (chim kent′) city in SC Kazakhstan, north of Tashkent: pop. 369,000

**Chi·na** (chī′nə) country in E Asia: before 1912, the CHINESE EMPIRE: *c.* 3,707,000 sq. mi. (9,600,000 sq. km); pop. 1,045,537,000; cap. Beijing: see also TAIWAN

**China Sea** *see* EAST CHINA SEA & SOUTH CHINA SEA

**Chin·chow, Chin·chou** (jin′jō′) *old form of* JINZHOU

**Chin·dwin** (chin′dwin) river in NW Myanmar, flowing southward into the Irrawaddy: over 500 mi. (800 km)

**Chinese Empire** empire in E Asia, from the founding of its first dynasty (*c.* 2200 B.C.) to the revolution of 1911, including China, Manchuria, Mongolia, Tibet, & Turkestan

**Chinese Turkestan** the part of Turkestan under Chinese control, now constituting the section of Xinjiang-Uygur region, China, south of the Tian Shan mountains: also called *Eastern Turkestan*

**Chinese Wall** GREAT WALL OF CHINA

**Ching·hai** (chiŋ′hī′) *old form of* QINGHAI

**Ching·tao** (chiŋ′dou′) *old form of* QINGDAO

**Chin Hills** (chin) mountain range in NW Myanmar, along the India border: highest peak, *c.* 10,000 ft. (3,050 m)

**Chin·ling Shan** (jē′liŋ′ shän) *old form of* QINLING SHAN

**Chi·no** (chē′nō) 〚< ? Sp *chino*, person of mixed blood: perhaps orig. landowner was a person of mixed blood〛 city in SW Calif., east of Los Angeles: pop. 60,000

**Chin·wang·tao** (chin′wäŋ dou′) *old form of* QINHUANGDAO

**Chi·os** (kī′äs′) *var. of* KHÍOS

**Chis·holm Trail** (chiz′əm) 〚after Jesse *Chisholm* (*c.* 1806-68), U.S. frontier scout who established it〛 cattle trail from San Antonio, Tex., to Abilene, Kans.: important from 1865 until 1880's

**Chi·ta** (chē tä′) city in SE Russia, near the Mongolian border: pop. 336,000

**Chit·ta·gong** (chit′ə gôŋ′, -gäŋ′) seaport in SE Bangladesh, near the Bay of Bengal: pop. 1,392,000

**Cho·lu·la** (chō lōō′lə) town in central Mexico, near Puebla: site of Toltec and Aztec ruins: pop. 21,000

**Chong·jin** (chôŋ′jin′) seaport in NE North Korea, on
the Sea of Japan: pop. 328,000

**Chong·qing** (chooŋ′chiŋ′) city in Sichuan province, SC
China, on the Chang River: pop. 2,650,000

**Cho·rzów** (kô′zhōōf) city in S Poland: pop. 145,000

**Cho·sen** (chō′sen′) *Jpn. name of* KOREA

**Christ·church** (krīst′chʉrch′) city on the E coast of
South Island, New Zealand: pop. 324,000

**Chris·ti·an·i·a** (kris′chē an′ē ə, -tē-; -än′-) *old name of*
OSLO

**Christ·mas Island** (kris′məs) 1 island in the Indian
Ocean, south of Java: a territory of Australia: 52 sq.
mi. (135 sq. km); pop. 3,000 2 KIRITIMATI

**Chu·chow** (jōō′jō′) *old form of* ZHUZHOU

**Chud·sko·ye** (chōōt skoi′yə), Lake lake on the border
between Estonia & Russia: *c.* 1,400 sq. mi. (3,625 sq.
km) (with its S extension, Lake Pskov)

**Chuk·chi Sea** (chook′chē) part of the Arctic Ocean,
north of the Bering Strait

**Chu·kot Range** (chōō kät′) mountain range in NE
Siberia: highest peak, *c.* 7,500 ft. (2,290 m)

**Chu·la Vis·ta** (chōō′lə vis′tə) 〚AmSp, lit., beautiful
view〛 city in SW Calif.: suburb of San Diego: pop.
135,000

**Chung·king** (chooŋ′kiŋ′) *old form of* CHONGQING

**Church·ill** (chʉr′chil) 〚after John *Churchill*, Duke of
Marlborough, gov. of Hudson Bay Co. (1685-91) 〛 river
in Canada flowing from N Saskatchewan eastward
through N Manitoba into Hudson Bay: *c.* 1,000 mi.
(1,600 km)

**Churchill Falls** waterfall on the upper Hamilton River,
W Labrador: *c.* 245 ft. (75 m) high

**Cic·e·ro** (sis′ər ō′) 〚after Marcus Tullius *Cicero* (106-43
B.C.), Roman orator〛 city in NE Ill.: suburb of Chicago: pop. 67,000

**Cien·fue·gos** (syen fwā′gōs) seaport on the S coast of
Cuba: pop. 235,000

**Ci·li·cia** (sə lish′ə) region in SE Asia Minor, on the
Mediterranean, under the domination of various kingdoms & rulers from the Assyrians in the 7th cent. B.C.
until conquered by the Turks in the 15th cent.

**Cilician Gates** pass in the Taurus Mts., S Turkey

**Cim·ar·ron** (sim'ə rän', -rōn') ⟦AmSp *cimarrón*, wild, unruly (< OSp *cimarra*, thicket): prob. orig. referring to the wild sheep (bighorn) found along its banks⟧ river flowing from NE N.Mex. eastward to the Arkansas River, near Tulsa, Okla.: *c.* 600 mi. (965 km)

**Cin·cin·nat·i** (sin'sə nat'ē, -ə) ⟦from the Society of the *Cincinnati*, formed (1783) by former Revolutionary officers, after Lucius Quinctius *Cincinnatus*, 5th-c. Roman statesman⟧ city in SW Ohio, on the Ohio River: pop. 364,000 (met. area 1,453,000; urban area, with parts of Ind. & Ky., 1,744,000)

**Cinque Ports** (siŋk) group of towns (orig. five: Hastings, Romney, Hythe, Dover, and Sandwich) on the SE coast of England: they formerly (11th-15th cent.) received privileges in return for providing naval defense at a time when England had no navy

**Ci·pan·go** (si paŋ'gō) *old name for* a group of islands east of Asia, prob. what is now Japan: used by Marco Polo & medieval geographers

**Cir·cas·sia** (sər kash'ə, -kash'ē ə) region in the NW Caucasus, on the Black Sea

**Cir·ci·nus** (sur'sə nəs) ⟦L⟧ a S constellation near Centaurus

**Circus Max·i·mus** (maks'i məs) ⟦L, lit., largest racecourse⟧ a large amphitheater built in Rome *c.* 329 B.C., used as for chariot races and games

**Cir·e·na·i·ca** (sir'ə nä'i kə; *It* chē're nä'ē kä) *It. name of* CYRENAICA

**Cis·kei** (sis'kī') black homeland in SE South Africa, on the Indian Ocean: granted independence in 1981: 3,205 sq. mi. (8,300 sq. km); pop. 2,100,000

**Cit·lal·te·petl** (sē'tläl tä'pet″l) ORIZABA

**Cit·tà del Va·ti·ca·no** (chēt tä' del vä'tē kä'nô) *It. name of* VATICAN CITY

**City, the** the financial and commercial district of Greater London

**city of God** heaven: Ps. 46:4

**City of Seven Hills** *name for* ROME

**Ciu·dad Bo·lí·var** (syōō däd' bō lē'vär') city in NE Venezuela, on the Orinoco: pop. 154,000

**Ciudad Juá·rez** (hwä'res') city in N Mexico, across the Rio Grande from El Paso, Tex.: pop. 567,000

**Ciudad Ma·de·ro** (mä der'ō') city in Tamaulipas state, EC Mexico, north of Tampico: pop. 133,000

**Ciudad Vic·to·ri·a** (vik tôr'ē ə, -ä') capital of Tamaulipas state, EC Mexico: pop. 153,000

**Clack·man·nan** (klak man'ən) former county in EC Scotland, now in the region of Tayside

**Clare** (kler) county in W Ireland, in Munster province: 1,231 sq. mi. (3,188 sq. km); pop. 86,000

**Clark Fork** (klärk) ⟦after William *Clark* (1770-1838), Am explorer⟧ river flowing from W Mont. northwest into Pend Oreille Lake in N Ida.: *c.* 300 mi. (480 km)

**Clarks·ville** (klärks'vil') ⟦after George Rogers *Clark* (1752-1818), Am frontiersman⟧ city in N Tenn., on the Cumberland River: pop. 75,000

**Clear·wa·ter** (klir'wôt'ər) ⟦descriptive⟧ city in WC Fla., on the Gulf of Mexico: suburb of St. Petersburg: pop. 99,000: see TAMPA

**Cle·o·pa·tra's Needle** (klē'ə pa'trez) either of two ancient Egyptian obelisks, one in London, the other in New York City, sent as gifts (1878) by the ruler of Egypt to England & the U.S.

**Cler·mont-Fer·rand** (kler mōn fe rän') city in central France, in the Auvergne region: pop. 151,000

**Cleve·land** (klēv'lənd) 1 ⟦after Moses *Cleaveland* (1754-1806), surveyor of the WESTERN RESERVE⟧ city and port in NE Ohio, on Lake Erie: pop. 506,000 (met. area 1,831,000; urban area, with Akron & Lorain, 2,760,000) 2 county of N England, on the North Sea: 225 sq. mi. (583 sq. km); pop. 563,000

**Cleveland Heights** city in NE Ohio: suburb of Cleveland: pop. 54,000

**Cli·chy** (klē shē') city in N France, on the Seine: suburb of Paris: pop. 47,000

**Clif·ton** (klif'tən) ⟦for the cliffs in the area⟧ city in NE N.J.: pop. 72,000

**Cling·man's Dome** (kliŋ'mənz) ⟦after U.S. senator from N.C., T. L. *Clingman* (1812-97)⟧ mountain on the Tenn.-N.C. border: highest peak of the Great Smoky Mountains, 6,642 ft. (2,025 m)

**Cluj-Na·po·ca** (klo͞ozh'nə pō'kə) city in Transylvania, NW Romania: pop. 271,000

**Clu·ny** (klo͞o'nē; *Fr* klü nē') town in EC France: site of a Benedictine monastery (910-1790): pop. 4,000

**Clw·yd** (klo͞o'id) county of N Wales, on the Irish Sea: 937 sq. mi. (2,427 sq. km); pop. 396,000

**Clyde** (klīd) 1 river in S Scotland, flowing northwestward into the Firth of Clyde: 106 mi. (171 km) **2 Firth** of estuary of the Clyde River, flowing southward into the North Channel: 64 mi. (103 km)

**Clyde·bank** (-baŋk′) city in SW Scotland, on the Clyde River, near Glasgow: pop. 52,000

**Cni·dus** (nī′dəs) ancient Dorian city in Caria, SW Asia Minor: taken by Persians (540 B.C.)

**Cnos·sus** (näs′əs) ancient city in N Crete, near modern Iraklion: center of ancient Minoan civilization

**CO** *abbrev. for* Colorado

**Co·a·hui·la** (kō′ə wē′lə) state of N Mexico, on the Tex. border: 57,908 sq. mi. (149,982 sq. km); pop. 1,696,000; cap. Saltillo

**Coal·sack** (kōl′sak′) either of two prominent dark clouds in the Milky Way, esp. one located near Crux: also **Coal Sack**

**Coast, the** [Colloq.] in the U.S., the Pacific coast

**Coast Mountains** mountain range in W British Columbia & S Alas.; N continuation of the Cascade Range: highest peak, 13,260 ft. (4,042 m)

**Coast Ranges** series of mountain ranges along the W coast of North America, extending from Alas. to Baja California: highest peak, Mount Logan

**Co·at·za·co·al·cos** (kō ät′sə kō äl′kōs′) city in EC Mexico, in Veracruz state: pop. 187,000

**Co·blenz** (kō′blents′) *alt. sp. of* KOBLENZ

**Co·burg** (kō′burg′) city in central Germany, in the state of Bavaria: 19th-cent. capital of the duchy of Saxe-Coburg Gotha: pop. 45,000

**Co·cha·bam·ba** (kō′chə bäm′bə) city in central Bolivia: pop. 282,000

**Co·chin China** (kō′chin′) historic region and former French colony in SE Indochina: the S part of Vietnam

**Cock·aigne** (käk än′) ⟦ME *cokaygne* < OFr (*pais de*) *cocaigne*, (land of) sugar cake < MLowG *kokenje*, sugar cake, cookie < *koke*, cake⟧ an imaginary land of luxurious and idle living

**Co·cos Islands** (kō′kōs) group of small coral islands in the Indian Ocean, south of Sumatra: a territory of Australia: 5.5 sq. mi. (14.2 sq. km)

**Co·cy·tus** (kō sīt′əs) ⟦L < Gr *Kōkytos*, lit., a shrieking, wailing < *kōkyein*, to wail, redupl. of IE base *\*kau-*, howl⟧ *Gr. Myth.* the river of wailing, a tributary of the Acheron in Hades

**Cod, Cape** ⟦< fish name⟧ hook-shaped peninsula in E Mass. from Buzzards Bay to Provincetown: 64 mi. (104 km) long

**Coim·ba·tore** (koim′bə tôr′) city in S India, in the state of Tamil Nadu: pop. 917,000

**Col·ches·ter** (kōl′ches′tər) city in SE England, in Essex: pop. 82,000

**Col·chis** (käl′kis) ancient country south of the Caucasus Mountains, on the Black Sea, in what is now Georgia

**Co·li·ma** (kə lē′mə) **1** state of SW Mexico, on the Pacific: 2,004 sq. mi. (5,191 sq. km); pop. 368,000 **2** its capital: pop. 58,000 **3** inactive volcano in Jalisco state, near the Colima border: c. 14,000 ft. (4,270 m): in full **Ne·va·do de Colima** (nə väd′ō de) **4** active volcano on the Jalisco-Colima border: c. 12,750 ft. (3,885 m)

**Col·i·se·um** (käl′ə sē′əm) ⟦ModL < L *colosseum*⟧ Col-OSSEUM

**Col·mar** (kōl′mär; *Fr* kôl mȧr′) city in NE France, near the Rhine: pop. 64,000

**Colo** *abbrev. for* Colorado

**Co·logne** (kə lōn′) ⟦Fr, after L *Colonia (Agrippina)*, the colony (of Agrippina)⟧ city in W Germany, on the Rhine, in the state of North Rhine-Westphalia: pop. 932,000: Ger. name KÖLN

**Co·lom·bi·a** (kə lum′bē ə; *Sp* kô lôm′byä) country in NW South America, on the Pacific Ocean & the Caribbean Sea: gained independence from Spain (1819): 439,737 sq. mi. (1,138,914 sq. km); pop. 29,956,000; cap. Bogotá

**Co·lom·bo** (kə lum′bō) capital of Sri Lanka: seaport on the W coast: pop. 588,000

**Co·lón** (kə lōn′) ⟦Sp, after Christopher Columbus⟧ seaport in Panama, at the Caribbean end of the Panama Canal: pop. 59,000

**Co·lón** (kô lôn′), **Ar·chi·pié·la·go de** (är′chē pyä′lä gô *the*) *Sp. name of* GALÁPAGOS ISLANDS

**Col·o·rad·o** (käl′ə rad′ō, -rä′dō) ⟦< Sp name of the river, *Río Colorado*, lit., reddish-brown river⟧ **1** Mountain State of the W U.S.: admitted 1876; 104,247 sq. mi. (270,000 sq. km); pop. 3,294,000; cap. Denver: abbrev. *CO* or *Colo* **2** river in SW U.S., flowing from the Rocky Mts. of N Colo. southwest through Utah & along the Ariz.-Nev. & Ariz.-Calif. borders into the

Gulf of California: 1,450 mi. (2,333 km) **3** river in Tex., flowing from the NW part southeast into the Gulf of Mexico: 840 mi. (1,352 km)

**Colorado Desert** desert in SE Calif., west of the Colorado River: *c.* 2,000 sq. mi. (5,180 sq. km)

**Colorado Springs** ⟦ for the mineral springs in the area ⟧ city in central Colo.: site of the U.S. Air Force Academy: pop. 281,000 (met. area 397,000)

**Co·los·sae** (kə läs′ē) city in ancient Phrygia, SW Asia Minor (fl. 5th cent. B.C.)

**Col·os·se·um** (käl′ə sē′əm) ⟦L, orig., neut. of *colosseus,* gigantic < *colossus,* fol.⟧ an amphitheater in Rome, built *c.* A.D. 75-80: much of it is still standing

**Co·los·sus** (kə läs′əs) the gigantic statue of Apollo set at the entrance to the harbor of Rhodes *c.* 280 B.C. and included among the Seven Wonders of the World

**Co·lum·ba** (kə lum′bə) a S constellation near Canis Major

**Co·lum·bi·a** (kə lum′bē ə, -byə) ⟦after Christopher *Columbus*; city names are all after *Columbia,* personification of the U.S.⟧ **1** [Old Poet.] the U.S. personified as a woman **2** capital of S.C., on the Congaree River: pop. 98,000 (met. area 453,000) **3** city in central Mo.: pop. 69,000 **4** city in NC Md., southwest of Baltimore: pop. 76,000 **5** ⟦after the name of the first ship to enter it (1792)⟧ river rising in SE British Columbia and flowing south & west through Wash., & along the Wash.-Oreg. border into the Pacific: 1,210 mi. (1,950 km)

**Co·lum·bus** (kə lum′bəs) ⟦after Christopher *Columbus*⟧ **1** capital of Ohio, in the central part: pop. 633,000 (met. area 1,377,000) **2** city in W Ga., on the Chattahoochee River: pop. 179,000

**Com·mon·wealth** (käm′ən welth′), **the** association of independent nations (50 since 1990), all former components of the British Empire, united for purposes of consultation and mutual assistance: all members acknowledge the British sovereign as symbolic head of the association: formerly called **the Commonwealth of Nations**

**Commonwealth of Independent States** a loose confederation of countries that were part of the U.S.S.R.: it includes Armenia, Belarus, Kazakhstan, Kyrgyzstan, Moldova, Russia, Tajikistan, Turkmenistan,

Ukraine, and Uzbekistan: abbrev. *CIS*

**Co·mo** (kō′mō) **1** commune in N Italy, on Lake Como: pop. 90,000 **2 Lake** lake in Lombardy, N Italy: 56 sq. mi. (145 sq. km)

**Com·o·rin** (käm′ə rin), **Cape** cape at the southernmost tip of India

**Com·o·ro Islands** (käm′ə rō′) country on a group of islands in the Indian Ocean, at the head of Mozambique Channel: formerly a French territory, it became independent (1975): 838 sq. mi. (2,171 sq. km); pop. 420,000; cap. Moroni

**Com·piègne** (kōn pyen′y′) town in N France, on the Oise River: the armistices between the Allies & Germany (1918) & between Germany & France (1940) were signed near here: pop. 43,000

**Comp·ton** (kämp′tən) ⟦ after G. D. *Compton,* a founder of the University of Southern Calif. ⟧ city in SW Calif.: suburb of Los Angeles: pop. 90,000

**Com·stock Lode** (käm′stäk′, kum′-) ⟦ after H. T. *Comstock* (1820-70), who held first claim to it ⟧ rich deposits of silver & gold discovered in 1859 in W Nev.: virtually depleted by 1890

**Co·na·kry** (kän′ə krē′; *Fr* kô nä krē′) capital of Guinea: seaport on the Atlantic: pop. 763,000

**Con·cep·ción** (kən sep′sē ōn′; *Sp* kôn sep′syôn′) city in SC Chile: pop. 210,000

**Con·cord** (kän′kôrd; *for 2 & 3* käŋ′kərd) ⟦ prob. alluding to the amity hoped for among the inhabitants and their neighbors ⟧ **1** city in W Calif., near Oakland: pop. 111,000 **2** capital of N.H., on the Merrimack River: pop. 36,000 **3** town in E Mass., near Boston: pop. 17,000: with Lexington, site of the first battles of the Revolutionary War (April 19, 1775)

**Co·ney Island** (kō′nē) ⟦ < Du *Konynen Eyland,* rabbit island ⟧ beach & amusement park in Brooklyn, N.Y., on a peninsula, formerly an island, at the SW end of Long Island

**Con·fed·er·a·cy** (kən fed′ər ə sē), **the** the league of Southern States that seceded from the U.S. in 1860 & 1861; Ala., Ark., Fla., Ga., La., Miss., N.C., S.C., Tenn., Tex., & Va.: official name, **Con·fed′er·ate States of America** (-it)

**Confederation, the** **1** the United States of America (1781-89) under the Articles of Confederation **2** the union of Ontario, Quebec, Nova Scotia, and New Brunswick in 1867 to form the Dominion of Canada

**Con·ga·ree** (käŋ′gər ē) 〚AmInd: meaning unknown〛 river in S.C., joining the Wateree to form the Santee River: 50 mi. (96 km)

**Con·go** (käŋ′gō) **1** river in central Africa flowing through Zaire into the Atlantic: c. 2,720 mi. (4,380 km) **2** old name of ZAIRE **3** country in WC Africa, west of Zaire: formerly a French territory, it became independent (1960): 132,046 sq. mi. (342,000 sq. km); pop. 1,853,000; cap. Brazzaville: in full **People's Republic of the Congo**

**Conn** abbrev. for Connecticut

**Con·nacht** (kän′ôt, -əkht) province of NW Ireland: 6,611 sq. mi. (17,122 sq. km); pop. 424,000

**Con·naught** (kän′ôt) alt. sp. of CONNACHT

**Con·nect·i·cut** (kə net′ə kət) 〚< Algonquin (Mahican), lit., place of the long river〛 **1** New England State of the U.S.: one of the 13 original States; 5,009 sq. mi. (13,023 sq. km); pop. 3,287,000; cap. Hartford: abbrev. CT or Conn **2** river in NE U.S., flowing from N N.H. across Mass. & Conn. into Long Island Sound: 407 mi. (655 km)

**Con·stance** (kän′stəns) **1** city in SW Germany, on Lake Constance, in the state of Baden-Württemberg: pop. 69,000: Ger. name KONSTANZ **2** Lake (of) lake bounded by Switzerland, Germany, & Austria: 208 sq. mi. (539 sq. km); c. 46 mi. (68 km) long: Ger. name BODENSEE

**Con·stan·ţa** (kôn stän′tsä) seaport in SE Romania, on the Black Sea: pop. 285,000

**Con·stan·tine** (kän′stən tēn′; Fr kôn stän tēn′) city in NE Algeria: pop. 446,000

**Con·stan·ti·no·ple** (kän′stan tə nō′pəl) old name (A.D. 330-1930) of ISTANBUL

**Continental Divide** ridge of the Rocky Mountains forming a North American watershed that separates rivers flowing in an easterly direction from those flowing in a westerly direction

**Cook** (kook), **Mount** mountain of the Southern Alps, New Zealand: highest peak in New Zealand: 12,349 ft. (3,764 m)

**Cook Inlet** arm of the Gulf of Alaska, in S Alas.

**Cook Islands** group of islands in the S Pacific, west of Society Islands: a self-governing territory of New Zealand: 90 sq. mi. (234 sq. km); pop. 22,000

**Cook Strait** strait between North Island & South Island, New Zealand: narrowest point, 16 mi. (26 km)

**Co·pán** (kō̂ pän′) town in W Honduras: site of a ruined Mayan city of perhaps 7th-8th cent. A.D.: pop. 1,000

**Co·pen·hag·en** (kōp′ən hā′gən, -hä′-) capital of Denmark: seaport on the E coast of Zealand: pop. 633,000 (met. area 1,358,000): Dan. name KØBENHAVN

**Cop·per·mine** (käp′ər mīn′) ⟦for the copper in the region⟧ river in Kitikmeot & Fort Smith regions of Northwest Territories, Canada, flowing northwest into the Arctic Ocean: 525 mi. (845 km)

**Coral Gables** ⟦orig. the name of the founder's residence, built of coral rock with a colorful tile roof⟧ city on the SE coast of Fla.: suburb of Miami: pop. 40,000

**Coral Sea** part of the S Pacific, northeast of Australia & south of the Solomon Islands

**Coral Springs** ⟦after the company (*Coral* Ridge Properties) that once owned the land, and the natural *springs* found there⟧ city in SE Fla.: pop. 79,000

**Cor·co·va·do** (kō̂r′kō̂ vä′*th*oo) mountain in SE Brazil, near Rio de Janeiro: 2,310 ft. (704 m): there is a gigantic statue of Christ on its top

**Cor·cy·ra** (kôr sī′rə) *old name of* CORFU

**Cor·dil·le·ras** (kôr′dil yer′əz) **1** mountain system of W North America, including all mountains between the E Rockies & the Pacific coast **2** mountain system of W South America; Andes

**Cór·do·ba** (kôr′də bə, -və; *Sp* kō̂r′*th*ô̂ bä) **1** city in NC Argentina: pop. 969,000 **2** city in S Spain, on the Guadalquivir River: pop. 285,000 **3** city in EC Mexico, in Veracruz state: pop. 126,000

**Cor·do·va** (kôr′də və) *Eng. name of* CÓRDOBA

**Cor·fu** (kôr′foo; kôr foo′, -fyoo′) **1** one of the Ionian Islands, off the W coast of Greece: 229 sq. mi. (593 sq. km) **2** its chief city, a seaport: pop. 34,000

**Cor·inth** (kôr′inth, kär′-) **1** ancient city in the NE Peloponnesus, at the head of the Gulf of Corinth, noted for its luxury: fl. 7th-2d cent. B.C. **2** modern city near the site of ancient Corinth: pop. 18,000: Gr. name KORINTHOS **3 Gulf of** arm of the Ionian Sea, between the Peloponnesus & central Greece: *c.* 80 mi. (130 km) long **4 Isthmus of** land strip, joining the Peloponnesus with central Greece: *c.* 4-8 mi. (6.4-13 km) wide & 20 mi. (32 km) long

**Cork** (kôrk) **1** county on the S coast of Ireland, in Munster province: 2,880 sq. mi. (7,460 sq. km); pop. 266,000 **2** its county seat, a seaport: pop. 136,000

**Corn Belt** region in the NC plains area of the Middle West where much corn and cornfed livestock are raised: it extends from W Ohio to E Nebr. and NE Kans.

**Corn·wall** (kôrn′wôl; *chiefly Brit*, -wəl) **1** county at the SW tip of England: 1,369 sq. mi. (3,546 sq. km); pop. 439,000: in full **Cornwall and Isles of Scilly 2** ⟦after the Duke of *Cornwall*, eldest son of George III⟧ city in SE Ontario, on the St. Lawrence River: pop. 51,000

**Cor·o·man·del Coast** (kôr′ə man′dəl) coastal region of SE India, on Bay of Bengal: has low shoreline with no good harbors

**Co·ro·na** (kə ro′nə) ⟦Sp & L, wreath, crown: for the circular boulevard around the city⟧ city in S Calif.: pop. 76,000

**Corona Aus·tra·lis** (ôs trā′lis, -tral′is) ⟦L, Southern Crown⟧ a S constellation near Sagittarius

**Corona Bo·re·a·lis** (bôr′ē ā′lis, -al′is) ⟦L, Northern Crown⟧ a N constellation between Hercules and Boötes

**Cor·pus Chris·ti** (kôr′pəs kris′tē) ⟦L, Body of Christ⟧ city in SE Tex., on the Gulf of Mexico: pop. 257,000 (met. area 350,000)

**Cor·reg·i·dor** (kə reg′ə dôr′) small fortified island in the Philippines, at the entrance to Manila Bay: in World War II, American-Filipino troops fought on gallantly for a month after the fall of Bataan; finally invaded & garrison forced to surrender (May, 1942); recaptured (Feb., 1945)

**Cor·rien·tes** (kôr ryen′tes) city in N Argentina, on the Paraná River: pop. 180,000

**Corse** (kôrs) *Fr. name of* CORSICA

**Cor·si·ca** (kôr′si kə) French island in the Mediterranean, north of Sardinia, forming a metropolitan region: 3,367 sq. mi. (8,754 sq. km); pop. 275,000; chief city, Ajaccio

**Coruña, La** *see* LA CORUÑA

**Co·run·na** (kə rum′ə) *Eng. name of* LA CORUÑA

**Cor·val·lis** (kôr val′əs) ⟦< L *cor*, heart + *vallis*, valley: so named (1850's) by J. C. Avery, landowner, who intended it to mean "heart of the valley"⟧ city in W Oreg., on the Willamette River: pop. 45,000

**Cor·vus** (kôr′vəs) ⟦L, raven⟧ a small S constellation near Virgo; Crow

**Co·sen·za** (kō zent′sə) city in S Italy, southeast of Naples: pop. 106,000

**Cos·ta Bra·va** (käs′tə brä′vä, kôs′-) coast of Catalonia, Spain, northeast of Barcelona: site of many resorts

**Cos·ta del Sol** (käs′tə *th*el sôl, kôs′-) coast region of S Spain, on the Mediterranean, east of Gibraltar: site of many resorts

**Cos·ta Me·sa** (kōs′tə mā′sə) ⟦Sp *costa mesa*, coast plateau⟧ city in SW Calif., near Long Beach: pop. 96,000

**Cos·ta Ri·ca** (käs′tə rē′kə, kôs′-, kōs′-) country in Central America, northwest of Panama: revolted against Spain in 1821; became independent republic (1848): 19,575 sq. mi. (50,700 sq. km); pop. 2,714,000; cap. San José

**Côte d'A·zur** (kōt dà zür′) the part of the Riviera that is in France

**Côte d'I·voire** (kōt dē vwàr′) *official name of* IVORY COAST

**Co·to·nou** (kỗ tỗ nōō′) seaport and the principal city of Benin: pop. 487,000

**Co·to·pax·i** (kō′tə pak′sē; *Sp* kỗ′tỗ pä′hē) volcano in the Andes, in N Ecuador: 19,344 ft. (5,896 m)

**Cots·wold Hills** (käts′wōld, -wəld) a range of hills in SW central England, mostly in Gloucestershire: also **Cotswolds**

**Cott·bus** (kät′bəs, -boos′) city in E Germany, on the Spree River, in the state of Brandenburg: pop. 123,000

**Cot·ti·an Alps** (kät′ē ən) a division of the W Alps, between France & Italy: highest peak, *c.* 12,600 ft. (3,840 m)

**Cotton Belt** region in S and SE U.S., extending from Texas to the Carolinas, where much cotton is grown

**Council Bluffs** ⟦scene of councils with the Indians by Meriwether Lewis (1774-1809) & William Clark (1770-1838), Am explorers⟧ city in SW Iowa, across the Missouri River from Omaha, Nebr.: pop. 54,000

**Cour·land** (koor′lənd) *see* KURLAND

**Cour·trai** (kōōr trā′) city in W Belgium, in West Flanders: pop. 76,000: Fl. name KORTRIJK

**Cov·en·try** (kuv′ən trē, käv′-) city in central England, in

West Midlands county: pop. 314,000

**Cov·ing·ton** (kuv′iŋ tən) ⟦after Gen. L. *Covington*, 1768-1813⟧ city in N Ky., on the Ohio River: pop. 43,000

**Cowes** (kouz) resort town & yachting center on the N shore of the Isle of Wight: pop. 19,000

**Crab** (krab) Cancer, the constellation and fourth sign of the zodiac

**Crab nebula** a crab-shaped, rapidly expanding cloud of gas in the constellation Taurus, containing a neutron-star pulsar: believed to be the remnants of the supernova of A.D. 1054

**Cra·cow** (kra′kou, krä′-; -kō) *alt. sp. of* KRAKÓW

**Cra·io·va** (krä yô′və) city in SW Romania: pop. 243,000

**Cran·ston** (kran′stən) ⟦after S. *Cranston* (1659-1727), colonial gov.⟧ city in R.I.: suburb of Providence: pop. 76,000

**Cra·ter** (krāt′ər) a S constellation between Hydra and Corvus

**Crater Lake National Park** ⟦descriptive⟧ national park in SW Oreg., containing a lake, **Crater Lake**, 6 mi. (10.2 km) long, 5 mi. (8 km) wide, 1,932 ft. (589 m) deep, in the crater of an extinct volcano: area of the park, 250 sq. mi. (647 sq. km)

**Crater Mound** a huge, circular depression in central Ariz., believed to have been made by a meteorite: depth, 600 ft. (183 m); diameter, .75 mi. (1.2 km)

**Cré·cy** (krā sē′; *E* kres′ē) village in N France: scene of an English victory (1346) over the French in the Hundred Years' War: also **Cré·cy-en-Pon·thieu** (-än pōn tyë′)

**Cre·mo·na** (kri mō′nə; *It* kre mô′nä) commune in Lombardy, N Italy, on the Po River: famous (fl. 16th-17th cent.) for making violins: pop. 74,000

**Cres·sy** (kres′ē) *Eng. name for* CRÉCY

**Crete** (krēt) **1** Greek island in the E Mediterranean: 3,218 sq. mi. (8,334 sq. km); pop. 502,000; cap. Canea: Gr. name KRETE **2 Sea of** S section of the Aegean Sea, between Crete and the Cyclades

**Cri·me·a** (krī mē′ə, krə-) **1** peninsula in SW Ukraine, extending into the Black Sea: *c.* 10,000 sq. mi. (25,899 sq. km): Russ. name KRIM **2** autonomous republic of Ukraine, coextensive with this peninsula

**Cris·to·bal** (kris tō′bəl) seaport in the Canal Zone, at

the Caribbean entrance to the canal: a part of the city of Colón, Panama: pop. 400

**Cro·a·tia** (krō ā′shə) country in SE Europe: at one time part of Austria-Hungary, it was a constituent republic of Yugoslavia (1946-91): 21,834 sq. mi. (56,524 sq. km); pop. 4,602,000; cap. Zagreb

**Croc·o·dile** (kräk′ə dil′) LIMPOPO

**Crom·well current** (kräm′wel, krum′-) a strong, equatorial, subsurface current flowing east across the Pacific Ocean under the weaker, western-flowing equatorial surface currents

**Cross** (krôs, kräs) 1 Northern Cross 2 Southern Cross

**Crow** (krō) the constellation Corvus

**Crown Point** ‖ mistransl. of Fr name *Pointe à la Chevelure*, scalping point ‖ town in NE N.Y., on Lake Champlain: site of a fort important in the French and Indian & the Revolutionary wars: pop. 2,000

**Croy·don** (kroid′'n) borough of S Greater London, England: pop. 319,000

**Crux** (kruks) a small S constellation near the celestial pole containing Coalsack; Southern Cross

**CT** *abbrev. for* Connecticut

**Ctes·i·phon** (tes′ə fän′) ancient ruined city on the Tigris, near Baghdad, in present-day Iraq (fl. 1st cent. B.C.-5th cent. A.D.)

**Cu·ba** (kyōō′bə; *Sp* kōō′bä) 1 island in the West Indies, south of Fla. 2 country comprising this island & several small nearby islands: gained independence from Spain (1898): 44,197 sq. mi. (114,471 sq. km); pop. 10,221,000; cap. Havana

**Cú·cu·ta** (kōō′kōō tä) city in N Colombia: pop. 441,000

**Cuen·ca** (kwen′kä) city in SC Ecuador: pop. 273,000

**Cu·ia·bá** (kōō′yä bä′) city in WC Brazil: capital of Mato Grosso state: pop. 168,000

**Cu·lia·cán** (kōōl′yə kän′) city in NW Mexico; capital of Sinaloa state: pop. 560,000

**Cu·mae** (kyōō′mē) ancient Greek city in Campania, SW Italy, near Naples: thought to have been the first Greek colony in Italy, founded 9th or 8th cent. B.C.

**Cu·ma·ná** (kōō′mə nä′) seaport of NE Venezuela, on the Caribbean: pop. 173,000

**Cum·ber·land** (kum′bər lənd) 1 former county in NW England, now part of Cumbria county 2 ‖ after William Augustus, Duke of *Cumberland* (1721-65), son of

George II; Eng general] river in S Ky. & N Tenn.,
flowing west into the Ohio at the S Ill. border: 687 mi.
(1,105 km) **3** [after the Duke of *Cumberland*] city in
NW Md., on the Potomac near the Pa. border: pop.
24,000 (met. area 102,000)

**Cumberland Gap** pass in the Cumberland Plateau, at
the juncture of the Va., Ky., & Tenn. borders: *c.* 1,700
ft. high (518 m)

**Cumberland Plateau** (or **Mountains**) [after William
Augustus, Duke of *Cumberland*: see CUMBERLAND (the
river)] division of the W Appalachians, extending
from S W.Va. to N Ala.

**Cum·bri·a** (kum′brē ə) county of NW England, on the
border of Scotland: 2,629 sq. mi. (6,809 sq. km); pop.
483,000

**Cu·nax·a** (kyōō nak′sə) ancient town in Babylonia, near
the Euphrates: site of a battle (401 B.C.) in which
Cyrus the Younger was killed

**Cu·ra·çao** (kyōōr′ə sō′, kōōr′ə sou′) **1** largest island of
the Netherlands Antilles, just north of the coast of
Venezuela: 171 sq. mi. (444 sq. km); pop. 165,000; cap.
Willemstad **2** *old name of* NETHERLANDS ANTILLES

**Cu·ri·ti·ba** (kōō′rē tē′bə) city in S Brazil: capital of
Paraná state: pop. 843,000

**Cus·co** (kōōs′kō) *alt. sp. of* CUZCO

**Cush** (kush) *Bible* the land inhabited by the descendants
of Cush, thought to be on the W shore of the Red Sea:
Gen. 10:8; 1 Chron. 1:10

**Cutch** (kuch) *alt. sp. of* KUTCH

**Cut·tack** (kut′ək) city in E India, in Orissa state: pop.
326,000

**Cuy·a·ho·ga Falls** (kī′ə hō′gə, -hô′-, -hä′-) [after the
*Cuyahoga* River < AmInd (? Iroquois)] city in NE
Ohio, south of Cleveland: pop. 49,000

**Cuz·co** (kōōs′kō) city in S Peru: cap. of the Inca empire,
12th-16th cent.: pop. 182,000

**Cyc·la·des** (sik′lə dēz′) group of islands of Greece, on
the S Aegean: 995 sq. mi. (2,578 sq. km); pop. 88,000

**Cyg·nus** (sig′nəs) [L < *cygnus*, swan < Gr *kyknos*] a N
constellation in the Milky Way near Lyra, containing
the star Deneb; Northern Cross

**Cy·no·sure** (sī′nə shoor′, sin′ə-) *old name for* the constellation Ursa Minor or the North Star, in this constellation

**Cy·press** (sī′prəs) ⟦for cypress trees planted there⟧ city in SW Calif., southeast of Los Angeles: pop. 43,000

**Cy·prus** (sī′prəs) country on an island at the E end of the Mediterranean, south of Turkey: colonized by Phoenicians and ancient Greeks; at various times ruled by Persian, Roman, Ptolemaic, Byzantine, & Ottoman Empires; British territory (1914), became independent & a member of the Commonwealth (1960): 3,572 sq. mi. (9,251 sq. km); pop. 673,000; cap. Nicosia

**Cyr·e·na·i·ca** (sir′ə nā′i kə, sī′rə-) 1 region of E Libya: *c.* 330,000 sq. mi. (855,000 sq. km); chief city, Benghazi 2 ancient Greek kingdom (7th-4th cent. B.C.) in the same general region, dominated by the city of Cyrene

**Cy·re·ne** (sī rē′nē) ancient Greek city in N Africa, on the Mediterranean: capital of Cyrenaica

**Cy·the·ra** (si thir′ə) ⟦L < Gr *Kythera*⟧ Greek island just south of the Peloponnesus, near which Aphrodite is fabled to have arisen full-grown from the sea

**Cyz·i·cus** (siz′i kəs) ancient Greek city in NW Asia Minor, on the S shore of the Sea of Marmara

**Czech·o·slo·va·ki·a** (chek′ə slō vä′kē ə) former country in central Europe, south of Poland and east of Germany: formed (1918) by the merger of Bohemia, Moravia, and parts of Silesia and Slovakia, in 1993 it was divided into Czech Republic and Slovakia: Czech name ČESKOSLOVENSKO

**Czech Republic** (chek) country in central Europe: formerly the W constituent republic of Czechoslovakia: 30,450 sq. mi. (78,864 sq. km); pop. 10,364,599; cap. Prague

**Czę·sto·cho·wa** (chan′stô Hô′vä) city in S Poland, on the Warta River: pop. 244,000

# D

**Dac·ca** (dä′kə, dak′ə) *old sp. of* DHAKA

**Da·chau** (dä′khou) city in S Germany, near Munich, in the state of Bavaria: pop. 34,000: site (1933-45) of a Nazi concentration camp & extermination center

**Da·cia** (dā′shə) ancient region in SE Europe, inhabited by a Thracian people; later, a Roman province (2d-3d cent.): it corresponded approximately to modern Romania

**Da·dra and Na·gar Ha·vel·i** (də drä′ ənd nə gŭr′ hä′vel ē) territory of India (formerly two territories) consisting of an enclave on the S coast of Gujarat state: 190 sq. mi. (491 sq. km); pop. 104,000

**Dag·en·ham** (dag′ən əm) former municipal borough of SE England: see BARKING

**Da Hing·gan Ling** (dä′ hiŋ′gän′ liŋ′) mountain range in NE China along the E border of the Mongolian People's Republic: highest peak, 5,670 ft. (1,728 m): cf. XIAO HINGGAN LING

**Da·ho·mey** (də hō′mē) *old name of* BENIN

**Da·kar** (də kär′, däk′är) seaport and capital of Senegal, in W Africa: pop. 979,000

**Da·ko·ta** (də kōt′ə) ⟦< Dakota *dakóta*, allies < *da*, to think of as + *koda*, friend⟧ former U.S. territory (1861-89), orig. including an area that is present-day N.Dak., S.Dak., and much of what is now Wyo. & Mont.

**Dakotas,** the North Dakota and South Dakota

**Da·lian** (dä′lyen′) seaport in Liaoning province, NE China: pop. 4,000,000: see LÜDA

**Dal·las** (dal′əs) ⟦after G. M. *Dallas* (1792-1864), U.S. vice president (1845-49)⟧ city in NE Tex.: pop. 1,007,000 (met. area, incl. Fort Worth, 3,885,000)

**Dal·ma·tia** (dal mä′shə) region along the Adriatic coast, mostly in Croatia

**Da·ly City** (dā′lē) ⟦after a prominent citizen, John *Daly*⟧ city in W Calif.: suburb of San Francisco: pop. 92,000

**Da·man** (də män′) small region on the coast of Gujarat state, NW India: formerly part of Portuguese India: 28 sq. mi. (72 sq. km): see GOA

**Da·man·hûr** (dä′män hōōr′) city in N Egypt, in the Nile delta: pop. 189,000

**Da·mas·cus** (də mas′kəs) capital of Syria, in the SW part: a very ancient city dating to *c.* 2,000 B.C.: pop. 1,251,000

**Da·ma·vand** (dä′mə vänd′, dam′ə vand′) highest peak of the Elburz Mountains, N Iran: 18,934 ft. (5,771 m)

**Dam·i·et·ta** (dam′ē et′ə) seaport in N Egypt, in the E Nile delta: pop. 93,000

**Dan** (dan) village in NE Israel: site of an ancient town at the northernmost extremity of Israelite territory: cf. BEERSHEBA

**Da Nang** (dä näŋ') seaport in central Vietnam, on the South China Sea: pop. 492,000

**Dan·bur·y** (dan'ber'ē, -bər ē) ⟦after *Danbury* (orig. *Danebury*, "camp of the Danes"), town in SE England⟧ city in SW Conn., near Bridgeport: pop. 66,000

**Dan·dong** (dän'dooŋ') seaport in Liaoning province, NE China, at the mouth of the Yalu River: pop. 450,000

**Dan·ish West Indies** (dän'ish) those islands of the Virgin Islands occupied by Denmark from the 17th cent. to 1917: now *Virgin Islands of the United States*

**Dan·mark** (dan'märk) *Dan. name for* DENMARK

**Dan·ube** (dan'yōōb) ⟦Celt *Dānuvius* < IE *dānus-*, stream (< base *\*dā-*, liquid, flow) > DNEPR, DNESTR, DON, DONETS, DOON⟧ river in S Europe, flowing from the Black Forest in S Germany eastward into the Black Sea: *c.* 1,770 mi. (2,850 km): Bulg. name *Dunav*, Czech name *Dunaj*, Ger. name *Donau*, Hung. name *Duna*, Romanian name *Dunǎ rea*, Russ. name *Dunai*

**Dan·ville** (dan'vil, -vəl) ⟦after *Dan* River (in allusion to the Biblical town of DAN)⟧ city in S Va., near the N.C. border: pop. 53,000

**Dan·zig** (dant'sig; *Ger* dän'tsiH) *Ger. name of* GDAŃSK

**Dar·da·nelles** (där'də nelz') strait joining the Sea of Marmara and the Aegean Sea, between European & Asiatic Turkey: *c.* 40 mi. (65 km) long; 1 to 4 mi. (1.5 to 6.5 km) wide

**Dar es Sa·laam** (där' es sə läm') seaport in Tanzania, on the Indian Ocean: pop. 757,000

**Dar·fur** (där foor') region in W Sudan, formerly a province & (early 19th cent.) a sultanate

**Da·rien** (dar'ē en', der'-; där yen') **1 Gulf of** wedge-shaped extension of the Caribbean, between N Colombia & E Panama **2 Isthmus of** *old name of* Isthmus of PANAMA

**Dark Continent** *old name for* Africa, especially before the late 19th cent. when little was known of it

**Dar·ling** (där'liŋ) river in SE Australia, flowing southwest into the Murray River: *c.* 1,700 mi. (2,735 km)

**Dar·ling·ton** (där'liŋ tən) city in Durham, N England: pop. 85,000

**Darm·stadt** (därm'stat; *Ger* därm'shtät) city in SW Germany, in the state of Hesse: pop. 136,000

**Dart·moor** (därt'moor, -môr) a prison in Devon, SW England

Dartmouth**Dartmouth** 98

**Dart·mouth** (därt'məth) ⟦named in honor of Sir Wm. Legge, 2d Earl of *Dartmouth* (1672-1750)⟧ city in S Nova Scotia, Canada, near Halifax: pop. 62,000

**Dar·win** (där'win) capital of Northern Territory, Australia: seaport on the Timor Sea: pop. 64,000

**Dasht-e-Ka·vir** (däsh'tē kə vir') large salt-desert plateau in NC Iran: *c.* 18,000 sq. mi. (46,600 sq. km)

**Dasht-e-Lut** (däsh'tē lo͞ot') vast desert region of central and SE Iran, extending southward from the Dasht-e-Kavir

**Dau·gav·pils** (dou'guv pils') city in SE Latvia, on the Western Dvina River: pop. 122,000

**Dau·phi·né** (dō fē nā') historic region of SE France, on the Italian border, north of Provence

**Da·vao** (dä vou') seaport in the Philippines, on the SE coast of Mindanao: pop. 610,000

**Dav·en·port** (dav'ən pôrt') ⟦after Col. G. *Davenport* (1783-1845), fur trader⟧ city in E Iowa, on the Mississippi: pop. 95,000

**Da·vis Strait** (dā'vis) arm of the Atlantic between Baffin Island, Canada, and W Greenland: *c.* 200-400 mi. (320-640 km) wide

**Daw·son** (dô'sən) ⟦after G. M. *Dawson* (1849-1901), Cdn geologist⟧ city in W Yukon, Canada, on the Yukon River: former gold-mining center: pop. 700

**Dawson Creek** city in E British Columbia, Canada: S terminus of the Alaska Highway: pop. 11,000

**Day·ton** (dāt''n) ⟦after Gen. Elias *Dayton* (1737-1807)⟧ city in SW Ohio: pop. 182,000 (met. area with Springfield, 951,000)

**Day·to·na Beach** (dā tō'nə) ⟦after M. *Day*, the founder⟧ resort city in NE Fla., on the Atlantic: pop. 62,000

**DC, D.C.** *abbrev. for* District of Columbia

**DE** *abbrev. for* Delaware

**Dead Sea** inland body of salt water on the Israel-Jordan border: *c.* 390 sq. mi. (1,010 sq. km); surface, *c.* 1,300 ft. (400 m) below sea level (the lowest known point on earth)

**Dear·born** (dir'bərn, -bôrn') ⟦after Gen. Henry *Dearborn*, U.S. Secretary of War (1801-09)⟧ city in SE Mich.: suburb of Detroit: pop. 89,000

**Dearborn Heights** ⟦see prec.⟧ city in SE Mich.: suburb of Detroit: pop. 61,000

**Death Valley** dry, hot desert basin in E Calif. & S Nev.: contains lowest point in Western Hemisphere, 282 ft. (86 m) below sea level

**Deau·ville** (dō′vil; *Fr* dō vēl′) resort town in NW France, on the English Channel: pop. 5,600

**De·bre·cen** (deb′rət sen′) city in E Hungary: pop. 210,000

**De·cap·o·lis** (di kap′ə lis) ancient region of NE Palestine, mostly east of the Jordan, occupied by a confederation (formed *c.* 65 B.C.) of ten Greek cities

**De·ca·tur** (di kāt′ər) ⟦after Stephen *Decatur* (1779-1820), U.S. naval officer⟧ **1** city in N Ala., on the Tennessee River: pop. 49,000 **2** city in central Ill.: pop. 84,000

**Dec·can Plateau** (dek′ən) triangular tableland occupying most of the peninsula of India, between the Eastern Ghats & Western Ghats & south of the Narbada River: also called **the Deccan**

**Dee** (dē) **1** river in NE Scotland, flowing east into the North Sea: 90 mi. (145 km) **2** river in N Wales and W England, flowing northeast into the Irish Sea: 70 mi. (113 km)

**deep South** that area of the U.S. regarded as most typically Southern and conservative, especially the southernmost parts of Ga., Ala., Miss., and La.

**Deh·ra Dun** (der′ə dōōn′) city in Uttar Pradesh, N India: pop. 294,000

**Dei·mos** (dī′məs, dā′-) ⟦Gr *deimos*, lit., panic, personified as an attendant of Ares⟧ the smaller of the two satellites of Mars: cf. PHOBOS

**Del** *abbrev. for* Delaware

**Del·a·go·a Bay** (del′ə gō′ə) inlet of the Indian Ocean, on the SE coast of Mozambique

**Del·a·ware** (del′ə wer′, -war′) ⟦after Baron *De La Warr* (1577-1618), 1st Eng colonial gov. of Va.⟧ **1** Eastern State of the U.S., on the Atlantic: one of the 13 original States; 2,057 sq. mi. (5,328 sq. km); pop. 666,000; cap. Dover: abbrev. *DE* or *Del* **2** river flowing from N.Y. along the Pa.-N.Y. and Pa.-N.J. borders into Delaware Bay: *c.* 280 mi. (450 km)

**Delaware Bay** estuary of the Delaware River, & an inlet of the Atlantic, between SW N.J. and E Del.: *c.* 55 mi. (88 km) long

**Delft** (delft) city in W Netherlands: pop. 87,000

**Del·hi** (del′ē) 1 territory in N India, including the cities of Delhi & New Delhi: 573 sq. mi. (1,484 sq. km); pop. 6,220,000 2 city in this territory, on the Jumna River: pop. 5,714,000: see also NEW DELHI

**Del·mar·va Peninsula** (del mär′və) peninsula in the E U.S., between Chesapeake Bay on the west & Delaware Bay & the Atlantic on the east, consisting of Del. & parts of Md. & Va.: *c.* 180 mi. (290 km) long

**De·los** (dē′läs) small island of the Cyclades in the Aegean: legendary birthplace of Artemis & Apollo

**Del·phi** (del′fī) town in ancient Phocis, on the slopes of Mount Parnassus: seat of the famous ancient oracle of Apollo (**Delphic oracle**)

**Del·phi·nus** (del fī′nəs) 〖L, lit., dolphin〗 a small N constellation between Pegasus and Aquila

**Dem·a·vend** (dem′ə vend′) *alt. sp. of* DAMAVAND

**Den·bigh·shire** (den′bi shir′, -shər; -bē-) former county of N Wales, now part of Clwyd and Gwynedd counties: also **Den′bigh** (-bi, -bē)

**Den·eb** (den′eb′) 〖Ar *dhanab* (*aldajāja*), tail (of the hen)〗 a supergiant star, the brightest star in the constellation Cygnus, with a magnitude of 1.25

**Den Hel·der** (dən hel′dər) seaport in NW Netherlands, on the North Sea: pop. 64,000

**De·niz·li** (den′əz lē′) city in SW Turkey, near ancient Laodicea: pop. 135,000

**Den·mark** (den′märk) 〖ME *Denemarche* < OE *Denemearce* < ON *Danir*, the Danes (pl.), akin to OE *Dene* (prob. "lowlanders") + OE *mearc*, orig., boundary < Gmc *\*marka*〗 country in Europe, occupying most of the peninsula of Jutland and several nearby islands in the North and Baltic seas: 16,632 sq. mi. (43,076 sq. km); pop. 5,124,000; cap. Copenhagen

**Denmark Strait** arm of the N Atlantic between SE Greenland & Iceland: *c.* 130 mi. (200 km) wide

**Den·pa·sar** (dən päs′är) seaport in S Bali, Indonesia: pop. 261,000

**Den·ton** (dent′′n) 〖after Rev. John B. *Denton*, a pioneer〗 city in NE Tex.: pop. 66,000

**D'En·tre·cas·teaux Islands** (dän′trə kas′tō) group of islands off SE New Guinea: part of the country of Papua New Guinea: *c.* 1,200 sq. mi. (3,110 sq. km)

**Den·ver** (den′vər) 〖after J. W. *Denver* (1817-92), gov. of Kans.〗 capital of Colo., in the NC part: pop. 468,000

(met. area, incl. Boulder, 1,848,000)

**Der·by** (dʉr′bē; *chiefly Brit,* där′bē) 1 city in Derby-shire, England: pop. 215,000 2 DERBYSHIRE

**Der·by·shire** (dʉr′bi shir, -shər; *chiefly Brit,* där′-) county in central England: 1,016 sq. mi. (2,631 sq. km); pop. 912,000

**Der·ry** (der′ē) LONDONDERRY

**Des·chutes** (dā shōōt′) ⟦ < Fr *rivière des chutes,* river of the falls ⟧ river in central and N Oreg., flowing from the Cascades north into the Columbia River: *c.* 250 mi. (400 km)

**Des Moines** (də moin′) ⟦Fr, lit., of the monks ⟧ 1 river in Iowa, flowing southeast into the Mississippi: *c.* 325 mi. (523 km) 2 capital of Iowa, in the central part: pop. 193,000

**Des Plaines** (des plānz′) ⟦prob. in allusion to the sugar maples (*plaines* in Miss. Valley Fr.) once there ⟧ city in NE Ill.: suburb of Chicago: pop. 53,000

**Des·sau** (des′ou) city in EC Germany, in the state of Saxony-Anhalt: pop. 104,000

**De·troit** (di troit′) ⟦ < Fr *détroit,* strait: first applied to the river ⟧ 1 city in SE Mich., on the Detroit River: pop. 1,028,000 (met. area 4,382,000; urban area, including Ann Arbor, 4,665,000) 2 river flowing south from Lake St. Clair into Lake Erie: *c.* 31 mi. (50 km)

**Deutsch·land** (doich′länt′) ⟦ Ger < *Deutsch,* German (< OHG *diutisc,* of the people < OHG *thioda,* akin to OE *theod* & OIr *tuoth,* people < IE *\*teutā-,* crowd < base *\*tēu-,* to swell + OHG *-isc,* -ish (adj. suffix) + Ger *land,* land ⟧ *Ger. name of* GERMANY

**De·ven·ter** (dā′vən tər) city in E Netherlands: medieval commercial & educational center: pop. 65,000

**Devil's Island** one of a group of French islands off the coast of French Guiana: site of a former penal colony (1851-1951)

**Dev·on** (dev′ən) 1 island of the Arctic Archipelago, north of Baffin Island in Baffin Region of Northwest Territories, Canada: 20,861 sq. mi. (54,030 sq. km) 2 county of SW England, extending from the Bristol Channel to the English Channel: 2,593 sq. mi. (6,715 sq. km); pop. 978,000

**Dev·on·shire** (dev′ən shir′, -shər) DEVON (the county)

**Dez·ful** (dez fōōl′) city in W Iran: pop. 141,000

**Dezh·nev** (dyezh′nyev), **Cape** cape at the northeasternmost point of Asia, in Russia, projecting into Bering Strait: also **Cape Dezh'nev·a** (-nye və)

**Dhak·a** (dä′kə, dak′ə) capital of Bangladesh, in the WC part: pop. 3,440,000

**Dhan·bad** (dän′bäd) city in Bihar state, NE India: pop. 677,000

**Dhau·la·gi·ri** (dɑu′lə gir′e) mountain of the Himalayas, in NC Nepal: 26,810 ft. (8,172 m)

**Diamond Head** promontory in SE Oahu, Hawaii, near Honolulu, consisting of the rim of an extinct volcanic crater

**Di·e·go Gar·ci·a** (dē ā′gō gär sē′ə) chief island of the Chagos Archipelago, British Indian Ocean Territory: 17 sq. mi. (44 sq. km)

**Dien Bien Phu** (dyen′ byen′ fōō′) village in NW Vietnam: besieged & captured by Vietminh forces (1954), marking the end of French occupation of Indochina

**Di·eppe** (dē ep′) city in N France, on the English Channel: pop. 35,000

**Di·jon** (dē zhōn′) city in EC France: pop. 146,000

**Di·li** (dil′ē) city in E Timor, Indonesia: before 1975, capital of Portuguese Timor: pop. 60,000

**Di·mashq** (dē mäshk′) *Ar. name of* DAMASCUS

**Di·nar·ic Alps** (di nar′ik) range of the E Alps, along the Adriatic coast of Croatia, Yugoslavia, & N Albania: highest peak, *c.* 8,800 ft. (2,680 m)

**Di·o·mede Islands** (dī′ə med′) 〚so named by Vitus Bering, Dan explorer who discovered them (1728) on St. *Diomede*'s Day (August 16)〛 two islands in the Bering Strait, between Siberia & Alaska; **Big Diomede**, Russia (Russ. name *Ratmanov*) & **Little Diomede**, U.S.: U.S.-Russia boundary passes between them

**Di·o·ne** (dī ō′nē) a satellite of Saturn, sharing an orbit with a smaller satellite (Dione B)

**Dipper** *see* BIG DIPPER, LITTLE DIPPER

**Di·re Da·wa** (dir′id ə wä′) city in E Ethiopia: pop. 98,000: also written **Di′re·da·wa′**

**Dis** (dis) 〚L, contr. < *dives*, rich, transl. of Gr *Ploutōn*, Pluto〛 the lower world; Hades

**Dismal Swamp** marshy, forested region between Norfolk, Va. & Albemarle Sound, N.C.: *c.* 30 mi. (48 km) long; traversed by a canal that is part of the Intracoastal Waterway

**District of Columbia** 〚after Christopher *Columbus*〛

federal district of the U.S., on the N bank of the Potomac River: 69 sq. mi. (179 sq. km); pop. 607,000; coextensive with the city of Washington: abbrev. *DC* or *D.C.*

**Di·u** (dē′oo) small island just off the coast of Gujarat state, NW India: formerly part of Portuguese India: see GOA

**Dix·ie** (dik′sē) 〚 < *Dixie* (earlier, *Dixie's Land*), title of song (1859) by Daniel D. Emmett (1815-1904), U.S. songwriter, after *Dixie*, orig. name of a Negro character in a minstrel play (1850) 〛 the Southern States of the U.S. collectively; Dixieland

**Dix·ie·land** (-land′) the South; Dixie: also **Dixie Land**

**Di·yar·ba·kir** (dē yär′bä kir′) city in SE Turkey, on the Tigris: pop. 236,000

**Dja·ja Peak** (jä′yə) mountain in West Irian, W New Guinea: *c.* 16,500 ft. (5,030 m)

**Dja·kar·ta** (jə kärt′ə) *alt. sp. of* JAKARTA

**Dja·wa** (jä′və) *Indonesian name of* JAVA

**Dji·bou·ti** (ji boot′ē) 1 country in E Africa, on the Gulf of Aden: 8,500 sq. mi. (22,000 sq. km); pop. *c.* 430,000: see FRENCH SOMALILAND 2 its capital, a seaport: pop. 200,000

**Dne·pr** (nē′pər; *Russ* dnye′pər) 〚 Russ: see DANUBE 〛 river in W Russia, Belarus, & Ukraine, flowing from the Valdai Hills south and southwest into the Black Sea: 1,420 mi. (2,285 km)

**Dne·pro·dzer·zhinsk** (dnye′prô dzer zhinsk′) city in SC Ukraine, on the Dnepr just west of Dnepropetrovsk: pop. 271,000

**Dne·pro·pe·trovsk** (-pye trôfsk′) city in SC Ukraine, on the Dnepr: pop. 1,153,000

**Dnes·tr** (nēs′tər; *Russ* dnyes′tər) 〚 Russ: see DANUBE 〛 river in SW Ukraine & Moldova, flowing from the Carpathian Mountains southeast into the Black Sea: *c.* 850 mi. (1,370 km)

**Dnie·per** (nē′pər) *alt. sp. of* DNEPR

**Dnies·ter** (nēs′tər) *alt. sp. of* DNESTR

**Do·bru·ja** (dō′broo jə) region in SE Europe, on the Black Sea: divided, since 1940, between Romania & Bulgaria

**Do·dec·a·nese** (do dek′ə nēz′, -nēs′) group of Greek islands in the Aegean, off the SW coast of Turkey: 1,028 sq. mi. (2,663 sq. km); pop. 145,000; cap. Rhodes

**Do·do·ma** (dōd′ə mä′) capital of Tanzania, in the central part: pop. 46,000

**Dog** (dôg, däg) the constellation Canis Major or Canis Minor

**Dog·ger Bank** (-er) extensive sand bank in the central North Sea, between England & Denmark, submerged at a depth of 60-120 ft. (18-36 m)

**Dog Star 1** SIRIUS **2** PROCYON

**Do·ha** (dō′hə) capital of Qatar, a seaport on the Persian Gulf: pop. 190,000

**Dol·lard–des–Or·meaux** (*Fr* dô lår dä zôr mō′) town in S Quebec, Canada: suburb of Montreal: pop. 43,000

**Do·lo·mites** (dō′lə mīts′, däl′ə-) division of the E Alps, in N Italy: highest peak, 10,965 ft. (3,342 m): also **Dolomite Alps**

**Dol·phin** (däl′fin, dôl′-) the constellation Delphinus

**Dom·i·ni·ca** (däm′ə nē′kə, də min′i kə) a country that is an island of the Windward group in the West Indies: a British-controlled territory from 1783 to 1978, when it became independent: a member of the Commonwealth: 290 sq. mi. (751 sq. km); pop. 74,000; cap. Roseau

**Do·min·i·can Republic** (dō min′i kən, də-) country occupying the E part of the island of Hispaniola, in the West Indies: independent since 1844: 18,816 sq. mi. (45,734 sq. km); pop. 6,785,000; cap. Santo Domingo

**Don** (dän; *Russ* dôn) [ Russ: see DANUBE ] river in SC European Russia, flowing southward into the Sea of Azov: *c.* 1,200 mi. (1,930 km)

**Do·nau** (dō′nou) *Ger. name of* the DANUBE

**Don·bas, Don·bass** (dôn bäs′) DONETS BASIN

**Don·cas·ter** (dän′kas tər, -kəs-) city in NC England, in South Yorkshire: pop. 82,000

**Don·e·gal** (dän′ə gôl′; *Ir* dun′ə gôl′) northernmost county of Ireland, in Ulster province: 1,865 sq. mi.; pop. 125,000

**Do·nets** (də nets′; *Russ* dô nyets′) [ Russ: see DANUBE ] river in SW Russia & Ukraine, flowing southeast into the Don: *c.* 650 mi. (1,050 km)

**Donets Basin** major industrial and coal-producing region in the lower valley of the Donets River

**Do·netsk** (dô nyetsk′) city in SE Ukraine, in the Donets Basin: pop. 1,073,000

**Dong·ting** (dooŋ'tiŋ') lake in Hunan province, SE China: *c.* 1,450 sq. mi. (3,755 sq. km); during floods, over 4,000 sq. mi. (10,400 sq. km)

**Don·ner Pass** (dän'ər) 〖after the ill-fated *Donner* party who wintered there 1846-47〗 mountain pass in E Calif., in the Sierra Nevada: *c.* 7,100 ft. (2,160 m) high

**Doon** (dōōn) 〖see DANUBE〗 river in SW Scotland, flowing north into the Firth of Clyde: *c.* 30 mi. (48 km)

**Do·ra·do** (dō rä'dō, də-) a S constellation between Pictor and Reticulum, containing part of the Larger Magellanic Cloud

**Dor·dogne** (dôr dôn'y') river in SW France, flowing southwest to unite with the Garonne and form the Gironde estuary: *c.* 300 mi. (480 km)

**Dor·drecht** (dôr'dreHt) city in SW Netherlands, on the Maas (Meuse) delta: pop. 107,000

**Dor·is** (dôr'is) ancient mountainous region in what is now WC Greece: regarded as the home of the Dorians

**Dor·set·shire** (dôr'sit shir, -shər) county in SW England, on the English Channel: 1,025 sq. mi. (2,654 sq. km); pop. 618,000: also **Dor'set**

**Dort** (dôrt) *var. of* DORDRECHT

**Dort·mund** (dôrt'mənd; *Ger* dôrt'moont) city in W Germany, in the valley of the Ruhr River in the state of North Rhine-Westphalia: pop. 585,000

**Do·than** (dō'thən) 〖after *Dothan*, city in ancient Palestine (see Gen. 37:17)〗 city in SE Ala.: pop. 54,000

**Dou·ai** (dōō ā') city in N France: pop. 45,000: formerly sp. **Dou·ay'**

**Dou·a·la** (dōō ä'lə) seaport in Cameroon, on the Bight of Biafra: pop. 637,000

**Doubs** (dōō) river in E France, flowing from the Jura Mountains generally southwest into the Saône: *c.* 270 mi. (435 km)

**Doug·las** (dug'ləs) capital of the Isle of Man: pop. 20,000

**Dou·ro** (dō'roo) river flowing from NC Spain across N Portugal into the Atlantic: *c.* 500 mi. (800 km)

**Do·ver** (dō'vər) **1** seaport in Kent, SE England, on the Strait of Dover: pop. 33,000 **2** 〖after the seaport〗 capital of Del., in the central part: pop. 28,000 **3 Strait (or Straits) of** strait between France and England, joining the North Sea and the English Channel: narrowest point, 21 mi. (34 km)

**Down** (doun) district in SE Northern Ireland, in the S

part of a former, much larger county also called **Down**

**Dow·ney** (dou′nē) ⟦after J. G. *Downey*, gov. of Calif., 1860-62⟧ city in SW Calif.: suburb of Los Angeles: pop. 91,000

**Down·ing Street** (doun′iŋ) ⟦after Sir George *Downing* (1623-84), who owned property there⟧ street in Westminster, London, location of some of the principal government offices of the United Kingdom, including the official residence of the prime minister (No. 10): often used figuratively of the British government

**Downs, the** 1 two parallel ranges of low, grassy hills (**North Downs** & **South Downs**) in SE England 2 naturally protected anchorage in the Strait of Dover, England

**Dra·co** (drā′kō) ⟦L < *draco*, dragon < Gr *drakōn*, serpent, lit., the seeing one < *derkesthai*, to see < IE base *derk-, to see⟧ a large N constellation containing the north pole of the ecliptic

**Drag·on** (drag′ən) the constellation Draco

**Dra·kens·berg** (drä′kənz bʉrg′) mountain range in E South Africa, extending *c.* 700 mi. (1,130 km) from S Cape Province through Lesotho to SE Transvaal: highest peak, 11,425 ft. (3,482 m): also **Drakensberg Mountains (or Range)**

**Drake Passage** (drāk) strait between Cape Horn & the South Shetland Islands: *c.* 400 mi. (645 km) wide

**Dran·cy** (drän sē′) city in NC France: suburb of Paris: pop. 60,000

**Dra·va** (drä′vä) river in SC Europe, flowing from the Alps of Austria southeastward through Slovenia & Croatia into the Danube: *c.* 450 mi. (725 km)

**Dres·den** (drez′dən) city in E Germany, on the Elbe: capital of the state of Saxony: pop. 520,000

**Dro·ghe·da** (drô′ə də) seaport in E Ireland, at the mouth of the Boyne River: captured (1649) by Cromwell, who massacred its Royalist garrison: pop. 23,000

**Dry Tor·tu·gas** (tôr too′gəz) group of small islands of Fla. in the Gulf of Mexico, west of Key West

**Du·bai** (də bī′) 1 one of the emirates that constitute the United Arab Emirates: 1,500 sq. mi. (3,885 sq. km); pop. 318,000 2 seaport in the United Arab Emirates, on the Persian Gulf: pop. 266,000

**Dub·lin** (dub′lən) 1 capital of Ireland: seaport on the Irish Sea: pop. 526,000 2 county in E Ireland, on the

Irish Sea: 356 sq. mi. (922 sq. km); pop. 1,003,000;
county seat, Dublin

**Du·brov·nik** (dōō'brôv nik) seaport in S Croatia, on the
Adriatic: pop. 33,000

**Du·buque** (də byōōk') [after J. *Dubuque* (1762-1810),
early lead miner] city in E Iowa, on the Mississippi:
pop. 58,000

**Dud·ley** (dud'lē) city in West Midlands county, WC
England, near Birmingham: pop. 187,000

**Due·ro** (dwe'rô) *Sp. name of* DOURO

**Duis·burg** (dyōōs'bʉrg; *Ger* dŭs'boork) city in W Germany, at the junction of the Rhine & Ruhr rivers, in
the state of North Rhine-Westphalia: pop. 528,000

**Du·luth** (də lōōth') [after Daniel G. *Du Lhut* (or *Du
Luth*), 1636-1710, Fr explorer] city and port in NE
Minn., on Lake Superior: pop. 85,000

**Dum·bar·ton** (dum bärt'ʼn) city in the Strathclyde
region of W Scotland, on the Clyde River: pop. 23,000

**Dum·fries** (dum frēs') former county of S Scotland, on
Solway Firth: now part of a region called **Dumfries and
Galloway**, 2,500 sq. mi. (6,475 sq. km); pop. 146,000

**Dum·yat** (doom'yät') *Ar. name of* DAMIETTA

**Du·na** (doo'nà) *Hung. name of* DANUBE

**Du·nai** (dōō'nī') *Russ. name of* DANUBE

**Du·nă·rea** (dōō'nər yä) *Romanian name of* DANUBE

**Du·nav** (dōō'näv') *Bulg. name of* DANUBE

**Dun·bar·ton** (dun bärt'ʼn) former county of W Scotland, now in the Strathclyde region

**Dun·dalk** (dun'dôk) suburb of Baltimore, in central
Md.: pop. 66,000

**Dun·dee** (dun dē') seaport in E Scotland, on the Firth
of Tay: pop. 180,000

**Dun·e·din** (də nēd'ʼn) city on the SE coast of South
Island, New Zealand: pop. (of urban area) 111,000

**Dun·ferm·line** (dən fʉrm'lin) city in Fife region, E
Scotland, on the Firth of Forth: pop. 52,000

**Dun·kerque** (dën kerk') *Fr. name of* DUNKIRK

**Dun·kirk** (dun'kʉrk') seaport in N France, on the North
Sea: scene of the evacuation of over 300,000 Allied
troops under fire (1940) as France fell to Germany:
pop. 74,000

**Dun Laoghai·re** (dən ler'ə) port in E Ireland, on the
Irish Sea, near Dublin: pop. 54,000

**Dun·si·nane** (dun'sə nān') hill in central Scotland:

ruined fortress at its summit is the reputed site of Macbeth's defeat as related in Shakespeare's play

**Du·ran·go** (də raŋ'gō; *Sp* dōō räŋ'gô) **1** state of NW Mexico: 47,560 sq. mi. (123,181 sq. km); pop. 1,228,000 **2** its capital: pop. 321,000: in full **Victoria de Durango**

**Dur·ban** (dur'bən) seaport in Natal, on the E coast of South Africa: pop. 506,000

**Dur·ga·pur** (door'gə poor') city in the state of West Bengal, NE India: pop. 306,000

**Durg-Bhi·lai·na·gar** (doorg'bi li nug'ər) city in Madhya Pradesh, EC India: pop. 490,000

**Dur·ham** (dur'əm) **1** county of N England, on the North Sea: 941 sq. mi. (2,436 sq. km); pop. 604,000 **2** its county seat, on the Wear River: pop. 87,000 **3** city in north central N.C.: pop. 137,000: see RALEIGH

**Dur·rës** (door'əs) seaport in W Albania, on the Adriatic: as *Epidamnus*, an ancient Corinthian colony: pop. 66,000

**Du·shan·be** (dōō shän'be) capital of Tajikistan, in the W part: pop. 552,000

**Düs·sel·dorf** (dōōs'əl dôrf') city in W Germany, on the Rhine: capital of North Rhine-Westphalia: pop. 571,000

**Dust Bowl** region in SC U.S., including parts of Okla. & Tex., where eroded topsoil was blown away by winds during a drought in the 1930's

**Dutch Borneo** formerly, the part of Borneo that belonged to the Netherlands: now Kalimantan, Indonesia

**Dutch East Indies** NETHERLANDS (EAST) INDIES

**Dutch Guiana** Suriname, when it was a dependent territory of the Netherlands (1667-1954)

**Dutch New Guinea** NETHERLANDS NEW GUINEA

**Dvi·na** (dvē nä') **1** river in NW Russia, flowing northwest into Dvina Bay near Arkhangelsk: 460 mi. (740 km): often called **Northern Dvina 2** river in W Russia, flowing from the Valdai Hills northwest through Belarus & Latvia into the Gulf of Riga: 635 mi. (1,020 km): Latvian name *Daugava*: often called **Western Dvina**

**Dvina Bay** arm of the White Sea, in NW Russia: *c.* 65 mi. (105 km) long

**Dvinsk** (dvēnsk) *Russ. name of* DAUGAVPILS

**Dy·fed** (div'əd) county of SW Wales, on the Bristol &

St. George's channels: 2,226 sq. mi. (5,765 sq. km); pop. 335,000

**Dzer·zhinsk** (dzir zhinsk′) city in central European Russia, near Gorki: pop. 274,000

**Dzham·bul** (jäm bōōl′) city in SE Kazakhstan: pop. 303,000

**Dzun·ga·ri·a** (zoon ger′ē ə) *old name of* JUNGGAR PENDI

# E

**Ea·ling** (ē′liŋ) borough of Greater London, England: pop. 289,000

**East Anglia 1** former Anglo-Saxon kingdom in E England **2** corresponding section in modern England, chiefly comprising the counties of Norfolk and Suffolk

**East Berlin** *see* BERLIN

**East China Sea** part of the Pacific Ocean east of China and west of Kyushu, Japan, and the Ryukyu Islands: *c.* 480,000 sq. mi. (1,243,000 sq. km)

**Eas·ter Island** (ēs′tər) ⟦from the fact that it was discovered *Easter* day, 1722⟧ island in the South Pacific, *c.* 2,000 mi. (3,200 km) west of Valparaiso, Chile, & governed as an integral part of Chile: 64 sq. mi. (118 sq. km); pop. *c.* 2,000

**Eastern Hemisphere** that half of the earth which includes Europe, Africa, Asia, and Australia

**Eastern Province** province of Saudi Arabia, on the Persian Gulf: *c.* 41,200 sq. mi. (106,700 sq. km)

**Eastern Roman Empire** Byzantine Empire, esp. so called from A.D. 395, when the Roman Empire was divided, until A.D. 476, when the Western Roman emperor was deposed

**Eastern Shore 1** E shore of Chesapeake Bay, including all of Md. and Va. east of the Bay **2** sometimes, the entire Delmarva Peninsula

**East Flanders** province of NW Belgium: 1,147 sq. mi. (2,971 sq. km); pop. 1,330,000; cap. Ghent

**East Germany** *see* GERMANY

**East Hartford** suburb of Hartford, Conn., on the Connecticut River opposite Hartford: pop. 50,000

**East Indies 1** Malay Archipelago; esp., the islands of Indonesia **2** [Historical] India, Indochina, and the Malay Archipelago: also **East India**

**East Lansing** city in SC Mich.: suburb of Lansing: pop.

51,000: see Lansing

**East London** seaport on the SE coast of South Africa, on the Indian Ocean: pop. 161,000

**East Lothian** former county of SE Scotland, now a district in Lothian region

**Eas·ton** (ēs′tən) 〚after *Easton* Neston in Northamptonshire, England, country estate of the father-in-law of a son of William Penn〛 city in EC Pa.: pop. 26,000: see Allentown

**East Orange** 〚after *Orange*, ruling family of the Netherlands (early 17th-c.) at the time the Dutch were settling colonies in North America〛 city in NE N.J., adjoining Newark: pop. 74,000

**East Pakistan** former province of Pakistan: since 1971, the country of Bangladesh

**East Providence** city in E R.I.: suburb of Providence: pop. 50,000

**East Prussia** former province of Prussia, in NE Germany, on the Baltic Sea, separated from the rest of Germany (1919-39) by the Polish Corridor: in 1945, divided between Poland and the U.S.S.R.

**East River** strait in SE N.Y., connecting Long Island Sound and upper New York Bay and separating Manhattan Island from Long Island: 16 mi. (25.5 km) long

**East Siberian Sea** part of the Arctic Ocean, off the NE coast of Russia, east of the New Siberian Islands

**East St. Louis** city in SW Ill., on the Mississippi, opposite St. Louis, Mo.: pop. 41,000

**East Sussex** county in SE England, on the English Channel: 693 sq. mi. (1,795 sq. km): pop. 679,000

**East York** 〚orig. the E portion of the county of *York*, after the House of York〛 metropolitan borough of Toronto, Canada: pop. 102,000

**Eau Claire** (ō′ kler′) 〚Fr, clear water, for the *Eau Claire* River which flows through the city〛 city in WC Wis.: pop. 57,000

**E·bo·ra·cum** (i bôr′ə kəm) *ancient name of* York: chief city of the Roman province of Britain

**E·bro** (ā′brō; *E* ē′brō) river in N Spain, flowing southeast into the Mediterranean: *c.* 575 mi. (925 km)

**Ec·bat·a·na** (ek bat′'n ə) capital of ancient Media, on the site of modern Hamadan (Iran)

**Ec·ua·dor** (ek′wə dôr′) country on the NW coast of South America: independent since 1830: 109,483 sq.

mi. (283,561 sq. km); pop. 9,647,000; cap. Quito

**Ed·dy·stone Light** (ed'i stən) lighthouse on dangerous rocks (**Eddystone Rocks**) just off the SE coast of Cornwall, in the English Channel

**E·de** (ā'də) city in central Netherlands: pop. 88,000

**E·den** (ēd''n) 〚LL < Heb, lit., delight〛 *Bible* the garden where Adam and Eve first lived; Paradise: Gen. 2:8

**E·des·sa** (ē des'ə; i-) ancient city in NW Mesopotamia, on the site of modern Urfa (Turkey)

**E·di·na** (e dī'nə, i-) 〚coined by Scot settlers as a diminutive of fol.〛 suburb of Minneapolis, in E Minn.: pop. 46,000

**Ed·in·burgh** (ed''n bur'ə, -ō) capital of Scotland, in the Lothian region, on the Firth of Forth; pop. 419,000

**E·dir·ne** (e dir'nə) city in NW European Turkey, near the Greek border, on the site of an ancient Roman city (*Adrianopolis*) founded by the emperor Hadrian (*c.* A.D. 125): pop. 72,000

**Ed·i·son** (ed'i sən) 〚after Thomas Alva *Edison* (1847-1931), U.S. inventor who had his first laboratory here〛 urban township in NC N.J.: pop. 89,000

**Ed·mon·ton** (ed'mən tən) 〚prob. after *Edmonton*, former borough of London, England〛 capital of Alberta, Canada, in the central part: pop. 573,000 (met. area 786,000)

**E·dom** (ē'dəm) ancient kingdom in SW Asia, south of the Dead Sea

**Ed·ward** (ed'wərd), **Lake** lake in EC Africa, between Zaire and Uganda: 830 sq. mi. (2,150 sq. km)

**E·gypt** (ē'jipt) country in NE Africa, on the Mediterranean and Red seas: ancient Egyptian dynasties may date back as far as 4500 B.C.; in modern times, occupied by the British in 1882 & achieved independence in 1922: 386,650 sq. mi. (1,001,420 sq. km); pop. 50,525,000; cap. Cairo: official name **Arab Republic of Egypt**

**Eif·fel Tower** (ī'fəl) 〚after A. G. *Eiffel* (1832-1923), Fr engineer who designed it〛 tower of iron framework in Paris, built for the International Exposition of 1889: 984 ft. (300 m) high

**Ei·lat** (ā lät') seaport in S Israel, at the head of the Gulf of Aqaba: pop. 13,000

**Eind·ho·ven** (int'hō'vən) city in North Brabant province, S Netherlands: pop. 192,000

**Eir·e** (er'ə) *Gael. name of* IRELAND; also, the former official name (1937-49) of the country of Ireland

**E·lam** (ē'ləm) ancient kingdom of SW Asia, at the head of the Persian Gulf (fl. 13th & 12th cent. B.C.)

**E·lat, E·lath** (ā lät') *alt. sp. of* EILAT

**E·la·zig** (el'ə zig') city in EC Turkey: pop. 143,000

**El·ba** (el'bə) Italian island in the Tyrrhenian Sea, between Corsica & Italy: site of Napoleon's first exile (1814-15): 86 sq. mi. (223 sq. km)

**El·be** (el'bə, elb) river in central Europe, flowing from NW Czech Republic through Germany into the North Sea at Hamburg: *c.* 725 mi. (1,170 km)

**El·bert** (el'bərt), **Mount** ⟦after S. H. *Elbert*, territorial gov. of Colo. (1873-74)⟧ peak of the Sawatch Range, central Colo.: highest peak of the Rocky Mts. of the conterminous U.S.: 14,443 ft. (4,400 m)

**El·brus** (el'broos, -brōōz'), **Mount** mountain of the Caucasus range, in SW Russia: highest peak in Europe, 18,481 ft. (5,633 m): also sp. **El'brus**

**El·burz Mountains** (el boorz') mountain range in N Iran, along the Caspian Sea: highest peak, Mount Damavand

**El Ca·jon** (el kə hōn') ⟦Sp, the box: the city is boxed in by hills⟧ city in S Calif.: suburb of San Diego: pop. 89,000

**El·che** (el'chā') city in SE Spain, near Alicante: pop. 163,000

**El Do·ra·do, El·do·ra·do** (el'də rä'dō, -rä'dō, -rad'ō) ⟦Sp, the gilded; *dorado*, pp. of *dorar*, to gild < LL *deaurare*, to gild + L *de-*, intens. + *aurum*, gold⟧ a legendary country in South America, supposed to be rich in gold and precious stones and sought by early Spanish explorers

**El·e·phan·ti·ne** (el'ə fan tī'nē, -tē'-) small island in the Nile, opposite Aswan: site of ancient ruins

**E·leu·sis** (e lōō'sis) town in Greece, northwest of Athens: site of an ancient Greek city (also *Eleusis*), seat of the Eleusinian mysteries

**El Faiyûm** *see* FAIYÛM

**El Fer·rol** (el' fə rōl') seaport in NW Spain, on the Atlantic: pop. 92,000: official name **El Ferrol del Cau·di·llo** (del' kou dē'yō)

**El·gin** (el'jin) ⟦after the title of a Scots hymn written in honor of the town of *Elgin*, Scotland⟧ city in NE Ill., near Chicago: pop. 77,000

**El·gon** (el'gän'), **Mount** extinct volcano on the border of Kenya & Uganda: 14,178 ft. (4,321 m): crater, 5 mi. (8 km) wide

**E·lis** (ē'lis) ancient country in the W Peloponnesus, in which Olympia was located

**E·liz·a·beth** (ē liz'ə bəth, i-) 〖after the wife of Sir George Carteret (1610?-80), proprietor of a colony in the region〗 city in NE N.J., adjacent to Newark: pop. 110,000

**Elk·hart** (elk'härt', el'kärt') 〖after the nearby *Elkhart* River, transl. of Indian name, allegedly given because of an island at its mouth shaped like an elk's heart〗 city in N Ind.: pop. 44,000

**Elles·mere** (elz'mir') 〖after F. Egerton (1800-57), 1st Earl of *Ellesmere*, Eng statesman〗 northernmost island of the Arctic Archipelago, in Baffin Region of Northwest Territories, Canada: 82,119 sq. mi. (212,687 sq. km)

**El·lice Islands** (el'is) group of islands in the WC Pacific, north of Fiji: under British control, 1892-1978; name changed to Tuvalu in 1976 and as such became independent in 1978

**El·lis Island** (el'is) 〖after S. *Ellis*, a former owner〗 small, government-owned island in Upper New York Bay: former (1892-1943) examination center for immigrants seeking to enter the U.S.: 27 acres (11 hectares)

**Elm·hurst** (elm'hurst') 〖after the many *elms* set out there + *hurst*〗 city in NE Ill.: suburb of Chicago: pop. 42,000

**El Mis·ti** (el mē'stē) dormant volcano in S Peru: *c.* 19,100 ft. (5,820 m)

**El Mon·te** (el män'tē) 〖Sp, the thicket: from a dense clump of willows there〗 city in SW Calif.: suburb of Los Angeles: pop. 106,000

**El Ni·ño** (el nēn'yō) 〖Sp, the (Christ) Child: because it occurs near Christmas〗 a warm inshore current annually flowing south along the coast of Ecuador and, about every seven to ten years, extending down the coast of Peru, where it has a devastating effect on weather, crops, fish, etc.

**El O·beid** (el ō bād') city in central Sudan: pop. 140,000

**El Pas·o** (el pas'ō) 〖Sp, after *El Paso del Norte*, ford (of the river) of the north; i.e., the Rio Grande〗 city in westernmost Tex., on the Rio Grande: pop. 515,000

**El Pro·gre·so** (el' prō gres'ō) city in NW Honduras: pop. 105,000

**El Sal·va·dor** (el sal'və dôr'; el' säl'və dôr') country in Central America, southwest of Honduras, on the Pacific: independent since 1841: 8,260 sq. mi. (21,393 sq. km); pop. 5,105,000; cap. San Salvador

**El·si·nore** (el'sə nôr') HELSINGØR: name used in Shakespeare's *Hamlet*

**E·ly** (ē'lē), **Isle of** former county in EC England, now part of Cambridgeshire

**E·lyr·i·a** (i lir'ē ə) ⟦after J. *Ely* (1775-1852), a founder of the town, and Ma*ria*, his wife: ? infl. by ILLYRIA⟧ city in N Ohio, near Cleveland: pop. 57,000

**E·ly·si·um** (ē lizh'əm, -liz'ē əm; i-) ⟦L < Gr *Ēlysion* (*pedion*), Elysian (plain), plain of the departed, of non-IE orig.⟧ *Gr. Myth.* the dwelling place of virtuous people after death: also **E·ly'si·an fields** (-ən)

**Emerald Isle** ⟦from its green landscape⟧ *name for* IRELAND

**E·mil·ia-Ro·ma·gna** (ā mēl'yä'rō män'yä') region in NC Italy, near the head of the Adriatic: 8,542 sq. mi. (22,123 sq. km); pop. 3,947,000; cap. Bologna

**Em·men** (em'ən) city in NE Netherlands: pop. 91,000

**Empire State** *name for* NEW YORK (State)

**Ems** (emz) river in NW Germany, flowing northward into the North Sea: *c.* 200 mi. (320 km)

**En·cel·a·dus** (en sel'ə dəs) ⟦L < Gr *Enkelados*⟧ a smooth satellite of Saturn having more reflective brightness than any other celestial body in the solar system

**En·der·by Land** (en'dər bē) region of Antarctica, opposite the tip of Africa: claimed by Australia

**En·field** (en'fēld) borough of Greater London, England: pop. 263,000

**En·ga·dine** (en'gə dēn') valley of the upper Inn River, E Switzerland: site of many resorts: *c.* 60 mi. (95 km) long

**En·gels** (eŋ'gəlz) city in SC European Russia, on the Volga, opposite Saratov: pop. 177,000

**Eng·land** (iŋ'glənd, -lənd) ⟦ME *Englonde, Yngelonde* < ME *weng* < OE *Engla land*, lit., land of the Angles (as opposed to the Saxons), hence England⟧ **1** division of the United Kingdom of Great Britain & Northern Ireland, occupying most of the southern half of the island of Great Britain: 50,331 sq. mi. (130,357 sq. km); pop. 46,363,000; cap. London **2** England & Wales, considered an administrative unit **3** UNITED KINGDOM

**Eng·lish Channel** (iŋ'glish, -lish) arm of the Atlantic, between S England & NW France: 21-150 mi. (34-240 km) wide; *c*. 350 mi. (560 km) long

**E·nid** (ē'nid) ⟦prob. from Tennyson's poem "Geraint and *Enid*" (1859): in Arthurian legend, Enid was the wife of Geraint, seen as a model of constancy⟧ city in NC Okla.: pop. 45,000

**En·i·we·tok** (en'ə wē'täk') atoll in the Marshall Islands: site of U.S. atomic & hydrogen bomb tests (1948-54)

**En·sche·de** (en'skə dā') city in E Netherlands, near the German border: pop. 145,000

**En·se·na·da** (en'sə näd'ə) seaport in N Baja California, Mexico, on the Pacific: pop. 175,000

**En·teb·be** (en teb'ə) city in S Uganda, on Lake Victoria: cap. of Uganda when it was a British protectorate (1894-1962): pop. 21,000

**Eph·e·sus** (ef'i səs) ancient Greek city in W Asia Minor, near what is now Izmir, Turkey: site of a large temple of Artemis (*c*. 550 B.C.-A.D. 260)

**E·phra·im** (ē'frā im, -frē əm) ⟦LL(Ec) < Gr(Ec) < Heb *efrayim*, lit., very fruitful⟧ *Bible* the kingdom of Israel

**Ep·i·dam·nus** (ep'ə dam'nəs) *see* DURRËS

**E·pi·rus** (i pī'rəs) **1** ancient kingdom on the E coast of the Ionian Sea, in what is now S Albania & NW Greece (fl. 3d cent. B.C.) **2** region of modern Greece, in the same general area

**Ep·som** (ep'səm) town in Surrey, England, southwest of London: site of **Epsom Downs**, where the Derby is run: now part of the borough of **Epsom and Ewell**, pop. 69,000

**Equatorial Guinea** country in WC Africa, consisting of a mainland section (unofficially *Río Muni*) between Gabon & Cameroon, & two islands (*Bioko* and *Annobón*), 370 mi. (595 km) apart, in the Gulf of Guinea: formerly (until 1968) a Spanish possession: 10,830 sq. mi. (28,051 sq. km); pop. 359,000; cap. Malabo

**E·quu·le·us** (ē kwool'ē əs) ⟦L, dim. of *equus*, horse⟧ a very small N constellation near the celestial equator and Pegasus

**Er·bil** (er′bil) IRBIL

**Er·e·bus** (er′ə bəs) ⟦L < Gr *Erebos* < IE base *\*regwos*-, darkness > Arm *erekoy*, evening, Goth *rigis*, darkness⟧ **1** *Gr. Myth.* the dark place under the earth through which the dead passed before entering Hades **2 Mount** volcanic mountain on Ross Island, near Victoria Land, Antarctica: *c.* 12,500 ft. (3,800 m)

**Er·ech·the·um** (er′ek thē′əm) ⟦Gr *Erechtheion* < *Erechtheus*, lit., the render, a mythical king of Athens supposedly entombed there < *erechthein*, to rend, break < IE base *\*rekth*-, to harm > Sans *ráksas*-, torment⟧ temple on the Acropolis in Athens, built 5th cent. B.C.: it contains famous examples of Ionic architecture

**Er·furt** (er′foort) city in central Germany: pop. 217,000

**E·rid·a·nus** (ē rid′ə nəs, -rid′′n əs) ⟦L < Gr *Ēridanos*, poetic name of the Po River⟧ a long S constellation extending from the celestial equator to Hydrus and including the bright star Achernar

**Er·ie** (ir′ē) ⟦NAmFr *Erie*, *Erié* < Huron name of the village called *Rigué* by the Iroquois⟧ **1** port on Lake Erie, in NW Pa.: pop. 109,000 **2 Lake** one of the Great Lakes, between Lake Huron & Lake Ontario: 9,940 sq. mi. (25,745 sq. km); 241 mi. (388 km) long

**Erie Canal** former barge canal between Buffalo, on Lake Erie, and Albany, on the Hudson, completed in 1825: *c.* 360 mi. (580 km) long: much of it is now part of New York State Barge Canal

**Er·in** (er′in) *old poet. name for* IRELAND

**Er·i·tre·a** (er′ə trē′ə) country in E Africa, on the Red Sea: formerly part of Ethiopia, it became independent (1993): 45,400 sq. mi. (117,600 sq. km); pop. 2,615,000; cap. Asmara

**Er·i·van** (er′ə vän′) *alt. sp. of* YEREVAN

**Er·lang·en** (er′läŋ ən) city in SE Germany, near Nuremberg, in the state of Bavaria: pop. 101,000

**E·rode** (i rōd′) city in Tamil Nadu state, S India, on the Cauvery River: pop. 275,000

**Er·y·man·thus** (er′ə man′thəs), **Mount** mountain in the NW Peloponnesus, Greece: 7,297 ft. (2,224 m): in Greek mythology, haunt of a savage boar captured by Hercules

**Erz·ge·bir·ge** (erts′gə bir′gə) mountain range along the border of Germany & Czech Republic: highest peak,

4,080 ft. (1,244 m)

**Er·zu·rum** (er′zə ro͞om′) city in NE Turkey: pop. 252,000

**Es·bjerg** (es′byer) seaport in SW Jutland, Denmark, on the North Sea: pop. 81,000

**Es·caut** (es kō′) *Fr. name of* SCHELDT (River)

**Es·con·di·do** (es′kən dē′dō) ⟦Sp, hidden: after nearby *Escondido* Creek, whose source was difficult to find⟧ city in S Calif., near San Diego: pop. 109,000

**Es·co·ri·al** (es kôr′ē əl; *Sp* es′kŏ ryäl′) ⟦Sp *escorial*, lit., place where a mine has been exhausted < *escoria* < L *scoria*, dross < Gr *skōria*, scoria⟧ huge quadrangle of granite buildings near Madrid, built (16th cent.) by Philip II of Spain: it encloses a palace, church, monastery, etc.

**Es·cu·ri·al** (es kyoor′ē əl) *alt. sp. of* ESCORIAL

**Es·dra·e·lon** (ez′drə ē′lən, es′-) plain in N Israel, extending from the Jordan River valley to a coastal plain near Mt. Carmel: also, & in the Bible always, called JEZREEL

**Es·fa·hán** (es′fä han′) city in WC Iran: cap. of Persia in the 17th cent.: pop. 927,000

**Es·ki·şe·hir** (es kē′she hir′) city in WC Turkey: pop. 367,000

**Es·pa·ña** (es pä′nyä) *Sp. name of* SPAIN

**Es·pí·ri·to San·to** (i spē′rē to͞o sän′to͞o) state of E Brazil, on the Atlantic: 17,605 sq. mi. (45,597 sq. km); pop. 2,287,000; cap. Vitória

**Es·poo** (es′pō) city in S Finland, just west of Helsinki: pop. 153,000

**Es·qui·line** (es′kwə līn′) ⟦L (*Mons*) *esquilinus*, after *Esquiliae*, name of the hill⟧ *see* SEVEN HILLS OF ROME

**Es·sen** (es′ən) city in W Germany, in the Ruhr valley, in the state of North Rhine-Westphalia: pop. 629,000

**Es·se·qui·bo** (es′ə kē′bō) river in Guyana, flowing from the Guiana highlands northward to the Atlantic: *c.* 600 mi. (965 km)

**Es·sex** (es′iks) **1** former Anglo-Saxon kingdom in E England **2** county of SE England, on the North Sea: 1,418 sq. mi. (3,674 sq. km); pop. 1,497,000

**Es·tes Park** (es′tēz) ⟦after Joel *Estes*, first settler (*c.* 1859)⟧ resort town in N Colo., at the entrance to Rocky Mountain National Park: pop. 3,200

**Es·tho·ni·a** (es tō′nē ə, -thō′-) *old sp. of* ESTONIA

**Es·to·ni·a** (es tō′nē ə) country in N Europe, on the Bal-

tic Sea: from 1940 to 1991 it was a republic of the
U.S.S.R.: 17,400 sq. mi. (45,000 sq. km); pop.
1,500,000; cap. Tallinn: formerly, **Estonian Soviet
Socialist Republic**

**Es·tre·ma·dur·a** (es'trə mə door'ə) **1** region of WC
Spain, on the Portuguese border: 16,063 sq. mi.
(41,602 sq. km); pop. 1,050,000 **2** region of W Portugal, on the Atlantic: chief city, Lisbon

**E·thi·o·pi·a** (ē'thē ō'pē ə) **1** ancient kingdom (possibly
dating to the 10th cent. B.C.) in NE Africa, on the Red
Sea, corresponding to modern Sudan & N Ethiopia
(the country) **2** country in E Africa, on the Red Sea:
established, 1855: 471,800 sq. mi. (1,221,900 sq. km);
pop. 43,882,000; cap. Addis Ababa

**Et·na** (et'nə), **Mount** volcanic mountain in E Sicily:
10,900 ft. (3,320 m)

**E·to·bi·coke** (i tō'bi kō') 〚ult. < Ojibwa (? *Wahdobe-
kaug* or *Wadopikang*), place where the black alders
grow 〛 city within metropolitan Toronto, Canada: pop.
303,000

**E·ton** (ēt''n) town in Buckinghamshire, on the Thames,
near London: pop. 5,000: site of a private preparatory
school for boys (Eton College)

**E·tru·ri·a** (i troor'ē ə) 〚L〛 ancient country (fl. 6th cent.
B.C.) occupying what is now Tuscany & part of Umbria
in WC Italy

**Eu·boe·a** (yoo bē'ə) large island in the Aegean Sea, off
the E coast of Greece: 1,467 sq. mi. (3,800 sq. km)

**Eu·clid** (yoo'klid) 〚so named (after *Euclid*, 3rd-c. Gr
mathematician) by its surveyors 〛 city in NE Ohio:
suburb of Cleveland: pop. 55,000

**Eu·gene** (yoo jēn') 〚after *Eugene* Skinner, early settler 〛
city in W Oreg.: pop. 113,000

**Eu·phra·tes** (yoo frāt'ēz) river flowing from EC Turkey
generally southward through Syria & Iraq, joining the
Tigris to form the Shatt-al-Arab: *c.* 1,700 mi. (2,735
km)

**Eur·a·sia** (yoo rā'zhə; *chiefly Brit*, -shə) land mass made
up of the continents of Europe & Asia

**Eu·roc·ly·don** (yoo räk'li dän', -dən) 〚Gr(Ec) *eurok-
lydōn*, prob. in error (as if < *euros*, east wind + *klydōn*,
wave, billow) for *eurakylōn*, a northeast wind < *euros*
+ L *aquilo*, the north (or north-by-east) wind < *aqui-
lus*, dark, stormy, orig., watery < *aqua*, water 〛 *Bible* a

stormy northeast wind of the Mediterranean, referred to in the account of Paul's voyage to Rome: Acts 27:14

**Eu·ro·pa** (yōō rō'pə) 〚L < Gr *Eurōpē*〛 the fourth largest satellite of Jupiter: discovered in 1610 by Galileo

**Eu·rope** (yoor'əp) 〚L *Europa* < Gr *Eurōpē*〛 continent between Asia & the Atlantic Ocean: the Ural Mountains & the Ural River are generally considered the E boundary: *c.* 4,000,000 sq. mi. (10,360,000 sq. km); pop. *c.* 688,000,000

**Eux·ine Sea** (yook'sən, -sin) 〚L *Pontus Euxinus*〛 *ancient name of* the BLACK SEA

**Ev·ans·ton** (ev'ən stən) 〚after Dr. John *Evans,* local philanthropist〛 city in NE Ill., on Lake Michigan: suburb of Chicago: pop. 73,000

**Ev·ans·ville** (ev'ənz vil') 〚after Gen. R. M. *Evans,* a founder, who served in the War of 1812〛 city in SW Ind., on the Ohio River: pop. 126,000

**Ev·er·est** (ev'ər ist, ev'rist), **Mount** peak of the Himalayas, on the border of Nepal & Tibet: highest known mountain in the world: 29,028 ft. (8,848 m)

**Ev·er·ett** (ev'ər it, ev'rit) 〚after *Everett* Colby, son of a founder〛 port in NW Wash., on Puget Sound: pop. 70,000: see SEATTLE

**Ev·er·glades** (ev'ər glādz'), **the** large tract of subtropical marshland in S Fla.: *c.* 40 mi. (65 km) wide

**Everglades National Park** national park in the S part of the Everglades: wildlife refuge & biosphere reserve: 2,185 sq. mi. (5,660 sq. km)

**Ev·voi·a** (ev'ē ə) *var. of* EUBOEA

**Executive Mansion** the White House (in Washington, D.C.), official home of the President of the U.S.

**Ex·e·ter** (eks'ə tər) city in Devonshire, SW England: pop. 96,000

**Ex·moor** (eks'moor) hilly region of moors in SW England, mostly in Somerset

**Ex·tre·ma·du·ra** (ek'strə mə door'ə) *Sp. name of* ESTREMADURA

**Eyre** (er), **Lake** shallow salt lake in NE South Australia, varying from occasionally dry to *c.* 3,600 sq. mi. (9,300 sq. km)

**Eyre Peninsula** peninsula in S South Australia, east of the Great Australian Bight: base, 250 mi. (400 km) across

# F

**Faer·oe Islands** (fer'ō) group of Danish islands in the N Atlantic, between Iceland & the Shetland Islands: 540 sq. mi. (1,400 sq. km); pop. 45,000: also **Faeroes**

**Fair·banks** (fer'baŋks') ⟦after C. W. *Fairbanks* (1852-1918), prominent political figure⟧ city in EC Alas.: pop. 31,000

**Fair·field** (fer'fēld') 1 ⟦after an Eng village of the same name⟧ city in SW Conn., near Bridgeport: pop. 53,000 2 ⟦after *Fairfield*, Conn.⟧ city in W Calif., near Vallejo: pop. 77,000

**Fair·weath·er** (fer'weth'ər), **Mount** ⟦named by James Cook (1728-79), Eng explorer, in allusion to the state of the weather⟧ mountain on the border between SE Alas. and NW British Columbia; 15,300 ft. (4,663 m)

**Fai·sa·la·bad** (fī'säl'ə bäd', -sal'ə bad') city in NE Pakistan, near Lahore: pop. 1,092,000

**Fai·yûm** (fī yōōm', fä-) city in N Egypt, just west of the Nile: pop. 168,000: also **El Faiyûm**

**Fal·kirk** (fôl'kərk, fô'-) city in Central Region, Scotland: site of a battle (1298) in which the Scots under Wallace were defeated by the English: pop. 38,000

**Falk·land Islands** (fôk'lənd) British crown colony consisting of a group of islands in the S Atlantic, east of the tip of South America: 4,700 sq. mi. (12,150 sq. km); pop. 2,000

**Fall River** ⟦transl. of Algonquian name of the Taunton River, which flows into the ocean here⟧ seaport in SE Mass.: pop. 93,000

**Fal·mouth** (fal'məth) seaport & resort in Cornwall, SW England, on an inlet (**Falmouth Bay**) of the English Channel: pop. 18,000

**Fal·ster** (fäl'stər) one of the islands of Denmark, in the Baltic Sea: 198 sq. mi. (513 sq. km)

**Far East** countries of E Asia, including China, Japan, Korea, & Mongolia: the term sometimes includes the countries of Southeast Asia & the Malay Archipelago

**Fare·well** (fer wel'), **Cape** southernmost tip of Greenland

**Far·go** (fär'gō) ⟦after W. G. *Fargo*, of Wells, Fargo & Co., express shippers⟧ city in E N.Dak., on the Red River of the North: pop. 74,000

**Far·ming·ton Hills** (fär′miŋ tən) ⟦after *Farmington,*
N.Y.⟧ city in SE Mich.: suburb of Detroit: pop. 75,000
**Far·oe Islands** (fer′ō) *alt. sp. of* FAEROE ISLANDS
**Fay·ette·ville** (fā′ət vil′) ⟦after the Marquis de (LA)FA-
YETTE ⟧ city in SC N.C.: pop. 76,000
**Fay·um, Fay·yum** (fī yōom′, fä-) *alt. sp. of* FAIYÛM
**Fear** (fir), **Cape** cape on an island off the SE coast of
N.C.
**Federal Republic of Germany** *see* GERMANY
**Fer·man·agh** (fər man′ə) district & former county of
SW Northern Ireland
**Fer·nan·do de No·ro·nha** (fer nän′doo də nô rô′nyə)
island in the S Atlantic, northeast of Natal, Brazil:
with neighboring islets it constitutes a territory of
Brazil: *c.* 10 sq. mi. (26 sq. km); pop. 1,400
**Fer·nan·do Pó·o** (fer nän′dô pô′ô) *old name of* BIOKO
**Fer·ra·ra** (fə rär′ə) commune in NC Italy, in the Emilia-
Romagna region: pop. 158,000
**Ferrol** *see* EL FERROL
**Fès** (fes) *var. of* FEZ
**Fez** (fez) city in NC Morocco: pop. 563,000
**Fez·zan** (fe zan′) region of SW Libya, in the Sahara: *c.*
200,000 sq. mi. (518,000 sq. km)
**Fife** (fīf) region, formerly a county, of E Scotland,
between the Firths of Tay & Forth: 505 sq. mi. (1,308
sq. km); pop. 345,000
**Fi·ji** (fē′jē) country occupying a group of islands (**Fiji
Islands**) in the SW Pacific, north of New Zealand: a
member of the Commonwealth: *c.* 7,000 sq. mi. (18,130
sq. km); pop. 672,000; cap. Suva
**Fin·gal's Cave** (fiŋ′gəlz) large cavern on an islet (called
*Staffa*) west of Mull in the Hebrides, W Scotland
**Finger Lakes** group of long, narrow glacial lakes in WC
N.Y.
**Fin·is·terre** (fin′is ter′), **Cape** promontory at the west-
ernmost point of Spain
**Fin·land** (fin′lənd) country in N Europe, northeast of
the Baltic Sea: 130,119 sq. mi. (337,000 sq. km); pop.
5,099,000; cap. Helsinki: Finn. name SUOMI
**Fins·bur·y** (finz′ber′ē; *Brit,* -bə ri) former metropolitan
borough of EC London, now part of Islington
**Fin·ster·aar·horn** (fin′stər är′hôrn) mountain in SC
Switzerland: highest peak in the Bernese Alps: 14,026
ft. (4,276 m)

**Fi·ren·ze** (fē ren'dze) *It. name of* FLORENCE

**Fish** Pisces, the constellation and twelfth sign of the zodiac: also **Fishes**

**Fiu·me** (fyōō'me) *It. name of* RIJEKA

**FL** *abbrev. for* Florida

**Fla** *abbrev. for* Florida

**Fla·min·i·an Way** (flə min'ē ən) ⟦after the Roman censor Gaius *Flaminius*⟧ ancient Roman paved highway from Rome to Ariminum (Rimini): *c.* 210 mi. (338 km)

**Flan·ders** (flan'dərz) region (in medieval times a county) in NW Europe, on the North Sea, including a part of NW France & the provinces of East Flanders & West Flanders in Belgium

**Fleet, the** (flēt) **1** a former small creek in London, now a covered sewer **2** a debtor's prison which stood near this creek: also **Fleet Prison**

**Fleet Street** ⟦after *the Fleet*, a former small creek, now a covered sewer, which crosses beneath it⟧ old street in central London, where several newspaper & printing offices are located

**Fle·vo·land** (flē'vō land') province of the WC Netherlands, on the IJsselmeer: 1,420 sq. mi. (549 sq. km); pop. 177,000

**Flint** (flint) ⟦after the nearby *Flint* River, so called from the flint stones in it⟧ city in SE Mich.: pop. 141,000 (met. area 430,000)

**Flint·shire** (flint'shir) former county of NE Wales, now part of Clwyd county

**Flod·den** (fläd''n) hilly field in N Northumberland, England: site of a battle (1513) in which the English defeated James IV of Scotland

**Flor·ence** (flôr'əns, flär'-) commune in Tuscany, central Italy, on the Arno River: pop. 430,000: It. name FIRENZE

**Flo·res** (flô'res) **1** island of Indonesia, west of Timor & south of Celebes: 5,500 sq. mi. (14,245 sq. km) **2** westernmost island of the Azores: 55 sq. mi. (143 sq. km)

**Flores Sea** part of the Pacific, between the islands of Celebes & Flores in Indonesia

**Flo·ri·a·nó·po·lis** (flôr'ē ə näp'ə lis) city on an island just off the SE coast of Brazil: capital of Santa Catarina state: pop. 154,000

**Flor·i·da** (flôr'ə də, flär'-) ⟦Sp < L, lit., abounding in flowers: so named by Ponce de León (*c.* 1460-1521), Sp explorer ‖ **1** Southern State of the SE U.S., mostly on a peninsula between the Atlantic & the Gulf of Mexico: admitted, 1845; 58,560 sq. mi. (151,670 sq. km); pop. 12,938,000; cap. Tallahassee: abbrev. **FL** or **Fla 2 Straits of** strait between the S tip of Fla. & Cuba on the south & the Bahamas on the southeast: it connects the Atlantic & the Gulf of Mexico: also called **Florida Strait**

**Florida Keys** chain of small islands extending southwest from the S tip of Fla.

**Flo·ris·sant** (flôr′ə sənt) ‖ Fr, flourishing, a prp. of *fleurir*, to bloom, flourish < L *florere* < *flos*, flower ‖ city in E Mo.: suburb of St. Louis: pop. 51,000

**Flush·ing** (flush′iŋ) ‖ altered < Du *Vlissingen*, town in the Netherlands ‖ section of N Queens borough, New York City, on the East River

**Fly** (flī) river in S New Guinea, flowing through Papua New Guinea into the Coral Sea: *c.* 650 mi. (1,050 km)

**Fog·gia** (fôd′jä) commune in Apulia, SE Italy: pop. 157,000

**Fo·mal·haut** (fō′məl hôt′, -məl ōt′) ‖ Fr < Ar *fum al-ḥūt*, lit., mouth of the fish ‖ the brightest star in the constellation Piscis Austrinus, with a magnitude of 1.2

**Fon·se·ca** (fôn sā′kä), **Gulf of** inlet of the Pacific in W Central America

**Fon·taine·bleau** (fōn ten blō′; *E* fänt′ʼn blō′, -bloo′) town in N France, near Paris: site of a palace of former kings of France: pop. 21,000

**Fon·tan·a** (fän tan′ə) ‖ < ? ‖ city in SW Calif.: pop. 88,000

**Foo·chow** (foo′chou′; *Chin* foo′jō′) *old form of* Fuzhou

**For·a·ker** (fôr′ə kər), **Mount** ‖ after J. B. *Foraker* (1846-1917), prominent politician ‖ mountain in the Alaska Range, SC Alas.: 17,395 ft. (5,300 m)

**For·far** (fôr′fər) *old name of* Angus: also **For′far·shire′** (-shir′)

**For·li** (fôr lē′) commune in Emilia-Romagna region, NC Italy: pop. 110,000

**For·mo·sa** (fôr mō′sə, -zə) *old* (*Port.*) *name of* Taiwan

**Formosa Strait** *old name of* Taiwan Strait

**For·nax** (fôr′naks′) ‖ L, lit., furnace ‖ a S constellation between Eridanus and Cetus

**For·ta·le·za** (fôr′tə lā′zə) seaport in NE Brazil, on the Atlantic: capital of Ceará state: pop. 649,000

**Fort Col·lins** (käl′inz) 〖after Lt. Col. Wm. O. *Collins*〗 city in N Colo., north of Denver: pop. 88,000

**Fort-de-France** (fôr də fräns′) seaport & capital of Martinique, in the Windward Islands: pop. 100,000

**Forth** (fôrth) **1** river in SE Scotland, flowing east into the Firth of Forth: 65 mi. (105 km) **2 Firth of** long estuary of the Forth River, flowing into the North Sea: 51 mi. (82 km)

**Fort Knox** (näks) 〖see KNOXVILLE〗 military reservation in N Ky., near Louisville: site of U.S. gold bullion depository

**Fort Lau·der·dale** (lô′dər dāl′) 〖after Maj. Wm. *Lauderdale*〗 city on the SE coast of Fla., near Miami: pop. 149,000 (met. area, incl. Hollywood and Pompano Beach, 1,255,000): see MIAMI

**Fort Mc·Hen·ry** (mək hen′rē) 〖after J. *McHenry*, U.S. Secretary of War, 1796-1800〗 fort in Baltimore harbor, Md., where the British were repulsed in 1814

**Fort Smith** (smith) **1** 〖after Gen. T. A. *Smith*, died 1865〗 city in NW Ark., on the Arkansas River: pop. 73,000 **2** Region of S Northwest Territories, Canada: 235,698 sq. mi. (610,456 sq. km)

**Fort Sum·ter** (sum′tər) fort in Charleston harbor, S.C., where Confederate troops fired the first shots of the Civil War (April 12, 1861): now site of **Fort Sumter National Monument**

**Fort Wayne** 〖after Anthony *Wayne* (1745-96), Am general〗 city in NE Ind.: pop. 173,000

**Fort Wil·liam** (wil′yəm) 〖after *William* McGillivray, a director of the North West Co.〗 see THUNDER BAY

**Fort Worth** (wurth) 〖after Wm. J. *Worth* (1794-1849)〗 city in N Tex.: pop. 448,000: see DALLAS

**For·um** (fôr′əm, fō′rəm), **the** the forum of ancient Rome

**Foun·tain Valley** (fount′n) 〖from the many artesian wells in the area〗 city in SW Calif., near Long Beach: pop. 54,000

**Foxe Basin** (fäks) arm of the Atlantic Ocean, in NE Canada, west of Baffin Island: *c.* 3,500 sq. mi. (9,065 sq. km)

**Fra·ming·ham** (frā′miŋ ham′) 〖prob. after *Framlingham*, town in England〗 suburb of Boston, in E Mass.: pop. 65,000

**France** (frans, fräns) country in W Europe, on the Atlantic & the Mediterranean Sea: 212,821 sq. mi.

(551,204 sq. km): pop. 54,335,000; cap. Paris: Fr. name **Ré·pub·lique Fran·çaise** (*rā pü blek′ frän sez′*)

**Franche–Com·té** (*fränsh kōn tā′*) historical region of E France, on the border of Switzerland

**Fran·co·ni·a** (*fraŋ kō′nē ə*) region of central Germany, a duchy in the Middle Ages

**Frank·fort** (*fraŋk′fərt*) 1 ⟦orig. *Frank's Ford*, after Stephen *Frank*, a pioneer killed there⟧ capital of Ky., in the NC part: pop. 26,000 2 FRANKFURT

**Frank·furt** (*fraŋk′fərt; Ger* fräŋk′foort) 1 city in W Germany, on the Main River, in the state of Hesse: pop. 604,000: also **Frankfurt am Main** (ä mīn′) 2 city in E Germany, on the Oder River, in the state of Brandenburg: pop. 70,000: also **Frankfurt an der O·der** (än dər ō′dər)

**Frank·lin** (*fraŋk′lin*) ⟦after Sir John *Franklin* (1786-1847), Eng arctic explorer⟧ former district of the Northwest Territories, Canada

**Franz Jo·sef Land** (*fränts jō′zəf*) group of islands of Russia, in the Arctic Ocean, north of Novaya Zemlya: *c.* 8,000 sq. mi. (20,720 sq. km)

**Fra·ser** (*frā′zər*) river in British Columbia, Canada, flowing southward into the Strait of Georgia: 850 mi. (1,368 km)

**Fred·er·icks·burg** (*fred′riks burg′*) ⟦after *Frederick* Louis (1707-51), father of George III of Great Britain⟧ city in NE Va., on the Rappahannock: scene of a Civil War battle (Dec., 1862) in which Confederate forces were victorious: pop. 19,000

**Fred·er·ic·ton** (*fred′ə rik tən*) capital of New Brunswick, Canada, on the St. John River: pop. 45,000

**Fred·er·iks·burg** (*fred′ə riks bŭrg′; Dan* freth′ə rēks be*rkh′*) borough on Zealand island, Denmark: suburb of Copenhagen: pop. 114,000

**Free·town** (*frē′toun′*) seaport & capital of Sierra Leone, on the Atlantic: pop. 470,000

**Frei·burg** (*frī′boork*) 1 city in SW Germany, in the state of Baden-Württemberg: pop. 182,000: also **Freiburg im Breis·gau** (im brīs′gou) 2 *Ger. name of* FRIBOURG

**Fre·man·tle** (*frē′mant′l*) seaport in Western Australia: suburb of Perth: pop. 22,000

**Fre·mont** (*frē′mänt*) ⟦after John Charles *Frémont* (1813-90), U.S. explorer⟧ city in W Calif., on San Francisco Bay: suburb of Oakland: pop. 173,000

**French Community** political union (formed in 1958) comprising France & several of its former territories, the countries of Central African Republic, Chad, Congo, Gabon, Madagascar, & Senegal: since 1962 the member countries have maintained bilateral agreements with France

**French Equatorial Africa** former federation of French colonies in central Africa

**French Guiana** French overseas department in NE South America, on the Atlantic: 35,135 sq. mi. (91,000 sq. km); pop. 73,000; chief town, Cayenne

**French Guinea** Guinea when it was under French control

**French India** former French territory in India

**French Indochina** Indochina when it was under French control

**French Morocco** the former (1912-56) French zone of Morocco, making up most of the country: with Spanish Morocco & Tangier, it became the country of Morocco

**French Polynesia** French overseas territory in the South Pacific, consisting principally of five archipelagoes: 1,545 sq. mi. (4,000 sq. km); pop. 138,000; cap. Papeete: formerly called **French (Settlements in) Oceania**

**French Somaliland** former French overseas territory in E Africa: called *French Territory of the Afars and the Issas* from 1967 to 1977, when it became the country of Djibouti

**French Sudan** former French overseas territory in W Africa: since 1960, the republic of Mali

**French Union** former political union (1946-58) of France, its overseas departments & territories, & its protectorates & associated states: succeeded by the FRENCH COMMUNITY

**French West Africa** former French overseas territory in W Africa, including the present countries of Senegal, Mali, Mauritania, Guinea, Ivory Coast, Burkina Faso, Benin, & Niger

**French West Indies** two overseas departments of France in the West Indies, including Martinique & Guadeloupe & the dependencies of Guadeloupe

**Fres·no** (frez′nō) ⟦ < Sp *fresno*, ash tree ⟧ city in central Calif.: pop. 354,000 (met. area 667,000)

**Fri·bourg** (frē boor´) canton of WC Switzerland: 645 sq. mi. (1,670 sq. km); pop. 185,000

**Friendly Islands** TONGA

**Fries·land** (frēz´lənd, -land´; *Du* frēs´länt´) province of the N Netherlands, on the North Sea: 1,310 sq. mi. (3,391 sq. km); pop. 598,000; cap. Leeuwarden

**Frigid Zone** either of two zones of the earth (**North Frigid Zone & South Frigid Zone**) between the polar circles and the poles

**Fris·co** (fris´kō) *name for* SAN FRANCISCO: not a local usage

**Fri·sian Islands** (frizh´ən, frē´zhən) island chain in the North Sea, extending along the coast of NW Europe: it is divided into three groups, one belonging to the Netherlands (**West Frisian Islands**), one belonging to Germany (**East Frisian Islands**), & one divided between Germany & Denmark (**North Frisian Islands**)

**Fri·u·li-Ve·ne·zia Giu·lia** (frē o͞o´lē ve ne´tsyä jo͞o´lyä) region of NE Italy, on the Adriatic: 3,030 sq. mi. (7,848 sq. km); pop. 1,233,000; cap. Trieste

**Front Range** range on the E edge of the Rockies, in SE Wyo. & NC Colo.: highest peak, 14,274 ft. (4,350 m)

**Frostbelt** SNOWBELT: also **Frost Belt**

**Frun·ze** (fro͞on´ze) *old name of* BISHKEK

**Fu·ji** (fo͞o´jē) dormant volcano on Honshu island, Japan, southwest of Tokyo: highest peak in Japan: 12,388 ft. (3,776 m): also **Fu·ji·ya·ma** (-yä´mə) or **Fu´ji·san´** (-sän´)

**Fu·jian** (fo͞o´jyän´) province of SE China, on Taiwan Strait: 47,490 sq. mi. (123,000 sq. km); pop. 27,000,000; cap. Fuzhou: old form **Fu·kien** (fo͞o´kyen´)

**Fu·ku·o·ka** (fo͞o´ko͞o ō´kə) seaport on the N coast of Kyushu island, Japan: pop. 1,160,000

**Ful·ham** (fo͞ol´əm) former metropolitan borough of SW London, now part of Hammersmith

**Ful·ler·ton** (fo͞ol´ər tən) ⟦after G. H. *Fullerton*, a founder⟧ city in SW Calif.: suburb of Los Angeles: pop. 114,000

**Fun·chal** (fo͞on shäl´) capital of Madeira: pop. 120,000

**Fun·dy** (fun´dē), **Bay of** arm of the Atlantic, between New Brunswick & Nova Scotia, Canada: *c.* 140 mi. (225 km) long: noted for its high tides of 60-70 ft. (18-22 m)

**Fü·nen** (fü´nən) *Ger. name of* FYN

**Fu·san** (fo͞o´sän´) *old* (*Jpn.*) *name of* PUSAN

**Fu·se** (foo'sä') *old name of* HIGASHIOSAKA

**Fu·shun** (foo'shoon') city in Liaoning province, NE China: pop. 1,019,000

**Fu·tu·na** (fə too'nə) *see* WALLIS AND FUTUNA

**Fu·zhou** (foo'jo') city in SE China: capital of Fujian province: pop. 1,142,000

**Fyn** (fün) a main island of Denmark, between Jutland & Zealand: 1,149 sq. mi. (2,975 sq. km)

# G

**GA, Ga** *abbrev. for* Georgia

**Ga·bon** (gȧ bōn') country in WC Africa, on the Gulf of Guinea: formerly a French territory, it became independent (1960): 103,346 sq. mi. (267,667 sq. km); pop. 1,017,000; cap. Libreville

**Ga·bo·ro·ne** (gä'bə rō'nā) capital of Botswana, in the SE part: pop. *c.* 80,000

**Gads·den** (gadz'dən) 〖after James *Gadsden* (1788-1858), U.S. diplomat〗 city in NE Ala.: pop. 43,000

**Gae·a** (jē'ə) 〖Gr *Gaia* < *gē*, earth〗 *Gr. Myth.* a goddess who is the personification of the earth, the mother of the Titans: identified with the Roman Tellus

**Gai·a** (gā'ə, gī'ə) *var. of* GAEA

**Gail·lard Cut** (gāl'yərd, gä'lärd) 〖after D. D. *Gaillard* (1859-1913), U.S. army engineer in charge of its excavation〗 S section of the Panama Canal cut through the continental divide: *c.* 8 mi. (12.9 km) long

**Gaines·ville** (gānz'vil) 〖after Gen. E. P. *Gaines* (1777-1849)〗 city in NC Fla.: pop. 85,000

**Ga·lá·pa·gos Islands** (gə lä'pə gōs') group of islands in the Pacific on the equator, belonging to Ecuador: 2,868 sq. mi. (7,428 sq. km); pop. 6,000: Sp. name *Archipélago de Colón*

**Ga·la·ta** (gal'ə tə) commercial section of Istanbul, Turkey, on the Golden Horn

**Ga·la·ţi** (ga läts') city in E Romania, on the Danube: pop. 254,600

**Ga·la·tia** (gə lā'shə) ancient kingdom in central Asia Minor, made a Roman province *c.* 25 B.C.

**gal·ax·y** (gal'ək sē) 〖ME *galaxie* < LL *galaxias* < Gr, Milky Way < *gala*, milk < IE base *glak-*〗 [*often* G-] MILKY WAY

**Ga·li·cia** (gə lish'ə) **1** region of SE Poland & NW

Ukraine: formerly, an Austrian crown land **2** region of NW Spain: 11,365 sq. mi. (29,434 sq. km); pop. 2,754,000: a former medieval kingdom

**Gal·i·lee** (gal′ə lē′) ⟦L *Galilaea* < Gr *Galilaia* < Heb *hagalil* < *gelil* (*hagoyim*), lit., district (of the Gentiles)⟧ **1** region of N Israel **2 Sea of** lake of NE Israel, on the Syria border: *c.* 13 mi. (21 km) long

**Galle** (gäl) seaport in SW Sri Lanka: pop. 77,000

**Gal·li·a** (gal′ē a, gäl′lē ä′) *Latin name of* GAUL

**Gal·lip·o·li** (gə lip′ə lē) *var. of* GELIBOLU

**Gallipoli Peninsula** peninsula in S European Turkey, forming the NW shore of the Dardanelles: *c.* 55 mi. (88 km) long

**Gal·lo·way** (gal′ə wā′) former district in SW Scotland, comprising the counties of Wigtown and Kirkcudbright: now part of the region of DUMFRIES & GALLO-WAY

**Gal·ves·ton** (gal′vis tən) ⟦< fol.⟧ seaport in SE Tex., on an island (**Galveston Island**) at the mouth of Galveston Bay: pop. 59,000

**Galveston Bay** ⟦after Bernardo de *Gálvez* (1746-86), gov. of Louisiana⟧ inlet of the Gulf of Mexico, in SE Tex.

**Gal·way** (gôl′wā) **1** county in Connacht province, W Ireland: 2,293 sq. mi. (5,939 sq. km); pop. 172,000 **2** its county seat, on an inlet of the Atlantic (**Galway Bay**): pop. 37,800

**Gam·bi·a** (gam′bē ə) **1** country on the W coast of Africa, surrounded on three sides by Senegal: formerly a British colony & protectorate, it became independent (1965) & a member of the Commonwealth: 3,451 sq. mi. (11,295 sq. km); pop. 695,800; cap. Banjul: official name **The Gambia 2** river in W Africa, flowing from N Guinea, through Senegal & Gambia, into the Atlantic: *c.* 700 mi. (1,120 km)

**Gand** (gän) *Fr. name of* GHENT

**Gan·ges** (gan′jēz) river in N India & Bangladesh, flowing from the Himalayas into the Bay of Bengal: *c.* 1,560 mi. (2,510 km)

**Gang·tok** (guŋ′täk′) capital of Sikkim, in the SE part: pop. 36,700

**Gan·su** (gän′sü′) province of NW China: *c.* 141,500 sq. mi. (366,480 sq. km): pop. 19,570,000: cap. Lanzhou

**Gan·y·mede** (gan′i mēd′) ⟦Gr *Ganymēdēs*⟧ the largest

satellite of Jupiter: discovered in 1610 by Galileo

**Gar·da** (gär'də), **Lake** lake in N Italy, on the Lombardy-Veneto border: 143 sq. mi. (370 sq. km)

**Gar·de·na** (gär dē'nə) city in SW Calif.: suburb of Los Angeles: pop. 50,000

**Garden Grove** city in SW Calif.: pop. 143,000

**Gar·land** (gär'lənd) 〚after A. H. *Garland*, U.S. attorney general (1885-89)〛 city in NE Tex.: suburb of Dallas: pop. 181,000

**Ga·ronne** (gà rôn') river in SW France, flowing from the Pyrenees into the Gironde: *c.* 400 mi. (640 km)

**Gar·y** (ger'ē, gar'-) 〚after E. H. *Gary* (1846-1927), U.S. industrialist〛 city in NW Ind., on Lake Michigan: pop. 117,000 (met. area, with Hammond, 605,000): see CHICAGO

**Gas·cogne** (gàs kôn'y') *Fr. name of* GASCONY

**Gas·co·ny** (gas'kə nē) 〚ME *Gascoyne* < OFr *Gascogne* < LL *Vasconia* < L *Vascones*, pl., the Basques〛 historical region in SW France, on the Bay of Biscay

**Gas·pé Peninsula** (gas pā') 〚Fr < Algonquian (Micmac) *gachepe*, the end〛 peninsula in S Quebec, Canada, extending into the Gulf of St. Lawrence: *c.* 150 mi. (240 km) long

**Gates·head** (gāts'hed') city in NE England: pop. 210,000

**Gath** (gath) 〚Heb, lit., wine press〛 *Bible* one of the cities of the Philistines: 2 Sam. 1:20

**Gat·i·neau** (gat''n ō; *Fr* gà tē nō') city in S Quebec, Canada, near Ottawa: pop. 81,000

**Ga·tun** (gä tōōn') town in Central Panama: site of a dam (**Gatun Dam**), which forms a lake (**Gatun Lake**), 163 sq. mi. (423 sq. km), that is part of the route of the Panama Canal

**Gaul** (gôl) 〚Fr < Frank *walha*, Romans, foreigners, orig., Celts < WGmc *walhos* < Celt name〛 **1** ancient region in W Europe, consisting of what is now mainly France & Belgium: after the 5th cent. B.C., also called **Trans·al·pine Gaul** (trans al'pīn', tranz-) **2** ancient region in N Italy, occupied by the Gauls (4th cent. B.C.): in full **Cis·al·pine Gaul** (sis al'pīn') **3** ancient division of the Roman Empire, including Cisalpine Gaul & Transalpine Gaul (1st-5th cent. A.D.)

**Ga·ya** (gä'yə) city in Bihar, NE India: pop. 345,000

**Ga·za** (gäz'ə, gaz'ə, gä'zə) city in SW Asia, at the SE end of the Mediterranean: in ancient times, one of the

chief cities of the Philistines; Biblical site of Samson's
death (Judg. 16:21-30): from 1949 to 1967, control of
the city and a surrounding strip of land (**Gaza Strip**),
alternately occupied by Egypt and Israel, was in dis-
pute: since 1967 under Israeli administration: pop.
118,000

**Ga·zi·an·tep** (gä′zē än tep′) city in S Turkey, near the
Syrian border: pop. 374,000

**Gdańsk** (g′dänsk′) seaport in N Poland, on the Baltic
Sea: pop. 464,000: Ger. name DANZIG

**Gdy·nia** (g′dēn′yä) seaport in N Poland, on the Baltic
Sea: pop. 240,000

**Gee·long** (jē lôŋ′) seaport in S Victoria, Australia: pop.
(with suburbs) 177,000

**Geel·vink Bay** (khāl′viŋk) *old name of* SARERA BAY

**Ge·hen·na** (gi hen′ə, gə-) ⟦LL(Ec) < Gr *Geenna*, hell <
Heb *gey hinnom*, where the kings Ahaz and Manasseh
were said to have sacrificed their sons to Moloch⟧ the
valley of Hinnom, near Jerusalem, where refuse was
burned in Biblical times

**Gel·der·land** (gel′dər land′; *Du* khel′dər länt′) province
of E Netherlands: 1,937 sq. mi. (5,016 sq. km); pop.
1,745,000 ; cap. Arnhem

**Ge·li·bo·lu** (gel′ē bô̄ lōō′) seaport in S European Turkey, on the Gallipoli Peninsula: strategic point in the
defense of the Dardanelles and Bosporus straits: pop.
13,000

**Gel·sen·kir·chen** (gel′zən kir′Hən) city in WC Germany, in the state of North Rhine-Westphalia: pop.
295,000

**Gem·i·ni** (jem′ə nī′, -nē′) ⟦L, twins⟧ **1** a N constellation between Cancer and Taurus, containing the
bright stars Castor and Pollux **2** the third sign of the
zodiac, entered by the sun about May 21

**Gen·e·see** (jen′ə sē′) ⟦< Iroquoian (Seneca); ? "beautiful valley"⟧ river flowing from N Pa. across W N.Y.
into Lake Ontario: c. 150 mi. (242 km)

**Ge·ne·va** (jə nē′və) **1** city in SW Switzerland, on Lake
Geneva: pop. 159,500 **2** canton of SW Switzerland,
largely the city of Geneva & its suburbs: 109 sq. mi.
(282 km); pop. 360,500 **3 Lake (of)** lake in SW Switzerland on the border of France: 224 sq. mi. (580 sq.
km): see LEMAN, Lake

**Ge·nève** (zhə nev′) *Fr. name of* GENEVA (the city & the

canton)

**Genf** (genf) *Ger. name of* GENEVA (the city & the canton)

**Gen·o·a** (jen'ə wə) **1** seaport in NW Italy, at the head of the Gulf of Genoa: pop. 738,000: It. name GENOVA **2** Gulf of N part of the Ligurian Sea, off NW Italy

**Ge·no·va** (je'nô vä') *It. name of* GENOA

**Gent** (khent) *Fl. name of* GHENT

**George** (jôrj), **Lake** lake in NE N.Y.: 33 mi. (53 km) long

**George·town** (-toun') **1** seaport & capital of Guyana, on the Atlantic: pop. 188,000 **2** section of Washington, D.C. **3** *old name of* PENANG: also **George Town**

**Geor·gia** (jôr'jə) **1** ⟦ *after George* II (1683-1760) of England ⟧ Southern State of the SE U.S.: one of the 13 original States; 58,876 sq. mi. (152,489 sq. km); pop. 6,478,000; cap. Atlanta: abbrev. *GA* or *Ga* **2** region in SE Europe on the Black Sea **3** GEORGIAN SOVIET SOCIALIST REPUBLIC **4** country in Transcaucasia, on the Black Sea: became independent upon the breakup of the U.S.S.R. (1991): 26,900 sq. mi. (69,670 sq. km); pop. *c.* 5,200,000; cap. Tbilisi: formerly, *Georgian Soviet Socialist Republic* **5 Strait of** arm of the Pacific, between Vancouver Island & British Columbia, Canada: *c.* 150 mi. (241 km) long: also **Georgia Strait**

**Georgian Bay** NE arm of Lake Huron, in Ontario, Canada

**Georgian Soviet Socialist Republic** a republic of the U.S.S.R.: now *Georgia*

**Ge·ra** (gā'rä) city in E Germany, in the state of Thuringia: pop. 132,000

**German Democratic Republic** *see* GERMANY

**German East Africa** former colony of the German Empire, in E Africa: it was the territory now consisting chiefly of Tanzania, Rwanda, & Burundi

**German Southwest Africa** *old name of* SOUTH WEST AFRICA

**Ger·man·town** (jʉr'mən toun') NW section of Philadelphia, Pa.: formerly a separate town, scene of an American defeat in a Revolutionary War battle (1777)

**Ger·ma·ny** (jʉr'mə nē') ⟦ L *Germania* ⟧ country in NC Europe, on the North & Baltic seas; since reunification in 1990, comprising 16 states: formerly divided (1945) into four zones of occupation, administered respectively by France, Britain, the U.S., & the U.S.S.R., and partitioned (1949-90) into the **Federal Republic of Germany**, made up of the three western zones (British, French, & U.S.), also called **West Germany;** and the **German Democratic Republic**, comprising the eastern (U.S.S.R.) zone, also called **East Germany**: 137,772 sq. mi. (356,828 sq. km); pop. 77,454,000; cap. Berlin: official name *Federal Republic of Germany*

**Ger·mis·ton** (jur'mis tən) city in S Transvaal, South Africa: pop. 155,000

**Geth·sem·a·ne** (geth sem'ə nē) ⟦ Gr *Gethsēmanē* < Aram *gat shemanin*, lit., oil press: ? because such a press was located there ⟧ *Bible* a garden on the Mount of Olives, east of Jerusalem, scene of the agony, betrayal, and arrest of Jesus: Matt. 26:36

**Get·tys·burg** (get'iz burg') ⟦after J. *Gettys*, its 18th-c. founder ⟧ town in S Pa.: site of a crucial battle (July, 1863) of the Civil War and of a famous address by Abraham Lincoln dedicating a National Cemetery: pop. 7,000

**Ge·zi·ra** (jə zir'ə) region in EC Sudan, between the Blue Nile & the White Nile

**Gha·na** (gä'nə) country in W Africa, on the Gulf of Guinea: formed (1957) by a merger of the Gold Coast & the territory of Togoland: it is a member of the Commonwealth: 92,010 sq. mi. (238,300 sq. km); pop. 12,200,000; cap. Accra

**Ghats** (gôts, gäts) two mountain ranges (**Eastern Ghats** and **Western Ghats**) forming the east & west edges of the Deccan Plateau, India: highest peak, 8,841 ft. (2,693 m)

**Ghent** (gent) city in NW Belgium: capital of East Flanders: pop. 234,000

**Giant's Causeway** headland in N Northern Ireland, consisting of thousands of small, vertical basaltic columns: *c.* 3 mi. (4.8 km) long

**Gi·bral·tar** (ji brôl'tər) **1** small peninsula at the southern tip of Spain, extending into the Mediterranean: 2.5 sq. mi. (6.4 sq. km); it consists mostly of a rocky hill (**Rock of Gibraltar**), 1,396 ft. (426 m) high **2** Brit. crown colony, including a port & naval base, on this peninsula: pop. 29,000 **3 Strait of** strait between Spain & Morocco, joining the Mediterranean & the Atlantic: *c.* 35 mi. (58 km) long

**Gib·son Desert** (gib'sən) central section of the vast

desert region of Western Australia

**Gi·fu** (gē'foō') city on central Honshu, Japan: pop. 408,000

**Gi·jón** (hē hôn') seaport in NW Spain: pop. 256,000

**Gi·la** (hē'lə) ⟦Sp < Yuman name, lit., salty water⟧ river in S Ariz., flowing southwest into the Colorado: 630 mi. (1,013 km) long

**Gil·bert Islands** (gil'bərt) group of islands in the WC Pacific which in 1979 became the independent nation of KIRIBATI

**Gil·e·ad** (gil'ē əd) mountainous region of ancient Palestine, east of the Jordan (Gen. 37:25)

**Gi·raffe** (jə raf', -räf') the constellation Camelopardus

**Gi·ronde** (jə ränd'; *Fr* zhē rônd') **1** estuary in SW France, formed by the juncture of the Garonne & Dordogne rivers & flowing into the Bay of Biscay: *c.* 45 mi. (73 km) long **2** historical region of France, on the Bay of Biscay

**Gi·za** (gē'zə) city in N Egypt, near Cairo: site of the Sphinx & three pyramids: pop. 1,246,000: also sp. **Gi'zeh**

**Gla·cier National Park** (glā'shər) national park in NW Mont., on the Canadian border: it contains over 200 lakes & 60 small glaciers: 1,560 sq. mi. (4,040 sq. km)

**Gla·mor·gan** (glə môr'gən) former county of SE Wales, on the Bristol Channel: now divided into three counties: *a*) **Mid Glamorgan** 393 sq. mi. (1,019 sq. km); pop. 534,000 *b*) **South Glamorgan** 161 sq. mi. (416 sq. km); pop. 394,000 *c*) **West Glamorgan** 315 sq. mi. (816 sq. km); pop. 365,000: also **Gla·mor'gan·shire'** (-shir')

**Glar·us** (glär'əs) canton in EC Switzerland: 264 sq. mi. (684 sq. km); pop. 36,400: Fr. name **Gla·ris** (glå rēs')

**Glas·gow** (glas'kō, glaz'gō) seaport in SC Scotland, on the Clyde: pop. 762,000

**Glen·dale** (glen'dāl) ⟦ModE *glen* + *dale*⟧ **1** city in SW Calif.: suburb of Los Angeles; pop. 180,000 **2** city in SC Ariz.: suburb of Phoenix: pop. 148,000

**Glen More** (glen môr') valley across N Scotland, traversed by the Caledonian Canal: 60½ mi. (97.3 km) long

**Gli·wi·ce** (gli vē'tse) city in S Poland: pop. 211,000

**Glom·ma** (glô'mə) river in SE Norway, flowing south into the Skagerrak: longest river in Scandinavia: 375 mi. (603 km)

**Glouces·ter** (gläs'tər, glôs'-) **1** city in SW England, on the Severn: pop. 92,000 **2** GLOUCESTERSHIRE

**Glouces·ter·shire** (-shir, -shər) county of SW England, on Severn estuary: 1,020 sq. mi. (2,638 sq. km); pop. 509,000; county seat, Gloucester

**Go·a** (gō′ə) small region on the SW coast of India: 1,350 sq. mi. (3,496 sq. km); formerly part of Portuguese India, since 1962 it has formed (with DAMAN & DIU) a territory of India (called GOA, DAMAN, and DIU), 1,472 sq. mi. (3,813 sq. km); pop. 1,140,000

**Goat** Capricorn, the constellation and tenth sign of the zodiac

**Go·bi** (gō′bē) desert plateau in E Asia, chiefly in Mongolia: *c.* 500,000 sq. mi. (1,294,000 sq. km)

**Go·da·va·ri** (gō dä′vər ē) river in central India, flowing from the Western Ghats into the Bay of Bengal: *c.* 900 mi. (1,440 km)

**Godt·haab** (gôt′hôp) capital of Greenland, on the SW coast: pop. 10,500

**God·win Aus·ten** (gäd′win ôs′tən) mountain in the Karakorum range, N Jammu & Kashmir, near the Xinjiang border: second highest mountain in the world: 28,250 ft. (8,611 m)

**Gog and Ma·gog** (gäg′ ənd mā′gäg′) ⟦Heb *gog, magog*: see Ezek. 38:2⟧ *Bible* *personification of* the nations that, under Satan, are to war against the kingdom of God: Rev. 20:8

**Goi·â·ni·a** (goi ä′nē ə) city in central Brazil: capital of Goiás state: pop. 703,000

**Goi·ás** (goi äs′) state of central Brazil: 247,900 sq. mi. (642,092 sq. km); pop. 4,450,000; cap. Goiânia

**Gol·con·da** (gäl kän′də) ancient city, now ruins, in SC India, near Hyderabad: noted for diamond cutting in the 16th cent.

**Gold Coast** former British territory in W Africa, on the Gulf of Guinea: see GHANA

**Golden Gate** ⟦so named (1846) by John Charles Frémont (1813-90), U.S. explorer, after the GOLDEN HORN in anticipation of the flow of Oriental riches through the strait⟧ strait between San Francisco Bay and the Pacific: 2 mi. (3.2 km) wide

**Golden Horn** arm of the Bosporus in European Turkey, forming the harbor of Istanbul

**Gol·go·tha** (gäl′gə thə, gôl′-) ⟦LL(Ec) < Gr(Ec) *golgotha* < Aram *gulgulta* < Heb *gulgolet,* skull, place of a skull ] *Bible* the place where Jesus was crucified; Calvary: Mark 15:22

**Go·mel** (gō′mel) city in SE Belarus: pop. 465,000

**Go·mor·rah** (gə môr′ə) [ Gr *Gomorrha* < Heb ] *see* SODOM

**Gon·dar** (gän′dər) city in NW Ethiopia: former capital: pop. 69,000

**Gond·wa·na** (gänd wä′nə) [ after the *Gondwana Series*, an extensive tillite deposit in *Gondwana*, region in central India ] a hypothetical ancient continent that included what are now India, Australia, Africa, South America, and Antarctica, supposed to have separated and moved apart from Pangea at about the end of the Paleozoic Era

**Good Hope 1 Cape of** cape at the SW tip of Africa, on the Atlantic **2 Cape of** *old name of* CAPE PROVINCE

**Go·pher State** (gō′fər) *name for* MINNESOTA

**Go·rakh·pur** (gôr′ək poor′) city in Uttar Pradesh, NE India: pop. 306,000

**Gor·ki, Gor·kiy, Gor·ky** (gôr′kē) *name* (1932-89) *for* NIZHNY NOVGOROD

**Gor·lov·ka** (gär lôf′kä) city in SE Ukraine, in the Donets Basin: pop. 342,000

**Go·shen** (gō′shən) [ Heb ] *Bible* the fertile land assigned to the Israelites in Egypt: Gen. 45:10

**Gos·port** (gäs′pôrt) seaport in Hampshire, S England, on Portsmouth harbor: pop. 82,000

**Gö·te·borg** (yö′tə bôr′y′) seaport in SW Sweden, on the Kattegat: pop. 424,000

**Goth·am** (gäth′əm; *for* 1, *Brit* gōt′əm) **1** a village near Nottingham, England, whose inhabitants, the "wise men of Gotham," were, according to legend, very foolish **2** *name for* New York City

**Got·land** (gät′lənd; *Swed* gôt′-) Swed. island in the Baltic, off the SE coast of Sweden: 1,225 sq. mi. (3,173 sq. km)

**Göt·ting·en** (göt′iŋ ən) city in central Germany, in the state of Lower Saxony: pop. 133,000

**Gra·ian Alps** (grā′ən) division of the W Alps, along the French-Italian border: highest peak *c.* 13,320 ft. (4,060 m)

**Gram·pi·an** (gram′pē ən) region of NE Scotland, on the North Sea: 3,360 sq. mi. (8,700 sq. km); pop. 497,000

**Grampian Mountains** mountain range across central &

N Scotland, dividing the Highlands from the Lowlands: highest peak, Ben Nevis: also **Grampian Hills** or **Grampians**

**Gra·na·da** (grə nä′də; *Sp* grä nä′*th*ä) 1 former Moorish kingdom in S Spain 2 city in this region: site of the Alhambra: pop. 262,000

**Gran Cha·co** (grän chä′kô) CHACO

**Grand Banks** (or **Bank**) large shoal in the North Atlantic, southeast of Newfoundland: noted fishing grounds: *c.* 500 mi. (800 km) long

**Grand Canal** 1 canal in NE China, extending from Tianjin to Hangzhou: *c.* 1,000 mi. (1,600 km) 2 main canal in Venice

**Grand Canyon** 1 deep gorge of the Colorado River, in NW Ariz.: over 200 mi. (320 km) long; 4-18 mi. (6-28 km) wide; 1 mi. (1.6 km) deep 2 national park (**Grand Canyon National Park**) including 105 mi. (169 km) of this gorge: 1,875 sq. mi. (4,850 sq. km)

**Grand Cou·lee** (ko͞o′lē) dam on the Columbia River, NE Wash.: 550 ft. (167 m) high; over 4,000 ft. (1,220 m) long

**Grande-Terre** (grän′ter′) E island of the two major islands of Guadeloupe, West Indies: also **Grand Terre**

**Grand Falls** 1 *old name of* CHURCHILL FALLS 2 *see* YELLOWSTONE FALLS

**Grand Forks** city in E N.Dak.: pop. 49,000

**Grand Ma·nan** (mə nan′) island of New Brunswick at the entrance to the Bay of Fundy: 57 sq. mi. (147 sq. km)

**Grand Prairie** city in NE Tex.: suburb of Dallas: pop. 100,000

**Grand Pré** (gran prä′; *Fr* grän prä′) village in central Nova Scotia, on Minas Basin: site of an early Acadian settlement & the setting of Longfellow's *Evangeline*

**Grand Rapids** ⟦ after the *rapids* on the *Grand* River ⟧ city in SW Mich.: pop. 189,000 (met. area 688,000)

**Grand Te·ton National Park** (tē′tän) ⟦ Fr, lit., big breast: from the contours of the mountains ⟧ national park in NW Wyo.; 472 sq. mi. (1,222 sq. km): it includes a section of a range (**Teton Range**) of the Rockies: highest peak, 13,766 ft. (4,195 m)

**Gra·ni·cus** (grə nī′kəs) river in ancient Mysia (W Asia Minor): site of a battle (334 B.C.) in which Alexander the Great defeated the Persians

**Grau·bün·den** (grou'bün'dən) easternmost canton of Switzerland: 2,745 sq. mi. (7,109 sq. km): pop. 164,800

**Gravenhage** *see* 's GRAVENHAGE

**Gray's Inn** (grāz) *see* INNS OF COURT

**Graz** (gräts) city in SE Austria: pop. 243,000

**Great Australian Bight** wide bay of the Indian Ocean, indenting S Australia: *c.* 720 mi. (1,150 km) wide

**Great Barrier Reef** coral reef off the NE coast of Queensland, Australia: 1,250 mi. (2,010 km) long

**Great Basin** vast inland region of the W U.S., between the Sierra Nevada & the Wasatch Mountains: the rivers & streams flowing into this region form lakes which have no outlet to the sea: *c.* 200,000 sq. mi. (518,000 sq. km)

**Great Bear** the constellation Ursa Major

**Great Bear Lake** lake in Fort Smith & Inuvik regions, Northwest Territories, Canada: 12,275 sq. mi. (31,792 sq. km)

**Great Britain** 1 principal island of the United Kingdom, including England, Scotland, & Wales, & administratively including adjacent islands except the Isle of Man & the Channel Islands 2 popularly, the United Kingdom of Great Britain and Northern Ireland

**Great Dividing Range** series of mountain ranges along the E coast of Australia: highest peak, Mt. Kosciusko

**Greater Antilles** group of islands in the West Indies, made up of the N & W Antilles, including the islands of Cuba, Jamaica, Hispaniola, & Puerto Rico

**Greater Wol·lon·gong** (wool'ən gäŋ', -gôŋ') city in SE New South Wales, Australia: pop. 234,000

**Great Falls** city in WC Mont., on the Missouri River: pop. 55,000

**Great Glen of Scotland** GLEN MORE

**Great Kar·roo** (kə rōō', ka-), the karroo in SC Cape Province, South Africa: *c.* 350 mi. (563 km) long & 2,000 to 3,000 ft. (610 to 915 m) high

**Great Lakes** chain of freshwater lakes in EC North America, emptying into the St. Lawrence River; Lakes Superior, Michigan, Huron, Erie, & Ontario

**Great Plains** sloping region of valleys & plains in WC North America, extending from Tex. north to S Alberta, Canada, & stretching east from the base of the Rockies for *c.* 400 mi. (644 km)

**Great Rift Valley** depression of SW Asia & E Africa,

extending from the Jordan River valley across Ethiopia & Somalia to the lakes region of E Africa

**Great Salt Lake** shallow saltwater lake in NW Utah, fluctuating greatly in size from *c.* 1,100 sq. mi. (2,500 sq. km) to *c.* 2,300 sq. mi. (5,950 sq. km)

**Great Sandy Desert** N section of the vast desert region of Western Australia

**Great Slave Lake** lake in S Fort Smith Region, Northwest Territories, Canada: 10,980 sq. mi. (28,440 sq. km)

**Great Smoky Mountains** mountain range of the Appalachians, along the Tenn.-N.C. border: highest peak, Clingman's Dome: site of a national park (**Great Smoky Mountains National Park**): 795 sq. mi. (2,060 sq. km)

**Great St. Ber·nard Pass** (sānt bər närd´) mountain pass in the Pennine Alps, on the border between SW Switzerland & Italy: 8,110 ft. (2,470 m) high

**Great Victoria Desert** S section of the vast desert region of Western Australia

**Great Wall of China** stone & earth wall extending across N China, built as a defense against invaders in the 3d cent. B.C., with later extensions: 15-30 ft. (4.5-9 m) high; 12-20 ft. (3.5-6 m) wide; *c.* 1,500 mi. (2,415 km) long

**Great White Way** the brightly lighted, former theater district in New York City, on Broadway near Times Square

**Great Yarmouth** seaport on the eastern coast of England, in Norfolk: pop. 82,000

**Greece** (grēs) country in the S Balkan Peninsula, including many islands in the Aegean, Ionian, & Mediterranean seas: 50,949 sq. mi. (131,950 sq. km); pop. 9,900,000; cap. Athens: in ancient times, the region comprised a number of small monarchies and city-states

**Gree·ley** (grē′lē) ⟦after Horace *Greeley* (1811-72), U.S. journalist⟧ city in NC Colo.: pop. 61,000

**Green** (grēn) river flowing from W Wyo. south into the Colorado River in SE Utah: 730 mi. (1,175 km)

**Green Bay** ⟦transl. of Fr *Baie Verte*⟧ **1** arm of Lake Michigan, extending into NE Wis.: *c.* 100 mi. (160 km) long **2** city & port in Wis., on this bay: pop. 96,000

**Green·land** (grēn′lənd) ⟦orig. so called (ON *Grönland*,

A.D. 986) to attract settlers ⟧ self-governing island northeast of North America, an integral part of Denmark: it is the world's largest island: 840,000 sq. mi. (2,175,600 sq. km): ice-free land 131,930 sq. mi. (341,700 sq. km); pop. 53,000; cap. Godthaab

**Greenland Sea** part of the Arctic Ocean east of Greenland

**Green Mountains** range of the Appalachians, extending the length of Vermont: highest peak 4,393 ft. (1,340 m)

**Greens·bor·o** (grēnz′bur′ō) ⟦after Nathanael *Greene* (1742-86), Am general⟧ city in NC N.C.: pop. 184,000 (met. area, with Winston-Salem & High Point, 942,000)

**Green·ville** (grēn′vil) ⟦after Nathanael *Greene* (1742-86), Am general⟧ city in NW S.C.: pop. 58,000 (met. area, with Spartanburg, 641,000)

**Green·wich** (gren′ich; *chiefly Brit*, grin′ij; *for 2, also* grēn′wich) 1 borough of Greater London, located on the prime meridian: pop. 216,000: formerly the site of an astronomical observatory: see Herstmonceux 2 suburb of Stamford, in SW Conn.: pop. 58,000

**Green·wich Village** (gren′ich) section of New York City, on the lower west side of Manhattan: noted as a center for artists, writers, etc.: formerly a village

**Gre·na·da** (grə nā′də) 1 southernmost island of the Windward group in the West Indies: 120 sq. mi. (311 sq. km) 2 country consisting of this island & the S Grenadines: formerly a British colony, it became independent (1974) & a member of the Commonwealth: 133 sq. mi. (345 sq. km); pop. 92,000

**Gren·a·dines** (gren′ə dēnz) chain of small islands of the Windward group in the West Indies: the northern group is part of the nation of St. Vincent & the southern group is part of Grenada: *c.* 30 sq. mi. (78 sq. km)

**Gre·no·ble** (grə nō′bəl; *Fr* grə nồ′bl′) city in SE France, in the Alps: pop. 159,000

**Gret·na Green** (gret′nə) border village in Scotland, where, formerly, many eloping English couples went to be married: used figuratively of any similar village or town

**Grims·by** (grimz′bē) seaport in Humberside, NE England, at the mouth of the Humber estuary: pop. 95,000

**Gri·sons** (grē zōn′) *Fr. name of* Graubünden

**Grod·no** (grôd′nô) city in W Belarus, on the Neman

River: pop. 247,000

**Gro·ning·en** (grō′niŋ ən; *Du* khrō′niŋ ən) **1** province of the N Netherlands: 898 sq. mi. (2,335 sq. km); pop. 562,000 **2** its capital: pop. 168,000

**Grøn·land** (grön′län) *Dan. name of* GREENLAND

**Groz·ny** (grôz′nē) city in SW Russia, at the northern foot of the Caucasus Mountains: pop. 393,000

**Grus** (grōōs) ⟦L, the crane⟧ a S constellation between Piscis Austrinus and Indus

**GU** *abbrev. for* Guam

**Gua·da·la·ja·ra** (gwäd″l ə här′ə; *Sp* gwä′thä lä hä′rä) city in W Mexico: capital of Jalisco: pop. 2,244,000

**Gua·dal·ca·nal** (gwäd″l kə nal′) largest island of the Solomon Islands, in the SW Pacific: *c.* 2,060 sq. mi. (5,336 sq. km)

**Gua·dal·quiv·ir** (gwäd″l kwiv′ər; *Sp* gwä′thäl kē vir′) river in S Spain, flowing into the Atlantic: *c.* 375 mi. (603 km)

**Gua·de·loupe** (gwä′də lōōp′) overseas department of France consisting of two islands (BASSE-TERRE & GRANDE-TERRE) and five island dependencies in the Leeward Islands: 657 sq. mi. (1,702 sq. km); pop. 328,000; cap. Basse-Terre

**Gua·di·a·na** (gwä′dē ä′nə) river flowing from SC Spain west & then south into the Atlantic, forming part of the Spanish-Portuguese border: *c.* 510 mi. (816 km)

**Guam** (gwäm) largest of the Mariana Islands, in the W Pacific: an unincorporated territory of the U.S.: 209 sq. mi. (541 sq. km); pop. 133,000; cap. Agana: abbrev. *GU*

**Gua·na·jua·to** (gwä′nä hwä′tô) **1** state of central Mexico: rich mining center, esp. for silver: 11,773 sq. mi. (30,491 sq. km); pop. 3,295,000 **2** its capital: pop. 45,000

**Guang·dong** (guäŋ′dōōŋ′) province of SE China, on the South China Sea: 89,344 sq. mi. (231,400 sq. km); pop. 61,000,000; cap. Guangzhou

**Guang·xi** (gwäŋ′sē′) autonomous region in S China: 85,097 sq. mi. (220,400 sq. km); pop. 38,000,000; cap. Nanning: also **Guang′xi′-Zhuang′** (-jwäŋ′)

**Guang·zhou** (gwäŋ′jō) seaport in SE China, in the Zhu River delta: capital of Guangdong province: pop. 3,120,000

**Guan·tá·na·mo** (gwän tä′nə mô′) city in SE Cuba: pop.

125,000

**Guantánamo Bay** inlet of the Caribbean, on the SE coast of Cuba: site of a U.S. naval station: 12 mi. (19 km) long

**Gua·po·ré** (gwä'pô re') river in central South America, flowing from central Brazil northwest along the Brazil-Bolivia border into the Mamoré: c. 750 mi. (1,210 km)

**Gua·te·ma·la** (gwä'tə mä'lə) country in Central America, south & east of Mexico: 42,042 sq. mi. (108,889 sq. km); pop. 8,335,000; cap. Guatemala City

**Guatemala City** capital of Guatemala, in the S part: pop. 1,300,000

**Guay·a·quil** (gwī'ä kēl') seaport in W Ecuador: pop. 1,300,000

**Guay·na·bo** (gwī nä'bô, -vô) city in NE Puerto Rico, near San Juan: pop. 73,000

**Guelph** (gwelf) city in SE Ontario, Canada: pop. 81,000

**Guern·sey** (gurn'zē) second largest of the Channel Islands of the United Kingdom, north and west of Jersey: 25 sq. mi. (65 sq. km); pop. 53,000

**Guer·re·ro** (ge re'rô) state of S Mexico: 24,887 sq. mi. (64,457 sq. km); pop. 2,110,000

**Gui·a·na** (gē an'ə, -ä'nə) 1 region in N South America, including Guyana, Suriname, and French Guiana 2 an area including this region, SE Venezuela, & part of N Brazil, bounded by the Orinoco, Negro, & Amazon rivers & the Atlantic Ocean

**Gui·enne** (güē yen') alt. sp. of GUYENNE

**Guild·hall** (gild'hôl'), **The** the hall of the City of London

**Gui·lin** (gwē'lin') city in Guangxi province, S China: pop. 170,000

**Guin·ea** (gin'ē) 1 coastal region of W Africa, between Senegal & Nigeria 2 country in this region: formerly a French colony, it became independent (1958): 94,925 sq. mi. (245,857 sq. km); pop. 5,400,000; cap. Conakry 3 Gulf of part of the Atlantic, off the W coast of Africa

**Guin·ea-Bis·sau** (-bi sou') country in W Africa, on the coast between Guinea & Senegal: formerly a Portuguese territory, it became independent (1973): 13,948 sq. mi. (36,125 sq. km); pop. 859,000; cap. Bissau

**Gui·yang** (gwē'yäŋ') city in S China: capital of Guizhou province: pop. 530,000

**Gui·zhou** (gwē'jō') province of S China: 67,181 sq. mi.

(173,998 sq. km); pop. 29,320,000; cap. Guiyang

**Gu·ja·rat** (gŏo′jə rät′) state of W India: 75,670 sq. mi. (195,984 sq. km); pop. 33,960,000; cap. Ahmedabad

**Guj·ran·wa·la** (gŏoj′rən wäl′ə) city in NE Pakistan: pop. 597,000

**Gulf·port** (gulf′pôrt′) seaport in S Miss., on the Gulf of Mexico: pop. 41,000

**Gulf States** States on the Gulf of Mexico; Fla., Ala., Miss., La., & Tex.

**Gulf Stream** warm ocean current flowing from the Gulf of Mexico along the E coast of the U.S., and turning east at the Grand Banks toward Europe: *c.* 50 mi. (80 km) wide

**Gun·tur** (gŏon tŏor′) city in Andhra Pradesh, SE India, in the Kistna River delta: pop. 367,000

**Guy·a·na** (gī an′ə, -än′ə) country in NE South America: formerly a British colony, it became independent & a member of the Commonwealth (1966): 83,000 sq. mi. (214,969 sq. km); pop. 965,000; cap. Georgetown

**Guy·enne** (güē yen′) historical region of SW France, roughly corresponding to earlier Aquitaine

**Gwa·li·or** (gwä′lē ôr′) city in Madhya Pradesh, NC India: pop. 560,000

**Gwent** (gwent) county of SE Wales, on the Severn estuary: 531 sq. mi. (1,376 sq. km); pop. 440,000

**Gwyn·edd** (gwin′əth) county of NW Wales, on the Irish Sea & St. George's Channel: 1,493 sq. mi. (3,868 sq. km); pop. 232,000

**Gyan·dzha** (gyän′jə) city in NC Azerbaijan, in Transcaucasia: pop. 261,000

**Györ** (dyör) city in NW Hungary: pop. 129,000

# H

**Haar·lem** (här′ləm) city in NW Netherlands: capital of North Holland province: pop. 152,000

**Haar·lem·mer·meer** (här′lə mər mer′) city in NW Netherlands, on the site of a former lake: pop. 85,000

**Ha·ba·na** (ä bä′nä), (La) *Sp. name of* HAVANA

**Ha·chi·o·ji** (häch′ē ō′jē) city in SE central Honshu, Japan: pop. 405,000

**Hack·en·sack** (hak′ən sak′) ⟦< Du < AmInd (Delaware) name⟧ city in NE N.J.: pop. 37,000

**Ha·des** (hā′dēz′) ⟦Gr *Haidēs*⟧ **1** *Gr. Myth.* the home of the dead, beneath the earth **2** *Bible* the state or rest-ing place of the dead: name used in some modern translations of the New Testament **3** [*often* **h-**] hell: a euphemism

**Ha·dhra·maut, Ha·dra·maut** (hä'drä môt') **1** region on the S coast of Arabia, on the Gulf of Aden: *c.* 58,500 sq. mi. (151,500 sq. km) **2** river valley (**Wadi Hadhramaut**) that crosses this region: *c.* 350 mi. (565 km)

**Ha·dri·an's Wall** (hā'drē ənz) stone wall across N Eng-land, from Solway Firth to the Tyne: built (A.D. 122-128) by the Rom. emperor Hadrian to protect Roman Britain from N tribes: 73.5 mi. (118.3 km)

**Ha·gen** (hä'gən) city in W Germany, in the Ruhr valley, in the state of North Rhine-Westphalia: pop. 209,500

**Ha·gers·town** (hā'gərz toun') ⟦after J. *Hager*, early set-tler⟧ city in N Md.: pop. 35,000

**Hague** (hāg), **The** city in W Netherlands: capital of South Holland province: seat of the government (cf. AMSTERDAM): pop. 672,000: Du. name 's GRAVENHAGE

**Hai·fa** (hī'fə) seaport in NW Israel, on the Mediterra-nean: pop. 225,000

**Hai·nan** (hī'nän') island south of China, in the South China Sea: part of Guangdong province: *c.* 13,500 sq. mi. (35,000 sq. km)

**Hai·naut** (e nō') province of SW Belgium: 1,437 sq. mi. (3,722 sq. km); pop. 1,280,000; cap. Mons

**Hai·phong** (hī'fäŋ') seaport in N Vietnam, in the delta of the Red River: pop. 1,300,000

**Hai·ti** (hāt'ē) **1** country occupying the W portion of the island of Hispaniola, West Indies: 10,714 sq. mi. (27,700 sq. km); pop. 5,250,000; cap. Port-au-Prince **2** *old name of* HISPANIOLA

**Ha·ko·da·te** (hä'kō dä'tä) seaport on the SW coast of Hokkaido, Japan: pop. 320,000

**Ha·le·a·ka·la National Park** (hä'lä ä'kä lä') national park on the island of Maui, Hawaii, including a dor-mant volcano (**Haleakala**), 10,023 ft. (3,100 m) high, with a crater of 19 sq. mi. (49 sq. km)

**Ha·leb** (hä leb') *Ar. name of* ALEPPO

**Hal·i·car·nas·sus** (hal'ə kär nas'əs) ancient city in SW Asia Minor, on the Aegean: site of the MAUSOLEUM

**Hal·i·fax** (hal'ə faks') ⟦after the 2d Earl of *Halifax* (1716-71)⟧ **1** capital of Nova Scotia, Canada: seaport

on the Atlantic: pop. 205,000 (met. area 296,000) **2**
city in West Yorkshire, England: pop. 95,000

**Hal·le** (häl'ə; *E* hal'ē) city in E Germany: capital of
Saxony-Anhalt: pop. 237,000

**Hal·ley's comet** (hal'ēz; *occas.* hô'lēz, hā'-) a famous
comet, last seen in 1986, whose reappearance about
every 76 years was predicted by Edmund Halley (1656-
1742), Eng. astronomer

**Hal·ma·he·ra** (häl'mə her'ə) largest of the Molucca
Islands, Indonesia, east of Celebes: 6,870 sq. mi.
(17,800 sq. km)

**Häl·sing·borg** (hel'siŋ bôr'y') seaport in SW Sweden, on
the Öresund, opposite Helsingør, Denmark: pop.
104,000

**Ha·ma, Ha·mah** (hä'mä) city in W Syria: pop. 176,000:
called, in the Bible, **Ha·math** (hā'math)

**Ha·ma·dan** (ham'ə dan') city in W Iran: noted for car-
pets and rugs made there: pop. 165,000

**Ha·ma·ma·tsu** (hä'mä mä'tsoo) city on the SC coast of
Honshu, Japan: pop. 510,000

**Ham·burg** (ham'bərg; *Ger* häm'boorkh) seaport and
state of N Germany, on the Elbe River: 292 sq. mi.
(755 sq. km); pop. 1,600,000

**Ham·den** (ham'dən) ⟦after J. *Hampden* (1594-1643),
Puritan leader⟧ suburb of New Haven, in S Conn.:
pop. 52,000

**Ham·e·lin** (ham'ə lin) city in NW Germany, in the state
of Lower Saxony: pop. 56,000: Ger. name **Ha·meln** (hä'
məln)

**Ham·hung** (häm'hooŋ') city in EC North Korea: pop.
420,000

**Ham·il·ton** (ham'əl tən) **1** ⟦after G. *Hamilton*, local
farmer (*c.* 1813)⟧ city & port in SE Ontario, Canada,
at the W end of Lake Ontario: pop. 307,000 (met. area
557,000) **2** ⟦after Alexander *Hamilton* (*c.* 1755-1804),
Am statesman⟧ city in SW Ohio, near Cincinnati: pop.
61,000 **3** city in N North Island, New Zealand: pop.
157,000 **4** city in SC Scotland, near Glasgow, on the
Clyde River: pop. 51,000 **5** capital of Bermuda, on the
main island: pop. 6,000 **6** ⟦after Sir Charles *Hamilton*, gov. of Newfoundland (1818-24)⟧ river in S Labrador, flowing east to **Hamilton Inlet**, an arm of the
Atlantic: 208 mi. (with upper course, 560 mi.)

**Ham·mer·fest** (häm'ər fest') seaport on an island in N

Norway: northernmost city in the world: pop. 7,500

**Ham·mer·smith** (ham'ər smith') borough of Greater London, England: pop. 150,000: in full **Hammersmith and Fulham**

**Ham·mond** (ham'ənd) 〚after G. H. *Hammond*, local meatpacker〛 city in NW Ind., near Chicago: pop. 84,000

**Hamp·shire** (hamp'shir, ham'-; -shər) **1** county on the S coast of England: 1,457 sq. mi.: (3,773 sq. km); pop. 1,509,000; county seat, Winchester **2** former county of England including present-day Hampshire & the Isle of Wight

**Hamp·stead** (-stid, -sted) former metropolitan borough of London, now part of borough of Camden

**Hamp·ton** (-tən) 〚after a town in England〛 seaport in SE Va., on Hampton Roads: pop. 134,000

**Hampton Roads** 〚prec. + *road(stead)*〛 channel & harbor in SE Va., linking the James River estuary with Chesapeake Bay

**Han** (hän) river in central China, flowing from Shaanxi province southeast into the Chang at Wuhan: *c.* 900 mi. (1,450 km)

**Han Cities** *see* WUHAN

**Hang·zhou** (hän'jō') port in E China: capital of Zhejiang province: pop. 4,020,000: old form **Hang·chow** (han'chou')

**Han·kow** (han'kou') former city in EC China: see WUHAN

**Ha·noi** (hä noi', ha-) capital of Vietnam, in the N part: pop. 1,440,000

**Han·o·ver** (han'ō vər) **1** former province (1886-1945) of Prussia, in NW Germany: earlier, an electorate (1692-1815) & a kingdom (1815-86): now part of the German state of Lower Saxony **2** city in NW Germany: capital of Lower Saxony: pop. 517,000

**Hanse** (hans), **the** a medieval league of free towns in N Germany and adjoining countries, formed to promote and protect their economic interests: the leading members were Bremen, Lübeck, and Hamburg: also **Han·se·at·ic League** (han'sē at'ik, -zē-) or **the Han·sa** (han'sə)

**Hants** (hants) *short for* HAMPSHIRE

**Han·yang** (hän'yäŋ') former city in EC China: see WUHAN

**Ha·ra·re** (hä rä'rē) capital of Zimbabwe, in the NE part:

pop. 656,000

**Har·bin** (här′bin) city in NE China, on the Songhua River; capital of Heilongjiang province: pop. 2,550,000

**Har·ia·na** (hər yä′nə) state of NW India: 17,274 sq. mi. (44,200 sq. km); pop. 12,850,000; cap. Chandigarh

**Har·in·gey** (hä′riŋ gā) borough of Greater London, England; pop. 200,000

**Har·lem** (här′ləm) section of New York City, in N Manhattan

**Harlem River** tidal river separating Manhattan Island from the Bronx &, with Spuyten Duyvil Creek, connecting the East River with the Hudson: *c.* 8 mi. (12 km)

**Harp** (härp) the constellation Lyra

**Har·pers Ferry** (här′pərz) town in W.Va., at the juncture of the Potomac & Shenandoah rivers: site of the U.S. arsenal captured by John Brown (1859): pop. 300

**Har·ris** (har′is) *see* LEWIS WITH HARRIS

**Har·ris·burg** (har′is bʉrg′) [[after John *Harris*, Jr., the founder]] capital of Pa., in the S part, on the Susquehanna: pop. 52,000

**Har·row** (har′ō) 1 borough of Greater London, England: pop. 201,000 2 private preparatory school for boys, in this borough

**Hart·ford** (härt′fərd) capital of Conn., in the central part, on the Connecticut River: pop. 140,000 (met. area 768,000)

**Har·ya·na** (hər yä′nə) *alt. sp. of* HARIANA

**Harz (Mountains)** (härts) mountain range in central Germany, extending from Lower Saxony to the Elbe River

**Ha·sa** (hä′sə) region of NE Saudi Arabia: now constituting the *Eastern Province*: also **Al Hasa**

**Has·selt** (häs′əlt) commune in NE Belgium: capital of Limburg province: pop. 65,000

**Has·tings** (hās′tiŋz) city in Sussex, SE England, on the English Channel: near the site of the decisive battle (Battle of Hastings, 1066) in the Norman Conquest of England: pop. 74,000

**Hat·ter·as** (hat′ər əs), **Cape** cape on an island (**Hatteras Island**) of N.C., between Pamlico Sound & the Atlantic: site of a national recreational area (**Cape Hatteras National Seashore**), 39 sq. mi. (113 sq. km)

**Hat·ties·burg** (hat′ēz bʉrg′) city in SE Miss.: pop.

42,000

**Haute-Nor·man·die** (ōt nôr män dē') metropolitan region of NW France: 4,700 sq. mi. (12,317 sq. km); pop. 1,671,000; chief city, Rouen

**Ha·van·a** (hə van'ə) capital of Cuba: seaport on the Gulf of Mexico: pop. 1,950,000: Sp. name HABANA

**Ha·vel** (hä'fəl) river in NE Germany, flowing southwest into the Elbe: *c.* 215 mi. (345 km)

**Ha·ver·ing** (hāv'riŋ) borough of Greater London: pop. 240,000

**Havre, Le** *see* LE HAVRE

**Ha·wai·i** (hə wä'ē, -wī'-) ⟦Haw *Hawai'i* > Proto-Polynesian *\*hawaiki*; akin to *Savai'i*, SAVAII⟧ 1 a State of the U.S., consisting of a group of islands (**Hawaiian Islands**) in the North Pacific: admitted, 1959; 6,450 sq. mi. (16,706 sq. km); pop. 1,108,000; cap. Honolulu: abbrev. *HI* 2 largest & southernmost of the islands of Hawaii, southeast of Oahu: 4,021 sq. mi. (10,420 sq. km); pop. 120,000

**Hawaii Volcanoes National Park** national park on the island of Hawaii, including Mauna Loa: 280 sq. mi. (725 sq. km)

**Hawk·eye State** (hôk'ī') *name for* IOWA

**Haw·thorne** (hô'thôrn') ⟦after Nathaniel *Hawthorne* (1804-64), U.S. writer⟧ city in SW Calif.: suburb of Los Angeles: pop. 71,000

**Hay·mar·ket Square** (hā'mär'kit) square in Chicago: site of a battle between police & workmen (Haymarket Riot) on May 4, 1886, following a demonstration for the eight-hour workday

**Hay·ward** (hā'wərd) ⟦after W. *Hayward*, local postmaster⟧ city in W Calif.: suburb of Oakland: pop. 111,000

**He·bei** (hə bā') province of NE China, on the gulf of Bo Hai: 84,865 sq. mi. (220,640 sq. km) pop. 53,000,000; cap. Shijiazhuang

**Heb·ri·des** (heb'rə dēz') group of islands off the W coast of Scotland: they are divided into the **Inner Hebrides**, nearer the mainland, & the **Outer Hebrides**: *c.* 2,800 sq. mi. (7,251 sq. km); pop. *c.* 80,000

**He·bron** (hē'brən) city in W Jordan, south of Jerusalem, dating from Biblical times: pop. 143,000

**He·fei** (he'fā') city in E China: capital of Anhui province: pop. 360,000

**Hei·del·berg** (hīd″'l bʉrg′; *Ger* hī′dəl berkh′) city in SW Germany, in the state of Baden-Württemberg: site of a famous university (founded 1386): pop. 133,000

**Hei·long·jiang** (hä′loʊŋ′jyäŋ′) province of NE China: 179,000 sq. mi. (463,600 sq. km); pop. 32,660,000; cap. Harbin: old form **Hei·lung·kiang** (hä′loʊŋ′jyäŋ′)

**He·jaz** (he jaz′, hē-; -jäz′) region of NW Saudi Arabia, formerly a kingdom: now constituting the *Western Province*

**Hel** (hel) ⟦ON: see HELL⟧ *Norse Myth.* the underworld to which the dead not killed in battle are sent: cf. VALHALLA

**Hel·e·na** (hel′i nə) ⟦said to be after the hometown of a settler from Minnesota⟧ capital of Mont., in the WC part: pop. 25,000

**Hel·go·land** (hel′gō land′; *Ger* hel′gō länt′) island of Germany, in the North Sea: one of the North Frisian Islands: *c.* .25 sq. mi. (.64 sq. km)

**Hel·i·con** (hel′i kän′, -kən) mountain group in SC Greece, on the Gulf of Corinth: in Greek mythology, the home of the Muses; highest peak, 5,735 ft. (1,750 m)

**He·li·op·o·lis** (hē′lē äp′ə lis) ⟦Gr *Hēliopolis*, lit., city of the sun < *hēlios*, sun + *polis*, city⟧ **1** ancient city in the Nile delta, just north of where Cairo now stands: center for the worship of the sun god Ra **2** ancient city on the site of modern BAALBEK

**hell** (hel) ⟦ME *helle* < OE *hel* (akin to Ger *hölle*, hell & ON *Hel*, the underworld goddess, HEL) < base of *helan*, to cover, hide < IE base *\*kel-*, to hide, cover up > L *celare*, to hide⟧ [*often* H-] **1** *Bible* the place where the spirits of the dead are: identified with SHEOL and HADES **2** *Theol. a)* a state or place of woe and anguish, arrived at by the wicked after death; specif., esp. in Christian theology, the state or place of total and final separation from God and so of eternal misery and suffering, arrived at by those who die unrepentant in grave sin *b)* popularly, this state or place as the abode of Satan and of all other devils and of all the damned

**Hel·las** (hel′əs) **1** in ancient times, Greece, including the islands & colonies **2** *modern Gr. name of* GREECE

**Hel·les** (hel′əs), **Cape** S tip of the Gallipoli Peninsula, Turkey, at the entrance to the Dardanelles

**Hel·les·pont** (hel′əs pänt′) ⟦Gr, lit., "sea of Helle"⟧

*ancient name of* DARDANELLES

**Hell Gate** 〚< Du *Helle Gat*, hell strait: from the whirl-pools formerly there〛 narrow channel of the East River, N.Y., between Manhattan & Queens

**Hel·sing·ør** (hel'siŋ ör') seaport in Denmark, on the Öresund, opposite Hälsingborg, Sweden: pop. 57,000

**Hel·sin·ki** (hel'siŋ kē, hel siŋ'-) capital of Finland: seaport on the Gulf of Finland: pop. 485,000: Swed. name **Hel·sing·fors** (hel'siŋ fôrs')

**Hel·ve·tia** (hel vē'shə) **1** ancient Celtic country in central Europe, in what is now W Switzerland **2** *Latin name of* SWITZERLAND

**Hemp·stead** (hemp'sted, hem'-; -stəd) 〚after *Heemstede*, town in Netherlands; form infl. by name HAMP-STEAD〛 town on W Long Island, N.Y.: pop. 49,000

**He·nan** (hu'nän') province of EC China: 64,479 sq. mi. (167,645 sq. km); pop. 74,422,000; cap. Zhengzhou

**Hen·don** (hen'dən) former urban district in Middlesex, SE England: now part of Barnet

**Heng·e·lo** (heŋ'ə lō) city in E Netherlands: pop. 76,000

**Hen·ley** (hen'lē) city in SE England, on the Thames: site of an annual rowing regatta; pop. 10,000: also **Henley-on-Thames**

**Hen·ry** (hen'rē) **1 Fort** Confederate fort in NW Tenn., on the Tennessee River: captured (1862) by Union forces **2 Cape** 〚after Prince *Henry*, son of James I〛 promontory in SE Va., at the entrance of Chesapeake Bay

**Hep·tar·chy, the** (hep'tär kē, -tär'kē) **1** orig., the supposed confederacy of seven Anglo-Saxon kingdoms **2** the kingdoms of Anglo-Saxon England before the 9th cent. A.D. A term used by historians

**He·ra·kli·on, He·ra·klei·on** (hi rak'lē ən) IRAKLION

**Her·at** (he rät') city in NW Afghanistan: pop. 140,000

**Her·ce·go·vi·na** (hert'sə gō vē'nə) *alt. sp. of* HERZEGO-VINA

**Her·cu·la·ne·um** (hur'kyə lā'nē əm) ancient city in S Italy, at the foot of Mt. Vesuvius: buried, together with Pompeii, in a volcanic eruption (A.D. 79)

**Herds·man** (hurdz'mən) the constellation Boötes

**Her·e·ford** (her'ə fərd) **1** city in WC England, on the Wye River: pop. 47,000 **2** former county of England (see HEREFORD AND WORCESTER): also **Her'e·ford·shire'** (-shir', -shər)

**Hereford and Worcester** county of WC England, comprising the former counties of Hereford and Worcester: 1,516 sq. mi. (3,927 sq. km); pop. 645,000

**Her·mon** (hur'mən), **Mount** mountain on the Syria-Lebanon border, in the Anti-Lebanon mountains: 9,232 ft. (2,814 m)

**Her·mo·sil·lo** (er'mô sē'yô) city in NW Mexico: capital of Sonora state: pop. 340,000

**Herst·mon·ceux** (hurst'mən sōō') village in East Sussex, S England: site of the Royal Greenwich Observatory

**Hert·ford·shire** (här'fərd shir', härt'-; -shər) county in SE England: 632 sq. mi. (1,634 sq. km); pop. 980,000: also called **Hert'ford** or **Herts** (härts)

**Hertogenbosch,** 's see 's HERTOGENBOSCH

**Her·ze·go·vi·na** (hert'sə gō vē'nə) see BOSNIA AND HERZEGOVINA

**Hes·per** (hes'pər) [Old Poet.] HESPERUS

**Hes·pe·ri·a** (hes pir'ē ə) ⟦ L < Gr *Hesperia* < *hesperos*: see HESPERUS ⟧ the Western Land: the ancient Greek name for Italy and the Roman name for Spain

**Hes·per·i·des** (hes per'i dēz') *Gr. Myth.* the garden where the apples grow

**Hes·per·us** (hes'pər əs) ⟦ L < Gr ⟧ the evening star, esp. Venus

**Hesse** (hes, hes'ə) **1** state of central Germany: 8,150 sq. mi. (21,110 sq. km); pop. 5,580,000; cap. Wiesbaden **2** former region in WC Germany embracing various political units historically: Ger. name **Hes·sen** (hes'ən)

**Hes·ton and I·sle·worth** (hes'tən ənd ī'zəl wurth') former municipal borough in Middlesex, England: now part of Hounslow

**HI** *abbrev. for* Hawaii

**Hi·a·le·ah** (hī'ə lē'ə) ⟦ < ? Seminole-Creek *haiyakpo hili*, lit., pretty prairie ⟧ city in SE Fla.: suburb of Miami: pop. 188,000

**Hi·ber·ni·a** (hī bur'nē ə) ⟦ L, altered < *Iverna, Juverna* < OCelt *Iveriu* > OIr *Ériu*, Eire ⟧ old poet. name for IRELAND

**Hi·dal·go** (hi dal'gō; *MexSp* ē däl'gô) state of central Mexico: 8,058 sq. mi. (20,870 sq. km); pop. 1,550,000; cap. Pachuca

**Hi·ga·shi·o·sa·ka** (hē gä'shē ō säk'ə) city in S Honshu, Japan, east of Osaka: pop. 502,000

**High·lands** (hī′ləndz), **the** mountainous region occupying nearly all of the N half of Scotland

**High Point** ⟦after its location, the highest point on the N.C. Railroad⟧ city in central N.C.: pop. 69,000: see GREENSBORO

**Hii·u·maa** (hē′o͞o mä′) island of Estonia, in the Baltic Sea: 373 sq. mi. (965 sq. km)

**Hill, the** the location of the U.S. Capitol, where the Congress holds sessions

**Hil·ling·don** (hil′iŋ dən) borough of Greater London: pop. 232,000

**Hil·ver·sum** (hil′vər səm) city in WC Netherlands, near Amsterdam: pop. 88,000

**Hi·ma·chal Pra·desh** (hi mä′chəl pre desh′) state of N India: 21,599 sq. mi. (55,940 sq. km); pop. 4,200,000; cap. Simla

**Hi·ma·la·yas** (him′ə lā′əz, hi mäl′yəz) mountain system of SC Asia, extending along the India-Tibet border and through Pakistan, Nepal, & Bhutan: highest peak, Mt. Everest: also **Himalaya Mountains**

**Him·a·vat** (him′ə vat′) ⟦Hindi⟧ *Hindu Myth.* the personification of the Himalayas and father of Devi

**Hi·me·ji** (hē′me jē′) city on the S coast of Honshu, Japan, near Kobe: pop. 450,000

**Hin·du Kush** (hin′do͞o′ ko͞osh) mountain range mostly in NE Afghanistan, extending to the Karakoram in NW Kashmir: highest peak, Tirich Mir

**Hin·du·stan** (hin′do͞o stan′, -stän′) ⟦ult. < Pers *Hindū-stān*, lit., country of the Hindus⟧ **1** kingdom in N India in the 15th & 16th cent. **2** region in N India, between the Vindhya Mountains & the Himalayas, where Hindi is spoken **3** the entire Indian subcontinent **4** the republic of India

**Hip·po** (hip′ō) HIPPO REGIUS

**Hip·po·crene** (hip′ō krēn′, hip′ō krē′nē) ⟦L < Gr *Hippokrēnē* < *hippos*, a horse + *krēnē*, a spring, fountain⟧ *Gr. Myth.* a fountain on Mt. Helicon, sacred to the Muses: its waters inspire poets

**Hippo Re·gi·us** (rē′jē əs) ancient city in N Africa, near modern Annaba, Algeria: capital of ancient Numidia &, later, a Roman colony

**Hi·ra·ka·ta** (hir′ə kät′ə) city in S Honshu, Japan, north of Osaka: pop. 373,000

**Hi·ro·shi·ma** (hir′ə shē′mə, hi rō′shi mə) seaport in SW

Honshu, Japan, on the Inland Sea: largely destroyed (Aug. 6, 1945) by a U.S. atomic bomb, the first ever used in warfare: pop. 907,000

**His·pa·ni·a** (hi spä′nē ə, -spä′-) 1 *Latin name for* IBERIAN PENINSULA 2 *old poet. name for* SPAIN

**His·pan·io·la** (his′pən yō′lə) island in the West Indies, between Cuba & Puerto Rico: divided between Haiti & the Dominican Republic: 29,979 sq. mi. (77,945 sq. km)

**Ho·bart** (hō′bərt, -bärt) capital of Tasmania: seaport on the SE coast: pop. 173,000

**Ho·bo·ken** (hō′bō′kən) ⟦ < Du < AmInd *hopoakan,* at the place of the tobacco pipe: infl. by *Hoboken,* town in Belgium ⟧ city in NE N.J., on the Hudson River opposite New York: pop. 33,000

**Ho Chi Minh City** (hō′chē′min′) seaport in S Vietnam: formerly (as *Saigon*) capital of South Vietnam, 1954-76: pop. 4,000,000

**Ho·dei·da** (hō dā′də) seaport in Yemen, on the Red Sea: pop. 126,000

**Ho·fei** (hu′fā′) *old form of* HEFEI

**Ho·fuf** (hoo foof′) city in E Saudi Arabia, near the Persian Gulf: pop. 102,000

**Hoh·en·zol·lern** (hō′ən tsôl′ərn; *E,* -zäl′ərn) historical region of SW Germany: formerly a province of Prussia

**Hoh·hot** (hō′hōt′) city in N China: capital of Inner Mongolian Autonomous Region: pop. 748,000

**Hok·kai·do** (hō ki′dō) one of the four main islands of Japan, north of Honshu: 30,364 sq. mi. (78,642 sq. km); chief city, Sapporo

**Hol·guín** (ôl gēn′) city in E Cuba: pop. 235,000

**Hol·land** (häl′ənd) 1 former county of the Holy Roman Empire on the North Sea, now divided into two provinces (NORTH HOLLAND & SOUTH HOLLAND) of the Netherlands 2 NETHERLANDS

**Hol·lan·di·a** (hä lan′dē ə) *old name of* KOTABARU

**Hol·ly·wood** (häl′ē wood′) ⟦ *holly* (the plant) + *wood* ⟧ 1 section of Los Angeles, Calif., once the site of many U.S. film studios; hence, the U.S. film industry or its life, world, etc. 2 city on the SE coast of Fla.: pop. 122,000: see FORT LAUDERDALE

**Hol·stein** (hōl′stīn′; *Ger* hôl′shtīn′) region of NW Germany, in the state of Schleswig-Holstein: formerly a duchy of Denmark

**Holy Cross, Mount of the** peak in WC Colo.: snow-filled crevices on it form a large cross: 13,996 ft. (4,265 m)

**Holy Land** PALESTINE (the region)

**Hol·yoke** (hōl′yōk) ⟦after Rev. E. *Holyoke* (1689-1769), president of Harvard⟧ city in SW Mass., on the Connecticut River: pop. 44,000

**Holy Roman Empire** empire of WC Europe, comprising the German-speaking peoples & N Italy: begun in A.D. 800 with the papal crowning of Charlemagne or, in an alternate view, with the crowning of Otto I in 962, it lasted until Francis II (who was Francis I of Austria) resigned the title in 1806

**Homs** (hômz) city in W Syria, on the Orontes; pop. 354,000

**Ho·nan** (hō′nän′) *old form of* HENAN

**Hon·du·ras** (hän door′əs, -dyoor′-) country in Central America, with coastlines on the Pacific & the Caribbean: 43,227 sq. mi. (112,088 sq. km); pop. 4,092,000; cap. Tegucigalpa

**Hong** (häŋ, hôŋ) *Annamese name of* the RED (river in Vietnam)

**Hong Kong, Hong·kong** (häŋ′käŋ′, hôŋ′kôŋ′) **1** British crown colony in SE China, on the South China Sea: it consists of a principal island (**Hong Kong Island**), nearby islands, Kowloon Peninsula, & an area of adjacent mainland leased from China (called *New Territories*): 405 sq. mi. (1,049 sq. km); pop. 5,109,000; cap. Victoria **2** *another name for* VICTORIA (the capital)

**Hon·o·lu·lu** (hän′ə loo′loo, hō′nə-) ⟦Haw., lit., sheltered bay⟧ capital of Hawaii: seaport on the SE coast of Oahu: pop. 365,000 (met. area 836,000)

**Hon·shu** (hän′shoo′) largest of the islands forming Japan: 88,946 sq. mi. (230,369 sq. km); chief city, Tokyo

**Hood** (hood), **Mount** mountain of the Cascade Range, in N Oreg.: a peak of volcanic origin: 11,245 ft. (3,427 m)

**Hoogh·ly** (hoog′lē) river in E India, flowing into the Bay of Bengal: westernmost channel of the Ganges delta: *c.* 160 mi. (257 km)

**Hoo·ver Dam** (hoo′vər) ⟦after Herbert *Hoover* (1874-1964), U.S. president⟧ dam on the Colorado River, on the Ariz.-Nev. border: 726 ft. (221 m) high

**Ho·pei, Ho·peh** (hō′pā′) *old form of* HEBEI

**Ho·reb** (hō′reb′, hôr′eb′) *Bible* a mountain usually identified with Mt. Sinai: Ex. 3:1

**Hor·muz** (hôr′muz), **Strait of** strait joining the Persian Gulf & the Gulf of Oman, between Arabia & Iran

**Horn, Cape** cape on an island (**Horn Island**) in Tierra del Fuego, Chile: southernmost point of South America

**Horn of Africa** easternmost part of NE Africa, on the Gulf of Aden and the Indian Ocean: it includes Somalia and SE Ethiopia

**Hor·o·log·i·um** (hôr′ə lō′jē əm) a S constellation near Eridanus: essentially a large area with few bright objects

**Hos·pi·ta·let** (ôs′pē tä let′) city in NE Spain: suburb of Barcelona: pop. 294,000

**Hot Springs** city in central Ark., adjoining a national park, **Hot Springs National Park**: 1.5 sq. mi. (3.8 sq. km): the park has 47 hot mineral springs: pop. 32,000

**Houns·low** (hounz′lō) borough of Greater London, England: pop. 197,000

**Hous·ton** (hyōōs′tən) 〚after Samuel *Houston* (1793-1863), U.S. statesman〛 city in SE Tex., a port on a ship canal connected with the Gulf of Mexico: pop. 1,631,000 (met. area 3,302,000)

**How·rah** (hou′rə) city in S West Bengal, India, on the Hooghly River, opposite Calcutta: pop. 745,000

**Hra·dec Krá·lo·vé** (hrä′dets krä′lồ ve) city in N Czech Republic: in a battle at nearby Sadová (1866), the Prussians defeated the Austrians; pop. 98,000

**Hsia·men** (shyä′mun′) *old form of* XIAMEN

**Huang Hai, Hwang Hai** (hwäŋ′ hī′) *Chin. name of* YELLOW SEA

**Huang He** (hwäŋ′hu′) river in N China, flowing from Tibet into the Gulf of Bo Hai: *c.* 3,000 mi. (4,828 km)

**Huas·ca·rán** (wäs′kä rän′) mountain of the Andes, in WC Peru: 22,205 ft. (6,768 m)

**Hub, the** *name for* Boston

**Hu·bei** (hōō′bā′) province in EC China: 72,394 sq. mi. (188,224 sq. km); pop. 47,804,000; cap. Wuhan

**Hu·bli–Dhar·war** (hōōb′lē där′wär′) city in Karnataka state, SW India; pop. 526,000

**Hud·ders·field** (hud′ərz fēld′) city in SW Yorkshire, NC England: pop. 132,000

**Hud·son** (hud′sən) 〚after Henry *Hudson* (d. 1611), Eng explorer〛 river in E N.Y. flowing southward into

Upper New York Bay: *c.* 315 mi. (565 km)

**Hudson Bay** ⟦after Henry *Hudson* (d. 1611), Eng explorer⟧ inland sea in NE Canada; arm of the Atlantic: *c.* 475,000 sq. mi. (1,230,200 sq. km)

**Hudson Strait** ⟦after Henry *Hudson* (d. 1611), Eng explorer⟧ strait in NE Canada, connecting Hudson Bay with the Atlantic: *c.* 430 mi. (691 km) long; 37-120 mi. (60-195 km) wide

**Hue** (hwā, wā) city in central Vietnam, on the South China Sea; pop. 209,000

**Hu·fuf** (hoo foof′) *alt. sp. of* HOFUF

**Hu·he·hot** (hoo′hä′hōt′) *old form of* HOHHOT

**Hull** (hul) **1** seaport in Humberside, England, on the Humber estuary: pop. 269,000: officially *Kingston upon Hull* **2** ⟦after district in Yorkshire, England⟧ city in SW Quebec, Canada; pop. 61,000

**Hull–House** (hul′hous′) a social settlement house founded in Chicago in 1889 by Jane Addams

**Hum·ber** (hum′bər) estuary in NE England, formed by the Ouse & Trent rivers: *c.* 40 mi. (64 km) long

**Hum·ber·side** (-sīd′) county of NE England, on the Humber estuary & the North Sea: 1,356 sq. mi. (3,512 sq. km); pop. 854,000

**Hum·boldt current** (hoom′bōlt; *E* hum′bōlt) ⟦after Baron Alexander von *Humboldt* (1769-1859), Ger explorer⟧ the cold ocean current flowing north along the coasts of Chile and Peru

**Hu·nan** (hoo′nän′) province of SE China: 81,274 sq. mi. (211,132 sq. km); pop. 54,008,000; cap. Changsha

**Hun·ga·ry** (hun′gər ē) country in SC Europe: 35,911 sq. mi. (93,032 sq. km); pop. 10,700,000; cap. Budapest: Hung. name MAGYARORSZÁG

**Hung·nam** (hoon′näm′) seaport in E North Korea, on the Sea of Japan: pop. 150,000

**Hun·ting·don·shire** (hun′tiŋ dən shir′, -shər) former county in EC England, now part of Cambridgeshire: also **Hun′ting·don** or **Hunts**

**Hun·ting·ton** (hun′tiŋ tən) ⟦after Collis Porter *Huntington* (1821-1900), its founder⟧ city in W W.Va., on the Ohio River: pop. 55,000

**Huntington Beach** ⟦after H. E. *Huntington*, U.S. railroad executive⟧ city in SW Calif.: suburb of Los Angeles: pop. 182,000

**Huntington Park** city in SW Calif.: pop. 56,000

**Hunts·ville** (hunts′vil) 〚after J. *Hunt*, its first settler (1805)〛 city in N Ala.: pop. 160,000

**Hu·peh, Hu·pei** (hōō′bä′, -pā′) *old form of* HUBEI

**Hu·ron** (hyoor′än′, -ən), **Lake** second largest of the Great Lakes, between Mich. & Ontario, Canada: 24,328 sq. mi. (63,000 sq. km); 247 mi. (398 km) long

**Hutt** (hut) urban area in S North Island, New Zealand, near Wellington: pop. 115,000

**Hwang Ho** (hwäŋ′ hō′) *old name of* HUANG HE

**Hy·a·des** (hī′ə dēz′) 〚L *Hyades* < Gr〛 an open cluster of more than 200 stars in the constellation Taurus, whose five brightest members form a V near Aldebaran

**Hyde Park** (hīd) **1** public park in London, noted for the public discussions on current issues that take place there **2** 〚after the London park〛 village in SE N.Y., on the Hudson: site of the estate & burial place of Franklin D. Roosevelt

**Hy·der·a·bad** (hī′dər ə bad′, -bäd′; hī′drə-) **1** city in SC India: capital of Andhra Pradesh state: pop. 2,500,000 **2** city in S Pakistan, on the Indus River: pop. 795,000 **3** former state of SC India

**Hy·dra** (hī′drə) 〚ME *ydre* (< OFr < L), *ydra* < L *Hydra* < Gr, water serpent〛 a long S constellation between Cancer and Libra: the largest constellation

**Hy·drus** (hī′drəs) 〚L < Gr *hydros*, water snake〛 a S constellation near the celestial pole

**Hy·met·tus** (hī met′əs) mountain range in EC Greece, near Athens: highest peak, 3,367 ft. (1,027 m)

**Hy·pe·ri·on** (hī pir′ē ən) 〚L < Gr *Hyperiōn*〛 a small, irregularly shaped satellite of Saturn having an unusual shifting orientation and rotation

**Hyr·ca·ni·a** (hər kā′nē ə) province of the ancient Persian & Macedonian empires, on the S & SE coast of the Caspian Sea

**I**

**IA, Ia** *abbrev. for* Iowa

**I·a·pe·tus** (ī ā′pə təs, ē-) a satellite of Saturn having an extreme contrast of low and high reflectiveness on its leading and trailing sides

**Ia·şi** (yäsh, yä′shē) city in NE Romania: pop. 265,000

**I·ba·dan** (ē bä′dän′) city in SW Nigeria: pop. 847,000

**I·be·ri·a** (ī bir′ē ə) 〚L〛 **1** ancient region in the S Caucasus, in what is now Georgia 2 IBERIAN PENINSULA

**Iberian Peninsula** peninsula in SW Europe, comprising Spain & Portugal

**I·çá** (ē sä′) *Brazilian name of* PUTUMAYO

**I·car·i·a** (ī ker′ē ə, i-) Greek island in the Aegean Sea, southwest of Samos: 99 sq. mi. (256 sq. km)

**Icarian Sea** *old name for* the S part of the Aegean Sea, between the Cyclades & Asia Minor

**Ice·land** (īs′lənd) **1** island in the North Atlantic, southeast of Greenland **2** country including this island & a few small nearby islands: settled by Norwegians in 9th cent. A.D.; united with Norway (1262), with Denmark (1380); became independent kingdom with a common sovereign with Denmark (1918), and an independent republic (1944): 39,768 sq. mi. (102,998 sq. km); pop. 240,000; cap. Reykjavik

**I·chi·ka·wa** (ē chē′kä wä′) city in SE Honshu, Japan, east of Tokyo: pop. 382,000

**I·chi·no·mi·ya** (ē′chē nō′mē yä′) city in SE Honshu, Japan, northwest of Nagoya: pop. 254,000

**I·co·ni·um** (ī kō′nē əm) *Latin name of* KONYA

**ID, Id** *abbrev. for* Idaho

**I·da** (ī′də) **1 Mount** highest mountain in Crete, in the central part: 8,058 ft. (2,456 m) **2 Mount** mountain in NW Asia Minor, in ancient Phrygia & Mysia near the site of Troy: *c.* 5,800 ft. (1,767 m): Turk. name KAZ-DAĞI

**Ida** *abbrev. for* Idaho

**I·da·ho** (ī′də hō′) 〚< tribal (Shoshonean) name < ?〛 Mountain State of the NW U.S.: admitted, 1890; 83,557 sq. mi. (217,248 sq. km); pop. 1,007,000; cap. Boise: abbrev. *ID, Id,* or *Ida*

**Idaho Falls** city in SE Ida., on the Snake River: pop. 44,000

**Id·u·mae·a, Id·u·me·a** (id′yōō mē′ə, i′jōō-; ī′dyōō-, ī′jōō-) *Gr. name of* EDOM

**Ie·per** (ē′pər) *Fl. name of* YPRES

**I·fe** (ē′fā′) city in SW Nigeria, near Ibadan: pop. 176,000

**If·ni** (ēf′nē) former Spanish province in NW Africa, ceded to Morocco in 1969: 580 sq. mi. (1,500 sq. km)

**I·gua·çú** (ē′gwä sōō′) river in S Brazil, flowing into the Paraná River on the border of NE Argentina: *c.* 800 mi. (1,290 km): contains **Iguacu Falls,** *c.* 2.5 mi. (3.5 km) wide, composed of more than 200 cataracts averaging 200 ft. (61 m) in height: also sp. **I'gua·zú'** or **I'guas·sú'**

**IJs·sel** (i'səl) river in the E Netherlands, flowing from the Rhine north into the IJsselmeer: 72 mi. (115 km): also sp. **Ijs'sel** or **Ij'sel**

**IJs·sel·meer** (-mer') shallow freshwater lake in N & central Netherlands: formerly part of the Zuider Zee, until cut off by a dam (1932): also sp. **Ijs'sel·meer'** or **Ij'sel·meer'**

**Il** *abbrev. for* Illinois

**Île-de-France** (ēl də fräns') **1** historical region of NC France, surrounding Paris **2** metropolitan region of modern France, in the same general area; 4,637 sq. mi. (12,012 sq. km); pop. 10,147,000; chief city, Paris

**Île du Dia·ble** (ēl dü dyȧ'bl') *Fr. name of* DEVIL'S ISLAND

**Il·i·am·na** (il'ē am'nə) ⟦ < Esk: named for a mythical great fish of the lake ⟧ lake in SW Alas., at the base of the Alaska Peninsula: 1,000 sq. mi. (2,589 sq. km)

**Il·i·um** (il'ē əm) ⟦ L < Gr *Ilios* ⟧ Latin name for TROY

**Ill** *abbrev. for* Illinois

**I·llam·pu** (ē yäm'pōō') mountain of the Andes, in WC Bolivia: highest peak, *c.* 21,500 ft. (6,553 m)

**I·lli·ma·ni** (ē'yē mä'nē) mountain of the Andes, in WC Bolivia: *c.* 21,200 ft. (6,461 m)

**Il·li·nois** (il'ə noi'; *occas.*, -noiz') ⟦ Fr, earlier also *Ilinoués* < name in an unidentified Algonquian language: perhaps orig. meaning ordinary speaker ⟧ **1** Middle Western State of the U.S.: admitted 1818; 56,400 sq. mi. (146,640 sq. km); pop. 11,431,000; cap. Springfield: abbrev. *IL* or *Ill* **2** river in Ill., flowing from southwest of Chicago into the Mississippi, near St. Louis: *c.* 273 mi. (437 km)

**Il·lyr·i·a** (i lir'ē ə) ancient region along the E coast of the Adriatic

**Il·lyr·i·cum** (i lir'i kəm) Roman province including Illyria; later, Roman prefecture including much of the Balkan Peninsula & some of the area north of the Adriatic

**I·lo·i·lo** (ē'lō ē'lō) seaport on S Panay, in the Philippines: pop. 245,000

**Im·pe·ri·al Valley** (im pir'ē əl) a rich agricultural region in S Calif. & N Baja California, Mexico, reclaimed from the Colorado Desert

**Imp·hal** (imp'hul') city in NE India: capital of Manipur state: pop. 156,000

**IN, In** *abbrev. for* Indiana

**In·chon** (in'chän') seaport in NW South Korea, on the Yellow Sea: pop. 1,295,000

**Ind** (ind) ⟦ME & OFr *Inde* < L *India*⟧ 1 [Old Poet.] India 2 [Obs.] the Indies

**Ind** *abbrev. for* Indiana

**In·de·pend·ence** (in'dē pen'dəns, -di-)' ⟦in honor of Andrew Jackson (1767-1845), U.S. president, in allusion to his *independence* of character⟧ city in W Mo.: suburb of Kansas City: pop. 112,000

**In·di·a** (in'dē ə) ⟦L < Gr < *Indos*, the Indus < OPers *Hindu*, India⟧ 1 region in S Asia, south of the Himalayas, including a large peninsula between the Arabian Sea & the Bay of Bengal: it contains India (the republic), Pakistan, Bangladesh, Nepal, & Bhutan 2 republic in central & S India: established by Act of British Parliament (1947), became a republic (1950): a member of the Commonwealth: 1,269,000 sq. mi. (3,287,590 sq. km); pop. 783,940,000; cap. New Delhi: see also JAMMU AND KASHMIR 3 INDIAN EMPIRE

**In·di·an·a** (in'dē an'ə) ⟦ModL, "land of the Indians"⟧ Middle Western State of the U.S.: admitted, 1816; 36,291 sq. mi. (94,357 sq. km); pop. 5,544,000; cap. Indianapolis: abbrev. *IN, In,* or *Ind*

**In·di·an·ap·o·lis** (in'dē ə nap'ə lis) ⟦INDIANA + Gr *polis*, city⟧ capital of Ind., in the central part of the State: pop. 742,000 (met. area 1,250,000; urban area with Anderson 1,380,000)

**Indian Desert** THAR DESERT

**Indian Empire** formerly, territories in & near India, under British control: dissolved in 1947

**Indian Ocean** ocean south of Asia, between Africa & Australia: 28,356,000 sq. mi. (73,441,000 sq. km)

**Indian States and Agencies** [Historical] the group of partly independent states and agencies of British India

**Indian Territory** [Historical] territory (1834-90) of the S U.S., reserved for Amerindian peoples: now a part of Oklahoma

**In·dies** (in'dēz') 1 [Historical] EAST INDIES 2 WEST INDIES 3 formerly, Southeast Asia & the Malay Archipelago

**In·do·chi·na** (in′dō chī′nə) **1** large peninsula south of China, including Myanmar, Thailand, Laos, Cambodia, Vietnam, & Malaya **2** E part of this peninsula, formerly under French control, consisting of Laos, Cambodia, & Vietnam   Also sp. **In′do–Chi′na** or **Indo China**

**In·do·ne·sia** (in′də nē′zhə, -shə) republic in the Malay Archipelago, consisting of Java, Sumatra, most of Borneo, West Irian, Celebes, & many smaller nearby islands: formerly, until 1945, the Netherlands East Indies, an overseas territory of the Netherlands: 736,510 sq. mi. (1,907,500 sq. km); pop. 176,764,000; cap. Jakarta

**In·dore** (in dôr′) **1** city in Madhya Pradesh, central India: pop. 827,000 **2** former state of central India

**In·dus**[1] (in′dəs) ⟦L, the Indian⟧ a S constellation between Pavo and Gʀus

**In·dus**[2] (in′dəs) river in S Asia, rising in SW Tibet and flowing west across Jammu and Kashmir, India, then southwest through Pakistan into the Arabian Sea: *c.* 1,900 mi. (3,060 km)

**in·fer·no** (in fur′nō′) ⟦It < L *infernus*, underground, lower, infernal < *inferus*, low, below < IE *\*ṇdheros* < base *\*ṇdhos*, under⟧ hell or any place suggesting hell, usually characterized by great heat or flames

**In·gle·wood** (iŋ′gəl wood′) ⟦after the home town in Canada of a relative of one of the promoters⟧ city in SW Calif.: suburb of Los Angeles: pop. 110,000

**Inland Passage** Inside Passage

**Inland Sea** arm of the Pacific surrounded by the Japanese islands of Honshu, Shikoku, & Kyushu

**Inn** (in) river flowing from E Switzerland, across W Austria & SE Bavaria, into the Danube: *c.* 320 mi. (512 km)

**Inner Hebrides** *see* Hebrides

**Inner Mongolia** region in NE China, south & southeast of the Mongolian People's Republic, comprising mainly the **Inner Mongolian Autonomous Region**, 456,757 sq. mi. (1,183,000 sq. km); pop. 19,274,000; cap. Hohhot

**Inner Temple** *see* Inns of Court

**Inns·bruck** (inz′brook′; *Ger* ins′brook) city in the Tyrol region, W Austria, on the Inn River: pop. 117,000

**Inns of Court** the four groups of buildings (*Gray's Inn,*

*Lincoln's Inn, Inner Temple,* and *Middle Temple*) belonging to the four legal societies in London having the exclusive right to admit persons to practice at the bar

**Inside Passage** protected sea route along the W coast of North America, from Seattle, Wash., to the N part of the Alas. panhandle: the route uses channels and straits between islands and the mainland: *c.* 950 mi. (1,530 km) long

**In·ter·lak·en** (in'tər lä'kən) resort town in the Bernese Alps, central Switzerland, on the Aar River: pop. 13,000

**international date line** [*often* I- D- L-] an imaginary line drawn north and south through the Pacific Ocean, largely along the 180th meridian: at this line, by international agreement, each calendar day begins at midnight, so that when it is Sunday just west of the line, it is Saturday just east of it

**In·tra·coast·al Waterway** (in'trə kōs'təl) waterway for small craft extending in two sections from Boston, Mass., to Brownsville, Tex.: it consists of natural and artificial channels within the U.S. coastline except for a stretch of open water along the W Fla. coast: 2,500 to 3,000 mi. (4,000 to 4,900 km) long

**In·u·vik** (in'ōō vik, -yōō-) Region of W Northwest Territories, Canada: 152,130 sq. mi. (394,015 sq. km)

**In·ver·ness** (in'vər nes') **1** former county of N Scotland, now part of the region of Highland: also **In'ver·ness'-shire** (-shir) **2** burgh at the head of Moray Firth: pop. 40,000

**I·o** (ī'ō', ē'ō') [[L < Gr *Iō*]] the third largest satellite of Jupiter: discovered in 1610 by Galileo and found to be volcanically active in 1979

**Io·an·ni·na** (yô ä'nē nä') city in Epirus, NW Greece: pop. 45,000

**I·o·ni·a** (ī ō'nē ə) ancient region in W Asia Minor, including a coastal strip & the islands of Samos & Khíos: colonized by the Greeks in the 11th cent. B.C.

**Ionian Islands** group of islands along the W coast of Greece, on the Ionian Sea: 891 sq. mi. (2,307 sq. km); pop. 183,000

**Ionian Sea** section of the Mediterranean, between Greece, Sicily, & the S part of the Italian peninsula

**I·o·wa** (ī'ə wə) [[Fr *ayoés,* earlier *aiou[h]ouea,* etc., prob.

via Illinois < Dakota *ayúxba*, lit., ? the sleepy ones ‖ 1
Middle Western State of NC U.S.: admitted, 1846;
56,290 sq. mi. (146,354 sq. km); pop. 2,777,000; cap.
Des Moines: abbrev. *IA* or *Ia* 2 river flowing from N
Iowa southeast into the Mississippi: *c.* 300 mi. (482
km)

**Iowa City** city in E Iowa: pop. 60,000

**I·poh** (ē′pō) city in Perak, NW Malaysia: pop. 248,000

**Ips·wich** (ip′swich) 1 river port in Suffolk, E England:
pop. 121,000 2 city in SE Queensland, Australia: pop.
68,000

**I·qui·que** (ē kē′ke) seaport in N Chile: pop. 113,000

**I·qui·tos** (ē kē′tôs) river port in NE Peru, on the Amazon: pop. 174,000

**I·rak·li·on** (ē räk′lē ôn′) seaport & largest city in Crete,
on the N coast: pop. 264,000

**I·ran** (i ran′, i rän′) 1 country in SW Asia, between the
Caspian Sea & the Persian Gulf: formerly an empire,
now an Islamic republic (1979): 636,296 sq. mi.
(1,648,000 sq. km); pop. 46,604,000; cap. Tehran:
former name PERSIA 2 **Plateau of** plateau extending
from the Tigris River to the Indus River, mostly in
Iran & Afghanistan

**I·raq** (i räk′, -rak′) country in SW Asia, at the head of
the Persian Gulf, coinciding more or less with ancient
Mesopotamia: formerly a kingdom, now a republic
(1958): 171,599 sq. mi. (444,439 sq. km); pop.
16,019,000; cap. Baghdad

**Ir·bil** (ur′bil) city in N Iraq, on the site of ancient
ARBELA: pop. 334,000

**Ire·land** (īr′lənd) ‖ OE *Īrland* < *Īra-land* < *Īras*, the
Irish (< OIr *Ériu*, Ireland) + *land*, land ‖ 1 island of
the British Isles, west of Great Britain: 32,595 sq. mi.
(84,420 sq. km) 2 republic comprising the S provinces
of this island & three counties of Ulster province:
established as a republic in 1922, it was a member of
the Commonwealth until 1949: 27,136 sq. mi. (70,282
sq. km); pop. 3,624,000; cap. Dublin: cf. NORTHERN
IRELAND

**Ir·i·an** (ir′ē än′) *Indonesian name of* NEW GUINEA: see
WEST IRIAN

**I·rish Free State** (ī′rish) *old name* (1922-37) *of* IRELAND
(the republic)

**Irish Sea** arm of the Atlantic between Ireland & Great

Britain

**Ir·kutsk** (ir kōōtsk′) city in S Asian Russia, near Lake Baikal: pop. 597,000

**I·ron·de·quoit** (i rän′də kwoit′, -kwät′) 〚< Seneca *onyiumdaondagwat*, lit., a turning aside from the lake〛 city in NW N.Y., near Rochester: pop. 52,000

**Ir·ra·wad·dy** (ir′ə wä′dē, -wô′-) river flowing from N Myanmar south into the Andaman Sea: *c.* 1,000 mi. (1,600 km)

**Ir·tysh** (ir tish′) river in central Asia, flowing from NW China, northwestward into the Ob: *c.* 1,850 mi. (2,970 km): also sp. **Ir·tish′**

**Ir·vine** (ʉr′vin′) 〚after the *Irvine* Company, the developers〛 city in SW Calif.: suburb of Los Angeles: pop. 110,000

**Ir·ving** (ʉr′viŋ) 〚prob. an arbitrary selection〛 city in NW Tex.: suburb of Dallas: pop. 155,000

**Ir·ving·ton** (ʉr′viŋ tən) 〚after Washington *Irving* (1783-1859), U.S. writer〛 town in NE N.J.: suburb of Newark: pop. 61,000

**Is·fa·han** (is′fä hän′) *var. of* ESFAHÁN

**I·sis** (ī′sis) *Eng. name of* the THAMES River, esp. at, & west of, Oxford

**Is·ken·de·run** (is ken′də rōōn′) seaport in S Turkey, on the Mediterranean: pop. 125,000

**Is·lam·a·bad** (is läm′ə bäd′) capital of Pakistan, in the NE part, near Rawalpindi: pop. 201,000

**Islands of the Blessed** *Gr. & Rom. Myth.* the islands of bliss in the Western Ocean, where heroes are sent after death

**Isle of France** ÎLE-DE-FRANCE

**Isle Roy·ale** (roi′əl) 〚Fr., lit., royal island〛 island in N Lake Superior: it is part of the State of Mich. and, with adjacent islets, constitutes a U.S. national park (**Isle Royale National Park**), 842 sq. mi. (2,180 sq. km)

**Is·ling·ton** (iz′liŋ tən) borough of N Greater London: pop. 165,200

**Is·ma·i·li·a** (is′mä ē lē′ä) city in NE Egypt: pop. 146,000

**Is·ra·el** (iz′rē əl, -rä-; *also* iz′rəl) **1** ancient land of the Hebrews at the SE end of the Mediterranean **2** kingdom in the N part of this region, formed (10th cent. B.C.) by the ten tribes of Israel that broke with Judah & Benjamin **3** country between the Mediterranean Sea & Jordan: established (1948) as a Jewish state according to the United Nations plan (1947) partitioning Palestine into Arab and Jewish states: 7,992 sq. mi. (20,699 sq. km); pop. 4,208,000; cap. Jerusalem

**Is·sus** (is'əs) ancient town in Cilicia, in SE Asia Minor: site of a battle (333 B.C.) in which Alexander the Great defeated Darius III of Persia

**Is·syk Kul** (is'ik kool') mountain lake in E Kyrgyzstan: *c.* 2,400 sq. mi. (6,216 sq. km): also **Issyk–Kul**

**Is·tan·bul** (is'tan bool', -tän-; -bool; *Turk* is täm'bool) [ altered < ModGr *'s ten poli* < Gr *eis tēn polin,* lit., into the city ] seaport in NW Turkey, on both sides of the Bosporus: pop. 2,773,000: old name CONSTANTINO-PLE: ancient name BYZANTIUM

**Is·tri·a** (is'trē ə) peninsula in W Slovenia & Croatia, projecting into the N Adriatic, formerly including part of the area around Trieste: also **Istrian Peninsula**

**I·tal·ia** (ē täl'yä) *It. name of* ITALY

**I·tal·ian East Africa** (i tal'yən) former Italian colony in E Africa, consisting of Ethiopia, Eritrea, & Italian Somaliland

**Italian Somaliland** former Italian colony on the E coast of Africa: merged with British Somaliland to form Somalia

**It·a·ly** (it''l ē) [ L *Italia,* altered, prob. by Greeks living in S Italy < earlier (prob. Oscan) *Víteliú;* orig. used only of the SW point of the peninsula ] country in S Europe mostly on a peninsula extending into the Mediterranean & including Sicily, Sardinia, and numerous other islands: formerly a kingdom created by the unification of various Italian monarchies & states (1861), became a republic (1946): 116,304 sq. mi. (301,223 sq. km); pop. 57,226,000; cap. Rome: It. name ITALIA

**I·tas·ca** (i tas'kə), **Lake** [ coined by Henry Rowe Schoolcraft (1793-1864), U.S. ethnologist < L (*ver*)*itas,* truth + *ca*(*put*), head, in ref. to other alleged sources ] lake in NW Minn., a source of the Mississippi: *c.* 2 sq. mi. (5.7 sq. km)

**I·té·nez** (ē tä'nes) *Bolivian name of* GUAPORÉ

**Ith·a·ca** (ith'ə kə) **1** one of the Ionian Islands, off the W coast of Greece: legendary home of Odysseus: 37 sq. mi. (95.8 sq. km): Gr. name **I·thá·ki** (ē thä'kē) **2** [ after the Ionian island ] city in WC N.Y., on Cayuga Lake: pop. 30,000

**Iva·no–Fran·kovsk** (i vän'ə frän kôfsk') city in SW

Ukraine: pop. 210,000

**I·va·no·vo** (ē vä′nô̂ vô̂) city in central European Russia: pop. 474,000

**Ivory Coast** 1 country in WC Africa, on the Gulf of Guinea, west of Ghana: formerly a French territory, it became independent (1960): 124,500 sq. mi. (322,463 sq. km); pop. 10,500,000; cap. Yamoussoukro 2 [Historical] the African coast in this region

**I·wa·ki** (i wäk′ē) city of NE Honshu, northeast of Tokyo: pop. 327,000

**I·wo** (ē′wō) city in SW Nigeria: pop. 214,000

**I·wo Ji·ma** (ē′wō jē′mə, ē′wə-) small island of the Volcano Islands in the W Pacific: captured from the Japanese by U.S. forces in World War II (1945); returned to Japan (1968); c. 8 sq. mi. (20.7 sq. km)

**Ix·ta·ci·huatl** (ēs′tä sē′wät′l) volcanic mountain in central Mexico, southeast of Mexico City: 17,343 ft. (5,286 m): also sp. **Ix′tac·ci′huatl** or **Iz′tac·ci′huatl**

**I·zhevsk** (i zhefsk′) city in EC European Russia: pop. 611,000

**Iz·mir** (iz mir′) seaport in W Turkey on the Aegean Sea: pop. 758,000: former name SMYRNA

**Iz·mit** (iz mit′) city & seaport in NW Turkey in Asia, on an inlet of the Sea of Marmara: pop. 191,000

# J

**Ja·bal·pur** (jub′əl poor′) city in central India, in Madhya Pradesh: pop. 758,000

**Jack·son** (jak′sən) 〚after Andrew *Jackson* (1767-1845), U.S. president〛 1 capital of Miss., in the SW part, on the Pearl River: pop. 197,000 (met. area 395,000) 2 city in W Tenn.: pop. 49,000

**Jack·son·ville** (jak′sən vil′) 〚after Andrew *Jackson* (1767-1845), U.S. president〛 port in NE Fla., on the St. Johns River: pop. 673,000 (met. area 907,000)

**Ja·dot·ville** (zhȧ dō vēl′) *old name of* LIKASI

**Jaf·fa** (yäf′ə, jaf′ə) seaport in central Israel: since 1950, incorporated with Tel Aviv

**Jaff·na** (jaf′nə) seaport in N Sri Lanka: pop. 118,000

**Jai·pur** (jī′poor′) 1 city in NW India: capital of Rajasthan state: pop. 1,005,000 2 former state of NW India: since 1950, included in Rajasthan state

**Ja·kar·ta** (jə kär′tə) capital of Indonesia, on the NW

coast of Java: pop. *c.* 6,500,000

**Ja·la·pa** (hä lä′pä) city in E Mexico: capital of Veracruz state: pop. 66,000: official name **Jalapa En·ri·quez** (en rē′kes)

**Ja·lis·co** (hä lēs′kô) state of W Mexico, on the Pacific: 31,258 sq. mi. (80,957 sq. km); pop. 4,371,000; cap. Guadalajara

**Ja·mai·ca** (jə mā′kə) country on an island in the West Indies, south of Cuba: a former colony, it became independent & a member of the Commonwealth (1962): 4,243 sq. mi. (10,991 sq. km); pop. 2,288,000; cap. Kingston

**James** (jāmz) **1** river in Va., flowing from the W part southeast into Chesapeake Bay: 340 mi. (547 km) **2** river in E N.Dak. & E S.Dak., flowing south into the Missouri: 710 mi. (1,143 km)

**James Bay** arm of Hudson Bay, extending south into NE Ontario & NW Quebec: *c.* 275 mi. (442 km) long

**James·town** (jāmz′toun′) 〚after *James* I (1566-1625) of England〛 **1** former village near the mouth of the James River, Va.: the 1st permanent English colonial settlement in America (1607) **2** city in SW N.Y.: pop. 35,000

**Jam·mu** (jum′ōō) **1** city in SW Jammu and Kashmir, India: winter capital of the state: pop. 135,000 **2** former kingdom in N India: merged with Kashmir, 1846

**Jammu and Kashmir** state of N India: its control is disputed by Pakistan, which occupies *c.* 27,000 sq. mi. (72,932 sq. km) in the NW part: NE border areas in Indian territory are occupied by China: 16,500 sq. mi. (42,735 sq. km): 85,805 sq. mi. (222,236 sq. km); pop. 5,987,000 in section controlled by India; caps. Srinagar and Jammu

**Jam·na·gar** (jäm nug′ər) city in W Gujarat state, W India: pop. 317,000

**Jam·shed·pur** (jum′shed poor′) city in NE India, in Bihar state: pop. 670,000

**Janes·ville** (jānz′vil) 〚after H. F. *Janes,* early settler〛 city in S Wis.: pop. 52,000

**Ja·ni·na** (yä′nē nä′) *Serb. name of* IOANNINA

**Jan May·en** (yän mī′ən) Norwegian island in the Arctic Ocean, between Greenland & N Norway: site of a meteorological station: 145 sq. mi. (375.5 sq. km)

**Ja·nus** (jā′nəs) [[L, lit., gate, arched passageway < IE base \*yǎ-, var. of \*ei-, to go ]] a small satellite of Saturn

**Ja·pan** (jə pan′) **1** island country in the Pacific, off the E coast of Asia, including Hokkaido, Honshu, Kyushu, Shikoku, & many smaller islands: 143,750 sq. mi. (372,313 sq. km); pop. 121,402,000; cap. Tokyo: Jpn. names NIHON, NIPPON **2 Sea of** arm of the Pacific, between Japan & E Asia: c. 405,000 sq. mi. (1,048,945 sq. km)

**Japan Current** a fast, warm ocean current flowing northeast from the Philippine Sea east of Taiwan: it moves along the southern coast of Japan

**Ja·pu·rá** (zhä′poo rä′) river in S Colombia & NW Brazil, flowing southeast into the Amazon: c. 1,500 mi. (2,413 km)

**Jas·per National Park** (jas′pər) Canadian national park in SW Alberta, in the E Rockies: 4,200 sq. mi. (10,877 sq. km)

**Jas·sy** (yä′sē) var. of IAŞI

**Ja·va** (jä′və, jav′ə) large island of Indonesia, southeast of Sumatra: 49,995 sq. mi. (129,486 sq. km); pop. (with Madura) 91,270,000

**Java Sea** part of the Pacific, between Java & Borneo: c. 600 mi. (961.8 km) long

**Ja·wa** (jä′və) Indonesian name of JAVA

**Jax·ar·tes** (jaks ärt′ēz′) ancient name of SYR DARYA

**Ja·ya·pu·ra** (jä′yə poor′ə) capital of West Irian, Indonesia: seaport on the NE coast; pop. 149,000

**Je·bel Druze** (jeb′əl drōōz) region in S Syria, on the N Jordan border, inhabited by the Druses: 2,584 sq. mi. (6,692 sq. km): also **Jebel ed Druz** (ed)

**Jebel Mu·sa** (mōō′sə) mountain in N Morocco, opposite Gibraltar: c. 2,700 ft. (822 m): cf. PILLARS OF HERCULES

**Jef·fer·son City** (jef′ər sən) [[after Thomas Jefferson ]] capital of Mo., on the Missouri River: pop. 35,000

**Je·hol** (jə hōl′) former province of NE China: divided (1955) between Hebei & Liaoning provinces & Inner Mongolia

**Je·na** (yā′nä′) city in central Germany, in the state of Thuringia: site of a battle (1806) in which the Prussian forces were routed by Napoleon: pop. 107,000

**Je·rez de la Fron·te·ra** (he reth′ the lä frôn te′rä) city in SW Spain, near Cádiz: noted for the sherry made there: pop. 176,000: also **Jerez**

**Jer·i·cho** (jer′i kō′) city in W Jordan, just north of the Dead Sea: site of an ancient Canaanite city whose walls, according to the Bible, were miraculously destroyed when trumpets were sounded: Josh. 6

**Jer·sey** (jʉr′zē) largest of the Channel Islands of the United Kingdom, 15 mi. (24 km) from the coast of France: 45 sq. mi. (117 sq. km); pop. 77,000

**Jersey City** ⟦after NEW JERSEY⟧ city in NE N.J., across the Hudson from New York City: pop. 229,000 (met. area 553,000)

**Je·ru·sa·lem** (jə rōōz′ə ləm, -rōō′sə-; -lem) capital of Israel (the country) in the central part: divided (1948-67) between Israel & Jordan: since 1967 Israel holds entire city and environs: pop. *c.* 250,000

**Jer·vis Bay** (jär′vis) inlet of the Pacific, on the SE coast of New South Wales, Australia: peninsula on its S shore is a detached part of Australian Capital Territory

**Jes·sel·ton** (jes′əl tən) *old name of* KOTA KINABALU

**Jez·re·el** (jez rē′əl, -rēl′) **1** ancient town in N Israel, on the plain of Esdraelon **2** Plain of ESDRAELON

**Jhan·si** (jän′sē) city in S Uttar Pradesh, N India: pop. 281,000

**Jhe·lum** (jā′ləm) river in India, flowing from the Himalayas in Kashmir through Pakistan into the Chenab: *c.* 480 mi. (772 km)

**Ji·ang·su** (jē äŋ′sōō′) province of SE China: 39,459 sq. mi. (102,198 sq. km); pop. 60,500,000; cap. Nanjing

**Ji·ang·xi** (-sē′) province of SE China: 63,629 sq. mi. (164,800 sq. km); pop. 33,185,000; cap. Nanchang

**Jid·da** (jid′ə) seaport in Hejaz, Saudi Arabia, on the Red Sea: pop. 561,000: also **Jed·da** (jed′ə)

**Ji·lin** (jē′lin′) **1** province of NE China: 72,201 sq. mi. (187,000 sq. km); pop. 212,502,000; cap. Changchun **2** city in this province, on the Songhua River: pop. 1,071,000

**Ji·nan** (jē′nän′) city in NE China: capital of Shandong province: pop. 1,333,000

**Jin·zhou** (jin′jō′) city in Liaoning province, NE China, at the head of Bo Hai; pop. 712,000

**Jo·ão Pes·so·a** (zhōō oun′ pə sō′ə) city in NE Brazil: capital of Paraíba state: pop. 291,000

**Jodh·pur** (jōd′poȯr′, jäd′-) **1** city in Rajasthan, NW

India: pop. 494,000 **2** former state of NW India, now part of Rajasthan

**Jog·ja·kar·ta** (jäg'yə kärt'ə) *var. of* YOGYAKARTA

**Jo·han·nes·burg** (jō han'is bʉrg', yō hän'is-) city in the Transvaal, NE South Africa: pop. 1,156,000

**John Bull** ⟦title character in John Arbuthnot's *History of John Bull* (1712)⟧ *personification of* England or an Englishman

**John·son City** (jän'sən) ⟦after H. *Johnson* (1809-74), early settler & first mayor⟧ city in NE Tenn., near the borders of Va. & N.C.: pop. 49,000 (urban area with nearby Va. 436,000)

**Johns·town** (jänz'toun') ⟦after Joseph *Johns*, owner of the town site⟧ city in SW Pa.: site of a disastrous flood (1889): pop. 28,000

**Jo·hore** (jə hôr') state of Malaysia, at the tip of the Malay Peninsula: 7,330 sq. mi. (18,985 sq. km); pop. 1,602,000

**Jok·ja·kar·ta** (jäk'yə kärt'ə) *var. of* YOGYAKARTA

**Jo·li·et** (jō'lē et', jō'lē et') ⟦after Louis *Joliet* (1645-1700), Fr-Cdn explorer⟧ city in NE Ill.: pop. 77,000

**Jo·lo** (hō lō', hō'lō') island in the Philippines, southwest of Mindanao: largest island in Sulu Archipelago: 345 sq. mi. (897 sq. km)

**Jon·quière** (zhōn kyer') ⟦after J. P. Taffanel, Marquis de la *Jonquière* (1685-1752), gov. of New France (1749-52)⟧ city in SC Quebec, Canada: pop. 58,000

**Jop·lin** (jäp'lin) ⟦after Rev. H. G. *Joplin*, first settler⟧ city in SW Mo.: pop. 41,000

**Jop·pa** (jäp'ə) *ancient name of* JAFFA

**Jor·dan** (jôrd'n) **1** river in the Near East, flowing from the Anti-Lebanon mountains south through the Sea of Galilee, through Jordan, into the Dead Sea: 200 mi. (322 km) **2** country in the Near East, east of Israel: 35,000 sq. mi. (90,650 sq. km); pop. 2,756,000; cap. Amman: official name **the Hashemite Kingdom of Jordan**

**Jo·tunn·heim, Jo·tun·heim** (yō'toon häm) ⟦ON *jǫtunheimar*, pl. < *jǫtunn* + *heimr*, home⟧ *Norse Myth.* the home of the giants

**Juan de Fu·ca Strait** (wän də fōōk'ə, -fyōōk'ə) ⟦after *Juan de Fuca*, a sailor, who reputedly discovered it for Spain (1592)⟧ strait between Vancouver Island and NW Wash.: *c.* 100 mi. (161 km) long: also called **Strait**

of Juan de Fuca

**Juan Fer·nán·dez Islands** (hwän′ fer nan′dez′) group of three islands in the South Pacific, *c.* 400 mi. (643 km) west of, & belonging to, Chile: *c.* 70 sq. mi. (181 sq. km)

**Juárez** *see* CIUDAD JUÁREZ

**Ju·ba** (jōō′bə) river in Africa, flowing from S Ethiopia south through Somalia into the Indian Ocean: *c.* 1,000 mi. (1,609 km)

**Ju·dah** (jōō′də) 〚Heb *yehūdhāh*, lit., praised〛 the kingdom in the S part of Palestine formed by the tribes of Judah and Benjamin after they broke with the other ten tribes: 1 Kings 11:31; 12: 17-21

**Ju·de·a** (jōō dē′ə) ancient region of S Palestine under Persian, Greek, & Roman rule: it corresponded roughly to the Biblical Judah

**Ju·go·sla·vi·a** (yōō′gō slä′vē ə) *alt. sp. of* YUGOSLAVIA

**Jul·ian Alps** (jōōl′yən, -ē ən) SE range of the Alps, mostly in Slovenia: highest peak, 9,395 ft. (2,863 m)

**Jul·lun·dur** (jul′ən dər) city in N India, in Punjab state: pop. 406,000

**Jum·na** (jum′nə) river in N India, flowing from the Himalayas southwest into the Ganges in SE Uttar Pradesh state: 860 mi. (1,384 km)

**Ju·neau** (jōō′nō′) 〚after J. *Juneau,* a prospector〛 capital of Alas.: seaport on the SE coast: pop. 27,000

**Jung·gar Pen·di** (zhooŋ′gär′ pen′dē) region in N Xinjiang-Uygur, China, between the Tian Shan & the Altai Mountains

**Ju·pi·ter** (jōō′pit ər) 〚L *Juppiter,* orig. a voc. < bases of *Jovis,* Jove & *pater,* father〛 the largest planet of the solar system and the fifth in distance from the sun: it has a ring composed of microscopic dustlike particles: diameter, *c.* 142,800 km (*c.* 88,740 mi.); period of revolution, 11.86 earth years; period of rotation, 9.92 hours; 16 satellites; symbol, ♃

**Ju·ra** (joor′ə) **1** canton in W Switzerland: 323 sq. mi. (837 sq. km); pop. 70,000 **2** mountain range along the border of Switzerland & France: highest peak, 5,652 ft.: also called **Jura Mountains**

**Ju·ruá** (zhoor wä′) river flowing from the Andes in Peru northeast across NW Brazil into the Amazon: *c.* 1,200 mi. (1,931 km)

**Jut·land** (jut′lənd) peninsula of N Europe, that forms

the mainland of Denmark & the N part of the German
state of Schleswig-Holstein
**Jyl·land** (yül'län) *Dan. name of* JUTLAND

# K

**Kaa·ba** (kä'bə, kä'ə bə) 〚Ar *kaʕba,* lit., square building
< *kaʕb,* a cube 〛 the sacred Muslim shrine at Mecca,
toward which believers turn when praying: it contains
a black stone venerated as holy

**Ka·bul** (kä'bool') capital of Afghanistan, in the NE part:
pop. 913,000

**Ka·desh** (kä'desh') oasis in the desert, south of Palestine: Gen. 14:7, 16:14; Num. 32:8; Deut. 1:46, 2:14

**Kâ·ği·tha·ne** (kä'yi tä'nä) city in NW Turkey: suburb of
Istanbul: pop. 175,000

**Ka·go·shi·ma** (kä'gō shē'mä) seaport on the S coast of
Kyushu, Japan: pop. 517,000

**Ka·ho·o·la·we** (kä hō'ō lä'wä, -vä) 〚Haw *Ka-ho'olawe,*
lit., the carrying away (by currents) 〛 island of Hawaii,
southwest of Maui: 45 sq. mi. (117 sq. km)

**Kai·e·teur Falls** (kī'ə toor') waterfall in WC Guyana: 741
ft. (226 m) high

**Kair·ouan** (ker wän') city in NE Tunisia: holy city of
the Muslims: pop. 72,000

**Ka·la·ha·ri** (kä'lä hä'rē) desert plateau in S Africa,
mostly in Botswana: *c.* 350,000 sq. mi. (906,490 sq.
km)

**Kal·a·ma·zoo** (kal'ə mə zōō') 〚< Fr < Ojibwa < ? 〛 city
in SW Mich.: pop. 80,000

**Ka·lat** (kə lät') division of Baluchistan, Pakistan, former
state of W British India: 99,000 sq. mi. (256,400 sq.
km)

**Kal·gan** (käl'gän') *old name of* ZHANGJIAKOU

**Ka·li·man·tan** (kä'lē män'tän') S part of the island of
Borneo, belonging to Indonesia: 208,286 sq. mi.
(539,460 sq. km); pop. 6,723,000; chief city,
Banjermasin

**Ka·li·nin** (kä lē'nin) *old name of* TVER

**Ka·li·nin·grad** (-grät') seaport in W European Russia, on
the Baltic: pop. 385,000

**Ka·lisz** (kä'lish) city in central Poland: one of the oldest
Polish towns: pop. 81,000

**Kal·mar** (käl'mär') seaport in SE Sweden: pop. 53,000

**Ka·lu·ga** (kə lōō'gə) city in WC European Russia, on the Oka: pop. 297,000

**Ka·ma** (kä'mə) river in European Russia, flowing from the Urals southwest into the Volga: 1,262 mi. (2,030 km)

**Ka·ma·ku·ra** (käm'ə koor'ə) city in SE Honshu, Japan, southeast of Yokohama: site of Daibutsu, the great bronze figure of Buddha (cast 1252): pop. 174,000

**Kam·chat·ka** (käm chät'kə) peninsula in NE Siberia, between the Sea of Okhotsk & the Bering Sea: *c.* 750 mi. (1,206 km) long; 104,200 sq. mi. (269,876 sq. km)

**Ka·mensk–U·ral·ski** (kä'mensk' ōō räl'skē) city in W Asian Russia, in the Urals: pop. 200,000

**Kam·loops** (kam'lōōps') ⟦< ? AmInd⟧ city in S British Columbia, Canada; pop. 62,000

**Kam·pa·la** (käm pä'lə) capital of Uganda, in the S part near Lake Victoria: pop. 330,000

**Kam·pu·che·a** (kam'pōō chē'ə) *see* CAMBODIA

**Ka·na·za·wa** (kä'nə zä'wə) city in WC Honshu, Japan, on the Sea of Japan: pop. 414,000

**Kan·chen·jun·ga** (kän'chən jooŋ'gə) mountain in the E Himalayas, on the Nepal-Sikkim border: 3d highest in the world: 28,168 ft. (8,586 m)

**Kan·da·har** (kän'də här') city in S Afghanistan: pop. 115,000

**Kan·dy** (kan'dē, kän'-) city in central Sri Lanka: pop. 98,000

**Ka·no** (kä'nō) city in N Nigeria: pop. 399,000

**Kan·pur** (kän'poor') city in N India, on the Ganges, in Uttar Pradesh: pop. 1,688,000

**Kans** *abbrev. for* Kansas

**Kan·sas** (kan'zəs) ⟦Fr *kansa* (prob. via Illinois) < a Siouan name⟧ **1** Middle Western State of the NC U.S.: admitted, 1861; 82,264 sq. mi. (213,064 sq. km); pop. 2,478,000; cap. Topeka: abbrev. *KS* or *Kans* **2** river in NE Kans., flowing east into the Missouri at Kansas City: *c.* 170 mi. (273 km)

**Kansas City** ⟦after prec.⟧ **1** city in W Mo., on the Missouri River: pop. 435,000 **2** city in NE Kans., on the Missouri & Kansas rivers, opposite Kansas City, Mo.: pop. 150,000 (both cities are in a single met. area, pop. 1,566,000)

**Kan·su** (gän'sōō') *old form of* GANSU

**Kao·hsiung** (kou'shooŋ') seaport on the SW coast of

Taiwan: pop. 1,290,000

**Ka·ra·chi** (kə rä′chē) seaport in S Pakistan, on the Arabian Sea: former capital: pop. 5,103,000

**Ka·ra·de·niz Bo·ga·zi** (kä′rä deŋ ēz′ bō′gä zē′) *Turk. name of* BOSPORUS

**Ka·ra·fu·to** (kä′rä fōō′tō) *Jpn. name of* SAKHALIN

**Ka·ra·gan·da** (kä′rə gän′də) city in EC Kazakhstan: pop. 617,000

**Ka·ra·ko·ram** (kä′rä kôr′əm, kar′ə-) mountain range in SC Asia between Xinjiang-Uygur, China and N Kashmir, India, extending *c.* 300 mi. (480 km) to the Pamir: NW extension of the Himalayas: highest peak, GODWIN AUSTEN

**Ka·ra Kum** (kä *rä*′ kōōm′; *E* kar′ə-) desert in Turkmenistan, east of the Caspian Sea: *c.* 110,000 sq. mi. (284,900 sq. km)

**Ka·ra Sea** (kä′rə) arm of the Arctic Ocean, between Novaya Zemlya & NW Siberia

**Ka·re·li·a** (kə rēl′yə; *Russ* kä *rē*′lē ä) region in N Europe between the Gulf of Finland and the White Sea, constituting an autonomous republic (**Karelian A.S.S.R.**) of Russia: 66,500 sq. mi. (172,240 sq. km); pop. 769,000

**Karelian Isthmus** isthmus in Karelia, NW Russia, between the Gulf of Finland & Lake Ladoga: 90 mi. (145 km) long

**Ka·ri·ba Dam** (kə rē′bə) dam on the Zambezi River, on the Zambia-Zimbabwe border: 420 ft. (128 m) high: it has created a lake (**Kariba Lake**): 2,000 sq. mi. (5,180 sq. km)

**Karl-Marx-Stadt** (kärl′ märks′ shtät′) *name* (1953-90) *for* CHEMNITZ

**Kar·lo·vy Var·y** (kär′lô vē vä′rē) city in W Czech Republic, famous for its hot springs: pop. 60,000

**Karls·bad** (kärls′bät; *E* kärlz′bad) *Ger. name of* KARLOVY VARY

**Karls·ruh·e** (-rōō ə; *E*, -rōō ə) city in SW Germany, on the Rhine, in the state of Baden-Württemberg: pop. 268,000

**Kar·nak** (kär′nak′) village in S Egypt, on the Nile: site of ancient Thebes

**Kar·nat·a·ka** (kär nät′ə kə) state of SW India: 74,043 sq. mi. (191,773 sq. km); pop. 25,403,000; cap. Bangalore

**Kärn·ten** (kern′tən) *Ger. name of* CARINTHIA

**Ka·sai** (kä sī′) river in SC Africa, flowing from Angola

northwest into the Congo River: *c.* 1,100 mi. (1,770 km)

**Kash·mir** (kash′mir, kash mir′) **1** region in S Asia, between Afghanistan & Tibet: since 1846, part of Jammu & Kashmir **2** Jammu and Kashmir **3 Vale of** valley of the Jhelum River, in W Kashmir

**Kas·sel** (käs′əl) city in central Germany, in the state of Hesse: pop. 186,000

**Kat·mai** (kat′mī′) [[Russ < ?]] volcano in SW Alas.: *c.* 7,000 ft. (2,133 m): included in a volcanic region (**Katmai National Monument**) of the S Alaska Range, 4,215 sq. mi. (10,920 sq. km)

**Kat·man·du** (kät′män dōō′) capital of Nepal, in the central part: pop. 235,000: also sp. **Kath′man·du′**

**Ka·to·wi·ce** (kä′tô vē′tse) city in S Poland: pop. 361,000

**Kat·rine** (ka′trin, kä′-), **Loch** lake in central Scotland: scene of Sir Walter Scott's *Lady of the Lake*: 8 mi. (12.9 km) long

**Kat·te·gat** (kat′i gat′) strait between SW Sweden & E Jutland, Denmark: *c.* 150 mi. (241 km) long

**Ka·u·a·i** (kä′ōō ä′ē, kou′ī′) [[< Haw, prob. desert]] an island of Hawaii, northwest of Oahu: 551 sq. mi. (1,443 sq. km): pop. 51,000

**Kau·nas** (kou′näs′) city in SC Lithuania, on the Neman River: pop. 405,000

**Ka·vir Desert** (kə vir′) Dasht-e-Kavir

**Ka·wa·gu·chi** (kä′wä gōō′chē) city in E Honshu, Japan, north of Tokyo: pop. 396,000

**Ka·wa·sa·ki** (kä′wä sä′kē) city in central Honshu, Japan, on Tokyo Bay: pop. 1,050,000

**Kay·se·ri** (kī′se rē′) city in central Turkey: pop. 281,000

**Ka·zakh Soviet Socialist Republic** (kä zäk′) a republic of the U.S.S.R.: now Kazakhstan

**Ka·zakh·stan** (kä′zäk stän′) **1** Kazakh Soviet Socialist Republic **2** country in W Asia: became independent upon the breakup of the U.S.S.R. (1991): 1,048,000 sq. mi. (2,715,000 sq. km); pop. 15,000,000; cap. Alma-Ata: formerly, *Kazakh Soviet Socialist Republic*

**Ka·zan** (kä zän′; *Russ* kȧ zän′y′) city in W Russia, on the Volga: pop. 1,048,000

**Kaz·bek** (käz bek′) volcanic mountain in the central Caucasus, N Georgia: 16,558 ft. (5,047 m)

**Kaz·da·ği** (käz′dä gē′) *Turk. name of* Mount Ida

**Ke·a** (kā′ä) island of the NW Cyclades, Greece, in the

Aegean Sea: 60 sq. mi. (156 sq. km)

**Kecs·ke·mét** (kech′ke māt′) city in central Hungary: pop. 102,000

**Ke·dah** (kā′dä) state of Malaysia, in NW Peninsular Malaysia, bordering on Thailand: 3,660 sq. mi. (9,480 sq. km); pop. 1,102,000

**Ke·dron** (kē′drən) *alt. sp.* of KIDRON

**Kee·ling Islands** (kē′liŋ) COCOS ISLANDS

**Kee·lung** (kē′looŋ′) *var.* of CHILUNG

**Kee·wa·tin** (kē wät′′n) ⟦coined < Cree *kiiweetin*, the north, north wind, lit., the wind that comes back < *kiiwee-*, come back + *-tin*, wind⟧ Region of E Northwest Territories, Canada: 228,702 sq. mi. (592,335 sq. km): formerly the Keewatin District

**Ke·fal·li·ni·a** (kä′fä lē nē′ä) *Gr. name of* CEPHALONIA

**Ke·lan·tan** (kə län′tän′) state of Malaysia, in NE Peninsular Malaysia, bordering on Thailand: 5,750 sq. mi. (14,892 sq. km); pop. 878,000

**Ke·low·na** (kə lō′nə) ⟦< ? AmInd⟧ city in S British Columbia, Canada: pop. 70,000

**Ke·me·ro·vo** (kem′ə rō vō′, -və) city in SC Russia, in the Kuznetsk Basin: pop. 507,000

**Ke·nai Peninsula** (kē′nī′) peninsula in S Alas. between Cook Inlet & the main body of the Gulf of Alaska: *c.* 150 mi. (240 km) long: site of the **Kenai Fjords National Park**, containing numerous fjords, jagged cliffs, & one of the world's largest ice fields: 9,172 sq. mi. (26,232 sq. km)

**Ken·dall** (ken′dəl) ⟦< ?⟧ city on the SE coast of Fla.: suburb of Miami: pop. 87,000

**Ken·il·worth** (ken′əl wurth′) urban district in Warwickshire, England, near Coventry: site of the ruins of a major castle celebrated by Sir Walter Scott in his novel *Kenilworth*: pop. 19,000

**Ken·ne·bec** (ken′ə bek′) ⟦E Abenaki *kìnəpekw* < *kin-*, large + *əpekw*, body of water⟧ river in W Me., flowing into the Atlantic: *c.* 150 mi. (242 km)

**Ken·ne·dy** (ken′ə dē), **Cape** ⟦after U.S. Pres. John F. *Kennedy*⟧ *old name* (1963-73) *of* Cape CANAVERAL

**Ken·ner** (ken′ər) ⟦after the *Kenner* family, sugar planters who founded it (1853)⟧ city in SE La., on the Mississippi: suburb of New Orleans: pop. 72,000

**Ken·ne·saw Mountain** (ken′ə sô′) ⟦prob. < Cherokee; meaning unknown⟧ mountain in NW Ga.: scene of an unsuccessful attack by Sherman on Confederate forces (1864): 1,800 ft. (550 m)

**Ke·no·sha** (kə nō′shə) ⟦prob. ult. < Ojibwa *ginoozhe*, northern pike⟧ city in SE Wis., on Lake Michigan: pop. 80,000

**Ken·sing·ton and Chel·sea** (ken′ziŋ tən ənd chel′sē) borough of W Greater London: pop. 136,000

**Kent** (kent) county of SE England: formerly, an Anglo-Saxon kingdom (6th-9th cent. A.D.): 1,441 sq. mi. (3,732 sq. km); pop. 1,491,000; county seat, Maidstone

**Ken·tuck·y** (kən tuk′ē) ⟦earlier (18th c.) *Kentucke* (River), of Iroquois or Shawnee orig.⟧ 1 EC State of the U.S.: admitted, 1792; 40,395 sq. mi. (104,623 sq. km); pop. 3,685,000; cap. Frankfort: abbrev. *KY* or *Ky* 2 river in E Ky., flowing northwest into the Ohio: 259 mi. (415 km)

**Kentucky Lake** ⟦after the state⟧ reservoir in SW Ky. & W Tenn., on the Tennessee River: 247 sq. mi. (639 sq. km); 184 mi. (296 km) long

**Ken·ya** (ken′yə, kēn′-) 1 country in EC Africa, on the Indian Ocean: formerly a British crown colony & protectorate, it became independent & a member of the Commonwealth (1963): 224,960 sq. mi. (582,649 sq. km); pop. 21,044,000; cap. Nairobi 2 **Mount** volcanic mountain in central Kenya: 17,040 ft. (5,198 m)

**Ke·os** (kā′äs′) *var. of* KEA

**Ker·a·la** (ker′ə lə) state of SW India, on the Malabar Coast: 15,002 sq. mi. (38,855 sq. km); pop. 25,403,000; cap. Trivandrum

**Kerch** (kerch) seaport in W Crimea, on a strait (**Kerch Strait**) connecting the Black Sea & the Sea of Azov: pop. 168,000

**Ker·gue·len Islands** (kɐr′gə lən) group of French islands in the S Indian Ocean, consisting of one large island & over 300 small ones: 2,700 sq. mi. (6,992 sq. km)

**Kerk·ra·de** (kerk′rä′də) city in SE Netherlands, on the German border: pop. 53,000

**Kér·ky·ra** (ker′kē rä′) *Gr. name of* CORFU

**Ker·man** (ker män′) city in SE Iran: pop. 239,000

**Ker·man·shah** (ker′män shä′) *old name of* BAKHTARAN

**Ker·ry** (ker′ē) county in Munster province, SW Ireland: 1,815 sq. mi. (4,700 sq. km); pop. 120,000

**Ket·ter·ing** (ket′ər iŋ) ⟦after Charles Franklin *Kettering*

(1876-1958), U.S. inventor ] city in SW Ohio: suburb
of Dayton: pop. 61,000

**Kew** (kyōō) parish in NE Surrey, England: now part of
the Greater London borough of Richmond-on-
Thames: site of the Royal Botanic Gardens (**Kew Gardens**)

**Key Lar·go** (lär′gō) [[ Sp *Cayo Largo*, lit., long islet ]] largest island of the Florida Keys: *c.* 40 sq. mi. (104 sq.
km)

**Key·stone State** (kē′stōn′) *name for* PENNSYLVANIA:
from its central position among the 13 original colonies

**Key West** [[ Sp *Cayo Hueso*, lit., island of bones, for
human bones found there ]] **1** westernmost island of
the Florida Keys: *c.* 4 mi. (6.4 km) long **2** seaport on
this island: southernmost city in the U.S.: pop. 24,000

**Kha·ba·rovsk** (kä bä′rôfsk′) **1** territory in E Siberia:
965,400 sq. mi. (2,500,400 sq. km); pop. 1,345,000 **2**
capital of this territory, on the Amur River: pop.
576,000

**Khal·ki·di·ki** (khäl′ki *the*′kē) *Gr. name of* CHALCIDICE

**Khal·kis** (khäl kēs′) *Gr. name of* CHALCIS

**Kha·ni·a** (khä nyä′) *Gr. name of* CANEA

**Kha·rag·pur** (kar′əg pŏŏr′) city in SW West Bengal,
India: pop. 233,000

**Khar·kov** (kär′kôf) city in NE Ukraine: pop. 1,554,000

**Khar·toum** (kär tōōm′) capital of Sudan, on the Nile:
pop. 476,000

**Kher·son** (ker sôn′) port in S Ukraine, on the Dnepr
near its mouth: pop. 346,000

**Khin·gan Mountains** (shiŋ′än′) *see* DA HINGGAN LING,
XIAO HINGGAN LING

**Khi·os** (kē′ôs′) Greek island in the Aegean, off the W
coast of Turkey

**Khi·va** (kē′və) former khanate in central Asia

**Khy·ber Pass** (kī′bər) mountain pass in a range of the
Hindu Kush, between Afghanistan & Pakistan: *c.* 33
mi. (55 km) long

**Kiang·si** (jē än′sē′) *old form of* JIANGXI

**Kiang·su** (-sōō′) *old form of* JIANGSU

**Ki·dron** (kē′drən, kī′-, kī′-) **1** valley in Jordan, east of
Jerusalem **2** brook in this valley, flowing to the Dead
Sea

**Kiel** (kēl) seaport in N Germany, on the Kiel Canal:

capital of the state of Schleswig-Holstein: pop. 247,000

**Kiel Canal** canal in N Germany, connecting the North Sea & the Baltic Sea: 61 mi. (98 km)

**Kiel·ce** (kyel′sə) city in S Poland: pop. 197,000

**Ki·ev** (kē′ef′, -ev′) capital of Ukraine, on the Dnepr: pop. 2,448,000

**Ki·ga·li** (kə gä′lē) capital of Rwanda: pop. 157,000

**Ki·lau·e·a** (kē′lou ā′ə) ⟦ < Haw, lit., spewing ⟧ active volcanic crater on the slope of Mauna Loa, Hawaii: *c.* 8 mi. (13 km) in circumference

**Kil·dare** (kil der′) county in Leinster province, E Ireland: 654 sq. mi. (1,694 sq. km); pop. 104,000

**Kil·i·man·ja·ro** (kil′ə män jär′ō) mountain in NE Tanzania: highest mountain in Africa: 19,340 ft. (5,895 m)

**Kil·ken·ny** (kil ken′ē) county in Leinster province, E Ireland: 796 sq. mi. (2,061 sq. km); pop. 70,000

**Kil·lar·ney** (ki lär′nē) **1** town in central Kerry county, SW Ireland: pop. 7,000 **2 Lakes of** three lakes near this town

**Kil·leen** (ki lēn′) ⟦ after F. P. *Killeen*, official of the Santa Fe Railroad & early settler ⟧ city in central Tex., north of Austin: pop. 64,000

**Kil·lie·cran·kie** (kil′ē kraŋ′kē) mountain pass in the Grampians, Tayside, Scotland: *c.* 1.5 mi. (2.5 km) long

**Kil·mar·nock** (kil mär′nək) city in Strathclyde, SC Scotland: pop. 46,000

**Kim·ber·ley** (kim′bər lē) city in N Cape Province, South Africa: diamond-mining center: pop. 144,000

**Kin·a·ba·lu** (kin′ə bə lōō′) mountain in NW Sabah: highest peak on Borneo: 13,455 ft. (4,100 m)

**Kin·car·dine** (kin kär′din) former county of E Scotland, now in the region of Grampian: also **Kin·car′dine·shire′** (-shir′, -shər)

**Kings Canyon National Park** ⟦ after *Kings* River, transl. shortening of Sp *Río de los Santos Reyes,* River of the Holy Kings ⟧ national park in EC Calif., in the Sierra Nevada Mountains: 709 sq. mi. (1,837 sq. km)

**Kings·ton** (kiŋz′tən, kiŋ′stən) **1** seaport & capital of Jamaica, on the SE coast: pop. *c.* 117,000 **2** ⟦ orig., King's Town (1784), in honor of George III of Great Britain ⟧ port in SE Ontario, Canada, at the outlet of Lake Ontario into the St. Lawrence: pop. 86,000

**Kingston upon Hull** Hull (in England)

**Kingston upon Thames** borough of SW Greater London: pop. 134,000

**Kin·ross** (kin rôs′) former county of EC Scotland, now in the region of Tayside: also **Kin·ross′-shire** (-shir)

**Kin·sha·sa** (kēn shä′sä) capital of Zaire, on the Congo River, in the W part: pop. 2,444,000

**Kio·to** (kē ōt′ō) *alt. sp. of* KYOTO

**Kir·ghi·zi·a** (kir gē′zhə, -zhē ə) KIRGHIZ SOVIET SOCIAL- IST REPUBLIC

**Kir·ghiz Soviet Socialist Republic** (kir gēz′) a republic of the U.S.S.R.: now KYRGYZSTAN

**Kir·i·bati** (kir′ə bas′) country consisting principally of three groups of atolls in the WC Pacific, east of the Solomon Islands: formerly a British territory, it became independent & a member of the Common- wealth (1979): 313 sq. mi. (811 sq. km); pop. 63,000; cap. Tarawa

**Ki·rik·ka·le** (kə rik′ə lä′) city in central Turkey; pop. 178,000

**Ki·rin** (kē′rin′) *old form of* JILIN

**Ki·riti·mati** (kə ris′məs) island in the central Pacific, in the country of Kiribati: 222 sq. mi. (575 sq. km); pop. 1,300

**Kirk·cal·dy** (kər kô′dē, -kôl′dē) seaport in E Scotland, on the Firth of Forth; pop. 51,000

**Kirk·cud·bright** (kər kōō′brē) former county of SW Scotland, now in the region of Dumfries and Galloway: also **Kir·cud′bright·shire′** (-shir′, -shər)

**Ki·rov** (kē′rôf′) city in NC European Russia: pop. 411,000

**Ki·rov·a·bad** (kē rō′və bad′) *old name of* GYANDZHA

**Ki·rov·o·grad** (-grad′) city in SC Ukraine: pop. 263,000

**Ki·san·ga·ni** (kē′sän gä′nē) city in NE Zaire, on the upper Congo River: pop. 340,000

**Kish** (kish) ancient Sumerian city on the Euphrates in what is now central Iraq: fl. *c.* 4000 B.C.

**Ki·shi·nev** (kish′ə nev′, -nef′) capital of Moldova, in the central part: pop. 624,000

**Kist·na** (kist′nə) *old name of* KRISHNA

**Ki·ta·kyu·shu** (kē′ta kyōō′shōō) seaport on the N coast of Kyushu, Japan: pop. 1,052,000

**Kitch·e·ner** (kich′ə nər) ⟦after Horatio Herbert *Kitch- ener* (1850-1916), Brit statesman⟧ city in SE Ontario, Canada: pop. 150,000

**Ki·tik·me·ot** (ki tik′mē ät′) Region of central Northwest

Territories, Canada: 243,899 sq. mi. (631,695 sq. km)

**Kitty Hawk** ⟦ < ? Algonquian language ⟧ village on the Outer Banks of N.C., near where the first controlled & sustained airplane flight was made by Orville & Wilbur Wright in 1903

**Ki·vu** (kē′vōō′), **Lake** lake in EC Africa, on the border of E Zaire & Rwanda: c. 1,100 sq. mi. (2,849 sq. km)

**Ki·zil** (ki zil′) river in NC Turkey, flowing into the Black Sea: c. 700 mi. (1,126 km): also **Kizil Ir·mak** (ir mäk′) or **Ki·zil′ir·mak′**

**Klai·pe·da** (klī′pi də) seaport in W Lithuania, on the Baltic: pop. 195,000

**Kla·math** (klam′əth) ⟦ < ? ⟧ river flowing from S Oreg. southwest across NW Calif., into the Pacific: c. 250 mi. (402 km)

**Klon·dike** (klän′dīk′) ⟦ Athabaskan < ? ⟧ **1** river in W Yukon Territory, Canada, flowing west into the Yukon River: c. 100 mi. (160 km) **2** gold-mining region surrounding this river: site of a gold rush, 1898

**Knos·sos** (näs′əs) alt. sp. of CNOSSUS

**Knox·ville** (näks′vil′) ⟦ after Gen. Henry Knox (1750-1806), 1st secretary of war ⟧ city in E Tenn., on the Tennessee River: pop. 165,000 (met. area 605,000)

**Ko·ba·rid** (kō′bä rēd′) see CAPORETTO

**Ko·be** (kō′bā′; E kō′bē) seaport on the S coast of Honshu, Japan, on the Inland Sea: pop. 1,381,000

**Kø·ben·havn** (kö′bən houn′) Dan. name of COPENHAGEN

**Ko·blenz** (kō′blents′) city in W Germany, on the Rhine, in the state of Rhineland-Palatinate: pop. 112,000

**Ko·chi** (kō′chē) seaport in S Shikoku, Japan: pop. 306,000

**Ko·di·ak** (kō′dē ak′) ⟦ < Russ < ? native name meaning "island" ⟧ island off the SW coast of Alas., in the Gulf of Alaska: 5,363 sq. mi. (13,890 sq. km); pop. 13,000

**Ko·ko·mo** (kō′kə mō′) ⟦ < Algonquian (Miami) name of local Indian chief ⟧ city in central Ind.: pop. 45,000

**Ko·ko Nor** (kō′kō nôr′) QINGHAI (lake)

**Ko·la Peninsula** (kō′lə) peninsula in NW Russia, between the White & Barents seas: c. 50,000 sq. mi. (129,500 sq. km)

**Kol·ha·pur** (kōl′hä pōōr′) city in W India, in Maharashtra state: pop. 351,000

**Köln** (köln) Ger. name of COLOGNE

**Ko·ly·ma** (kä′lē mä′) river in far E Russia, flowing north into the East Siberian Sea: *c.* 1,500 mi. (2,410 km): also sp. **Ko'li·ma'**

**Kom·so·molsk-on-A·mur** (käm'sə môlsk' än' ä moor') city in SE Russia, on the Amur River: pop. 300,000

**Kö·nig·grätz** (kö'niH grets') old (*Ger.*) *name of* HRADEC KRÁLOVÉ

**Kö·nigs·berg** (-niHs berk') old (*Ger.*) *name of* KALININ-GRAD

**Kon·stanz** (kôn'stänts') *Ger. name of* CONSTANCE (the city)

**Kon·ya** (kôn'yä') city in SW central Turkey: pop. 329,000

**Koo·te·nay** (kōōt''n ā') ‖< a native name < ? ‖ **1** river flowing from SE British Columbia, through Mont. & Ida. into Kootenay Lake, thence into the Columbia River: 407 mi. (655 km) **2** elongated lake in the valley of this river, SE British Columbia: 168 sq. mi. (435 sq. km)

**Kor·do·fan** (kôr'də fän') region of central Sudan, west & south of Khartoum: 56,731 sq. mi. (146,932 sq. km); pop. 3,093,000; chief city, El Obeid

**Ko·re·a** (kə rē'ə, kô-) peninsula & country in E Asia, extending south from NE China: divided (1948) into *a*) **Korean People's Democratic Republic (North Korea)** occupying the N half of the peninsula: 46,768 sq. mi. (121,129 sq. km); pop. 20,543,000; cap. Pyongyang, and *b*) **Republic of Korea (South Korea)** occupying the S half of the peninsula: 38,030 sq. mi. (98,500 sq. km); pop. 43,285,000; cap. Seoul: war (1950-53) between the two countries ended in a cease-fire & reaffirmation of the division

**Korea Strait** strait between Korea & Japan, connecting the Sea of Japan & the East China Sea: *c.* 110 mi. (177 km) wide

**Ko·rin·thos** (kô'rēn thôs') *Gr. name of modern* CORINTH

**Ko·ri·ya·ma** (kôr'ē yäm'ə) city in NC Honshu, Japan: pop. 293,000

**Kort·rijk** (kôrt'rīk') *Fl. name of* COURTRAI

**Kos** (käs, kôs) Greek island in the Dodecanese, off the SW coast of Turkey: 111 sq. mi. (287 sq. km)

**Kos·ci·us·ko** (käs'ē us'kō), **Mount** mountain of the Australian Alps, in SE New South Wales: highest peak in Australia: 7,316 ft. (2,230 m)

**Ko·ši·ce** (kô'shē tse) city in E Slovakia: pop. 214,000

**Ko·stro·ma** (kä'strō mä') city in WC Russia, on the
   Volga: pop. 269,000

**Ko·ta·ba·ru** (kōt'ə bär'o͞o) *old name of* JAYAPURA

**Ko·ta Kin·a·ba·lu** (kōt'ə kin'ə bə lo͞o') seaport in N Borneo: capital of Sabah, Malaysia: pop. 109,000

**Kov·no** (kôv'nô) *Russ. name of* KAUNAS

**Kow·loon** (kou'lo͞on') **1** peninsula in SE China, opposite Hong Kong island & part of Hong Kong colony: 3
   sq. mi. (7.8 sq. km) **2** city on this peninsula: pop.
   1,350,000

**Ko·zhi·kode** (kō'zhi kōd') *old name of* CALICUT

**Kra** (krä), **Isthmus of** narrow strip of land connecting the
   Malay Peninsula with the Indochinese peninsula

**Kra·ka·tau** (krä'kä tou') small island & volcano of Indonesia, between Java & Sumatra: 2,667 ft. (813 m): also
   **Kra'ka·to'a** (-tō'ə)

**Kra·ków** (kra'kou', krä-; -kō; *Pol* krä'ko͝of) city in S
   Poland, on the Vistula: pop. 735,000

**Kra·ma·torsk** (kräm'ə tôrsk') city in E Ukraine: pop.
   192,000

**Kras·no·dar** (kräs'nō där') **1** territory in SW Russia, in
   the N Caucasus: 34,200 sq. mi. (88,579 sq. km); pop.
   4,511,000 **2** capital of this territory, on the Kuban
   River: pop. 609,000

**Kras·no·yarsk** (kräs'nō yärsk') **1** territory in SC Russia:
   928,000 sq. mi. (2,404,000 sq. km); pop. 2,960,000 **2**
   capital of this territory, on the Yenisei River: pop.
   872,000

**Kre·feld** (krā'felt') city in W Germany, on the Rhine, in
   the state of North Rhine-Westphalia: pop. 220,000

**Kre·men·chug** (krem'ən cho͞ok', -cho͞og') city in EC
   Ukraine: pop. 224,000

**Krem·lin** (krem'lin), **the** the citadel of Moscow, in which
   some government offices of the Soviet Union were
   located: it now contains some offices of the Russian
   government

**Kre·te**, **Kri·ti** (krē'tē) *Gr. name of* CRETE

**Krim** (krim) *Russ. name of* CRIMEA

**Krish·na** (krish'nə) river in S India, flowing from the
   Western Ghats eastward into the Bay of Bengal: *c.* 800
   mi. (1,287 km)

**Kri·voi Rog** (kri voi' rôg') city in SC Ukraine: pop.
   684,000

**Kron·shtadt** (krun shtät') city & naval fortress on an

island in NW Russia, on the Gulf of Finland: pop.
59,000: Ger. sp. **Kron·stadt** (krôn'shtät')

**Kru·gers·dorp** (krōō'gərz dôrp') city in the SW Transvaal, South Africa: pop. 141,000

**Krung Thep** (kroon' tāp') *Thai name of* BANGKOK

**KS** *abbrev. for* Kansas

**K2** (kā'tōō') GODWIN AUSTEN

**Kua·la Lum·pur** (kwä'lə loom poor') city in WC Peninsular Malaysia: its capital & capital of Malaysia: pop.
938,000

**Kuang-chou** (kwäŋ'jō') *var. of* GUANGZHOU

**Ku·ban** (kōō ban'; *Russ* kōō bän'y') river in the N Caucasus, flowing northwest into the Sea of Azov: c. 570
mi. (920 km)

**Ku·ching** (kōō'chiŋ) capital of Sarawak, Malaysia: seaport in the W part: pop. 300,000

**Kui·by·shev** (kwē'bi shef') *name* (1935-91) *for* SAMARA

**Ku·ma·mo·to** (kōō'mä mō'tō) city in W Kyushu, Japan:
pop. 527,000

**Ku·mas·i** (koo mä'sē) city in SC Ghana: capital of
Ashanti region: pop. 352,000

**Ku·may·ry** (kōō mä'rē) city in NW Armenia: pop.
223,000

**Kun·lun Mountains** (koon'loon') mountain system in W
China, between Tibet & Xinjiang: highest peak, c.
25,300 ft. (7,712 m)

**Kun·ming** (koon'miŋ') city in S China: capital of Yunnan province: pop. 1,430,000

**Ku·ra** (koo rä') river flowing from NE Turkey west
across Transcaucasia, into the Caspian Sea: c. 940 mi.
(1,512 km)

**Ku·ra·shi·ki** (kōō rä'shē kē) city in SW Honshu, Japan:
pop. 411,000

**Kur·dis·tan** (kur'di stan', koor'-; -stän') region in SW
Asia inhabited chiefly by Kurds, occupying SE Turkey, N Iraq, & NW Iran

**Ku·re** (kōō'rä') seaport in SW Honshu, Japan: pop.
231,000

**Kur·gan** (koor gän') city in SW Siberian Russia: pop.
343,000

**Ku·ril** (or **Ku·rile**) **Islands** (kōō'ril, kōō rēl') chain of
islands belonging to Russia, between N Hokkaido,
Japan, and Kamchatka Peninsula: formerly Japanese
(1875-1945): c. 6,000 sq. mi. (15,540 sq. km)

**Kur·land** (koor′lənd) historical name for a region in W Latvia: see KURZEME

**Ku·ro·shi·o** (koo rō′shē ō′) JAPAN CURRENT

**Kursk** (koorsk) city in SW Russia, near the Ukrainian border: pop. 420,000

**Kur·ze·me** (koor′ze mə) state of Latvia: it occupies the historical region of KURLAND

**Kush** (kush) *alt. sp. of* CUSH

**Kus·ko·kwim** (kus′kə kwim′) 〚 < Esk 〛 river in SW Alas., flowing from the Alaska Range southwest into the Bering Sea: 550 mi. (885 km)

**Kutch** (kuch) **1** former state of W India, on the Arabian Sea, now part of the state of Gujarat **2 Rann of** (run əv) large salt marsh in W India & S Pakistan: *c.* 9,000 sq. mi. (23,310 sq. km)

**Ku·te·nai, Ku·te·nay** (koot′′n ā′) *alt. sp. of* KOOTENAY

**Ku·wait** (koo wāt′, -wīt′) **1** independent Arab state in E Arabia, at head of Persian Gulf between Iraq & Saudi Arabia: 7,000 sq. mi. (17,818 sq. km); pop. 1,771,000 **2** its capital, a seaport on the Persian Gulf: pop. 168,000

**Kuz·netsk Basin** (kooz netsk′) industrial & coal-mining region in SC Asian Russia, including the cities of Kemerovo, Prokopyevsk, and Novokuznetsk: *c.* 10,000 sq. mi. (25,900 sq. km)

**Kwa·ja·lein** (kwä′jə lān′) atoll in the W Pacific, in the Marshall Islands: 6.5 sq. mi. (16.9 sq. km)

**Kwang·chow** (kwäŋ′chō′; *Chin* gwäŋ′jō′) *old form of* GUANGZHOU

**Kwang·ju** (gwäŋ′joo′) city in SW South Korea: pop. 870,000

**Kwang·si** (gwäŋ′sē′) *old form of* GUANGXI

**Kwang·tung** (kwaŋ′tooŋ′; *Chin* gwäŋ′dooŋ′) *old form of* GUANGDONG

**Kwei·chow** (kwā′chou′; *Chin* gwā′jō′) *old form of* GUIZHOU

**Kwei·lin** (kwā′lin′; *Chin* gwā′lin′) *old form of* GUILIN

**Kwei·yang** (kwā′yäŋ′; *Chin* gwā′yäŋ′) *old form of* GUIYANG

**KY, Ky** *abbrev. for* Kentucky

**Kyong·song** (kyôŋ′sôŋ′) SEOUL

**Kyo·to** (kē′ōt′ō) city in S Honshu, Japan: former capital of Japan (794-1869): contains many fine Buddhist & Shinto temples, shrines, & other buildings: pop. 1,464,000

**Kyr·gyz·stan** (kir'gi stan') country in SC Asia: became independent upon the breakup of the U.S.S.R. (1991): 76,460 sq. mi. (198,500 sq. km); pop. 4,000,000; cap. Bishkek: formerly, *Kirghiz Soviet Socialist Republic*

**Ky·the·ra** (kē'thi rä') *Gr. name of* CYTHERA

**Kyu·shu** (kyoo'shoo') one of the four main islands of Japan, south of Honshu: 13,760 sq. mi. (35,640 sq. km); chief city, Nagasaki

# L

**LA, La** *abbrev. for* Louisiana

**Laa·land** (lô'län) *var. of* LOLLAND

**La·be** (lä'be) *Czech name of* the ELBE

**Lab·ra·dor** (lab'rə dôr') 〚prob. < Port *lavrador*, landholder, for 15th-c. Port explorer João Fernandes, a landholder in the Azores: the name was first applied to Greenland〛 1 region along the Atlantic coast of NE Canada, constituting the mainland part of the province of Newfoundland: 112,826 sq. mi. (292,218 sq. km) 2 large peninsula between the Atlantic & Hudson Bay, containing Quebec & Labrador (the region)

**Labrador Current** icy arctic current flowing south from Baffin Bay past Labrador into the Gulf Stream

**La·bu·an** (lä'boo än') island of Malaysia, off the NW coast of Sabah: 35 sq. mi. (90.6 sq. km)

**Lab·y·rinth** (lab'ə rinth') *Gr. Myth.* the labyrinthine structure built by Daedalus for King Minos of Crete, to house the Minotaur

**Lac·ca·dive Islands** (lak'ə dīv') islands in the Arabian Sea, off the west coast of Kerala, India: 11 sq. mi. (29 sq. km)

**Lac·e·dae·mon** (las'ə dē'mən) SPARTA

**La·cer·ta** (lə surt'ə) 〚L < *lacerta*, lizard〛 a N constellation in the Milky Way, between Cygnus and Andromeda

**La·chine** (lə shēn') 〚< Fr *chine*, China: derisive name applied to the land grant of Fr explorer Robert La Salle (1643-87), in ref. to his failure to find a westward passage to China〛 city in S Quebec, Canada, on Montreal Island: pop. 37,000

**La·co·ni·a** (lə kō'nē ə) 1 ancient country on the SE coast of the Peloponnesus, Greece: dominated by the city of Sparta 2 region of modern Greece in the same general area: also sp. **Lakonia**

**La Co·ru·ña** (lä′ kô̄ rōō′nyä) seaport in NW Spain, on the Atlantic: pop. 232,000

**La Crosse** (lə krôs′) city in W Wis., on the Mississippi: pop. 51,000

**La·do·ga** (lä′dô gä′), **Lake** lake in NW Russia, near the border of Finland: largest lake in Europe: *c.* 7,000 sq. mi. (18,130 sq. km)

**La·fa·yette** (laf′ē et′; lä′fē-, -fä-; *also, for 1,* lä′fē et′, &, *for 2,* lə fä′it) 〚after the Marquis de *Lafayette* (1757-1834), Fr statesman〛 **1** city in WC Ind.: pop. 44,000 **2** city in SC La.: pop. 94,000

**La·gos** (lä′gäs′, -gəs) seaport in Nigeria, on the Bight of Benin: former capital: pop. 1,061,000

**La Ha·bra** (lə häb′rə) 〚< Sp *la,* the + *abra,* gorge, mountain pass〛 city in SW Calif.: pop. 51,000

**La·hore** (lə hôr′, lä-) city in NE Pakistan: pop. 2,922,000

**Lake Charles** (chärlz) 〚after *Charles* Sallier, an early settler〛 city in SW La.: pop. 71,000

**Lake District** (or **Country**) lake & mountain region in Cumbria county, NW England: see CUMBERLAND, WESTMORLAND, LANCASHIRE

**Lake·land** (lāk′lənd) 〚descriptive〛 city in WC Fla.: pop. 71,000

**Lake of the Woods** 〚descriptive〛 lake in N Minn. & in Ontario & Manitoba, Canada: 1,485 sq. mi. (3,846 sq. km)

**Lake·wood** (lāk′wood′) 〚descriptive〛 **1** city in NC Colo.: suburb of Denver: pop. 126,000 **2** city in SW Calif.: suburb of Los Angeles: pop. 74,000 **3** city in NE Ohio, on Lake Erie: suburb of Cleveland: pop. 60,000

**Lak·shad·weep** (luk shäd′wēp′) territory of India comprising the Laccadive, Minicoy, and Amindivi islands: 12.4 sq. mi. (32 sq. km); pop. 40,000

**La La·gu·na** (lä lə gōō′nə) city in Tenerife, Canary Islands: pop. 112,000

**La Man·cha** (lä män′chä′) flat region in SC Spain

**Lam·beth** (lam′bəth) borough of S Greater London: site of the official residence (Lambeth Palace) of the archbishops of Canterbury since 1197: pop. 244,000

**La Me·sa** (lä mā′sə, lə-) 〚Sp., lit., the mesa〛 city in SW Calif.: suburb of San Diego: pop. 53,000

**La Mi·ra·da** (lä′mə rä′də) 〚Sp, lit., the gaze, glance〛 city in SW Calif.: pop. 40,000

**Lam·pe·du·sa** (läm′pə dōōs′ə, -dōōz′ə) Italian island in the Mediterranean, between Malta & Tunisia: 8 sq. mi. (21 sq. km)

**La·na·i** (lä nä′ē, -nī′; lə-) 〖Haw *Lā-na'i*, lit., day of conquest < Proto-Polynesian *la'ā*, day + *ngaki*, conquer〗 an island of Hawaii, west of Maui: 141 sq. mi. (365 sq. km); pop. 2,400

**Lan·ark** (lan′ərk) former county of SC Scotland, now in the region of Strathclyde: also **Lan′ark·shire′** (-shir′, -shər)

**Lan·ca·shire** (laŋ′kə shir′, -shər) county on the NW coast of England: 1,175 sq. mi. (3,043 sq. km); pop. 1,379,000; county seat, Lancaster

**Lan·cas·ter** (laŋ′kə stər; *for 3 & 4 also*, laŋ′kas′tər) **1** city in N Lancashire: pop. 126,000 **2** LANCASHIRE **3** 〖after city in England〗 city in SE Pa.: pop. 56,000 (met. area 422,000) **4** 〖prob. after a railroad official〗 city in SW Calif.: suburb of Los Angeles: pop. 97,000

**Lan·chow** (lan′chou′; *Chin* län′jō′) *old form of* LANZHOU

**Land of Nod** (näd) **1** *Bible* the country to which Cain journeyed after slaying Abel: Gen. 4:16 **2** [l- of N-] the imaginary realm of sleep and dreams

**Land of Promise** PROMISED LAND

**Land's End** cape in Cornwall at the southwesternmost point of England: also **Lands End**

**Lang·ley** (laŋ′lē) city in SW British Columbia, Canada: suburb of Vancouver: pop. 69,000

**Langue·doc** (läng dôk′) historical region of S France, between the E Pyrenees & the lower Rhone

**Langue·doc–Rous·sil·lon** (läng dôk rōō sē yōn′) metropolitan region of France incorporating part of the Languedoc region and the Roussillon; 10,570 sq. mi. (127,376 sq. km); pop. 1,963,000; chief city, Montpellier

**Lan·sing** (lan′siŋ) 〖ult. after J. *Lansing* (1751-c. 1829), U.S. jurist〗 capital of Mich., in the SC part: pop. 127,000 (met. area with East Lansing 433,000)

**La·nús** (lä nōōs′) city in E Argentina: suburb of Buenos Aires: pop. 466,000

**Lan·zhou** (län′jō′) city in NW China, on the Huang He: capital of Gansu province: pop. 1,430,000

**La·od·i·ce·a** (lā äd′i sē′ə, lā′ə də-) **1** ancient city in Phrygia, SW Asia Minor **2** *ancient name of* LATAKIA (the seaport)

**Laoigh·is** (lā′ish) county in Leinster province, central Ireland: 664 sq. mi. (1,719 sq. km); pop. 52,000

**La·os** (lä′ōs, lous) country in the NW part of the Indochinese peninsula: formerly a French protectorate, it became an independent kingdom (1949) & a republic (1975): 91,429 sq. mi. (236,804 sq. km); pop. 3,679,000; cap. Vientiane

**La Paz** (lä päs′; *E* lə päz′) **1** city in W Bolivia: actual seat of government (cf. SUCRE): pop. 881,000 **2** seaport in NW Mexico, on the Gulf of California; capital of Baja California Sur: pop. 46,000

**Lap·land** (lap′land′) region of N Europe, including the N parts of Norway, Sweden, & Finland, & the NW extremity of European Russia, inhabited by the Lapps

**La Pla·ta** (lä plä′tä) seaport in E Argentina, on the Río de la Plata, southeast of Buenos Aires: pop. 455,000

**Lap·tev Sea** (läp′tef′, -tev′) arm of the Arctic Ocean, between the New Siberian Islands & the Taimyr Peninsula

**La·pu·ta** (lə pyōōt′ə) in Jonathan Swift's *Gulliver's Travels*, a flying island inhabited by impractical, visionary philosophers who engage in various absurd activities

**Lar·a·mie** (lar′ə mē) ⟦after J. *Laramie* (died *c.* 1821), trapper & explorer⟧ city in SE Wyo.: pop. 27,000

**La·re·do** (lə rä′dō) ⟦after *Laredo*, town in Spain⟧ city in S Tex., on the Rio Grande: pop. 123,000

**Lar·go** (lär′gō) ⟦after nearby *Lake Largo* (< Sp *largo*, long), now drained⟧ city in WC Fla.: pop. 66,000

**La·ri·sa** (lä′rē sä′; *E* lə ris′ə) city in E Thessaly, Greece: pop. 102,000: also sp. **La·ris′sa**

**La Ro·chelle** (là rô shel′) seaport in W France, on the Bay of Biscay: pop. 78,000

**La·Salle** (lə sal′; *Fr* là sål′) ⟦after Robert *La Salle* (1643-87), Fr explorer⟧ city in S Quebec, Canada, on Montreal island: pop. 76,000

**Las·caux** (las kō′) cave in the Dordogne region, SW France, containing Upper Paleolithic paintings and engravings

**Las Cru·ces** (läs krōō′sis) ⟦Sp, lit., the crosses: prob. from crosses marking an early burial spot⟧ city in S N.Mex., on the Rio Grande: pop. 62,000

**Las Pal·mas** (läs päl′məs) seaport in the Canary Islands: pop. 366,000

**La Spe·zia** (lä spät'sē ä') seaport in NW Italy, on the Ligurian Sea: pop. 111,000

**Las·sen Volcanic National Park** (läs'ən) ⟦after P. *Lassen* (fl. 1845), Dan pioneer⟧ national park in N Calif.: it contains volcanic peaks, lava flows, hot springs, & an active volcano, **Lassen Peak**, 10,457 ft. (3,187 m) high: 166 sq. mi. (430 sq. km)

**Las Ve·gas** (läs vā'gəs) ⟦Sp, the fertile plains (or meadows)⟧ city in SE Nev.: pop. 258,000 (met. area 741,000)

**La·ta·ki·a** (lät'ə kē'ə, lat'-) **1** seaport in W Syria, on the Mediterranean: pop. 197,000 **2** coastal region of NW Syria, bordering on the Mediterranean

**Lat·er·an** (lat'ər ən) ⟦< L *Lateranus*, pl. *laterani*, name of the Roman family (the *Plautii Laterani*) whose palace once occupied the same site⟧ **1** the church of St. John Lateran, the cathedral of the pope as bishop of Rome **2** the palace, now a museum, adjoining this church

**Lat·in America** (lat''n) that part of the Western Hemisphere south of the U.S., in Mexico, Central America, the West Indies, & South America, where Spanish, Portuguese, & French are the official languages

**Latin Quarter** a section of Paris, south of the Seine, where many artists and students live

**La·ti·um** (lā'shəm, -shē əm) ⟦L⟧ **1** region of central Italy, on the Tyrrhenian Sea: 6,642 sq. mi. (17,203 sq. km); pop. 5,080,000; chief city, Rome **2** ancient country in the part of this region southeast of Rome

**Lat·vi·a** (lat'vē ə) country in N Europe, on the Baltic Sea: from 1940 to 1991 it was a republic of the U.S.S.R.: 24,594 sq. mi. (63,698 sq. km); pop. 2,600,000; cap. Riga: formerly, **Latvian Soviet Socialist Republic**

**Lau·ra·sia** (lô rā'zhə, -shə) ⟦*Laur(entian)*, designating a series of Precambrian rocks in E Canada + (*Eur)asia*⟧ a hypothetical ancient continent that included what are now North America and Eurasia, supposed to have separated and moved apart from Pangea at about the end of the Paleozoic Era

**Lau·ren·tian Mountains** (lô ren'shən) mountain range in S Quebec, Canada, extending along the St. Lawrence River valley: highest peak, 3,905 ft. (1,360 m): also **Laurentian Highlands**

**Laurentian Plateau** CANADIAN SHIELD

**Lau·sanne** (lō zan') city in W Switzerland, on Lake Geneva: pop. 127,000

**La·val** (là vàl'; *E* lə val') ⟦after François de *Laval* (1623-1708), 1st bishop of Quebec⟧ city in SW Quebec, on an island just northwest of Montreal: pop. 284,000

**Law·rence** (lôr'əns, lär'-) **1** ⟦after Abbot *Lawrence* (1792-1855), Boston merchant, founder of the town⟧ city in NE Mass.: pop. 70,000: see BOSTON **2** ⟦after Amos A. *Lawrence* (1814-86), Boston manufacturer; active in antislavery group that founded the town⟧ city in NE Kans., on the Kansas River: pop. 66,000

**Law·ton** (lôt'′n) ⟦after Maj. Gen. H. W. *Lawton* (1843-99)⟧ city in SW Okla.: pop. 81,000

**Leaning Tower of Pisa** bell tower in Pisa, Italy, which leans approx. 10° from the vertical

**Leav·en·worth** (lev'ən wurth') ⟦ult. after U.S. Army Col. H. *Leavenworth* (1783-1834)⟧ city in NE Kans., on the Missouri River: site of a Federal prison: pop. 38,000

**Leb·a·non** (leb'ə nän', -nən) **1** country in SW Asia, at the E end of the Mediterranean: a former French mandate (1920-41), declared independent by British & Free French forces (1941); became independent after elections (1944): *c.* 4,000 sq. mi. (10,360 sq. km); pop. 2,675,000; cap. Beirut **2** mountain range extending nearly the entire length of Lebanon: highest peak, 10,131 ft. (3,087 m)

**Leeds** (lēdz) city in N England, in West Yorkshire: pop. 442,000

**Leeu·war·den** (lā'vär'dən) city in N Netherlands: capital of Friesland province: pop. 86,000

**Lee·ward Islands** (lē'wərd) **1** N group of islands in the Lesser Antilles of the West Indies, extending from Puerto Rico southeast to the Windward Islands **2** former British colony in this group (dissolved 1962), now separate countries or territories

**Left Bank** a district in Paris on the left bank of the Seine, associated with artists, bohemians, etc.

**Le·ga·nés** (le'gä nes') city in central Spain: suburb of Madrid: pop. 163,000

**Leg·horn** (leg'hôrn', leg'ərn) ⟦altered by folk etym. < It *Livorno*⟧ seaport in Tuscany, W Italy, on the Ligurian Sea: pop. 175,000: It. name LIVORNO

**Le Ha·vre** (lə häv′rə, lə häv′ər; *Fr* lə à′vr′) seaport in NW France, on the English Channel: pop. 200,000

**Le·high** (lē′hī′) ⟦ < ? Algonquian ⟧ river in E Pa., flowing into the Delaware: *c*. 120 mi. (193 km)

**Leices·ter** (les′tər) city in central England: county seat of Leicestershire: pop. 282,000

**Leices·ter·shire** (-shir′, -shər) county of central England: 986 sq. mi. (2,553 sq. km); pop. 866,000

**Lei·den** (līd′'n) city in W Netherlands: pop. 105,000

**Lein·ster** (len′stər) province of E Ireland: 7,580 sq. mi. (19,632 sq. km); pop. 1,790,000

**Leip·zig** (līp′sig, -sik) city in E Germany, in the state of Saxony: pop. 556,000

**Lei·trim** (lē′trəm) county in Connacht province, N Ireland: 589 sq. mi. (1,525 sq. km); pop. 28,000

**Leix** (lāsh, lēsh) *var. sp. of* LAOIGHIS

**Lei·zhou** (lā′jō′) peninsula in Guangdong province, SE China, opposite Hainan island: *c*. 90 mi. (145 km) long

**Le·man** (lē′mən), **Lake** Lake (of) GENEVA: Fr. name **Lac Lé·man** (làk lā män′)

**Le Mans** (lə män′) city in W France: pop. 150,000

**Lem·nos** (lem′näs′, -nōs′) Greek island in the N Aegean: 186 sq. mi. (483 sq. km)

**Le·na** (lē′nə, lā′-) river in EC Siberian Russia, rising near Lake Baikal and flowing northeast into the Laptev Sea: *c*. 2,680 mi. (4,300 km)

**Le·nin·a·kan** (len′in ə kän′) *old name of* KUMAYRY

**Len·in·grad** (len′in grad′) *name* (1924-91) *of* ST. PETERSBURG (Russia)

**Len·in Peak** (len′in) mountain located on the border between Kyrgyzstan & Tajikistan: *c*. 23,400 ft. (7,132 m)

**Le·o** (lē′ō) ⟦ L < *leo*, lion ⟧ **1 a** N constellation between Cancer and Virgo, containing the star Regulus **2** the fifth sign of the zodiac, entered by the sun about July 21

**Leo Minor** ⟦ L, lit., the Lesser Lion ⟧ a small N constellation between Leo and Ursa Major

**Le·ón** (le ôn′) **1** region in NW Spain: from the 10th cent., a kingdom which united with Castile (1037-1157), separated (1157-1230), and permanently united with Castile (1230) **2** city in this region: pop. 132,000 **3** city in central Mexico, in Guanajuato state: pop. 656,000: in full **León de los Al·da·mas** (de lôs äl dä′

mäs) **4** city in W Nicaragua: pop. 63,000

**Lé·o·pold·ville** (lē′ə pōld vil′; lā-) *old name of* KINSHASA

**Le·pan·to** (li pan′tō, -pän′-), **Gulf of** *old name of* Gulf of CORINTH; site of naval battle (Battle of Lepanto, 1571) in which the European powers defeated Turkey

**Le·pon·tine Alps** (li pän′tin) division of the W Alps between Switzerland & Italy: highest peak, 11,684 ft. (3,560 m)

**Le·pus** (lē′pəs) ⟦L, the Hare⟧ a S constellation between Eridanus and Canis Major

**Lé·ri·da** (lā′rē dä′) city in NE Spain: pop. 110,000

**Les·bos** (lez′bäs, -bəs) Greek island in the Aegean, off the coast of Asia Minor: *c.* 630 sq. mi. (1,630 sq. km)

**Le·sot·ho** (le sōō′tōō, le sō′tō) country in SE Africa, surrounded by South Africa: formerly the British protectorate of Basutoland, it became an independent member of the Commonwealth in 1966: 11,716 sq. mi. (30,462 sq. km); pop. 1,552,000; cap. Maseru

**Lesser Antilles** group of islands in the West Indies, southeast of Puerto Rico, including the Leeward Islands, the Windward Islands, & the islands off the N coast of Venezuela

**Leth·bridge** (leth′brij′) ⟦after W. *Lethbridge* (1824-1901), president of local coal-mining company⟧ city in S Alberta, Canada: pop. 59,000

**Le·the** (lē′thē) ⟦L < Gr *lēthē*, forgetfulness, oblivion⟧ *Gr. & Rom. Myth.* the river of forgetfulness, flowing through Hades, whose water produces loss of memory in those who drink of it

**Leu·ven** (lö′vən) city in central Belgium: pop. 85,000

**Le·val·lois–Per·ret** (lə vál lwá pe re′) city in NC France, on the Seine: suburb of Paris: pop. 54,000

**Le·vant** (lə vant′) ⟦Fr *levant* < It *levante* (< L *levans*, rising, raising, prp. of *levare*, to raise), applied to the East, from the "rising" of the sun⟧ region on the E Mediterranean, including all countries bordering the sea between Greece & Egypt

**Lev·it·town** (lev′it toun′) ⟦after *Levitt* & Sons, Inc., builders of planned towns⟧ **1** city in SE N.Y., on Long Island: pop. 53,000 **2** city in SE Pa., northeast of Philadelphia: pop. 55,000

**Lev·kás** (lef käs′) one of the Ionian Islands, in the Ionian Sea, off the W coast of Greece: 114 sq. mi. (295 sq. km)

**Lew·i·sham** (loo'i shəm, -səm) borough of SE Greater London, England: pop. 232,000

**Lew·is·ton** (loō'is tən) [[prob. < a personal name]] city in SW Me.: pop. 40,000

**Lew·is with Har·ris** (loō'is with har'is) northernmost island of the Outer Hebrides, Scotland, consisting of a larger N part (**Lewis**) & a S part (**Harris**): 770 sq. mi. (2,002 sq. km): also called **Lewis**

**Lex·ing·ton** (leks'iŋ tən) **1** [[after the Boston suburb]] city in NC Ky., in Fayette county, with which it constitutes a metropolitan government (**Lexington–Fayette**): pop. 225,000 (met. area 348,000) **2** [[after Robt. Sutton (1661-1723), 2d Baron of *Lexington*]] suburb of Boston, in E Mass.: pop. 29,000: see CONCORD (town in Mass.)

**Ley·den** (līd''n) *alt. sp.* of LEIDEN

**Ley·te** (lāt'ē; *Sp* lā'tā) island of EC Philippines, between Luzon & Mindanao: 2,785 sq. mi. (7,241 sq. km)

**Lha·sa** (lä'sə) capital of Tibet, China, in the SE part: it is a Buddhist holy city: pop. *c.* 105,000

**Liao** (lē ou') river in NE China, flowing from Inner Mongolia west & south into the Yellow Sea: *c.* 900 mi. (1,448 km)

**Liao·dong** (-dooŋ') peninsula in Liaoning province, NE China, extending into the Yellow Sea

**Liao·ning** (-niŋ') province of NE China: 58,301 sq. mi. (151,000 sq. km); pop. 35,722,000; cap. Shenyang

**Liao·yang** (-yäŋ') city in central Liaoning province, NE China: pop. 200,000

**Li·ard** (lē'ärd', lē är') river in W Canada, flowing from S Yukon in a SE direction to British Columbia, then north & east into the Mackenzie River: 755 mi. (1,215 km)

**Li·be·rec** (lē'bə rets') city in Bohemian region of N Czech Republic: pop. 100,000

**Li·ber·i·a** (li bir'ē ə) country on the W coast of Africa: founded (1821) by the American Colonization Society as settlement for freed U.S. slaves; established as independent republic (1847): 43,000 sq. mi. (111,370 sq. km): pop. 2,307,000; cap. Monrovia

**Lib·er·ty** (lib'ər tē) island in SE N.Y., in New York Bay: site of the Statue of Liberty: *c.* 10 acres or 0.015 sq. mi. (0.038 sq. km)

**Li·bra** (lē'brə, lī'-) [[L, a balance]] **1** a S constellation

between Virgo and Scorpio; the Scales **2** the seventh
sign of the zodiac, entered by the sun about September
23

**Library of Congress** the national library in Washington,
D.C., established in 1800 by the U.S. Congress for the
use of its members: it is now one of the largest public
reference libraries in the world

**Li·bre·ville** (lē′brə vēl′) capital of Gabon: seaport on the
Gulf of Guinea: pop. 350,000

**Lib·y·a** (lib′ē ə, lib′yə) **1** ancient Greek & Roman name
of N Africa, west of Egypt **2** country in N Africa, on
the Mediterranean under Turkish domination since
16th cent.; occupied by Italy (1911-43); placed under
British and French military rule, it became an independent kingdom (1951) and a republic (1969):
679,359 sq. mi. (1,759,540 sq. km); pop. 3,876,000; cap.
Tripoli

**Libyan Desert** E part of the Sahara, in Libya, Sudan, &
Egypt west of the Nile

**Liech·ten·stein** (lik′tən stīn′; *Ger* liH′tən shtīn′) country in WC Europe, on the Rhine: a principality: 61 sq.
mi. (158 sq. km); pop. 27,000; cap. Vaduz

**Li·ège** (lē ezh′, -āzh′; *Fr* lyezh′) **1** province of E Belgium:
1,526 sq. mi. (3,953 sq. km); pop. 992,000 **2** its capital,
on the Meuse River: pop. 203,000

**Lie·pā·ja** (lē′ə pä′yə) seaport in W Latvia, on the Baltic:
pop. 109,000

**Li·gu·ri·a** (li gyoor′ē ə) region of NW Italy, on the Ligurian Sea: 2,091 sq. mi. (5,416 sq. km); pop. 1,778,000;
chief city, Genoa

**Ligurian Sea** part of the Mediterranean, between Corsica & NW Italy

**Li·ka·si** (li käs′ē) city in SE Zaire: pop. 185,000

**Lille** (lēl) city in N France: pop. 174,000

**Lil·li·put** (lil′ə put′, -pət) in Jonathan Swift's *Gulliver's
Travels*, a land inhabited by tiny people about six
inches tall

**Li·long·we** (li lôŋ′wā) capital of Malawi, in the W part:
pop. 187,000

**Li·ma** (lē′mə; *for 2,* lī′-) **1** capital of Peru, in the WC
part: pop. 5,257,000 **2** ⟦after *Lima*, Peru⟧ city in NW
Ohio: pop. 46,000

**Lim·bo** (lim′bō′) ⟦ME < L, abl. of *limbus*, edge, border
(in *in limbo*, in or on the border) < IE *(s)lemb-, to

hand down ] [*often* l-] in some Christian theologies, the eternal abode or state, neither heaven nor hell, of the souls of infants or others dying in original sin but free of grievous personal sin, or, before the coming of Christ, the temporary abode or state of all holy souls after death

**Lim·burg** (lim′bʉrg′) 1 province of NE Belgium: 930 sq. mi. (2,408 sq. km); pop. 730,000; cap. Hasselt: also **Limbourg** (*Fr* laɴ bōōr′) 2 province of SE Netherlands: 837 sq. mi. (2,169 sq. km); pop. 1,085,000; cap. Maastricht 3 former duchy occupying the general area of these two provinces

**Lime·house** (līm′hous′) district in the E London borough of Tower Hamlets, on the Thames: former Chinese quarter

**Lim·er·ick** (lim′ər ik, lim′rik) 1 county in SW Ireland, in Munster province: 1,037 sq. mi. (2,685 sq. km); pop. 101,000 2 its county seat: pop. 61,000

**Li·moges** (lē mōzh′; *Fr* lē môzh′) city in WC France: pop. 144,000

**Li·mou·sin** (lē mōō zan′) 1 historical region of WC France, west of Auvergne 2 metropolitan region of modern France in the same general area: 6,541 sq. mi. (16,942 sq. km); pop. 738,000; chief city, Limoges

**Lim·po·po** (lim pō′pō) river in SE Africa, flowing from Transvaal, South Africa across Mozambique into the Indian Ocean: *c.* 1,000 mi. (1,609 km)

**Lin·coln** (liŋ′kən) 1 [ after Pres. Abraham *Lincoln* ] capital of Nebr., in the SE part: pop. 192,000 2 Lincolnshire 3 city in Lincolnshire, England: pop. 78,000

**Lincoln Park** [ after Pres. Abraham *Lincoln* ] city in SE Mich.: pop. 42,000

**Lin·coln·shire** (liŋ′kən shir′, -shər) county in NE England, on the North Sea: 2,272 sq. mi. (5,885 sq. km); pop. 556,000

**Lincoln's Inn** *see* Inns of Court

**Line Islands** (līn) group of coral atolls of Kiribati in the central Pacific, south of Hawaii, formerly divided between the U.S. and Great Britain

**Lin·kö·ping** (lin′shö′piŋ) city in SE Sweden: pop. 116,000

**Lin·lith·gow** (lin lith′gō) *old name of* West Lothian

**Linz** (lints) city in N Austria, on the Danube: pop.

200,000

**Li·on** (lī′ən) Leo, the constellation and fifth sign of the zodiac

**Lions, Gulf of** (the) part of the Mediterranean, on the S coast of France, between Toulon & Spain: Fr. name **Golfe du Lion** (gôlf dü lyôn′)

**Li·pa·ri Islands** (lip′ə rē′) group of volcanic islands of Italy in the Tyrrhenian Sea, northeast of Sicily: *c.* 45 sq. mi. (117 sq. km)

**Li·petsk** (lē′petsk′) city in SW European Russia: pop. 447,000

**Lip·pe** (lip′ə) region in W Germany, in the state of North Rhine-Westphalia: formerly a principality

**Lis·bon** (liz′bən) capital of Portugal: seaport on the Tagus estuary: pop. 817,000: Port. name **Lis·bo·a** (lēzh bô′ə)

**Lith·u·a·ni·a** (lith′ōō ā′nē ə, lith′ə wā′-) country in N Europe, on the Baltic Sea: from 1940 to 1991 it was a republic of the U.S.S.R.: 25,170 sq. mi. (65,200 sq. km); pop. 3,572,000; cap. Vilnius: formerly, **Lithuanian Soviet Socialist Republic**

**Little America** five operational bases established by the Admiral Byrd expeditions, on the Ross Ice Shelf, Antarctica

**Little Bear** the constellation Ursa Minor

**Little Bighorn** river in N Wyo., flowing north into the Bighorn in S Mont.: *c.* 90 mi. (145 km): in a battle near here (Battle of the Little Bighorn, 1876) General Custer's troops attacked Dakota and Cheyenne Indians and were annihilated

**Little Diomede** *see* DIOMEDE ISLANDS

**Little Dipper** a dipper-shaped group of stars in the constellation Ursa Minor

**Little Missouri** river in the NW U.S., flowing from NE Wyo. into the Missouri in N.Dak.: 560 mi. (901 km)

**Little Rock** ⟦after a rocky promontory in the river⟧ capital of Ark., on the Arkansas River: pop. 176,000

**Little St. Ber·nard Pass** (bər närd′, bʉr′nərd) mountain pass in the Graian Alps, between France & Italy: 7,178 ft. (2,188 m) high

**Liv·er·more** (liv′ər môr′) ⟦after R. *Livermore*, an English sailor who settled there (*c.* 1838)⟧ city in W Calif., east of San Francisco: pop. 57,000

**Liv·er·pool** (liv′ər pool′) seaport in NW England, in

Merseyside, on the Mersey estuary: pop. 497,000

**Li·vo·ni·a** (li vō'nē ə) **1** former province (1783-1918) of Russia, on the Gulf of Riga: divided (1918) between Latvia & Estonia **2** ⟦after Russian province⟧ city in SE Mich.: suburb of Detroit: pop. 101,000

**Li·vor·no** (lə vôr'nō; *It* lē vôr'nô) *It. name of* LEGHORN

**Liz·ard Head** (or **Point**) (liz'ərd) promontory at the tip of a peninsula (**The Lizard**) in SW Cornwall, England: southernmost point of Great Britain

**Lju·blja·na** (lōō'blē ä'nä', lyōō'-) capital of Slovenia, in the central part: pop. 326,000

**Lla·nel·ly** (lä nel'ē) seaport in Dyfed, SW Wales: pop. 41,000

**Lla·no Es·ta·ca·do** (lä'nō es'tə kä'dō) ⟦Sp, lit., staked plain⟧ extensive high plain in W Tex. & SE N.Mex.: S extension of the Great Plains: *c.* 40,000 sq. mi. (103,600 sq. km)

**Lo·car·no** (lō kär'nō) town in S Switzerland, on Lake Maggiore: site of peace conference (1925): pop. 15,000

**Lo·cris** (lō'kris) region of ancient Greece, north of the Gulf of Corinth

**Lod** (lōd) city in central Israel: pop. 31,000

**Lo·di** (lō'dē) city in Lombardy, NW Italy: scene of Napoleon's defeat of the Austrians (1796): pop. 37,000

**Łódź** (lōōj) city in central Poland: pop. 845,000

**Lo·fo·ten Islands** (lō'fōōt'n) group of Norwegian islands within the Arctic Circle, off the NW coast of Norway: *c.* 550 sq. mi. (1,425 sq. km)

**Lo·gan** (lō'gən), **Mount** ⟦after Sir W. E. *Logan* (1798-1875), Cdn geologist⟧ mountain in the St. Elias range, SW Yukon, Canada: highest mountain in Canada: 19,850 ft. (6,050 m)

**Lo·gro·ño** (lə grōn'yō') city in N Spain: pop. 110,000

**Loire** (lə wär'; *Fr* lwȧr) river flowing from S France north & west into the Bay of Biscay: 625 mi. (1,006 km)

**Lol·land** (läl'ənd; *Dan* lôl'än) island of Denmark, in the Baltic Sea, south of Zealand: 479 sq. mi. (1,240 sq. km)

**Lo·mas** (lō'mäs') city in E Argentina: suburb of Buenos Aires: pop. 509,000: in full **Lo·mas de Za·mo·ra** (lō'mäz' də zə mōr'ə, -môr-)

**Lom·bar·dy** (läm'bər dē) ⟦the region was invaded and settled by Lombards in the 6th-c. A.D.⟧ region of N Italy, on the border of Switzerland: 9,210 sq. mi.

(23,856 sq. km); pop. 8,885,000; chief city, Milan: It. name **Lom·bar·dia** (lôm bär′dyä)

**Lom·bok** (läm bäk′) island of Indonesia, between Bali & Sumbawa: 1,825 sq. mi. (4,725 sq. km)

**Lo·mé** (lô mā′) capital of Togo: seaport on the Bight of Benin: pop. 366,000

**Lo·mond** (lō′mənd), **Loch** lake in WC Scotland, between Strathclyde & Central regions: *c.* 27 sq. mi. (70 sq. km)

**Lon·don** (lun′dən) **1** administrative area in SE England, consisting of the City of London and 32 boroughs: capital of England, the United Kingdom, & the Commonwealth: 610 sq. mi. (1,580 sq. km); pop. 6,754,000: called **Greater London 2** ⟦after *London, England*⟧ city in SE Ontario, Canada: pop. 275,000 **3 City of** historic center of London, with its ancient boundaries: 677 acres or 1.06 sq. mi.

**Lon·don·der·ry** (-der′ē) **1** district in NW Northern Ireland, in the E part of a former, much larger county (also called **Londonderry**) **2** seaport in this district, on an inlet of the Atlantic: pop. 63,000

**Lone Star State** *name for* TEXAS

**Long Beach** ⟦descriptive⟧ seaport in SW Calif., on the Pacific: see LOS ANGELES

**Long·ford** (lôŋ′fərd) county in Leinster province, EC Ireland: 403 sq. mi. (1,043 sq. km); pop. 31,000

**Long Island** ⟦descriptive⟧ island in SE N.Y. between Long Island Sound & the Atlantic: 1,411 sq. mi. (3,655 sq. km)

**Long Island Sound** arm of the Atlantic, between N Long Island & S Conn.: *c.* 100 mi. (161 km) long

**Long·mont** (lôŋ′mänt) ⟦after fol. + Fr *mont*, mountain⟧ city in NC Colo.: pop. 52,000

**Longs Peak** (lôŋz) ⟦after S. H. *Long* (1784-1864), U.S. engineer⟧ peak in Rocky Mountain National Park, NC Colo.: 14,255 ft. (4,345 m)

**Lon·gueuil** (lôŋ gāl′; *Fr* lōn gë′y′) ⟦after Charles Le Moyne de *Longueuil* (1626-85), Fr colonist⟧ city in S Quebec, on the St. Lawrence: suburb of Montreal: pop. 124,000

**Long·view** (lôŋ′vyo͞o′) ⟦from the "view" afforded by its altitude⟧ city in NE Tex.: pop. 70,000

**Look·out Mountain** (look′out′) ⟦descriptive⟧ mountain ridge in Tenn., Ga., & Ala.: the section near Chattanooga was the site of a Civil War battle (1863) in

which Union forces defeated the Confederates: highest
point, 2,125 ft. (647 m)

**Loop, the** the main business and shopping district in
downtown Chicago

**Lo·rain** (lô rān´) ⟦ult. after LORRAINE⟧ city in N Ohio,
on Lake Erie: pop. 71,000: see CLEVELAND

**Lo·rient** (lô ryän´) seaport in NW France, on the Bay of
Biscay: pop. 65,000

**Lor·raine** (lô rān´; *Fr* lô ren´) historical region of NE
France: see ALSACE-LORRAINE

**Los Al·a·mos** (lôs al´ə mōs´, läs-) ⟦Sp, lit., the poplars⟧
town in NC N.Mex., near Santa Fe: site of atomic
energy facility where the atomic bomb was developed:
pop. 11,000

**Los An·ge·les** (lôs an´jə ləs, -lēz; läs an´-; *also*, -aŋ´gə-)
⟦Sp, short for *Reina de los Angeles*, lit., Queen of the
Angels⟧ city & seaport on the SW coast of Calif.: pop.
3,485,000 (met. area with Long Beach 8,863,000; urban
area, with Anaheim & Riverside, 14,532,000)

**Lot** (lôt) river in S France, flowing west into the
Garonne: *c.* 300 mi. (483 km)

**Lo·thi·an** (lō´*th*ē ən, -*th*ē-) region of SE Scotland,
including the former counties of East Lothian, Midlo-
thian, & West Lothian: 677 sq. mi. (1,756 sq. km); pop.
745,000

**Lou·ise** (lōō ēz´), **Lake** ⟦after Princess *Louise* Alberta,
daughter of Queen Victoria of Great Britain & wife of
the Marquess of Lorne, Cdn gov. gen. (1878-83)⟧
small lake in SW Alberta, Canada, in Banff National
Park

**Lou·i·si·an·a** (lōō ē´zē an´ə, lōō´ə zē-) ⟦Fr *La Loui-
sianne*, name for the Mississippi Valley, after *Louis*
XIV of France (1638-1715)⟧ Southern State of the
U.S., on the Gulf of Mexico: admitted, 1812; 48,523 sq.
mi. (126,160 sq. km); pop. 4,220,000; cap. Baton
Rouge: abbrev. *LA* or *La*

**Louisiana Purchase** land bought by the U.S. from
France in 1803 for $15,000,000: it extended from the
Mississippi to the Rocky Mountains & from the Gulf
of Mexico to Canada

**Lou·is·ville** (lōō´ē vil; *locally* lōō´ə vəl) ⟦after *Louis* XVI
of France (1754-93)⟧ city in N Ky., on the Ohio River:
pop. 269,000 (met. area 953,000)

**Lou·ren·ço Mar·ques** (lō ren´sō mär´kes; *Port* lô ren´

soo mär′kezh) *old name of* MAPUTO

**Louth** (louth) county in Leinster province, E Ireland: 317 sq. mi. (821 sq. km); pop. 88,000

**Lou·vain** (lōō van′; *E* lōō vān′) *Fr. name of* LEUVEN

**Low Countries** the Netherlands, Belgium, & Luxembourg

**Low·ell** (lō′əl) [after F. C. *Lowell* (1775-1817), industrialist] city in NE Mass.: pop. 103,000

**Lower California** BAJA CALIFORNIA

**Lower Canada** *old name* (1791-1841) *of* QUEBEC

**lower forty–eight** the forty-eight conterminous States of the United States: a term used mainly by Alaskans: usually written **lower 48**

**Lower Saxony** state of NW Germany, on the North Sea: 18,319 sq. mi. (47,447 sq. km); pop. 7,230,000; cap. Hanover

**Lowes·toft** (lōs′tôft) city in Suffolk, E England, on the North Sea: pop. 57,000

**Low·lands** (lō′ləndz), **the** lowland region of SC Scotland, between the Highlands & the Southern Uplands

**Lo·yang** (lō′yäŋ′) *old form of* LUOYANG

**Lu·a·la·ba** (lōō′ə lä′bə) upper course of the Congo, rising in SE Zaire & flowing north

**Lu·an·da** (lōō än′də, -an′-) capital of Angola: seaport on the Atlantic: pop. 700,000

**Lu·ang Pra·bang** (lōō äŋ′ prə bäŋ′) city in NC Laos, on the Mekong River: pop. 44,000

**Lub·bock** (lub′ək) [after T. S. *Lubbock*, Confederate officer] city in NW Tex.: pop. 186,000

**Lü·beck** (lōō′bek′; *Ger* lü′bek′) city & port in N Germany, in the state of Schleswig-Holstein: pop. 213,000

**Lub·lin** (lōō′blin; *Pol* lōō′blēn′) city in SE Poland: pop. 320,000

**Lu·bum·ba·shi** (lōō′bōōm bä′shē) city in SE Zaire, near the border of Zambia: pop. 451,000

**Lu·ca·ni·a** (lōō kā′nē ə) **1** ancient district in S Italy, now in the Italian region of BASILICATA **2 Mount** mountain in the St. Elias range, SW Yukon, Canada: 17,150 ft. (5,227 m)

**Luc·ca** (lōō′kä′) city in Tuscany, W Italy: pop. 90,000

**Lu·cerne** (lōō sʉrn′; *Fr* lü sʉrn′) **1** canton in central Switzerland: 577 sq. mi. (1,494 sq. km); pop. 302,000 **2** its capital: pop. 73,000 **3 Lake of** lake in central Switzerland: 44 sq. mi. (113 sq. km)

**Lu·chow** (lōō'jō') *old form of* LUZHOU

**Lu·ci·fer** (lōō'sə fər) ⟦ME < OE < L, morning star (in ML, Satan), lit., light-bringing < *lux* (gen. *lucis*), light + *ferre*, to bear⟧ the planet Venus when it is the morning star

**Luck·now** (luk'nou') city in N India: capital of Uttar Pradesh: pop. 1,007,000

**Lü·da** (lōō'dä') urban complex in NE China, at the tip of the Liaodong Peninsula: it consists of the seaports of Dalian (formerly *Dairen*) & Lüshun (formerly *Port Arthur*): pop. 7,000,000

**Lu·dhi·a·na** (lōō'dē ä'nə) city in N India, in Punjab: pop. 607,000

**Lud·wigs·ha·fen** (lood'vigz hä'fən) city in SW Germany, on the Rhine, in the state of Rhineland-Palatinate: pop. 156,000

**Lu·ga·no** (lōō gä'nō) **1** city in S Switzerland: pop. 28,000 **2 Lake** lake on the border between Switzerland and Italy: *c.* 20 sq. mi. (51 sq. km)

**Lu·gansk** (lōō gänsk') city in E Ukraine, in the Donets Basin: pop. 497,000: see VOROSHILOVGRAD

**Lui·chow** (lə wē'jō') *old form of* LEIZHOU

**Luik** (loik) *Fl. name of* LIÈGE

**Lun·dy's Lane** (lun'dēz) ⟦< ?⟧ road near Niagara Falls, Ontario, Canada: site of an indecisive battle (1814) between British & American forces

**Lu·né·ville** (lü nā vēl') city in NE France: treaty signed here (1801) between France & Austria: pop. 22,000

**Luo·yang** (lə wō'yäŋ') city in Henan province, EC China, near the Huang He: pop. 750,000

**Lu·pus** (lōō'pəs) ⟦L < *lupus*, wolf⟧ a S constellation near the Milky Way between Centaurus and Scorpius

**Lu·sa·ka** (lōō sä'kä) capital of Zambia, in the central part: pop. 538,000

**Lu·sa·ti·a** (lōō sā'shə, -shē ə) region in E Germany & SW Poland

**Lü·shun** (lōō'shoon') seaport in Liaoning province, NE China: pop. 200,000

**Lu·si·ta·ni·a** (lōō'sə tā'nē ə) ancient Roman province in the Iberian Peninsula, corresponding to most of modern Portugal & part of W Spain

**Lut Desert** (lōōt) DASHT-E-LUT

**Lu·te·tia** (lōō tē'shə) *ancient Rom. name of* PARIS

**Lu·ton** (lōōt'n) city in Bedfordshire, SC England: pop.

165,000

**Lux·em·bourg** (luk'səm burg'; *Fr* lük sän bōōr') **1** grand duchy in W Europe, bounded by Belgium, Germany, & France: 998 sq. mi. (2,586 sq. km); pop. 366,000 **2** its capital, in the S part: pop. 76,000 **3** province of SE Belgium: 1,714 sq. mi. (4,440 sq. km); pop. 224,000: also **Lux'em·burg'**

**Lux·or** (luk'sôr, look'-) city in S Egypt, on the Nile, near the ruins of ancient Thebes: pop. 93,000

**Lu·zern** (lōōt sern') *Ger. name of* LUCERNE

**Lu·zhou** (lōō'jō') city in Sichuan province, SC China, on the Chiang: pop. 289,000

**Lu·zon** (lōō zän') main island of the Philippines: 40,420 sq. mi. (104,647 sq. km); chief city, Manila

**Lviv** (ly'vēf) city in W Ukraine: pop. 742,000: Russ. name **Lvov** (ly'vôf)

**Lwów** (lə vōōf') *Pol. name of* LVIV

**Ly·all·pur** (lī'əl poor') *old name of* FAISALABAD

**Ly·ce·um** (lī sē'əm) ⟦L < Gr *Lykeion*, the Lyceum: so called from the neighboring temple of *Apollōn Lykeios*⟧ the grove at Athens where Aristotle taught

**Ly·ci·a** (lish'ə, -ē ə) ancient country in SW Asia Minor, on the Mediterranean: settled in early times, came under Persian and Syrian rule; annexed as a province by Rome (1st cent. A.D.)

**Lyd·da** (lid'ə) LOD

**Lyd·i·a** (lid'ē ə) ancient kingdom in W Asia Minor: fl. 7th-6th cent. B.C.; conquered by Persians and absorbed into Persian Empire (6th cent. B.C.)

**Lynch·burg** (linch'burg') ⟦after J. *Lynch*, reputed founder⟧ city in central Va., on the James River: pop. 66,000

**Lynn** (lin) city in NE Mass., on Massachusetts Bay: suburb of Boston: pop. 81,000

**Lyn·wood** (lin'wood') ⟦ult. after *Lynn Wood* Sessions, wife of a local dairy owner⟧ city in SW Calif.: pop. 62,000

**Lynx** (liŋks) a N constellation between Auriga and Ursa Major

**Lyon** (lyôn) city in EC France, at the juncture of the Rhone & Saône rivers: pop. 418,000

**Ly·on·nais** (lē ô ne') historical region of SE central France

**Ly·on·nesse** (lī'ə nes') ⟦OFr *Leonois*, earlier *Loonois*,

ult., after ? *Lothian,* former division of Scotland ]
*Arthurian Legend* a region in SW England, apparently
near Cornwall, supposed to have sunk beneath the sea

**Ly·ons** (lī′ənz) *Eng. name of* LYON

**Ly·ra** (lī′rə) [[ L < *lyra,* lyre < Gr ]] a N constellation
between Hercules and Cygnus containing the star
Vega; Harp

**Lys** (lēs) river in N France & W Belgium, flowing northwest into the Scheldt: *c.* 130 mi. (209 km)

# M

**M** *abbrev. for* Manitoba

**MA** *abbrev. for* Massachusetts

**Maas** (mäs) *Du. name of* MEUSE

**Maas·tricht** (mäs′triHt) city in SE Netherlands, on the
Maas River: pop. 114,000

**Ma·cao** (mə kou′) 1 Chinese territory under Portuguese
administration forming an enclave in Guangdong
Province, SE China: it consists of a peninsula & two
small adjacent islands at the mouth of the Zhu River,
west of Hong Kong: 6 sq. mi. (16 sq. km); pop. 343,000
2 its capital, a seaport coextensive with the peninsula:
Port. sp. **Ma·cau′**

**Ma·ca·pá** (mak′ə pä′) seaport in N Brazil, on the Amazon delta: capital of Amapá state: pop. 115,000

**Ma·cas·sar** (mə kas′ər) *alt. sp. of* MAKASSAR

**Mac·e·don** (mas′ə dän′) ancient Macedonia

**Mac·e·do·ni·a** (mas′ə dō′nē ə, -dōn′yə) 1 ancient kingdom in SE Europe: now a region divided among
Greece, the country of Macedonia, & Bulgaria 2 country in the Balkan Peninsula: formerly (1946-91) a constituent republic of Yugoslavia: 9,928 sq. mi. (25,713
sq. km); pop. 1,909,000; cap. Skopje

**Ma·ce·ió** (mä′sā yô′) seaport in NE Brazil, on the Atlantic: capital of Alagoas state: pop. 375,000

**Ma·chi·da** (mə chē′də, mäch′i dä′) city in SE Honshu,
Japan, near Tokyo: pop. 307,000

**Ma·chu Pic·chu** (mä′chōō pēk′chōō) site of ruins of an
ancient Incan city in SC Peru

**Mac·ken·zie** (mə ken′zē) [[ after explorer Sir Alexander
*Mackenzie* (*c.* 1763-1820) ]] 1 river in W Northwest
Territories, Canada, flowing from the Great Slave
Lake northwest into the Beaufort Sea: 2,635 mi. (4,216

km) 2 former district of Northwest Territories, Canada

**Mack·i·nac** (mak′ə nô′) 〖CdnFr *Mackinac* < Ojibwa *mitchimakinak*, big turtle〗 small island in the Straits of Mackinac: a Mich. State park: 6 sq. mi. (15.5 sq. km): formerly a center of trade with the Indians of the Northwest

**Mack·i·nac** (mak′ə nô′), **Straits of** 〖see prec.〗 channel connecting Lake Huron & Lake Michigan, separating the upper & lower peninsulas of Mich.: *c.* 4 mi. (6.4 km) wide

**Ma·con** (mā′kən) 〖after N. *Macon* (1758-1837), N.C. patriot〗 city in central Ga.: pop. 107,000

**Mac·quar·ie** (mə kwôr′ē, -kwär′-) river in SE Australia, flowing northwest into the Darling: *c.* 600 mi. (965 km)

**Mad·a·gas·car** (mad′ə gas′kər) 1 large island in the Indian Ocean, off the SE coast of Africa 2 country comprising this island and nearby islands: discovered by the Portuguese (1500), it became a French protectorate (1895), colony (1896), & a republic (*Malagasy Republic*) of the French Community; it became fully independent (1960); since 1975, the **Democratic Republic of Madagascar**: 228,919 sq. mi. (592,900 sq. km); pop. 7,604,000; cap. Antananarivo

**Ma·deir·a** (mə dir′ə) 1 group of Portuguese islands in the Atlantic, off the W coast of Morocco: 308 sq. mi. (798 sq. km); pop. 268,000; chief city, Funchal 2 largest island of this group: 286 sq. mi. (740 sq. km) 3 river in NW Brazil, flowing northeast into the Amazon: *c.* 2,100 mi. (3,379 km)

**Mad·hya Pra·desh** (mud′yə prä′desh) state of central India: 172,985 sq. mi. (442,841 sq. km); pop. 52,178,000; cap. Bhopal

**Mad·i·son** (mad′ə sən) 〖after U.S. Pres. James *Madison* (1751-1836)〗 capital of Wis., in the SC part: pop. 191,000

**Madison Avenue** a street in New York City, regarded as the center of the U.S. advertising industry

**Ma·dras** (mə dras′, -dräs′; mad′rəs, mäd′-) 1 *old name of* TAMIL NADU 2 capital of Tamil Nadu: seaport on the Coromandel Coast: pop. 4,277,000

**Ma·dre de Di·os** (mä′drе de dyŏs′) river in SE Peru & N Bolivia, flowing east into the Beni: *c.* 900 mi. (1,448 km)

**Ma·drid** (mə drid'; *Sp* mä thrēth') capital of Spain, in the central part: pop. 3,200,000

**Ma·du·ra** (mä door'ä) island of Indonesia, just off the NE coast of Java: 1,770 sq. mi. (4,584 sq. km): see JAVA

**Ma·du·rai** (mä də rī') city in S India, in the state of Tamil Nadu: pop. 904,000

**Mae·an·der** (mē an'dər) *ancient name of* MENDERES (river flowing into the Aegean)

**Mae·ba·shi** (mä'yə bäsh'ē, mē bäsh'ē) city in central Honshu, Japan: pop. 272,000

**Mael·strom** (māl'strəm) ⟦17th-c. Du (now *maalstroom*) < *malen*, to grind, whirl round + *stroom*, a stream: first applied by 16th-c. Du geographers⟧ a famous strong, swirling tidal current off the W coast of Norway, hazardous to safe navigation

**Maf·i·keng** (mäf'ə kiŋ) city in NC Bophuthatswana, near the Botswana border, South Africa: scene of famous siege of British garrison by the Boers, lasting 217 days: pop. 6,500: old name **Maf·e·king**

**Ma·gal·la·nes** (mä'gä yä'nes) *old name of* PUNTA ARENAS

**Mag·da·le·na** (mäg'dä le'nä) river in W Colombia, flowing north into the Caribbean: *c.* 1,000 mi. (1,609 km)

**Mag·de·burg** (mäg'də boorkh; *E* mag'də bʉrg') city & port in E Germany, on the Elbe, in the state of Saxony-Anhalt: pop. 288,000

**Ma·gel·lan** (mə jel'ən), **Strait of** channel between the South American mainland & Tierra del Fuego: *c.* 350 mi. (563 km) long

**Mag·el·lan·ic cloud** (maj'ə lan'ik) ⟦after Ferdinand *Magellan* (*c.* 1480-1521), Port navigator⟧ either of two (the Large and the Small) irregular galaxies visible to the naked eye in the S constellations Dorado, Mensa, and Tucana: the nearest of the external galaxies to the Milky Way

**Mag·gio·re** (mə jôr'ē; *It* mäd jô're), **Lake** lake in NW Italy & S Switzerland: 82 sq. mi. (212 sq. km)

**Ma·ghreb** (mu'grəb) NW Africa, chiefly Morocco, Algeria, & Tunisia: the Arabic name

**Ma·gi·not line** (mazh'ə nō') ⟦after A. *Maginot* (1877-1932), Fr minister of war⟧ a system of heavy fortifications built before World War II on the E frontier of France: it failed to prevent invasion by the Nazi armies

**Mag·na Grae·ci·a** (mag′nə grē′shē ə) ancient Greek colonies in S Italy

**Mag·ne·sia** (mag nē′zhə, -shə) *ancient name of* MANISA

**Mag·ni·to·gorsk** (mäg′ni tô gôrsk′) city in SW Russia, on the Ural River: pop. 422,000

**Ma·gyar·or·szág** (mô̆d′yär ôr′säg) *Hung. name of* HUNGARY

**Ma·hal·la el Ku·bra** (mä hä′lä el kōō′brä) city in N Egypt, in the Nile delta: pop. 292,000

**Ma·ha·rash·tra** (mə hä′räsh′trə) state of W India: 118,717 sq. mi. (307,475 sq. km); pop. 62,693,000; cap. Bombay

**Ma·hé** (mä hā′) chief island of the Seychelles, in the Indian Ocean: 56 sq. mi. (145 sq. km)

**Mai·da·nek** (mī′də nek′) Nazi concentration camp & extermination center in E Poland, near Lublin

**Maid·stone** (mād′stən, -stōn′) city in SE England: county seat of Kent: pop. 72,000

**Main** (mīn; *E* mān) ⟦G < Gaul *Moenus* < IE *\*moin-*, river name < base *\*mei-*, to go, wander > L *meare*, to go ⟧ river in SW Germany, flowing west into the Rhine at Mainz: 307 mi. (494 km)

**Maine** (mān; *for 2, Fr* men) ⟦orig. after *Maine*, region in NW France, but later interpreted as signifying its status as the *main* part of the New England region ⟧ 1 New England State of the U.S.: admitted, 1820; 33,215 sq. mi. (86,027 sq. km); pop. 1,228,000; cap. Augusta: abbrev. *ME* or *Me* 2 historical region of NW France, south of Normandy

**Main·land** (mān′land′, -lənd) 1 chief island of Japan: see HONSHU 2 largest of the Orkney Islands: *c.* 190 sq. mi. (492 sq. km) 3 largest of the Shetland Islands: 407 sq. mi. (1,055 sq. km)

**Mainz** (mīnts) city in W Germany, on the Rhine: capital of the state of Rhineland-Palatinate: pop. 187,000

**Ma·jor·ca** (mə jôr′kə) island of Spain, largest of the Balearic Islands: 1,405 sq. mi. (3,653 sq. km); chief city, Palma: Sp. name MALLORCA

**Ma·kas·sar** (mə kas′ər) *old name of* UJUNG PANDANG

**Ma·key·ev·ka** (mä kā′yif kä′) city in SE Ukraine, in the Donets Basin: pop. 451,000

**Ma·khach·ka·la** (mə käch′kə lä′) city and seaport of SW Russia, on the Caspian Sea: pop. 301,000

**Mal·a·bar Coast** (mal′ə bär′) coastal region in SW India

on the Arabian Sea, extending from Cape Comorin to Goa & inland to the Western Ghats: *c.* 450 mi. (725 km) long: also **Malabar**

**Ma·la·bo** (mä lä′bō) capital of Equatorial Guinea: seaport on the island portion of the country: pop. 37,000

**Ma·lac·ca** (mə lak′ə) **1** state of Malaysia in W Peninsular Malaysia, on the strait of Malacca: 637 sq. mi. (1,650 sq. km); pop. 453,000 **2** seaport in this state: its capital: pop. 88,000 **3 Strait of** strait between Sumatra & the Malay Peninsula: *c.* 500 mi. (805 km) long

**Má·la·ga** (mä′lä gä′; *E* mal′ə gə) seaport in S Spain, on the Mediterranean: pop. 503,000

**Mal·a·gas·y Republic** (mal′ə gas′ē) *old name of* MADAGASCAR (the country)

**Ma·lang** (mä läŋ′) city in E Java, Indonesia: pop. 511,000

**Mäl·ar** (mel′är) lake in SE Sweden: 440 sq. mi. (1,140 sq. km): Swed. name **Mäl·ar·en** (mel′ä rən)

**Ma·la·tya** (mä′lä tyä′) city in EC Turkey: pop. 179,000

**Ma·la·wi** (mä′lä wē) **1** country in SE Africa, on Lake Malawi: a former British protectorate, it became independent & a member of the Commonwealth (1964); a republic since 1966: 45,746 sq. mi. (118,484 sq. km); pop. 7,293,000; cap. Lilongwe **2 Lake** lake in SE central Africa bounded by Malawi, Tanzania, & Mozambique: *c.* 11,600 sq. mi. (30,040 sq. km)

**Ma·lay·a** (mə lā′ə) **1** MALAY PENINSULA **2 Federation of** former federation of states on the S end of the Malay Peninsula: formerly a British colony, it became independent & a member of the Commonwealth (1957); since 1963 a territory of Malaysia called PENINSULAR MALAYSIA: see MALAYSIA

**Ma·lay Archipelago** (mä′lä′) large group of islands between SE Asia & Australia, including Indonesia, the Philippines, &, sometimes, New Guinea

**Malay Peninsula** peninsula in SE Asia, extending from Singapore to the Isthmus of Kra: it includes Peninsular Malaysia & part of Thailand: *c.* 700 mi. (1,100 km) long

**Ma·lay·sia** (mə lā′zhə, -shə) **1** MALAY ARCHIPELAGO **2** country in SE Asia, a union (1963) of the former Federation of MALAYA, Sabah, Sarawak, & Singapore (which seceded in 1965 to become an independent nation); a member of the Commonwealth: *c.* 129,000

sq. mi. (334,000 sq. km); pop. 15,270,000; cap. Kuala Lumpur

**Mal·den** (môl′dən) 〖after *Maldon,* town in England〗 city in E Mass.: suburb of Boston: pop. 54,000

**Mal·dives** (mal′dīvz) country on a group of islands in the Indian Ocean, southwest of Sri Lanka: a former sultanate under British protection, it became independent in 1965, a republic in 1968, & a member of the Commonwealth in 1982: 115 sq. mi. (298 sq. km); pop. 184,000; cap. Malé

**Ma·lé** (mä′lā) chief island and capital of the Maldives: pop. 42,000: also **Ma·le** (mä′lē)

**Ma·li** (mä′lē) country in W Africa, south & east of Mauritania: a former French territory (FRENCH SUDAN), it joined the French Community as the autonomous *Sudanese Republic* (1958); it joined with Senegal to form the **Mali Federation** (1959); union dissolved & full independence proclaimed (1960): 478,786 sq. mi. (1,240,000 sq. km); pop. 7,898,000; cap. Bamako

**Ma·lines** (má lēn′) *Fr. name of* MECHELEN

**Mal·lor·ca** (mäl yôr′kä, mä-) *Sp. name of* MAJORCA

**Malm·ö** (mälm′ö; *E* mal′mō) seaport in S Sweden, on the Öresund: pop. 229,000

**Mal·ta** (môl′tə) **1** country on a group of islands in the Mediterranean, south of Sicily: a former British colony, it became independent & a member of the Commonwealth (1964); 122 sq. mi. (317 sq. km); pop. 354,000; cap. Valletta **2** main island of this group: 95 sq. mi. (247 sq. km)

**Ma·lu·ku** (mə lōō′kōō′) *Indonesian name of* MOLUCCAS

**Mal·vern Hill** (mal′vərn) 〖after *Malvern Hills,* England〗 plateau near Richmond, Va.: site of a battle (1862) of the Civil War in which Union troops repulsed Confederate attacks but withdrew the next day

**Mam·moth Cave National Park** (mam′əth) national park in SW Ky., containing enormous limestone caverns: 79 sq. mi. (205 sq. km)

**Ma·mo·ré** (mä′mô re′) river in NC Bolivia, flowing north to join the Beni & form the Madeira: *c.* 1,200 mi. (1,931 km)

**Man** (man), **Isle of** one of the British Isles, between Northern Ireland & England: 227 sq. mi. (587 sq. km); pop. 60,000; cap. Douglas

**Man** *abbrev. for* Manitoba

**Ma·na·gua** (mä nä′gwä) **1** lake in W Nicaragua: *c.* 390 sq. mi. (1,010 sq. km) **2** capital of Nicaragua, on this lake: pop. 650,000

**Ma·na·ma** (mə nam′ə) capital of Bahrain: pop. 121,000

**Ma·nas·sas** (mə nas′əs) ⟦ < ? ⟧ city in NE Va., near Bull Run: site of two Civil War battles in which Union forces were defeated: pop. 28,000

**Ma·naus** (mä nous′) city in NW Brazil, on the Negro River: capital of Amazonas state: pop. 175,000

**Man·ches·ter** (man′ches′tər, -chi stər) **1** city & port in NW England, connected by canal (**Manchester Ship Canal**), 35 mi. (56 km) long, with the Irish Sea: pop. 458,000 **2** county of NW England, surrounding this city: 497 sq. mi. (1,287 sq. km); pop. 2,588,000: in full **Greater Manchester** **3** ⟦after Eng city⟧ city in S N.H., on the Merrimack River: pop. 100,000

**Man·chu·kuo** (man chōō′kwō) former country (1932-45), a Japanese puppet state consisting mainly of Manchuria

**Man·chu·ri·a** (man choor′ē ə) region & former administrative division of NE China coextensive with the provinces of Heilongjiang, Jilin, & Liaoning, & the NE section of Inner Mongolia

**Man·da·lay** (man′də lā′, man′də lā′) city in central Myanmar, on the Irrawaddy River: pop. 417,000

**Man·ga·lore** (mäŋ′gə lôr′) city in SW Karnataka, India, on Malabar Coast: pop. 306,000

**Man·hat·tan** (man hat′′n, mən-) ⟦ < Du prob. < the native name < *manah,* island + *atin,* hill ⟧ **1** island in SE N.Y., between the Hudson & East rivers, forming part of New York City: 13 mi. (21 km) long: also **Manhattan Island** **2** borough of New York City, consisting of this island, some small nearby islands, & a small bit of the mainland: 22 sq. mi. (57 sq. km); pop. 1,488,000

**Ma·nil·a** (mə nil′ə) capital & seaport of the Philippines, in SW Luzon, on an inlet (**Manila Bay**) of the South China Sea: pop. 1,630,000 (met. area 5,926,000)

**Man·i·pur** (mun′ə poor′) state of NE India, on the Myanmar border: 8,631 sq. mi. (22,356 sq. km); pop. 1,434,000; cap. Imphal

**Ma·ni·sa** (mä′ni sä′) city in W Turkey: as Magnesia, site of a battle (190 B.C.) in which the Romans defeated Antiochus the Great: pop. 94,000

**Man·i·to·ba** (man'ə tō'bə) ⟦Cree *manitoowapaaw*, the narrows (of Lake Manitoba), lit., god narrows⟧ **1** province of SC Canada: 251,000 sq. mi. (652,000 sq. km); pop. 1,064,000; cap. Winnipeg: abbrev. *MB* or *Man* **2 Lake** lake in S Manitoba: 1,817 sq. mi. (4,706 sq. km)

**Man·i·tou·lin Island** (man'ə tōō'lin) ⟦earlier *Manitoualin* < 18th-c. Ojibwa dial. *manitoowaalink*, lit., at the god's den⟧ Canadian island in N Lake Huron: 1,068 sq. mi. (2,766 sq. km)

**Ma·ni·za·les** (mä'nē sä'les) city in WC Colombia: pop. 328,000

**Mann·heim** (man'hīm; *Ger* män'-) city in SW Germany, on the Rhine, in the state of Baden-Württemberg: pop. 297,000

**Mans·field** (manz'fēld', mans'-) **1** city in Nottingham-shire, NC England: pop. 58,000 **2** ⟦after J. *Mansfield* (1759-1830), surveyor⟧ city in NC Ohio: pop. 51,000

**Man·su·ra** (man sōōr'ə) city in N Egypt, on the Nile delta: pop. 256,000

**Man·tu·a** (man'choo wə, -too wə) commune in Lom-bardy, N Italy: birthplace of Virgil: pop. 62,000: It. name **Man·to·va** (män'tô vä)

**Ma·pu·to** (mə pōōt'ō) capital of Mozambique: seaport on the Indian Ocean: pop. 785,000

**Mar·a·cai·bo** (mar'ə kī'bō; *Sp* mä'rä kī'bô) **1** seaport in NW Venezuela: pop. 929,000 **2 Gulf of** Gulf of VEN-EZUELA **3 Lake** lake in NW Venezuela, connected by channel with the Gulf of Venezuela: largest lake in South America: *c.* 5,000 sq. mi. (12,950 sq. km)

**Mar·a·can·da** (mer'ə kan'də) *ancient name of* SAMAR-KAND

**Ma·ra·cay** (mä'rä kī') city in N Venezuela: pop. 440,000

**Ma·ra·nh·ão** (mä'rə nyoun') state of NE Brazil: 126,897 sq. mi. (328,663 sq. km); pop. 4,640,000 cap. São Luís

**Ma·ra·ñón** (mä'rä nyôn') river that rises in the Andes in WC Peru, flows northwest to N Peru, then east & joins the Ucayali to form the Amazon: *c.* 1,000 mi. (1,600 km)

**Mar·a·thon** (mar'ə thän') ancient Greek village in E Attica, or a plain nearby, where the Athenians under Miltiades defeated the Persians under Darius I (490 B.C.)

**Marche** (mársh) historical region of central France

**Mar·che** (mär′ke), **Le** (le) region of central Italy, on the Adriatic: 3,742 sq. mi. (9,692 sq. km); pop. 1,425,000; chief city, Ancona: Eng. name **(The) Marches**

**March·es** (märch′əz), the borderlands between England & Scotland and between England & Wales

**Mar·cy** (mär′sē), **Mount** ⟦after Wm. L. *Marcy*, gov. of New York (1833-39)⟧ mountain in N N.Y.: highest peak of the Adirondacks: 5,344 ft. (1,629 m)

**Mar del Pla·ta** (mär′del plät′ə) seaport & resort in E Argentina, south of Buenos Aires: pop. 424,000

**Mare** (mer) ⟦transl. of Sp *Isla de la Yegua*: said to be for a *mare* that swam to the island and joined a herd of elk⟧ island at the N end of San Francisco Bay, Calif.: site of a U.S. navy yard

**Ma·ren·go** (mə reŋ′gō) village in the Piedmont, NW Italy: site of a victory (1800) by Napoleon over the Austrians

**Mar·ga·ri·ta** (mär′gə rēt′ə) island of Venezuela, just off the N coast: 444 sq. mi. (1,150 sq. km)

**Mar·gate** (mär′gāt, -git) seaport & summer resort in Kent, SE England: pop. 53,000

**Ma·ri·an·a Islands** (mer′ē an′ə, mar′-) group of islands in the W Pacific, east of the Philippines: formerly (except Guam) a Japanese possession and (1947-78) part of the U.S. Trust Territory of the Pacific Islands; since 1978, a commonwealth (called **Northern Marianas**) of the U.S. with its own internal self-government: pop. 43,000

**Ma·ri·na·o** (mä′ryä nä′ô) city in NW Cuba: suburb of Havana: pop. 128,000

**Mar·i·anne** (mer′ē an′, mar′-) *a personification of* the French Republic: a woman in French Revolutionary costume

**Ma·ri·bor** (mär′i bôr′) city in N Slovenia: pop. 186,000

**Ma·rie Byrd Land** (mə rē′ bʉrd) region in W Antarctica, on the Amundsen Sea

**Ma·rie Ga·lante** (mȧ rē′ gȧ länt′) island in the Leeward group of the West Indies: a dependency of Guadeloupe: 58 sq. mi. (151 sq. km); pop. 16,000

**Mar·i·et·ta** (mer′ē et′ə, mar′-) ⟦after *Marie* Antoinette (1755-93), Fr queen⟧ city in SE Ohio, on the Ohio River: 1st permanent settlement (1788) in the Northwest Territory: pop. 15,000

**Maritime Alps** S division of the W Alps, along the

French-Italian border: highest peak, 10,817 ft. (3,297 m)

**Maritime Provinces** Canadian provinces of Nova Scotia, New Brunswick, & Prince Edward Island

**Ma·ri·u·pol** (mä′rē ōō′pôl) city in SE Ukraine, on the Sea of Azov: pop. 522,000: see ZHDANOV

**Mark·ham** (mär′kəm) **1** ⟦after Rev. W. *Markham* (1720-1806), Archbishop of York (England)⟧ city in SE Ontario, Canada, northeast of Toronto: pop. 115,000 **2 Mount** mountain in Antarctica, near the SW edge of the Ross Ice Shelf: 14,270 ft. (4,349 m)

**Mar·ma·ra** (mär′mə rə), **Sea of** sea between European & Asiatic Turkey, connected with the Black Sea by the Bosporus & with the Aegean by the Dardanelles: *c.* 4,300 sq. mi. (11,137 sq. km)

**Mar·mo·la·da** (mär′mô lä′dä) highest peak of the Dolomites, N Italy: 10,965 ft. (3,342 m)

**Marne** (märn) river in NE France, flowing northwest & west into the Seine near Paris: scene of two World War I battles in which German offensives were checked

**Ma·roc** (mȧ rôk′) *Fr. name of* MOROCCO

**Mar·que·sas Islands** (mär kā′zəz, -səz) group of islands in French Polynesia, in E South Pacific: 492 sq. mi. (1,275 sq. km); pop. 5,100

**Mar·ra·kech, Mar·ra·kesh** (mə rä′kesh, mar′ə kesh′) city in WC Morocco: pop. 483,000

**Mar·rue·cos** (mär′we′kôs) *Sp. name of* MOROCCO

**Mars** (märz) ⟦L⟧ the seventh largest planet of the solar system and the fourth in distance from the sun: diameter, *c.* 6,790 km (*c.* 4,220 mi.); period of revolution, 1.88 earth years; period of rotation, 24.6 hours; two satellites; symbol, ♂

**Mar·seille** (mȧr se′y′; *E* mär sā′) seaport in SE France, on the Gulf of Lions: pop. 879,000

**Mar·seilles** (mär sā′, -sālz′) *Eng. sp. of* MARSEILLE

**Mar·shall Islands** (mär′shəl) ⟦after John *Marshall*, Brit explorer (1788)⟧ group of islands in the W Pacific, east of the Caroline Islands: formerly a Japanese mandate, since 1947 part of the U.S. Trust Territory of the Pacific Islands: *c.* 70 sq. mi. (181 sq. km); pop. 31,000

**Mar·shal·sea** (mär′shəl sē′) a prison in Southwark, London, for debtors, etc., abolished in 1842

**Mar·ston Moor** (mär′stən) moor in Yorkshire, N Eng-

land: site of a battle (July, 1644) of the English civil
war in which Royalist forces were routed by the Par-
liamentarians

**Mar·ta·ban** (mär′tə bän′), **Gulf of** part of the Andaman
Sea, on the S coast of Myanmar

**Mar·tha's Vineyard** (mär′thəz) ⟦after a *Martha* Gos-
nold and the wild grapes there ⟧ island off the SE coast
of Mass., south of Cape Cod: *c.* 100 sq. mi. (258 sq.
km)

**Mar·ti·nique** (mär′tə nēk′) island in the Windward
group of the West Indies: overseas department of
France: 420 sq. mi. (1,087 sq. km); pop. 328,000; cap.
Fort-de-France

**Mar·y·land** (mer′ə lənd) ⟦after Queen Henrietta *Maria*,
wife of Charles I of England (1600-49) ⟧ E State of the
U.S., on the Atlantic: one of the 13 original States;
10,577 sq. mi. (27,394 sq. km); pop. 4,781,000; cap.
Annapolis: abbrev. *MD* or *Md*

**Ma·sa·da** (mə sä′də, mä sä dä′) ancient Jewish fortress
in Israel, near the Dead Sea: site of a prolonged
Roman siege (A.D. 72-73) resulting in a mass suicide by
the Jews to avoid capture

**Mas·ba·te** (mäs bä′tē) island of the EC Philippines,
west of Samar: 1,562 sq. mi. (4,046 sq. km)

**Mas·ca·rene Islands** (mas′kə rēn′) group of islands in
the W Indian Ocean, east of Madagascar, including
Mauritius & Réunion

**Ma·se·ru** (maz′ə rōō′) capital of Lesotho, in the NW
part: pop. *c.* 45,000

**Mash·had** (mə shäd′) city in NE Iran: site of a Shiite
shrine: pop. 668,000

**Ma·son-Dix·on line** (mā′sən dik′sən) ⟦after C. *Mason*
& J. *Dixon*, who surveyed it, 1763-67 ⟧ boundary line
between Pa. & Md., regarded, before the Civil War, as
separating the free States from the slave States or,
now, the North from the South: also **Mason and Dixon's line**

**Mass** *abbrev. for* Massachusetts

**Mas·sa·chu·setts** (mas′ə chōō′sits) ⟦after *Massachusett*, Massachusett Indian name of Great Blue Hill
(SW of Boston), lit., at the large hill ⟧ New England
State of the U.S.: one of the 13 original States; 8,257
sq. mi. (21,386 sq. km); pop. 6,016,000; cap. Boston:
abbrev. *MA* or *Mass*

**Massachusetts Bay** inlet of the Atlantic, on the E coast of Mass.

**Ma·su·ri·a** (mə zoor′ē ə) region with many lakes, in NE Poland: formerly in East Prussia

**Ma·ta·di** (mä tä′dē) main port of Zaire, on the Congo River: pop. 162,000

**Ma·ta·mo·ros** (mä′tä mô′rôs; *E* mat′ə môr′əs) city in NE Mexico, on the Rio Grande, opposite Brownsville, Tex.: pop. 239,000

**Ma·tan·zas** (mə tan′zəs; *Sp* mä tän′säs) seaport on the NW coast of Cuba: pop. 103,000

**Ma·ta·pan** (mat′ə pan′), **Cape** promontory of the S Peloponnesus, Greece

**Ma·thu·ra** (mut′oo rə) city in N India, in Uttar Pradesh, on the Jumna River: sacred Hindu city, reputed birthplace of Krishna: pop. 159,000

**Ma·to Gros·so** (mät′oo grô′soo) state of WC Brazil: 340,155 sq. mi. (881,000 sq. km); pop. 1,139,000; cap. Cuiabá

**Ma·to Gros·so do Sul** (mät′oo grô′soo dō sool) state of WC Brazil: 135,347 sq. mi. (350,548 sq. km); pop. 1,370,000; cap. Campo Grande

**Mats·qui** (mäts′kē) ⟦< ? AmInd⟧ city in SW British Columbia, Canada: near Vancouver: pop. 51,000

**Mat·su** (mät′soo′, mat′-) island of a small group in Taiwan Strait, administered by Taiwan: pop. 11,000

**Mat·su·do** (mät soo′dō′) city in SE Honshu, Japan: suburb of Tokyo: pop. 416,000

**Ma·tsu·ya·ma** (mä′tsoo yä′mə) seaport on W Shikoku, Japan, on the Inland Sea: pop. 418,000

**Mat·ter·horn** (mat′ər hôrn′) mountain of the Pennine Alps, on the Swiss-Italian border: *c.* 14,700 ft. (4,480 m)

**Mau·i** (mou′ē) ⟦Haw⟧ an island of Hawaii, southeast of Oahu: 728 sq. mi. (1,896 sq. km); pop. 91,000

**Mau·na Ke·a** (mou′nə kā′ə) ⟦Haw, lit., ? white mountain⟧ extinct volcano on the island of Hawaii: 13,796 ft. (4,205 m)

**Mauna Lo·a** (lō′ə) ⟦Haw, lit., long mountain⟧ active volcano in Hawaii Volcanoes National Park, on the island of Hawaii: 13,680 ft. (4,170 m)

**Mau·re·ta·ni·a** (môr′ə tā′nē ə, -tän′yə) ancient country & Roman province in NW Africa, including areas now in NE Morocco & W Algeria

**Mau·ri·ta·ni·a** (môr′ə tā′nē ə, -tän′yə) country in NW
Africa, on the Atlantic: formerly a French protectorate
& colony, it became independent (1960): 419,230 sq.
mi. (1,085,763 sq. km); pop. 1,690,000; cap. Nouak-
chott: official name **Islamic Republic of Mauritania**

**Mau·ri·ti·us** (mô rish′ē əs, -rish′əs) **1** island in the
Indian Ocean, east of Madagascar: 720 sq. mi. (1,865
sq. km) **2** country consisting of this island & several
nearby islands: discovered by the Portuguese in the
16th cent., it was in turn occupied by the Dutch, the
French, & the British; became independent & a member of the Commonwealth in 1968: 787 sq. mi. (2,040
sq. km); pop. 851,000; cap. Port Louis

**Mau·so·le·um** (mô′sə lē′əm, -zə-) 〚L < Gr *Mausōleion* 〛
the tomb of Mausolus, king of Caria, at Halicarnassus:
included among the Seven Wonders of the World

**May** (mā), **Cape** 〚after C. J. *Mey*, 17th-c. Du explorer 〛
peninsula at the southernmost point of N.J.: *c.* 20 mi.
(32 km) long

**Ma·ya·güez** (mä′yä gwes′) 〚prob. after *Mayagüa*, legendary local Indian chief 〛 seaport in W Puerto Rico:
pop. 100,000

**May·fair** (mā′fer′) a fashionable residential district of
the West End, London

**May·o** (mā′ō) county in NW Ireland, in Connacht province: 2,084 sq. mi. (5,397 sq. km); pop. 116,000

**Ma·yon** (mä yōn′) active volcano in SE Luzon, Philippines: *c.* 8,000 ft. (2,440 m)

**Ma·za·tlán** (mä′sät län′) seaport & resort on the Pacific
coast of Mexico, in the state of Sinaloa: pop. 250,000

**MB** *abbrev. for* Manitoba

**Mba·ba·ne** (əm bä bä′nä) capital of Swaziland, in the
NW part: pop. 23,000

**Mban·da·ka** (em′bän däk′ə) city in WC Zaire, on the
Congo River: pop. 149,000

**Mbi·ni** (em bē′nē) mainland portion of Equatorial
Guinea, on the Gulf of Guinea: 10,045 sq. mi. (26,016
sq. km)

**Mbu·ji-Ma·yi** (em bōō′jē mī′yē) city in SC Zaire: pop.
383,000

**Mc·Al·len** (mə kal′ən) 〚after J. *McAllen*, local rancher 〛
city in S Tex., in the Rio Grande valley: pop. 84,000

**Mc·Kin·ley** (mə kin′lē), **Mount** 〚after U.S. Pres. William *McKinley* (1843-1901) 〛 mountain of the Alaska

Range, SC Alas.: highest peak in North America: 20,320 ft. (6,194 m): in a national park (**Mount McKinley National Park**), 3,030 sq. mi. (7,770 sq. km)

**Mc·Mur·do Sound** (mək mur′dō) arm of the Ross Sea, off the coast of Victoria Land, Antarctica

**MD, Md** *abbrev. for* Maryland

**ME, Me** *abbrev. for* Maine

**Mead** (mēd), **Lake** ⟦after E. *Mead* (1858-1936), U.S. engineer⟧ lake in SE Nev. & NW Ariz., formed by the Hoover Dam on the Colorado River: *c.* 250 sq. mi. (648 sq. km)

**Me·an·der** (mē an′dər) *alt. sp. of* MAEANDER

**Meath** (mēth) county in E Ireland, in Leinster province: 903 sq. mi. (2,340 sq. km); pop. 95,000

**Mec·ca** (mek′ə) city in W Saudi Arabia, near the Red Sea: birthplace of Mohammed & hence a holy city of Islam: pop. *c.* 367,000

**Mech·e·len** (mek′ə lən) city in NC Belgium, in Antwerp province: pop. 65,000

**Mech·lin** (mek′lin) *Eng. name of* MECHELEN

**Meck·len·burg** (mek′lən burg′) historical region in NE Germany, formerly a German state and now part of the state of Mecklenburg-Western Pomerania

**Mecklenburg–Western Pomerania** state of NE Germany: 8,842 sq. mi. (22,900 sq. km); pop. 2,100,000; cap. Schwerin

**Me·dan** (mā dän′, mä′dän′) city in N Sumatra, Indonesia, near the Strait of Malacca: pop. 1,379,000

**Me·de·llín** (mä′dä yēn′) city in NW Colombia: pop. 2,069,000

**Med·ford** (med′fərd) **1** ⟦prob. after an English place name⟧ city in E Mass.: suburb of Boston: pop. 57,000 **2** ⟦after the city in Mass.⟧ city in SW Oreg.: pop. 47,000

**Me·di·a** (mē′dē ə) ancient kingdom in the part of SW Asia that is now NW Iran: cap. Ecbatana

**Medicine Hat** ⟦prob. transl. of Blackfoot *saamis*, headdress of a medicine man⟧ city in SE Alberta, Canada: pop. 42,000

**Me·di·na** (mə dē′nə) city in Hejaz, NW Saudi Arabia: site of Mohammed's tomb & hence a holy city of Islam: pop. *c.* 198,000

**Med·i·ter·ra·ne·an Sea** (med′i tə rā′nē ən) large sea surrounded by Europe, Africa, & Asia: *c.* 2,300 mi.

(3,700 km) long; *c.* 965,000 sq. mi. (2,499,000 sq. km)

**Mee·rut** (mē′rət) city in N India, in Uttar Pradesh: pop. 538,000

**Meg·a·ra** (meg′ə rə) city on the Isthmus of Corinth, central Greece: capital of ancient Megaris: pop. 15,000

**Meg·a·ris** (meg′ə ris) ancient district on the E part of the Isthmus of Corinth

**Me·gha·la·ya** (mā′gə lā′ə) state of NE India: 8,785 sq. mi. (22,489 sq. km); pop. 1,328,000

**Me·gid·do** (mə gid′ō) ancient town in N Palestine, on the plain of Esdraelon, dating from *c.* 3500 B.C.: thought to be the Biblical Armageddon

**Meis·sen** (mī′sən) city in EC Germany, on the Elbe, in the state of Saxony: noted for its porcelain: pop. 50,000

**Mé·ji·co** (me′hē kô′) *Sp. name of* MEXICO

**Mek·nès** (mek nes′) city in NC Morocco: pop. 386,000

**Me·kong** (mā′käŋ′, -kôŋ′) river in SE Asia, flowing from Tibet through SW China & the Indochinese peninsula into the South China Sea: *c.* 2,600 mi. (4,184 km)

**Mel·a·ne·sia** (mel′ə nē′zhə, -shə; *Brit,* -zē ə) ⟦ModL < Gr *melas*, black + *nēsos*, island + suffix *-ia*: in reference to the dark skin of the inhabitants⟧ one of the three major divisions of the Pacific islands, south of the equator and including groups from the Bismarck Archipelago to the Fiji Islands

**Mel·bourne** (mel′bərn) **1** seaport in SE Australia: capital of Victoria: pop. 2,864,000 **2** ⟦after the Austral city⟧ city in E Fla.: pop. 60,000

**Me·li·lla** (mə lē′yə) seaport in NW Africa: Spanish enclave in NE Morocco: pop. 59,000

**Me·li·to·pol** (mel′ə tō′pəl) city in S Ukraine: pop. 170,000

**Me·los** (mē′läs′) *var. of* MÍLOS

**Mel·rose** (mel′rōz) village in SE Scotland: site of the ruins of a Cistercian abbey

**Mel·ville** (mel′vil) ⟦after R. Saunders, Viscount *Melville* (1771-1851), First Lord of the Admiralty⟧ **1** island of Canada in the Arctic Ocean, north of Victoria Island: 16,141 sq. mi. (41,805 sq. km) **2** island of Australia, off the N coast: *c.* 2,400 sq. mi. (6,216 sq. km)

**Melville Peninsula** ⟦after Viscount *Melville:* see prec.⟧ peninsula in NE Canada, opposite Baffin Island: *c.* 250 mi. (402 km) long

**Me·mel** (mā′məl; *E* mem′əl) *Ger. name of* KLAIPEDA

**Mem·non** (mem′nän′) 〖L < Gr *Memnōn*〗 a gigantic statue of an Egyptian king at Thebes, said to have emitted a musical sound at sunrise

**Mem·phis** (mem′fis) **1** capital of ancient Egypt, on the Nile just south of Cairo **2** 〖after the ancient Egypt city〗 city in SW Tenn., on the Mississippi: pop. 610,000 (met. area 982,000)

**Mem·phre·ma·gog** (mem′fri mā′gäg) 〖AmInd, lit., beautiful water〗 lake in N Vt. & S Quebec, Canada: *c.* 30 mi. (48 km) long; 2-4 mi. (3-6.5 km) wide

**Me·na·do** (me nä′dō) seaport in NE Celebes, Indonesia: pop. 217,000

**Men·ai Strait** (men′ī) narrow channel between the NW mainland of Wales & Anglesey island: 14 mi. (22.5 km) long

**Me·nam** (me näm′) CHAO PHRAYA

**Men·de·res** (men′də res′) **1** river in W Turkey in Asia, flowing west into the Aegean: *c.* 250 mi. (403 km): ancient name MAEANDER **2** river in NW Turkey in Asia, flowing west into the Dardanelles: 60 mi. (96 km): ancient name SCAMANDER

**Men·do·ci·no** (men′də sē′nō), **Cape** 〖Sp, prob. after *Mendoza*, surname of a viceroy of New Spain〗 cape in NW Calif.: westernmost point of the State

**Men·do·za** (men dō′zə) city in W Argentina: pop. 597,000

**Men·lo Park** (men′lō) 〖after *Menlo Park*, Calif., in turn after *Menlough*, town in GALWAY〗 village in NE N.J. that was the site of Thomas Edison's workshop (1876-87)

**Me·nor·ca** (me nôr′kä) *Sp. name of* MINORCA

**Men·sa** (men′sə) 〖L, lit., table〗 a S constellation between Dorado and Octans, containing part of the Large Magellanic Cloud

**Men·ton** (män tōn′) seaport & resort town on the French Riviera: pop. 25,000

**Men·tor** (men′tər) 〖prob. after H. *Mentor*, early settler〗 city in NE Ohio, near Cleveland: pop. 47,000

**Mer·ci·a** (mur′shə; -shē ə, -sē ə) former Anglo-Saxon kingdom in central & S England

**Mer·cu·ry** (mur′kyoo rē) 〖L *Mercurius*, Mercury, of Etr orig.〗 the eighth largest planet in the solar system and the one nearest to the sun: diameter, *c.* 4,880 km (*c.*

3,030 mi.); period of revolution, 88 earth days; period of rotation, 58.65 earth days; symbol, ☿

**Mé·ri·da** (me′rē dä′) city in SE Mexico: capital of Yucatán state: pop. 425,000

**Mer·i·den** (mer′i dən) ⟦prob. after *Meriden,* England⟧ city in central Conn.: pop. 59,000: see NEW HAVEN

**Me·rid·i·an** (mə rid′ē ən) ⟦named for its location at a railroad junction, from the idea that *meridian* meant "junction"⟧ city in E Miss.: pop. 41,000

**Mer·i·on·eth·shire** (mer′ē än′ith shir′, -shər) former county of NW Wales, now part of Gwynedd county: also **Merioneth**

**Mer·o·ë** (mer′ō ē′) ruined city in N Sudan, on the Nile: capital of ancient Ethiopia

**Mer·ri·mack, Mer·ri·mac** (mer′ə mak′) ⟦< AmInd, ? place of swift current⟧ river flowing from S N.H. through NE Mass. into the Atlantic: 110 mi. (177 km)

**Mer·sey** (mur′zē) river in NW England, flowing into the Irish Sea through an estuary at Liverpool: 70 mi. (113 km)

**Mer·sey·side** (-sīd′) county of NW England, on the Mersey River & the Irish Sea: 251 sq. mi. (652 sq. km); pop. 1,490,000

**Mer·thyr Tyd·fil** (mur′thər tid′vil) city in Mid Glamorgan, SE Wales: pop. 60,000

**Mer·ton** (murt′'n) borough of SW Greater London: pop. 164,000

**Me·sa** (mā′sə) ⟦< Sp *mesa,* mesa⟧ city in SC Ariz., on the Salt River, near Phoenix: pop. 288,000

**Me·sa·bi Range** (mə sä′bē) ⟦< Ojibwa *missabe wudjiu,* giant mountain⟧ range of hills in NE Minn., containing rich iron ore deposits

**Me·sa Ver·de National Park** (mā′sə vurd′, -vur′dē, -ver′dä) ⟦Sp *mesa verde,* green plateau⟧ national park in SW Colo., with ruins of early cliff dwellings: 80 sq. mi. (207 sq. km)

**Me·shed** (mə shed′) *var. of* MASHHAD

**Mes·o·a·mer·i·ca** (mes′ō ə mer′i kə, mez′-; mē′sō-, -zō-) region that includes parts of Mexico and Central America, inhabited by various ancient and pre-Columbian Indian civilizations

**Mes·o·po·ta·mi·a** (mes′ə pə tā′mē ə) ⟦Gr *mesopotamia* (*chōra*), lit., (land) between rivers < *mesos,* mid + *potamos,* river, orig., rapids < IE base *\*pet-,* to fall,

rush at ] ancient country in SW Asia, between the
upper Tigris & Euphrates rivers: a part of modern Iraq

**Mes·quite** (mə skēt′, me-) [ after the *mesquite* trees
found there ] city in NE Tex.: suburb of Dallas: pop.
101,000

**Mes·se·ne** (me sē′nē) town in Messenia: it was the capital of the region in ancient times

**Mes·se·ni·a** (mə sē′nē ə, -sēn′yə) 1 ancient region in
the SW Peloponnesus bordering on the Ionian Sea 2
region of modern Greece in the same general area

**Mes·si·na** (mə sē′nə, me-) 1 seaport in NE Sicily, on
the Strait of Messina: pop. 265,000 2 **Strait of** strait
between Sicily & Italy: 2-12 mi. (3-19 km) wide; 20 mi.
(32 km) long

**Me·tai·rie** (met′ə rē) [ < Fr, lit., sharecropping farm, for
nearby farms owned by Jesuits ] city in SE La.: suburb
of New Orleans: pop. 149,000

**Metz** (mets) city in NE France, on the Moselle River:
pop. 118,000

**Meuse** (myo͞oz; *Fr* möz) river flowing from NE France,
through Belgium & the Netherlands, into the North
Sea: *c.* 575 mi. (925 km): Du. name, MAAS

**Mex·i·ca·li** (meks′i kä′lē) city in NW Mexico, on the
U.S. border: capital of Baja California: pop. 510,000

**Mex·i·co** (meks′i kō′) [ < Sp *Méjico* < Nahuatl *Mexìtli*,
name of the war god ] 1 country in North America,
south of the U.S.: 756,198 sq. mi. (1,958,201 sq. km);
pop. 66,846,000; cap. Mexico City 2 state of SC Mexico: 8,284 sq. mi. (21,455 sq. km); pop. 7,565,000; cap.
Toluca 3 **Gulf of** arm of the Atlantic, east of Mexico
& south of the U.S.: *c.* 700,000 sq. mi. (1,813,000 sq.
km) Spanish name MÉJICO; Mexican sp. **Mé·xi·co**
(me′hē kō′)

**Mexico City** capital of Mexico, in a federal district, 573
sq. mi. (1,485 sq. km), in the SC part of Mexico: pop.
9,377,000 (met. area *c.* 14,000,000): official name **Mexico, D(istrito) F(ederal)**

**MI** *abbrev. for* Michigan

**Mi·am·i** (mī am′ē, -ə) [ < Sp *Mayaimi*, name for Lake
Okeechobee, infl. by name of the Miami Indian people ] city on the SE coast of Fla.: pop. 359,000 (met.
area 1,937,000; urban area with Fort Lauderdale
3,193,000)

**Miami Beach** resort city in SE Fla., on an island opposite Miami: pop. 93,000

**Mich** *abbrev. for* Michigan

**Mich·i·gan** (mish′i gən) ⟦ < Fr < Algonquian, lit., great water ⟧ 1 Middle Western State of the U.S.: admitted, 1837; 58,216 sq. mi. (150,780 sq. km); pop. 9,295,000; cap. Lansing: abbrev. *MI* or *Mich* 2 **Lake** one of the Great Lakes, between Mich. & Wis.: 22,178 sq. mi. (57,440 sq. km)

**Mi·cho·a·cán** (mē′chô ä kän′) state of WC Mexico: 23,138 sq. mi. (59,928 sq. km); pop. 2,869,000; cap. Morelia

**Mi·cro·ne·sia** (mī′krə nē′zhə, -shə) ⟦ ModL < Gr *mikro-*, small + *nēsos*, island + suffix *-ia* ⟧ one of the three major divisions of the Pacific islands, north of the equator, east of the Philippines, & west of the international date line

**Mi·cro·sco·pi·um** (mī′krə skō′pē əm) a S constellation between Capricornus and Indus

**Middle America** the part of America that includes Mexico, Central America, &, sometimes, the West Indies

**Middle Atlantic States** New York, New Jersey, Pennsylvania, Delaware, and Maryland

**Middle East** 1 orig., those regions between the Far East & the Near East 2 area from Afghanistan to Libya, including Arabia, Cyprus, & Asiatic Turkey

**Middle Kingdom** Chinese name for the Chinese Empire, considered as the center of the world

**Mid·dles·brough** (mid′′lz brə) city in NE England, in Cleveland county, on the Tees River: pop. 148,000

**Mid·dle·sex** (mid′′l seks′) former county of SE England, now mostly a part of Greater London

**Middle States** those eastern States between the New England States and the South; New York, New Jersey, Pennsylvania, Delaware, and Maryland

**Middle Temple** *see* INNS OF COURT

**Mid·dle·town** (mid′′l toun′) ⟦ each name descriptive of the city's location in relation to nearby communities ⟧ 1 city in central Conn., on the Connecticut River: pop. 43,000 2 city in SW Ohio: pop. 46,000 3 city in EC N.J.: pop. 68,000

**Middle West** region of the NC U.S. between the Rocky Mountains & the E border of Ohio, north of the Ohio River & the S borders of Kans. & Mo.

**Mid·gard** (mid′gärd′) [ON *mithgarthr* < *mithr*, mid + *garthr*, yard] *Norse Myth.* the earth, regarded as midway between Asgard and the underworld and encircled by a huge serpent: also **Mid′garth′** (-gärth′)

**Mid Gla·mor·gan** (mid′ glə môr′gən) county of SW Wales: 393 sq. mi. (1,019 sq. km); pop. 536,000

**Mi·di** (mē dē′) [Fr, south, lit., midday < *mi-*, half (< L *medius*, middle) + *di* (< L *dies*), day] the south of France

**Mi·di–Pyr·é·nées** (mē dē′ pir′ə nēz′) metropolitan region of SW France: 17,509 sq. mi. (45,348 sq. km); pop. 2,325,000; chief city, Toulouse

**Mid·land** (mid′lənd) [from being about midway between Fort Worth and El Paso] city in WC Tex.: pop. 89,000

**Mid·lands** (-ləndz) highly industrialized region of central England, usually considered to include the present counties of Derbyshire, Leicestershire, Northamptonshire, Nottinghamshire, Staffordshire, Warwickshire, West Midlands, & E Hereford and Worcester: with *the*

**Mid·lo·thi·an** (mid lō′thē ən) former county of SE Scotland, now in the region of Lothian

**Mid·way Islands** (mid′wā) coral atoll & two islets at the end of the Hawaiian chain: administered by the U.S. Navy: 2 sq. mi. (5.2 sq. km)

**Mid·west City** (mid′west) [after *Midwest* Air Depot, nearby U.S. Air Force installation] city in central Okla.: suburb of Oklahoma City: pop. 52,000

**Mi·lan** (mi lan′) commune in NW Italy, in Lombardy: pop. 1,520,000: It. name **Mi·la·no** (mē lä′nô)

**Mi·le·tus** (mī lēt′əs) ancient city in Ionia, SW Asia Minor

**Mil·ford** (mil′fərd) [? after *Milford,* town in England] city in SW Conn., on Long Island Sound, near Bridgeport: pop. 50,000

**Milk·y Way** (mil′kē) [transl. of L *via lactea,* transl. of Gr *galaxias kyklos:* see GALAXY] the spiral galaxy containing our sun: seen from the earth as a broad, faintly luminous band of stars and interstellar gas, arching across the night sky with the constellation Sagittarius marking the direction to its center

**Mi·los** (mē′läs′) Greek island of the SW Cyclades, in the Aegean Sea: 61 sq. mi. (157 sq. km): It. name **Mi·lo** (mē′lô)

**Mil·wau·kee** (mil wô′kē) ⟦ < Fr < Algonquian, lit., good land, council place ⟧ city & port in SE Wis., on Lake Michigan: pop. 628,000 (met. area 1,432,000; urban area with Racine 1,607,000)

**Mi·mas** (mī′mas′) a small satellite of Saturn with a gigantic crater

**Mi·nas Basin** (mī′nəs) ⟦ < Fr *Le Bassin des Mines,* lit., basin of mines, for nearby copper mines ⟧ NE arm of the Bay of Fundy, Nova Scotia, Canada: *c.* 60 mi. (96.5 km) long

**Mi·nas Ge·rais** (mē′nəs zhi rīs′) state of EC Brazil: 226,708 sq. mi. (587,172 sq. km); pop. 13,378,000; cap. Belo Horizonte

**Mi·na·ti·tlán** (mē′nə ti tlän′) city in SE Mexico: pop. 145,000

**Min·da·na·o** (min′də nou′, -nä′ō) 2d largest island of the Philippines, at the S end of the group: 36,906 sq. mi. (95,586 sq. km)

**Min·do·ro** (min dôr′ō) island of the Philippines, south of Luzon: 3,759 sq. mi. (9,735 sq. km)

**Min·i·coy** (min′i koi′) southernmost island of the Laccadives, off the W coast of Kerala, India: 1.8 sq. mi. (4.7 sq. km); pop. 7,000

**Minn** *abbrev. for* Minnesota

**Min·ne·ap·o·lis** (min′ē ap′ə lis) ⟦ after nearby *Minnehaha* Falls (< Dakota *mní,* water + *xaxa,* waterfall) + Gr *polis,* city ⟧ city in E Minn., on the Mississippi, adjacent to St. Paul: pop. 368,000 (met. area with St. Paul 2,464,000)

**Min·ne·so·ta** (min′ə sōt′ə) ⟦ < Dakota *mnisóta,* Minnesota River, lit., whitish (cloudy or milky) water ⟧ Middle Western State of the U.S., adjoining the Canadian border: admitted, 1858; 84,068 sq. mi. (217,736 sq. km); pop. 4,375,000; cap. St. Paul: abbrev. *MN* or *Minn*

**Mi·nor·ca** (mi nôr′kə) 2d largest island of the Balearic Islands, east of Majorca: 264 sq. mi. (684 sq. km): Sp. name MENORCA

**Minsk** (minsk) capital of Belarus, in the central part: pop. 1,472,000

**Min·ya** (min′yə), **Al** (al) city in central Egypt, on the Nile: pop. 147,000

**Mi·que·lon** (mik′ə län′; *Fr* mē klō*n*′) island in the Atlantic, off the S coast of Newfoundland: part of the

French overseas territory of St. Pierre and Miquelon: 83 sq. mi. (215 sq. km)

**Mish·a·wa·ka** (mish ə wô′kə, -wä′kə) city in N Ind.: pop. 43,000

**Mis·kolc** (mish′kôlts′) city in NE Hungary: pop. 212,000

**Miss** *abbrev. for* Mississippi

**Mis·sion·ar·y Ridge** (mish′ən er′ē) ⟦after the Brainerd *Mission* there⟧ ridge in SE Tenn. & NW Ga.: site of a Union victory (1863) in the Civil War

**Mis·sion Vie·jo** (mish′ən vē ā′hō) ⟦< Sp *misión*, mission + *viejo*, old⟧ city in SW Calif.: pop. 73,000

**Mis·sis·sau·ga** (mis′ə sô′gə) ⟦< Ojibwa < *misi*, large + *sauk*, river mouth⟧ city in S Ontario, Canada, southwest of Toronto: pop. 374,000

**Mis·sis·sip·pi** (mis′ə sip′ē) ⟦< Fr < Illinois *missisipioui*, lit., big river⟧ **1** river in central U.S., flowing from NC Minn. south into the Gulf of Mexico: 2,348 mi. (3,757 km): see also Missouri **2** Southern State of the U.S., on the Gulf of Mexico: admitted, 1817; 47,716 sq. mi. (123,584 sq. km); pop. 2,573,000; cap. Jackson: abbrev. *MS* or *Miss*

**Mis·sou·ri** (mi zoor′ē, -ə) ⟦< Fr, earlier *ouemessourit*, for an Indian people orig. living on the Missouri River in Nebraska < Illinois, lit., person who has a canoe⟧ **1** river in WC U.S., flowing from SW Mont. southeast into the Mississippi: 2,714 mi. (4,342 km) **2** Middle Western State of the central U.S.: admitted, 1821; 69,686 sq. mi. (180,486 sq. km); pop. 5,117,000; cap. Jefferson City: abbrev. *MO* or *Mo*

**Mis·tas·si·ni** (mis′tə sē′nē) ⟦< Cree *mista-assini*, lit., the great stone lake⟧ lake in SC Quebec, Canada: 840 sq. mi. (2,176 sq. km)

**Misti** *see* El Misti

**Mitch·ell** (mich′əl), **Mount** ⟦after Elisha *Mitchell* (1793-1857), Am geologist⟧ mountain of the Black Mountains, W N.C.: highest peak of the E U.S.: 6,684 ft. (2,037 m)

**Mit·i·li·ni** (mit″l ē′nē) **1** chief city of Lesbos, on the SE coast: pop. 26,000 **2** Lesbos

**Mit·tel·eu·ro·pa** (mit″l yōō rō′pə, -yə-; -oi rō′-) Central Europe, esp. with reference to its culture, style, or customs: also **Mit′tel–Eu·ro′pa** or **Mit′tel Eu·ro′pa**

**Mi·ya·za·ki** (mē′yä zä′kē) city in SE Kyushu, Japan: pop. 268,000

**Mi·zar** (mī'zär') ⟦Ar *mīzār*, lit., waist-cloth, apron⟧ a multiple star with a magnitude of 2.2: it is the brighter companion of an optical double star at the middle of the Big Dipper's handle

**Mi·zo·ram** (mə zôr'əm) territory of NE India, between Myanmar & Bangladesh: 8,142 sq. mi. (21,087 sq. km); pop. 488,000

**MN** *abbrev. for* Minnesota

**MO, Mo** *abbrev. for* Missouri

**Mo·ab** (mō'ab') ancient kingdom east & south of the Dead Sea, now the SW part of Jordan

**Mo·bile** (mō bēl', mō'bēl') ⟦< Fr < AmInd < ?⟧ **1** seaport in SW Ala., on Mobile Bay: pop. 196,000 **2** river in SW Ala., formed by the Alabama & Tombigbee rivers & flowing into Mobile Bay: *c.* 45 mi. (73 km)

**Mobile Bay** arm of the Gulf of Mexico, extending into SW Ala.: *c.* 35 mi. (56 km) long

**Mo·çam·bi·que** (moo'səm bē'kə) *Port. name of* MOZAMBIQUE

**Mo·cha** (mō'kə) seaport in SW Yemen, on the Red Sea: pop. 6,000

**Mo·de·na** (mōd'n ə, môd'-; -ä') commune in N Italy, in Emilia-Romagna: pop. 180,000

**Mo·des·to** (mə des'tō) ⟦Sp, lit., modest: said to be with reference to Wm. C. Ralston's modest refusal to have the place named after him⟧ city in central Calif.: pop. 165,000

**Moe·si·a** (mē'shē ə, -shə) ancient Roman province in SE Europe, between the Danube & the Balkan Mountains

**Mo·ga·di·shu** (mō'gä dē'shōō) capital of Somalia: seaport on the Indian Ocean: pop. 371,000: It. name **Mo'ga·di'scio** (-shō)

**Mo·gi·lev** (mō'gə lef') city in E Belarus, on the Dnepr: pop. 343,000

**Mo·ha·ve Desert** (mō hä'vē) *alt. sp. of* MOJAVE DESERT

**Mo·hawk** (mō'hôk') ⟦after *Mohawk* (the North American Indian people) < Narragansett *mohowawog*, lit., man-eaters: orig. so named by enemy peoples⟧ river in central & E N.Y., flowing into the Hudson: *c.* 140 mi. (225 km)

**Mo·hen·jo-Da·ro** (mō hen'jō dä'rō) an archaeological site in the Indus valley of Pakistan, NE of Karachi, containing ruins of cities from *c.* 3000 to *c.* 1500 B.C.

**Mo·ja·ve Desert** (mō hä′vē) desert in SE Calif.: *c.* 15,000 sq. mi. (38,850 sq. km)

**Mol·dau** (môl′dou′) *Ger. name of* VLTAVA

**Mol·da·vi·a** (mäl dā′vē ə, -dāv′yə) **1** region & former principality in E Europe, east of the Carpathians: merged with Walachia (1861) to form Romania **2** MOLDAVIAN SOVIET SOCIALIST REPUBLIC

**Moldavian Soviet Socialist Republic** a republic of the U.S.S.R.: now MOLDOVA

**Mol·do·va** (môl dō′və) country in E Europe: became independent upon the breakup of the U.S.S.R. (1991): 13,000 sq. mi. (33,670 sq. km); pop. 4,100,000; cap. Kishinev: formerly, *Moldavian Soviet Socialist Republic*

**Mo·line** (mō lēn′) ⟦ < Sp *molino*, mill ⟧ city in NW Ill., on the Mississippi: pop. 43,000

**Mo·li·se** (mō′lē zā′) region of SC Italy: 4,438 sq. mi. (1,713 sq. km); pop. 329,000

**Mo·lo·kai** (mō′lə kī′, mäl′ə-) ⟦ Haw ⟧ an island of Hawaii, southeast of Oahu: 259 sq. mi. (671 sq. km); pop. 6,800

**Mo·luc·cas** (mō luk′əz, mə-) group of islands of Indonesia, between Celebes & New Guinea: *c.* 32,000 sq. mi. (82,880 sq. km); pop. 1,412,000: also **Molucca Islands**

**Mom·ba·sa** (mäm bä′sə, -bas′ə) seaport on the SE coast of Kenya, partly on an offshore island: pop. 341,000

**Mon·a·co** (män′ə kō, mə nä′kō) **1** country in S Europe on the Mediterranean: an independent principality & an enclave in SE France: .5 sq. mi. (1.3 sq. km); pop. 27,000 **2** its capital, a commune

**Mon·a·ghan** (män′ə gən) county in NE Ireland, in Ulster province: 499 sq. mi. (1,293 sq. km); pop. 51,000

**Mon·as·tir** (mō′nä stir′) *Turk. name of* BITOLJ

**Mön·chen–Glad·bach** (mön′Hən glät′bäkh′) city in WC Germany, in the state of North Rhine-Westphalia: pop. 256,000

**Monc·ton** (muŋk′tən) ⟦ orig. *Monckton*, after R. *Monckton* (1726-82), Lt.-Governor of Nova Scotia ⟧ city in SE New Brunswick, Canada: pop. 63,000

**Mon·go·li·a** (mäŋ gō′lē ə, män-; -gōl′yə) **1** region in EC Asia, consisting of Inner Mongolia & the Mongolian People's Republic **2** MONGOLIAN PEOPLE'S REPUBLIC

**Mongolian People's Republic** country in EC Asia, north of China: 592,280 sq. mi. (1,564,000 sq. km);

pop. 1,942,000; cap. Ulan Bator

**Mon·mouth·shire** (män'məth shir', -shər) former county of SE Wales: also **Mon'mouth**

**Mo·noc·er·os** (mə näs'ər əs) ⟦L, the unicorn < Gr *monokeras*⟧ a S constellation between Orion and Canis Minor

**Mo·non·ga·he·la** (mə nän'gə hē'lə, -näŋ'-; -hä'-) ⟦< Algonquian⟧ river in N W.Va. & SW Pa., flowing north to join the Allegheny at Pittsburgh & form the Ohio: 128 mi. (206 km)

**Mon·roe** (mən rō') ⟦after U.S. Pres. James *Monroe* (1758-1831)⟧ city in N La.: pop. 55,000

**Mon·ro·vi·a** (mən rō'vē ə) capital of Liberia: seaport on the Atlantic: pop. 425,000

**Mons** (mōns') city in SW Belgium: pop. 95,000

**Mont** *abbrev. for* Montana

**Mon·tan·a** (män tan'ə) ⟦L *montana*, mountainous regions⟧ Mountain State of the NW U.S.: admitted, 1889; 147,138 sq. mi. (381,087 sq. km); pop. 799,000; cap. Helena: abbrev. *MT* or *Mont*

**Mon·tauk Point** (män'tôk') ⟦< Algonquian tribal name + *point*⟧ promontory at the easternmost tip of Long Island, N.Y.

**Mont Blanc** *see* BLANC, Mont

**Mont Cervin** *see* CERVIN, Mont

**Mon·te·bel·lo** (mänt'ə bel'ō) ⟦It, lit., beautiful mountain⟧ city in SW Calif.: suburb of Los Angeles: pop. 60,000

**Mon·te Car·lo** (mänt'ə kär'lō) town in Monaco: gambling resort: pop. 12,500

**Mon·te·ne·gro** (mänt'ə nē'grō, -neg'rō) constituent republic of S Yugoslavia: formerly a kingdom: 5,333 sq. mi. (13,812 sq. km); pop. 584,000; cap. Podgorica

**Mon·te·rey** (mänt'ə rā') ⟦< Sp *Puerto de Monterrey*, lit., port of *Monterrey*, after the viceroy of New Spain (1602)⟧ city on the coast of central Calif.: former capital (until 1846) of Calif. region: pop. 32,000

**Monterey Park** ⟦see prec.⟧ city in SW Calif.: suburb of Los Angeles: pop. 61,000

**Mon·ter·rey** (mänt'ə rā'; *Sp* môn'ter rā') city in NE Mexico: capital of Nuevo Léon: pop. 1,006,000 (met. area 1,916,000)

**Mon·te·vi·de·o** (mänt'ə və dā'ō) capital & seaport of Uruguay: pop. 1,360,000

**Mont·gom·er·y** (munt gum′ər ē) capital of Ala., in the SC part, on the Alabama River: pop. 187,000

**Mont·gom·er·y·shire** (-shir′, -shər) former county of central Wales, now mostly in Powys county: also **Montgomery**

**Mon·ti·cel·lo** (män′tə sel′ō, -chel′ō) [[It, little mountain]] home & burial place of Thomas Jefferson, near Charlottesville, Va.

**Mont·mar·tre** (mōn mår′tr′) district of Paris, in the N part, noted for its cafés and as an artists' quarter

**Mont·par·nasse** (mōn pår nås′) section of Paris, on the left bank of the Seine

**Mont·pel·ier** (mänt pēl′yər) [[after fol.]] capital of Vt., in the NC part: pop. 8,200

**Mont·pel·lier** (mōn pəl yā′) city in S France, near the Gulf of Lions: pop. 201,000

**Mon·tre·al** (män′trē ôl′, mun′-) [[Fr *Montréal,* after *Mont Royal,* Mount Royal, at its center]] **1** city & seaport in SW Quebec, Canada, on an island in the St. Lawrence River: pop. 980,000 (met. area 2,921,000) **2** this island: 201 sq. mi. (520 sq. km)  Fr. name **Mont·ré·al** (mōn rā àl′)

**Montreal North** city in SW Quebec, Canada: suburb of Montreal, on Montreal Island: pop. 90,000: Fr. name **Montréal Nord** (nôr)

**Mon·treuil** (mōn trë′y′) city in NC France: suburb of Paris: pop. 93,000

**Mont·ser·rat** (mänt′sə rat′) British island of the Leeward group, in the West Indies: 33 sq. mi. (86 sq. km); pop. 12,000

**Mont–St–Mi·chel** (mōn san mē shel′) islet just off the NW coast of France, noted for its fortified abbey

**Mon·za** (mȏn′tsä) commune in N Italy: pop. 123,000

**Moose·head Lake** (mōōs′hed′) [[transl. of AmInd name]] lake in WC Me.: 117 sq. mi. (303 sq. km)

**Mo·rad·a·bad** (mə räd′ə bäd′) city in N India, in Uttar Pradesh: pop. 348,000

**Mo·ra·va** (mor′ə və) **1** *Czech name of* MORAVIA **2** river in Moravia flowing south along the Austrian border, into the Danube: *c.* 230 mi. (368 km) **3** river in E Yugoslavia, flowing north into the Danube: 134 mi. (216 km)

**Mo·ra·vi·a** (mô rā′vē ə, mə-) region in E Czech Republic: chief city, Brno

**Mo·rav·ská Ostrava** (mô′räf skä) *see* OSTRAVA

**Mor·ay** (mur′ē) former county of NE Scotland, now in the region of Grampian: also **Mor′ay·shire′** (-shir′, -shər)

**Moray Firth** inlet of the North Sea, on the NE coast of Scotland

**Mo·re·a** (mô re′ə) *old name of* PELOPONNESUS

**Mo·re·li·a** (mô re′lyä) city in central Mexico: capital of Michoacán state: pop. 353,000

**Mo·re·los** (mô re′lôs) state in SC Mexico: 1,911 sq. mi. (4,950 sq. km); pop. 947,000; cap. Cuernavaca

**Mo·re·no Valley** (mə rē′nō) city in S Calif.: pop. 119,000

**Mo·roc·co** (mə rä′kō) kingdom on the NW coast of Africa, bordering on the Atlantic & the Mediterranean; a Muslim kingdom since the 11th cent., from 1912-56 was divided into a French protectorate (**French Morocco**), a Spanish protectorate (**Spanish Morocco**), & the **International Zone** of Tangier (established in 1923); 254,815 sq. mi. (659,970 sq. km); pop. 23,667,000; cap. Rabat

**Mo·ro·ni** (mô rō′nē) capital of the Comoro Islands; pop. 20,000

**Mor·ris Jes·sup** (môr′is jes′əp, mär′-), **Cape** cape at the N tip of Greenland: northernmost point of land in the world

**Mos·cow** (mäs′kō, -kou′) capital of Russia, in the W part: pop. 8,642,000: Russ. name MOSKVA

**Mo·selle** (mō zel′; *Fr* mô zel′) ⟦*Fr* < L *Mosella*⟧ river in NE France & SW Germany, flowing north into the Rhine at Koblenz: *c.* 320 mi. (515 km): Ger. name **Mo·sel** (mō′zəl)

**Mos·kva** (môs kvä′) *Russ. name of* Moscow

**Mos·qui·to Coast** (mə skēt′ō) region on the Caribbean coast of Honduras & Nicaragua: also **Mos·qui·ti·a** (môs kē′tē ä)

**Mós·to·les** (môs′tô les) city in central Spain: suburb of Madrid: pop. 150,000

**Mo·sul** (mō sōōl′) city in N Iraq, on the Tigris, opposite the site of ancient Nineveh: pop. 293,000

**Moth·er·well and Wi·shaw** (muth′ər wel′ ənd wish′ô) city in SC Scotland: pop. 76,000

**Moul·mein** (mool mān′, mōl-) seaport in S Myanmar, on the Gulf of Martaban: pop. 203,000

**Mountain State** *n.* any of the eight States of the W U.S. through which the Rocky Mountains pass; Mont., Ida., Wyo., Nev., Utah, Colo., Ariz., & N.Mex.

**Mountain View** ⟦descriptive⟧ city in WC Calif., near San Jose: pop. 67,000

**Mount Desert** ⟦< Fr *Isle des Monts Deserts*, lit., island of desert mountains⟧ island off the S coast of Me.: resort: *c.* 100 sq. mi. (259 sq. km)

**Mount McKinley National Park** *see* McKinley, Mount

**Mount Pros·pect** (prä′spekt) ⟦after a high ridge in the area⟧ village in NE Ill.: suburb of Chicago: pop. 53,000

**Mount Rainier National Park** *see* Rainier, Mount

**Mount Ver·non** (vur′nən) ⟦after Brit Admiral Edward *Vernon* (1684-1757)⟧ 1 home & burial place of George Washington in N Va., on the Potomac, near Washington, D.C. 2 ⟦after the historic site⟧ city in SE N.Y.: suburb of New York City: pop. 67,000

**Mo·zam·bique** (mō′zəm bēk′) country in SE Africa, on Mozambique Channel: formerly a Portuguese territory, it became independent in 1975: 302,329 sq. mi. (783,030 sq. km); pop. 14,022,000; cap. Maputo

**Mozambique Channel** part of the Indian Ocean, between Mozambique & Madagascar: *c.* 1,000 mi. (1,609 km) long

**MP** *abbrev. for* Northern Marianas

**MS** *abbrev. for* Mississippi

**MT** *abbrev. for* Montana

**Muk·den** (mook′dən, mook den′) *old name of* Shenyang

**Mul·ha·cén** (mool′ä then′) highest mountain in Spain, in the S part, near Granada: 11,420 ft. (3,480 m)

**Mül·heim** (mül′hīm′) city in W Germany, on the Ruhr, in the state of North Rhine-Westphalia: pop. 175,000: also **Mülheim an der Ruhr** (än der rōōr′)

**Mul·house** (mü lōōz′) city in E France, near the Rhine: pop. 113,000

**Mull** (mul) island of the Inner Hebrides, Scotland: 351 sq. mi. (909 sq. km); pop. (with small nearby islands) 1,700

**Mul·tan** (mool tän′) city in NE Pakistan, near the Chenab River: pop. 730,000

**Mün·chen** (mün′Hən) *Ger. name of* Munich

**Mün·chen–Glad·bach** (-glät′bäkh′) *var. of* Mönchen-Gladbach

**Mun·cie** (mun′sē) ⟦after the *Munsee* (Delaware) Indians ‖ city in EC Ind.: pop. 71,000

**Mu·nich** (myōō′nik) city in SE Germany: capital of the state of Bavaria: pop. 1,277,000: Ger. name MÜNCHEN

**Mun·ster** (mun′stər) province of SW Ireland: 9,315 sq. mi. (24,125 sq. km); pop. 998,000

**Mün·ster** (mün′stər) city in WC Germany, in the state of North Rhine-Westphalia: pop. 274,000

**Mur·ci·a** (mur′shə, -shē ə; *Sp* mōōr′thyä) 1 region & ancient kingdom of SE Spain: 4,370 sq. mi. (11,317 sq. km); pop. 958,000 2 its capital: pop. 288,000

**Mu·reş** (mōō resh′) river flowing west from the Carpathian Mountains into the Tisza in SE Hungary: 470 mi. (756 km)

**Mur·frees·bor·o** (mur′frēz bur′ō, -ə) ‖ after Col. H. *Murfree* (1752-1809) ‖ city in central Tenn.: site of a Union victory over Confederate forces during the Civil War (1863): pop. 45,000

**Mur·mansk** (mōōr mänsk′) seaport in Russia on the NW coast of Kola Peninsula, on the Barents Sea: pop. 419,000

**Mur·ray** (mur′ē) river in SE Australia, flowing from the Australian Alps into the Indian Ocean: 1,596 mi. (2,568 km)

**Mur·rum·bidg·ee** (mur′əm bij′ē) river in SE Australia, flowing west into the Murray: *c.* 1,000 mi. (1,609 km)

**Mus·ca** (mus′kə) ‖ L, a fly ‖ a S constellation near Crux

**Mus·cat** (mus kat′) capital of Oman: seaport on the Gulf of Oman: pop. 7,500

**Muscat and Oman** *old name of* OMAN (the country)

**Mus·co·vy** (mus′kə vē) 1 former grand duchy, surrounding and including Moscow, that expanded into the Russian Empire under Ivan IV (16th cent.) 2 *old name of* RUSSIA

**Mus·ke·gon** (mus kē′gən) ‖ < Algonquian tribal name ‖ city & port in SW Mich.: pop. 40,000

**Mus·ko·gee** (mus kō′gē) ‖ < Creek *maaskóoki*, the Muskogean language of the Creek Indians ‖ city in E Okla.: pop. 38,000

**Mut·tra** (mut′rə) *old name of* MATHURA

**Mwe·ru** (mwä′rōō) lake between SE Zaire & NE Zambia: *c.* 1,700 sq. mi. (4,403 sq. km)

**Myan·mar** (myun′mä, -mär) country in SE Asia, on the Indochinese peninsula: modern state founded in 18th cent.; under British control from 1885 to 1948: 261,789

sq. mi. (678,030 sq. km); pop. 37,651,000; cap. Yangon: officially, a federation of states called **Union of Myanmar**

**My·ce·nae** (mī sē′nē) ancient city in Argolis, in the NE Peloponnesus

**My·si·a** (mish′ē ə) ancient region in NW Asia Minor, on the Propontis

**My·sore** (mī sôr′) 1 *old name of* KARNATAKA state 2 city in S India, in the state of Karnataka: pop. 476,000

**Myt·i·le·ne** (mit″l ē′nē) *alt. sp. of* MITILÍNI

# N

**Nab·a·te·a, Nab·a·tae·a** (nab′ə tē′ə) ancient Arab kingdom in SW Asia, now in W Jordan

**Na·be·rezh·niy·e Chel·ny** (nä′bi *ri*zh nē yi chēl nē′) city in E European Russia, on the Kama River: pop. 437,000

**Nab·lus** (nab′ləs, näb′-) city in W Jordan: capital (as *Shechem*) of ancient Samaria: pop. 202,000

**Na·fud** (nə fōod′) desert in the N Arabian Peninsula: *c.* 180 mi. (290 km) long; 140 mi. (225 km) wide

**Na·ga·land** (nä′gə land′) state of NE India, on the Myanmar border: 6,381 sq. mi. (16,527 sq. km); pop. 774,000

**Na·ga·no** (nä gä′nō) city in WC Honshu, Japan: pop. 330,000

**Na·ga·sa·ki** (nä′gə sä′kē) seaport on the W coast of Kyushu, Japan: partly destroyed (Aug. 9, 1945) by a U.S. atomic bomb, the second ever used in warfare: pop. 446,000: cf. HIROSHIMA

**Na·gor·no-Ka·ra·bakh** (nä gôr′nō kär′ä bäk′) autonomous region in Azerbaijan, mostly populated by Armenians: 1,700 sq. mi. (4,400 sq. km); pop. 180,000; cap. Stepanakert

**Na·go·ya** (nä′gô̂ yä′) seaport in S Honshu, Japan, on an inlet of the Pacific: pop. 2,066,000

**Nag·pur** (näg′poor′) city in EC India, in Maharashtra state: pop. 1,298,000

**Na·ha** (nä′hä′) seaport on Okinawa: pop. 304,000

**Nairn** (nern) former county of NE Scotland, now in the region of Highland: also **Nairn′shire** (-shir, -shər)

**Nai·ro·bi** (nī rō′bē) capital of Kenya, in the SW part: pop. 828,000

**Na·ma·qua·land** (nə mä'kwə land') region in SW Africa divided by the Orange River into **Great Namaqualand** in Namibia & **Little Namaqualand** in Cape Province, Republic of South Africa: also **Na·ma·land** (nä'mə land')

**Nam Co** (näm' tsō') salt lake in E Tibet: *c.* 700 sq. mi. (1,813 sq. km); 15,200 ft. (4,650 m) above sea level

**Na·men** (nä'mən) *Fl. name of* NAMUR

**Na·mib·i·a** (nə mib'ē ə) country in S Africa, on the Atlantic: a former mandate of South Africa; administered by South Africa until full independence (1990): 318,261 sq. mi. (824,292 sq. km); pop. 1,033,000; cap. Windhoek

**Na·mur** (nȧ mür') **1** province of S Belgium: 1,413 sq. mi. (3,660 sq. km); pop. 412,000 **2** its capital, on the Meuse River: pop. 102,000

**Na·nai·mo** (nə nī'mō) city in SE Vancouver Island, British Columbia, Canada: pop. 49,000

**Nan·chang** (nän'chäŋ') city in SE China: capital of Jianxi province: pop. 1,046,000

**Nan·cy** (nä*n* sē'; *E* nan'sē) city in NE France: pop. 99,000

**Nan·da De·vi** (nun'dä dā'vē) mountain of the Himalayas, in N Uttar Pradesh, India: 25,645 ft. (7,817 m)

**Nan·ga Par·bat** (nuŋ'gə pʉr'bət) mountain of the Himalayas, in W Kashmir: 26,660 ft. (8,126 m)

**Nan·jing** (nän'jiŋ') city in E China, on the Chang: capital of Jiangsu province: pop. 2,000,000

**Nan·king** (nan'kiŋ', nän'-) *old form of* NANJING

**Nan·ning** (nän'niŋ') city in S China: capital of Guangxi autonomous region: pop. 866,000

**Nan Shan** (nän'shän') mountain system in NW China, in N Qinghai & S Gansu provinces: highest peak, *c.* 20,000 ft. (6,096 m)

**Nan·terre** (nä*n* ter') city in NC France: suburb of Paris: pop. 91,000

**Nantes** (nä*n*t; *E* nänts, nants) city in W France, on the Loire River: pop. 247,000

**Nan·tuck·et** (nan tuk'it) 〚Massachusett〛 island of Mass., south of Cape Cod: summer resort: 46 sq. mi. (119 sq. km); pop. 6,000

**Nap·a** (nap'ə) 〚< AmInd < ? *napa*, grizzly bear or *napo*, house 〛 city in W Calif., north of Oakland: pop. 62,000

**Na·per·ville** (nä'pər vil') 〚after Captain J. *Naper*, its founder ] city in NE Ill., west of Chicago: pop. 85,000

**Na·ples** (nā′pəlz) **1** seaport in S Italy, on the Bay of Naples: pop. 1,212,000 **2** former kingdom occupying the S half of Italy **3 Bay of** inlet of the Tyrrhenian Sea, on the S coast of Italy: *c.* 10 mi. (16 km) wide

**Na·po·li** (nä′pô̇ lē′) *It. name of* NAPLES

**Na·ra** (nä′rä) city in S Honshu, Japan, east of Osaka: oldest permanent capital of Japan & chief early Buddhist center (fl. 8th cent. A.D.): pop. 316,000

**Nar·ba·da** (nər bud′ə) river in central India, flowing west into the Arabian Sea: *c.* 800 mi. (1,288 km)

**Na·rew** (nä′ref) river in NE Poland, flowing west & southwest into the Bug River, near Warsaw: *c.* 270 mi. (435 km)

**Nar·ra·gan·sett Bay** (nar′ə gan′sit) [ earlier (17th c.) *Nanhiggansett, Nanohigganset*, etc. < a Narragansett place name of uncert. meaning ] inlet of the Atlantic, extending into R.I.: *c.* 30 mi. (48 km)

**Nar·rows** (nar′ōz, ner′ōz), **The** strait between Upper & Lower New York Bay, separating Staten Island & Long Island

**Nase·by** (nāz′bē) village in Northamptonshire, England: site of a decisive Royalist defeat (1645)

**Nash·u·a** (nash′o͞o ə, nash′ə wə) [ < Massachusett or a closely related language: meaning uncert. ] city in S N.H., on the Merrimack River: pop. 80,000

**Nash·ville** (nash′vil; *locally,* -vəl) [ after Gen. Francis *Nash* (1720-77) ] capital of Tenn., on the Cumberland River: pop. 511,000 (met. area 985,000)

**Nas·sau** (nä′sou′; *for 2,* na′sô′) **1** region in W Germany: formerly a duchy **2** capital of the Bahamas, on New Providence Island: pop. 135,000

**Na·tal** (nə tal′; -täl′) **1** province of E South Africa, on the Indian Ocean: 33,578 sq. mi. (86,967 sq. km); pop. 5,722,000; cap. Pietermaritzburg **2** seaport in NE Brazil: capital of Rio Grande de Norte state: pop. 376,000

**Natch·ez Trace** (nach′iz) early 19th-cent. road following an old Indian trail from Natchez, Miss., to Nashville, Tenn.

**National City** [ located on part of Rancho de la Nacion, lit., *National* Ranch ] city in SW Calif.: suburb of San Diego: pop. 54,000

**Natural Bridge** a limestone formation in WC Va., over a tributary of the James River: 215 ft. (65.6 m) high;

span *c.* 90 ft. (27 m)

**Nau·cra·tis** (nô′krə tis) ancient Greek city in the Nile delta

**Na·u·ru** (nä ōō′rōō) country on an island in the W Pacific, just south of the equator: formerly, a UN trust territory (1947-68): 8 sq. mi. (21 sq. km); pop. 7,254

**Na·varre** (nə vär′) **1** historical region & former kingdom in NE Spain & SW France **2** region in NE Spain: 4,023 sq. mi. (10,421 sq. km); pop. 507,000; cap. Pamplona  Sp. name **Na·var·ra** (nä vär′rä)

**Nax·os** (naks′äs′; *Gr* näks′ôs′) largest island of the Cyclades, in the SC Aegean: *c.* 170 sq. mi. (440 sq. km)

**Na·ya·rit** (nä′yä *r*ēt′) state of W Mexico: 10,417 sq. mi. (26,979 sq. km); pop. 726,000; cap. Tepic

**Naz·a·reth** (naz′ə rəth, -rith) 〚Heb *natzērath*〛 town in Galilee, N Israel, where Jesus lived as a child: pop. 33,000

**NB** *abbrev. for* New Brunswick

**NC, N.C.** *abbrev. for* North Carolina

**ND, N.D.** *abbrev. for* North Dakota

**N Dak** *abbrev. for* North Dakota

**N'Dja·me·na** (ən jä′mə nə) capital of Chad, on the Shari river: pop. 303,000

**NE** *abbrev. for* Nebraska

**Near East 1** countries near the E end of the Mediterranean, including those of SW Asia, the Arabian Peninsula, & NE Africa **2** [Historical] the lands occupied by the former Ottoman Empire, including the Balkans

**Neb** *abbrev. for* Nebraska

**Ne·bo** (nē′bō′), **Mount** *Bible* mountain from which Moses saw the Promised Land; summit Pisgah (Deut. 34:1)

**Nebr** *abbrev. for* Nebraska

**Ne·bras·ka** (nə bras′kə) 〚< Omaha *nibdhathka,* name of Platte River, lit., flat river〛 Middle Western State of the NC U.S.: admitted, 1867; 77,227 sq. mi. (20,017 sq. km); pop. 1,578,000; cap. Lincoln: abbrev. *NE, Neb,* or *Nebr*

**Nech·es** (nech′iz) 〚prob. < AmInd tribal name〛 river in E Tex., flowing southeast into Sabine Lake: 280 mi. (450 km): see SABINE

**Ne·der·land** (nā′dər länt′) *Du. name of* the NETHERLANDS

**Ne·fud** (nə fōōd′) *alt. sp. of* NAFUD

**Neg·ev** (neg'ev') region in S Israel of partially reclaimed desert: *c.* 4,000 sq. mi. (10,360 sq. km): also **Nég'eb'** (-eb')

**Ne·gri Sem·bi·lan** (ne'grē sem bē'lən) state of Malaysia in W Peninsular Malaysia: 2,565 sq. mi. (6,643 sq. km); pop. 480,000; cap. Seremban

**Ne·gro** (nā'grō; *Port* nā'grōō; *Sp* nā'grô) **1** river in N Brazil, flowing southeast into the Amazon, near Manaus: *c.* 1,400 mi. (2,253 km) **2** river in SC Argentina, flowing east into the Atlantic: *c.* 700 mi. (1,126 km)

**Ne·gros** (nā'grōs'; *Sp* nā'grôs') island of the central Philippines, between Cebu & Panay: 4,905 sq. mi. (12,704 sq. km)

**Neis·se** (nī'sə) river in N Europe, flowing from N Czech Republic into the Oder River on the Polish-German border: *c.* 140 mi. (225 km): see ODER

**Nejd** (nezhd) region in central & E Saudi Arabia, formerly a sultanate, now administered as a viceroyalty & constituting the *Central Province*; chief city, Riyadh

**Nel·son** (nel'sən) ⟦ so named by Sir T. Button on an expedition into Hudson Bay (1612), after R. *Nelson*, a crew member who died there ⟧ river in Manitoba, Canada, flowing from Lake Winnipeg northeast into Hudson Bay: 400 mi. (644 km)

**Ne·man** (nye'mən; *E* nem'ən) river flowing west through Belarus & Lithuania into the Baltic: 597 mi. (961 km)

**Ne·me·a** (nē'mē ə) valley in Argolis, Greece, in the NE Peloponnesus

**Ne·pal** (nə pôl', -päl') country in the Himalayas, between India & Tibet: 54,300 sq. mi. (140,791 sq. km); pop. 17,422,000; cap. Katmandu

**Nep·tune** (nep'tōōn', -tyōōn') ⟦ ModL < L *Neptunus*, prob. < IE *\*nebhtus* < base *\*nebh-*, moist ⟧ the fourth largest planet of the solar system and normally the eighth in distance from the sun: diameter, *c.* 50,450 km (*c.* 31,350 mi.); period of revolution, 164.78 earth years; period of rotation, 16.05 hours; eight satellites; symbol Ψ

**Ness** (nes), **Loch** lake in Highland region in NW Scotland: 23 mi. (37 km) long

**Neth·er·lands** (ne*th*'ər ləndz) **1** country in W Europe, on the North Sea: 15,770 sq. mi. (40,844 sq. km); pop. 14,536,000; cap. Amsterdam; seat of government, The

Hague **2** kingdom consisting of the independent states of the Netherlands & Netherlands Antilles  Du. name NEDERLAND

**Netherlands Antilles** islands in the West Indies, constituting a part of the kingdom of the Netherlands & comprising two of the Leeward Islands & part of another & three islands off the coast of Venezuela: 394 sq. mi. (1,020 sq. km); pop. 260,000; cap. Willemstad

**Netherlands (East) Indies** former island possessions of the Netherlands, in the East Indies: now part of Indonesia

**Netherlands Guiana** *old name of* SURINAME

**Netherlands New Guinea** *old name of* WEST IRIAN

**nether world** *Theol., Myth.* the world of the dead or of punishment after death; hell

**Né·thou** (nā tōō′), **Pic de** (pēk də) *Fr. name of* Pico de ANETO

**Neu·châ·tel** (nö shä tel′; *E* nōō′shə tel′) **1** canton of W Switzerland, on the French border: 308 sq. mi. (797 sq. km); pop. 158,000  **2** its capital, on the Lake of Neuchâtel: pop. 32,000  **3 Lake of** lake in W Switzerland: 84 sq. mi. (217 sq. km)

**Neu·en·burg** (noi′ən boork′) *Ger. name of* NEUCHÂTEL

**Neuil·ly–sur–Seine** (nö yē′ sür sen′) city in NC France: suburb of Paris: pop. 73,000

**Neuss** (nois) city in W Germany, in the state of North Rhine-Westphalia: pop. 145,000

**Neus·tri·a** (nōōs′trē ə, nyōōs′-) W part of the kingdom of the Merovingian Franks in what is now N & NW France

**Nev** *abbrev. for* Nevada

**Ne·va** (nē′və) river in NW Russia, flowing from Lake Ladoga through St. Petersburg into the Gulf of Finland: 46 mi. (74 km)

**Ne·vad·a** (nə vad′ə, -väd′ə) ⟦ after (SIERRA) NEVADA ⟧ Mountain State of the W U.S.: admitted, 1864; 110,540 sq. mi. (286,300 sq. km); pop. 1,202,000; cap. Carson City: abbrev. *NV* or *Nev*

**Ne·vis** (nē′vis, nev′is) island of St. Kitts and Nevis: 36 sq. mi. (93 sq. km); pop. 9,500

**New Amsterdam** Dutch colonial town on Manhattan Island: renamed (1664) New York by the British

**New·ark** (nōō′ərk, nyōō-) **1** ⟦ after *Newark*, England ⟧ city in NE N.J.: pop. 275,000 (met. area 1,824,000)  **2**

⟦after *Newark*, N.J.⟧ city in central Ohio: pop. 44,000

**New Bedford** ⟦after *Bedford*, England⟧ seaport in SE Mass.: pop. 100,000

**New Britain 1** largest island of the Bismarck Archipelago, east of New Guinea: (with small nearby islands) 14,100 sq. mi. (36,519 sq. km); pop. 227,000 **2** city in central Conn.: pop. 75,000

**New Brunswick 1** ⟦named to honor George III, who was also elector of *Brunswick*-Lüneburg⟧ province of SE Canada, on the Gulf of St. Lawrence: 27,834 sq. mi. (72,090 sq. km); pop. 709,000; cap. Fredericton: abbrev. *NB* **2** ⟦in honor of George I, elector of *Brunswick*-Lüneburg⟧ city in NC N.J.: pop. 42,000

**New Caledonia** French island in the SW Pacific, east of Australia: with nearby islands an overseas territory of France: 7,172 sq. mi. (18,576 sq. km); pop. 145,000; cap. Nouméa

**New Castile** *see* CASTILE

**New·cas·tle** (nōō′kas′əl, nyōō′-; -käs′-) **1** seaport in N England, north of Leeds: pop. 277,000: in full **New′cas′tle-up·on′-Tyne′** (-tīn′) **2** city in Staffordshire, WC England: pop. 120,000: in full **New′cas′tle-un′der-Lyme′** (-līm′) **3** seaport in E New South Wales, Australia, on the Pacific: pop. 146,000

**New Delhi** capital of India, in Delhi territory, adjacent to the old city of Delhi: pop. 302,000

**New England** ⟦so named by Captain John Smith (*c.* 1580-1631), Eng colonist⟧ the six NE States of the U.S.: Me., Vt., N.H., Mass., R.I., & Conn.: abbrev. **New Eng**

**Newf** *abbrev. for* Newfoundland

**New Forest** partially wooded rural district in SW Hampshire, England: 144 sq. mi. (373 sq. km)

**New·found·land** (nōō′fənd lənd, -land′; -foond-; nyōō′-; nōō′found land′, -fənd-, -foond-; nyōō′-; nōō found′ lənd, -land′; nyōō-) ⟦descriptive⟧ **1** island of Canada, off the E coast: 42,734 sq. mi. (110,680 sq. km) **2** province of Canada, including this island & Labrador: 156,185 sq. mi. (406,000 sq. km); pop. 568,000; cap. St. John's: abbrev. *NF, Nfld, Newf,* or *Nfd*

**New France** French possessions in North America, from the end of the 16th cent. to 1763, including E Canada, the Great Lakes region, & the Mississippi valley

**New·gate** (nōō′gāt′, nyōō′-) former prison in London:

torn down in 1902

**New Georgia 1** group of islands in central Solomon Islands, in the SW Pacific: *c.* 2,170 sq. mi. (5,621 sq. km) **2** largest island of this group: *c.* 1,300 sq. mi. (3,365 sq. km)

**New Granada 1** former Spanish possessions, mostly in NW South America, including what is now Colombia, Venezuela, Ecuador, & Panama **2** former country consisting of present-day Colombia & Panama

**New Guinea 1** large island in the East Indies, north of Australia: divided between West Irian (in Indonesia) and Papua New Guinea: *c.* 330,000 sq. mi. (854,700 sq. km): Indonesian name IRIAN **2 Trust Territory of** former Australian trust territory including NE New Guinea, the Bismarck Archipelago, Bougainville, Buka, & smaller adjacent islands of the Solomons: see PAPUA NEW GUINEA

**New·ham** (nōō'əm, nyōō'-) borough of E Greater London, England, on the Thames: formed by the merger of the former cities of East Ham & West Ham: pop. 227,000

**New Hampshire** [after HAMPSHIRE] New England State of the U.S.: one of the 13 original States: 9,304 sq. mi. (24,190 sq. km); pop. 1,109,000; cap. Concord: abbrev. *NH* or *N.H.*

**New Ha·ven** (hā'vən) city in S Conn., on Long Island Sound: pop. 130,000 (met. area with Meriden 530,000)

**New Hebrides** *old name of* VANUATU

**New Ireland** island in the Bismarck Archipelago, north of New Britain: 3,340 sq. mi. (8,650 sq. km); pop. (with small nearby islands) 77,000

**New Jersey** [after JERSEY (the Channel Island)] Eastern State of the U.S. on the Atlantic: one of the 13 original States; 7,836 sq. mi. (20,296 sq. km); pop. 7,730,000; cap. Trenton: abbrev. *NJ* or *N.J.*

**New Jerusalem** *Bible* the holy city of heaven: Rev. 21:2

**New London** city in SE Conn., on Long Island Sound: site of U.S. Coast Guard Academy: pop. 29,000

**New·mar·ket** (nōō'mär'kit, nyōō'-) rural district in Suffolk, E England: scene of many horse-racing events: pop. 14,000

**New Mexico** [transl. of Sp *Nuevo Méjico*] Mountain State of the SW U.S.: admitted, 1912; 121,666 sq. mi. (316,410 sq. km); pop. 1,515,000; cap. Santa Fe:

abbrev. *NM, N.M.,* or *N Mex*

**New Netherland** Dutch colony (1613-64) on Manhattan Island & along the Hudson River: taken by England & divided into the colonies of New York & New Jersey

**New Or·le·ans** (ôr′lē ənz, -lənz; ôr lēnz′) 〚< Fr *Nouvelle Orléans,* in honor of Philippe II, Duc d'*Orléans* (1674-1723), and of *Orléans,* France 〛 city & port in SE La., on the Mississippi: pop. 497,000 (met. area 1,289,000)

**New·port** (nōō′pôrt′, nyōō′-) **1** seaport in SE Wales, on the Usk River, near Bristol: pop. 130,000 **2** 〚after Eng towns of the same name 〛 city in SE R.I., on Narragansett Bay: pop. 28,000

**Newport Beach** 〚see prec.〛 city in SW Calif., on the Pacific, near Long Beach: pop. 67,000

**Newport News** 〚orig. obscure 〛 seaport in SE Va., on the James River at Hampton Roads: pop. 170,000

**New Providence** island of the NC Bahamas: 58 sq. mi. (151 sq. km): see NASSAU

**New Ro·chelle** (rō shel′) 〚after *La Rochelle,* in France 〛 city in SE N.Y., on Long Island Sound, north of New York City: pop. 67,000

**New Siberian Islands** group of islands of Russia, in the Arctic Ocean, between the Laptev & East Siberian seas: *c.* 11,000 sq. mi. (28,490 sq. km)

**New South Wales** state of SE Australia, on the Pacific: 309,433 sq. mi. (801,429 sq. km); pop. 5,378,000; cap. Sydney

**New Spain** former Spanish viceroyalty (1535-1821) including, at its greatest extent, Mexico, SW U.S., Central America north of Panama, the West Indies, & the Philippines

**New·ton** (nōōt′'n, nyōōt′'n) 〚after *New Towne,* orig. name of Cambridge, Mass. 〛 city in E Mass.: suburb of Boston: pop. 83,000

**New World** the Western Hemisphere

**New York** 〚after the Duke of *York* and Albany〛 **1** State of the NE U.S.: one of the 13 original States: 49,576 sq. mi. (128,402 sq. km); pop. 17,990,000; cap. Albany: abbrev. *NY* or *N.Y.* **2** city & port in SE N.Y., at the mouth of the Hudson: divided into five boroughs (the Bronx, Brooklyn, Manhattan, Queens, Staten Island) 365 sq. mi. (946 sq. km); pop. 7,323,000

(met. area 8,547,000; urban area with Long Island, N
New Jersey, & parts of SE Conn., 18,087,000): often
**New York City**

**New York Bay** inlet of the Atlantic, south of Manhattan, divided by the Narrows into a N section (**Upper
Bay**) & a S section (**Lower Bay**)

**New York State Barge Canal** system of waterways connecting Lake Erie & the Hudson River, with branches
to Lakes Ontario, Champlain, Cayuga, & Seneca: *c.*
525 mi. (845 km): cf. ERIE CANAL

**New Zealand** country made up of two large & several
small islands in the S Pacific, southeast of Australia:
discovered in 1642, became a British colony (1841), &
achieved complete independence (1931): a member of
the Commonwealth: 103,736 sq. mi. (268,676 sq. km);
pop. 3,305,000; cap. Wellington

**NF** *abbrev. for* Newfoundland

**Nfd, Nfld** *abbrev. for* Newfoundland

**NH, N.H.** *abbrev. for* New Hampshire

**Ni·ag·a·ra** (nī ag′ə rə, -ag′rə) ⟦< Fr < Iroquoian town
name⟧ river between W N.Y. & SE Ontario, Canada,
flowing from Lake Erie into Lake Ontario: *c.* 36 mi.
(58 km)

**Niagara Falls 1** large waterfall on the Niagara River: it
is divided by an island into two falls, Horseshoe, or
Canadian, Falls, *c.* 160 ft. (48 m) high, & American
Falls, *c.* 167 ft. (51 m) high **2** city in W N.Y., near
Niagara Falls: pop. 62,000 **3** city in SE Ontario, Can-
ada, opposite Niagara Falls: pop. 72,000

**Nia·mey** (nyä mā′) capital of Niger, in the SW part, on
the Niger River: pop. 399,000

**Ni·cae·a** (nī sē′ə) ancient city in Bithynia, NW Asia
Minor: the Nicene Creed was formulated here in A.D.
325

**Nic·a·ra·gua** (nik′ə rä′gwə) **1** country in Central America, on the Caribbean & the Pacific: declared itself
independent from Spain (1821); frequent interventions by Great Britain and the U.S. (1821-50); renewed
U.S. interventions (1912-25; 1926-33); since 1970's
political unrest escalated to a virtual state of civil war:
54,342 sq. mi. (140,750 sq. km); pop. 3,342,000; cap.
Managua **2 Lake** lake in S Nicaragua: *c.* 3,100 sq. mi.
(8,990 sq. km)

**Nice** (nēs) seaport & resort in SE France: pop. 338,000

**Nic·o·bar Islands** (nik′ō bär′, nik′ō bär′) group of islands in the Bay of Bengal: 635 sq. mi. (1,645 sq. km): see ANDAMAN ISLANDS

**Ni·cop·o·lis** (ni käp′ō lis, nī-) city in ancient Epirus

**Nic·o·si·a** (nik′ō sē′ə) capital of Cyprus, in the NC part: pop. 161,000

**Nid·wal·den** (nēd′väl′dən) canton of central Switzerland: 106 sq. mi. (276 sq. km); pop. 28,000

**Nie·der·sach·sen** (nē′dər zäkh′zən) *Ger. name of* LOWER SAXONY

**Ni·fl·heim** (niv′əl hām′) 〚ON *Niflheimr*〛 *Norse Myth.* the regions of darkness and cold, or realm of the dead

**Ni·ger** (nī′jər) **1** river in W Africa, flowing from Guinea through Mali, Niger, & Nigeria into the Gulf of Guinea: *c.* 2,600 mi. (4,185 km) **2** country in WC Africa, north of Nigeria: formerly a French territory, it became independent (1960): 489,191 sq. mi. (1,267,000 sq. km); pop. 6,715,000; cap. Niamey

**Ni·ger·i·a** (nī jir′ē ə) country in WC Africa, on the Gulf of Guinea: formerly a British colony & protectorate, it became independent & a member of the Commonwealth (1960); a republic since 1963: 356,668 sq. mi. (923,768 sq. km); pop. 105,448,000; cap. Abuja

**Ni·hon** (nē′hôn′) 〚short for *Nihon koku* < *Nihon* (< Sino-Jpn *hi no moto*, lit., where the sun rises) + *koku*, country〛 *Jpn. name of* JAPAN: in full **Nihon ko·ku** (kō′ kōō)

**Ni·i·ga·ta** (nē′ē gä′tä) seaport in N Honshu, Japan, on the Sea of Japan: pop. 459,000

**Ni·i·ha·u** (nē′ē hä′ōō, nē′hou′) 〚Haw〛 an island of Hawaii, west of Kauai: 72 sq. mi. (187 sq. km)

**Nij·me·gen** (nī′mā′gən; *Du* nī′mā′khən) city in the E Netherlands, on the Waal river: pop. 147,000

**Nik·ko** (nē′kō, nik′ō) town in EC Honshu, Japan: Buddhist religious center: pop. 33,000

**Ni·ko·la·yev** (nik′ə lä′yev′) seaport in S Ukraine, on the Bug River: pop. 486,000

**Nile** (nīl) river in NE Africa, formed at Khartoum, Sudan, by the juncture of the **Blue Nile**, flowing from N Ethiopia, *c.* 1,000 mi. (1,610 km) & the **White Nile**, flowing from Lake Victoria, *c.* 1,650 mi. (2,655 km), & flowing north through Egypt into the Mediterranean: with the White Nile & a headstream south of Lake Victoria, over 4,000 mi. (6,437 km)

**Nîmes** (nēm) city in S France: pop. 130,000

**Nin·e·veh** (nin′ə və) capital of ancient Assyria, on the Tigris: ruins opposite modern Mosul in N Iraq

**Ning·bo** (niŋ′bō′) city in Zhejiang province, E China: pop. 350,000: also sp. **Ning·po**

**Ning·xia-Hui** (niŋ′shyä′wē′) autonomous region in NW China, on the border of Inner Mongolia: *c.* 65,638 sq. mi. (170,000 sq. km); pop. 3,896,000; cap. Yinchuan: old form **Ning′sia′ Hui′** (-shyä′-)

**Ni·nus** (nī′nəs) *Latin name of* NINEVEH

**Ni·o·brar·a** (nī′ə brer′ə) 〚< Siouan (Omaha), lit., broad, flat river〛 river flowing from E Wyo. east through N Nebr. into the Missouri: 431 mi. (694 km)

**Nip·i·gon** (nip′i gän′), **Lake** 〚< 18th-c. Fr (*Lac*) *Alimipigon* < Ojibwa (unattested); lit. meaning ? where the water begins〛 lake in WC Ontario, Canada, north of Lake Superior: 1,870 sq. mi. (4,844 sq. km)

**Nip·is·sing** (nip′ə siŋ′), **Lake** 〚< Fr < Ojibwa; lit. meaning prob. at the lake〛 lake in SE Ontario, Canada, between Georgian Bay & the Ottawa River: 350 sq. mi. (906 sq. km)

**Nip·pon** (nēp′pôn′; *E* nip′än′, ni pän′) *var. of* NIHON

**Nip·pur** (ni poor′) ancient city of Sumer, southeast of Babylon on the Euphrates, in what is now SE Iraq

**Niš** (nēsh) city in Serbia, E Yugoslavia: pop. 230,000

**Ni·shi·no·mi·ya** (nē′shē nō′mē yä′) city in S Honshu, Japan, west of Osaka: pop. 404,000

**Ni·te·rói** (nē′tə roi′) seaport in SE Brazil, opposite Rio de Janeiro: pop. 383,000

**Ni·u·e** (nē ōō′ā) island in the SC Pacific, east of Tonga, a territory of New Zealand: 100 sq. mi. (259 sq. km); pop. 5,000

**Ni·ver·nais** (nē ver ne′) historical region of central France, southeast of Paris

**Nizh·niy Ta·gil** (nēzh′nē tä gēl′) city in W Russia, in the EC Urals: pop. 419,000

**Nizh·ny Nov·go·rod** (nēzh′nē nôv′gu rət) city in central European Russia, at the Volga & Oka rivers: pop. 1,400,000: see GORKI

**NJ, N.J.** *abbrev. for* New Jersey

**NM, N.M.** *abbrev. for* New Mexico

**N Mex** *abbrev. for* New Mexico

**Nod** (näd) *see* LAND OF NOD

**Nome** (nōm) 〚after nearby Cape *Nome*, prob. < "?

*name*," query on an early map, misread as *C. Nome* ⟧ city in W Alas., on S coast of Seward Peninsula: pop. 3,500

**Noord·bra·bant** (nôrt′brä bänt′) *Du. name of* NORTH BRABANT

**Noord·hol·land** (-hô′länt′) *Du. name of* NORTH HOLLAND

**Nor·den·skjöld** (noor′dən shüld′) *old name of* LAPTEV SEA

**Nord·kyn** (nôr′kün′), **Cape** cape in NE Norway: northernmost point of the European mainland

**Nord-Pas-de-Ca·lais** (nôr pät kä le′) metropolitan region of NE France: 4,793 sq. mi. (12,414 sq. km); pop. 3,932,000; chief city, Lille

**Nor·folk** (nôr′fək) **1** ⟦ after the county in England ⟧ seaport in SE Va., on Hampton Roads & Chesapeake Bay: pop. 261,000 (met. area incl. Newport News & Virginia Beach, 1,396,000) **2** ⟦ OE *Northfolc* < *north*, north + *folc*, folk, people ⟧ county of E England, on the North Sea: 2,068 sq. mi. (5,356 sq. km); pop. 644,000; county seat, Norwich

**Norfolk Island** Australian island in the SW Pacific, east of New South Wales: 13 sq. mi. (36 sq. km); pop. *c.* 1,700

**Nor·ge** (nôr′gə) *Norw. name of* NORWAY

**No·ri·cum** (nō′rē koom′, nôr′i kəm) ancient Roman province south of the Danube, in the region of modern Austria

**Nor·ma** (nôr′mə) ⟦ L < *norma*, carpenter's square, rule ⟧ a S constellation in the Milky Way between Lupus and Ara

**Nor·man** (nôr′mən) ⟦ ult. after A. *Norman*, railroad surveyor ⟧ city in central Okla., near Oklahoma City: pop. 80,000

**Nor·man·dy** (nôr′mən dē) historical region in NW France, on the English Channel

**Norr·kö·ping** (nôr′shö′piŋ) seaport in SE Sweden, on an inlet of the Baltic Sea: pop. 118,000

**North, the** that part of the U.S. which is bounded on the south by Md., the Ohio River, and Mo.; specif., the States opposed to the Confederacy in the Civil War

**North America** N continent in the Western Hemisphere: 9,366,000 sq. mi. (24,258,000 sq. km); pop. 366,628,000

**North·amp·ton** (nôrth amp'tən, -hamp'-; nôr thamp'-)
   1 NORTHAMPTONSHIRE 2 county seat of Northamptonshire: pop. 163,000

**North·amp·ton·shire** (-shir', -shər) county of central
   England: 914 sq. mi. (2,367 sq. km); pop. 540,000;
   county seat, Northampton

**North Bay** city in SE Ontario, Canada: pop. 50,000

**North Ber·gen** (bʉr'gən) city in NE N.J.: pop. 48,000

**North Borneo** *old name of* SABAH

**North Brabant** province of the S Netherlands, between
   the Meuse River & the Belgian border: 1,913 sq. mi.
   (4,956 sq. km); pop. 2,112,000; cap. 's Hertogenbosch

**North Canadian** river flowing from NE N.Mex. east &
   southeast into the Canadian River in E Okla.: 760 mi.
   (1,223 km)

**North Carolina** ⟦see CAROLINA[1]⟧ Southern State of the
   SE U.S.: one of the 13 original States; 52,712 sq. mi.
   (136,523 sq. km); pop. 6,629,000; cap. Raleigh: abbrev.
   *NC* or *N.C.*

**North Cascades National Park** national park in the N
   Cascade Range, N Wash.: 789 sq. mi. (2,044 sq. km)

**North Channel** strait between Northern Ireland & SW
   Scotland: *c.* 80 mi. (128 km) long

**North Charleston** city in E S.C., north of Charleston:
   pop. 70,000

**North Dakota** ⟦see DAKOTA⟧ Middle Western State of
   the NC U.S.: admitted, 1889; 70,665 sq. mi. (183,022
   sq. km); pop. 639,000; cap. Bismarck: abbrev. *ND,*
   *N.D.,* or *N Dak*

**North Downs** *see* DOWNS, the

**Northeast, the** the northeastern part of the U.S., esp.
   New England, but sometimes including New York City

**North East Frontier Agency (or Tract)** *old name of*
   ARUNACHAL PRADESH

**Northeast Passage** water route from the Atlantic to the
   Pacific through the seas north of Europe & Asia

**Northern Cross** the five brightest stars in Cygnus forming a cross: often used to mean Cygnus

**Northern Crown** the constellation Corona Borealis

**Northern Hemisphere** that half of the earth north of
   the equator

**Northern Ireland** division of the United Kingdom, in
   the NE part of the island of Ireland: 5,462 sq. mi.
   (14,147 sq. km); pop. 1,573,000; cap. Belfast

**Northern Province** province of Saudi Arabia, bordering on Jordan & Iraq: *c.* 183,000 sq. mi. (473,000 sq. km)

**Northern Rhodesia** *old name of* ZAMBIA

**Northern Sporades** group of islands in the NW Aegean, west of Thessaly & Evvoia

**Northern Territory** territory of N Australia, on the Arafura Sea: 519,770 sq. mi. (1,346,200 sq. km); pop. 137,000; cap. Darwin

**North Holland** province of the W Netherlands, on the North Sea: 1,029 sq. mi. (2,667 sq. km); pop. 2,311,000; cap. Haarlem

**North Island** N island of the two main islands of New Zealand: 44,297 sq. mi. (114,729 sq. km); pop. 2,439,000

**North Las Vegas** city in SE Nev.: pop. 48,000

**North Little Rock** city in central Ark., on the Arkansas River opposite Little Rock: pop. 62,000

**North Miami** city on the SE coast of Fla: suburb of Miami: pop. 43,000

**North Platte** river flowing from N Colo. north into Wyo. & then southeast through W Nebr., joining the South Platte to form the Platte: 618 mi. (994 km)

**North Pole** the place on the earth where its northern rotational axis intersects its surface: in full **North Terrestrial Pole**

**North Rhine–Westphalia** state of W Germany: 13,151 sq. mi. (34,061 sq. km); pop. 16,775,000; cap. Düsseldorf

**North Rid·ing** (rīd'iŋ) former division of Yorkshire county, England, now part of the county of North Yorkshire

**North River** lower course of the Hudson River, between New York City & NE N.J.

**North Saskatchewan** river flowing from SW Alberta east through Saskatchewan, joining the South Saskatchewan to form the Saskatchewan: 760 mi. (1,224 km)

**North Sea** arm of the Atlantic, between Great Britain & the N European mainland: *c.* 222,000 sq. mi. (574,978 sq. km)

**North Star** POLARIS

**North·um·ber·land** (nôrth um'bər lənd, nôr thum'-) northernmost county of England: 1,943 sq. mi. (5,033 sq. km); pop. 300,000; county seat, Newcastle-upon-

Tyne

**North·um·bri·a** (nôrth um′brē ə, nôr thum′-) former Anglo-Saxon kingdom in Great Britain, south of the Firth of Forth

**Northwest, the** 1 NORTHWEST TERRITORY 2 the northwestern part of the U.S., esp. Wash., Oreg., and Ida. 3 the northwestern part of Canada

**Northwest Passage** water route from the Atlantic to the Pacific, through the arctic islands of Canada

**Northwest Territories** division of N Canada, subdivided into five Regions (Baffin, Fort Smith, Inuvik, Keewatin, & Kitikmeot): 1,253,437 sq. mi. (3,246,389 sq. km): abbrev. *NT* or *NWT* or *NWTer*

**Northwest Territory** region north of the Ohio River, between Pa. & the Mississippi (established 1787): it now forms Ohio, Ind., Ill., Mich., Wis., & part of Minn.

**North York** city in SE Ontario, Canada: part of metropolitan Toronto: pop. 556,000

**North Yorkshire** county of N England: 3,211 sq. mi. (8,317 sq. km); pop. 691,000

**Nor·walk** (nôr′wôk′) 1 〚prob. contr. < *North Walk*, a trail from Anaheim Landing〛 city in SW Calif.: suburb of Los Angeles: pop. 94,000 2 〚< AmInd < ?〛 city in SW Conn., on Long Island Sound: pop. 78,000

**Nor·way** (nôr′wā′) 〚OE *Norweg* < ON *Norvegr* < *northr*, north + *vegr*, way〛 country in N Europe, occupying the W & N parts of the Scandinavian Peninsula: 125,064 sq. mi. (323,877 sq. km); pop. 4,165,000; cap. Oslo: Norw. name NORGE

**Nor·we·gian Sea** (nôr wē′jən) part of the Atlantic between Norway & Iceland

**Nor·wich** (nôr′ij, -ich) 〚OE *northwic* < *north*, north + *wic*, village〛 county seat of Norfolk, E England: known for its cathedral (founded 1096): pop. 119,000

**No·tre Dame** (nō′trə däm′, -dām′; nōt′ər-; Fr nô trə dàm′) 〚Fr, lit., Our Lady (Mary, mother of Jesus)〛 a famous early Gothic cathedral in Paris, built 1163-1257: in full **Notre Dame de Paris**

**Not·ting·ham** (nät′iŋ əm) 〚< OE *Snotingaham* < *Snoting*, people of *Snot* (< *Snot*, personal name < *snotor*, wise + *-inga*, patronymic suffix) + *ham*, home〛 1 NOTTINGHAMSHIRE 2 county seat of Nottinghamshire: pop. 271,000

**Not·ting·ham·shire** (-shir′, -shər) 〚< OE *Snotingham-*

---

*scir*: see prec. + *scir*, office, charge ‖ county of central England: 835 sq. mi. (2,164 sq. km); pop. 1,000,000: county seat, Nottingham

**Nouak·chott** (nwäk shät′) capital of Mauritania, in the W part: pop. 135,000

**Nou·me·a** (nōō′mä ä′) capital of New Caledonia: seaport on the SE coast: pop. 60,000

**No·va I·gua·çu** (nô′və ē′gwə sōō′) city in SE Brazil: suburb of Rio de Janeiro: pop. 492,000

**No·va·ra** (nô vä′rä) commune in the Piedmont, NW Italy: pop. 102,000

**No·va Sco·tia** (nō′və skō′shə) ‖ ModL, New Scotland ‖ province of SE Canada, consisting of a peninsula on the Atlantic, & Cape Breton Island: 21,425 sq. mi. (55,490 sq. km); pop. 873,000; cap. Halifax: abbrev. *NS*

**No·va·to** (nō vät′ō) ‖ after a local Indian chief baptized for St. *Novatus* ‖ city in W Calif., north of San Francisco: pop. 48,000

**No·va·ya Zem·lya** (nô′vä yä zem lyä′) ‖ Russ, lit., new land ‖ archipelago of two large islands & several small ones in NW Russia, between the Barents & Kara seas: *c.* 36,000 sq. mi. (93,240 sq. km)

**Nov·go·rod** (nôv′gu rət) city in NW Russia: former political & commercial center (11th-15th cent.): pop. 220,000

**No·vi Sad** (nô′vē säd′) city in N Yugoslavia, on the Danube: pop. 258,000

**No·vo·kuz·netsk** (nô′vô kōōz nyetsk′) city in SC Russia, in the Kuznetsk Basin: pop. 577,000

**No·vo·si·birsk** (nô′vô sē birsk′) city in SC Russia, on the Ob River: pop. 1,393,000

**NS** *abbrev. for* Nova Scotia

**NT** *abbrev. for* Northwest Territories

**Nu·bi·a** (nōō′bē ə, nyōō′-) ‖ ML < L *Nubae*, the Nubians < Gr *Noubai* ‖ region & ancient kingdom in NE Africa, west of the Red Sea, in Egypt & Sudan

**Nubian Desert** desert in NE Sudan, between the Nile & the Red Sea

**Nu·e·ces** (nōō ā′sās′, -səs) ‖ Sp, nuts, for the pecan trees there ‖ river in S Tex., flowing SE into the Gulf of Mexico at Corpus Christi: 315 mi. (507 km)

**Nue·vo La·re·do** (nwä′vô lä *rä*′dô) city in N Mexico, on the Rio Grande, opposite Laredo, Tex.: pop. 203,000

**Nuevo Le·ón** (lā ôn′) state in NE Mexico: 25,136 sq. mi.

(65,101 sq. km); pop. 2,513,000; cap. Monterrey

**Nu·ku·a·lo·fa** (nōō'kōō ə lô'fə) capital of Tonga: pop. 28,000

**Nu·man·ti·a** (nōō man'shē ə; nyōō-; -shə) ancient city in what is now NC Spain: besieged & captured by Scipio the Younger (133 B.C.)

**Nu·mid·i·a** (nōō mid'ē ə, nyōō-) [L < *Numidae*, the Numidians, pl. of *numida*, a nomad < Gr *noumada*, acc. of *nomas*, nomad] ancient country in N Africa, mainly in what is now E Algeria

**Nur·em·berg** (noor'əm burg', nyoor'-) city in SE Germany, in the state of Bavaria: pop. 472,000: Ger. name **Nürn·berg** (nürn'berk')

**NV** *abbrev. for* Nevada

**NWT, NWTer** *abbrev. for* Northwest Territories

**NY, N.Y.** *abbrev. for* New York

**Nya·sa** (nyä'sä, nī as'ə), **Lake** *old name of* Lake MALAWI

**Nya·sa·land** (-land') *old name of* MALAWI

# O

**O** *abbrev. for* **1** Ohio **2** Ontario

**O·a·hu** (ō ä'hōō) [Haw] chief island of Hawaii: 589 sq. mi. (1,526 sq. km); pop. 836,000; chief city, Honolulu

**Oak·land** (ōk'lənd) [after the *oak* groves orig. there] seaport in W Calif., on San Francisco Bay, opposite San Francisco: pop. 372,000

**Oak Lawn** [after the many *oak* trees there] village in NE Ill.: suburb of Chicago: pop. 56,000

**Oak Park** [see prec.] village in NE Ill.: suburb of Chicago: pop. 53,000

**Oak Ridge** [see OAK LAWN] city in E Tenn., near Knoxville: center for atomic research: pop. 27,000

**Oak·ville** (ōk'vil) [named for an oak stave industry there] town in SE Ontario, Canada, on Lake Ontario, near Toronto: pop. 87,000

**Oa·xa·ca** (wä hä'kä) **1** state of SE Mexico: 36,275 sq. mi. (93,952 sq. km); pop. 2,369,000 **2** its capital: pop. 157,000

**Ob** (ōb; *Russ* ôb'y') **1** river in W Siberia, flowing from the Altai Mountains northwest & north into the Gulf of Ob: 2,495 mi. (4,015 km) **2 Gulf of** arm of the Kara Sea, in NW Siberia: *c.* 600 mi. (966 km) long

**O·ber·am·mer·gau** (ō'bər äm'ər gou') village in S Germany, in the state of Bavaria: site of a Passion play performed usually every ten years: pop. 4,700

**O·ber·hau·sen** (ō′bər hou′zən) city in WC Germany, in the state of North Rhine-Westphalia: pop. 224,000

**O·ber·land** (ō′bər länt′) BERNESE ALPS

**Ob·wal·den** (ôp′väl′dən) canton of central Switzerland: 189 sq. mi. (491 sq. km); pop. 26,000

**Oc·ci·dent** (äk′sə dənt, -dent′) the part of the world west of Asia, esp. Europe and the Americas

**O·ce·an·i·a** (ō′shē an′ē ə) islands in the Pacific, including Melanesia, Micronesia, & Polynesia (incl. New Zealand) &, sometimes, Australia & the Malay Archipelago: also **O′ce·an′i·ca** (-i kə)

**O·cean·side** (ō′shən sīd′) ⟦descriptive⟧ city in SW Calif., near San Diego: pop. 128,000

**O·ce·a·nus** (ō sē′ə nəs) ⟦L < Gr *Ōkeanos*, the outer sea (in contrast to the Mediterranean)⟧ *Gr. Myth.* the great outer stream supposedly encircling the earth

**Oc·tans** (äk′tanz) ⟦ModL < LL *octans*, eighth part < L *octo*, eight⟧ a S constellation containing the celestial pole

**O·den·se** (ō′thən sə, -dən-) seaport on N Fyn island, Denmark: pop. 171,000

**O·der** (ō′dər) river in central Europe, flowing north through Czech Republic & Poland into the Baltic: *c.* 560 mi. (900 km): it forms, with the Neisse, the boundary (**Oder-Neisse Line**) between Germany & Poland

**O·des·sa** (ō des′ə) **1** seaport in S Ukraine, on the Black Sea: pop. 1,126,000 **2** ⟦after the Ukrainian city⟧ city in WC Tex.: pop. 90,000

**O·dra** (ô′drä) *Pol. name of* ODER

**Of·fa·ly** (äf′ə lē) county in Leinster province, central Ireland: 771 sq. mi. (1,996 sq. km); pop. 58,000

**Of·fen·bach** (ôf′ən bäkh′) city in SW Germany, on the Main River, in the state of Hesse: pop. 107,000

**Og·bo·mo·sho** (äg′bə mō′shō) city in SW Nigeria: pop. 432,000

**Og·den** (äg′dən, ôg′) ⟦after P. S. *Ogden*, a fur trader who explored the region in 1820⟧ city in N Utah: pop. 64,000: see SALT LAKE CITY

**OH** *abbrev. for* Ohio

**O·hi·o** (ō hī′ō) ⟦after the river⟧ **1** Middle Western State of the NC U.S.: admitted, 1803; 41,222 sq. mi.

(106,765 sq. km); pop. 10,847,000; cap. Columbus: abbrev. *OH* or *O* 2 〚< Fr < Iroquoian, lit., fine (or large) river〛 river formed by the junction of the Monongahela & the Allegheny at Pittsburgh, flowing southwestward into the Mississippi: 981 mi. (1,579 km)

**Oise** (wàz) river flowing from S Belgium southwest through N France into the Seine: 186 mi. (299 km)

**Oi·ta** (ɔi'tä'; ō ēt'ə) city in NE Kyushu, Japan: pop. 373,000

**OK** *abbrev. for* Oklahoma

**O·ka** (ô kä') river in central European Russia, flowing northeast into the Volga: *c.* 950 mi. (1,529 km)

**O·ka·van·go** (ō'kə väŋ'gō) *alt. sp. of* OKOVANGGO

**O·ka·ya·ma** (ô kä yä'mä) seaport in SW Honshu, Japan, on the Inland Sea: pop. 555,000

**O·kee·cho·bee** (ō'kē chō'bē), **Lake** 〚< AmInd〛 lake in SE Fla. at the N edge of the Everglades: 700 sq. mi. (1,813 sq. km): main element of **Okeechobee Waterway**, a system of connected canals, rivers, & lakes across the Fla. peninsula: 155 mi. (250 km)

**O·ke·fe·no·kee Swamp** (ō'kə fə nō'kē) 〚< AmInd name, lit., trembling earth + *swamp*〛 swamp in SE Ga. & NE Fla.: *c.* 700 sq. mi. (1,813 sq. km)

**O·khotsk** (ō kätsk'; *Russ* ô khôtsk'), **Sea of** arm of the Pacific, off the E coast of Siberia: 590,000 sq. mi. (1,528,000 sq. km)

**O·ki·na·wa** (ō'kə nä'wə) largest island of the Ryukyus, in the W Pacific northeast of Taiwan: 454 sq. mi. (1,176 sq. km); cap. Naha City

**Okla** *abbrev. for* Oklahoma

**O·kla·ho·ma** (ō'klə hō'mə) 〚< Choctaw *okla,* people + *homma,* red〛 State of the SC U.S.: admitted, 1907; 69,919 sq. mi. (181,100 sq. km); pop. 3,146,000; cap. Oklahoma City: abbrev. *OK* or *Okla*

**Oklahoma City** capital of Okla., in the central part: pop. 445,000 (met. area 959,000)

**O·ko·vang·go** (ō'kə väŋ'gō) river in SW Africa, flowing from central Angola southeast into a marshy basin (**Okovanggo Basin**) in N Botswana: *c.* 1,000 mi. (1,609 km)

**Ö·land** (ö länd') Swedish island in the Baltic Sea, off the SE coast of Sweden: *c.* 520 sq. mi. (1,344 sq. km)

**Old Bai·ley** (bā'lē) historic criminal court in London on

Old Bailey Street

**Old Castile** *see* CASTILE

**Old Delhi** *see* DELHI (the city)

**Old Dominion** *name for* VIRGINIA

**Ol·den·burg** (ōl′dən bʉrg′; *Ger* ōl′dən boͦorkh′) **1** former state of NW Germany, earlier a grand duchy **2** city in NW Germany, in the state of Lower Saxony: pop. 138,000

**Old Faithful** a noted geyser in Yellowstone National Park, which erupts about every 67 minutes

**Old·ham** (ōl′dəm) city in NW England, in the county of Greater Manchester: pop. 95,000

**Old Man River** *name for* MISSISSIPPI (the river)

**Old South** *name for* the South before the Civil War

**Ol·ives** (äl′ivz), **Mount of** ridge of hills east of Jerusalem: also **Mount Ol·i·vet** (äl′ə vet′, -vət)

**O·lym·pi·a** (ō lim′pē ə, ə-) **1** plain in ancient Elis, W Peloponnesus: site of the ancient Olympic games **2** ⟦after fol.⟧ capital of Wash.: seaport on Puget Sound: pop. 34,000

**Olym·pic Mountains** (-pik) one of the Coast Ranges on Olympic Peninsula, NW Wash.: highest peak, Mt. Olympus

**Olympic National Park** national park in NW Wash., around Mount Olympus: 1,389 sq. mi. (3,598 sq. km)

**Olympic Peninsula** peninsula in NW Wash., between Puget Sound & the Pacific

**O·lym·pus** (-pəs) ⟦L < Gr *Olympos*⟧ **1 Mount** mountain in N Greece, between Thessaly & Macedonia: *c.* 9,580 ft. (2,920 m): in Greek mythology, the home of the gods **2 Mount** ⟦after the mountain in Greece⟧ highest peak of the Olympic Mountains, NW Wash.: 7,965 ft. (2,428 m)

**O·lyn·thus** (ō lin′thəs) city in ancient Greece, on the Chalcidice Peninsula

**O·ma·ha** (ō′mə hô, -hä) ⟦< Fr < Siouan tribal name; lit., ? upstream people⟧ city in E Nebr., on the Missouri River: pop. 336,000 (met. area 618,000)

**O·man** (ō män′) **1** SE coastal region of Arabia, on the Arabian Sea **2** country in this region: an independent sultanate: 82,000 sq. mi. (212,380 sq. km); pop. 1,270,000; cap. Muscat **3 Gulf of** arm of the Arabian Sea, between Iran & Oman in Arabia: *c.* 350 mi. (*c.* 564 km) long

**Om·dur·man** (äm′door män′) city in WC Sudan, on the Nile, opposite Khartoum: pop. 305,000

**Omsk** (ômsk) city in S Asian Russia on the Irtysh river: pop. 1,108,000

**On** (än) *Biblical name of* HELIOPOLIS

**ON** *abbrev. for* Ontario

**O·ne·ga** (ō nē′gə; *Russ* ô nye′gä), **Lake** lake in NW European Russia: *c.* 3,800 sq. mi. (9,842 sq. km)

**Onega Bay** S arm of the White Sea, extending into NW European Russia: *c.* 100 mi. (160 km) long

**O·nei·da Lake** (ō nī′də) ⟦ after *Oneida*, an Indian people orig. living nearby < Iroquois *Oneiute*, lit., standing rock ⟧ lake near Syracuse, N.Y.: part of the New York State Barge Canal system: *c.* 80 sq. mi. (208 sq. km)

**On·on·da·ga Lake** (än′ən dô′gə, -dä′-) ⟦ < AmInd (Iroquois) *Ononta'ge'*, lit., on top of the hill (name of the principal village of the Onondaga Indians) ⟧ salt lake northwest of Syracuse, N.Y.: *c.* 5 sq. mi. (13 sq. km)

**Ont** *abbrev. for* Ontario

**On·tar·i·o** (än ter′ē ō) **1** ⟦ after Lake *Ontario* ⟧ province of SC Canada, between the Great Lakes & Hudson Bay: 412,582 sq. mi. (1,068,000 sq. km); pop. 9,102,000: cap. Toronto: abbrev. *ON* or *Ont* **2** ⟦ after the Cdn province ⟧ city in S Calif.: pop. 133,000 **3 Lake** ⟦ < Fr < Iroquoian, lit., fine lake ⟧ smallest & easternmost of the Great Lakes, between N.Y. & Ontario, Canada: 7,540 sq. mi. (19,529 sq. km)

**Oost·en·de** (ōs ten′də) *Fl. name of* OSTEND

**O·phir** (ō′fər) ⟦Heb *ōphīr* ⟧ Bible a land rich in gold: 1 Kings 9:28; 10:11; 2 Chron. 8:18

**Oph·i·u·chus** (äf′ē yōō′kəs, ō′fē-) ⟦L < Gr *ophiouchos*, lit., holding a serpent < *ophis*, a snake + base of *echein*, to hold ⟧ a large N and S constellation between Hercules and Scorpius

**O·por·to** (ō pôr′tō) seaport in N Portugal, on the Douro River: pop. 330,000: Port. name PôRTO

**OR** *abbrev. for* Oregon

**O·ra·dea** (ô räd′yä) city in NW Romania, near the Hungarian border: pop. 198,000

**O·ran** (ō ran′; *Fr* ô rän′) seaport in N Algeria, on the Mediterranean: pop. 660,000

**Or·ange** (ôr′inj, är′-; *also, for 3 & 4, Fr* ô ränzh′) **1** ⟦prob. named for the *orange* groves there ⟧ city in SW Calif.: suburb of Los Angeles: pop. 111,000 **2** river in

South Africa, flowing from NE Lesotho west into the Atlantic: *c.* 1,300 mi. (2,092 km) **3** former principality of W Europe (12th-17th cent.), now in SE France **4** city in SE France: pop. 27,000

**Orange Free State** province of South Africa, west of Lesotho: formerly a Boer republic (1854-1900) & then a British colony (**Orange River Colony**, 1900-10): 49,418 sq. mi. (127,993 sq. km); pop. 1,932,000; cap. Bloemfontein

**Or·cus** (ôr′kəs) *Rom. Myth.* the lower world; Hades

**Or·dzho·ni·kid·ze** (ôr′jô ni kēd′ze) *old name of* VLADI-KAVKAZ

**Ö·re·bro** (ö′rə brōō′) city in SC Sweden: pop. 118,000

**Oreg** *abbrev. for* Oregon

**Or·e·gon** (ôr′i gən, är′-; *also, but not locally,* -gän′) ⟦prob. < AmInd *ouragan* (lit., birch-bark dish), native name of the COLUMBIA (River)⟧ NW coastal State of the U.S.: admitted, 1859; 96,981 sq. mi. (251,181 sq. km); pop. 2,842,000; cap. Salem: abbrev. *OR* or *Oreg*

**Oregon Trail** former route extending from the Missouri River in Mo., northwest to the Columbia River in Oreg., much used by westward migrants (*c.* 1840-60): *c.* 2,000 mi. (3,218 km)

**O·rel** (ô rel′, ôr yôl′) city in W European Russia, on the Oka: pop. 328,000

**Or·em** (ôr′əm) ⟦after W. C. *Orem* (died 1951), pres. of a former interurban railroad in the area⟧ city in NC Utah: pop. 68,000

**O·ren·burg** (ô̂r′yən boorkh) city in SE European Russia: pop. 519,000

**Ö·re·sund** (*Swed* ö′rə sund′) strait between Sweden and the Danish island of Zealand: *c.* 80 mi. (129 km) long: Dan. sp. **Ø′re·sund′** (*Dan*, -soon′)

**O·ri·ent** (ôr′ē ənt) the East, or Asia; esp., the Far East

**O·ri·no·co** (ôr′ə nō′kō) river in Venezuela, flowing from the Brazil border into the Atlantic: *c.* 1,700 mi. (2,736 km)

**O·ri·on** (ō rī′ən, ə-) ⟦ME < L < Gr *Ōríōn*⟧ an equatorial constellation between Taurus and Lepus, containing the bright stars Rigel and Betelgeuse

**O·ris·sa** (ō ris′ə) state of E India, on the Bay of Bengal: 60,118 sq. mi. (155,707 sq. km); pop. 26,272,000; cap. Bhubaneswar

**O·ri·za·ba** (ô̂′rē sä′bä) **1** volcanic mountain in SE Mex-

ico, highest mountain in Mexico: 18,700 ft. (5,700 m)
**2** city at the foot of this mountain, in Veracruz state:
pop. 115,000

**Ork·ney Islands** (ôrk′nē) 〚< ON *Orkneyjar*, lit., seal
islands < *orkn*, a seal + *ey*, island〛 group of islands
north of Scotland, constituting a region of Scotland:
376 sq. mi. (974 sq. km); pop. 19,000

**Or·lan·do** (ôr lan′dō) 〚after *Orlando* Reeves, a soldier
killed there in an Indian attack〛 city in central Fla.:
pop. 165,000 (met. area 1,073,000)

**Or·lé·a·nais** (ôr lā à ne′) historical region in NC
France: chief city, Orléans

**Or·lé·ans** (ôr lā än′; *E* ôr′lē ənz) city in NC France, on
the Loire: pop. 84,000

**Or·muz** (ôr′muz′), **Strait of** see HORMUZ, Strait of

**O·ron·tes** (ō rän′tēz) river in SW Asia, flowing from
Lebanon through Syria & Turkey into the Mediterranean: *c.* 240 mi. (386 km)

**Orsk** (ôrsk) city in SE European Russia, on the Ural
River: pop. 266,000

**Or·te·gal** (ôr′te gäl′), **Cape** cape in NW Spain,
extending into the Bay of Biscay

**Ort·les** (ôrt′lās) range of the E Alps, in N Italy: highest
peak (**Ortles**), 12,792 ft. (3,900 m): Ger. name **Ort·ler**
(ôrt′lər)

**O·ru·ro** (ô rŏŏr′ō) city in W Bolivia: pop. 132,000

**O·sage** (ō sāj′, ō′sāj′) 〚after *Osage* (an Indian people) <
Osage *Wazhazhe*〛 river in central Mo. & E Kans.,
flowing east into the Missouri: *c.* 500 mi. (804 km)

**O·sa·ka** (ō sä′kə, ō′sä kä′) seaport in S Honshu, Japan:
pop. 2,648,000

**Osh·a·wa** (äsh′ə wə, -wô) city in SE Ontario, Canada,
on Lake Ontario: pop. 124,000

**Osh·kosh** (äsh′käsh) 〚after *Oshkosh* (1795-1858),
Menomini chief〛 city in E Wis., on Lake Winnebago:
pop. 55,000

**Os·lo** (äs′lō, äz′-; *Norw* ōŏs′lŏŏ) capital of Norway: seaport on an inlet (**Oslo Fjord**) of the Skagerrak: pop.
447,000

**Os·na·brück** (ôs′nä brük′; *E* äz′nə brook′) city in NW
Germany, in the state of Lower Saxony: pop. 155,000

**Os·sa** (äs′ə) mountain in Thessaly, NE Greece: 6,490 ft.
(1,978 m): see PELION

**Ost·end** (äs tend′, äs′tend) seaport in NW Belgium, on

the North Sea: pop. 69,000: Fr. name **Ost·ende** (ô stäⁿd′)

**Ös·ter·reich** (ös′tər rīH′) *Ger. name of* AUSTRIA

**Os·ti·a** (äs′tē ə) ancient city in Latium, at the mouth of the Tiber, that was the port of Rome

**Os·tra·va** (ôs′trä vä) city in NE Czech Republic: pop. 324,000

**Oś·wię·cim** (ôsh vyaⁿ′tsim) *Pol. name of* AUSCHWITZ

**O·ta·ru** (ô′tä rōō′) seaport on the W coast of Hokkaido, Japan: pop. 180,000

**O·tran·to** (ō trän′tō; *It* ô trän′tô), **Strait of** strait between Albania & Italy, connecting the Adriatic & Ionian seas: *c.* 45 mi. (73 km) wide

**Ot·ta·wa** (ät′ə wə, -wä′, -wô′) ⟦after *Ottawa* (an Indian people) < Fr *Outaouois* < Ojibwa *odaawaa*⟧ 1 river in SE Canada, forming the border between Ontario & Quebec, flowing southeast into the St. Lawrence: 696 mi. (1,120 km) 2 capital of Canada, in SE Ontario, on the Ottawa River: pop. 567,000 (met. area 819,000)

**Ot·to·man Empire** (ät′ə mən) empire (*c.* 1300-1918) of the Turks, including at its peak much of SE Europe, SW Asia, & NE Africa: cap. (after 1453) Constantinople

**Ötz·tal Alps** (öts′täl) division of the E Alps, along the Austro-Italian border: highest peak, 12,379 ft. (3,774 m)

**Ouach·i·ta** (wäsh′i tô, wôsh′-) ⟦< Fr < ?⟧ river flowing from W Ark. southeast & south into the Red River in La.: 605 mi. (974 km)

**Oua·ga·dou·gou** (wä′gə dōō′gōō) capital of Burkina Faso, in the central part: pop. 375,000

**Ouj·da** (ōōj dä′) city in NE Morocco: pop. 262,000

**Ouse** (ōōz) 1 river in E England, flowing north into The Wash: 156 mi. (251 km): also **Great Ouse** 2 river in N England, joining the Trent to form the Humber: 60 mi. (96 km)

**Outer Banks** chain of long, narrow, sandy islands, along the coast of N.C.

**Outer Hebrides** *see* HEBRIDES

**Outer Mongolia** *old name of* MONGOLIAN PEOPLE'S REPUBLIC

**O·ver·ijs·sel** (ō′və rī′səl) province of the E Netherlands, bordering on Germany; 1,469 sq. mi. (3,805 sq. km); pop. 1,044,000

**O·ver·land Park** (ō'vər lənd) ⟦after the *Overland,* or Santa Fe, Trail which passed through the area⟧ city in NE Kans.: suburb of Kansas City: pop. 112,000

**O·vie·do** (ô vye'thô) city in NW Spain: pop. 190,000

**O·wens·bor·o** (ō'ənz bur'ō) ⟦after Col. A. *Owen* (1769-1811)⟧ city in NW Ky., on the Ohio: pop. 54,000

**Ow·en Stan·ley Range** (ō'ən stan'lē) mountain range in SE New Guinea, in Papua New Guinea: highest peak, 13,363 ft. (4,073 m)

**Ox·ford** (äks'fərd) ⟦OE *Oxenaford* < *oxan,* gen. pl. of *oxa,* ox + *ford,* ford: originally, place where oxen forded the river⟧ 1 city in SC England; county seat of Oxfordshire & the site of Oxford University: pop. 116,000 2 OXFORDSHIRE

**Ox·ford·shire** (-shir', -shər) county of SC England: 1,008 sq. mi. (2,611 sq. km); pop. 558,000; county seat, Oxford

**Ox·nard** (äks'närd) ⟦after H. T. *Oxnard,* local businessman⟧ city in SW Calif., near Los Angeles: pop. 142,000 (met. area with Ventura, 669,000)

**Ox·us** (äk'səs) *ancient name of* AMU DARYA

**O·zark Mountains** (ō'zärk) ⟦< Fr *aux Arcs,* to the (region of the) Arc (Arkansa) Indians⟧ highland region in NW Ark., SW Mo., & NE Okla.: 1,500-2,500 ft. (450-760 m) high

**Ozarks** 1 OZARK MOUNTAINS 2 **Lake of the** artificial lake in central Mo., formed by a dam on the Osage River: 130 mi. (209 km) long

# P

**PA, Pa** *abbrev. for* Pennsylvania

**Pa·chu·ca** (pä chōō'kä) city in EC Mexico: capital of Hidalgo state: pop. 135,000

**Pa·cif·ic** (pə sif'ik) ⟦< ModL (*mare*) *Pacificum,* peaceful sea: so called by Ferdinand Magellan (c. 1480-1521), Port navigator, because of its tranquil appearance⟧ largest of the earth's oceans, between Asia and the American continents: c. 64,186,000 sq. mi. (166,241,000 sq. km); greatest known depth, 35,809 ft. (10,915 m)

**Pacific Islands, Trust Territory of the** U.S. trust territory in the W Pacific, consisting of the Caroline & Marshall Islands: c. 420 sq. mi. (1,090 sq. km); pop.

105,000

**Pacific Rim 1** the coastal regions bordering the Pacific Ocean **2** the countries of these regions, esp. with respect to their trade relations, political alliances, etc. with each other

**Pa·dang** (pä däŋ′) seaport on the W coast of Sumatra, Indonesia: pop. 481,000

**Pad·ding·ton** (pad′iŋ tən) former borough of London, now part of Westminster

**Pa·der·born** (pä′dər bôrn′) city in WC Germany, in the state of North Rhine-Westphalia: pop. 110,000

**Pa·do·va** (pä′dô vä) *It. name of* PADUA

**Pad·u·a** (paj′o͞o ə, pad′yo͞o ə) commune in N Italy, in Veneto: pop. 235,000: It. name PADOVA

**Pa·dus** (pā′dəs) *ancient name of* Po

**Paes·tum** (pes′təm) ancient Greek city in S Italy

**Pa·go Pa·go** (päŋ′ō päŋ′ō, pä′gō pä′gō) seaport on the S coast of Tutuila Island: capital of American Samoa: pop. 3,500

**Pa·hang** (pä häŋ′) state of Malaysia, in Peninsular Malaysia, on the South China Sea: 13,886 sq. mi. (35,906 sq. km); pop. 771,000

**Painted Desert** ‖so named from the colorful rock strata‖ desert plateau in NC Ariz., east of the Colorado River

**Pais·ley** (pāz′lē) city in SC Scotland, near Glasgow: pop. 84,000

**Pa·ki·stan** (pak′i stan′, pä′ki stän′) country in S Asia, on the Arabian Sea: formed from parts of former British India, it became a dominion (1947-56) & a republic (1956-72) of the Commonwealth: 310,403 sq. mi. (803,943 sq. km); pop. 101,855,000; cap. Islamabad: see also JAMMU AND KASHMIR

**Pa·lat·i·nate** (pə lat′'n āt′, -it) a historical region now part of Germany: in two parts: **Lower Palatinate** or **Rhine Palatinate** (on the Rhine east of Saarland) and the **Upper Palatinate** (in E Bavaria on the Danube): see RHINELAND-PALATINATE

**Pal·a·tine** (pal′ə tīn′, -tin) *see* SEVEN HILLS OF ROME

**Pa·lau Islands** (pä lou′) *see* BELAU

**Pa·la·wan** (pä lä′wän′) island in the W Philippines, southwest of Mindoro: 4,550 sq. mi. (11,785 sq. km)

**Pa·lem·bang** (pä′lem bäŋ′) seaport in SE Sumatra, Indonesia: pop. 787,000

**Pa·len·que** (pä leŋ′kā′) village in N Chiapas state, Mexico: site of ancient Mayan ruins

**Pa·ler·mo** (pə ler′mō; *It* pä ler′mô) capital of Sicily: seaport on the N coast: pop. 700,000

**Pal·es·tine** (pal′əs tīn′) 1 historical region in SW Asia at the E end of the Mediterranean comprising parts of modern Israel, Jordan, & Egypt: also known as the HOLY LAND 2 British mandated territory in this region, west of the Jordan River, from 1923 to the establishment of the state of Israel (1948) according to the United Nations partition plan (1947)

**Pal·i·sades** (pal′ə sādz′, pal′ə sādz′), **the** the line of steep cliffs in NE N.J. & SE N.Y. on the west shore of the Hudson: *c.* 15 mi. (24.14 km) long

**Pal·las** (pal′əs) ⟦ModL: so named (1802) by H. W. M. Olbers (1758-1840), Ger astronomer, after L *Pallas*, the goddess⟧ the second asteroid discovered (1802), and the second largest (*c.* 610 km or *c.* 380 mi. in diameter)

**Pal·ma** (päl′mä) seaport on Majorca: capital of Baleares, Spain: pop. 305,000: in full **Palma de Mal·lor·ca** (*the* mä lyôr′kä)

**Palm Beach** (päm) ⟦descriptive⟧ town in SE Fla., on the Atlantic; winter resort: pop. 10,000

**Pal·mer Peninsula** (päm′ər) *old name of* ANTARCTIC PENINSULA

**Palm Springs** ⟦descriptive⟧ resort city in SW Calif. east of Los Angeles: pop. 40,000

**Pal·my·ra** (pal mī′rə) ancient city in central Syria, northeast of Damascus: now the site of a village

**Pal·o Al·to** (pal′ō al′tō) ⟦Sp, lit., tall tree (the redwood)⟧ city in W Calif., near San Francisco: pop. 56,000

**Pal·o·mar** (pal′ə mär′), **Mount** ⟦Sp, lit., dovecote⟧ mountain in SW Calif., near San Diego: site of an astronomical observatory: 6,140 ft. (1,872 m)

**Pa·los** (pä′lôs) village & former port in SW Spain, from which Columbus embarked on his 1st voyage

**Pa·mirs** (pä mirz′) mountain system mostly in Tajikistan: highest peak, *c.* 25,000 ft. (7,650 m): also **Pa·mir′**

**Pam·li·co Sound** (pam′li kō′) ⟦earlier *Pampticough* < Algonquian tribal name⟧ inlet of the Atlantic between the coast of N.C. and narrow offshore islands: *c.* 80 mi. (129 km) long

**Pam·phyl·i·a** (pam fil′ē ə) ancient region in S Asia

Minor, on the Mediterranean

**Pam·plo·na** (päm plô′nä) city in Navarre, NE Spain: pop. 183,000

**Pan·a·ma** (pan′ə mä′, -mô′) 〚< AmSp *Panamá* < native Ind word〛 **1** country in Central America, on the Isthmus of Panama: formerly a part of Colombia, it became independent (1903); in 1979 assumed sovereignty over CANAL ZONE: 29,760 sq. mi. (77,080 sq. km); pop. 2,227,000 **2** its capital: seaport on the Gulf of Panama: pop. 386,000 **3 Gulf of** arm of the Pacific, on the S coast of Panama: *c.* 115 mi. (185 km) wide **4 Isthmus of** strip of land connecting South America & Central America: 31 mi. (50 km) wide at its narrowest point

**Panama Canal** ship canal across the Isthmus of Panama, connecting the Caribbean Sea (hence, Atlantic Ocean) and the Pacific Ocean: 50.7 mi. (82 km) long

**Panama Canal Zone** CANAL ZONE

**Panama City** PANAMA (the capital)

**Pan·a·mint Range** (pan′ə mint) 〚< name of a division of the Shoshonean Indians〛 mountain range in SE Calif., forming the W rim of Death Valley: highest peak, 11,045 ft. (3,367 m)

**Pa·nay** (pä nī′, pə-) island of the central Philippines, between Mindoro & Negros: 4,446 sq. mi. (11,515 sq. km)

**Pan·de·mo·ni·um** (pan′də mō′nē əm) 〚ModL < Gr *pan,* all + *daimōn,* demon〛 **1** the capital of Hell in Milton's *Paradise Lost* **2** HELL

**Pan·ge·a** (pan jē′ə) 〚coined (1912) by A. L. Wegener (1880-1930), Ger geologist: < Gr *pan,* all + *gē,* the earth〛 the hypothetical single landmass that split apart about 200 million years ago and formed Gondwana and Laurasia: also **Pan·gae′a**

**Pang·o Pang·o** (päŋ′ō päŋ′ō) *var. of* PAGO PAGO

**Pan·no·ni·a** (pə nō′nē ə) ancient Roman province in central Europe, between the Danube & Sava rivers

**Pan·tel·le·ri·a** (pän tel′le rē′ä) Italian island in the Mediterranean, between Sicily & Tunisia: 32 sq. mi. (83 sq. km)

**Pan·thal·as·sa** (pan′thə lä′sə) the hypothetical ocean surrounding Pangea

**Pan·the·on** (pan′thē än′, -ən; *also, chiefly Brit,* pan thē′-) a temple built by Agrippa in Rome in 27 B.C., and rebuilt in the 2d cent. A.D. by Hadrian: used since A.D. 609 as a Christian Church

**Pao·tou** (bou'dō') *old form of* BAOTOU

**Pa·pal States** (pā'pəl) former territory in central & NC Italy, ruled by the papacy from the 8th cent. until 1870

**Pa·pe·e·te** (pä'pē ā'tā) seaport & chief town on Tahiti: capital of French Polynesia: pop. 23,000

**Paph·la·go·ni·a** (paf'lə gō'nē ə) ancient region of N Asia Minor, on the Black Sea

**Pa·phos** (pā'fäs') ancient city in SW Cyprus, founded by the Phoenicians

**Pap·u·a** (pap'yōō ə) **1** PAPUA NEW GUINEA **2 Gulf of** arm of the Coral Sea, on the SE coast of New Guinea: *c.* 225 mi. wide (362 km) **3 Territory of** former UN trust territory consisting of the SE section of New Guinea, and nearby islands, administered by Australia

**Papua New Guinea** country occupying the E half of the island of New Guinea, & nearby islands, including the former Territory of Papua & the Trust Territory of New Guinea: independent since 1975: *c.* 180,000 sq. mi. (466,190 sq. km); pop. 3,395,000; cap. Port Moresby

**Pa·rá** (pä rä') **1** river in NE Brazil, the S estuary of the Amazon: *c.* 200 mi. (321 km) **2** state of N Brazil, on the Atlantic: 482,906 sq. mi. (1,250,722 sq. km); pop. 3,403,000; cap. Belém

**Par·a·dise** (par'ə dīs'; *also,* -dīz') ⟦ME *paradis* < OE & OFr, both < LL(Ec) *paradisus,* heaven, abode of the blessed < L, park, orchard < Gr *paradeisos,* park, garden (in N.T. & LXX, Paradise) < Iran *\*pardez,* akin to Avestan *pairi-daēza,* enclosure < *pairi,* around + *daēza,* a wall < IE base *\*dheigh-,* to knead clay ⟧ **1** the garden of Eden **2** the abode of the righteous after death; abode of God and the blessed; heaven **3** ⟦descriptive⟧ city in SE Nev., near Las Vegas: pop. 125,000

**Par·a·guay** (par'ə gwā', -gwī'; *Sp* pä rä gwī') **1** inland country in SC South America: 157,046 sq. mi. (406,750 sq. km); pop. 4,119,000; cap. Asunción **2** river in SC South America, flowing from S Brazil south through Paraguay into the Paraná: *c.* 1,500 mi. (2,414 km)

**Pa·ra·i·ba** (pä rä ē'bä) state of NE Brazil: 21,765 sq. mi. (56,372 sq. km); pop. 2,770,000; cap. João Pessoa

**Par·a·mar·i·bo** (par'ə mar'i bō') seaport & capital of

Suriname: pop. 103,000

**Pa·ra·ná** (pä′rä nä′) **1** state of S Brazil: 77,040 sq. mi. (199,550 sq. km): pop. 7,629,000; cap. Curitiba **2** river port in NE Argentina, on the Paraná River: pop. 174,000 **3** river in S South America, flowing from S Brazil along the SE boundary of Paraguay, through NE Argentina into the Río de la Plata: *c.* 2,000 mi. (3,218 km)

**Pa·ri·cu·tín** (pä *r*ē kōō tēn′) volcanic mountain in WC Mexico, formed by eruptions starting 1943 & now dormant: *c.* 7,500 ft. (2,286 m): also **Pa·ri·cu·tin** (pä *r*ē′kōō tēn′)

**Par·is** (par′is; *Fr* pà′rē′) capital of France, in the NC part, on the Seine: pop. 2,189,000 (urban area 8,707,000)

**Park Avenue** a wealthy residential street in New York City, regarded as a symbol of high society, fashion, etc.

**Par·kers·burg** (pär′kərz burg′) 〚after A. *Parker,* early owner of the site〛 city in NW W.Va., on the Ohio River: pop. 34,000

**Park Range** 〚descriptive〛 range of the Rockies, in NC Colo. & S Wyo.: highest peak, 14,284 ft. (4,354 m)

**Par·ma** (pär′mə; *for 1, also It* pär′mä) **1** commune in N Italy, in Emilia-Romagna: pop. 177,000 **2** 〚ult. after the commune in Italy〛 city in NE Ohio: suburb of Cleveland: pop. 88,000

**Par·na·i·ba** (pär′nə ē′bə) river in NE Brazil, flowing north into the Atlantic: *c.* 900 mi. (1,448 km)

**Par·nas·sus** (pär nas′əs) 〚L < Gr *Parnasos*〛 mountain in central Greece, near the Gulf of Corinth: 8,061 ft. (2,457 m): sacred to Apollo and the Muses in ancient times

**Par·os** (per′äs′; *Gr* pä′rôs′) island of the Cyclades, in the SC Aegean, west of Naxos: 81 sq. mi. (210 sq. km)

**Par·ra·mat·ta** (par′ə mat′ə) city in E New South Wales, SE Australia: suburb of Sydney: pop. 131,000

**Par·sip·pa·ny–Troy Hills** (pär sip′ə nē troi′) 〚< AmInd + *Troy* (< ?)〛 township in N N.J.: pop. 48,000

**Par·the·non** (pär′thə nän′, -nən) 〚L < Gr *Parthenōn* < *parthenos,* a virgin (i.e., Athena)〛 the Doric temple of Athena built (5th cent. B.C.) on the Acropolis in Athens: sculpture is attributed to Phidias

**Par·thi·a** (pär′thē ə) ancient country in SW Asia, southeast of the Caspian Sea

**Pas·a·de·na** (pas′ə dē′nə) ⟦< Ojibwa *pasadinaa*, valley⟧ **1** city in SW Calif., near Los Angeles: pop. 132,000 **2** ⟦after the city in Calif.⟧ city in SE Tex., near Houston: pop. 119,000

**Pa·sar·ga·dae** (pə sär′gə dē′) ancient capital of Persia, built by Cyrus the Great: near modern Shiraz, Iran

**Pas·cua** (päs′kwä), **Is·la de** (ēs′lä *the*) *Sp. name of* EASTER ISLAND

**Pas·sa·ic** (pə sā′ik) ⟦< Delaware *énta pahsá·e·k*, where there is a valley⟧ **1** river in NE N.J., flowing south into Newark Bay: *c.* 100 mi. (160 km) **2** city on this river: pop. 52,000

**Pas·sa·ma·quod·dy Bay** (pas′ə mə kwäd′ē) ⟦< Micmac *pestəmokati*, lit., place where pollock are plentiful⟧ arm of the Bay of Fundy between Maine & New Brunswick, Canada: *c.* 15 mi. (24 km) long

**Pat·a·go·ni·a** (pat′ə gō′nē ə, -gōn′yə) dry, grassy region in S South America, east of the Andes, including the S parts of Argentina and Chile: often restricted to the portion, *c.* 250,000 sq. mi. (647,450 sq. km), in Argentina

**Pat·er·son** (pat′ər sən) ⟦after Wm. *Paterson* (1745-1806), State gov.⟧ city in NE N.J., on the Passaic River: pop. 141,000

**Pa·ti·a·la** (put′ē ä′lə) former state of N India: since 1956, part of Punjab

**Pat·mos** (pat′məs, pät′-) island of the Dodecanese, in the SE Aegean: traditionally where St. John wrote the Book of Revelation (Rev. 1:9): 13 sq. mi. (34 sq. km)

**Pat·na** (put′nə, pat′-) city in NE India, on the Ganges: capital of Bihar state: pop. 916,000

**Pa·tras** (pä träs′) **1** seaport in W Greece, on the Gulf of Patras: pop. 142,000 **2 Gulf of** arm of the Ionian Sea, in the NW Peloponnesus: Gr. name **Pá·trai** (pä′trē)

**Pau** (pō) city in SW France: pop. 86,000

**Pa·vi·a** (pä vē′ä) commune in NW Italy, on the Ticino River: pop. 90,000

**Pa·vo** (pā′vō) ⟦L, peacock⟧ a S constellation near the celestial pole between Octans and Telescopium

**Paw·tuck·et** (pə tuk′it) ⟦< Narragansett, at the falls⟧ city in R.I.: pop. 73,000: see PROVIDENCE

**Pays de la Loire** (pā ē′ de lä lwàr′) metropolitan region of NW France: 12,404 sq. mi. (32,126 sq. km); pop. 2,930,000; chief city, Nantes

**PE** *abbrev. for* Prince Edward Island

**Pea·bod·y** (pē′bäd′ē, -bə dē) ⟦after George *Peabody* (1795-1869), U.S. merchant⟧ city in NE Mass., near Boston: pop. 47,000

**Peace** (pēs) ⟦after *Peace Point,* where Cree & Beaver Indians made a peace pact⟧ river in W Canada, flowing from N British Columbia east & northeast into the Slave river in NE Alberta: 945 mi. (1,521 km)

**Pearl** (purl) ⟦named for pearls found there⟧ **1** river in central Miss., flowing south into the Gulf of Mexico: 490 mi. (789 km) **2** *see* ZHU

**Pearl Harbor** ⟦after the *pearl* oysters once there⟧ inlet on the S coast of Oahu, Hawaii, near Honolulu: site of a U.S. naval base bombed by Japan, Dec. 7, 1941

**Pearly Gates** the gates of heaven: cf. Rev. 21:21

**Pe·cho·ra** (pe chôr′ə; *Russ* pye chô′rä) river in N European Russia, flowing from the Urals north into the Barents Sea: 1,110 mi. (1,786 km)

**Pe·cos** (pā′kōs′, -kəs) ⟦< ? AmInd⟧ river in SW U.S., flowing from N N.Mex. through Tex. into the Rio Grande: 735 mi. (1,183 km)

**Pécs** (pāch) city in SW Hungary: pop. 175,000

**Pee·bles** (pē′bəlz) former county of SC Scotland, now in the Borders region: also **Pee′bles·shire′** (-shir′, -shər)

**Pee Dee** (pē′ dē′) ⟦< AmInd tribal name⟧ river flowing through N.C. & S.C. into the Atlantic: 233 mi. (374 km): see YADKIN

**Peg·a·sus** (peg′ə səs) ⟦L < Gr *Pēgasos*⟧ a large N constellation between Andromeda and Pisces

**PEI** *abbrev. for* Prince Edward Island

**Pei·ping** (bā′piŋ′) *old form of* BEIJING

**Peip·si** (pāp′sē) *Estonian name of* Lake CHUDSKOYE

**Pei·pus** (pī′poos) *Ger. name of* Lake CHUDSKOYE

**Pei·rai·évs** (pē′re efs′) *modern Gr. name of* PIRAEUS

**Pe·king** (pē′kiŋ′; *Chin* bā′jiŋ′) *old form of* BEIJING

**Pe·lée** (pə lā′), **Mount** volcanic mountain on Martinique, in the West Indies: erupted 1902: 4,429 ft. (1,350 m)

**Pe·li·on** (pē′lē ən) mountain in E Thessaly, NE Greece: 5,252 ft. (1,601 m)

**Pel·o·pon·ne·sus, Pel·o·pon·ne·sos** (pel′ə pə nē′səs) peninsula forming the S part of the mainland of Greece

**Pem·ba** (pem′bə) island of Tanzania in the Indian

Ocean, off the E coast of Africa: 380 sq. mi. (984 sq. km)

**Pem·broke** (pem′brook′; *also,* -brōk′) PEMBROKESHIRE

**Pem·broke·shire** (-shir′, -shər) former county of SW Wales, now part of Dyfed county

**Pe·nang** (pi naŋ′) **1** island off the NW coast of the Malay Peninsula: 110 sq. mi. (285 sq. km) **2** state of Malaysia, in Peninsular Malaysia, including this island & a section of the mainland opposite it: 398 sq. mi. (1,030 sq. km); pop. 912,000 **3** its capital: seaport on the NE coast of Penang island: pop. 250,000

**Pen·chi** (bun′chē′) *old form of* BENXI

**Pen·del·i·kón** (pen del′ē kōn′) mountain in Attica, Greece, northeast of Athens: known for its fine marble: 3,638 ft. (1,109 m)

**Pend O·reille** (pän′ də rā′) ⟦Fr *pend(re)*, to hang + *oreille*, ear: name given by the Fr to local Salishan Indians who wore ear pendants⟧ **1** river in N Ida. & NE Wash., flowing from Pend Oreille Lake into the Columbia River: 100 mi. (160 km): see CLARK FORK **2** lake in N Ida.: 148 sq. mi. (383 sq. km)

**Pe·ne·us** (pi nē′əs) *ancient name of* PINIÓS

**Peninsular Malaysia** territory of Malaysia comprising the former federation of states on the S end of the Malay Peninsula: see MALAYA, Federation of

**Penn** *abbrev. for* Pennsylvania

**Penna** *abbrev. for* Pennsylvania

**Pen·nine Alps** (pen′in′, -in) division of the W Alps, along the Swiss-Italian border, northeast of the Graian Alps: highest peak, *c.* 15,200 ft. (4,632 m)

**Pennine Chain** range of hills in N England, extending from the Cheviot Hills southward to Derbyshire & Staffordshire: highest point, *c.* 3,000 ft. (914 m)

**Penn·syl·va·ni·a** (pen′səl vān′yə, -vā′nē ə) ⟦after its founder, William *Penn* (1644-1718), Eng Quaker leader, or his father + L *sylvania*, wooded (land)⟧ Middle Atlantic State of the NE U.S.: one of the 13 original States; 45,333 sq. mi. (117,412 sq. km); pop. 11,882,000; cap. Harrisburg: abbrev. *PA, Pa, Penn,* or *Penna* .

**Pe·nob·scot** (pi näb′skät′, -skət) ⟦< Abenaki *panáwahpskek*, lit., where the rocks widen⟧ river in central Me., flowing south into an arm (**Penobscot Bay**) of the Atlantic: *c.* 350 mi. (107 km)

**Pen·sa·co·la** (pen′sə kō′lə) 〚Fr < a tribal name; ? equiv. to Choctaw *pǫši*, hair + *okla*, people〛 seaport in NW Fla., on an inlet (**Pensacola Bay**) of the Gulf of Mexico: pop. 58,000

**Pen·ta·gon** (pen′tə gän′), **the** a five-sided building in Arlington, Va., in which the main offices of the U.S. Department of Defense are located

**Pen·tel·i·cus** (pen tel′i kəs) *Latin name of* PENDELIKÓN

**Pen·tel·i·kon** (pen tel′i kän′) *var. of* PENDELIKÓN

**Pent·land Firth** (pent′lənd) channel between the mainland of Scotland & the Orkney Islands: 6-8 mi. (9.5-13 km) wide

**Pen·za** (pen′zä) city in central European Russia: pop. 527,000

**Pen·zance** (pen zans′) city in SW Cornwall, England, on the English Channel: pop. 19,000

**People's Republic of China** *official name of* CHINA

**Pe·or·i·a** (pē ôr′ē ə) 〚Fr *Peouarea*, a tribal name < Illinois *Peouareoua*〛 city in central Ill., on the Illinois River: pop. 114,000

**Pe·rae·a** (pə rē′ə) in Roman times, a region in Palestine east of the Jordan, roughly the same as ancient Gilead

**Pe·rak** (pä′rak′; *Malay* pä′rä) state of Malaysia, in W Peninsular Malaysia, on the strait of Malacca: 8,110 sq. mi. (21,019 sq. km); pop. 1,765,000

**Perche** (persh) historical region in NW France, in Maine & Normandy

**Per·di·do** (per *th*ē′*th*ō), **Mon·te** (môn′te) mountain in the central Pyrenees, NE Spain: 11,007 ft. (3,354 m)

**Per·du** (per dü′), **Mont** (môn) *Fr. name of* Monte PERDIDO

**Per·ga·mum** (pur′gə məm) **1** ancient Greek kingdom occupying most of W Asia Minor (fl. 2d cent. B.C.): later a Roman province **2** ancient capital of this kingdom, the present site of Bergama, Turkey

**Per·lis** (per′lis) state of Malaysia, in NW Peninsular Malaysia, bordering on Thailand: 310 sq. mi. (803 sq. km); pop. 148,000

**Perm** (perm) city in E European Russia, on the Kama River: pop. 1,056,000

**Per·nam·bu·co** (pur′nəm bōō′kō; *Port* per′nänm bōō′koo) **1** state of NE Brazil: 37,940 sq. mi. (98,263 sq. km); pop. 6,140,000; cap. Recife **2** *old name of* RECIFE

**Per·pi·gnan** (per pē nyän′) city in S France, near the

Gulf of Lions & the Spanish border: pop. 114,000

**Per·sep·o·lis** (pər sep′ə lis) capital of the ancient Persian Empire, near the modern city of Shiraz, Iran

**Per·se·us** (pur′sē əs, -syŏŏs′) ⟦L < Gr⟧ a N constellation between Andromeda and Auriga, containing Algol

**Per·sia** (pur′zhə, -shə) ⟦L < Gr *Persais* < OPers *Pārsa*⟧ 1 *old name of* IRAN 2 PERSIAN EMPIRE

**Persian Empire** ancient empire in SW Asia, including at its peak (*c.* 500 B.C.) the area from the Indus River to the W borders of Asia Minor & Egypt: it was founded by Cyrus the Great (6th cent. B.C.) & conquered by Alexander the Great (*c.* 328 B.C.)

**Persian Gulf** arm of the Arabian Sea, between SW Iran & Arabia: *c.* 90,000 sq. mi. (233,000 sq. km)

**Persian Gulf States** group of Arab sheikdoms along the Persian Gulf: Kuwait, Bahrain, Qatar, & United Arab Emirates

**Perth** (purth) 1 former county of central Scotland: also **Perth′shire′** (-shir′, -shər) 2 city in central Scotland on the Tay: pop. 42,000 3 capital of Western Australia, in the SW part: pop. 80,000 (met. area 969,000)

**Pe·ru** (pə rŏŏ′) country in W South America, on the Pacific: 496,222 sq. mi. (1,285,210 sq. km); pop. 17,000,000; cap. Lima

**Peru current** HUMBOLDT CURRENT

**Pe·ru·gia** (pe rŏŏ′jä) commune in Umbria, central Italy: pop. 142,000

**Pes·ca·do·res** (pes′kə dôr′ēz, -is) group of islands in Taiwan Strait, a dependency of Taiwan: *c.* 50 sq. mi. (129 sq. km)

**Pes·ca·ra** (pās kä′rä) commune & seaport in central Italy, on the Adriatic: pop. 131,000

**Pe·sha·war** (pe shä′wər) city in N Pakistan, near the Khyber Pass: pop. 555,000

**Pe·tah Tiq·wa** (pe tä′ tēk′vä) city in WC Israel: pop. 124,000

**Pe·ter·bor·ough** (pēt′ər bur′ō, -ə) 1 county seat of the Soke of Peterborough 2 city in SE Ontario, Canada, near Toronto: pop. 62,000 3 **Soke of** former county in EC England, now part of Cambridgeshire

**Pe·ters·burg** (pēt′ərz burg′) ⟦after Capt. *Peter* Jones⟧ city in SE Va., near Richmond: pop. 38,000: see RICHMOND

**Pe·tra** (pē′trə) ancient Edomite city in SW Jordan

**Petrified Forest National Park** national park in EC Ariz., containing petrified trunks of several coniferous forests dating from the Triassic Period: 147 sq. mi. (380 sq. km)

**Pet·ro·grad** (pe′trə grad′; *Russ* pyet′rô grät′) *name* (1914-24) *of* St. Petersburg (Russia)

**Pet·ro·pav·lovsk** (pe′trə päv′ləfsk) city in N Kazakhstan: pop. 226,000

**Pet·ro·pav·lovsk-Kam·chat·skiy** (-käm chät′skē) seaport in E Asian Russia, on Kamchatka Peninsula: pop. 245,000

**Pe·tró·po·lis** (pə trô′pə lis) city in EC Rio de Janeiro state, Brazil, near Rio de Janeiro: pop. 242,000

**Pet·ro·za·vodsk** (pe′trə zä vôtsk′) city in NW Russia, on Lake Onega: pop. 255,000

**Pforz·heim** (pfôrts′him) city in SW Germany, northwest of Stuttgart, in the state of Baden-Württemberg: pop. 105,000

**Pha·ros** (fer′äs′) small peninsula at Alexandria, Egypt: in ancient times it was an island with a large lighthouse (also called **Pharos**) on it: this lighthouse was one of the Seven Wonders of the World

**Phar·sa·li·a** (fär sā′lē ə) district in ancient Thessaly, surrounding Pharsalus

**Phar·sa·lus** (fär sā′ləs) city in S Thessaly, Greece: site of an ancient city near which Caesar decisively defeated Pompey (48 B.C.): pop. 6,000: modern name **Phar·sa·la** (fär′sə lə)

**Phe·ni·cia** (fə nish′ə, -nē′shə) *alt. sp. of* Phoenicia

**Phil·a·del·phi·a** (fil′ə del′fē ə, -fyə) ⟦Gr *philadelphia*, brotherly love < *philos*, loving + *adelphos*, brother⟧ 1 city & port in SE Pa., on the Delaware River: pop. 1,586,000 (met. area 4,857,000; urban area with Wilmington, Del. & Trenton, N.J., 5,899,000) 2 ancient city in Lydia, W Asia Minor

**Phi·lip·pi** (fi lip′ī′) ancient city in Macedonia, where, in 42 B.C., Mark Antony & Octavius defeated Brutus & Cassius: site of Paul's first preaching of the Gospel in Europe (Acts 16:12)

**Phil·ip·pines** (fil′ə pēnz′) country occupying a group of *c.* 7,100 islands (**Philippine Islands**) in the SW Pacific off the SE coast of Asia: discovered by Magellan (1521); formerly a Spanish possession (1565-1898) & U.S. possession (1898-1946), it became independent

(1946): *c.* 116,000 sq. mi. (300,440 sq. km); pop. 58,000,000; cap. Manila

**Philippine Sea** part of the W Pacific, between the Philippines & the Mariana Islands, south of Japan

**Phil·ip·pop·o·lis** (fil'ə päp'ə lis) *Gr. name of* PLOVDIV

**Phi·lis·ti·a** (fə lis'tē ə) country of the Philistines (fl. 12th-4th cent. B.C.), in ancient SW Palestine

**Phleg·e·thon** (fleg'i thän, flej'-) [[ L < Gr *Phlegethōn,* orig. prp. of *phlegethein,* to blaze ]] *Gr. Myth.* a river of fire in Hades

**Phnom Penh** (pə näm'pen', näm'pen') capital of Cambodia, at the junction of the Mekong & Tonle Sap rivers: pop. *c.* 500,000

**Pho·bos** (fō'bəs) [[ Gr *phobos,* lit., fear, personified as an attendant of Ares ]] the larger of the two satellites of Mars: cf. DEIMOS

**Pho·cae·a** (fō sē'ə) ancient Ionian city in W Asia Minor, on the Aegean

**Pho·cis** (fō'sis) ancient region in central Greece, on the Gulf of Corinth: chief city, Delphi

**Phoe·be** (fē'bē) [[ L < Gr *Phoibē,* fem. of *Phoibos,* bright one < *phoibos,* bright ]] the small outermost satellite of Saturn, having an unusual retrograde orbit

**Phoe·ni·cia** (fə nish'ə, -nē'shə) ancient region of city-states at the E end of the Mediterranean, in the region of present-day Syria & Lebanon

**Phoe·nix** (fē'niks) [[ altered (infl. by L) < OE & OFr *fenix* < L *phoenix* < Gr *phoinix,* phoenix, dark-red, Phoenician, akin to *phoinos,* blood-red, deadly ]] a S constellation between Eridanus and Grus

**Phoe·nix** (fē'niks) [[ in allusion to the *Phoenix,* the mythical bird that rises anew from the ashes of its self-destruction by fire ]] capital of Ariz., in the SC part, near the Salt River: pop. 983,000 (met. area 2,122,000)

**Phos·phor** (fäs'fər, -fôr') [[ L *Phosphorus,* morning star < Gr *phōsphoros,* bringer of light < *phōs,* a light, contr. < *phaos* < IE base *\*bhā-,* to shine ]] [Old Poet.] the morning star, esp. Venus

**Phryg·i·a** (frij'ē ə) ancient country in WC Asia Minor

**Pia·cen·za** (pyä chen'tsä) commune in N Italy, in Emilia-Romagna, on the Po River: pop. 109,000

**Piau·i** (pyʊu ē') state of NE Brazil: 96,886 sq. mi. (250,934 sq. km); pop. 2,139,000; cap. Terezina

**Pic·ar·dy** (pik′ər dē) **1** historical region of N France **2** metropolitan region of modern N France: 7,494 sq. mi. (19,410 sq. km); pop. 1,740,000; chief city, Amiens: Fr. name **Pi·car·die** (pē kàr dē′)

**Pic·ca·dil·ly** (pik′ə dil′ē) street in London, a traditional center of fashionable shops, clubs, & hotels

**Pick·er·ing** (pik′ər iŋ) city in S Ontario, Canada: part of Toronto metropolitan area: pop. 49,000

**Pi·co Ri·ver·a** (pē′kō rə ver′ə) ⟦after Pío *Pico*, last governor of Mexican Calif. + *Rivera*, in allusion to its being between two rivers⟧ city in SW Calif.: suburb of Los Angeles: pop. 59,000

**Pic·tor** (pik′tər) ⟦L, painter⟧ a S constellation between Carina and Dorado

**Pied·mont** (pēd′mänt) **1** hilly, upland region of the E U.S., between the Atlantic coastal plain & the Appalachians, stretching from SE N.Y. to central Ala. **2** region of NW Italy, on the borders of Switzerland & France: 9,807 sq. mi. (25,399 sq. km); pop. 4,479,000; chief city, Turin: It. name **Pie·mon·te** (pye môn′te)

**Pi·er·i·a** (pī ir′ē ə) ancient region of Macedonia, N Greece

**Pierre** (pir) ⟦after *Pierre* Chouteau, early fur trader⟧ capital of S.Dak., on the Missouri River: pop. 13,000

**Pie·ter·mar·itz·burg** (pē′tər mer′its bʉrg′) capital of Natal province, South Africa: pop. 165,000

**Pikes Peak** (pīks) ⟦after Zebulon Montgomery *Pike* (1779-1813), U.S. explorer⟧ mountain of the Front Range, central Colo.: 14,110 ft. (4,341 m)

**Pil·co·ma·yo** (pēl′kô mä′yô) river flowing from S Bolivia southeast along the Argentine-Paraguay border into the Paraguay River, near Asunción: *c.* 1,000 mi. (1,069 km)

**Pillars of Her·cu·les** (hʉr′kyōō lēz′) two headlands on either side of the Strait of Gibraltar, one at Gibraltar (ancient CALPE) & the other at Ceuta (ancient ABYLA) or Jebel Musa, on the coast of Africa

**Pil·sen** (pil′zən) *Ger. name of* PLZEŇ

**Pi·nar del Rio** (pē när′ del rē′ō) city in W Cuba: pop. 149,000

**Pin·dus** (pin′dəs) mountain range in central & NW Greece: highest peak, 8,650 ft. (2,636 m)

**Pine Bluff** ⟦descriptive⟧ city in central Ark., on the Arkansas River: pop. 57,000

**Pines, Isle of** *old name of* Isle of YOUTH

**Pi·ni·ós** (pēn yôs′) river in Thessaly, E Greece, flowing eastward to the Gulf of Salonika: 125 mi. (201 km)

**Pinsk** (pēnsk; *E* pinsk) city in SW Belarus: pop. 77,000

**Pi·rae·us** (pī rē′əs) seaport in SE Greece, on the Saronic Gulf: part of Athens′ metropolitan area: pop. 184,000: ModGr name PEIRAIÉVS

**Pi·sa** (pē′zə; *It* pē′sä) commune in Tuscany, W Italy, on the Arno River: famous for its Leaning Tower: pop. 105,000

**Pis·cat·a·way** (pis kat′ə wā′) 〚< AmInd〛 township in NE N.J.: pop. 47,000

**Pis·ces** (pī′sēz′; *also* pis′ēz′) 〚ME < L, pl. of *piscis*, fish〛 1 a N constellation between Aries and Aquarius; Fishes 2 the twelfth sign of the zodiac, entered by the sun about February 21

**Pis·cis Aus·tri·nus** (pis′is ôs trī′nəs, pī′sis-) a S constellation between Grus and Aquarius containing Fomalhaut: also **Piscis Aus·tra·lis** (ôs trā′lis)

**Pis·gah** (piz′gə) 〚Heb *pisga*, lit., peak, summit〛 *Bible* mountain ridge east of the N end of the Dead Sea: Deut. 3:27: see NEBO, Mount

**Pi·sid·i·a** (pi sid′ē ə) ancient country in SC Asia Minor, south of Phrygia

**Pit·cairn** (pit′kern) British island in Polynesia, South Pacific: settled by mutineers of the British ship *Bounty* in 1790: *c.* 2 sq. mi. (5 sq. km); pop. 67

**Pitts·burgh** (pits′burg′) 〚after William *Pitt* (1708-78), Eng statesman〛 city in SW Pa., at the juncture of the Allegheny & Monongahela rivers: pop. 370,000 (met. area 2,057,000)

**Pitts·field** (pits′fēld′) 〚after William *Pitt* (1708-78), Eng statesman〛 city in W Mass.: pop. 49,000

**Plac·id** (plas′id), **Lake** 〚descriptive〛 lake in NE N.Y., in the Adirondacks: resort center: *c.* 4 mi. long (6.5 km)

**Plain·field** (plān′fēld′) 〚after a local resident′s estate〛 city in NE N.J.: suburb of Newark: pop. 47,000

**Plains of A·bra·ham** (ā′brə ham′) 〚after *Abraham* Martin (1589-1664), an early settler〛 a plain near Quebec: site of a battle (1759) of the French and Indian War, in which the British under Wolfe defeated the French under Montcalm

**Pla·no** (plā′nō) 〚Sp *plano*, plane, flat surface: misunderstood as "plain," for the plains in the area〛 city in NE

Tex.: suburb of Dallas: pop. 129,000

**Plan·ta·tion** (plan tā′shən) ⟦prob. named for the large town lots, called *plantations* by early settlers⟧ city in SE Fla., near Fort Lauderdale: pop. 67,000

**Plas·sey** (plä′sē) village in West Bengal, India, north of Calcutta: scene of a decisive victory (1757) by which the British established their rule in India

**Pla·ta** (plä′tä), **Río de la** (rē′ô̄ de lä) estuary of the Paraná & Uruguay rivers, between Argentina & Uruguay: *c.* 200 mi. (321 km): Eng. name **River Plate** (plāt)

**Pla·tae·a** (plə tē′ə) ancient city in Boeotia, EC Greece: site of a battle (479 B.C.) in which the Greeks defeated the Persians: also **Pla·tae′ae** (-ē)

**Platte** (plat) ⟦< Fr *Rivière Platte*, lit., flat river⟧ river formed in central Nebr. by the North Platte & the South Platte, & flowing eastward into the Missouri: 310 mi. (499 km)

**Platt National Park** (plat) ⟦after O. H. *Platt* (1827-1905), U.S. senator from Conn.⟧ national park in S Okla., containing sulfur springs: *c.* 1.5 sq. mi. (3.8 sq. km)

**Platts·burgh** (plats′bʉrg) ⟦after Z. *Platt*, early settler, *c.* 1784⟧ city in NE N.Y., on Lake Champlain: scene of a British invasion (1814) repulsed by the U.S.: pop. 21,000

**Ple·ia·des** (plē′ə dēz′, plī′-; -yə-) ⟦ME *Pliades* < L *Pleiades* < Gr⟧ a cluster of stars in the constellation Taurus, six of which are now readily visible and represent six daughters of Atlas: a seventh bright star (the **Lost Pleiad**) has apparently faded from sight since the original sightings

**Plev·en** (plev′ən) city in N Bulgaria: pop. 150,000: also **Plev′na** (-nä)

**Plo·eşti** (plô̄ yesht′) city in SC Romania, north of Bucharest: pop. 215,000: also sp. **Plo·ieşti′**

**Plov·div** (plôv′dif) city in SC Bulgaria: pop. 373,000

**Plow 1** the constellation Ursa Major **2** Big Dipper

**Plu·to** (plōōt′ō) ⟦L < Gr *Ploutōn* < *ploutos*, wealth⟧ the smallest planet of the solar system and the ninth in average distance from the sun: diameter, *c.* 2,290 km (*c.* 1,420 mi.); period of revolution, *c.* 248.4 earth years; period of rotation, 6.39 earth days; one satellite; symbol ♇

**Ply·mouth** (plim′əth) **1** seaport in Devonshire, SW

England, on the English Channel: pop. 244,000 **2**
⟦after the English seaport⟧ town on the SE coast of
Mass.: settled by the Pilgrims (1620) as the 1st permanent colonial settlement (**Plymouth Colony**) in New
England: pop. 46,000

**Plymouth Rock** boulder at Plymouth, Mass., where the
Pilgrims who sailed on the *Mayflower* are said to have
landed in 1620

**Plzeň** (pul'zen yə) city in W Czech Republic: pop.
174,000

**Pnom-Penh** (pə näm'pen', näm'pen') *alt. sp. of* PHNOM
PENH

**Po** (pō) river in N Italy, flowing from the Cottian Alps
east into the Adriatic: 405 mi. (651 km)

**Po·ca·tel·lo** (pō'kə tel'ō) ⟦after an Indian chief who
helped railroad builders⟧ city in SE Ida.: pop. 46,000

**Po·co·no Mountains** (pō'kə nō') ⟦< ? AmInd⟧ ridge of
the Appalachians, in E Pa.: resort area: *c.* 2,000 ft.
high (610 m)

**Pod·go·ri·ca** (pôd'gô rē tsä) city in S Yugoslavia: capital of Montenegro: pop. 54,000: see TITOGRAD

**Po·dolsk** (pə dôlsk') city in W European Russia, south
of Moscow: pop. 208,000

**Po Hai** (bō' hī') *old form of* BO HAI

**Pointers, the** the two stars in the Big Dipper that are
almost in a direct line with the North Star, Polaris

**Poi·tiers** (pwȧ tyā') city in WC France: pop. 83,000

**Poi·tou** (pwȧ tōō') historical region of WC France

**Poi·tou-Cha·rente** (-shə ränt') metropolitan region of
W France: 9,957 sq. mi. (25,790 sq. km); pop.
1,568,000; chief city, Poitiers

**Po·land** (pō'lənd) country in EC Europe, on the Baltic
Sea: a kingdom in the Middle Ages reaching from the
Baltic to the Black Sea: partitioned successively (1772,
1793, 1795) between Russia, Prussia, & Austria; was
restored as kingdom (1815-30); lost autonomy, becom-
ing Russian province (1830-1918); proclaimed independent republic (1918): 120,727 sq. mi. (312,683 sq.
km); pop. 37,546,000; cap. Warsaw: Pol. name, POLSKA

**Po·la·ris** (pō lar'is) ⟦ModL < ML (*stella*) *polaris,* polar
(star) < Gr *polos,* axis of the sphere, firmament <
*pelein,* to be in motion < IE base *\*kwel-,* to turn⟧ a
slightly variable, supergiant, binary star, the brightest
star in the constellation Ursa Minor, with a magnitude

of 2.1; North Star; Pole Star: used for navigation, since it is the closest star to the north celestial pole and remains nearly stationary throughout the night

**pole·star** (pōl'stär') Polaris, the North Star: also **Pole Star**

**Pol·ish Corridor** (pōl'ish) strip of Poland, between Germany & East Prussia, giving Poland an outlet to the Baltic Sea (1919-39): *c.* 120 mi. (193 km) long; 20-70 mi. (32-113 km) wide

**Pol·lux** (päl'əks) 〚L, earlier *Polluces* < Gr *Polydeukēs*〛 a red giant star, actually the brightest star in the constellation Gemini although it is considered the twin of Castor, with a magnitude of 1.2

**Pol·ska** (pôl'skä) *Pol. name of* POLAND

**Pol·ta·va** (pôl tä'vä) city in EC Ukraine: scene of a battle (1709) in which the Russians under Peter the Great defeated Sweden: pop. 302,000

**Pol·y·ne·sia** (päl'ə nē'zhə, -shə) 〚ModL < Gr *poly-*, many + *nēsos*, island + suffix *-ia*〛 a major division of the Pacific islands east of the international date line, including Hawaii, Samoa, Tonga, the Society Islands, Marquesas Islands, etc.: cf. MELANESIA, MICRONESIA

**Pom·er·a·ni·a** (päm'ər ā'nē ə) region in central Europe, on the Baltic, now divided between Poland & Germany

**Pom·mern** (pôm'ərn) *Ger. name of* POMERANIA

**Po·mo·na** (pō mō'nə) 〚after the Roman goddess〛 1 city in S Calif., east of Los Angeles: pop. 132,000 2 MAINLAND (Orkney Islands)

**Pom·pa·no Beach** (päm'pə nō') 〚after ModE *pompano* (a kind of fish) < Sp *pámpano*〛 city on the SE coast of Fla.: pop. 72,000: see FORT LAUDERDALE

**Pom·pei·i** (päm pā'ē, -pā') ancient city in S Italy, on the Bay of Naples: destroyed by the eruption of Mount Vesuvius (A.D. 79)

**Pon·ce** (pôn'se) 〚after Juan *Ponce* de León y Loaiza (great-grandson of Ponce de León), who founded it (*c.* 1692)〛 seaport in S Puerto Rico: pop. 188,000

**Pon·di·cher·ry** (pän'di cher'ē) 1 territory of SE India, chiefly on the Coromandel Coast: before 1954 a part of French India: 185 sq. mi. (480 sq. km); pop. 472,000 2 its capital: pop. 251,000 Fr. name **Pon·di·ché·ry** (pōn dē shä rē')

**Pon·ta Del·ga·da** (pôn'tə *th*el gä'*th*ə; *E* pän'tə del gä'

də) seaport on São Miguel Island, the Azores: pop. 75,000

**Pont·char·train** (pän'chər trān'), **Lake** ⟦after Louis, Comte de *Pontchartrain* (1643-1727), Fr statesman & explorer⟧ shallow, saltwater lake in SE La.: 625 sq. mi. (1,619 sq. km)

**Pon·ti·ac** (pän'tē ak') ⟦after *Pontiac* (*c.* 1720-69), Ottawa Indian chief⟧ city in SE Mich., north of Detroit: pop. 71,000

**Pon·ti·a·nak** (pän'tē ä'näk') seaport in W Kalimantan, Indonesia, on the South China Sea: pop. 305,000

**Pon·tine Marshes** (pän'tēn, -tīn') region in central Italy, southeast of Rome: formerly swampy, now reclaimed

**Pon·tus** (pän'təs) ⟦L < Gr *Pontos* < *pontos*, sea (esp. the Black Sea)⟧ ancient kingdom in NE Asia Minor, on the Pontus Euxinus

**Pontus Eux·i·nus** (yŏŏks ī'nəs) *Latin name of* BLACK SEA

**Poole** (pōōl) seaport in Dorsetshire, SE England: pop. 123,000

**Poo·na** (pōō'nə) city in W India, in Maharashtra state: pop. 1,685,000

**Po·o·pó** (pô'ô pô'), **Lake** shallow, saltwater lake in WC Bolivia: 970 sq. mi. (2,512 sq. km); altitude, *c.* 12,000 ft. (3,658 m)

**Pop·lar** (päp'lər) former metropolitan borough of E London, now part of Tower Hamlets

**Po·po·ca·té·petl** (pô pô'kä te'pet''l; *E* pō'pə kat'ə pet' 'l) volcano in SC Mexico, in W Puebla state: 17,887 ft. (5,452 m)

**Por·cu·pine** (pôr'kyōō pīn', -kyə-) ⟦descriptive⟧ river in N Yukon Territory, Canada, flowing into the Yukon River in NE Alas.: 590 mi. (950 km)

**Port Ar·thur** (är'thər) **1** *old name of* LÜSHUN **2** ⟦after *Arthur* Stilwell, local philanthropist⟧ seaport in SE Tex., on Sabine Lake: pop. 59,000 **3** *see* THUNDER BAY

**Port-au-Prince** (pôrt'ō prins'; *Fr* pôr tō prans') capital of Haiti: seaport on the Caribbean: pop. 450,000

**Port Elizabeth** seaport in S Cape Province, South Africa, on the Indian Ocean: pop. 492,000

**Port Jackson** inlet of the Pacific, in E New South Wales, Australia: harbor of Sydney: 21 sq. mi. (54.5 sq. km)

**Port·land** (pôrt'lənd) **1** ⟦after the city in Maine⟧ city and port in NW Oreg., at the confluence of the Colum-

bia & Willamette rivers: pop. 437,000 (met. area
1,240,000) **2** ⟦after the town and island in England⟧
seaport in SW Me., on the Atlantic: pop. 64,000

**Port Lou·is** (lōō′is, lōō′ē) capital of Mauritius: seaport on
the NW coast: pop. 134,000

**Port Mores·by** (môrz′bē) seaport in SE New Guinea:
capital of Papua New Guinea: pop. 123,000

**Pôr·to** (pôr′tŏŏ) *Port. name of* OPORTO

**Pôrto A·le·gre** (ä le′grə) seaport in S Brazil: capital of
Rio Grande do Sul state: pop. 1,115,000

**Port-of-Spain** (pôrt′əv spān′) seaport on NW Trinidad:
capital of Trinidad and Tobago: pop. 56,000: also **Port
of Spain**

**Por·to No·vo, Por·to-No·vo** (pôr′tō nō′vō) capital of
Benin: seaport on the Gulf of Guinea: pop. 208,000

**Por·to Ri·co** (pôr′tə rē′kō) *old name of* PUERTO RICO

**Pôr·to Ve·lho** (pôr′tŏŏ vä′lyō) city in W Brazil: capital
of Rondônia state: pop. 150,000

**Port Phil·lip Bay** (fil′ip) inlet of Bass Strait, in S
Victoria, Australia: harbor of Melbourne: 762 sq. mi.
(1,973 sq. km)

**Port Roy·al** (roi′əl) town in Jamaica, at the entrance to
Kingston harbor: the original town, former capital,
was destroyed by an earthquake in 1692

**Port Sa·id** (sä ēd′, sä′id) seaport in NE Egypt, at the
Mediterranean end of the Suez Canal: pop. 263,000

**Ports·mouth** (pôrts′məth) **1** seaport in Hampshire, S
England, on the English Channel: pop. 179,000 **2**
⟦after the city in England⟧ seaport in SE Va., on
Hampton Roads: pop. 104,000

**Por·tu·gal** (pôr′chə gəl; *Port* pôr′tŏŏ gäl′) country in SW
Europe, on the Atlantic: a kingdom until 1910, now a
republic: 34,340 sq. mi. (88,941 sq. km); pop. 9,336,000;
with the Azores & Madeira, 35,553 sq. mi. (92,082 sq.
km); pop. 9,834,000; cap. Lisbon

**Por·tu·guese East Africa** (pôr′chə gēz′, -gēs′) *old alt.
name of* MOZAMBIQUE

**Portuguese Guinea** *old name of* GUINEA-BISSAU

**Portuguese India** former Portuguese overseas territory
consisting of three enclaves in India: see GOA

**Portuguese Timor** former Portuguese territory in the
Malay Archipelago, consisting principally of the E half
of Timor: since 1976, a province of Indonesia

**Portuguese West Africa** *old alt. name of* ANGOLA

**Po·to·mac** (pə tō'mək) 〚< Algonquian; meaning unknown〛 river in the E U.S., forming a boundary of W.Va., Md., & Va., and flowing into Chesapeake Bay: 285 mi. (459 km)

**Po·to·sí** (pô'tô sē') **1** city in SW Bolivia, on the slopes of Cerro de Potosí: altitude *c.* 13,340 ft. (4,067 m); pop. 103,000 **2 Cer·ro de** (ser'rô de) mountain of the Andes, in SW Bolivia: 15,843 ft. (4,828 m)

**Pots·dam** (päts'dam'; *Ger* pôts däm') city in E Germany: capital of the state of Brandenburg: pop. 138,000

**Pow·ys** (pō'is, pou'is) county of central Wales: 1,960 sq. mi. (5,077 sq. km); pop. 110,000

**Po·yang Hu** (pô'yäŋ' hōō') lake in N Jianxi province, SE China: *c.* 1,000 sq. mi. (2,589 sq. km)

**Poz·nań** (pôz'nän'y') city in W Poland, on the Warta River: pop. 571,000

**PQ** *abbrev. for* Quebec

**PR, P.R.** *abbrev. for* Puerto Rico

**Prague** (präg) capital of Czech Republic, on the Vltava River: pop. 1,186,000: Czech name **Pra·ha** (prä'hä)

**Prai·a** (prä'yə) capital of Cape Verde: pop. 37,000

**Prairie Provinces** Canadian provinces of Manitoba, Saskatchewan, & Alberta

**Pra·to** (prä'tô) commune in Tuscany, central Italy, near Florence: pop. 160,000

**Pres·ton** (pres'tən) city in Lancashire, NW England: pop. 125,000

**Pre·to·ri·a** (prē tôr'ē ə, pri-) capital of the Transvaal, in the S part: seat of the government of South Africa: pop. 574,000

**Prib·i·lof Islands** (prib'ə läf') 〚after Gavril *Pribylov*, Russ sea captain, *c.* 1786〛 group of four Alaskan islands in the Bering Sea, north of the Aleutian Islands: noted as a breeding place of seals

**prime meridian** the meridian from which longitude is measured both east and west; 0° longitude: it passes through Greenwich, England

**Prince Albert** city in central Saskatchewan, Canada: pop. 41,000

**Prince Albert National Park** Canadian national park in central Saskatchewan: 1,496 sq. mi. (3,875 sq. km)

**Prince Edward Island** 〚after Prince *Edward*, Duke of Kent (1767-1820), father of Queen Victoria〛 island province of SE Canada, in the S Gulf of St. Lawrence: 2,184 sq. mi. (5,656 sq. km); pop. 127,000; cap. Charlottetown: abbrev. *PE* or *PEI*

**Prince George** 〚after King *George* III of Great Britain〛 city in EC British Columbia, Canada: pop. 68,000

**Prince of Wales** 1 〚after George, *Prince of Wales*, future George IV of Great Britain〛 island of SE Alas., largest in the Alexander Archipelago: 2,230 sq. mi. (5,776 sq. km) 2 〚after Albert Edward, *Prince of Wales*, future Edward VII〛 island in central Northwest Territories, Canada, divided between Baffin & Kitikmeot regions: 12,830 sq. mi. (33,230 sq. km)

**Prince of Wales, Cape** 〚after George, *Prince of Wales*, future George IV of Great Britain〛 promontory of the Seward Peninsula, NW Alas., on the Bering Strait: westernmost point of North America

**Prince·ton** (prins′tən) 〚after the *Prince* of Orange, later William III of England〛 borough in central N.J., near Trenton: scene of a battle (1777) of the Revolutionary War in which troops led by Washington defeated the British: pop. 12,000

**Prin·ci·pe** (prin′se pē′) island in the Gulf of Guinea, off the W coast of Africa: 42 sq. mi. (110 sq. km); pop. 5,200: see SÃO TOMÉ AND PRÍNCIPE

**Pri·pet** (prē′pet) river in Ukraine & Belarus, flowing through the **Pripet Marshes** into the Dnepr: *c.* 500 mi. (805 km): Russ. name **Pri·pyat** (prē′pyät′y′)

**Pro·cy·on** (prō′sē än′) 〚L < Gr *Prokyōn* < *pro-*, before + *kyōn*, dog: it rises before the Dog Star〛 a binary star, the brightest star in the constellation Canis Minor, with a magnitude of 0.35

**Pro·ko·pyevsk** (prä kô′pyifsk) city in the Kuznetsk Basin, in SC Russia: pop. 274,000

**Promised Land** *Bible* Canaan, promised by God to Abraham and his descendants: Gen. 17:8

**Pro·pon·tis** (prə pän′tis) *ancient name of* Sea of MARMARA

**Pro·vence** (prô väns′) 〚Fr < L *provincia*, province〛 historical region of SE France, on the Mediterranean

**Pro·vence–Côte d'A·zur** (-kōt′ dà zür′) metropolitan region of SE France: 12,137 sq. mi. (31,435 sq. km); pop. 3,965,000; chief city, Marseille

**Prov·i·dence** (präv′ə dəns) 〚named by Eng colonist Roger Williams (*c.* 1603-83)〛 capital of R.I., on Narragansett Bay: pop. 161,000 (met. area with Pawtucket & Fall River, 1,142,000)

**Prov·ince·town** (präv′ins toun′) 〚after *Province Lands*, title of public land at the end of Cape Cod〛 resort town in Mass., at the N tip of Cape Cod: pop. 3,600

**Pro·vo** (prō′vō) 〚after Étienne *Provot*, early fur trader〛 city in NC Utah: pop. 87,000

**Pru·dhoe Bay** (prōōd′ō) inlet of the Beaufort Sea, in N Alas.: site of large oil fields

**Prus·sia** (prush′ə) 1 historical region of N Germany, on the Baltic 2 former kingdom in N Europe (1701-1871) & the dominant state of the German Empire (1871-1919): formally dissolved in 1947

**Prut** (prōōt) river in Europe, flowing from SW Ukraine southeastward along the Romania-Moldova border into the Danube: *c.* 600 mi. (966 km)

**Pskov** (pskôf) 1 lake in W European Russia, connected with Chudskoye Lake by a strait: see CHUDSKOYE, Lake 2 city near the SE end of this lake: pop. 194,000

**Pue·bla** (pwe′blä) 1 state of SE Mexico: 13,125 sq. mi. (33,993 sq. km); pop. 3,348,000 2 its capital: pop. 836,000

**Pueb·lo** (pweb′lō) 〚Sp, village, people < L *populus*, people〛 city in SC Colo., on the Arkansas River: pop. 99,000

**Puer·to Ri·co** (pwer′tə rē′kō, pôr′-) 〚Sp, lit., rich port〛 island in the West Indies which, with small nearby islands, constitutes a commonwealth associated with the U.S.: 3,425 sq. mi. (8,897 sq. km); pop. 3,522,000; cap. San Juan: abbrev. *PR* or *P.R.*

**Pu·get Sound** (pyōō′jit) 〚after Lt. Peter *Puget* of the Vancouver expedition (1792)〛 inlet of the Pacific in NW Wash.: *c.* 100 mi. (160 km) long

**Pu·glia** (pōō′lyä) *It. name of* APULIA

**Pun·jab** (pun jäb′; pun′jäb, -jab) 〚Hindi *Panjāb*, lit., (land of) five rivers < Sans *panj*, five + *ab*, river, water〛 1 region in NW India & NE Pakistan, between the upper Indus & Jumna rivers: formerly, a state of India; divided between India & Pakistan (1947): *c.* 99,000 sq. mi. (256,410 sq. km); chief city, Lahore (now in Pakistan) 2 a state of India, in this region: 19,445 sq. mi. (50,362 sq. km); pop. 16,670,000; cap. Chandigarh

**Pun·ta A·re·nas** (pōōn′tä ä re′näs) seaport in S Chile,

on the Strait of Magellan: southernmost city in the world: pop. 99,000

**Pup·pis** (pup'is) 〖L, poop of a ship〗 a S constellation between Vela and Columba: see ARGO

**Pu·rús** (pōō rōōs') river in South America, flowing from E Peru through NW Brazil into the Amazon: c. 2,000 mi. (3,218 km)

**Pu·san** (pōō'sän') seaport in SE South Korea, on Korea Strait: pop. 3,495,000

**Pu·tu·ma·yo** (pōō'tōō mä'yô) river in NW South America, flowing from SW Colombia along the Colombia-Peru border into the Amazon in NW Brazil: c. 1,000 mi. (1,609 km)

**PW** *abbrev. for* Belau

**Pyd·na** (pid'nə) ancient city in Macedonia, near the Gulf of Salonika: scene of a battle (168 B.C.) of the final Roman defeat of the Macedonians

**Pyong·yang** (pyuŋ'yäŋ') capital of North Korea, in the W part: pop. 1,280,000

**Pyramids, the** the three large pyramids at Giza, Egypt: the largest is the Pyramid of Khufu: also **the Great Pyramids**

**Pyr·e·nees** (pir'ə nēz') mountain range along the border between France & Spain: c. 300 mi. (483 km) long; highest peak, Pico de Aneto

**Pyx·is** (piks'is) 〖ModL, short for *Pyxis nautica*, mariner's compass〗 a S constellation between Puppis and Antlia: see ARGO

# Q

**Q** *abbrev. for* Quebec

**Qa·tar** (ke tär', kä'tär') country occupying a peninsula of E Arabia, on the Persian Gulf: entered into treaty relations with Great Britain (1878); became independent emirate (1971): c. 6,000 sq. mi. (15,540 sq. km); pop. 305,000; cap. Doha

**Qing·dao** (chiŋ'dou') seaport in Shandong province, NE China, on the Yellow Sea: pop. 1,144,000

**Qing·hai** (chiŋ'hī') **1** province of NW China, northeast of Tibet: 278,378 sq. mi. (721,000 sq. km); pop. 3,896,000; cap. Xining **2** salt lake in the NE part of this province: c. 2,200 sq. mi. (5,698 sq. km)

**Qin·huang·dao** (chin'hwäŋ'dou') seaport in NE Hebei

province, NE China: pop. 400,000

**Qin·ling Shan** (chin′liŋ′ shän′) mountain range in NC China, extending across Gansu, Shaanxi, & Henan provinces: highest peak, *c.* 13,500 ft. (4,100 m)

**Qi·qi·har** (chē′chē′här′) city in Heilongjiang province, NE China: pop. 1,222,000

**Qishm** (kish′əm) island of SE Iran, in the Strait of Hormuz: 516 sq. mi. (1,337 sq. km)

**Quai d'Or·say** (kā dôr sā′; *Fr* kā dôr se′) a street along the bank of the Seine in Paris, on which are located the offices of the French Ministry of Foreign Affairs

**Que** *abbrev. for* Quebec

**Que·bec** (kwi bek′, kwə-) 〖Fr, earlier *Quebecq*, *Kébec*, prob. < Algonquian name of region where the city was built〗 **1** province of E Canada, between Hudson Bay & the Gulf of St. Lawrence: 594,860 sq. mi. (1,540,668 sq. km); pop. 6,530,000: abbrev. *PQ* or *Que* **2** capital of this province: seaport on the St. Lawrence River: pop. 164,000 (met. area 603,000): Fr. name **Qué·bec** (kā bek′)

**Queen Charlotte Islands** 〖after an explorer's ship, the *Queen Charlotte*〗 group of islands in British Columbia, Canada, off the W coast: 3,970 sq. mi. (10,283 sq. km); pop. 4,500

**Queen Maud Land** (môd) region in Antarctica, south of Africa: it is claimed by Norway

**Queen Maud Range** mountain range in Antarctica, south of the Ross Ice Shelf: peaks over 13,000 ft. (3,950 m)

**Queens** (kwēnz) 〖after *Queen* Catherine, wife of Charles II of England〗 borough of New York City, on W Long Island, east of Brooklyn: pop. 1,952,000

**Queens·land** (kwēnz′land′, -lənd) state of NE Australia: 667,000 sq. mi. (1,727,200 sq. km); 2,488,000; cap. Brisbane

**Que·moy** (kē moi′) island of a small group in Taiwan Strait, held by the government on Taiwan: pop. 49,000

**Que·ré·ta·ro** (kə rāt′ə rō′; *Sp* ke re′tä rô′) **1** state of central Mexico: 4,420 sq. mi. (11,449 sq. km); pop. 740,000 **2** its capital: pop. 294,000

**Quet·ta** (kwet′ə) city in N Baluchistan, Pakistan: pop. 285,000

**Que·zon City** (kā′sän′) former capital of the Philippines: absorbed into Manila in 1975: pop. 1,165,000

**Quil·mes** (kēl'mes') city in E Argentina, on the Río de la
   Plata: suburb of Buenos Aires: pop. 150,000
**Quin·cy** (kwin'zē; *for 2*, -sē) **1** ⟦after Col. John *Quincy*
   (1689-1767), a local official⟧ city in E Mass.: suburb of
   Boston: pop. 85,000 **2** ⟦after U.S. Pres. John *Quincy*
   Adams (1767-1848)⟧ city in W Ill., on the Mississippi:
   pop. 40,000
**Quin·ta·na Ro·o** (kin tän'ə rō'ō'; *Sp* kēn tä'nä *rô'ô*) territory of SE Mexico, on E Yucatán Peninsula: 19,387
   sq. mi. (50,212 sq. km); pop. 226,000
**Quir·i·nal** (kwir'ə nəl, kwi ri'nəl) ⟦L *Quirinalis*, after
   *Quirinus*, a god of war in early Roman mythology,
   later identified with Romulus, mythical founder and
   first king of Rome⟧ one of the SEVEN HILLS OF ROME:
   site of a palace used (1870-1946) as a royal residence,
   later as the presidential residence
**Qui·to** (kē'tō) capital of Ecuador, in the NC part: pop.
   1,110,000
**Qum** (koom) city in NC Iran: pop. 247,000
**Qum·ran** (koom rän') region in NW Jordan, near the
   Dead Sea: site of the caves in which the Dead Sea
   Scrolls were found

# R

**Ra·bat** (rə bät'; *Fr* rȧ bȧ') capital of Morocco, in the
   NW part, on the Atlantic: pop. 517,000
**Rab·bah** (rab'ə) *Bible* chief city of the Ammonites: site
   now occupied by Amman, Jordan: also **Rab'bath** (-əth)
**Ra·cine** (rə sēn') ⟦Fr, root, after Fr name of the nearby
   Root River < ?⟧ city in SE Wis., on Lake Michigan:
   pop. 84,000: see MILWAUKEE
**Rad·nor·shire** (rad'nər shir', -shər) former county of EC
   Wales, now part of Powys county: also called **Rad'nor**
**Ra·dom** (rä'dôm') city in EC Poland: pop. 199,000
**Rae·ti·a** (rē'shə, -shē ə) *alt. sp. of* RHAETIA
**Ra·gu·sa** (rə gōō'zə) **1** commune in SE Sicily: pop.
   60,000 **2** *It. name of* DUBROVNIK
**Rain·bow Bridge** (rān'bō') natural sandstone bridge in
   S Utah: a national monument: 278 ft. (84 m) long; 309
   ft. (94 m) high
**Rai·nier** (rā nir', rə-), **Mount** ⟦after an 18th-c. Brit
   Adm. *Rainier*⟧ mountain of the Cascade Range, in
   WC Wash.: 14,410 ft. (4,392 m): the central feature of

a national park (**Mount Rainier National Park**): 378 sq. mi. (979 sq. km)

**Rai·pur** (rī′poor′) city in SE Madhya Pradesh: pop. 339,000

**Ra·jah·mun·dry** (rä′jä mun′drē) city in NE Andhra Pradesh, E India: pop. 268,000

**Ra·jas·than** (rä′jäs tän′) state of NW India, on the border of Pakistan: 132,152 sq. mi. (342,250 sq. km); pop. 25,765,000; cap. Jaipur

**Raj·kot** (räj′kōt′) city in Gujarat state, NW India: pop. 444,000

**Raj·pu·ta·na** (räj′pōō tä′nä) region in NW India, mostly in the state of Rajasthan

**Ra·leigh** (rô′lē, rä′lē) ⟦after Eng statesman & explorer Sir Walter *Raleigh* (c. 1552-1618)⟧ capital of N.C., in the central part: pop. 208,000 (met. area with Durham, 735,000)

**Ram** Aries, the constellation and first sign of the zodiac

**Ra·mat Gan** (rä′mät′ gän′) city in W Israel, northeast of Tel Aviv: pop. 117,000

**Rams·gate** (ramz′gāt′) seaport & resort in Kent, SE England, on the English Channel: pop. 38,000

**Ran·chi** (rän′chē) city in S Bihar, NE India: pop. 500,000

**Ran·cho Cu·ca·mon·ga** (ran′chō kōō′kə mäŋ′gə) ⟦< AmSp *rancho*, small farm + Shoshonean *kukamonga*, sandy place⟧ city in S Calif., near San Bernardino: pop. 101,000

**Rand** (rand), the WITWATERSRAND

**Ran·ders** (rän′ərs) seaport in NE Jutland, Denmark: pop. 61,000

**Range·ley Lakes** (rānj′lē) ⟦after an early owner of the region⟧ chain of lakes in W Me. & NE N.H.

**Ran·goon** (ran gōōn′, raŋ-) *old name of* YANGON

**Ra·pa Nu·i** (rä′pä nōō′ē) *local name of* EASTER ISLAND

**Rap·i·dan** (rap′i dan′) ⟦< ?⟧ river in NC Va., flowing eastward from the Blue Ridge Mountains into the Rappahannock: *c.* 90 mi. (145 km)

**Rapid City** ⟦from its location on the *Rapid* River⟧ city in W S.Dak., in the Black Hills: pop. 55,000

**Rap·pa·han·nock** (rap′ə han′ək) ⟦< Virginia Algonquian, prob. lit., the river that flows back again⟧ river in NE Va., flowing southeastward into Chesapeake Bay: *c.* 185 mi. (297 km)

**Ra·ro·ton·ga** (rä'rō tôŋ'gə) largest of the Cook Islands, in the S Pacific: 26 sq. mi. (67 sq. km); pop. 10,000

**Rasht** (räsht, rasht) city in NW Iran: pop. 189,000

**Ra·ven·na** (rə ven'ə) commune in NC Italy, in Emilia-Romagna: pop. 138,000

**Ra·wal·pin·di** (rä'wəl pin'dē) city in NE Pakistan: pop. 928,000

**Read·ing** (red'iŋ) **1** city in SC England: county seat of Berkshire: pop. 125,000 **2** ⟦after the city in England⟧ city in SE Pa., on the Schuylkill River: pop. 78,000

**Re·ci·fe** (rə sē'fə) seaport in NE Brazil, on the Atlantic: capital of Pernambuco state: pop. 1,183,000

**Reck·ling·hau·sen** (rek'liŋ hou'zən) city in W Germany, in the state of North Rhine-Westphalia: pop. 118,000

**Red 1** river flowing southeast along the Tex.-Okla. border, through SW Ark. & central La. into the Mississippi: 1,018 mi. (1,638 km) **2** river flowing north along the N.Dak.-Minn. border into Lake Winnipeg in Manitoba, Canada: c. 310 mi. (499 km): in full **Red River of the North 3** river in SE Asia, flowing from Yunnan province, China, southeast across Vietnam, into the Gulf of Tonkin: c. 500 mi. (804 km): Annamese name HONG, Chin. name YUAN

**Red·bridge** (red'brij') borough of NE Greater London: pop. 226,000

**Red Deer** city in SC Alberta, Canada: pop. 54,000

**Red·ding** (red'iŋ) city in N Calif.: pop. 66,000

**Red·lands** (red'ləndz) ⟦from the reddish soil in the area⟧ city in S Calif., near San Bernardino: pop. 60,000

**Re·don·do Beach** (rə dän'dō) ⟦< Sp *redondo*, circular, round + *beach*⟧ city in SW Calif., on the Pacific: suburb of Los Angeles: pop. 60,000

**Red Sea** sea between NE Africa & W Arabia, connected with the Mediterranean Sea by the Suez Canal & with the Indian Ocean by the Gulf of Aden: c. 1,400 mi. (2,253 km) long: c. 178,000 sq. mi. (461,000 sq. km)

**Red·wood City** (red'wood') city in W Calif., on San Francisco Bay: suburb of San Francisco: pop. 66,000

**Redwood National Park** national park in NW Calif., containing groves of redwood trees: 170 sq. mi. (440 sq. km)

**Re·gens·burg** (rä'gəns boork', -gənz burg') city in SE Germany, on the Danube, in the state of Bavaria: pop.

128,000

**Reg·gio di Ca·la·bri·a** (re'jō dē kə lä'brē ə) seaport in Calabria, S Italy, on the Strait of Messina: pop. 173,000: also **Reggio Calabria**

**Reg·gio nel·l'E·mi·lia** (re'jō nel'ä mēl'yə) commune in NC Italy, in Emilia-Romagna: pop. 130,000: also **Reggio Emilia**

**Re·gi·na** (ri jī'nə) ⟦after Queen Victoria of Great Britain, called Victoria *Regina*⟧ capital of Saskatchewan, Canada, in the S part: pop. 187,000

**Reg·u·lus** (reg'yə ləs) ⟦ModL < L, dim. of *rex*, a king⟧ a variable, multiple star, the brightest star in the constellation Leo, with a magnitude of 1.3

**Reims** (rēmz; *Fr* rans) city in NE France: scene of Germany's surrender to the Allies (1945): pop. 182,000

**Rein·deer Lake** (rān'dir') ⟦? transl. of AmInd name⟧ lake in NE Saskatchewan & NW Manitoba, Canada: 2,467 sq. mi. (6,389 km)

**Rem·scheid** (rem'shīt') city in W Germany, in the Ruhr Basin, in the state of North Rhine-Westphalia: pop. 123,000

**Ren·frew** (ren'froo') former county of SW Scotland, now in the region of Strathclyde: also **Ren'frew·shire'** (-shir', -shər)

**Rennes** (ren) city in NW France: pop. 200,000

**Re·no** (rē'nō) ⟦after U.S. Gen. J. L. *Reno* (1823-62)⟧ city in W Nev.: pop. 134,000

**Re·pen·ti·gny** (*Fr* rə pän tē nyē') town in S Quebec, Canada: suburb of Montreal: pop. 41,000

**Re·pub·li·can** (ri pub'li kən) ⟦after the "*Republican* Pawnees," so called from their form of government⟧ river flowing from E Colo. east & southeast through Nebr. & Kans., joining the Smoky Hill River to form the Kansas River: 445 mi. (716 km)

**Resht** (resht) *var. of* RASHT

**Re·sis·ten·cia** (rä'sēs ten'sē ä') city in N Argentina, on the Paraná River: pop. 218,000

**Re·tic·u·lum** (ri tik'yə ləm) a S constellation between Dorado and Horologium

**Ré·u·nion** (rā ü nyōn'; *E* rē yoon'yən) island in the Indian Ocean, east of Madagascar: overseas department of France: 969 sq. mi. (2,509 sq. km); pop. 515,000; cap. St-Denis

**Re·vere** (rə vir') ⟦after Am patriot Paul *Revere* (1735-

1818) ]] city in E Mass.: suburb of Boston: pop. 43,000

**Rey·kja·vik** (rā′kyə vēk′, -vik′) capital of Iceland: seaport on the SW coast: pop. 89,000

**Rey·no·sa** (rā nō′sä′) city in N Mexico, on the Rio Grande, opposite McAllen, Tex.: pop. 211,000

**Rhae·ti·a** (rē′shə, -shē ə) ancient Roman province in the region of modern Bavaria, E Switzerland, & the N Tirol

**Rhaetian Alps** division of the central Alps, mostly in E Switzerland: highest peak, *c.* 13,300 ft. (4,053 m)

**Rhe·a** (rē′ə) [[ L < Gr ]] a large satellite of Saturn

**Rheims** (rēmz; Fr rans) *old sp. of* REIMS

**Rhein** (rīn) *Ger. name of* RHINE

**Rhein·land–Pfalz** (rīn′länt′pfälts′) *Ger. name of* RHINE-LAND–PALATINATE

**Rhin** (ran) *Fr. name of* RHINE

**Rhine** (rīn) [[ Ger *Rhein* < Celt *Rēnos* < IE *erei-* < base *er-*, set in motion ]] river in W Europe, flowing from E Switzerland north through Germany, then west through the Netherlands into the North Sea: *c.* 820 mi. (1,320 km): Ger. name RHEIN, Fr. name RHIN, Du. name RIJN

**Rhine·land** (rīn′land′, -lənd) 1 that part of Germany west of the Rhine 2 RHINE PROVINCE

**Rhine·land–Pa·lat·i·nate** (-pə lat′n āt′, -it) state of SW Germany: 7,663 sq. mi. (19,848 sq. km); pop. 3,628,000; cap. Mainz

**Rhine Province** former province of Prussia, now divided between North Rhine-Westphalia & Rhineland-Palatinate

**Rhode Island** (rōd) [[ < ? Du *Roodt Eylandt,* red island or < ? fol. ]] New England State of the U.S.: one of the 13 original States; 1,214 sq. mi. (3,144 sq. km); pop. 1,003,000; cap. Providence: abbrev. *RI* or *R.I.*

**Rhodes** (rōdz) [[ Gr *Rhodos* ]] 1 largest island of the Dodecanese, in the Aegean: 545 sq. mi. (1,411 sq. km) 2 seaport on this island: capital of the Dodecanese: pop. 41,000

**Rho·de·si·a** (rō dē′zhə, -zhē ə; *also, chiefly Brit,* -dē′shə, -dē′zē ə) former region in S Africa, including NORTHERN RHODESIA (now ZAMBIA) & SOUTHERN RHODESIA (now ZIMBABWE)

**Rhod·o·pe** (räd′ə pē) mountain system in S Bulgaria extending into NE Greece: highest peak, 9,595 ft.

(2,924 m)

**Rhond·da** (rän′thə, hrän′-; rän′də) city in Mid Glamorgan, SE Wales: pop. 82,000

**Rhone, Rhône** (rōn) 〚Fr *Rhône*, prob. < Celt *Rodanos*, stream name, lit., the flowing one < IE *\*ered-*, to flow < base *\*er-* > run 〛 river flowing from SW Switzerland south through France into the Gulf of Lions: 505 mi. (812 km)

**RI, R.I.** *abbrev. for* Rhode Island

**Ri·al·to** (rē al′tō) a theater district, as on Broadway, in New York City

**Ri·bei·rão Prê·to** (rē′bā roun′ prā′tōō) city in SE Brazil, in São Paulo state: pop. 300,000

**Rich·ard·son** (rich′ərd sən) 〚after A. S. *Richardson*, 19th-c. railroad official〛 city in NE Tex.: suburb of Dallas: pop. 75,000

**Rich·mond** (rich′mənd) 〚Richmond, N.Y., named after the Duke of *Richmond*, son of Charles II of England; other U.S. cities after the London borough〛 **1** *old name of* STATEN ISLAND (the borough) **2** capital of Va.: seaport on the James River: pop. 203,000 (met. area with Petersburg, 866,000) **3** seaport in W Calif., on San Francisco Bay: pop. 87,000 **4** city in E Ind.: pop. 39,000 **5** borough of SW Greater London, England: pop. 160,000: also **Richmond–on–Thames**

**Richmond Hill** town in SE Ontario, Canada: suburb of Toronto: pop. 47,000

**Rif** (rif) mountain range along the NE coast of Morocco, extending from the Strait of Gibraltar to the Algerian border: highest peak, *c.* 8,000 ft. (2,440 m): also **Er Rif** (er rif′)

**Riff** (rif) *alt. sp. of* RIF

**Rift Valley** GREAT RIFT VALLEY

**Ri·ga** (rē′gə) **1** capital of Latvia: seaport on the Gulf of Riga: pop. 883,000 **2 Gulf of** inlet of the Baltic Sea, between NW Latvia & SW Estonia: *c.* 100 mi. (160 km) long; *c.* 60 mi. (96 km) wide

**Ri·gel** (rī′jəl, -gəl) 〚Ar *rijl*, foot: so called because in the left foot of Orion 〛 a supergiant, multiple star, usually the brightest star in the constellation Orion, with a magnitude of 0.14: see BETELGEUSE

**Ri·je·ka** (rē yek′ə) seaport in W Croatia, on the Adriatic: pop. 193,000

**Rijn** (rān) *Du. name of* RHINE

**Rijs·wijk** (ris'vĭk'; *Du* räs'vāk') town in the W Netherlands, near The Hague: pop. 49,000

**Ri·mi·ni** (rim'ə nē; *It* rē'mē nē') seaport in NC Italy, on the Adriatic: pop. 128,000

**Ri·o Bran·co** (rē'ōō brun'kōō) city in W Brazil: capital of Acre state: pop. 118,000

**Rí·o Bra·vo** (rē'ō brä'vō) *Mex. name of* RIO GRANDE: also **Río Bravo del Nor·te** (del nôr'te)

**Ri·o de Ja·nei·ro** (rē'ō dä' zhə ner'ō; *Port* rē'ōō də zhə nä'rōō) **1** state of SE Brazil: 17,091 sq. mi. (44,268 sq. km); pop. 11,291,000; cap. Rio de Janeiro **2** its capital: seaport in SE Brazil, on the Atlantic: pop. 5,090,000

**Río de la Plata** *see* PLATA, Río de la

**Ri·o de O·ro** (rē'ō dä ôr'ō) *old name of* SPANISH SAHARA

**Ri·o Gran·de** (rē'ō grand'; -gran'dē, -grän'dä; *for 2 & 3, Port* rē'ōō grun'də) 〚Sp, lit., great river〛 **1** river flowing from S Colo. south through N.Mex., then southeast as the boundary between Texas and Mexico into the Gulf of Mexico: 1,885 mi. (3,033 km) **2** river in SE Brazil in the states of Minas Gerais & São Paulo; headstream of the Paraná: *c.* 650 mi. (1,046 km) **3** seaport in SE Brazil, on the Atlantic: pop. 125,000

**Ri·o Gran·de do Nor·te** (rē'ōō grun'də dōō nôr'tə) state of NE Brazil: 20,465 sq. mi. (53,015 sq. km); pop. 1,898,000; cap. Natal

**Rio Grande do Sul** (-sōōl') southernmost state of Brazil: 108,935 sq. mi. (282,141 sq. km); pop. 7,773,000; cap. Pôrto Alegre

**Rí·o Mu·ni** (rē'ō mōō'nē) *old name of* MBINI

**Riv·er·side** (riv'ər sīd') 〚after Santa Ana *River*, near which it is located〛 city in S Calif.: pop. 227,000: see SAN BERNARDINO

**Riv·i·er·a** (riv'ē er'ə) coastal strip along the Mediterranean from La Spezia, Italy, to west of Cannes, France: a famous resort area

**Ri·yadh** (rē yäd') capital of Saudi Arabia: pop. 667,000

**Ro·a·noke** (rō'ə nōk') 〚< Carolina Algonquian: meaning unknown〛 **1** river flowing from SW Va. southeast through NE N.C. into Albemarle Sound: *c.* 380 mi. (611 km) **2** city in SW Va., on this river: pop. 96,000 **3** island off the coast of N.C.: site of abortive English colony (1585-87)

**Rob·son** (räb'sən), **Mount** 〚prob. after C. *Robertson* (1793-1842), an officer of the Hudson's Bay Company in the region ] mountain in E British Columbia; highest peak of the Canadian Rockies: 12,972 ft. (3,954 m)

**Ro·ca** (rō'kə), **Cape** cape in SW Portugal, near Lisbon: westernmost point of continental Europe: Port. **Ca·bo da Ro·ca** (kä'bōō də rô'kə)

**Roch·dale** (räch'dāl') borough of Greater Manchester in NW England: one of the earliest English cooperative societies was founded there (1844): pop. 212,000

**Roch·es·ter** (räch'əs tər, rä'ches'-; *for 3* räch'is-) **1** [ after N. *Rochester* (1752-1831), Revolutionary officer ] city & port in W N.Y., on Lake Ontario: pop. 232,000 (met. area 1,002,000) **2** [ after the city in N.Y. ] city in SE Minn.: pop. 71,000 **3** city in Kent, SE England: pop. 52,000

**Rochester Hills** city in SE Mich., near Detroit: pop. 62,000

**Rock·ford** (räk'fərd) [ in allusion to the *rocky*-bottomed *ford* there ] city in N Ill.: pop. 139,000

**Rock·ies** (räk'ēz) ROCKY MOUNTAINS

**Rock Island** [ from the *rocky island* in the river ] city in NW Ill., on the Mississippi: pop. 41,000

**Rock·ville** (räk'vil', -vəl) [ *rock* + *-ville* ] city in central Md.: suburb of Washington, D.C.: pop. 45,000

**Rocky Mount** [ descriptive ] city in NE N.C.: pop. 49,000

**Rocky Mountain National Park** national park in the Front Range of the Rockies, NC Colo.: highest peak, 14,255 ft. (4,344 m); 400 sq. mi. (1,036 sq. km)

**Rocky Mountains** [ transl. < Fr *Montaignes Rocheuses* ] mountain system in W North America, extending from central N.Mex. to N Alas.: over 3,000 mi. (4,828 km) long; highest peak, Mt. McKinley

**Ro·ma** (rô'mä) *It. name of* ROME

**Ro·man Empire** (rō'mən) empire established (27 B.C.) by Augustus, succeeding the Roman Republic: at its peak it included W & S Europe, Britain, Asia Minor, N Africa, & the lands of the E Mediterranean: divided (A.D. 395) into the EASTERN ROMAN EMPIRE & the WESTERN ROMAN EMPIRE

**Ro·ma·ni·a, Ro·mâ·ni·a** (rō mā'nē ə, -mān'yə; rô-, rōō-; *Romanian* rô mu'nē ə) country in SE Europe, on the Black Sea: 91,700 sq. mi. (237,499 sq. km); pop. 22,830,000; cap. Bucharest

**Rome** (rōm) [ L *Roma*, of Etr orig. ] **1** capital of Italy, on the Tiber River: formerly, the capital of the Roman Republic, the Roman Empire, & the Papal States: pop. 2,840,000: It. name ROMA **2** [after the It city] city in central N.Y., on the Mohawk River, near Utica: pop. 44,000

**Rom·ford** (räm′fərd, rum′-) former municipal borough in Essex, SE England: now part of Havering, near London: pop. 115,000

**Ron·dô·nia** (rôn dô′nyə) state in W Brazil, on the border of Bolivia: 93,820 sq. mi. (242,992 sq. km) pop. 491,000; cap. Pôrto Velho

**Ro·sa** (rō′zə; *It* rô′zä), **Mon·te** (mänt′ē; *It* môn′te) mountain in the Pennine Alps, on the Swiss-Italian border: 15,217 ft. (4,638 m)

**Ro·sa·ri·o** (rō zär′ē ō′; *Sp* rô sä′ryô) city & port in EC Argentina, on the Paraná River: pop. 935,000

**Ros·com·mon** (räs käm′ən) county in Connacht province, WC Ireland: 951 sq. mi. (2,463 sq. km); pop. 56,000

**Rose·mead** (rōz′mēd′) [after L. J. *Rose*, local horse breeder] city in SW Calif.: suburb of Los Angeles: pop. 52,000

**Rose·ville** (rōz′vil′) [after Wm. *Rose*, first local postmaster (1836)] city in SE Mich.: suburb of Detroit: pop. 51,000

**Ross and Crom·ar·ty** (rôs′ and kräm′ər tē) former county in N Scotland, now in the region of Highland

**Ross Dependency** [see Ross SEA] region in Antarctica, south of New Zealand and south of 60° latitude: claimed by Great Britain & administered by New Zealand: area, *c.* 160,000 sq. mi. (414,000 sq. km)

**Ross Ice Shelf** frozen S section of the Ross Sea, between Victoria Land & Marie Byrd Land: also called **Ross Shelf Ice**

**Ross Sea** [after Brit explorer Sir James Clark *Ross* (1800-62), who discovered it] arm of the Pacific, along the coast of Antarctica, east of Victoria Land

**Ros·tock** (räs′täk′; *Ger* rôs′tôk′) seaport in NE Germany, on the Baltic, in the state of Mecklenburg-Western Pomerania: pop. 242,000

**Ros·tov** (rä′stäv′, -stôf′; *Russ* rô stôf′) city in SW Russia, at the mouth of the Don: pop. 986,000: also called **Rostov–on–Don**

**Roth·er·ham** (räth′ər əm) city in W South Yorkshire,

NC England: pop. 253,000

**Rot·ter·dam** (rät′ər dam′; *Du* rô̂′tər däm′) seaport in SW Netherlands, in the Rhine delta: pop. 571,000

**Rou·baix** (rōō bā′; *Fr* rōō be′) city in N France: pop. 101,000

**Rou·en** (rōō än′; *Fr* rwän) city & port in NW France, on the Seine: pop. 105,000

**Rou·ma·ni·a** (rōō mä′nē ə, -mān′yə) *var. of* ROMANIA

**Rou·me·li·a** (rōō mē′lē ə, -mēl′yə) *alt. sp. of* RUMELIA

**Rous·sil·lon** (rōō sē yōn′) historical region of S France bordering on the Pyrenees & the Gulf of Lions

**Rov·no** (räv′nō′, -nə; rôv′-) city in W Ukraine: pop. 221,000

**Rox·burgh** (räks′bə rə) former county of S Scotland, now in the region of the Borders: also **Rox′burgh·shire′** (-shir′, -shər)

**Royal Oak** 〚in allusion to an oak in which Charles II of England is said to have hidden〛 city in SE Mich.: suburb of Detroit: pop. 65,000

**Ru·an·da-U·run·di** (rōō an′də ōō rōon′dē) former Belgian-administered UN trust territory in EC Africa: divided (1962) into the independent countries of RWANDA & BURUNDI

**Rub′ al Kha·li** (rōōb′ äl kä′lē) large desert of S & SE Arabia: *c.* 300,000 sq. mi. (777,000 sq. km)

**Ru·bi·con** (rōō′bi kän′) 〚L *Rubico* (gen. *Rubiconis*)〛 small river in N Italy that formed the boundary between Cisalpine Gaul & the Roman Republic: when Caesar crossed it (49 B.C.) at the head of his army to march on Rome, he began the civil war with Pompey

**Ru·dolf** (rōō′dôlf′, -dälf′), **Lake** lake in NW Kenya, on the border of Ethiopia: *c.* 3,500 sq. mi. (9,065 sq. km); *c.* 185 mi. (298 km) long

**Rug·by** (rug′bē) **1** city in Warwickshire, central England: pop. 59,000 **2** famous school for boys located there: founded 1567

**Ruhr** (rōor; *Ger* rōō′ər) **1** river in WC Germany, flowing west into the Rhine: 145 mi. (234 km) **2** major coal-mining & industrial region centered in the valley of this river: also called **Ruhr Basin**

**Ru·ma·ni·a** (rōō mä′nē ə, -mān′yə) *var. of* ROMANIA

**Ru·me·li·a** (rōō mē′lē ə, -mēl′yə) former Turkish possessions in the Balkan Peninsula, including Macedonia, Thrace, & an autonomous province (**Eastern**

**Rumelia**) that was annexed to Bulgaria in 1885

**Run·ny·mede** (run'i mēd') meadow on the S bank of the Thames, southwest of London: site of the granting of the Magna Carta

**Ru·se** (rōo'sē) city in Bulgaria, on the Danube: pop. 181,000

**Rush·more** (rush'môr'), **Mount** ⟦after Chas. E. *Rushmore*, N.Y. mining attorney⟧ mountain in the Black Hills, W S.Dak., on which are carved huge heads (60 ft., 18 m, high) of Washington, Jefferson, Lincoln, & Theodore Roosevelt: 6,200 ft. (1,889 m): it constitutes a national memorial (**Mount Rushmore National Memorial**), *c.* 2 sq. mi. (5.2 sq. km)

**Rus·sia** (rush'ə) ⟦< Russ *Rus'*, name of land & people⟧ 1 former empire (**Russian Empire**) in E Europe & N Asia, 1547-1917, ruled by the czars: cap. St. Petersburg 2 loosely, the UNION OF SOVIET SOCIALIST REPUBLICS 3 RUSSIAN SOVIET FEDERATED SOCIALIST REPUBLIC, esp. the European part 4 country in E Europe and N Asia, stretching from the Baltic Sea to the Pacific & from the Arctic Ocean to the Chinese border: established in 1991 upon the breakup of the U.S.S.R.: 6,592,800 sq. mi. (17,075,286 sq. km); pop. 149,469,000; cap. Moscow: official name **Russian Federation**

**Rus·sian Soviet Federated Socialist Republic** (rush'ən) a republic of the U.S.S.R.: now RUSSIA

**Russian Turkestan** the part of Turkestan formerly under Soviet control comprising the Kirghiz, Tadzhik, Turkmen & Uzbek republics and sometimes Kazakhstan: also called *Western Turkestan*

**Rust Belt** [*also* **r- b-**] that part of the U.S. comprising many of the States of the Midwest and the Northeast, regarded as an area marked by decreasing production of such items as steel and automobiles, aging factories, diminishing population, etc.

**Ru·the·ni·a** (rōo thē'nē ə, -thēn'yə) ⟦ML, Russia⟧ region in W Ukraine, a former province of Czechoslovakia

**Rut·land** (rut'lənd) former county of EC England, now part of Leicestershire: also **Rut'land·shire'** (-shir', -shər)

**Ru·wen·zo·ri** (rōo'wen zôr'ē) group of mountains in EC Africa, on the Zaire-Uganda border: identified with the

"Mountains of the Moon" referred to by ancient writers: highest peak, Mt. Stanley

**Rwan·da** (rōō än′də) country in EC Africa, east of Zaire: formerly part of Ruanda-Urundi: 10,169 sq. mi. (26,338 sq. km); pop. 4,819,000; cap. Kigali

**Ry·a·zan** (rē′ə zän′, -zän′y′) city in W European Russia, near the Oka River: pop. 494,000

**Ry·binsk** (ri′binsk′) 1 city in W European Russia, on Rybinsk Reservoir: pop. 251,000 2 artificial lake on the upper Volga: c. 1,800 sq. mi. (4,661 sq. km): in full **Rybinsk Reservoir**

**Ry·u·kyu** (rē yōō′kyōō′, rē ōō′-) chain of Japanese islands in the W Pacific, between Kyushu & Taiwan: c. 1,800 sq. mi. (4,661 sq. km); pop. 1,200,000: chief island, Okinawa

# S

**Saar** (sär, zär) 1 river flowing from the Vosges Mountains, NE France, north into the Moselle River, SW Germany: c. 150 mi. (240 km) 2 rich coal-mining region (also called **Saar Basin**) in the valley of this river: administered by France (1919-35) & Germany (1935-47) until set up as an autonomous government having a customs union with France (1947-57): since 1957, the SAARLAND

**Saar·brück·en** (sär′brook′ən, zär′-; Ger zär′brük′ən) city in SW Germany, on the Saar: capital of the Saarland: pop. 190,000

**Saa·re·maa** (sä′rə mä′) island of Estonia in the Baltic Sea, at the entrance to the Gulf of Riga: 1,048 sq. mi. (2,715 sq. km)

**Saar·land** (sär′land, zär′-; Ger zär′länt′) state of SW Germany, in the Saar River Basin: 991 sq. mi. (2,566 sq. km); pop. 1,054,000; cap. Saarbrücken

**Sa·ba** (sä′bə; for 2 sä′bə, sab′ə) 1 island of the Leeward group, in the Netherlands Antilles: 5 sq. mi. (13 sq. km); pop. 1,000 2 ancient kingdom in S Arabia in the region of modern Yemen: Biblical name SHEBA

**Sa·ba·dell** (sä′bä del′) city in NE Spain, near Barcelona: pop. 185,000

**Sa·bah** (sä′bä) state of Malaysia, occupying NE Borneo & several offshore islands, including Labuan: formerly, until 1963, a British colony (called *North Borneo*):

28,460 sq. mi. (73,711 sq. km); pop. 1,012,000; cap. Kota Kinabalu

**Sa·bine** (sə bēn′) ⟦Fr < Sp *sabina,* red cedar: named for the trees along its banks⟧ river flowing from E Tex. south along the Tex.-La. border into the Gulf of Mexico: *c.* 550 mi. (886 km): lower course is part of a system of channels (**Sabine-Neches Waterway**) connecting Beaumont, Tex., & Lake Charles, La., with the Gulf of Mexico

**Sabine Lake** shallow lake formed by the widening of the Sabine River just above its mouth: *c.* 17 mi. (27 km) long

**Sable** (sā′bəl) ⟦< Fr, sand < L *sabulum,* sand⟧ **1 Cape** cape at the S tip of Fla.: southernmost point of the U.S. mainland: *c.* 20 mi. (32 km) long **2 Cape** cape at the S tip of Nova Scotia

**Sach·sen** (zäk′sən) *Ger. name of* SAXONY

**Sac·ra·men·to** (sak′rə men′tō) ⟦Sp, sacrament⟧ **1** river in central Calif., flowing south into an E arm of San Francisco Bay: *c.* 400 mi. (644 km) **2** capital of Calif., on this river: pop. 369,000 (met. area 1,481,000)

**Sa·do·vá** (sä′dô vä′) village in N Czech Republic: see HRADEC KRÁLOVÉ

**Sa·fi** (sä fē′, saf′ē) seaport in W Morocco, on the Atlantic: pop. 129,000

**Sag·i·naw** (sag′ə nô′) ⟦< Ojibwa *sa·gi·na·ng,* lit., at the place of the Sauks⟧ city in central Mich.: pop. 70,000

**Sa·git·ta** (sə jit′ə) ⟦L, lit., arrow⟧ a small N constellation between Vulpecula and Aquila

**Sag·it·tar·i·us** (saj′ə ter′ē əs) ⟦ME < L *sagittarius,* archer < *sagitta,* arrow⟧ **1** a large S constellation in the brightest part of the Milky Way, beyond which lies the center of our galaxy **2** the ninth sign of the zodiac, entered by the sun about November 21

**Sag·ue·nay** (sag′ə nā′) ⟦< ? AmInd⟧ river in SC Quebec, Canada, flowing southeastward from Lake St. John into the Gulf of St. Lawrence: *c.* 120 mi. (193 km), incl. principal headstream north of Lake St. John, 475 mi. (765 km)

**Sa·ha·ra** (sə har′ə, -her′ə, -hä′rə) ⟦Ar *ṣaḥrāʔ* (pl. *ṣaḥārā*), desert⟧ vast desert region in N Africa, extending from the Atlantic to the Nile (or to the Red Sea): *c.* 3,500,000 sq. mi. (9,100,000 sq. km)

**Sa·ha·ran·pur** (sə här′ən poor′) city in NW Uttar

Pradesh, N India: pop. 294,000

**Sa·hel** (sä hel') region in NC Africa, south of the Sahara, characterized by periodic drought

**Sa·i·da** (sä'ē dä') seaport in SW Lebanon, on the site of ancient Sidon: pop. 25,000

**Sai·gon** (sī'gän', sī gän') *old name of* Ho Chi Minh City

**Sainte-Foy** (sant fwä') city in S Quebec, Canada: suburb of Quebec: pop. 70,000

**Saint-Hu·bert** (san tü ber') town in S Quebec, Canada: part of metropolitan Montreal: pop. 66,000

**Saint John** ⟦named after the river⟧ 1 seaport in S New Brunswick, Canada, at the mouth of the Saint John River: pop. 76,000 2 ⟦named for the date of its discovery, June 24, 1604, the feast of St. John the Baptist⟧ river flowing from N Maine through New Brunswick, Canada, into the Bay of Fundy: 418 mi. (673 km)

**Saint-Lau·rent** (san lô ran') town in S Quebec, Canada: part of metropolitan Montreal: pop. 67,000

**Saint-Lé·o·nard** (san lä ô nar') town in S Quebec, Canada: part of metropolitan Montreal: pop. 79,000

**Sai·pan** (sī pan', -pän') island in the W Pacific: seat of government of the Northern Marianas: 47 sq. mi. (122 sq. km)

**Sa·ïs** (sā'is) ancient city in the Nile delta: capital of Egypt (718-712 B.C.; 663-525 B.C.)

**Sa·kai** (sä'kī) city in S Honshu, Japan: pop. 810,000

**Sa·kha·lin** (sä'khä lēn'; *E* sak'ə lēn') island of Russia off the E coast of Siberia: *c.* 29,000 sq. mi. (75,100 sq. km)

**Sa·la·do** (sä lä'thô) river in N Argentina, flowing from the Andes southeast into the Paraná: *c.* 1,100 mi. (1,770 km)

**Sal·a·man·ca** (sal'ə man'kə; *Sp* sä'lä män'kä) 1 city in Léon, WC Spain: pop. 167,000 2 city in central Mexico: pop. 160,000

**Sal·a·mis** (sal'ə mis; *Gr* sä'lä mēs') island of Greece, in the Saronic Gulf: 36 sq. mi. (93 sq. km)

**Sa·lé** (sa lä') city & seaport in NW Morocco: suburb of Rabat: pop. 290,000

**Sa·lem** (sā'ləm) 1 ⟦after Biblical place name: see Gen. 14:18, Ps. 76:2⟧ capital of Oreg., in the NW part, on the Willamette River: pop. 108,000 2 ⟦after the Biblical *Salem*⟧ city in NE Mass., on Massachusetts Bay: suburb of Boston: pop. 38,000: see Boston 3 city in N

Tamil Nadu state, S India: pop. 515,000

**Sa·ler·no** (sä ler′nô; *E* sə lur′nō) seaport in S Italy, on an inlet (**Gulf of Salerno**) of the Tyrrhenian Sea: pop. 157,000: ancient name **Sa·ler·num** (sə lur′nəm)

**Sal·ford** (sôl′fərd, sal′-) city in NW England, in Greater Manchester: pop. 130,000

**Sa·li·na** (sə lī′nə) ⟦< L *salina*, pl. of *salinae*, salt pits: for the salt deposits found there⟧ city in central Kans.: pop. 42,000

**Sa·li·nas** (sə lē′nəs) ⟦after the nearby *Salinas* River < L *salina* (see prec.): for the salt marshes at its mouth⟧ city in WC Calif., near Monterey: pop. 109,000

**Salis·bur·y** (sôlz′ber′ē, -bə rē; salz′-) ⟦OE *Searoburh*⟧ 1 city in Wiltshire, SC England: noted for its 13th-cent. cathedral: pop. 36,000 2 *old name of* HARARE

**Salisbury Plain** rolling plateau in S Wiltshire, England: site of Stonehenge

**Salm·on** (sam′ən) river in central Ida., flowing into the Snake River: 420 mi. (676 sq. km)

**Sa·lo·ni·ka** (sal′ə nī′kə, -nē′-; sə län′i kə) 1 seaport in Macedonia, N Greece, at the head of the Gulf of Salonika: pop. 406,000: Gr. name THESSALONIKI 2 **Gulf of** N arm of the Aegean Sea: *c.* 70 mi. (113 km) long Also sp. **Sa′lo·ni′ca**

**Sal·op** (sal′əp) ⟦short for Early ME *Salopescira* < OE *Scropscir*, contr. < *Scrobbesbyrigscir*, Shropshire⟧ *old name* (1974-80) *of* SHROPSHIRE

**Salt** ⟦because of the saltiness of the lower stream⟧ river in SC Ariz., flowing into the Gila River: *c.* 200 mi. (322 km)

**Sal·ta** (säl′tə) city in NW Argentina: pop. 260,000

**Sal·til·lo** (säl tē′yô) city in N Mexico: capital of Coahuila state: pop. 321,000

**Salt Lake City** capital of Utah, near the SE end of Great Salt Lake: pop. 160,000 (met. area incl. Ogden 1,072,000)

**Sal·ton Sea** (sôlt′'n) ⟦prob. coined < ModE *salt*⟧ shallow saltwater lake, orig. a salt-covered depression (**Salton Sink**), in the Imperial Valley, S Calif., kept filled by runoff water from irrigation ditches fed by the Colorado River: *c.* 350 sq. mi. (907 sq. km); *c.* 280 ft. (86 m) below sea level

**Sal·va·dor** (sal′və dôr′; *Port* säl′və dô̄r′) seaport in E Brazil: capital of Bahia state: pop. 1,490,000

**Sal·ween** (sal wēn′) river in SE Asia, flowing from E Tibet through E Myanmar into the Gulf of Martaban: *c.* 1,750 mi. (2,816 km)

**Salz·burg** (zälts′boork′; *E* sôlz′bʉrg′) city in central Austria: scene of annual music festivals: pop. 140,000

**Sa·mar** (sä′mär′) island of the EC Philippines, southeast of Luzon: 5,181 sq. mi. (13,415 sq. km)

**Sa·ma·ra** (su mä′rə) city in SE European Russia, on the Volga: pop. 1,257,000: see KUIBYSHEV

**Sa·mar·i·a** (sə mer′ē ə, -mar′-) 1 region in W Jordan, west of the Jordan River 2 in ancient times, N kingdom of the Hebrews; Israel 3 the capital of this kingdom 4 district of Palestine between Galilee & Judea, later a part of the Roman province of Judea

**Sam·ar·kand** (sam′ər kand′; *Russ* sä mär känt′) city in E Uzbekistan: capital (as MARACANDA) of Tamerlane's empire (1370-1405): pop. 371,000

**Sam·ni·um** (sam′nē əm) ancient country in SC Italy

**Sa·mo·a** (sə mō′ə) group of islands in the South Pacific, north of Tonga: see AMERICAN SAMOA & WESTERN SAMOA

**Sa·mos** (sä′mäs′; *Gr* sä′môs) Greek island in the Aegean, off W Turkey: *c.* 180 sq. mi. (479 sq. km)

**Sam·o·thrace** (sam′ə thrās′) Greek island in the NE Aegean: *c.* 70 sq. mi. (181 sq. km): Gr. name **Sa·mo·thrá·ki** (sä′mô thrä′kē)

**Sa·na** (sä′nä, sä nä′) capital of the Republic of Yemen, in the W part: pop. 278,000: also sp. **Sa′n′a** or **Sa′naa**

**San An·dre·as fault** (san an drā′əs) ⟦after *San Andreas* valley, through which the fault runs: orig. Sp, *San Andrés*, St. Andrew⟧ active fault in the earth's crust extending northwest from S California for about 600 miles (966 km)

**San An·ge·lo** (san an′jə lō′) ⟦masc. of earlier name *Santa Angela*, after a Mex nun⟧ city in central Tex.: pop. 84,000

**San An·to·ni·o** (san′ ən tō′nē ō′, an-) ⟦Sp, *St. Anthony* of Padua (1195-1231)⟧ city in SC Tex.: site of the Alamo: pop. 936,000 (met. area 1,302,000)

**San Ber·nar·di·no** (san′ bʉr′nər dē′nō, -nə-) ⟦Sp, after *St. Bernardino* of Siena⟧ 1 city in S Calif.: pop. 164,000 (met. area incl. Riverside 2,589,000) 2 mountain range in S Calif., south of the Mojave Desert: highest peak, 11,502 ft. (3,506 m): in full **San Bernar-**

dino Mountains

**San·dal·wood** (san′dəl wood′) *old name of* SUMBA

**Sand·hurst** (sand′hurst′) village in Berkshire, England: nearby is the Royal Military Academy

**San Di·e·go** (san′ dē ā′gō) 〚after *San Diego* (St. Didacus), 15th-c. Sp friar〛 seaport in S Calif.: pop. 1,111,000 (met. area 2,498,000)

**Sand·wich** (sand′wich) 〚OE *Sandwic* < *sand*, sand + *wic*, village〛 town in Kent, SE England, near the Strait of Dover: one of the Cinque Ports: pop. 4,000

**Sandwich Islands** 〚after John Montagu (1718-92), the 4th Earl of *Sandwich*〛 *old name of* the Hawaiian Islands: see HAWAII

**Sand·y City** (san′dē) 〚< ? the *sandy* soil there or after the nickname of A. Kinghorn, railroad engineer (19th-c.)〛 city in NW Utah: pop. 75,000

**Sandy Hook** narrow, sandy peninsula in E N.J., at the S entrance to Lower New York Bay

**San Fer·nan·do Valley** (san′ fər nan′dō) 〚after a mission named for *Ferdinand III*, 13th-c. king of Castile〛 valley in SW Calif., partly in NW Los Angeles: *c.* 260 sq. mi. (673 sq. km)

**San·ford** (san′fərd), **Mount** 〚after the namer's family〛 mountain in SE Alas.: 16,208 ft. (4,940 m)

**San Fran·cis·co** (san′ frən sis′kō) 〚Sp, name of old mission there, after *St. Francis* of Assisi (*c.* 1181-1226), It friar〛 seaport on the coast of central Calif., separated from Oakland by an inlet (**San Francisco Bay**) of the Pacific: pop. 724,000 (met. area incl. Oakland 3,687,000; urban area with Oakland & San Jose, 6,253,000)

**San Francisco Peaks** 〚Sp, after *St. Francis* of Assisi (*c.* 1181-1226), It friar〛 three peaks of an eroded volcano in NC Ariz.: highest peak, *c.* 12,700 ft. (3,870 m)

**San·gre de Cris·to Mountains** (saŋ′grē də kris′tō) 〚Sp, lit., blood of Christ〛 range of the Rocky Mountains, in S Colo. & N N.Mex.: highest point, BLANCA PEAK

**San Ja·cin·to** (san′ jə sin′tō) 〚Sp, *St. Hyacinth* (13th c.)〛 river in SE Tex., flowing into Galveston Bay: in a battle (1836) near its mouth, troops under Sam Houston won Tex. from Mexico: 100 mi. (161 km)

**San Joa·quin** (san′ wô kēn′, wä-) 〚Sp, *St. Joachim*, reputed father of the Virgin Mary〛 river in central Calif., flowing from the Sierra Nevada into the Sacramento River: *c.* 350 mi. (563 km)

**San Jo·se** (san′ hō zā′, -ə zā′) 〚Sp, *San José,* St. Joseph〛 city in WC Calif.: pop. 782,000 (met. area 1,498,000): see SAN FRANCISCO

**San Jo·sé** (sän′ hô se′) capital of Costa Rica, in the central part: pop. 241,000

**San Juan** (san′ hwän′, wôn′; *Sp* sän hwän′) 〚Sp, *St. John*〛 capital of Puerto Rico: seaport on the Atlantic: pop. 438,000 (met. area 1,689,000)

**San Juan Hill** hill near Santiago de Cuba: captured by U.S. troops in a battle (1898) of the Spanish-American War

**San Juan Islands** group of islands in NW Wash., between the Strait of Georgia & Puget Sound

**San Juan Mountains** range of the Rocky Mountains in SW Colo. & N N.Mex.: highest peaks, over 14,000 ft. (4,270 m)

**Sankt Mo·ritz** (zäŋkt mō′rits) *Ger. name of* ST. MORITZ

**San Le·an·dro** (san′ lē an′drō′) 〚Sp, *St. Leander,* 6th-c. archbishop of Seville〛 city in W Calif., near Oakland: pop. 68,000

**San Lu·is Po·to·sí** (sän′ lwēs′ pô′tô sē′) 1 state of NC Mexico: 24,417 sq. mi. (63,240 sq. km); pop. 1,674,000 2 its capital, in the SW part: pop. 407,000

**San Ma·ri·no** (sän′ mä rē′nō; *E* san′ mə rē′nō) 1 independent country within E Italy: 23 sq. mi. (60 sq. km); pop. 21,000 2 its capital

**San Ma·te·o** (san′ mə tā′ō) 〚Sp, *St. Matthew*〛 city in W Calif., on San Francisco Bay: suburb of San Francisco: pop. 85,000

**San Ra·fael** (san′ rə fel′) 〚Sp, short for *La Mision de San Rafael Arcangel,* mission of the Holy Archangel Raphael〛 city in W Calif., on San Francisco Bay: pop. 48,000

**San Re·mo** (sän re′mô; *E* san rē′mō) resort town in Liguria, NW Italy, on the Riviera: pop. 70,000

**San Sal·va·dor** (san sal′və dôr′; *Sp* sän säl′vä dôr′) 〚Sp, Holy Savior〛 1 capital of El Salvador, in the central part: pop. 440,000 2 island of the E Bahamas: prob. the place of Columbus' landing (1492) in the New World: 60 sq. mi. (155 sq. km)

**San Se·bas·tian** (sän′ se bäs tyän′; *E* san′ si bas′chən) seaport in the Basque Provinces, N Spain: pop. 176,000

**San Ste·fa·no** (sän ste′fä nō′) village in European Turkey, site of the signing of a peace treaty (1878) between Russia & Turkey, at the end of the Russo-Turkish War

**San·ta An·a** (san′tə an′ə; *also, for 3, Sp* sän′tä ä′nä) [Sp, *St. Anne*] **1** hot desert wind from the east or northeast in S Calif. **2** city in SW Calif.: pop. 294,000: see ANAHEIM **3** city in W El Salvador: pop. 208,000

**San·ta Bar·ba·ra** (san′tə bär′bə rə, -bär′brə) [Sp, *St. Barbara*, early Christian martyr] city on the coast of SW Calif.: pop. 86,000

**Santa Barbara Islands** group of nine islands, & many islets, off the SW coast of Calif.

**San·ta Cat·a·li·na** (san′tə kat′ʰl ē′nə) [Sp, *St. Catherine* (of Alexandria)] one of the Santa Barbara Islands, a tourist resort: *c.* 20 mi. (32 km) long

**San·ta Cat·a·ri·na** (sän′tə kä′tə rē′nə) state of S Brazil: 37,055 sq. mi. (95,973 sq. km); pop. 3,627,000; cap. Florianópolis

**San·ta Cla·ra** (san′tə kler′ə; *for 1, Sp* sän′tä klä′rä) **1** city in central Cuba: pop. 189,000 **2** [Sp, *St. Clare* (of Assisi), 13th-c. It nun] city in W Calif., near San Jose: pop. 94,000

**San·ta Cla·ri·ta** (san′tə klə rēt′ə) city in SW Calif., near Los Angeles: pop. 111,000

**San·ta Cruz** (san′tə krōōz′; *Sp* sän′tä krōōs′) [Sp, holy cross] **1** city in central Bolivia: pop. 377,000 **2** city in W Calif., south of San Jose: pop. 49,000 **3** one of the Santa Barbara Islands: *c.* 23 mi. (37 km) long **4** ST. CROIX

**Santa Cruz de Te·ne·ri·fe** (də ten′ə rif′; *Sp* de te′ne rē′ fe) seaport on Tenerife Island, Canary Islands: pop. 191,000

**San·ta Fe** (san′tə fā′) [Sp, holy faith] capital of N.Mex., in the NC part: pop. 56,000

**San·ta Fé** (sän′tä fe′) city in central Argentina: pop. 287,000

**Santa Fe Trail** trade route between Santa Fe, N.Mex., & Independence, Mo.: important from 1821 to 1880

**San·ta Is·a·bel** (sän′tä ē sä bel′) *old name of* MALABO

**San·ta Ma·ri·a** (san′tə mə rē′ə; *Sp* sän′tä mä rē′ä) active volcano in SW Guatemala: 12,362 ft. (3,768 m)

**San·ta Mon·i·ca** (san′tə män′i kə) [Sp, *St. Monica*, mother of St. Augustine (of Hippo)] city in SW Calif., on the Pacific: suburb of Los Angeles: pop. 87,000

**San·tan·der** (sän'tän der') seaport in N Spain, on the Bay of Biscay: pop. 180,000

**San·ta Ro·sa** (san'tə rō'zə) ⟦Sp, *St. Rose* (of Lima) (1586-1617): 1st New World saint⟧ **1** one of the Santa Barbara Islands: 17 mi. (27 km) long **2** city in W Calif., north of San Francisco: pop. 113,000

**San·tee** (san tē') **1** ⟦< ? AmInd tribal name⟧ river in E S.C., flowing southeast into the Atlantic: 143 mi. (230 km) **2** ⟦after M. *Santee*, 1st postmaster⟧ city in SW Calif., near San Diego: pop. 53,000

**San·ti·a·go** (sän'tē ä'gô; *E* san'tē ä'gō) capital of Chile, in the central part: pop. 3,615,000 (met. area 4,133,000)

**Santiago de Cu·ba** (de kōō'bä) seaport in SE Cuba, on the Caribbean: pop. 404,000

**San·to Do·min·go** (sän'tô dô miŋ'gô; *E* san'tō dō miŋ' gō) **1** capital of the Dominican Republic, a seaport on the S coast: pop. 1,313,000 **2** *old name of* DOMINICAN REPUBLIC **3** *old name of* HISPANIOLA

**San·tos** (sän'toos) seaport in S Brazil: pop. 411,000

**São Fran·cis·co** (soun' frän sēs'koo) river in E Brazil, flowing northeast and east into the Atlantic: *c.* 1,800 mi. (2,897 km)

**São Lu·ís** (lwēs') capital of Maranhão state, Brazil: seaport on an island off the N coast: pop. 350,000

**São Mi·guel** (mē gel') largest island of the Azores: 290 sq. mi. (751 sq. km); chief city, Ponta Delgada

**Saône** (sōn) river in E France, flowing south into the Rhone at Lyon: *c.* 280 mi. (451 km)

**São Pau·lo** (soun pou'loo) **1** state of SE Brazil: *c.* 95,750 sq. mi. (247,990 sq. km); pop. 25,040,000 **2** its capital: pop. 7,032,000

**São Sal·va·dor** (säl'və dôr') *var. of* SALVADOR

**São To·mé and Prin·ci·pe** (tô me' ənd prin'sə pē') country off the W coast of Africa, comprising two islands (*São Tomé* and *Príncipe*) in the Gulf of Guinea: formerly a Portuguese territory, it became independent (1975): 372 sq. mi. (964 sq. km); pop. 74,000

**Sap·po·ro** (sä'pô rô') chief city on the island of Hokkaido, Japan, in the SW part: pop. 1,479,000

**Saq·qar·a, Sak·kar·a** (sə kär'ə) village in N Egypt, near the ruins of Memphis: site of many pyramids

**Sa·ra·gos·sa** (sar'ə gäs'ə) *Eng. name of* ZARAGOZA

**Sa·ra·je·vo** (sä'rä'ye vô; *E* sar'ə yā'vō) capital of Bosnia and Herzegovina: scene of the assassination of Archduke Francis Ferdinand (June 28, 1914), which precipitated World War I: pop. 449,000

**Sar·a·nac Lake** (sar'ə nak') ⟦< ? Iroquoian name⟧ **1** any of three connected lakes (*Upper, Middle, & Lower*) in the Adirondacks, NE N.Y. **2** resort village on Lower Saranac Lake: pop. 5,400

**Sa·ransk** (sə ränsk', -ransk') city in central European Russia: pop. 307,000

**Sar·a·so·ta** (sar'ə sōt'ə) ⟦Sp *Sarazota* < unidentified AmInd language⟧ city on the W coast of Fla., near Tampa: pop. 51,000

**Sar·a·to·ga** (sar'ə tō'gə) ⟦prob. of Mohawk orig.⟧ *old name of* SCHUYLERVILLE: scene of two Revolutionary War battles (1777) in which American forces led by Gates defeated the British under Burgoyne

**Saratoga Springs** ⟦see prec.⟧ city in NE N.Y.: a resort with mineral springs: pop. 25,000

**Sa·ra·tov** (sä rä'tôf) city & port in SC European Russia, on the Volga: pop. 899,000

**Sa·ra·wak** (sə rä'wäk) state of Malaysia, occupying NC & NW Borneo: 48,250 sq. mi. (124,449 sq. km); pop. 1,295,000; cap. Kuching

**Sar·din·i·a** (sär din'ē ə, -din'yə) ⟦L < Gr *Sardō*⟧ **1** Italian island in the Mediterranean, south of Corsica: *c.* 9,196 sq. mi. (23,818 sq. km) **2** region of Italy, comprising this island & small nearby islands: 9,300 sq. mi. (24,000 sq. km); pop. 1,594,000; cap. Cagliari **3** former kingdom (1720-1860) including this region, Piedmont, Nice, Savoy (by which the kingdom was ruled), etc. It. name **Sar·de·gna** (sär dā'nyä)

**Sar·dis** (sär'dis) ⟦L < Gr *Sardeis*⟧ capital of ancient Lydia

**Sa·re·ma** (sä'rə mä') *alt. sp. of* SAAREMAA

**Sa·re·ra Bay** (sə re'rə) large inlet on the NW coast of New Guinea: *c.* 200 mi. (322 km) wide

**Sar·gas·so Sea** (sär gas'ō) region of calms in the N Atlantic, northeast of the West Indies, noted for its abundance of sargassum

**Sar·go·dha** (sər gōd'ə) city in Punjab, N Pakistan: pop. 294,000

**Sar·ma·ti·a** (sär mā'shə, -shē ə) ancient region in E

Europe, between the Vistula & Volga rivers, occupied by the Sarmatians (c. 300 B.C.-c. A.D. 200)

**Sar·ni·a** (sär′nē ə) city & port in SE Ontario, Canada, opposite Port Huron, Mich.: pop. 72,000

**Sa·ron·ic Gulf** (sə rän′ik) inlet of the Aegean Sea, in SE Greece, between Attica & the Peloponnesus: c. 50 mi. (80 km) long

**Sa·se·bo** (sä′se bô′) seaport in E Kyushu, Japan, on the East China Sea: pop. 252,000

**Sask** abbrev. for Saskatchewan

**Sas·katch·e·wan** (sas kach′ə wän′, -wən) ⟦earlier *Keiskatchewan*, name of the river < Cree *kisiskatchewani sipi*, lit., swift-flowing river⟧ 1 province of SC Canada: 251,700 sq. mi. (651,900 sq. km); pop. 1,010,000; cap. Regina: abbrev. *SK* or *Sask* 2 river in central Saskatchewan flowing east into Lake Winnipeg: 340 mi. (547 km); with principal headstream 1,205 mi. (1,939 km)

**Sas·ka·toon** (sas′kə tōōn′) city in central Saskatchewan, Canada, on the South Saskatchewan River: pop. 178,000 (met. area 200,000)

**Sat·urn** (sat′ərn) ⟦ME *Saturne* < OE < L *Saturnus* < Etr⟧ the second largest planet of the solar system and the sixth in distance from the sun: it has a thin, icy ring system around its equator: diameter, c. 120,660 km (c. 74,980 mi.); period of revolution, 29.46 earth years; period of rotation, 10.67 hours; 18 satellites; symbol, ♄

**Sa·u·di Arabia** (sou′dē, sô′-) kingdom occupying most of Arabia: 849,400 sq. mi. (2,200,000 sq. km); pop. c. 12,400,000; cap. Riyadh (Mecca is the religious cap.)

**Sault Ste. Ma·rie** (sōō′ sänt′ mə rē′) ⟦< Fr *Sault de Sainte Marie*, lit., falls of St. Mary⟧ city in central Ontario, Canada, on the St. Marys River: pop. 81,000: also **Sault Sainte Marie**

**Sa·va** (sä′vä) river in S Europe, flowing from Slovenia eastward into the Danube: c. 450 mi. (724 km)

**Sa·vai·i** (sä vī′ē) largest & westernmost island of Western Samoa: 662 sq. mi. (1,715 sq. km)

**Sa·van·nah** (sə van′ə) ⟦< ? a name for the Shawnees in an unidentified Amerindian language⟧ 1 river forming the border between Ga. & S.C., flowing southeast into the Atlantic: 314 mi. (506 km) 2 seaport in SE Ga., near the mouth of this river: pop. 138,000

**Sa·voie** (så vwå′) *Fr. name of* SAVOY

**Sa·voy** (sə voi′) region in SE France, on the borders of Italy & Switzerland: a former duchy & part of the kingdom of Sardinia: annexed by France (1860)

**Sa·watch Mountains** (sə wäch′) 〖< ? AmInd name〗 range of the Rocky Mountains, in central Colo.: highest peak, Mount ELBERT

**Saxe** (såks; *E* saks) *Fr. name of* SAXONY: used in the names of several former duchies of the German Empire, now mostly in Thuringia, as **Saxe–Co·burg Go·tha** (saks′kō′bʉrg gō′thə), a duchy of central Germany, divided (1920) between Thuringia & Bavaria

**Sax·on·y** (sak′sə nē) 〖LL *Saxonia*〗 1 region in E Germany: formerly an electorate, kingdom, Prussian province, & state of the Weimar Republic 2 state of E Germany: 6,564 sq. mi. (17,000 sq. km); pop. 4,900,000; cap. Dresden 3 medieval duchy at the base of the Jutland peninsula in what is now Lower Saxony

**Sax·on·y-An·halt** (-än′hält′) state of E Germany: 9,653 sq. mi. (25,000 sq. km); pop. 3,000,000; cap. Halle

**Sa·yan Mountains** (sä yän′) mountain system in central Asia, partially along the Mongolian-Russian border: highest peak, 11,453 ft. (3,490 m)

**SC, S.C.** *abbrev. for* South Carolina

**Sca·fell Pike** (skô′fel) peak of a mountain in Cumberland, NW England, the highest in England: 3,210 ft. (978 m)

**Scales** Libra, the constellation and seventh sign of the zodiac

**Sca·man·der** (skə man′dər) *ancient name of* MENDERES (river in NW Turkey)

**Scan·di·na·vi·a** (skan′də nā′vē ə, -vyə) 1 region in N Europe, including Norway, Sweden, & Denmark and, sometimes, Iceland & the Faeroe Islands 2 SCANDINAVIAN PENINSULA

**Scandinavian Peninsula** large peninsula in N Europe, consisting of Norway & Sweden

**Scap·a Flow** (skap′ə) sea basin in the Orkney Islands, off N Scotland: British naval base: *c.* 50 sq. mi. (129 sq. km)

**Scar·bor·ough** (skär′bʉr′ō, -ə; -bə rə) 〖OE *Scartheborc* < ON *Skarthaborg* < *Skarthi* (lit., harelip, nickname of Thorgils, Norw founder of the town, *c.* 966) + -*borg*; akin to OE *burg*, borough〗 1 city & seaside resort in

NE England, in North Yorkshire: pop. 50,000 **2** city in SE Ontario, Canada: part of metropolitan Toronto: pop. 485,000

**Schaff·hau·sen** (shäf'hou'zən) canton of Switzerland, in the northernmost part: 115 sq. mi. (298 sq. km); pop. 71,000

**Schaum·burg** (shôm'bərg, shäm'-) 〚after *Schaumburg*-Lippe, former state in Germany whence many settlers emigrated〛 village in NE Ill., near Chicago: pop. 69,000

**Scheldt** (skelt) river flowing from N France through Belgium and the Netherlands into the North Sea: *c.* 270 mi. (434 km): Du. name **Schel·de** (skhel'də)

**Sche·nec·ta·dy** (skə nek'tə dē') 〚Du *Schanhectade* < Mohawk *skahnéhtati*, Albany, lit., on the other side of the pines: the pines were between the communities; the Dutch transferred the name〛 city in E N.Y., on the Mohawk River: pop. 66,000 (met. area with Albany & Troy, 874,000)

**Schie·dam** (skhē däm') city in SW Netherlands: pop. 69,000

**Schles·wig** (shles'wig; *Ger* shläs'viH) region in the S Jutland peninsula, divided between Denmark & Germany: Dan. name SLESVIG

**Schles·wig–Hol·stein** (-hōl'stīn; *Ger*, -hôl'shtīn) state of N Germany: 6,069 sq. mi. (15,721 sq. km); pop. 2,615,000; cap. Kiel

**Schuy·ler·ville** (skī'lər vil') 〚after Philip John *Schuyler* (1733-1804), Am statesman〛 resort village in E N.Y., on the Hudson: pop. 1,360: cf. SARATOGA

**Schuyl·kill** (skool'kil) 〚< Du *Schuilkil*, lit., hidden channel < *schuilen*, to hide, skulk + *kil*, stream〛 river in SE Pa., flowing southeast into the Delaware River at Philadelphia: 130 mi. (209 km)

**Schwa·ben** (shvä'bən) *Ger. name of* SWABIA

**Schwarz·wald** (shvärts'vält') *Ger. name of* BLACK FOREST

**Schweiz** (shvīts) *Ger. name of* SWITZERLAND

**Schwe·rin** (shver'in; *Ger* shvä rēn') city in N Germany: capital of the state of Mecklenburg-Western Pomerania: pop. 105,000

**Schwyz** (shvēts) canton of EC Switzerland, on Lake Lucerne: 351 sq. mi. (909 sq. km); pop. 97,000

**Scil·ly Isles** (or **Islands**) (sil'ē) group of about 140 islets off Cornwall, England: *c.* 6 sq. mi. (16 sq. km); pop. 2,400: also called **Isles of Scilly**

**Scone** (skōōn, skōn) village in E Scotland northeast of Perth: site of an abbey that contained the stone (**Stone of Scone**) on which Scottish kings before 1296 were crowned: removed by Edward I and placed under the coronation chair at Westminster Abbey

**Scor·pi·o** (skôr′pē ō′) ⟦L, lit., scorpion⟧ 1 *old name of* SCORPIUS 2 the eighth sign of the zodiac, entered by the sun about October 24

**Scor·pi·on** (skôr′pē ən) SCORPIO

**Scor·pi·us** (skôr′pē əs) a S constellation in the Milky Way between Ophiuchus and Ara, containing the bright star Antares

**Sco·tia** (skō′shə) ⟦LL⟧ *old poet. name for* SCOTLAND

**Scot·land** (skät′lənd) division of the United Kingdom, occupying the N half of Great Britain & nearby islands: 30,410 sq. mi. (78,761 sq. km); pop. 5,130,000; cap. Edinburgh

**Scotland Yard** ⟦so named because orig. the residence of the kings of Scotland when in London⟧ 1 short street in London, off Whitehall, orig. the site of police headquarters 2 headquarters of the metropolitan London police, on the Thames embankment since 1890: officially **New Scotland Yard**

**Scotts·dale** (skäts′dāl′) ⟦after Winfield *Scott* (1837-1910), early settler⟧ city in SC Ariz.: suburb of Phoenix: pop. 130,000

**Scran·ton** (skrant′'n) ⟦family name of the founders of a local ironworks⟧ city in NE Pa.: pop. 82,000

**Sculp·tor** (skulp′tər) a S constellation between Cetus and Phoenix containing the S galactic pole

**Scun·thorpe** (skun′thôrp) city in Humberside, E England: pop. 69,000

**Scu·ta·ri** (skōō′tä rē), **Lake** lake on border of S Yugoslavia & NW Albania: 140-200 sq. mi. (362-520 sq. km)

**Scu·tum** (skyōōt′əm) a small S constellation between Aquila and Sagittarius

**Scyl·la** (sil′ə) ⟦L < Gr *Skylla*⟧ a dangerous rock on the Italian side of the Straits of Messina, opposite the whirlpool Charybdis: in classical mythology both Scylla and Charybdis were personified as female monsters

**Scy·ros** (sī′rəs) *Latin name of* SKÍROS

**Scyth·i·a** (sith'ē ə) ancient region in SE Europe, centered about the N coast of the Black Sea

**SD, S.D.** *abbrev. for* South Dakota

**S Dak** *abbrev. for* South Dakota

**Sea Islands** chain of islands off the coasts of S.C., Ga., & N Fla.

**Se·at·tle** (sē at″l) 〚after *Seathl*, an Indian chief〛 seaport in WC Wash., on Puget Sound: pop. 516,000 (met. area incl. Tacoma 2,559,000)

**Se·bas·to·pol** (si bas′tə pōl′) *var. of* SEVASTOPOL

**Se·dan** (si dan′; *Fr* sə dän′) city in N France, on the Meuse River: scene of a decisive French defeat (1870) in the Franco-Prussian War: pop. 20,000

**Se·go·via** (se gô′vyä) city in central Spain: pop. 41,000

**Seine** (sān; *Fr* sen) river in N France, flowing northwest through Paris into the English Channel: 482 mi. (775 km)

**Se·lan·gor** (se län′gôr) state of Malaysia, in SW Peninsular Malaysia: 3,167 sq. mi. (8,202 sq. km); pop. 1,467,000

**Se·leu·ci·a** (sə lo͞o′shē ə, -shə) any of several ancient cities of SW Asia, founded by Seleucus I; esp., the chief city of the Seleucid Empire, on the Tigris

**Sel·kirk** (sel′kʉrk) former county of S Scotland, now in the region of the Borders: also **Sel′kirk·shire′** (-shir′, -shər)

**Selkirk Mountains** range of the Rocky Mountain system, in SE British Columbia: highest peak, 11,590 ft. (3,533 m)

**Se·ma·rang** (sə mär′äŋ) seaport in NC Java, Indonesia, on the Java Sea: pop. 1,027,000

**Se·mi·pa·la·tinsk** (sye′mē pə lä′tinsk) city in NE Kazakhstan, on the Irtysh River: pop. 317,000

**Sen·dai** (sen′dī′) seaport in NE Honshu, Japan: pop. 663,000

**Sen·e·gal** (sen′i gôl′, sen′ə gəl) **1** country in W Africa, on the Atlantic: formerly a territory of French West Africa, it became independent (1960) (see MALI): 75,750 sq. mi. (196,192 sq. km); pop. 6,540,000; cap. Dakar **2** river flowing from W Mali northwest into the Atlantic: *c.* 1,000 mi. (1,609 km)

**Sen·e·gam·bi·a** (sen′i gam′bē ə) region in W Africa, comprising the basins of the rivers Senegal & Gambia

**Sen·lac** (sen′lak) hill in Sussex, SE England: site of the

Battle of Hastings

**Se·oul** (sōl; *Kor* syŏ′ōōl′) capital of South Korea, in the NW part: pop. 9,500,000

**Se·quoi·a National Park** (si kwoi′ə) national park in EC Calif., containing giant sequoias: 602 sq. mi. (1,560 sq. km)

**Se·ra·je·vo** (ser′ə yä′vō) *var. of* SARAJEVO

**Se·ram** (si ram′) *alt. sp. of* CERAM

**Ser·bi·a** (sur′bē ə) the major constituent republic of Yugoslavia, formerly a kingdom: 34,116 sq. mi. (88,360 sq. km); pop. 9,720,000; cap. Belgrade

**Serbs, Croats, and Slovenes, Kingdom of the** see YUGOSLAVIA

**Ser·em·ban** (sur′əm bän′) city in SW Peninsular Malaysia, Malaysia: capital of Negri Sembilan state: pop. 136,000

**Ser·gi·pe** (sər zhē′pə) state of E Brazil: 8,490 sq. mi. (21,989 sq. km); pop. 1,140,000; cap. Aracajú

**Ser·pens** (sur′penz) an equatorial constellation split into two separate regions, **Serpens Ca·put** (kā′pət, kap′ət) (head) and **Serpens Cau·da** (kô′də) (tail), on opposite sides of Ophiuchus

**Ses·tos** (ses′täs) town in ancient Thrace, on the Hellespont opposite Abydos

**Se·vas·to·pol** (sə vas′tə pōl; *Russ* se′väs tô′pəl y′) seaport in SW Crimea, on the Black Sea: pop. 341,000

**Seven Hills of Rome** seven low hills on the E bank of the Tiber, on & about which Rome was originally built; Aventine, Caelian, Capitoline, Esquiline, Palatine (approximately in the center), Quirinal, & Viminal

**seven seas** all the oceans of the world

**Seven Wonders of the World** seven remarkable landmarks of ancient times: the Egyptian pyramids, the walls and hanging gardens of Babylon, the Mausoleum at Halicarnassus, the temple of Artemis at Ephesus, the Colossus of Rhodes, the statue of Zeus by Phidias at Olympia, and the Pharos (or lighthouse) at Alexandria

**Sev·ern** (sev′ərn) river flowing from central Wales through England & into the Bristol Channel: c. 200 mi. (322 km)

**Se·ver·na·ya Zem·lya** (sev′ər nə yä′ zem lyä′) group of Russian islands in N Asian Russia north of the Taimyr Peninsula, between the Kara & Laptev seas: *c.* 14,500 sq. mi. (37,555 sq. km)

**Se·ville** (sə vil′) city in SW Spain, on the Guadalquivir River: pop. 654,000: Sp. name **Se·vil·la** (sā vē′lyä)

**Sew·ard Peninsula** (sōō′ərd) ⟦after William H. *Seward*, U.S. statesman who directed the purchase of Alaska from Russia (1867) ⟧ peninsula of W Alas. on the Bering Strait: *c.* 200 mi. (321 km) long

**Sex·tans** (sek′stənz) an equatorial constellation between Leo and Hydra

**Sey·chelles** (sā shel′, -shelz′) country on a group of islands in the Indian Ocean, northeast of Madagascar: formerly a British colony, it became independent as a republic within the Commonwealth (1976): *c.* 100 sq. mi. (259 sq. km); pop. 64,000; cap. Victoria (on Mahé Island)

**Sfax** (sfäks) seaport on the E coast of Tunisia: pop. 232,000

**'s Gra·ven·ha·ge** (skhrä′vən hä′khə) *Du. name of* The HAGUE

**Shaan·xi** (shän′shē′) province of NC China: 75,598 sq. mi. (195,798 sq. km); pop. 28,900,000; cap. Xian

**Sha·che** (shä′chu′) city in W Xinjiang, China: a trading center: pop. 80,000

**Shakh·ty** (shäkh′tē) city in SW European Russia, in the Donets Basin: pop. 221,000

**Shan·dong** (shän′dooŋ′) province of NE China, including a peninsula (**Shandong Peninsula**) which projects between the Yellow Sea & Bo Hai: 59,189 sq. mi. (153,300 sq. km); pop. 74,420,000; cap. Jinan

**Shang·hai** (shaŋ′hī′, shäŋ′-) seaport in Jiangsu province, E China, near the mouth of the Chang: pop. *c.* 6,270,000 (met. area 12,000,000)

**Shan·gri-La** (shaŋ′gri lä′) *n.* ⟦< the scene of James Hilton's novel *Lost Horizon* (1933) ⟧ any imaginary, idyllic utopia or hidden paradise

**Shan·non** (shan′ən) river in WC Ireland, flowing southwestward into the Atlantic: *c.* 220 mi. (354 km)

**Shan State** (shän, shan) administrative division of EC Myanmar, occupying a plateau region (**Shan Plateau**), inhabited by Shans

**Shan·tou** (shän′tō′) seaport in Guangdong province, SE China, on the South China Sea: pop. 400,000

**Shan·tung** (shan′tuŋ′) *old form of* SHANDONG

**Shan·xi** (shän′shē′) province of NE China, between the Huang He and Inner Mongolia: 60,656 sq. mi. (157,100 sq. km); pop. 25,290,000; cap. Taiyuan: old form **Shan′si′**

**Sha·ri** (shä′rē) river in central Africa, flowing northwest through the Central African Republic & Chad into Lake Chad: *c.* 500 mi. (804 km)

**Shar·on** (sher′ən), **Plain of** coastal plain in W Israel, extending from Tel Aviv to Mount Carmel <

**Shas·ta** (shas′tə), **Mount** ⟦< a tribal name < ?⟧ volcanic mountain in the Cascade Range, N Calif.: 14,162 ft. (4,317 m)

**Shatt-al-A·rab** (shat′əl ä′räb) river in SE Iraq, formed by the confluence of the Tigris & Euphrates rivers & flowing southeast into the Persian Gulf: 120 mi. (193 km)

**She·ba** (shē′bə) *Biblical name of* SABA (the ancient kingdom)

**She·boy·gan** (shi boi′gən) ⟦< Menomini *saapi-iweehekaneh*, lit., at a hearing distance through the woods⟧ city & port in E Wis., on Lake Michigan: pop. 50,000

**Shef·field** (shef′ēld) city in NC England, in South Yorkshire: pop. 477,000

**Shen·an·do·ah** (shen′ən dō′ə) ⟦prob. of Iroquoian orig.⟧ river in N Va., flowing through a valley (**Shen-andoah Valley**) between the Blue Ridge & Allegheny mountains, into the Potomac: *c.* 200 mi. (321 km)

**Shenandoah National Park** national park in the Blue Ridge Mountains of N Va.: 302 sq. mi. (782 sq. km)

**Shen·si** (shen′sē′; *Chin* shun′shē′) *old form of* SHAANXI

**Shen·yang** (shun′yäŋ′) city in NE China: capital of Liaoning province: pop. 4,020,000

**She·ol** (shē′ōl′) ⟦Heb < ? *shaal*, to dig⟧ *Bible* a place in the depths of the earth conceived of as the dwelling of the dead

**Sher·brooke** (shur′brook′) city in S Quebec, Canada: pop. 76,000

**'s Her·to·gen·bosch** (ser′tō khən bôs′) city in SC Netherlands: capital of North Brabant province: pop. 78,000

**Sher·wood Forest** (shur′wood) forest in Nottinghamshire, England, made famous in the Robin Hood legends

**Shet·land** (shet'lənd) 〖ON *Hjaltland*〗 region of NE
Scotland, consisting of a group of islands (**Shetland
Islands**) in the Atlantic, northeast of the Orkney
Islands: 551 sq. mi. (1,427 sq. km); pop. 23,000

**Shi·be·li** (shə bel'ē) river in E Africa, flowing from SE
Ethiopia through Somalia into a swamp near the Juba
River: *c.* 1,200 mi. (1,932 km)

**Shi·jia·zhuang** (shu'jyä'jwäŋ') city in Hebei province,
NE China: pop. 1,118,000: old form **Shih'chia'chuang**

**Shi·ko·ku** (shē'kô kōō') island of Japan, south of Honshu: *c.* 6,860 sq. mi. (17,768 sq. km)

**Shi·loh** (shī'lō) 〖after an ancient town in Israel: see
Josh. 18:1〗 national military park in SW Tenn., on
the Tennessee River: scene of a Civil War battle (1862)

**Shi·mo·no·se·ki** (shē'mô nô sä'kē) seaport at the SW
tip of Honshu, Japan: pop. 262,000

**Shi·nar** (shī'när) region mentioned in the Bible, prob.
corresponding to Sumer, in Babylonia

**Ship** the constellation Argo

**Shi·raz** (shē räz') city in SC Iran: pop. 426,000

**Shi·re** (shē're) river in SE Africa, flowing from Lake
Malawi south into the Zambezi: *c.* 250 mi. (402 km)

**Shires, the** the counties of EC England, esp. Cambridgeshire & Lincolnshire

**Shi·zu·o·ka** (shē'zōō ô'kä) city on the S coast of Honshu, Japan: pop. 463,000

**Sho·la·pur** (shō'lə poor') city in Maharashtra state, W
India: pop. 514,000

**Sho·sho·ne** (shō shō'nē) river in NW Wyo., flowing
northeast into the Bighorn River: *c.* 100 mi. (160 km)

**Shoshone Falls** waterfall on the Snake River, in S Ida.:
*c.* 200 ft. (61 m)

**Shreve·port** (shrēv'pôrt') 〖after H. M. *Shreve* (1785-
1851), Mississippi River steamboat captain〗 city in
NW La.: pop. 199,000

**Shrews·bur·y** (shrōōz'ber'ē, shrōz'-; -bə rē) city in
Shropshire, W England: pop. 51,000

**Shrop·shire** (shräp'shir', -shər) county of W England:
1,347 sq. mi. (3,488 sq. km); pop. 388,000; county seat,
Shrewsbury

**Shu·shan** (shōō'shän') *Biblical name of* SUSA

**Si** (shē) *old form of* XI

**Si·al·kot** (sē äl'kōt) city in the Punjab region of NE
Pakistan: pop. 296,000

**Si·am** (sī am′) **1** *old name of* THAILAND **2 Gulf of** *old name of* Gulf of THAILAND

**Si·an** (shē′än′) *old form of* XI'AN

**Siang** (shyäŋ) *old form of* XIANG

**Si·ber·i·a** (sī bir′ē ə) region in N Asia, between the Urals & the Pacific: Asian section of Russia: *c.* 5,000,000 sq. mi. (12,950,000 sq. km)

**Si·biu** (sē byōō′) city in central Romania: pop. 160,000

**Si·chuan** (sē′chwän′) province of SC China: 219,691 sq. mi. (569,000 sq. km); pop. 99,700,000; cap. Chengdu

**Si·ci·lia** (sē chēl′yä) *It. name of* SICILY

**Sicilies, Two** *see* TWO SICILIES

**Sic·i·ly** (sis′ə lē) **1** island of Italy, off its S tip **2** region of Italy, comprising this island & small nearby islands: 9,926 sq. mi. (25,709 sq. km); pop. 4,907,000; cap. Palermo

**Si·di-bel-Ab·bès** (sē′dē bel′ä bes′) city in NW Algeria, near Oran: pop. 187,000

**Si·don** (sīd′n) ⟦L < Gr *Sidōn* < Heb *tsidon* or Phoen *ṣdn*, prob. < or akin to Sem root *ṣyd*, to hunt, fish⟧ chief city of ancient Phoenicia: site of modern SAIDA

**Sid·ra** (sid′rə), **Gulf of** inlet of the Mediterranean, on the NC coast of Libya

**Sieg·fried line** (sig′frēd, sēg′-) a system of heavy fortifications built before World War II on the W frontier of Germany

**Si·en·a** (sē en′ə; *It* sye′nä) commune in Tuscany, central Italy: pop. 62,000

**Si·er·ra Le·one** (sē er′ə lē ōn′) country in W Africa, on the Atlantic, between Guinea & Liberia: formerly a British colony, it became independent & a member of the Commonwealth (1961): a republic since 1971: 27,925 sq. mi. (72,326 sq. km); pop. 3,354,000; cap. Freetown

**Si·er·ra Ma·dre** (sē er′ə mä′drä; *Sp* sye′rä mä′dre) mountain system of Mexico, consisting of three ranges bordering the central plateau: highest peak, Orizaba

**Si·er·ra Ne·vad·a** (sē er′ə nə vad′ə, -vä′də) ⟦Sp, lit., snowy range⟧ mountain range in E Calif.: highest peak, Mt. Whitney: also **the Sierras**

**Sik·kim** (sik′im) state, formerly a protectorate, of India, in the E Himalayas: 2,818 sq. mi. (7,299 sq. km); pop. 316,000; cap. Gangtok

**Si·le·sia** (sī lē′shə, si-; -zhə) region in E Europe, on both sides of the upper Oder, mainly in what is now SW Poland

**Sil·i·con Valley** (sil′i kän′, -kən) ⟦after the principal material used for electronic chips ⟧ *name for* a valley in California, southeast of San Francisco, a center of high-technology activities, esp. ones involving microelectronics

**Si·lo·am** (si lō′əm, sī-) ⟦LL(Ec) < Gr(Ec) *Silōam* < Heb *shiloach*, lit., sending forth < *shalach*, to send⟧ *Bible* a spring and pool outside Jerusalem: John 9:7

**Sim·fe·ro·pol** (sim′fe rô′pôl y′) capital of the Crimea: pop. 331,000

**Si·mi Valley** (sē′mē) ⟦prob. < a Hokan place name ⟧ city in SW Calif., northwest of Los Angeles: pop. 100,000

**Sim·la** (sim′lə) capital of Himachal Pradesh, N India: pop. 56,000

**Sim·plon** (sim′plän′; *Fr* saṅ plôn′) **1** mountain pass in the Alps of S Switzerland: 6,589 ft. (2,008 m) **2** railway tunnel near this pass: 12.4 mi. (19.9 km) long

**Si·nai** (sī′nī′), **Mount** the mountain (probably in the S Sinai Peninsula but not identified) where Moses received the law from God: Ex. 19

**Sinai Peninsula** broad peninsula in NE Egypt, between the Gulf of Suez & the Gulf of Aqaba

**Si·na·lo·a** (sē′nä lô′ä) state of NW Mexico, on the Gulf of California: 22,582 sq. mi. (58,487 sq. km); pop. 1,849,000; cap. Culiacán

**Sind** (sind) province of Pakistan, in the lower Indus River valley: chief city, Karachi

**Sin·ga·pore** (siŋ′ə pôr′, -gə-) **1** island off the S tip of the Malay Peninsula **2** country comprising this island & nearby islets: a former British colony, it became a state of Malaysia (1963-65) & an independent republic & member of the Commonwealth (1965): 238 sq. mi. (616 sq. km); pop. 2,558,000 **3** its capital, a seaport on the S coast: pop. *c.* 2,000,000 **4 Strait of** channel between Singapore & a group of Indonesian islands to the south: 65 mi. (104 km) long: also **Singapore Strait**

**Sing Sing** (siŋ′ siŋ′) ⟦ < Du *Sintsing* < *Ossinsing*, earlier form of the village name, apparently < a Delaware word meaning "at the small stones"⟧ a N.Y. State penitentiary at Ossining

**Si·ning** (shē′niŋ′) *old form of* XINING

**Sin·kiang** (sin′kyaŋ′; *Chin* shin′jyäŋ′) *old form of* XIN-

JIANG

**Sin·tra** (sēn′trə, sin′-) city in W Portugal, northwest of Lisbon: pop. 225,000

**Si·on** (sī′ən) *var. of* ZION

**Sioux City** (sōō) city in W Iowa, on the Missouri River: pop. 81,000

**Sioux Falls** city in SE S.Dak.: pop. 101,000

**Si·ra·cu·sa** (sē′rä kōō′zä) *It. name of* SYRACUSE (the seaport in Sicily)

**Si·ret** (si ret′) river in SE Europe, flowing from the Carpathian mountains southeast into the Danube: 280 mi. (450 km)

**Sir·i·us** (sir′ē əs) ⟦ME < L < Gr *Seirios*, lit., scorcher⟧ a binary star in the constellation Canis Major, the brightest star in the sky, with a magnitude of -1.45; Dog Star

**Sis·tine Chapel** (sis′tēn, -tin) the principal chapel in the Vatican at Rome, famous for its frescoes by Michelangelo and other artists: built by order of Sixtus IV

**Sit·ka** (sit′kə) ⟦Tlingit *sheet'ka* < *ŝì·-t'i-ka*, on the seaward side of Baranof Island⟧ city in SE Alas., on Baranof Island: pop. 8,600

**Sit·twe** (sit′wē′) seaport in W Myanmar: pop. 143,000

**Si·vas** (sē väs′) city in central Turkey: pop. 173,000

**Sjæl·land** (shel′län) *Dan. name of* ZEALAND

**SK** *abbrev. for* Saskatchewan

**Ska·gen** (skä′yən), **Cape** The SKAW

**Skag·er·rak** (skag′ə rak′) arm of the North Sea, between Norway & Denmark: 150 mi. (241 km) long; 70-90 mi. (112-145 km) wide

**Skaw** (skô), **The** cape at the N tip of the Jutland peninsula, Denmark

**Ski·ros** (skē′rôs) Greek island of the N Sporades, in the Aegean Sea: *c.* 80 sq. mi. (207 sq. km)

**Sko·kie** (skō′kē) ⟦< ? AmInd⟧ village in NE Ill.: suburb of Chicago: pop. 59,000

**Sko·pje** (skô′pye) capital of MACEDONIA (the country): pop. 172,000: also **Skop·lje** (skôp′lye)

**Skye** (skī), **Isle of** island off the W coast of Scotland: largest of the Inner Hebrides: 643 sq. mi. (1,665 sq. km)

**Ský·ros** (skē′rôs) *alt. sp. of* SKÍROS

**Slave** river in NE Alberta & S Northwest Territories, Canada, flowing from Lake Athabasca northwest into

Great Slave Lake: 258 mi. (415 km)

**Slave Coast** W African coast between the Volta & Niger rivers, on the Bight of Benin: its ports were the former centers of the African slave trade

**Slav·kov** (släf′kôf) *Czech name of* AUSTERLITZ

**Sla·vo·ni·a** (slə vō′nē ə) region in S Europe bounded by the Sava, Drava, & Danube rivers

**Sles·vig** (sles′vikh) *Dan. name of* SCHLESWIG

**Sli·go** (slī′gō) **1** county in Connacht province, NW Ireland: 694 sq. mi. (1,798 sq. km); pop. 55,000 **2** its county seat: a seaport: pop. 17,000

**Slo·va·ki·a** (slō vä′kē ə, -vak′ē ə) country in central Europe: formerly the E constituent republic of Czechoslovakia: 18,933 sq. mi. (49,035 sq. km); pop. 5,310,154; cap. Bratislava

**Slo·ve·ni·a** (slō vē′nē ə, -vēn′yə) country in SE Europe: formerly a constituent republic of Yugoslavia (1946-91): 7,821 sq. mi. (20,256 sq. km); pop. 1,975,000; cap. Ljubljana

**Slo·ven·sko** (slô′ven skô′) *Czech name of* SLOVAKIA

**Smeth·wick** (smeth′ik) city in Staffordshire, central England, near Birmingham: pop. 56,000

**Smith·so·ni·an Institution** (smith sō′nē ən) institution & museum founded in 1846 in Washington, D.C. by a bequest of James Smithson (*c.* 1765-1829), Eng. scientist: branches of the Institution cover a wide range of fields in the arts and sciences: also, unofficially, **Smithsonian Institute**

**Smok·ies** (smō′kēz) GREAT SMOKY MOUNTAINS

**Smoky Hill** ⟦ named for the haze on the nearby hills ⟧ river flowing from E Colo. eastward through Kans., joining the Republican River to form the Kansas River: 540 mi. (869 km)

**Smoky Mountains** GREAT SMOKY MOUNTAINS

**Smo·lensk** (smō lensk′, smä-; *Russ* smô lyensk′) city in W European Russia, on the Dnepr: pop. 331,000

**Smyr·na** (smur′nə) *old name of* IZMIR

**Snake** ⟦ transl. (prob. erroneous) of earlier *Shoshone River* ⟧ river in NW U.S., flowing from Yellowstone National Park into the Columbia River in Wash.: 1,038 mi. (1,670 km)

**Sno·qual·mie Falls** (snō kwäl′mē) ⟦ < Salish tribal name ⟧ waterfall, 270 ft. (82.2 m), in WC Wash., on a river (**Snoqualmie**) that flows west out of the Cascades

**Snow·belt** (snō′belt′) that part of the U.S. comprising States of the Midwest and Northeast, characterized by cold, snowy winters: also **Snow Belt**

**Snow·don** (snōd′ʼn) mountain in NW Wales: highest peak, 3,560 ft. (1,085 m)

**So·che** (sō′che′) *old form of* SHACHE

**So·chi** (sô′chē) seaport & resort in S Russia, on the Black Sea: pop. 310,000

**Society Islands** ⟦so named (1769) by James Cook, Eng explorer⟧ group of islands in the South Pacific, constituting a division of French Polynesia: *c.* 650 sq. mi. (1,683 sq. km); pop. 142,000; chief town, Papeete

**So·co·tra** (sō kō′trə) island of the Republic of Yemen, in the Indian Ocean, off the E tip of Africa: 1,400 sq. mi. (3,625 sq. km); pop. *c.* 12,000

**Sod·om** (säd′əm) ⟦LL(Ec) *Sodoma* < Gr(Ec) < Heb *sedom*⟧ *Bible* a city destroyed by fire together with a neighboring city, Gomorrah, because of the sinfulness of the people: Gen. 18-19

**So·fi·a** (sō′fē ə, sō fē′ ə; *Bulg* sô′fē yä′) capital of Bulgaria, in the W part: pop. 1,173,000: also sp. **So′fi·ya′**

**Sog·di·a·na** (säg′dē an′ə) ancient region in central Asia, between the Oxus & Jaxartes rivers

**So·ho** (sō′hō′, sō hō′) district in Westminster, central London

**So·Ho** (sō′hō′) ⟦< *so(uth of) Ho(uston)* (street in Manhattan), prob. echoing *Soho* (see prec.)⟧ district in the lower west side of Manhattan: noted as a center for artists, art galleries, etc.

**So·ko·tra** (sō kō′trə) *alt. sp. of* SOCOTRA

**So·lent** (sō′lənt), **The** W part of the channel between the Isle of Wight & the mainland of Hampshire, England: *c.* 15 mi. (24 km) long: the E part is called *Spithead*

**So·leure** (sô lër′) *Fr. name of* SOLOTHURN

**So·li·mões** (sô′li moins′) the upper Amazon, between the Peruvian border & the Negro River

**So·ling·en** (zō′liŋ ən) city in W Germany, in the Ruhr Basin, in the state of North Rhine-Westphalia: pop. 175,000

**Sol·o·mon Islands** (säl′ə mən) **1** country on a group of islands in the SW Pacific, east of New Guinea: formerly a British protectorate, it became independent (1978): *c.* 11,500 sq. mi. (29,785 sq. km); pop. 283,000; cap. Honiara **2** group of islands including both the islands of this country and Bougainville, Buka, and other islands belonging to Papua New Guinea: *c.* 16,000 sq. mi. (41,438 sq. km)

**So·lo·thurn** (zō′lô̅ toorn′) **1** canton of NW Switzerland: 305 sq. mi. (790 sq. km); pop. 218,000 **2** its capital: pop. 19,000

**Sol·way Firth** (säl′wā) arm of the Irish Sea, between England & Scotland: *c.* 40 mi. (64 km) long

**So·ma·li·a** (sō mä′lē ə, sə-; -mäl′yə) country of E Africa, on the Indian Ocean & the Gulf of Aden: formed by merger of British Somaliland & Italian Somaliland (1960): 246,201 sq. mi. (637,658 sq. km); pop. 7,825,000; cap. Mogadishu

**So·ma·li·land** (sō mä′lē land′, sə-) region in E Africa, including NE Somalia, Djibouti, & E Ethiopia

**Som·er·set** (sum′ər set′) ⟦OE *Sumersaete*, contr. < *Sumortun sæte*, lit., the people of Somerton (< *sumor*, summer + *tun*, town) + *sæte*, residents, pl. of *sæta*, akin to *sæti*, seat⟧ county of SW England, on Bristol Channel: 1,335 sq. mi. (3,458 sq. km); pop. 441,000; county seat, Taunton: also **Som′er·set·shire′** (-shir′, -shər)

**Som·er·ville** (sum′ər vil′) ⟦? after Capt. R. *Somers* (1778-1804)⟧ city in E Mass.: suburb of Boston: pop. 76,000

**Somme** (sum; *Fr* sôm) river in N France: *c.* 150 mi. (241 km)

**Song·hua** (sooŋ′hwä′) river in Manchuria, NE China, flowing into the Amur River: *c.* 1,150 mi. (1,850 km)

**So·no·ra** (sô nô′rä) state of NW Mexico, on the Gulf of California & the S Ariz. border: 70,484 sq. mi. (182,552 sq. km); pop. 1,513,000; cap. Hermosillo

**Soo** (soō) ⟦alteration of *Sault*⟧ region in N Mich. & S Ontario, Canada, at the St. Marys Falls Canals, including the city of Sault Ste. Marie

**Soo·chow** (soō′chou′; *Chin* soō′jō′) *old form of* SUZHOU

**Soo Locks** locks of St. Marys Falls Canals

**Sor·bonne** (sôr bän′; *Fr* sôr bôn′) ⟦Fr, after the founder, Robert de *Sorbon* (1201-74), chaplain of Louis IX of France⟧ **1** orig., a theological college in Paris, established about the middle of the 13th cent. **2** the University of Paris; specif., the seat of the faculties of letters and science

**Sor·ren·to** (sə ren′tō; *It* sôr ren′tô) resort town in S

Italy, on the Bay of Naples: pop. 13,000

**Sos·no·wiec** (sôs nô′vyets) city in SW Poland: pop. 252,000

**Sound** (sound), **The** ÖRESUND

**South, the** that part of the U.S. which is bounded on the north by the southern border of Pa., the Ohio River, and the eastern and northern borders of Mo.; specif., in the Civil War, the Confederacy

**South Africa** country in southernmost Africa: until 1961, as the **Union of South Africa**, a member of the Commonwealth: 472,358 sq. mi. (1,223,000 sq. km); pop. 33,241,000; caps. Cape Town (legislative), Pretoria (administrative), & Bloemfontein (judicial)

**South African Republic** *old name of* TRANSVAAL

**South America** S continent in the Western Hemisphere: *c.* 6,881,000 sq. mi. (17,823,000 sq. km); pop. 241,000,000

**South·amp·ton** (south amp′tən, south hamp′-) **1** seaport in S England, on an inlet (**Southampton Water**) of The Solent: pop. 209,000 **2** ⟦after Henry Wriothesley (1573-1624), 3d Earl of *Southampton*⟧ island in N Hudson Bay, Canada: 15,700 sq. mi. (40,660 sq. km)

**South Australia** state of SC Australia: 380,070 sq. mi. (984,000 sq. km); pop. 1,347,000; cap. Adelaide

**South Bend** ⟦from its being at a southernmost bend in the St. Joseph River⟧ city in N Ind.: pop. 106,000

**South Carolina** ⟦see CAROLINA¹⟧ Southern State of the SE U.S., on the Atlantic: one of the 13 original States: 31,055 sq. mi. (80,432 sq. km); pop. 3,487,000; cap. Columbia: abbrev. *SC* or *S.C.*

**South China Sea** arm of the W Pacific, touching Taiwan, the Philippines, Borneo, the Malay Peninsula, Indochina, & China: *c.* 895,000 sq. mi. (2,318,000 sq. km)

**South Dakota** ⟦see DAKOTA⟧ Middle Western State of the NC U.S.: admitted, 1889; 77,047 sq. mi. (199,550 sq. km); pop. 696,000; cap. Pierre: abbrev. *SD, S.D.,* or *S Dak*

**South Downs** *see* DOWNS, the

**Southeast, the** the southeastern part of the U.S.

**Southeast Asia** region comprising the Malay Archipelago, the Malay Peninsula, & Indochina

**South·end-on-Sea** (south′end′än sē′) seaport in Essex, SE England, on the Thames estuary: pop. 157,000

**Southern Alps** mountain range on South Island, New Zealand: highest peak, Mt. Cook

**Southern Cross** the constellation Crux

**Southern Crown** the constellation Corona Australis

**Southern Hemisphere** that half of the earth south of the equator

**Southern Ocean** that part of the Indian Ocean south of Australia: name used by Australians

**Southern Province** province of Saudi Arabia, on the Red Sea: *c.* 40,130 sq. mi. (103,937 sq. km)

**Southern Rhodesia** *old name of* ZIMBABWE

**Southern Sporades** SPORADES (islands along Turkish coast)

**Southern Up·lands** (up'ləndz) hilly moorland region in S Scotland, between the English border & the Lowlands

**Southern Yemen** *old name of* YEMEN (People's Democratic Republic)

**South·field** (south'fēld') [descriptive] city in SE Mich.: suburb of Detroit: pop. 76,000

**South Gate** [after *South Gate Gardens* south of Los Angeles] city in SW Calif.: suburb of Los Angeles: pop. 86,000

**South Georgia** island in the South Atlantic: former dependency of the Falkland Islands: 1,600 sq. mi. (4,143 sq. km)

**South Glamorgan** county of S Wales: 160 sq. mi. (416 sq. km); pop. 395,000

**South Holland** province of the W Netherlands, on the North Sea: 1,121 sq. mi. (2,905 sq. km); pop. 3,151,000; cap. The Hague

**South Island** S island of the two main islands of New Zealand: 59,439 sq. mi. (153,946 sq. km); pop. 850,000

**South Orkney Islands** group of British islands in the South Atlantic, southeast of South America: 240 sq. mi. (621 sq. km)

**South Platte** river flowing from central Colo. through W Nebr., joining the North Platte to form the Platte: 424 mi. (682 km)

**South Pole** the place on the earth where its northern rotational axis intersects its surface: in full **South Terrestrial Pole**

**South·port** (south'pôrt') city in Merseyside, NW England, on the Irish Sea: pop. 90,000

**South San Francisco** city in W Calif.: pop. 54,000

**South Saskatchewan** river flowing from SW Alberta east & northeast through Saskatchewan, joining the North Saskatchewan to form the Saskatchewan: 865 mi. (1,392 km)

**South Sea Islands** islands in temperate or tropical parts of the South Pacific

**South Seas 1** the South Pacific **2** all the seas south of the equator

**South Shetland Islands** group of British islands in the South Atlantic, south of South America: 1,800 sq. mi. (4,661 sq. km)

**South Shields** seaport in N England, on the Tyne estuary, in the county of Tyne and Wear: pop. 93,000

**South·wark** (su*th*ʹərk) borough of Greater London, England: pop. 221,000

**Southwest, the** the southwestern part of the U.S., esp. Okla., Tex., N.Mex., Ariz., and S Calif.

**South West Africa** *old name of* NAMIBIA

**South Yorkshire** county of N England: 602 sq. mi. (1,560 sq. km); pop. 1,305,000

**So·vi·et Union** (sōʹvē ət) UNION OF SOVIET SOCIALIST REPUBLICS: also **Soviet Russia**

**Spain** (spān) ⟦ME *Spaine,* aphetic < Anglo-Fr *Espaigne* < OFr < LL *Spania,* for L *Hispania* (prob. infl. by Gr *Spania*)⟧ country in SW Europe, on the Iberian peninsula: 194,346 sq. mi. (503,354 sq. km); pop. 39,000,000; cap. Madrid: Sp. name ESPAÑA

**Span·ish America** (spanʹish) Mexico and those countries in Central and South America and islands in the Caribbean in which Spanish is the chief language

**Spanish Guinea** *old name of* EQUATORIAL GUINEA

**Spanish Main 1** orig., the coastal region of the Americas along the Caribbean Sea; esp., the N coast of South America between the Isthmus of Panama & the mouth of the Orinoco **2** later, the Caribbean Sea itself, or that part of it adjacent to the N coast of South America, traveled in the 16th-18th cent. by Spanish merchant ships, which were often harassed by pirates

**Spanish Morocco** the former Spanish zone of Morocco, constituting a coastal strip along the Mediterranean

**Spanish Sahara** *old name of* WESTERN SAHARA

**Spar·ta** (spärtʹə) ancient city in the S Peloponnesus,

Greece, a powerful military city in Laconia

**Spar·tan·burg** (spärt′′n burg′) 〚after the "Spartan Regiment" raised there in the Am Revolution〛 city in NW S.C.: pop. 43,000

**Spezia** *see* LA SPEZIA

**Sphinx** (sfiŋks) a huge statue having the body of a lion and the head of a man, at Gîza, near Cairo, Egypt

**Spi·ca** (spī′kə) the brightest star in the constellation Virgo, with a magnitude of 1.03

**Spice Islands** (spīs) *old name of* MOLUCCAS

**Spit·head** (spit′hed′) *see* SOLENT, The

**Spits·ber·gen** (spits′bur′gən) **1** group of Norwegian islands in the Arctic Ocean, constituting the major part of Svalbard: 23,658 sq. mi. (61,273 sq. km) **2** SVALBARD

**Split** (splēt) seaport in Croatia, on the Adriatic: pop. 235,000

**Spo·kane** (spō kan′) 〚< ? Salish *spokanee,* sun〛 city in E Wash.: pop. 177,000

**Spo·le·to** (spə lāt′ō) commune in central Italy, near Perugia: pop. 37,000

**Spo·ra·des** (spôr′ə dēz; *Gr* spô *rä*′thes) **1** all the Greek islands in the Aegean Sea except the Cyclades **2** the Greek islands along the W coast of Turkey, esp. the Dodecanese: also *Southern Sporades* See also NORTHERN SPORADES

**Spree** (shprā) river in E Germany, flowing northwest through Berlin into the Havel: c. 250 mi. (402 km)

**Spring·field** (spriŋ′fēld′) 〚first sense after *Springfield,* village in Essex, England: others prob. after first sense〛 **1** city in SW Mass., on the Connecticut River: pop. 157,000 (met. area 530,000) **2** city in SW Mo.: pop. 140,000 **3** capital of Ill., in the central part: pop. 105,000 **4** city in WC Ohio: pop. 70,000

**Spuy·ten Duy·vil** (spīt′′n dī′vəl) 〚Du, lit., spouting devil, nickname for a dangerous ford〛 ship canal between N Manhattan Island & the mainland, connecting the Hudson & Harlem rivers

**Squaw Valley** (skwô) 〚?〛 valley in the Sierra Nevada Mountains, E Calif., near Lake Tahoe: a ski resort

**Sri Lan·ka** (srē läŋ′kə) country coextensive with an island off the SE tip of India: a former British colony, it became independent & a member of the Commonwealth (1948): a republic since 1972: 24,959 sq. mi.

(64,643 sq. km); pop. 14,850,000; cap. Colombo

**Sri·nag·ar** (srē nug′ər) city in W Kashmir, on the Jhelum River: summer capital of Jammu & Kashmir: pop. 533,000

**Staf·ford** (staf′ərd) **1** county seat of Staffordshire, in the central part: pop. 63,000 **2** STAFFORDSHIRE

**Staf·ford·shire** (-shir′, -shər) county of WC England: 1,049 sq. mi. (2,716 sq. km); pop. 1,019,000; county seat, Stafford

**Staked Plain** *see* LLANO ESTACADO

**St. Al·bans** (ôl′bənz) city in Hertfordshire, SE England: pop. 55,000

**Sta·lin·a·bad** (stä′li nä bät′) *old name of* DUSHANBE

**Sta·lin·grad** (stä′lin grät′; *E* stä′lin grad′) *old name of* VOLGOGRAD

**Sta·li·no** (stä′li nô′) *old name of* DONETSK

**Sta·linsk** (stä′linsk) *old name of* NOVOKUZNETSK

**Stam·boul, Stam·bul** (stäm bōōl′) **1** *old name of* ISTANBUL **2** the old section of Istanbul

**Stam·ford** (stam′fərd) ⟦after *Stamford*, town in NE England⟧ city in SW Conn.: pop. 108,000

**Stan·ley** (stan′lē), **Mount** mountain in EC Africa, highest peak of the Ruwenzori group: 16,795 ft. (5,119 m)

**Stanley Falls** series of seven cataracts of the upper Congo River, just south of Kisangani

**Stanley Pool** broad, lakelike expansion of the Congo River between Congo & Zaire: *c.* 320 sq. mi. (828 sq. km)

**Stan·ley·ville** (stan′ lē vil′) *old name of* KISANGANI

**Sta·ra Za·go·ra** (stä′rä zä gô′rä) city in central Bulgaria: pop. 130,000

**star of Bethlehem** *Bible* the bright star over Bethlehem at the birth of Jesus, guiding the Magi: Matt. 2:1-10

**Stat·en Island** (stat′′n) ⟦< Du *Staaten Eylandt*, States Island, referring to the States-General of the Dutch Republic⟧ **1** island in New York Bay: 60 sq. mi. (155 sq. km) **2** borough of New York City, comprising this island & small nearby islands: pop. 379,000

**States, the** the United States

**Statue of Liberty** a colossal copper statue personifying Liberty in the form of a crowned woman holding a torch in her upraised hand: it was given to the U.S. by France and is located on Liberty Island in New York harbor: official name *Liberty Enlightening the World*

**St. Au·gus·tine** (ô′gəs tēn′) ⟦after *St. Augustine* (of Hippo)⟧ seaport in NE Fla.: oldest city (founded 1565) in the U.S.: pop. 12,000

**Sta·vang·er** (stä vaŋ′ər) seaport in SW Norway, on the North Sea: pop. 92,000

**Stav·ro·pol** (stäv′rô pôl′y’) city in Russia, in the N Caucasus: pop. 293,000

**St. Bernard** *see* GREAT ST. BERNARD PASS and LITTLE ST. BERNARD PASS

**St. Bon·i·face** (bän′ə fəs) city in S Manitoba, Canada: pop. 43,000

**St. Cath·ar·ines** (kath′ər inz) city in SE Ontario, Canada, on the Welland Canal: pop. 124,000

**St. Chris·to·pher** (kris′tə fər) ST. KITTS

**St. Clair** (kler) ⟦after Fr *Sainte Claire* (St. Clare of Assisi, 1194-1253)⟧ **1 Lake** lake between SE Mich. & Ontario, Canada: 460 sq. mi. (1,191 sq. km) **2** river between Mich. & Ontario, connecting this lake & Lake Huron: 40 mi. (65 km)

**St. Clair Shores** city in SE Mich., on Lake St. Clair: suburb of Detroit: pop. 68,000

**St-Cloud** (sa*n* klōō′) city in NC France: suburb of Paris: pop. 26,000

**St. Cloud** (sānt kloud) ⟦after prec.⟧ city in central Minn., on the Mississippi: pop. 49,000

**St. Croix** (krɔi) ⟦Fr, holy cross⟧ **1** largest island of the Virgin Islands of the U.S.: 80 sq. mi. (208 sq. km); pop. 50,000 **2** river flowing from NW Wis. south along the Wis.-Minn. border into the Mississippi: *c.* 165 mi. (265 km)

**St-De·nis** (sa*n*d nē′) **1** city in NC France: suburb of Paris: pop. 94,000 **2** capital of Réunion Island: pop. 126,000

**Ste-Anne-de-Beau·pré** (sānt an′də bō prā′; *Fr* sa*n* tán də bō prā′) village in S Quebec, Canada, on the St. Lawrence: site of a Rom. Catholic shrine (established 1620): pop. 3,300

**Stei·er·mark** (shtī′ər märk′) *Ger. name of* STYRIA

**St. E·li·as** (ə lī′əs) **1** range of the Coast Ranges, in SW Yukon & SE Alas.: highest peak, Mt. Logan **2 Mount** mountain in this range, on the Canada-Alas. border: 18,008 ft. (5,488 m)

**Step·ney** (step′nē) former metropolitan borough of E London, now part of Tower Hamlets

**Ster·ling Heights** (stur'lin) ⟦after A. W. *Sterling,* early settler⟧ city in SE Mich.: suburb of Detroit: pop. 118,000

**St-É·tienne** (san tā tyen') city in SE France: pop. 207,000

**Stet·tin** (shte tēn') *Ger. name of* SZCZECIN

**Stew·art** (stōō'ərt, styōō'-) island of New Zealand, just south of South Island: 670 sq. mi. (1,735 sq. km)

**St. Gal·len** (gäl'ən) **1** canton of NE Switzerland, on the Rhine: 777 sq. mi. (2,014 sq. km); pop. 392,000 **2** its capital, in the N part: pop. 74,000 Fr. name **St–Gall** (san gál')

**St. George's Channel** strait between Ireland & Wales, connecting the Irish Sea with the Atlantic: *c.* 100 mi. (160 km) long

**St. Gott·hard** (gät'ərd, gäth'-) **1** mountain group in the Lepontine Alps, SC Switzerland: highest peak, 10,490 ft. (3,198 m) **2** pass through these mountains: *c.* 6,935 ft. (2,114 m) high Fr. name **St–Got·hard** (san gô tár')

**St. He·le·na** (hə lē'nə, hel'ə nə) **1** British island in the South Atlantic, *c.* 1,200 mi. (1,931 km) from Africa: site of Napoleon's exile (1815-21): 47 sq. mi. (121 sq. km); pop. 5,500 **2** British colony including this island, Ascension, & the Tristan da Cunha group: *c.* 120 sq. mi. (310 sq. km); pop. 5,800

**St. Hel·ens** (hel'ənz), **Mount** ⟦after Baron A. F. *St. Helens* (1753-1839), Brit diplomat⟧ volcanic mountain in the Cascade Range, SW Wash.: dormant since 1857, it erupted in 1980: 8,364 ft. (2,549 m)

**Stir·ling** (stur'lin) former county of central Scotland, now in the region called Central: also **Stir'ling·shire'** (-shir', -shər)

**St. James's Palace** palace in Westminster, London: the royal residence from 1697 to 1837

**St. John 1** island of the Virgin Islands of the U.S.: 20 sq. mi. (52 sq. km); pop. 3,500 **2 Lake** lake in SC Quebec, Canada: 321 sq. mi. (831 sq. km): Fr. name **Lac St–Jean** (lák san zhän')

**St. Johns** river in E & NE Fla., flowing into the Atlantic near Jacksonville: 276 mi. (444 km)

**St. John's 1** capital of Newfoundland: seaport on the SE coast: pop. 76,000 (met. area 121,000) **2** seaport & chief town of Antigua, on the N coast: capital of Antigua and Barbuda: pop. 25,000

**St. Joseph** ⟦after *St. Joseph*, husband of Mary⟧ city in
NW Mo., on the Missouri River: pop. 72,000

**St. Kitts** (kits) island of St. Kitts and Nevis: 65 sq. mi.
(169 sq. km); pop. 50,500

**St. Kitts and Nevis** country in the Leeward Islands of
the West Indies, consisting of two islands, St. Kitts
and Nevis: formerly a British colony, it became an
independent state (1983) & a member of the Commonwealth; cap. Basseterre

**St-Lau·rent** (san lô rän′) city in SW Quebec, Canada,
on Montreal Island: suburb of Montreal: pop. 64,000

**St. Lawrence** ⟦[ < Fr *St. Laurent*, Rom. martyr (died A.D.
258) ]⟧ **1** river flowing from Lake Ontario northeast
into the Gulf of St. Lawrence: *c.* 750 mi. (1,206 km) **2**
**Gulf of** large inlet of the Atlantic in E Canada: *c.*
100,000 sq. mi. (259,000 sq. km)

**St. Lawrence Seaway** inland waterway for oceangoing
ships, connecting the Great Lakes with the Atlantic:
operated jointly by the U.S. & Canada, it consists of
the Welland Canal, the St. Lawrence River, & several
locks & canals between Montreal & Lake Ontario

**St. Lou·is** (lo͞o′is, lo͞o′ē) ⟦prob. after *Louis* IX of France⟧
city & port in E Mo., on the Mississippi: pop. 397,000
(met. area 2,444,000)

**St. Louis Park** ⟦prob. after *Louis* IX of France⟧ city in
SE Minn.: pop. 44,000

**St. Lu·ci·a** (lo͞o′shē ə, -shə; lo͞o sē′ə) country on an island
of the Windward group, West Indies, south of Martinique: a former British colony, it became independent
& a member of the Commonwealth (1979): 238 sq. mi.
(616 sq. km); pop. 120,000; cap. Castries

**St-Ma·lo** (san mà lô′) **1** seaport & resort town on an
island in the Gulf of St-Malo, NW France: pop. 47,000
**2 Gulf of** inlet of the English Channel, on the N coast
of Brittany, NW France, *c.* 60 mi. (97 km) wide

**St. Martin** island of the Leeward group, West Indies,
south of Anguilla: the N part belongs to Guadeloupe,
the S part to the Netherlands Antilles: 33 sq. mi. (88
sq. km); pop. 23,000: Fr. name **St-Mar·tin** (san màr
tan′), Du. name **St. Maar·ten** (sint märt′'n)

**St. Mar·y·le·bone** (mer′i lə bōn′) former metropolitan
borough of London: since 1965, part of Westminster

**St. Marys 1** river flowing from the Okefenokee Swamp

along the Ga.-Fla. border into the Atlantic: *c.* 180 mi.
(289 km) **2** river flowing from Lake Superior into
Lake Huron, between NE Mich. & Ontario, Canada:
63 mi. (101 km)

**St. Marys Falls Canals** three ship canals (two U.S., one
Canadian) bypassing a rapids of the St. Marys River
at Sault Ste. Marie

**St. Mo·ritz** (sänt′ mō rits′; *Fr* san mô *r*ēts′) mountain
resort town in SE Switzerland: pop. 5,900

**St-Na·zaire** (san nə zer′) seaport in NW France, at the
mouth of the Loire: pop. 69,000

**Stock·holm** (stäk′hōm′, -hōlm′; *Swed* stôk′hôlm′) capital
of Sweden: seaport on the Baltic Sea: pop. 635,000
(met. area 1,420,000)

**Stock·port** (stäk′pôrt′) city in NW England, in the
county of Greater Manchester: pop. 141,000

**Stock·ton** (stäk′tən) ⟦after R. F. *Stockton* (1795-1866),
U.S. naval officer⟧ city in central Calif.: pop. 211,000

**Stock·ton-on-Tees** (-än tēz′) seaport in N England, on
the Tees River: pop. 83,000

**Stoke New·ing·ton** (stōk nōō′iŋ tən) former metropolitan borough of London, now part of Hackney

**Stoke-on-Trent** (stōk′än trent′) city in Staffordshire,
WC England, on the Trent River: pop. 253,000

**Stone·henge** (stōn′henj′) ⟦ME *stonheng* < *ston,* stone
+ OE *henge,* (something) hanging⟧ a circular arrange-
ment of prehistoric megaliths on Salisbury Plain, England, probably set up in the Neolithic period

**Stone Mountain** ⟦descriptive⟧ mountain near Atlanta,
Ga., on which a huge Confederate memorial is carved:
*c.* 2,000 ft. (609 m) high

**Stones** river in central Tenn., flowing into the Cumberland: *c.* 60 mi. (97 km)

**Stony Point** ⟦descriptive⟧ village in SE N.Y., on the
Hudson: site of a British fort in the Revolutionary
War

**St-Ouen** (san twän′) city in NC France, on the Seine:
suburb of Paris: pop. 52,000

**St. Paul** ⟦after the Apostle *Paul*⟧ capital of Minn., on
the Mississippi: pop. 272,000: see MINNEAPOLIS

**St. Pe·ters·burg** (pēt′ərz bʉrg′) **1** seaport in NW Russia, on the Gulf of Finland: former capital of the Russian Empire (1712-1917): pop. 4,867,000: see
LENINGRAD, PETROGRAD **2** ⟦after the Russian city⟧

city in WC Fla., on Tampa Bay: pop. 239,000: see TAMPA

**St-Pierre** (san pyer′) town in NW Martinique, West Indies, on the site of a city destroyed (1902) by eruption of Mount Pelée: pop. 6,000

**St. Pierre and Mi·que·lon** (san pē ər′ ən mik′ə län′) French overseas department in the Atlantic, south of Newfoundland, consisting of the islands of St. Pierre, c. 10 sq. mi. (25 sq. km) & Miquelon & six islets: 93 sq. mi. (240 sq. km); pop. 6,000

**Straits Settlements** former British crown colony in SE Asia, comprising Singapore, Malacca, Penang, Labuan, Christmas Island, & the Cocos Islands

**Stras·bourg** (stras′bɛrg; *Fr* sträz bo͞or′) city & port in NE France, on the Rhine: pop. 252,000

**Strat·ford** (strat′fərd) ‖ after fol. ‖ town in SW Conn., on Long Island Sound: suburb of Bridgeport: pop. 49,000

**Strat·ford-on-A·von** (-än ā′vän) town in S Warwickshire, England, on the Avon River: birthplace & burial place of Shakespeare: pop. 25,000: also **Stratford-up·on-Avon**

**Strath·clyde** (strath klīd′) region of SW Scotland, on the Firth of Clyde, including the former counties of Ayr, Lanark, Renfrew, and most of Dunbarton & Argyll: 5,348 sq. mi. (13,856 sq. km); pop. 2,373,000; cap. Glasgow

**Street, the** WALL STREET

**Stri·mon** (strē mỗn′) *Gr. name of* STRUMA

**Strom·bo·li** (strôm′bô lē′) **1** northernmost of the Lipari Islands, north of Sicily, c. 5 sq. mi. (12 sq. km) **2** active volcano on this island: 3,040 ft. (927 m)

**Stru·ma** (stro͞o′mä) river in SE Europe, flowing from W Bulgaria across NE Greece into the Aegean Sea: c. 220 mi. (354 km)

**St. Thomas** second largest island of the Virgin Islands of the U.S.: 32 sq. mi. (82 sq. km); pop. 48,000

**St-Tro·pez** (san trô pā′) commune and seaside resort in SE France, on the Mediterranean: pop. 4,500

**Stutt·gart** (stut′gärt; *Ger* shto͞ot′gärt) city in SW Germany: capital of the state of Baden-Württemberg: pop. 563,000

**St. Vincent** island of the Windward group in the West Indies: 133 sq. mi. (345 sq. km)

**St. Vincent and the Grenadines** country consisting of

St. Vincent & the N Grenadines: formerly a British colony, it became independent & a member of the Commonwealth (1979): 150 sq. mi. (388 sq. km); pop. 108,000; cap. Kingstown

**Styr** (stir) river in NW Ukraine & S Belarus, flowing north into the Pripet River: *c.* 290 mi. (467 km)

**Styr·i·a** (stir′ē ə) region of central & SE Austria: Ger. name STEIERMARK

**Styx** (stiks) [L < Gr, lit., the Hateful, orig., icy cold, prob. akin to Russ *stygnut'*, to freeze, grow stiff] *Gr. Myth.* the river encircling Hades over which Charon ferries the souls of the dead

**Su·chow** (shōō′jō′) *old form of* XUZHOU

**Su·cre** (sōō′kre) city in SC Bolivia: legal capital & seat of the judiciary: pop. 58,000: cf. LA PAZ

**Su·dan** (sōō dan′, -dän′) **1** vast semiarid region in NC Africa, south of the Sahara, extending from the Atlantic to the Red Sea **2** country in the E part of this region, south of Egypt: formerly a British & Egyptian condominium called ANGLO-EGYPTIAN SUDAN, it became an independent republic (1956): 967,500 sq. mi. (2,505,815 sq. km); pop. 20,000,000; cap. Khartoum  Often preceded by *the*

**Sud·bur·y** (sud′ber′ē, -bər ē) city in SE Ontario, Canada: pop. 89,000

**Su·de·ten** (sōō dāt′′n; *Ger* zōō dā′tən) **1** SUDETES MOUNTAINS **2** SUDETENLAND

**Su·de·ten·land** (-land′; *Ger,* -länt′) region in the Sudetes Mountains, N Czech Republic: annexed by Germany (1938): returned to Czechoslovakia (1945): *c.* 8,900 sq. mi. (23,050 sq. km)

**Su·de·tes Mountains** (sōō dēt′ēz) mountain range along the borders of N Czech Republic & SW Poland: highest peak, 5,259 ft. (8,463 m)

**Su·ez** (sōō ez′, sōō′ez) **1** seaport in NE Egypt, on the Suez Canal: pop. 193,000 **2 Gulf of** N arm of the Red Sea: *c.* 180 mi. (290 km) long **3 Isthmus of** strip of land connecting Asia & Africa, between the Mediterranean & the Gulf of Suez: narrowest point, 72 mi. (116 km)

**Suez Canal** ship canal across the Isthmus of Suez, joining the Mediterranean & the Gulf of Suez: *c.* 107 mi. (172 km) long

**Suf·folk** (suf′ək) **1** county of E England, on the North

Sea: 1,467 sq. mi. (3,800 sq. km); pop. 616,000; county seat, Ipswich **2** ⟦ after the English county ⟧ city in SE Va.: pop. 52,000

**Sugar Loaf Mountain** granite mountain at the entrance to the harbor of Rio de Janeiro: 1,296 ft. (395 m)

**Suisse** (süēs) *Fr. name of* SWITZERLAND

**Su·la·we·si** (sō͞o′lä wä′sē) *Indonesian name of* CELEBES

**Su·lu Archipelago** (sō͞o′lō͞o) group of islands in the Philippines, southwest of Mindanao: 1,038 sq. mi. (2,688 sq. km); pop. 427,000

**Sulu Sea** arm of the W Pacific, between the SW Philippines & NE Borneo

**Su·ma·tra** (sō͞o mä′trə) large island of Indonesia, just south of the Malay Peninsula: *c.* 165,000 sq. mi. (427,333 sq. km); pop. (with small nearby islands) 28,000,000

**Sum·ba** (sō͞om′bə) island of Indonesia, west of Timor & south of Flores: *c.* 4,300 sq. mi. (11,130 sq. km)

**Sum·ba·wa** (sō͞om bä′wä) island of Indonesia, between Lombok & Flores: *c.* 5,500 sq. mi. (14,200 sq. km)

**Su·mer** (sō͞o′mər) ancient region in the lower valley of the Euphrates River

**summer triangle** a group of three first-magnitude stars (Deneb, Vega, and Altair) visible during the summer in the N skies

**Sumter, Fort** *see* FORT SUMTER

**Sunbelt** that part of the U.S. comprising most of the States of the South and the Southwest, characterized by a warm, sunny climate and regarded as an area of rapid population and economic growth: also **Sun Belt**

**Sun City** ⟦ descriptive ⟧ city in SW central Ariz.: pop. 38,000

**Sun·da Islands** (sun′də; *Du* sō͞on′dä) group of islands in the Malay Archipelago, consisting of two smaller groups: **Greater Sunda Islands** (Sumatra, Java, Borneo, Celebes, & small nearby islands) & **Lesser Sunda Islands** (Bali & islands stretching east through Timor)

**Sun·der·land** (sun′dər lənd) seaport in N England, on the North Sea: pop. 299,000

**Sun·flow·er State** (sun′flou′ər) *name for* KANSAS

**Sun·ga·ri** (sō͞oŋ′gä rē′) *old form of* SONGHUA

**Sun·ny·vale** (sun′ē väl′) ⟦ descriptive ⟧ city in W Calif.: suburb of San Jose: pop. 117,000

**Suo·mi** (swô′mē) *Finn. name of* FINLAND

**Su·pe·ri·or** (sə pir′ē ər), **Lake** ⟦orig. so called in Fr (*Supérieur*), from its position above Lake Huron⟧ largest & westernmost of the Great Lakes, between Mich. & Ontario, Canada: 32,483 sq. mi. (84,130 sq. km)

**Su·ra·ba·ja**, **Su·ra·ba·ya** (soo′rä bä′yä) seaport in NE Java, Indonesia, opposite Madura: pop. 2,028,000

**Su·ra·kar·ta** (soo′rä kär′tä) city in central Java, Indonesia: pop. 470,000

**Su·rat** (soo rat′, soor′ət) seaport in Gujarat state, W India, on the Arabian Sea: pop. 913,000

**Su·ri·name** (soor′i näm′, soor′i nam′; *Du* soor′ə nä′mə) country in NE South America: a former territory of the Netherlands, it became an independent republic (1975): 63,036 sq. mi. (163,265 sq. km); pop. 381,000; cap. Paramaribo: earlier **Su′ri·nam′** (-näm′, soor′ə nam′)

**Sur·rey** (sur′ē) county of SE England: 638 sq. mi. (1,652 sq. km); pop. 1,014,000

**Su·sa** (soo′sä) capital of ancient Elam, now a ruined city in W Iran

**Sus·que·han·na** (sus′kwi han′ə) ⟦< earlier *Sasquesahanough*, name of an Iroquoian tribe in an unidentified Eastern Algonquian language < name of the river: meaning of name unknown⟧ river flowing from central N.Y. through Pa. & Md. into Chesapeake Bay: 444 mi. (715 km)

**Sus·sex** (sus′iks) ⟦ME *Suth-sæxe* < OE *Suth-Seaxe*, South Saxon (land or people)⟧ **1** former Anglo-Saxon kingdom in SE England: see HEPTARCHY, THE **2** former county in SE England, on the English Channel: now divided into two counties: EAST SUSSEX & WEST SUSSEX

**Suth·er·land** (su*th*′ər lənd) former county of N Scotland, now in the region of Highland: also **Suth′er·land·shire′** (-shir′, -shər)

**Sut·lej** (sut′lej) river flowing from SW Tibet across the Punjab into the Indus River in Pakistan: *c.* 900 mi. (1,448 km)

**Sut·ter's Mill** (sut′ərz) a mill, owned by John Sutter (1803-80), northeast of Sacramento, Calif.: discovery of gold near there led to the gold rush of 1849

**Sut·ton** (sut′n) borough of S Greater London, England: pop. 170,000

**Su·va** (sōō′vä) capital of the Fiji Islands: seaport on Viti Levu Island: pop. 71,000

**Su·wan·nee** (sə wän′ē, swä′-) ⟦ < Creek < Sp *San Juan,* name of a Sp mission on the river ⟧ river flowing from the Okefenokee Swamp across N Fla. into the Gulf of Mexico: *c.* 250 mi. (402 km)

**Su·zhou** (sü′jō′) city in S Jiangsu province, E China, on the Grand Canal: pop. 635,000

**Sval·bard** (sväl′bär) group of Norwegian islands, including Spitsbergen, in the Arctic Ocean, between Greenland & Franz Josef Land: 23,979 sq. mi. (62,106 sq. km)

**Sverd·lovsk** (sferd lôfsk′) *old name* (1924-91) *of* YEKATERINBURG

**Sve·ri·ge** (sve′rē ə) *Swed. name of* SWEDEN

**Swa·bi·a** (swā′bē ə) region in SW Germany, formerly a duchy: Ger. name SCHWABEN

**Swan** the constellation Cygnus

**Swa·nee** (swä′nē) *var. of* SUWANNEE

**Swan·sea** (swän′sē, -zē) seaport in West Glamorgan, S Wales, on Bristol Channel: pop. 170,000

**Swat** (swät) region in NE Pakistan, on the Indus River: a former princely state of India

**Swat·ow** (swä′tou′) *old form of* SHANTOU

**Swa·zi·land** (swä′zē land′) country in SE Africa, surrounded on three sides by South Africa: a former British protectorate, it became an independent kingdom & member of the Commonwealth (1968): 6,705 sq. mi. (17,365 sq. km); pop. 626,000; cap. Mbabane

**Swe·den** (swēd′′n) country in N Europe, in the E part of the Scandinavian Peninsula: 173,620 sq. mi. (449,674 sq. km); pop. 8,320,000; cap. Stockholm: Swed. name SVERIGE

**Swit·zer·land** (swit′sər lənd) country in WC Europe, in the Alps: 15,941 sq. mi. (41,287 sq. km); pop. 6,365,000; cap. Bern: Ger. name SCHWEIZ, Fr. name SUISSE

**Syb·a·ris** (sib′ə ris) ancient Greek city in S Italy, famed as a center of luxury: destroyed 510 B.C.

**Syd·ney** (sid′nē) seaport in SE Australia: capital of New South Wales: pop. (met. area) 3,300,000

**Sy·e·ne** (sī ē′nē) *ancient name of* ASWAN

**Syr·a·cuse** (sir′ə kyōōs′, -kyōōz′) **1** ⟦ after the seaport in Sicily ⟧ city in central N.Y.: pop. 164,000 (met. area

660,000) **2** seaport on the SE coast of Sicily: in ancient times, a Greek city-state: pop. 119,000: It. name SIRACUSA

**Syr Dar·ya** (sir där′yä) river in central Asia, flowing from the Tian Shan Mountains into the Aral Sea: *c.* 1,700 mi. (2,736 km)

**Syr·i·a** (sir′ē ə) **1** region of ancient times at the E end of the Mediterranean **2** country in the NW part of this region, south of Turkey: formerly a French mandate, it became an independent republic (1944-58); united with Egypt to form the UNITED ARAB REPUBLIC (1958-61); union dissolved (1961); 71,227 sq. mi. (184,480 sq. km); pop. 10,900,000; cap. Damascus

**Syz·ran** (siz′rän) city in SE European Russia, on the Volga, near Samara: pop. 173,000

**Szcze·cin** (shche tsēn′) river port in NW Poland, on the Oder: pop. 390,000

**Sze·chwan** (se′chwän′; *Chin* su′-) *old form of* SICHUAN

**Sze·ged** (se′ged) city in SE Hungary, at the junction of the Mures & Tisza rivers: pop. 175,000

# T

**Ta·bas·co** (tə bas′kō; *Sp* tä bäs′kô) state of SE Mexico, west of Yucatán: 9,783 sq. mi. (25,337 sq. km); pop. 1,062,000; cap. Villahermosa

**Tab·er·nac·le** (tab′ər nak′əl) the Jewish Temple

**Table Mountain** flat-topped mountain in SE Cape Province, South Africa: 3,549 ft. (1,082 m)

**Ta·bor** (tā′bər), **Mount** mountain in N Israel, east of Nazareth: *c.* 1,900 ft. (579 m)

**Ta·briz** (tä brēz′) city in NW Iran: pop. 598,000

**Tac·na** (täk′nə, tak′-) **1** city in S Peru: pop. 43,000 **2** region in S Peru which, with an adjacent region (ARICA) in Chile, was divided between the two countries in 1929

**Ta·co·ma** (tə kō′mə) ⟦< ? AmInd⟧ seaport in W Wash., on Puget Sound: pop. 177,000

**Ta·dzhik Soviet Socialist Republic** (tä′jik′, tä jik′) a republic of the U.S.S.R.: now TAJIKISTAN

**Tae·gu** (tī′go͞o′, tī go͞o′) city in SE South Korea: pop. 2,012,000

**Tae·jon** (tī′jän′, tī jän′) city in EC South Korea: pop. 842,000

**Ta·gan·rog** (tä'gən räg'; *Russ* tä'gän rôk') seaport in SW Russia, on the Sea of Azov, near Rostov: pop. 289,000

**Ta·gus** (tä'gəs) river flowing west across central Spain & Portugal into the Atlantic through a broad estuary: *c.* 600 mi. (966 km): Sp. name Tajo, Port. name Tejo

**Ta·hi·ti** (tə hēt'ē) ⟦ < Proto-Polynesian *\*tafiti*, distant, remote ⟧ one of the Society Islands, in the South Pacific: *c.* 402 sq. mi. (1,042 sq. km); pop. 116,000; chief town, Papeete

**Ta·hoe** (tä'hō), **Lake** ⟦ < Washo (a Hokan language) *dá?aw*, lake ⟧ lake between Calif. & Nev.: a resort: 193 sq. mi. (499 sq. km)

**Tai·chung** (tī' cho͞oŋ') city in WC Taiwan: pop. 660,000

**Tai·myr Peninsula** (tī mir') large peninsula in N Asian Russia, between the Kara & Laptev seas: *c.* 700 mi. (1,126 km) wide at its base: also sp. **Tay·myr'**, **Tai·mir'**, or **Tay·mir'**

**Tai·nan** (tī nän') city in SW Taiwan: pop. 633,000

**Tai·pei, Tai·peh** (tī pā') capital of Taiwan, in the N part: pop. 2,500,000

**Tai·wan** (tī wän') **1** island of China, off the SE coast: a Japanese territory (1895-1945) **2** province of China coextensive with this island: together with the Pescadores Islands and Quemoy Island it forms the Republic of China, the Kuomintang (Nationalist) government since 1949: 13,885 sq. mi. (35,962 sq. km); pop. 14,118,000; cap. Taipei

**Taiwan Strait** strait between Taiwan & Fujian province, China, joining the East & South China seas: *c.* 100 mi. (160 km) wide

**Tai·yu·an** (tī'yo͞o än') city in N China: capital of Shanxi province: pop. 1,750,000

**Ta·jik·i·stan** (tä jik'i stan', -stän') country in WC Asia: became independent upon the breakup of the U.S.S.R. (1991): 55,240 sq. mi. (143,071 sq. km); pop. 4,400,000; cap. Dushanbe: formerly, *Tadzhik Soviet Socialist Republic*

**Taj Ma·hal** (täzh' mə häl', täj'-) ⟦Pers, best of buildings ⟧ famous mausoleum at Agra, India, built (*c.* 1630-*c.* 1648) by Shah Jahan for his favorite wife

**Ta·jo** (tä'hō) *Sp. name of* Tagus

**Tal·ca** (täl'kä') city in central Chile: pop. 138,000

**Tal·ca·hua·no** (täl'kä wä'nō) seaport in SC Chile, near Concepción: pop. 209,000

**Ta·lien** (täl yen', däl-) *old form of* DALIAN

**Tal·la·has·see** (tal'ə has'ē) 〚< Creek *talwahasi* < *talwa*, town + *hasi*, old〛 capital of Fla., in the N part: pop. 125,000

**Tal·linn** (täl'in) capital of Estonia, on the Gulf of Finland: pop. 465,000: also sp. **Tal'lin**

**Ta·mau·li·pas** (tä'mou lē'päs) state of NE Mexico, on the Gulf of Mexico: 30,734 sq. mi. (79,000 sq. km); pop. 1,935,000

**Tam·bov** (täm bôf') city in central European Russia, southeast of Moscow: pop. 296,000

**Tamil Na·du** (tam'əl nä'do͞o, nä do͞o'; täm'-, tum'-) state of S India: 50,331 sq. mi. (130,356 sq. km); pop. 48,297,000; cap. Madras

**Tam·pa** (tam'pə) 〚Sp < name of a town of the Calusa, an extinct Indian people of S Florida〛 seaport in WC Fla., on an arm (**Tampa Bay**) of the Gulf of Mexico: pop. 280,000 (met. area with Clearwater & St. Petersburg, 2,068,000)

**Tam·pe·re** (täm'pə re') city in SW Finland: pop. 167,000

**Tam·pi·co** (täm pē'kō) seaport in E Mexico, in Tamaulipas state: pop. 268,000

**Ta·na** (tä'nə) **1** lake in N Ethiopia: source of the Blue Nile: *c.* 1,400 sq. mi. (3,625 sq. km) **2** river in E Kenya, flowing southeast into the Indian Ocean: *c.* 500 mi. (804 km)

**Tan·a·gra** (tan'ə grə, tə näg'rə) ancient Greek town in Boeotia, known for the terra cotta figurines made there

**Tan·a·na** (tan'ə nä', -nô') river in E Alas., flowing northwest into the Yukon River: 800 mi. (1,287 km)

**Ta·na·na·rive** (tə nan'ə rēv'; *Fr* tà nà nà rēv') *old name of* ANTANANARIVO

**Tan·gan·yi·ka** (tan'gən yē'kə) **1** mainland region of Tanzania, on the E coast of Africa: a former British territory, it became a member of the Commonwealth as an independent republic (1961): united with Zanzibar to form Tanzania (1964): 361,800 sq. mi. (937,058 sq. km) **2 Lake** lake in EC Africa, between Tanganyika & Zaire: 12,700 sq. mi. (32,892 sq. km)

**Tan·gier** (tan jir') seaport in N Morocco, on the Strait of Gibraltar: pop. 215,000: formerly part of an internationalized zone: Fr. name **Tan·ger** (tän zhā')

**Tang·shan** (täŋ shän', däŋ-) city in Hebei province, NE

China, near Tianjin: pop. 1,200,000

**Ta·nis** (tā′nis) city in ancient Egypt, in the Nile delta: probable capital of the Hyksos kings

**Tan·ta** (tän′tə) city in N Egypt, in the center of the Nile delta: pop. 278,000

**Tan–tung** (tän′ toon′, dän doon′) *old form of* DANDONG

**Tan·za·ni·a** (tan′zə nē′ə) country in E Africa, formed by the merger of Tanganyika & Zanzibar (1964): it is a member of the Commonwealth: 362,820 sq. mi. (939,700 sq. km); pop. 19,730,000; cap. Dodoma

**Ta·os** (tä′ōs, tous) ⟦Sp (orig. pl.) < Taos (a Tanoan language) *tôotʰo*, pueblo name, lit., in the village⟧ resort town in N N.Mex.: pop. 4,000

**Ta·pa·jós, Ta·pa·joz** (tä′pə zhôsh′, -zhôs′) river in N Brazil, flowing northeast into the Amazon: *c.* 500 mi. (804 km): with principal headstream, *c.* 1,200 mi. (1,931 km)

**Ta·ran·to** (tä′rän tō′; *also* tə rant′ō) ⟦L *Tarentum* < Gr *Taras*, said to be named after *Taras*, son of Poseidon⟧ 1 seaport in SE Italy, on the Gulf of Taranto: pop. 244,000 2 **Gulf** of arm of the Ionian Sea, in SE Italy: *c.* 85 mi. (136 km) long

**Ta·ra·wa** (tə rä′wə; tär′ə wə) coral atoll in the WC Pacific, near the equator: capital of Kiribati: 7.5 sq. mi. (19.4 sq. km); pop. 22,000

**Ta·ren·tum** (tə rent′əm) *ancient name of* TARANTO

**Tar·heel State** (tär′hēl′) *name for* NORTH CAROLINA

**Ta·rim** (tä rēm′, dä-) river in NW China flowing from the Tian Shan into E Xinjiang region: *c.* 1,300 mi. (2,092 km)

**Tar·shish** (tär′shish′) seaport or maritime region of uncertain location, mentioned in the Bible: cf. 1 Kings 10:22

**Tar·sus** (tär′səs) city in S Turkey, near the Mediterranean: in ancient times, the capital of Cilicia & birthplace of the Apostle Paul: pop. 51,000

**Tar·ta·rus** (tär′tə rəs) ⟦L < Gr *Tartaros*⟧ *Gr. Myth.* 1 an infernal abyss below Hades, where Zeus hurls the rebel Titans, later a place of punishment for the wicked after death 2 HADES (sense 1)

**Tar·ta·ry** (tärt′ər ē) *var. of* TATARY

**Tar·tu** (tär′tōō) city in E Estonia: pop. 106,000

**Tash·kent** (tash kent′, täsh-) capital of Uzbekistan, on a branch of the Syr Darya: pop. 2,030,000

**Tas·ma·ni·a** (taz mā′nē ə, -mān′yə) **1** island south of Victoria, Australia: *c.* 24,450 sq. mi. (63,325 sq. km) **2** state of Australia comprising this island & smaller nearby islands: 26,383 sq. mi. (68,331 sq. km); pop. 427,000; cap. Hobart

**Tas·man Sea** (taz′mən) section of the South Pacific, between SE Australia & New Zealand

**Ta·tar Strait** (tät′ər) strait between Sakhalin Island & the Asia mainland: *c.* 350 mi. (563 km) long

**Ta·ta·ry** (tät′ə rē) vast region in Europe & Asia under the control of Tatar tribes in the late Middle Ages: its greatest extent was from SW Russia to the Pacific

**Ta·tra Mountains** (tä′trə) range of the Carpathian Mountains in N Slovakia & S Poland: highest peak, 8,737 ft. (2,663 m)

**Taun·ton** (tônt′'n, tänt′'n) **1** ⟦after the English city⟧ city in SE Mass.: pop. 50,000 **2** county seat of Somerset, SW England: pop. 56,000

**Tau·rus** (tô′rəs) ⟦ME < L bull, ox⟧ **1** a N constellation between Aries and Orion containing the Hyades and the Pleiades star clusters, the Crab nebula, and Aldebaran **2** the second sign of the zodiac, entered by the sun about April 21

**Taurus Mountains** mountain range along the S coast of Asia Minor, Turkey: highest peak, *c.* 12,250 ft. (3,735 m)

**Tax·co** (täks′kō) city in Guerrero state, S Mexico: resort & silver manufacturing center: pop. 64,000

**Tay** (tā) **1** river in EC Scotland, flowing into the North Sea: *c.* 120 mi. (193 km) **2 Firth of** estuary of this river: 25 mi. (33 km)

**Tay·lor** (tā′lər) ⟦after Zachary *Taylor* (1784-1850), U.S. president⟧ city in SE Mich.: suburb of Detroit: pop. 71,000

**Tay·side** (tā′sīd′) region of EC Scotland, on the Firth of Tay, including the former counties of Angus, Clackmannan, Kinross, & most of Perth

**Tbi·li·si** (tə bi′lē sē′; tu′bi lē′sē; tə bil′i sē′) capital of Georgia, on the Kura River: pop. 1,158,000

**Tees** (tēz) river in N England, flowing into the North Sea: 70 mi. (112 km)

**Te·gu·ci·gal·pa** (te gōō′sē gäl′pä) capital of Honduras, in the SC part: pop. 533,000

**Teh·ran** (te rän′, tə-; -ran′) capital of Iran, in the NC part: pop. 4,530,000: also **Te·he·ran** (te rän′, tǝ-; te′ǝ rän′, te′he rän′; -ran′)

**Te·huan·te·pec** (tǝ wänt′ǝ pek′) 1 Gulf of arm of the Pacific, off the S coast of Mexico: *c.* 300 mi. (483 km) wide 2 **Isthmus** of narrowest part of Mexico, between this gulf & the Gulf of Campeche: *c.* 125 mi. (201 km) wide

**Tei·de** (tād′ǝ), **Pi·co de** (pē′kō dǝ) volcanic mountain on Tenerife, Canary Islands: *c.* 12,200 ft. (3,718 m)

**Te·jo** (te′zhōō) *Port. name of* TAGUS

**Tel A·viv** (tel′ ǝ vēv′) seaport in W Israel, incorporating the former city of Jaffa: pop. 394,000

**Tel·e·sco·pi·um** (tel′ǝ skō′pē ǝm) a S constellation between Sagittarius and Pavo

**Tel·lus** (tel′ǝs) 〚 L < *tellus*, earth 〛 *Rom. Myth.* the goddess of the earth: identified with the Greek Gaea

**Tem·pe** (tem pē′; *also* tem′pē; *for 2* tem′pē) 〚 after the sacred Greek valley 〛 1 city in SC Ariz., on the Salt River: suburb of Phoenix: pop. 142,000 2 **Vale of** valley of the Piniós River in NE Thessaly, Greece, between Mounts Olympus & Ossa: anciently regarded as sacred to Apollo

**Tem·per·ate Zone** (tem′pǝr it; *often*, -prit) either of the two zones of the earth (**North Temperate Zone** and **South Temperate Zone**) between the tropics and the polar circles

**Tem·ple** (tem′pǝl) 〚 after Maj. B. M. *Temple*, construction engineer for the railroad (1880-81) 〛 city in central Tex., south of Waco: pop. 46,000

**Temple Bar** a former London gateway before the Temple buildings: the heads of executed traitors and criminals were exhibited on it

**Ten·der·loin** (ten′dǝr loin′) a former district in New York City, in which there was much graft and corruption: so called because regarded as a choice assignment for police seeking graft

**Ten·e·dos** (ten′ǝ däs′) *ancient name of* BOZCAADA

**Te·ne·ri·fe** (ten′ǝ rē′fä, -rēf′; *Sp* te′ne rē′fe) largest island of the Canary Islands: 795 sq. mi. (2,059 sq. km)

**Teng·ri Nor** (teŋ′rē nôr′, teŋ′grē-) NAM CO

**Tenn** *abbrev. for* Tennessee

**Ten·nes·see** (ten′ǝ sē′) 〚 < *Tanasi*, Cherokee village name 〛 1 EC State of the U.S.: admitted, 1796; 42,244 sq. mi. (109,412 sq. km); pop. 4,877,000; cap. Nashville: abbrev. *TN* or *Tenn* 2 river flowing from NE Tenn. through N Ala. & W Tenn. into the Ohio River: 652 mi. (1,005 km)

**Te·pic** (tä pēk′) city in Nayarit state, W Mexico: pop. 177,000

**Ter·cei·ra** (tər sā′rə) island of the central Azores: 153 sq. mi. (396 sq. km)

**Te·re·zi·na** (ter′ə zē′nə) city in NE Brazil, on the Parna-íba River: capital of Piauí state: pop. 339,000

**Ter·ni** (ter′nē) commune in central Italy, northeast of Rome: pop. 112,000

**Ter·re Haute** (ter′ə hōt′) [Fr, lit., high land] city in W Ind., on the Wabash: pop. 57,000

**Tes·sin** (*Fr* tä san′; *Ger* te sēn′) *Fr. & Ger. name of* TICINO

**Te·thys** (tē′this) [L < Gr *Tēthys*] 1 a satellite of Saturn having long trenchlike valleys and sharing its orbit with other satellites 2 a hypothetical ancient sea and geosyncline that separated Laurasia from Gondwana

**Te·tu·án** (te′tōō än′, -twän′) seaport in NE Morocco, on the Mediterranean: former cap. of Spanish Morocco: pop. 364,000

**Teu·to·burg Forest** (tōōt′ə bʉrg′, tyōōt′-) region of low, forested mountains, mostly in North Rhine-Westphalia, Germany: highest point, *c.* 1,500 ft. (450 m): Ger. name **Teu·to·bur·ger Wald** (toi′tŏ boor′gər vält′)

**Te·ve·re** (te′ve re) *It. name of* TIBER

**Tewkes·bur·y** (tyōōks′bə rē, -brē; tōōks′-; -ber′ē) town in N Gloucestershire, England, on the Severn: site of a battle (1471) in the Wars of the Roses, reestablishing Edward IV on the English throne: pop. 9,500

**Tex** *abbrev. for* Texas

**Tex·ar·kan·a** (teks′är kan′ə, -ər-) [< TEX(AS), ARK(AN-SAS), (LOUISI)ANA] city on the Tex.-Ark. border, having a separate municipal government in each State: pop. (Tex.) 32,000, (Ark.) 23,000

**Tex·as** (teks′əs) [Sp *Texas*, earlier pronounced (tä·shäs), orig. an ethnic name < Caddo *tayša*, friends, allies] SW State of the U.S., on the Gulf of Mexico & the Mexican border: admitted, 1845; 267,339 sq. mi. (692,405 sq. km); pop. 16,987,000; cap. Austin: abbrev. *TX* or *Tex*

**Texas City** [promotional name] city in SE Tex., on Galveston Bay: pop. 41,000

**Tey·de** (tād′ə), **Pi·co de** (pē′kō də) *alt. sp. of* Pico de
TEIDE

**Thai·land** (tī′land′; -lənd) **1** country in SE Asia, on the
Indochinese & Malay peninsulas: 198,456 sq. mi.
(514,000 sq. km); pop. 50,100,000; cap. Bangkok:
abbrev. **Thai 2 Gulf of** arm of the South China Sea,
between the Malay & Indochinese peninsulas

**Thames** (temz; *for 3* thāmz, tāmz, temz) **1** river in S
England, flowing from Gloucestershire east through
London into the North Sea: 210 mi. (338 km) **2** ⟦after
the English river⟧ river in SE Ontario, Canada, flowing southwest into Lake St. Clair: 163 mi. (261 km) **3**
⟦after the English river⟧ estuary in SE Conn., flowing
south into Long Island Sound: 15 mi. (24 km)

**Thap·sus** (thap′səs) ancient town in N Africa: its site is
on the NE coast of Tunisia

**Thar Desert** (tär′, tʉr′) desert in NW India & E Pakistan

**Tha·sos** (thā′säs′, thä′sôs′) island of Greece in the N
Aegean, a part of Macedonia: *c.* 170 sq. mi. (440 sq.
km)

**Thebes** (thēbz) **1** ancient city in S Egypt, on the Nile,
on the site of modern Luxor and Karnak **2** chief city
of ancient Boeotia, EC Greece

**Ther·ma** (thʉr′mə) *ancient name of* SALONIKA

**Ther·mop·y·lae** (thər mäp′ə lē′) in ancient Greece, a
mountain pass in Locris, near an inlet of the Aegean
Sea: scene of a battle (480 B.C.) in which the Persians
under Xerxes destroyed a Spartan army under Leoni-
das

**Thes·sa·li·a** (thə säl′yə; the′sə lē′ə) *Gr. name of* THES-
SALY

**Thes·sa·lon·i·ca** (thes′ə län′i kə, -ə lō nī′kə) *ancient
name of* SALONIKA

**Thes·sa·lo·ni·ki, Thes·sa·lo·ni·ke** (thes′ä lô′nē′kē) *Gr.
name of* SALONIKA

**Thes·sa·ly** (thes′ə lē) region of E Greece, between the
Pindus Mountains & the Aegean Sea

**Thi·bet** (tə bet′) *alt. sp. of* TIBET

**Thon·bu·ri** (tun bʊr′ē, tän-; tän′bʊ̄ō rē′) city in Thailand, on the Chao Phraya River, opposite Bangkok:
pop. 628,000

**Thorn·ton** (thôrnt′′n) ⟦after Dan *Thornton*, gov. of
Colo. (1956)⟧ city in NE Colo., north of Denver: pop.

55,000

**Thou·sand Islands** (thou'zənd) group of over 1,500 islands in the St. Lawrence River at the outlet of Lake Ontario, some part of N.Y. State & some of Ontario, Canada

**Thousand Oaks** ⟦after the many *oak* trees there⟧ city in SW Calif., northwest of Los Angeles: pop. 104,000

**Thrace** (thrās) 1 ancient region in the E Balkan Peninsula 2 modern region in the SE Balkan Peninsula divided between Greece & Turkey

**Thu·le** (thoo′lē, thyoo′-; too′-, tyoo′-; *for 2* too′lē) ⟦L < Gr *Thoulē, Thylē*⟧ 1 among the ancients, the northernmost region of the world, possibly taken to be Norway, Iceland, Jutland, etc.: also *ultima Thule* 2 Eskimo settlement on the NW coast of Greenland: pop. *c.* 1,000: site of U.S. air base

**Thun** (toon) 1 city in central Switzerland, on the Aar River where it leaves the Lake of Thun: pop. 37,000 2 **Lake of** lake in Bern canton, central Switzerland: *c.* 18 sq. mi. (46 sq. km)

**Thun·der Bay** (thun′dər) ⟦after the bay on which it is located: the bay was named for the thunderbird of Indian legend⟧ city & port in W Ontario, Canada, on Lake Superior: formed in 1970 by the merger of Fort William and Port Arthur: pop. 118,000

**Thur·gau** (toor′gou′) canton of NE Switzerland, on Lake Constance: 388 sq. mi. (1,005 sq. km); pop. 183,000: Fr. name **Thur·go·vie** (tür gō vē′)

**Thu·rin·gi·a** (thoo rin′jē ə, thyoo-; -jə) state of central Germany: 5,985 sq. mi. (15,500 sq. km); pop. 2,500,000; cap. Erfurt: Ger. name **Thü·ring·en** (tü′riŋ ən)

**Thuringian Forest** forested mountain range in Thuringia, Germany: highest peak, 3,222 ft.: Ger. name **Thü·ring·er Wald** (tü′riŋ ər vält′)

**Thurs·day** (thurz′dā) Australian island in Torres Strait: 1.25 sq. mi. (3.23 sq. km)

**Ti·a Jua·na** (tē′ə wän′ə, -hwän′ə; *Sp* tē′ä hwä′nä) *old name of* Tijuana

**Tian·jin** (tyen jin′) seaport in NE China: capital of Hebei province: pop. 5,100,000

**Tian Shan** (tyen shän′) mountain system in central Asia, extending across Kyrgyzstan & Xinjiang, China, to the Altai Mountains: highest peak, 24,406 ft. (7,450 m)

**Ti·ber** (tī′bər) ⟦L *Tiberis*⟧ river in central Italy, flowing from the Apennines south through Rome into the Tyrrhenian Sea: *c.* 250 mi. (402 km): It. name TEVERE

**Ti·be·ri·as** (tī bir'ē əs), **Sea of** Sea of GALILEE

**Ti·bes·ti** (ti bes'tē) mountain group of the Sahara, mostly in NW Chad: highest peak, 11,204 ft. (3,414 m)

**Ti·bet** (ti bet') autonomous region of SW China, occupying a high plateau area north of the Himalayas: 471,660 sq. mi. (1,221,000 sq. km); pop. 1,892,000; cap. Lhasa

**Ti·bur** (tī'bər) *ancient name of* TIVOLI (Italian city)

**Ti·ci·no** (tē chē'nō) **1** canton of S Switzerland, on the Italian border: 1,085 sq. mi. (2,811 sq. km); pop. 265,000 **2** river flowing from this canton south into the Po River: *c.* 160 mi. (258 km)

**Ti·con·der·o·ga** (tī kän'dər ō'gə, tī'kän-), **Fort** [[Mohawk *tekontaró:ken*, lit., at the junction of two waterways]] former fort in NE N.Y., taken from the British by the Green Mountain Boys in 1775

**Tide·wa·ter** (tīd'wôt'ər) the eastern part of Virginia

**Tien Shan** (tyen shän') *alt. sp. of* TIAN SHAN

**Tien·tsin** (tyen tsin', tin-) *old name of* TIANJIN

**Ti·er·ra del Fue·go** (tē er'ə del fwā'gō) **1** group of islands at the tip of South America, separated from the mainland by the Strait of Magellan: they are divided between Argentina & Chile: *c.* 27,500 sq. mi. (71,225 sq. km) **2** chief island of this group, divided between Argentina & Chile: *c.* 18,500 sq. mi. (47,915 sq. km)

**Tif·lis** (tif'lis) *old name of* TBILISI

**Ti·gré** (tē grā') [[< ?]] region of N Ethiopia, on the Eritrea border

**Ti·gris** (tī'gris) river flowing from EC Turkey through Iraq, joining the Euphrates to form the Shatt-al-Arab: 1,150 mi. (1,850 km)

**Ti·jua·na** (tē wän'ə, -hwän'ə; *Sp* tē hwä'nä) city in Baja California, NW Mexico, on the U.S. border: pop. 461,000

**Til·burg** (til'bərg; *Du* til'bürkh) city in the S Netherlands, in North Brabant province: pop. 154,000

**Tim·buk·tu** (tim'buk tōō') *old name of* TOMBOUCTOU

**Ti·mi·şoa·ra** (tē'mē shwä'rə) city in the Banat region of W Romania: pop. 262,000

**Tim·mins** (tim'inz) city in NE Ontario, Canada, north of Sudbury: pop. 46,000

**Ti·mor** (tē′môr′, tē môr′, tī′môr′) island of Indonesia, in the SE Malay Archipelago: *c.* 13,000 sq. mi. (33,670 sq. km)

**Timor Sea** arm of the Indian Ocean, between Timor & the NW coast of Australia: *c.* 300 mi. (483 km) wide

**Tin Pan Alley** a district of New York, where there are many songwriters, publishers of popular music, etc.

**Tin·sel·town** (tin′səl toun′) *name for* HOLLYWOOD, California

**Tin·tag·el Head** (tin taj′əl) cape of NW Cornwall, England: legendary birthplace of King Arthur

**Tip·pe·ca·noe** (tip′i kə nōō′) ⟦earlier *Kithtipecanunk* < Miami *Kitapkwanunk* (exact form uncert.), lit., buffalo-fish place⟧ river in N Ind. flowing southwest into the Wabash: *c.* 180 mi. (289 km): scene of a battle (1811) in which U.S. forces under William Henry Harrison defeated a band of Tecumseh's Indians

**Tip·per·ar·y** (tip′ər er′ē) county of S Ireland, in Munster province: 1,643 sq. mi. (4,255 sq. km); pop. 138,000

**Ti·ra·na** (tə rän′ə) capital of Albania, in the central part: pop. 194,000: also **Ti·ra′në** (-rän′ə)

**Ti·rich Mir** (tir′ich mir′) mountain in N Pakistan: highest peak of the Hindu Kush: 25,230 ft. (7,690 m)

**Ti·rol** (ti rōl′, -räl′; tir′ōl′, -äl′) E Alpine region in W Austria & N Italy

**Tir·u·chi·ra·pal·li** (tir′ə chir′ə päl′ē, -pul′ē) city in Tamil Nadu state, S India: pop. 363,000

**Ti·sza** (tē′sə, -sä) river in E Europe, flowing from W Ukraine southwest through Hungary & Yugoslavia into the Danube: *c.* 800 mi. (1,287 km): Romanian name **Ti·sa** (tē′sə)

**Ti·tan** (tīt′ʼn) ⟦ME < L < Gr (pl. *Titanes*)⟧ the largest of the satellites of Saturn: the only one in the solar system known to have a permanent atmosphere

**Ti·ti·ca·ca** (tit′i kä′kə; *Sp* tē′tē kä′kä), **Lake** lake of South America, on the border of SE Peru & W Bolivia: *c.* 3,500 sq. mi. (9,064 sq. km); altitude, 12,500 ft. (3,810 m)

**Ti·to·grad** (tēt′ō grad′, -gräd′) *name* (1946-92) *of* PODGORICA

**Ti·vo·li** (tiv′əl ē) **1** city in central Italy, near Rome: pop. 43,000 **2** famous recreational & cultural garden center in Copenhagen, Denmark

**Tlax·ca·la** (tläs′käl′ə) state of central Mexico: 1,555 sq.

mi. (4,027 sq. km); pop. 557,000

**TN** *abbrev. for* Tennessee

**To·ba·go** (tō bā′gō, tə-) island in the West Indies, north-east of Trinidad: 116 sq. mi. (300 sq. km); pop. 40,000: see TRINIDAD

**To·bol** (tō′bôl′, tō bôl′; *Russ* tô bôl′yə) river in W Siberia, flowing from the S Urals into the Irtysh: 1,042 mi. (1,676 km)

**To·can·tins** (tō′kən tēns′; *Port* tô′kän tēnsh′, -tēns′) river flowing from central Brazil north into the Pará River: *c.* 1,700 mi. (2,735 km)

**To·gliat·ti** (tōl yät′ē) ⟦after P. *Togliatti* (1893-1964), It communist leader⟧ city in SE European Russia, near Samara: pop. 594,000

**To·go** (tō′gō) country in W Africa, on the Gulf of Guinea, east of Ghana: a former French mandate, it became independent (1960): 21,853 sq. mi. (56,560 sq. km); pop. 2,700,000; cap. Lomé

**To·go·land** (tō′gō land′) former German protectorate (until 1919); it was divided between France & Great Britain: the British part is now part of Ghana (since 1957), & the French part is now Togo (since 1958)

**To·ku·shi·ma** (tō′kōō shē′mə) seaport in E Shikoku, Japan, on the Inland Sea: pop. 252,000

**To·ky·o** (tō′kē ō′) capital of Japan: seaport on an inlet (**Tokyo Bay**) of the Pacific, on S Honshu: pop. 8,991,000 (met. area 11,620,000)

**To·le·do** (tə lēd′ō; *for 2, also Sp* tô lā′thô) **1** ⟦after the city in Spain⟧ city & port in NW Ohio, on Lake Erie: pop. 333,000 (met. area 614,000) **2** city in central Spain, on the Tagus River: pop. 44,000

**To·li·ma** (tə lē′mə; *Sp* tô lē′mä) volcanic mountain of the Andes, in WC Colombia: 16,207 ft. (4,940 m)

**To·lu·ca** (tə lōō′kə; *Sp* tô lōō′kä) **1** city in S Mexico; capital of Mexico state: pop. 357,000: in full **Toluca de Lerido 2** volcanic mountain near this city: 15,020 ft. (4,578 m)

**Tom·big·bee** (täm big′bē) ⟦< Choctaw, coffin maker < *itombi*, box, coffin + *ikbi*, maker: referring to burial boxes used by Choctaws⟧ river flowing from NE Miss. through Ala., joining the Alabama River to form the Mobile River: 409 mi. (658 km)

**Tom·bouc·tou** (tôn′bōōk tōō′; *Fr* tôn bōōk tōō′) town in central Mali, near the Niger River: pop. 21,000

**Tomsk** (tämsk) city in SW Siberia: pop. 475,000

**Ton·ga** (täŋ′gə) kingdom occupying a group of islands (**Tonga Islands**) in the SW Pacific, east of Fiji: a member of the Commonwealth: 289 sq. mi. (748 sq. km); pop. 98,700; cap. Nukualofa

**Ton·kin** (tän′kin) **1** historical region and former French protectorate in NE Indochina: the N part of Vietnam **2 Gulf of** arm of the South China Sea between Hainan Island & the coasts of S China & N Vietnam

**Ton·le Sap** (tän′lä säp′, -sap′) **1** lake in central Cambodia: area varies from 1,000-9,500 sq. mi. (2,500-24,000 sq. km) according to season **2** river flowing from this lake into the Mekong River: *c.* 70 mi. (113 km)

**To·pe·ka** (tə pē′kə) ⟦prob. < Kansa (a Siouan language) *toppik'e*, lit., dig good Indian potatoes⟧ capital of Kans., in the NE part, on the Kansas River: pop. 120,000

**To·phet, To·pheth** (tō′fet′) ⟦ME < Heb *tofet*⟧ **1** *Bible* a place near Jerusalem where human sacrifices were made to Molech: 2 Kings 23:10 **2** hell

**To·ri·no** (tə rē′nō; *It* tô rē′nô) *It. name of* TURIN

**To·ron·to** (tə ränt′ō) ⟦< an Iroquoian language: meaning unknown⟧ capital of Ontario, Canada: port on Lake Ontario: pop. 633,000 (met. area 3,000,000)

**Tor·rance** (tôr′əns) ⟦after Jared S. *Torrance*, local landowner⟧ city in SW Calif.: suburb of Los Angeles: pop. 133,000

**Tor·rens** (tôr′ənz), **Lake** shallow salt lake in SE South Australia: *c.* 2,230 sq. mi. (5,775 sq. km)

**Tor·re·ón** (tôr′ē ōn′; *Sp* tôr *r*ā ôn′) city in NC Mexico, in Coahuila state: pop. 364,000

**Tor·res Strait** (tör′iz) strait between New Guinea & NE Australia: *c.* 95 mi. (152 km) wide

**Torrid Zone** the area of the earth's surface between the Tropic of Cancer & the Tropic of Capricorn, divided by the equator

**Tor·to·la** (tôr tō′lə) chief island of the British Virgin Islands: 21 sq. mi. (54 sq. km); pop. 9,000

**Tor·tu·ga** (tôr tōō′gə) island of Haiti, off the NW coast: *c.* 70 sq. mi. (181 sq. km): pop. 14,000: Fr. name **La Tortue** (lä tôr tü′)

**To·ruń** (tō′rōōn′; *Pol* tô′rōōn yə) city in NC Poland, on the Vistula: pop. 183,000

**Tos·ca·na** (tôs kä′nə; *It* tôs kä′nä) *It. name of* TUSCANY

**Tot·ten·ham** (tät′′n əm) city in Middlesex, SE England: suburb of London: pop. 113,000

**Tou·lon** (tōō lōn′; *E* tōō lōn′, -län′) seaport in SE France, on the Mediterranean: pop. 182,000

**Tou·louse** (tōō lōōz′) city in S France, on the Garonne river: pop. 354,000

**Tou·raine** (tōō rān′, too-; *Fr* tōō ren′) historical region of WC France: chief city, Tours

**Tour·coing** (tōōr kwan′) city in N France, near the Belgian border: pop. 97,000

**Tour·nai** (tōōr ne′) city in W Belgium: pop. 67,000

**Tours** (toor; *Fr* tōōr) city in WC France, on the Loire: site of a battle (A.D. 732) in which the Franks under Charles Martel defeated the Saracens: pop. 136,000

**Tower Hamlets** borough of E Greater London: pop. 145,000

**Tower of London** a fortress made up of several buildings on the Thames in London, serving in historic times as a palace, prison, etc.

**Towns·ville** (tounz′vil′) seaport on the E coast of Queensland, Australia: pop. 104,000

**Tow·son** (tou′sən) ‖after the *Towson* family, early settlers‖ town in central Maryland, near Baltimore: pop. 49,000

**To·ya·ma** (tō yä′mə) seaport on the N coast of central Honshu, Japan: pop. 309,000

**To·yo·ha·shi** (tō′yō hä′shē) seaport on the S coast of Honshu, Japan: pop. 315,000

**To·yo·na·ka** (tō′yō nä′kə) city in S Honshu, Japan, near Osaka: pop. 398,000

**To·yo·ta** (tō yōt′ə, toi ōt′ə) city in S Honshu, Japan, near Nagoya: pop. 294,000

**Trab·zon** (trab zän′, trab′zän′) *Turk. name of* TREBIZOND

**Tra·fal·gar** (trə fal′gər; *Sp* trä′fäl gär′), **Cape** cape on the SW coast of Spain, between Cádiz & the Strait of Gibraltar: site of a naval battle (1805) in which Nelson's British fleet defeated Napoleon's fleet

**Tra·lee** (trə lē′) county seat of Kerry, SW Ireland: pop. 16,000

**Trans·cau·ca·sia** (trans′kô kā′zhə) the region directly south of the Caucasus Mountains, containing the Asian countries of Armenia, Azerbaijan, & Georgia

**Trans·jor·dan** (trans jôrd′′n, tranz-) *old name for* JOR-

DAN: also **Trans′jor·da′ni·a**

**Trans·kei** (trans kā′, -kī′) homeland of the Xhosa nation in E Cape Province, South Africa: granted independence in 1976: 16,500 sq. mi. (42,735 sq. km); pop. *c.* 2,500,000; cap. Umtata

**Trans·vaal** (trans väl′, tranz-) province of South Africa, in the NE part: 109,621 sq. mi. (283,917 sq. km); pop. 8,350,000; cap. Pretoria: see SOUTH AFRICAN REPUBLIC

**Tran·syl·va·ni·a** (tran′sil vā′nē ə, -vān′yə) plateau region in central & NW Romania: *c.* 24,000 sq. mi. (62,159 sq. km); chief city, Cluj

**Transylvanian Alps** range of the Carpathian Mountains, in central & SW Romania, between Transylvania & Walachia: highest peak, 8,361 ft. (2,548 m)

**Tra·si·me·no** (traz′ə mē′nō, trä′zə-) lake in central Italy: scene of a victory by Hannibal over the Romans (217 B.C.): Latin name **Tra′si·me′nus** (-nəs)

**Trav·an·core** (trav′ən kôr′) former native state of SW India: now part of the state of Kerala

**Treb·bia** (treb′yə, treb′ē ə) river in NW Italy, flowing north into the Po: scene of a victory by Hannibal over the Romans (218 B.C.): ancient name **Tre·bi·a** (trē′bē ə)

**Treb·i·zond** (treb′i zänd′) **1** Greek empire (1204-1461) on the SE coast of the Black Sea **2** seaport in NE Turkey: former capital of the empire of Trebizond: pop. 53,000: Turk. name TRABZON

**Treng·ga·nu** (treŋ gä′nōō′) state of Malaysia, on the E coast of Peninsular Malaysia: 5,027 sq. mi. (12,955 sq. km); pop. 543,000

**Trent** (trent) **1** commune in N Italy, on the Adige River: pop. 100,000 **2** river in central England, flowing from Staffordshire northeast to the Humber: 170 mi. (273 km)

**Tren·ti·no-Al·to A·di·ge** (tren tē′nō äl′tō ä′dē jā′) region of N Italy: the N part (*Alto Adige*) is in the S Tirol: 5,256 sq. mi. (13,612 sq. km); pop. 873,000; cap. Trent

**Tren·to** (tren′tô) *It. name of* TRENT

**Tren·ton** (trent′'n) 〖after Wm. *Trent* (1655-1724), colonist〗 capital of N.J., on the Delaware River: pop. 89,000: see PHILADELPHIA

**Tri·an·gu·lum** (trī aŋ′gyōō ləm) a N constellation between Aries and Andromeda

**Triangulum Aus·tra·le** (ôs trā'lē) a S constellation between Apus and Norma

**Tri·Be·Ca** (trī bek'ə) [[ *tri*angle *be*low *Ca*nal (street in Manhattan) ]] in Manhattan, the area between Broadway and the Hudson River south of Greenwich Village: noted as a center for artists, art galleries, etc.: also **Tri·be·ca**

**Trier** (trir) city in W Germany, on the Moselle River, in the state of Rhineland-Palatinate: pop. 94,000

**Tri·este** (trē est'; *It* trĕ es'te) **1** seaport in NE Italy, on an inlet (**Gulf of Trieste**) of the Adriatic: pop. 243,000 **2 Free Territory of** former region surrounding this city, administered by the United Nations and divided between Italy & Yugoslavia in 1954: 285 sq. mi. (738 sq. km)

**Tri·na·cri·a** (trī nā'krē ə; trē-, trə-) *ancient Rom. name of* SICILY

**Trin·i·dad** (trin'i dad') island in the West Indies, off the NE coast of Venezuela: 1,864 sq. mi. (4,827 sq. km): see TRINIDAD AND TOBAGO

**Trinidad and Tobago** country in the West Indies, comprising the islands of Trinidad & Tobago: formerly a British colony, it became independent & a member of the Commonwealth (1962): 1,980 sq. mi. (5,128 sq. km); pop. 1,055,000; cap. Port-of-Spain

**Trip·o·li** (trip'ə lē') **1** former Barbary State on the N coast of Africa **2** capital of Libya: seaport on the NW coast: pop. (met. area) 980,000 **3** seaport on the NW coast of Lebanon: pop. *c.* 175,000

**Trip·ol·i·ta·ni·a** (trip'ə lə tā'nē ə) region of NW Libya, on the Mediterranean: 110,000 sq. mi. (284,898 sq. km); chief city, Tripoli

**Trip·u·ra** (trip'oo rə) state of NE India: 4,036 sq. mi. (10,453 sq. km); pop. 1,556,000

**Tris·tan da Cu·nha** (tris'tən də kōōn'yə) group of four British islands in the South Atlantic, administered as a dependency of St. Helena: 45 sq. mi. (116 sq. km); pop. *c.* 325

**Tri·ton** (trīt''n) [[ L < Gr *Tritōn*; ? akin to OIr *triath*, sea ]] the largest of Neptune's eight satellites

**Tri·van·drum** (tri van'drəm) seaport on the Malabar Coast of S India, in Kerala state: pop. 520,000

**Tro·as** (trō'əs, trō'as') region surrounding ancient Troy, in NW Asia Minor: also called **the Tro'ad'** (-ad')

**Tro·bri·and Islands** (trō'brē ənd; -and', -änd') group of small islands off SE New Guinea: part of Papua New Guinea: *c.* 170 sq. mi. (440 sq. km)

**Trois–Ri·viè·res** (trwä rē vyer') ⟦descriptive⟧ city in S Quebec, Canada, on the St. Lawrence: pop. 58,000: Eng. name *Three Rivers*

**Trond·heim** (trän'hām') seaport in central Norway, on an inlet (**Trondheim Fjord**) of the Norwegian Sea: pop. 134,000

**tropic 1** either of two circles of the celestial sphere parallel to the celestial equator, one, the **Tropic of Cancer,** *c.* 23° 26' north, and the other, the **Tropic of Capricorn,** *c.* 23° 26' south: they are the limits of the apparent north-and-south journey of the sun and are determined by the obliquity of the ecliptic **2** *Geog.* either of two parallels of latitude (**Tropic of Cancer and Tropic of Capricorn**) situated on either side of the earth's equator that correspond to the astronomical tropics **3** [*also* T-] [*pl.*] the region of the earth lying between these latitudes; Torrid Zone

**Tropical Zone** TORRID ZONE

**Tropic of Cancer** (or **Capricorn**) *see* TROPIC

**Tros·sachs** (träs'əks) valley in SW Perth, Scotland

**Trou·ville** (trōō vēl') resort town in NW France, on the English Channel: pop. 7,000: also **Trou·ville–sur–Mer** (trōō vēl sür mer')

**Troy** (troi) **1** ancient Phrygian city in Troas, NW Asia Minor: scene of the Trojan War **2** ⟦after ancient *Troy*⟧ city in E N.Y., on the Hudson: pop. 54,000: see SCHENECTADY **3** ⟦after ancient *Troy*⟧ city in SE Mich.: suburb of Detroit: pop. 73,000

**Troyes** (trwà) city in NE France, on the Seine: pop. 67,000

**Tru·cial O·man** (trōō'shəl ō män') region in E Arabia, on the coast (**Trucial Coast**) of the Persian Gulf: see UNITED ARAB EMIRATES

**Trucial States** seven semi-independent Arab sheikdoms in Trucial Oman, under British protection: since 1971, an independent country called UNITED ARAB EMIRATES

**Tru·ji·llo** (trōō hē'yō) city in NW Peru: pop. 356,000

**Trujillo Al·to** (äl'tō) city in NE Puerto Rico: pop. 44,000

**Truk Islands** (truk, trook) island group in the E Caroline Islands, W Pacific: *c.* 40 sq. mi. (103 sq. km); pop. 37,000

**Tsang·po** (tsäŋ′pō′) *old form of* Zangbo

**Tsa·ri·tsyn** (tsä rē′tsin) *old name of* Volgograd

**Tsi·nan** (tse′nän′, jē′-) *old form of* Jinan

**Tsing·hai** (tsiŋ′hī′, chiŋ′-) *old form of* Qinghai

**Tsing·tao** (tsiŋ′tou′, -dou′; chiŋ′-) *old form of* Qingdao

**Tsin·ling Shan** (tsin′liŋ′ shän′; chin′-, jin′-) *old form of* Qinling Shan

**Tsi·tsi·har** (tse′tse′här′, chē′chē′-) *old form of* Qiqihar

**Tsu·shi·ma** (tsoo′she mä′; tsoo she′mə) islands of Japan in the Korea Strait, between Kyushu & Korea: 271 sq. mi. (702 sq. km)

**Tu·a·mo·tu Archipelago** (too′ə mōt′oo) group of islands of French Polynesia: 330 sq. mi. (854 sq. km)

**Tu·ca·na** (too kä′nə) a S constellation between Indus and Phoenix containing the Small Magellanic Cloud

**Tuc·son** (too′sän′, too sän′) ⟦Sp < Piman *tu-uk-so-on*, black base, referring to a dark stratum, in a nearby mountain⟧ city in S Ariz.: pop. 405,000 (met. area 667,000)

**Tu·cu·mán** (too′koo män′) city in N Argentina: pop. 497,000: in full **San Mi·guel de Tucumán** (sän′ mē gel′ de)

**Tu·la** (too′lə) city in W European Russia: pop. 532,000

**Tul·sa** (tul′sə) ⟦< Creek town name; akin to Tallahassee⟧ city in NE Okla., on the Arkansas River: pop. 367,000 (met. area 709,000)

**Tun·bridge Wells** (tun′brij′) city & spa in Kent, SE England: pop. 96,000

**Tung·ting** (tooŋ′tiŋ′, dooŋ′-) *old form of* Dongting

**Tun·gus·ka Basin** (toon goos′kä) large coal basin in central Siberia, between the Yenisei & Lena rivers: it is drained by three rivers, the **Lower Tunguska, Stony Tunguska, & Upper Tunguska** (usually called the *Angara River*), which flow west into the Yenisei

**Tu·nis** (too′nis, tyoo′-) **1** capital of Tunisia: seaport near the site of ancient Carthage: pop. 557,000 **2** a former Barbary State, which became Tunisia

**Tu·ni·si·a** (too nē′zhə, -zhē ə; tyoo-) country in N Africa, on the Mediterranean: a French protectorate since 1883, it became independent (1956): a monarchy (1956-57) & a republic since 1957: 48,332 sq. mi. (125,179 sq. km); pop. 7,424,000; cap. Tunis

**Tu·pun·ga·to** (too′poon gät′ō) mountain of the Andes on the border between Argentina and Chile: 22,310 ft.

(6,800 m)

**Tu·rin** (toor'in, tyoor'-) commune in the Piedmont, NW Italy, on the Po River: pop. 1,117,000: It. name TORINO

**Tur·ke·stan** (tur'ki stan', -stän') region in central Asia, extending from the Caspian Sea to the Gobi Desert, inhabited by Turkic-speaking peoples: divided into RUSSIAN TURKESTAN & CHINESE TURKESTAN

**Tur·key** (tur'kē) country occupying Asia Minor & a SE part of the Balkan Peninsula: 301,381 sq. mi. (780,573 sq. km); pop. 51,819,000; cap. Ankara

**Turk·ish Empire** (turk'ish) OTTOMAN EMPIRE

**Turk·men·i·stan** (tərk men'i stan', -stän') **1** TURKMEN SOVIET SOCIALIST REPUBLIC **2** country in central Asia, on the Caspian Sea, north of Iran: became independent upon the breakup of the U.S.S.R. (1991): 188,455 sq. mi. (488,100 sq. km); pop. 3,192,000; cap. Ashkhabad: formerly, *Turkmen Soviet Socialist Republic*

**Turk·men Soviet Socialist Republic** (turk'mən) a republic of the U.S.S.R.: now TURKMENISTAN: also **Turk·me·ni·a** (tərk mē'nē ə, -mēn'yə)

**Turks and Cai·cos Islands** (turks' ən kāk'əs) British crown colony in the West Indies, consisting of two groups of small islands southeast of the Bahamas: 166 sq. mi. (430 sq. km); pop. 7,500

**Tur·ku** (toor'kōō') seaport in SW Finland: pop. 160,000

**Tus·ca·loo·sa** (tus'kə lōō'sə) ⟦< Choctaw, name of a chief, lit., Black Warrior < *taska*, warrior + *lusa*, black ⟧ city in WC Ala., near Birmingham: pop. 78,000

**Tus·ca·ny** (tus'kə nē) region of central Italy, formerly a grand duchy: 8,876 sq. mi. (22,989 sq. km); pop. 3,581,000; chief city, Florence: It. name TOSCANA

**Tu·tu·i·la** (tōōt'ōō ē'lə) chief island of American Samoa, in the South Pacific: with nearby islets, 53 sq. mi. (138 sq. km); pop. 30,000; chief town, Pago Pago

**Tu·va·lu** (tōō'və lōō') country consisting of a group of nine islands in the WC Pacific: a British protectorate since 1892, it became independent & a member of the Commonwealth (1978): 10 sq. mi. (26 sq. km); pop. 8,000; cap. Fongafale

**Tux·tla** (tōōst'lä') city in Chiapas state, SE Mexico: pop. 166,000: in full **Tuxtla Gu·tiér·rez** (gōō tyer'ās')

**Tver** (tvyer) city in W European Russia, on the Volga: pop. 438,000

**Tweed** (twēd) river in SE Scotland flowing east through NE England into the North Sea: 97 mi. (156 km)

**Tweed·dale** (twēd'dāl') PEEBLES

**Twick·en·ham** (twik'ən əm) former borough in Middlesex, England, near London: now part of Richmond-on-Thames: pop. 102,000

**Twin Cities** *name for* Minneapolis & St. Paul, Minn.

**Twins** Gemini, the constellation and third sign of the zodiac

**Two Sic·i·lies** (sis'ə lēz') a former kingdom including Naples (with lower Italy) and Sicily: united with the Kingdom of Italy in 1861

**TX** *abbrev. for* Texas

**Ty·ler** (tī'lər) 〚after John *Tyler* (1790-1862), U.S. president〛 city in E Tex.: pop. 75,000

**Tyne** (tīn) river in N England, flowing east into the North Sea: *c.* 30 mi. (48 km)

**Tyne and Wear** county of N England, on the Tyne River & the North Sea: 209 sq. mi. (540 sq. km); pop. 1,145,000

**Tyne·mouth** (tīn'mouth'; tin'-) seaport in Tyne and Wear, N England, at the mouth of the Tyne: pop. 72,000

**Tyre** (tīr) 〚ME < L *Tyrus* < Gr *Tyros*〛 seaport in SW Lebanon, on the Mediterranean: center of ancient Phoenician culture: pop. 12,000

**Ty·rol** (ti rōl', -räl'; tīr'ōl', -äl') *alt. sp. of* TIROL

**Ty·rone** (ti rōn') former county of W Northern Ireland

**Tyr·rhe·ni·an Sea** (ti rē'nē ən) part of the Mediterranean, between the W coast of Italy & the islands of Corsica, Sardinia, & Sicily

**Tyu·men** (tyōō men') city in W Asian Russia, near the Urals: pop. 425,000

**Tzu·kung** (tsōō'koong'; dzōō'goong') *old form of* ZIGONG

**Tzu·po** (tsōō'pō'; dzōō'bō') *old form of* ZIBO

# U

**U·ban·gi** (yōō baŋ'gē, -bäŋ'-; ōō-) river in central Africa, formed on the N Zaire border by the juncture of the Uele & Bomu rivers & flowing west & south into the Congo River: *c.* 700 mi. (1,126 km)

**U·ca·ya·li** (ōō'kä yä'lē) river in E Peru, flowing north to join the Marañón & form the Amazon: *c.* 1,200 mi.

(1,931 km)

**U·di·ne** (o͞o′dē ne) commune in NE Italy: pop. 102,000

**Ue·le** (wā′lə) river flowing from NE Zaire west to join the Bomu & form the Ubangi: *c.* 700 mi. (1,126 km)

**U·fa** (o͞o fä′) city in E European Russia, in the W foothills of the Urals: pop. 1,064,000

**U·gan·da** (yo͞o gan′də, -gän′-; o͞o-) country in EC Africa: a former British protectorate, it became independent & a member of the Commonwealth (1962): 93,981 sq. mi. (243,409 sq. km); pop. 15,158,000; cap. Kampala

**U·in·ta Mountains** (yo͞o in′tə) ⟦after the *Uinta* Indians, a division of the Utes < ?⟧ range of the Rockies, in NE Utah: highest peak, 13,498 ft. (4,115 m)

**U·jung Pan·dang** (o͞o′jo͞oŋ′ pän däŋ′) seaport on the SW coast of Celebes, Indonesia: pop. 709,000

**U·kraine** (yo͞o krān′, -krīn′; yo͞o′krān) 1 region in SE Europe, north of the Black Sea 2 UKRAINIAN SOVIET SOCIALIST REPUBLIC 3 country in SE Europe: became independent upon the breakup of the U.S.S.R. (1991): 231,990 sq. mi. (600,851 sq. km); pop. 50,000,000; cap. Kiev: formerly, *Ukrainian Soviet Socialist Republic*

**U·krain·i·an Soviet Socialist Republic** (yo͞o krā′nē ən) a republic of the U.S.S.R.: now *Ukraine*

**U·lan Ba·tor** (o͞o′län′ bä′tôr′) capital of the Mongolian People's Republic, in the NC part: pop. 400,000

**U·lan-U·de** (o͞o län′o͞o dä′) city in S Siberia, near Lake Baikal: pop. 325,000

**Ulm** (o͝olm) city in S Germany, on the Danube, in the state of Baden-Württemberg: pop. 100,000

**Ul·ster** (ul′stər) 1 former province of Ireland, divided in 1920, with six of its counties forming Northern Ireland & the other three forming a province of the Republic of Ireland 2 province of the Republic of Ireland, in the N part; 3,094 sq. mi. (8,010 sq. km); pop. 230,000 3 loosely, NORTHERN IRELAND

**ul·ti·ma Thule** (ul′ti mə) ⟦L, farthest Thule⟧ THULE (northernmost region)

**Ul·ya·novsk** (o͞ol yä′nôfsk′) river port in central European Russia, on the Volga: pop. 544,000

**Um·bri·a** (um′brē ə; *It* o͞om′brē ä′) ⟦L, after *Umbri*, the Umbrians⟧ region in central Italy: in ancient times a district extending from the Tiber to the Adriatic: 3,270 sq. mi. (8,469 sq. km); pop. 807,000; chief city, Perugia

**Um·ta·ta** (o͞om tät′ə) capital of Transkei, in the central part: pop. 29,000

**Un·a·las·ka** (ōō′nə las′kə, un′ə-) [[Russ *Unalashka* < Aleut (*n*)*aw*(*a*)*n alaxsxa*(ẑ), lit., this Alaska]] island of Alas., in the E Aleutians: *c.* 75 mi. (120 km) long

**Uncle Sam** [[extended < abbrev. *U.S.*]] [Colloq.] the U.S. (government or people), personified as a tall, spare man with chin whiskers, dressed in a red, white, and blue costume of swallow-tailed coat, striped trousers, and tall hat with a band of stars

**Un·ga·va** (uŋ gä′və, -gä′-) region in N Quebec, Canada, between Labrador & Hudson Bay: 351,780 sq. mi. (911,106 sq. km)

**Union, the** 1 the United States of America, specif. when regarded as a Federal union 2 the North in the Civil War

**Union City** [[formed by the union of two older towns]] city in NE N.J.: suburb of Jersey City: pop. 58,000

**Union of South Africa** *see* SOUTH AFRICA

**Union of Soviet Socialist Republics** former country in E Europe & N Asia, extending from the Arctic Ocean to the Black Sea & from the Baltic Sea to the Pacific: formed in 1922 as a union of fifteen constituent republics, it was disbanded in 1991: 8,649,000 sq. mi. (22,402,000 sq. km); cap. Moscow

**United Arab Emirates** country in E Arabia, on the Persian Gulf, consisting of seven Arab sheikdoms (formerly called TRUCIAL STATES): *c.* 32,000 sq. mi. (82,880 sq. km); pop. 1,326,000; cap. Abu Dhabi

**United Arab Republic** 1 *old name of* Egypt and Syria, united as a single nation (1958-61) 2 *old name of* Egypt (1961-71)

**United Kingdom** 1 country in W Europe, consisting of Great Britain & Northern Ireland: 94,217 sq. mi. (244,021 sq. km); pop. 56,458,000; cap. London: in full **United Kingdom of Great Britain and Northern Ireland** 2 country (1801-1921) consisting of Great Britain & Ireland: in full **United Kingdom of Great Britain and Ireland**

**United States of America** country made up of the North American area extending from the Atlantic Ocean to the Pacific Ocean between Canada and Mexico, together with Alas. & Hawaii; 3,615,211 sq. mi. (9,376,614 sq. km); pop. 248,710,000; cap. Washington: also called **the United States**

**University City** [named for its proximity to Washington University] city in E Mo., near St. Louis: pop. 40,000

**Un·ter·wal·den** (oon′tər väl′dən) former canton of central Switzerland: now divided into two cantons, NID-WALDEN & OBWALDEN

**Up·land** (up′lənd) [descriptive] city in SW Calif., near San Bernardino: pop. 63,000

**U·po·lu** (o͞o pō′lo͞o) smaller of the two main islands of Western Samoa: 435 sq. mi. (1,126 sq. km); pop. 109,000: cf. SAVAII

**Upper Canada** *old name of* (1791-1841) ONTARIO (Canada)

**Upper Peninsula** NW section of Mich., a peninsula separated from the rest of the State by the Straits of Mackinac: 16,538 sq. mi. (42,833 sq. km)

**Upper Vol·ta** (väl′tə, vôl′-, vōl′-) *old name of* BURKINA FASO

**Upp·sa·la** (up′sə lə, o͞op′-; -sä lä′, -sä′lä) city in EC Sweden: pop. 156,000: also sp. **Up′sa·la**

**Ur** (oor, ur) ancient Sumerian city on the Euphrates River, in what is now S Iraq

**U·ral** (yoor′əl) **1** [*pl.*] mountain system in Russia, extending from the Arctic Ocean south to the N border of Kazakhstan: traditionally regarded as the boundary between Europe & Asia: highest peak, *c.* 6,180 ft. (1,884 m): also **Ural Mountains 2** river flowing from the S section of these mountains into the N end of the Caspian Sea: 1,575 mi. (2,534 km)

**U·ra·nus** (yoor′ə nəs, yo͞o rān′əs) [ModL < LL *Uranus* < Gr *Ouranos*, lit., heaven] the third largest planet of the solar system and the seventh in distance from the sun: it has a system of thin rings around the equator: diameter, *c.* 52,400 km (*c.* 32,560 mi.); period of revolution, *c.* 84.02 earth years; period of rotation, *c.* 17.24 hours around an axis tilted 98° to its orbital plane; fifteen satellites; symbol, ♅

**U·ra·wa** (o͞o rä′wä) city in EC Honshu, Japan, north of Tokyo: pop. 369,000

**Ur·fa** (oor fä′) city in SE Turkey, near the Syrian border: pop. 147,000: cf. EDESSA

**U·ri** (o͞o′rē) canton of EC Switzerland: 415 sq. mi. (1,075 sq. km); pop. 34,000

**Ur·mi·a** (o͞or′mē ə), **Lake** large saltwater lake in NW

Iran: *c.* 1,500 to 2,300 sq. mi. (3,800 to 6,000 sq. km)

**Ur·sa Major** (ʉr′sə) 〚L, lit., Great Bear〛 a most conspicuous N constellation between Lynx and Draco: it contains more than 50 visible stars, seven of which form the Big Dipper

**Ursa Minor** 〚L, lit., Little Bear〛 a N constellation surrounded by Draco and containing the N celestial pole and the Little Dipper: see POLARIS

**U·ru·a·pan** (o͞o′ro͞o ä′pän′; *Sp* o͞o rwä′pän′) city in Michoacán state, SW Mexico: pop. 147,000

**U·ru·guay** (yoor′ə gwā′, -gwī′; oor′ə-; *Sp* o͞o′ro͞o gwī′) **1** country in SE South America, on the Atlantic: 72,171 sq. mi. (186,922 sq. km); pop. 2,974,000; cap. Montevideo **2** river in SE South America flowing from S Brazil into the Río de la Plata: *c.* 1,000 mi. (1,609 km)

**Ü·rüm·qi** (o͞o′ro͞om′chē′) city in NW China; capital of Xinjiang region: pop. *c.* 940,000: old form **U′rum′chi′**

**U·run·di** (oo roon′dē) the S portion of the former Ruanda-Urundi that is now Burundi

**Usk** (usk) river flowing from S Wales through W England into the Severn estuary: 60 mi. (96 km)

**Üs·kü·dar** (o͞os′ko͞o där′) section of Istanbul, Turkey, on the Asian side of the Bosporus

**Us·pa·lla·ta Pass** (o͞os′pä yä′tä) mountain pass in the Andes, on the Chile-Argentina border: *c.* 12,650 ft. (3,855 m) high

**Us·su·ri** (o͞o so͞o′rē) river in SE Asian Russia, flowing north along the Manchurian border into the Amur River: 365 mi. (587 km)

**Us·ti·nov** (yo͞os′tə nôf′) *old name of* IZHEVSK

**UT, Ut** *abbrev. for* Utah

**U·tah** (yo͞o′tô′, -tä′) 〚< Sp *Yutta* < Ute name, lit. ? hill dwellers〛 Mountain State of the W U.S.: admitted, 1896; 84,916 sq. mi. (219,931 sq. km); pop. 1,723,000; cap. Salt Lake City: abbrev. *UT* or *Ut*

**U·ti·ca** (yo͞ot′i kə) **1** 〚after the ancient African city〛 city in central N.Y., on the Mohawk River: pop. 69,000 **2** city of ancient times in N Africa, north of modern Tunis

**U·to·pi·a** (yo͞o tō′pē ə) 〚ModL < Gr *ou*, not + *topos*, a place〛 an imaginary island described in a book of the same name by Sir Thomas More (1516) as having a perfect political and social system

**U·trecht** (yo͞o′trekt′) **1** province of the central Netherlands: 513 sq. mi. (1,329 sq. km); pop. 936,000 **2** its capital: pop. 230,000

**U·tsu·no·mi·ya** (ōōt'sōō nō mē'yä) city in central Honshu, Japan, north of Tokyo: pop. 395,000

**Ut·tar Pra·desh** (ōōt'ər prə desh', -däsh') state of N India: 113,654 sq. mi. (294,363 sq. km); pop. 110,858,000; cap. Lucknow

**Ux·bridge** (uks'brij') former borough in Middlesex, SE England: now a district of Greater London

**Ux·mal** (ōōz mäl') ruined Mayan city in the NW Yucatán Peninsula, Mexico

**Uz·bek·i·stan** (ooz bek'i stan', -stän') **1** UZBEK SOVIET SOCIALIST REPUBLIC **2** country in central Asia: became independent upon the breakup of the U.S.S.R. (1991): 172,741 sq. mi. (447,397 sq. km); pop. 17,989,000; cap. Tashkent: formerly, *Uzbek Soviet Socialist Republic*

**Uz·bek Soviet Socialist Republic** (ooz'bek') a republic of the U.S.S.R.: now UZBEKISTAN

# V

**VA, Va** *abbrev. for* Virginia

**Vaal** (väl) river in South Africa, flowing from SE Transvaal into the Orange River in N Cape Province: *c.* 700 mi. (1,126 km)

**Vac·a·ville** (vak'ə vil') ⟦after a family named *Vaca*, early settlers⟧ city in WC Calif., northeast of San Francisco: pop. 71,000

**Va·do·da·ra** (vä dō dä'rə) **1** former state of W India, now part of Gujarat state **2** city in SE Gujarat state, W India: pop. 745,000

**Va·duz** (vä dōōts') capital of Liechtenstein: pop. 4,900

**Va·lais** (và le') canton of SW Switzerland: 2,020 sq. mi. (5,231 sq. km); pop. 218,000

**Val·dai Hills** (väl dī') range of hills in W European Russia, between St. Petersburg & Moscow, forming a watershed for rivers flowing to the Baltic & those flowing south & southeast, esp. the Volga

**Val d'A·os·ta** (väl' dä ôs'tä) *var. of* VALLE D'AOSTA

**Val·dez** (val dēz') ⟦after A. *Valdés*, 18th-c. Sp naval officer⟧ port in S Alas., on the Gulf of Alaska: southern terminus of oil pipeline originating at Prudhoe Bay: pop. 4,100

**Va·lence** (và läns') city in SE France: pop. 68,000

**Va·len·ci·a** (və len'shē ə, -shə, -sē ə; *Sp* vä len'thyä) **1** region & ancient kingdom in E Spain, on the Mediterranean **2** seaport in this region: pop. 752,000 **3** city in N Venezuela: pop. 568,000

**Valencian Community** region comprising three provinces of E Spain: 8,998 sq. mi. (23,304 sq. km); pop. 3,646,000; cap. Valencia

**Va·len·ci·ennes** (və len'sē enz'; *Fr* và län syen') city in N France, near the Belgian border: pop. 41,000

**Val·hal·la** (val hal'ə, väl häl'ə) ⟦ModL < ON *valhöll* (gen. *valhallar*), hall of the slain < *valr*, slaughter, the slain + *höll*, hall⟧ *Norse Myth.* the great hall where Odin receives and feasts the souls of heroes fallen bravely in battle: also **Val·hall** (val hal', väl häl')

**Val·la·do·lid** (val'ə dō lid'; *Sp* vä'lyä *th*ō lē*th*') city in NC Spain: pop. 330,000

**Val·le d'A·os·ta** (väl'ā dä ôs'tä) region of NW Italy: 1,260 sq. mi. (3,263 sq. km); pop. 112,000

**Val·le·jo** (və lā'hō, -lā'ō) ⟦after Mariano G. *Vallejo* (1808-90), owner of the site⟧ seaport in W Calif., near Oakland: pop. 109,000

**Val·let·ta** (vä let'ä) seaport & capital of Malta, on the island of Malta: pop. 18,000

**Valley Forge** ⟦after an iron *forge* located on *Valley* Creek⟧ village in SE Pa., on the Schuylkill River: scene of Washington's winter encampment (1777-78)

**Valley of Ten Thousand Smokes** region in Katmai National Monument, SW Alas., in which steam and gases are emitted from thousands of earth vents

**Va·lois** (và lwà') former duchy in NC France

**Val·pa·rai·so** (val'pə rā'zō, -rī'sō) seaport in central Chile: pop. 267,000: also **Val·pa·ra·í·so** (*Sp* väl'pä *r*ä ē' sô)

**Van** (vän) salt lake in E Turkey: *c.* 1,450 sq. mi. (3,755 sq. km)

**Van Al·len radiation belt** (van al'ən) ⟦after James A. *Van Allen* (1914- ), U.S. physicist⟧ a broad, doughnut-shaped region surrounding the earth and composed of high-energy electrons and protons trapped in the earth's magnetic field at heights between *c.* 400 km (*c.* 250 mi.) and *c.* 64,370 km (*c.* 40,000 mi.)

**Van·cou·ver** (van kōō'vər) ⟦after Capt. George *Vancouver* (1757-98), Brit explorer⟧ **1** island of British Columbia, Canada, off the SW coast: 12,408 sq. mi.

(32,136 sq. km) **2** seaport in SW British Columbia, opposite this island, on the Strait of Georgia: pop. 410,000 (met. area 1,268,000) **3** city in SW Wash., on the Columbia River, opposite Portland, Oreg.: pop. 46,000 **4 Mount** mountain of the St. Elias Range, on the Alas.-Yukon border: 15,700 ft. (4,785 m)

**Van Die·men's Land** (van dē′mənz) *old name of* TAS-MANIA

**Vä·nern** (ve′nərn), **Lake** largest lake in Sweden, in the SW part: *c.* 2,150 sq. mi. (5,568 sq. km): also **Vä′ner** (-nər)

**Va·nu·a Le·vu** (vä noo′ä lev′oo) second largest of the Fiji Islands, northeast of Viti Levu: 2,137 sq. mi. (5,534 sq. km)

**Va·nua·tu** (vän′wä too′) country on a group of islands in the SW Pacific, west of Fiji: formerly an Anglo-French condominium, it became an independent republic (1980): 5,700 sq. mi. (14,762 sq. km); pop. 136,000; cap. Vila

**Va·ra·na·si** (və rän′ə sē′) city in Uttar Pradesh, NE India, on the Ganges: pop. 794,000

**Var·dar** (vär′där) river in Macedonia & N Greece, flowing into the Gulf of Salonika: *c.* 230 mi. (370 km)

**Var·na** (vär′nä) seaport in NE Bulgaria, on the Black Sea: pop. 295,000

**Vas·con·ga·das** (väs′kôn gä′*th*äs) *Sp. name of* The BASQUE COUNTRY

**Väs·te·rås** (ves′tə rôs′) city in SC Sweden, on Lake Malar: pop. 117,000

**Vat·i·can** (vat′i kən) 〚L *Vaticanus* (*mons*), Vatican (hill)〛 the papal residence, consisting of a group of buildings in Vatican City

**Vatican City** independent papal state constituted in 1929 as an enclave in Rome: it includes the Vatican & St. Peter's Basilica: 108 acres (0.438 sq. km); pop. *c.* 1,000

**Vat·ter** (vet′ər), **Lake** lake in SC Sweden: 733 sq. mi. (1,898 sq. km): Swed. name **Vät·tern** (vet′tərn)

**Vaud** (vō) canton of W Switzerland: 1,240 sq. mi. (3,216 sq. km); pop. 529,000; cap. Lausanne

**Ve·ga** (vē′gə, vā′-) 〚ML < Ar (*ar nasr*) *al wāqiʕ*, the falling (vulture)〛 the brightest star in the constellation Lyra, with a magnitude of 0.05

**Ve·gas** (vā′gəs) *short for* LAS VEGAS

**Ve·ii** (vē′yī) ancient Etruscan city northwest of Rome: destroyed by the Romans in 396 B.C.

**Ve·la** (vē′lə, vā′-) ⟦ModL < L *vela*, veil⟧ a constellation in the S Milky Way between Carina and Antlia: see ARGO

**Vel·sen** (vel′sən) city in W Netherlands: outer port of Amsterdam: pop. 57,000

**Ven·dée** (vän dā′) region of W France, south of Brittany: scene of peasant insurrections against the French Revolutionary government (1793-96)

**Ve·ne·ti·a** (və nē′shē ə, -shə) ⟦L < *Veneti*, a people living in the ancient district⟧ 1 ancient district at the head of the Adriatic, north of the Po River: with Istria it formed a Roman province 2 former region of NE Italy, the E portion of which was ceded to Yugoslavia in 1947 3 VENETO

**Ve·ne·to** (ve′ne tō′) region of N Italy, on the Adriatic: 7,095 sq. mi. (18,375 sq. km); pop. 4,345,000; chief city, Venice

**Ve·ne·zi·a** (ve ne′tsyä) 1 *It. name of* VENICE 2 former region of N Italy, generally corresponding to ancient Venetia: it now forms most of Veneto

**Ven·e·zue·la** (ven′ə zwä′lə, -zwē′-; *Sp* ve′ne swe′lä) 1 country in N South America: 352,143 sq. mi. (912,047 sq. km); pop. 17,791,000; cap. Caracas 2 Gulf of inlet of the Caribbean, on the NW coast of Venezuela: c. 150 mi. (241 km) wide

**Ven·ice** (ven′is) 1 seaport in N Italy built on more than 100 small islands in the Lagoon of Venice: formerly a maritime city-state extending over most of Venetia & Dalmatia: pop. 346,000: It. name VENEZIA 2 Gulf of N end of the Adriatic: c. 60 mi. (96 km) wide 3 Lagoon of arm of this gulf, on the coast of Veneto: c. 180 sq. mi. (466 sq. km)

**Ven·lo** (ven′lō) city in SE Netherlands, near the German border: pop. 63,000

**Ven·tu·ra** (ven toor′ə) ⟦< (*San Buena*)*ventura* (the official name) < Sp, lit., saint of good fortune⟧ city in SW Calif., northwest of Los Angeles: pop. 93,000: see OXNARD

**Ve·nus** (vē′nəs) ⟦ME < L, lit., love < IE *wenos*, desire < base *wen-*, to strive for, attain⟧ the brightest, sixth-largest planet in the solar system and the second in distance from the sun, with a dense atmosphere of carbon dioxide and a very high surface temperature: diameter, *c.* 12,100 km (*c.* 7,520 mi.); period of revolution, *c.* 225 earth days; period of rotation (retrograde), 243.01 earth days; symbol, ♀

**Ve·nus·berg** (vē′nəs burg′; *Ger* vä′noos berk′) ⟦ Ger, Venus mountain ⟧ *Medieval Legend* a mountain somewhere in Germany where Venus held court in a cavern, enticing travelers, who became reluctant to leave

**Ver·a·cruz** (ver′ə krōōz′; *Sp* ve′rä krōōs′) ⟦ Sp, lit., true cross ⟧ **1** state of Mexico, on the E coast: 27,759 sq. mi. (71,895 sq. km); pop. 5,387,000; cap. Jalapa **2** seaport in this state: pop. 305,000

**Verde** (vurd), **Cape** promontory on the coast of Senegal: westernmost point of Africa

**Ver·dun** (ver dun′, vər-; *Fr* ver dën′) **1** city in NE France, on the Meuse River: scene of much battle in World War I: pop. 22,000 **2** ⟦ var. of *Savardun*, town in France, birthplace of an early settler ⟧ city on Montreal Island, SW Quebec, Canada: suburb of Montreal: pop. 62,000

**Ve·ree·ni·ging** (fə rä′nə giŋ) city in S Transvaal, South Africa: pop. 170,000

**Ver·mont** (vər mänt′) ⟦ < Fr *Verd Mont* (1647), green mountain ⟧ New England State of the U.S.: admitted, 1791; 9,609 sq. mi. (24,887 sq. km); pop. 563,000; cap. Montpelier: abbrev. *VT* or *Vt*

**Ve·ro·na** (və rō′nə; *It* ve rô′nä) commune in Veneto, N Italy: pop. 266,000

**Ver·sailles** (vər sī′; *Fr* ver sä′y′) city in NC France, near Paris: site of a palace built by Louis XIV: the Allies & Germany signed a peace treaty here (1919) ending World War I: pop. 95,000

**Ve·su·vi·us** (və sōō′vē əs) active volcano in S Italy, on the Bay of Naples: eruption of A.D. 79 destroyed Pompeii & Herculaneum: *c.* 4,000 ft. (1,220 m): It. name **Ve·su·vio** (ve zōō′vyô)

**VI** *abbrev. for* Virgin Islands

**Vi·borg** (vē′bôr y′) *Swed. name of* VYBORG

**Vi·cen·za** (vē chen′tsä) commune in N Italy: pop. 115,000

**Vi·chy** (vish′ē, vē′shē; *Fr* vē shē′) city in central France: capital of unoccupied France (1940-44): pop. 31,000

**Vicks·burg** (viks′burg′) ⟦ after Rev. Newitt *Vick* (?-1819), early settler ⟧ city in W Miss., on the Mississippi River: besieged by Grant in the Civil War (1863): pop. 21,000

**Vic·to·ri·a** (vik tôr′ē ə) **1** state of Australia, in the SE part: 87,884 sq. mi. (227,619 sq. km); pop. 4,053,000; cap. Melbourne **2** capital of Hong Kong; seaport on Hong Kong Island: pop. *c.* 1,000,000 **3** ⟦after Queen *Victoria* of Great Britain⟧ capital of British Columbia, Canada: seaport on SE Vancouver Island: pop. 64,000 **4** capital of the Seychelles, on Mahé island: pop. 15,000 **5** ⟦orig. name Sp *Guadalupe Victoria,* after the 1st president (1824-28) of the Mexican Republic⟧ city in SE Tex.: pop. 55,000 **6 Lake** lake in E Africa, bounded by Kenya, Uganda, & Tanzania: 26,828 sq. mi. (69,484 sq. km) **7** ⟦after Queen *Victoria* of Great Britain⟧ island of the Northwest Territories, Canada, east of Banks Island: 81,930 sq. mi. (237,588 sq. km)

**Victoria Falls** waterfall of the Zambezi River, between Zimbabwe & Zambia: *c.* 350 ft. (107 m) high; *c.* 1 mi. (1.6 km) wide

**Victoria Land** mainland region of Antarctica, along the Ross Sea: part of the Ross Dependency

**Victoria Nile** upper course of the Nile, flowing from Lake Victoria into Lake Albert: *c.* 250 mi. (403 km)

**Vi·en·na** (vē en′ə) capital of Austria, on the Danube: pop. 1,531,000: Ger. name WIEN

**Vienne** (vyen) **1** city in SE France: pop. 27,000 **2** river in WC France, flowing into the Loire: 230 mi. (370 km)

**Vien·tiane** (vyen tyän′) administrative capital of Laos, on the Mekong River: pop. *c.* 125,000

**Vi·et·nam** (vē′et näm′, -nam′; vyet′-) ⟦Vietnamese *Viet,* name of people + *nam,* south⟧ country on the E coast of the Indochinese Peninsula: ruled by the French from mid-19th cent. until 1945; partitioned into two republics (**North Vietnam & South Vietnam**) in 1954, and reunified in 1976 under the name of **Socialist Republic of Vietnam**: 127,300 sq. mi. (329,707 sq. km); pop. 61,994,000; cap. Hanoi

**Vi·go** (vē′gô) seaport in NW Spain: pop. 259,000

**Vii·pu·ri** (vē′pŏŏ rē′) *Finn. name of* VYBORG

**Vi·ja·ya·wa·da** (vē′jə yə wä′də) city in Andhra Pradesh, SE India, on the Krishna River: pop. 545,000

**Vi·la** (vē′lə) capital of Vanuatu: pop. 14,000

**Vi·lla·her·mo·sa** (vē′yä er mō′sä) city in SE Mexico: capital of Tabasco state: pop. 133,000

**Ville·ur·banne** (vĕl ür bản′) city in EC France: suburb of Lyon: pop. 118,000

**Vil·ni·us** (vil′nē əs′) capital of Lithuania: pop. 544,000: Russ. name **Vil·na** (vĕl′nä; *E* vil′nə)

**Vim·i·nal** (vim′ə nəl) *see* SEVEN HILLS OF ROME

**Vi·my** (vē mē′) town in N France, near the site of a fierce battle (1917) of World War I: pop. 2,700

**Vi·ña del Mar** (vē′nyä del mär′) seaport in central Chile, near Valparaiso: pop. 298,000

**Vind·hya Pra·desh** (vind′yä prä′desh) former state of central India: since 1956, part of Madhya Pradesh

**Vindhya Range** chain of hills across central India, north of the Narbada River, marking the N edge of the Deccan Plateau: also called **Vindhya Mountains** (or **Hills**)

**Vine·land** (vīn′lənd) [after the vineyards there] city in S N.J.: pop. 55,000

**Vin·land** (vin′lənd) [ON, lit., wine-land (after the wild berries or grapes discovered there)] region, now believed to be part of North America, discovered by Norsemen led by Leif Ericson in *c.* A.D. 1000

**Vir·gin** (vur′jən) VIRGO

**Vir·gin·i·a** (vər jin′yə) [after Elizabeth I of England, the *"Virgin* Queen"] Southern State of the U.S., on the Atlantic: one of the 13 original States; 40,815 sq. mi. (105,710 sq. km); pop. 6,187,000; cap. Richmond: abbrev. *VA* or *Va*

**Virginia Beach** city in SE Va., on the Atlantic: pop. 393,000: see NORFOLK

**Virginia City** [after "Old *Virginny*", nickname of an early miner, a local eccentric] township in W Nev., near Reno: formerly a center of gold & silver mining (site of the Comstock Lode): pop. 1,800

**Virgin Islands** [< Sp *Las Virgenes*, the virgins, so named (1493) by Christopher Columbus in honor of the legendary 11,000 followers of St. Ursula] group of islands of the Leeward group in the West Indies, east of Puerto Rico comprising the **British Virgin Islands**, easternmost islands of this group, constituting a British colony: 59 sq. mi. (152 sq. km); pop. 12,000 & the **Virgin Islands of the United States**, the islands of this group closest to Puerto Rico, constituting a territory of the U.S.: 132 sq. mi. (342 sq. km); pop. 102,000; cap. Charlotte Amalie: abbrev. *VI*

**Virgin Islands National Park** national park on the

island of St. John in the Virgin Islands: 8 sq. mi. (20 sq. km)

**Vir·go** (vur'gō') ⟦ME < L, lit., virgin⟧ **1** a large equatorial constellation between Leo and Libra, including the bright star Spica **2** the sixth sign of the zodiac, entered by the sun about August 22

**Vi·sa·kha·pat·nam** (vi sä'kə put'nəm) seaport in Andhra Pradesh, E India, on the Bay of Bengal: pop. 594,000

**Vi·sa·lia** (vi sāl'yə, vī-) ⟦prob. after *Visalia*, Ky.⟧ city in SC Calif.: pop. 76,000

**Vi·sa·yas** (vi sä'yəz) group of islands in the central Philippines, including Cebu, Leyte, Negros, Panay, Samar, & many smaller islands: also called **Vi·sa'yan Islands** (-yən)

**Vis·tu·la** (vis'choo lə) river in Poland, flowing from the Carpathians into the Baltic: 677 mi. (1,089 km): Pol. name WISLA

**Vi·tebsk** (vē'tepsk') city in NE Belarus, on Western Dvina River: pop. 335,000

**Vi·ti Le·vu** (vē'tē le'vōō) largest island of the Fiji Islands: 4,010 sq. mi. (10,385 sq. km); chief city, Suva

**Vi·to·ria** (vē tô'ryä) city in the Basque Provinces, N Spain: pop. 193,000

**Vi·tó·ria** (vē tô'ryə) seaport in E Brazil, on the Atlantic: capital of Espírito Santo state: pop. 144,000

**Vi·try-sur-Seine** (vē trē sür sen') city in N France: suburb of Paris: pop. 85,000

**Vlaar·ding·en** (vlär'diŋ ən) seaport in SW Netherlands, west of Rotterdam: pop. 76,000

**Vla·di·kav·kaz** (vlä'dē käf'käz') city in S European Russia, in the Caucasus: pop. 303,000

**Vlad·i·mir** (vlä dē'mir) city in central European Russia, east of Moscow: pop. 331,000

**Vla·di·vos·tok** (vlad'i väs'täk; *Russ* vlä'di vôs tôk') seaport in SE Siberia, on the Sea of Japan: the E terminus of the Trans-Siberian Railroad: pop. 600,000

**Vl·ta·va** (vul'tə və) river in W Czech Republic, flowing from the Bohemian Forest into the Elbe: *c.* 265 mi. (426 km)

**Vo·lans** (vō'lanz) a S constellation between Mensa and Carina

**Vol·ca·no Islands** (väl kā'nō) group of small Japanese islands, including Iwo Jima, in the W Pacific: 11 sq.

mi. (28 sq. km)

**Vol·ga** (väl′gə, vōl′-; *Russ* vôl′gä) river in European Russia, flowing from the Valdai Hills into the Caspian Sea: 2,290 mi. (3,686 km)

**Vol·go·grad** (väl′gə grad′, vōl′-; *Russ* vôl gä grät′) city in SC European Russia, on the Volga: scene of a decisive Soviet victory (1943) over German troops in World War II: pop. 720,000: old names *Stalingrad, Tsaritsyn*

**Vo·log·da** (vô′lôg dä) city in NC European Russia: pop. 269,000

**Vol·ta** (väl′tə, vôl′-, vōl′-) river in Ghana, flowing south into the Bight of Benin: *c.* 300 mi. (482 km): formed by the confluence of the **Black Volta**, *c.* 500 mi. (804 km) & the **White Volta**, *c.* 550 mi. (885 km)

**Vol·tur·no** (vôl tōōr′nô) river in SC Italy, flowing from the Apennines into the Tyrrhenian Sea: *c.* 110 mi. (177 km)

**Vo·ro·nezh** (vô rô′nesh) city in SW European Russia, near the Don: pop. 850,000

**Vo·ro·shi·lov·grad** (vô′rô shē′lôf grät′) *name* (1935-91) *of* LUGANSK

**Vosges (Mountains)** (vōzh) mountain range in NE France, west of the Rhine: highest peak, *c.* 4,700 ft. (1,430 m)

**Vo·ya·geurs National Park** (voi′ə jʉrz′) national park in a lake region of northernmost Minn., on the border of Ontario, Canada: 343 sq. mi. (888 sq. km)

**VT, Vt** *abbrev. for* Vermont

**Vul·pec·u·la** (vul pek′yōō lə) a N constellation in the Milky Way between Delphinus and Cygnus

**Vy·borg** (vē′bôrg) seaport in NW European Russia, on the Gulf of Finland: pop. 65,000

# W

**W** *abbrev. for* Washington

**WA, Wa** *abbrev. for* Washington

**Waadt** (vät) *Ger. name of* VAUD

**Waal** (väl) southernmost of two arms of the Rhine, flowing west through the Netherlands & joining the Meuse in the Rhine delta on the North Sea: *c.* 50 mi. (80 km)

**Wa·bash** (wô′bash′) ⟦Fr *Ouabache*, altered < Illinois *ouabouskigou*, of unknown meaning⟧ river flowing

from W Ohio across Ind. into the Ohio River: 475 mi.
(764 km)

**Wa·co** (wā′kō) ⟦Sp *Hueco* < Wichita (a Caddoan language) *we·koh*, name of a tribe later absorbed into the Wichita people⟧ city in EC Tex., on the Brazos River: pop. 104,000

**Wad·den·zee, Wad·den Zee** (väd′ən zā′) shallow section of the North Sea, in the Netherlands, between the West Frisian Islands & the IJsselmeer

**Wag·on** (wag′ən) CHARLES'S WAIN

**Wag·on·er** (-ər) AURIGA

**Wa·gram** (vä′gräm′) town in NE Austria, near Vienna: site (1809) of a Napoleonic victory over the Austrians

**Wai·ki·ki** (wī′kē kē′) ⟦Haw < *wai*, water (< Proto-Polynesian \**wai*) + *kikī* (< ?): said to mean, lit., spouting water⟧ beach and resort section in Honolulu, Hawaii

**Wail·ing Wall** (wā′liŋ) WESTERN WALL

**Wain** (wān), the CHARLES'S WAIN

**Wa·ka·ya·ma** (wä′kä yä′mä) seaport on the S coast of Honshu, Japan: pop. 403,000

**Wake·field** (wāk′fēld′) city in NC England, in West Yorkshire: pop. 60,000

**Wake Island** (wāk) coral atoll in the N Pacific between Midway & Guam: a U.S. possession: 3 sq. mi. (7.7 sq. km); pop. 300

**Wa·la·chi·a** (wä lā′kē ə) region in E Europe, south of the Transylvanian Alps: merged with Moldavia (1861) to form Romania

**Wal·den Pond** (wôl′dən) ⟦prob. < a family name⟧ pond in E Mass., near Concord: site of Thoreau's cabin (1845-47)

**Wales** (wālz) ⟦OE *Wealas, walas* < PGmc \**walhos* < \**walh-*, Celt⟧ division of the United Kingdom, occupying a peninsula of WC Great Britain: 8,016 sq. mi. (20,761 sq. km); pop. 2,792,000; chief city, Cardiff

**Wal·hal·la** (wäl häl′ə) *var. of* VALHALLA

**Wal·la·chi·a** (wä lā′kē ə) *alt. sp. of* WALACHIA

**Wal·la·sey** (wäl′ə sē) seaport in Merseyside, NW England, on the Mersey River opposite Liverpool: pop. 93,000

**Wal·lis** (väl′is) *Ger. name of* VALAIS

**Wal·lis and Futuna** (wôl′is) French overseas territory in the South Pacific, northeast of the Fiji Islands: it consists of two groups of islands (**Wallis Islands** and

**Futuna Islands**: *c.* 105 sq. mi. (274 sq. km); pop. 12,000

**Walls·end** (wôlz'end') city in N England, on the Tyne: pop. 50,000

**Wall Street** [from a defensive wall built there by the Dutch in 1653 ] street in lower Manhattan, New York City: the main financial center of the U.S.

**Walnut Creek** [transl. of Sp *Arroyo de los Nogales*, Creek of the Walnuts, after the native black walnuts ] city in W Calif., near Oakland: pop. 61,000

**Wal·sall** (wôl'sôl') city in WC England, near Birmingham: pop. 266,000

**Wal·tham** (wôl'tham', -thəm) [? after *Waltham* Abbey in England, home of some of the first settlers ] city in E Mass., on the Charles River: pop. 58,000

**Wal·tham Forest** (wôl'thəm, -təm) borough of NE Greater London, England: pop. 220,000

**Wal·vis Bay** (wôl'vis) [ < Du *walvis*, whale < MDu *walvisc* < *wal*, whale + *visc*, akin to OE *fisc*, fish ] **1** inlet of the Atlantic, on the coast of Namibia **2** seaport on this inlet: pop. 25,000 **3** small exclave of Cape Province, South Africa, surrounding this seaport: 434 sq. mi. (1,124 sq. km)

**Wands·worth** (wändz'wurth') borough of SW Greater London: pop. 258,000

**Wan·hsien** (wän'shyen') *old form of* WANXIAN

**Wan·ne-Ei·ckel** (vän'ə i'kəl) city in the Ruhr Basin of North Rhine-Westphalia, Germany: pop. 108,000

**Wan·xian** (wän'shyän') city in Sichuan province, central China, on the Chang: pop. *c.* 300,000

**Wa·ran·gal** (wô'rəŋ gəl) city in N Andhra Pradesh, S India: pop. 336,000

**War·ren** (wôr'ən, wär'-) **1** [after Dr. Joseph *Warren* (1741-75), killed at Bunker Hill ] city in SE Mich.: suburb of Detroit: pop. 145,000 **2** [after Moses *Warren*, 19th-c. U.S. surveyor ] city in NE Ohio: pop. 51,000: see YOUNGSTOWN

**War·ring·ton** (wôr'iŋ tən, wär'-) city in Cheshire, NW England, on the Mersey River: pop. 173,000

**War·saw** (wôr'sô') capital of Poland, on the Vistula River: pop. 1,628,000: Pol. name **War·sza·wa** (vär shä'vä)

**War·ta** (vär'tä) river in Poland, flowing from the S part northwest into the Oder: 445 mi. (716 km)

**Wart·burg** (värt'boork) medieval castle in Thuringia,

Germany, where Martin Luther completed his translation of the New Testament (1521-22)

**War·wick** (wôr'ik, wär'-; *for 2, usually* wôr'wik') 1 WARWICKSHIRE 2 ⟦after the Earl of *Warwick*, friend of the founder⟧ city in central R.I., on Narragansett Bay: pop. 85,000

**War·wick·shire** (wôr'ik shir', -shər; wär'-) county of central England: 765 sq. mi. (1,981 sq. km); pop. 478,000

**Wa·satch Range** (wô'sach') ⟦< AmInd (Ute), lit., mountain pass⟧ range of the Rockies, extending from central Utah to SE Ida.: highest peak, 12,008 ft. (3,660 m)

**Wash** (wôsh, wäsh), **The** shallow inlet of the North Sea, on the E coast of England: *c.* 20 mi. (32 km) long

**Wash** *abbrev. for* Washington

**Wash·ing·ton** (wôsh'iŋ tən, wäsh'-) ⟦after George *Washington*⟧ 1 NW coastal State of the U.S.: admitted, 1889; 68,192 sq. mi. (176,617 sq. km); pop. 4,867,000; cap. Olympia: abbrev. *WA, Wash,* or *Wa* 2 capital of the U.S., coextensive with the District of Columbia: pop. 607,000 (met. area incl. parts of Md. & Va. 3,924,000) 3 **Lake** lake in WC Wash., near Seattle: *c.* 20 mi. (32 km) long 4 **Mount** mountain of the White Mountains, in N N.H.: highest peak in New England: 6,288 ft. (1,916 m)

**Wash·i·ta** (wäsh'i tô', wôsh'-) *alt. sp. of* OUACHITA

**Water Bearer** Aquarius, the constellation and eleventh sign of the zodiac

**Wa·ter·bur·y** (wôt'ər ber'ē, wät'-) city in WC Conn.: pop. 109,000

**Wa·ter·ee** (wôt'ər ē') ⟦AmInd tribal name < ?⟧ river in NW S.C., flowing south to join the Congaree & form the Santee: *c.* 300 mi. (482 km)

**Wa·ter·ford** (wôt'ər fərd) 1 county of Munster province, S Ireland, on the Atlantic: 709 sq. mi. (1,837 sq. km); pop. 50,000 2 its county seat: a seaport: pop. 38,000

**Wa·ter·loo** (wôt'ər lōō', wät'-; wôt'ər lōō', wät'-) 1 ⟦after the town in Belgium⟧ city in NE Iowa: pop. 66,000 2 town in eentral Belgium, south of Brussels: scene of Napoleon's final defeat (June 18, 1815) by the Allies under Wellington & Blücher: pop. 25,000

**Wa·ter·ton Lakes National Park** (wôt'ər tən, wät'-)

national park in S Alberta, Canada: 203 sq. mi. (526 sq. km): with Glacier National Park of Mont., it forms **Waterton–Glacier International Peace Park**

**Wau·ke·gan** (wô kē′gən) ⟦prob. < Ojibwa *waakaaʔigan*, fort ⟧ city in NE Ill., on Lake Michigan: pop. 69,000

**Wau·ke·sha** (wô′ki shô′) ⟦ < Algonquian dial., ? lit., fox ⟧ city in SE Wis., near Milwaukee: pop. 57,000

**Wau·wa·to·sa** (wô′wə tō′sə) ⟦ < AmInd *wawatosi*, ? fire-fly ⟧ city in SE Wis.: suburb of Milwaukee: pop. 49,000

**Wayne** (wān) ⟦after Anthony *Wayne* (1745-96), Am general ⟧ city in NE N.J., near Paterson: pop. 47,000

**Wa·zir·i·stan** (wä zir′i stän′) mountainous region in W Pakistan, on the Afghanistan border: *c.* 5,000 sq. mi. (12,950 sq. km)

**Weald** (wēld), **The** region in SE England, in Surrey, Kent, & Sussex: formerly heavily forested

**Wear** (wir) river in Durham, N England, flowing north-east into the North Sea: 67 mi. (107 km)

**Wed·dell Sea** (wed′əl, wə del′) ⟦after James *Weddell* (1787-1834), Brit whaler who discovered it (1823)⟧ section of the Atlantic east of Antarctic Peninsula

**Wei** (wā) river in NC China, flowing from Gansu prov-ince east into the Huang He: *c.* 500 mi. (805 km)

**Wei·mar** (vī′mär′; *E* vī′mär′, wī′-) city in central Ger-many, near Erfurt, in the state of Thuringia: pop. 64,000

**Weiss·horn** (vīs′hôrn′) mountain of the Pennine Alps, S Switzerland: *c.* 14,800 ft. (4,512 m)

**Wel·land** (wel′ənd) port in SE Ontario, Canada, on the Welland Canal: pop. 45,000

**Welland (Ship) Canal** ⟦ult. after *Welland* River, in England⟧ canal of the St. Lawrence Seaway, in Ontario, Canada between Lake Ontario & Lake Erie: 27.5 mi. (45 km) long

**Wel·ling·ton** (wel′iŋ tən) capital of New Zealand: sea-port in S North Island, on Cook Strait: pop. 135,000

**Wem·bley** (wem′blē) district of NW London, part of Greater London borough of Brent

**We·ser** (vā′zər) river in NW Germany, flowing from S Lower Saxony north into the North Sea: *c.* 300 mi. (483 km)

**Wes·sex** (wes′iks) **1** former Anglo-Saxon kingdom in S England: see HEPTARCHY, THE **2** corresponding sec-tion in modern England, chiefly in Dorsetshire, as the locale of Hardy's novels

**West** the Western Roman Empire

**West, the 1** the western part of the earth; esp., the Western Hemisphere, or the Western Hemisphere and Europe; Occident **2** the western part of the U.S.; specif., *a)* [Historical] the region west of the Allegheny Mountains *b)* the region west of the Mississippi, esp. the northwestern part of this region **3** the U.S. and its non-Communist allies in Europe and the Western Hemisphere

**West Al·lis** (al'is) [[ after the *Allis*-Chalmers Co. there ]] city in SE Wis.: suburb of Milwaukee: pop. 63,000

**West Bank** area in Jordan, on the W bank of the Jordan River: occupied by Israel since 1967

**West Bengal** state of NE India: 33,920 sq. mi. (87,853 sq. km); pop. 54,485,000; cap. Calcutta

**West Berlin** *see* BERLIN

**West Brom·wich** (brum'ich, -ij; bräm'ich) city in West Midlands, England, near Birmingham: pop. 155,000

**West Co·vi·na** (kō vē'nə) city in SW Calif., near Los Angeles: pop. 96,000

**West End** W section of London, England: a fashionable residential district

**Western Australia** state of Australia, in the W third of the continent: 975,100 sq. mi. (2,525,500 sq. km); pop. 1,374,000; cap. Perth

**Western Hemisphere** that half of the earth which includes North & South America

**Western Isles** region of W Scotland comprising the Outer Hebrides: 1,120 sq. mi. (2,901 sq. km); pop. 31,400

**Western Ocean** *ancient name of* the ATLANTIC

**Western Province** province of Saudi Arabia: *c.* 135,000 sq. mi. (349,648 sq. km); pop. *c.* 2,000,000; chief cities, Mecca & Jiddah

**Western Reserve** section of the Northwest Territory, on Lake Erie: reserved by Conn. for settlers when its other W lands were ceded to the Federal government in 1786: incorporated into the Ohio territory in 1800

**Western Roman Empire** the W part of the Roman Empire, after it was divided in A.D. 395 by Theodosius until it was overthrown by Odoacer in A.D. 476

**Western Sahara** former Spanish province (*Spanish Sahara*) in NW Africa: divided (1975) between Mauri-

tania & Morocco: Mauritania renounced its claim to
its territory (1979) which was subsequently occupied
by Morocco

**Western Samoa** country in the South Pacific, consisting of two large islands & several small ones: became
independent in 1962 & a member of the Commonwealth of Nations in 1970: 1,132 sq. mi. (2,934 sq. km);
pop. 165,000; cap. Apia

**Western Wall** a high wall in Jerusalem believed to be
part of the western section of the wall surrounding
Herod's Temple: Jews have traditionally gathered at
this site for prayer

**West Flanders** province of NW Belgium, on the North
Sea: 1,151 sq. mi. (2,981 sq. km); pop. 1,054,000

**West Germany** *see* GERMANY

**West Glamorgan** county of SE Wales: 315 sq. mi. (815
sq. km); pop. 364,000; chief city, Swansea

**West Ham** *see* NEWHAM

**West Hartford** city in central Conn.: suburb of Hartford: pop. 60,000

**West Ha·ven** (hā′vən) city in SW Conn., on Long Island
Sound: suburb of New Haven: pop. 54,000

**West Indies** large group of islands between North
America & South America: it includes the Greater
Antilles, Lesser Antilles, & Bahamas

**West Indies Associated States** Antigua and Barbuda,
Dominica, St. Kitts and Nevis, St. Lucia, & St. Vincent and the Grenadines: countries associated with the
United Kingdom in matters of foreign relations &
defense

**West Ir·i·an** (ir′ē ən) territory of Indonesia, occupying
the W half of the island of New Guinea: a Dutch territory until 1963: *c.* 160,000 sq. mi. (414,398 sq. km);
pop. 1,174,000; cap. Jayapura

**West·land** (west′lənd, -land′) ⟦from its location in the
W part of the county⟧ city in SE Mich.: suburb of
Detroit: pop. 85,000

**West Lothian** former county of SC Scotland, now in
Lothian region

**West·meath** (west′mēth′) county in Leinster province,
EC Ireland: 681 sq. mi. (1,764 sq. km); pop. 62,000

**West Midlands** county of central England: 347 sq. mi.
(899 sq. km); pop. 2,647,000

**West·min·ster** (west′min′stər) **1** metropolitan borough of W central Greater London: site of the Houses of Parliament: pop. 182,000 **2** ⟦from the sympathy of its settlers with the Presbyterian principles of the *Westminster* Assembly (1643-49)⟧ city in SW Calif.: pop. 78,000 **3** ⟦after *Westminster* University (1907-17), located there⟧ city in NC Colo.: suburb of Denver: pop. 75,000

**Westminster Abbey** Gothic church (orig. a Benedictine abbey) in Westminster where English monarchs are crowned: it is also a burial place for English monarchs and famous statesmen, writers, etc.

**West·mor·land** (west′mər lənd) former county of NW England, now part of Cumbria county

**West Orange** town in NE N.J.: suburb of Newark: pop. 39,000

**West Pakistan** former province of Pakistan: it now constitutes the country of Pakistan: cf. EAST PAKISTAN

**West Palm Beach** city in SE Fla., on a lagoon opposite Palm Beach: winter resort: pop. 68,000 (met. area 864,000)

**West·pha·li·a** (west fā′lē ə, -fāl′yə) region in NW Germany, a part of the state of North Rhine-Westphalia: formerly a duchy, a kingdom, & a province of Prussia (1816-1945); chief city, Münster

**West Point** ⟦from its location on the *west* bank of the Hudson River⟧ military reservation in SE N.Y.: site of the U.S. Military Academy

**West Prussia** former province of Prussia, since 1945 part of Poland: chief city, Gdansk

**West Rid·ing** (rīd′iŋ) former division of Yorkshire, England, now part of the counties of North Yorkshire & West Yorkshire

**West Sussex** county in SE England, on the English Channel: 778 sq. mi. (2,016 sq. km); pop. 683,000

**West Valley City** city in Utah, near Salt Lake City: pop. 87,000

**West Virginia** ⟦see VIRGINIA⟧ E state of the U.S., northwest of Va.: admitted, 1863; 24,181 sq. mi. (62,628 sq. km); pop. 1,793,000; cap. Charleston: abbrev. *WV* or *WVa*

**West Yorkshire** county of N England: 787 sq. mi. (2,039 sq. km); pop. 2,056,000

**Wet·ter·horn** (vet′ər hôrn′) ⟦Ger < *wetter*, weather + *horn*, peak⟧ mountain of the Bernese Alps, SC Switzerland: *c.* 12,150 ft. (3,700 m)

**Wex·ford** (weks′fərd) county of Leinster province, SE
Ireland: 908 sq. mi. (2,352 sq. km); pop. 99,000

**Wey·mouth** (wā′məth) 〚prob. after *Weymouth,* town in
England〛 suburb of Boston, in E Mass.: pop. 54,000

**Whales** (hwālz, wālz), **Bay of** inlet of the Ross Sea, near
Little America

**Whea·ton** (hwēt′'n, wēt′-) 〚after W. L. *Wheaton,* early
settler〛 city in NE Ill., near Chicago: pop. 51,000

**Wheel·ing** (hwēl′iŋ, wēl′-) 〚said to be < Delaware
*wi·link,* lit., at the place of the head (of a slain enemy
exhibited there)〛 city in N W.Va., on the Ohio River:
pop. 35,000

**White** (hwīt, wīt) river flowing from NW Ark. through S
Mo. into the Mississippi: 690 mi. (1,110 km)

**White·chap·el** (-chap′əl) district of E London, part of
Greater London borough of Tower Hamlets

**White·fri·ars** (-frī′ərz) district of central London, near
Fleet Street: formerly the site of a Carmelite monastery

**White·hall** (-hôl′) **1** former royal palace in Westmin-
ster, London, destroyed by fire (1698): also **Whitehall
Palace 2** street in Westminster, south of Trafalgar
Square, site of several government offices

**White·horse** (-hôrs′) 〚after the *Whitehorse* Rapids
nearby, which were so named from a fancied resemblance to the tossing mane of a white horse〛 capital of
the Yukon Territory, Canada, in the S part: pop.
14,000

**White House, the** official residence of the President of
the U.S.: a white mansion in Washington, D.C.

**White Mountains** 〚from the appearance of the higher
peaks〛 range of the Appalachian system, in N N.H.:
highest peak, Mt. Washington

**White Nile** *see* NILE

**White Plains** 〚< ?〛 city in SE N.Y., near New York
City: scene of a battle (1776) of the Revolutionary
War: pop. 49,000

**White Russia** BELORUSSIA

**White Sea** arm of the Barents Sea, extending into NW
European Russia: *c.* 36,000 sq. mi. (93,240 sq. km)

**White Volta** *see* VOLTA

**Whit·ney** (hwit′nē, wit′-), **Mount** 〚after J. D. *Whitney*
(1819-96), U.S. geologist〛 mountain of the Sierra

Nevada Range, EC Calif., in Sequoia National Park: highest peak in the U.S. outside of Alas.: 14,495 ft. (4,419 m)

**Whit·ti·er** (hwit′ē ər, wit′-) ⟦so named (1887) by Quaker settlers, after John Greenleaf *Whittier* (1807-92), U.S. poet⟧ city in SW Calif.: suburb of Los Angeles: pop. 78,000

**WI** *abbrev. for* Wisconsin

**Wich·i·ta** (wich′ə tô′) ⟦after the *Wichita* (cf. Caddo *wíˑc'ita*, Osage *wícita*), a Caddoan people who relocated in a village at the site of the city in Kansas as Civil War refugees (1862-67)⟧ city in S Kans., on the Arkansas River: pop. 304,000

**Wichita Falls** ⟦see prec.: the Wichita had lived near the site of this city from late 18th c. to the Civil War⟧ city in NC Tex.: pop. 96,000

**Wick·low** (wik′lō) county of Leinster province, SE Ireland, on the Irish Sea: 782 sq. mi. (2,025 sq. km); pop. 87,000

**Wien** (vēn) *Ger. name of* VIENNA

**Wies·ba·den** (vēs′bäd′'n) resort city in W Germany, on the Rhine: capital of the state of Hesse: pop. 269,000

**Wig·an** (wig′ən) city in NW England, in the county of Greater Manchester: pop. 81,000

**Wight** (wīt), **Isle of** island in the English Channel, off the S coast of Hampshire, constituting a county of England: 147 sq. mi. (381 sq. km); pop. 121,000

**Wig·town** (wig′tən) former county of SW Scotland, now in the region of Dumfries & Galloway

**Wil·der·ness** (wil′dər nis), **the** woodland region in NE Va., south of the Rapidan River: scene of a Civil War battle (May, 1864) between the armies of Grant and Lee

**Wild West** [*also* w- W-] the western U.S. in its early frontier period of lawlessness

**Wil·helms·ha·ven** (vil′helms hä′fən) seaport in NW Germany, on the North Sea, in the state of Lower Saxony: pop. 101,000

**Wilkes-Bar·re** (wilks′bar′ə, -bar′, -bar′ē) ⟦after John *Wilkes* (1727-97), Brit political reformer & Col. Isaac *Barré*, (1726-1802), Brit soldier & politician⟧ city in NE Pa., on the Susquehanna River: pop. 48,000

**Wilkes Land** (wilks) region of Antarctica, on the Indian Ocean south of Australia

**Wil·lam·ette** (wi lam'it) 〖< ? AmInd place name〗 river in W Oreg., flowing north into the Columbia River near Portland: *c.* 190 mi. (306 km)

**Wil·lem·stad** (wil'əm stät', vil'-) capital of the Netherlands Antilles, on the island of Curaçao: pop. 50,000

**Willes·den** (wilz'dən) former municipal borough in SE England: now part of Brent, Greater London

**Wil·liams·burg** (wil'yəmz burg') 〖after *William* III of England (1650-1702)〗 city in SE Va.: colonial capital of Va., now restored to its 18th-cent. appearance: pop. 12,000

**Wil·ming·ton** (wil'miŋ tən) 〖after Spencer Compton (*c.* 1673-1743), Earl of *Wilmington*〗 1 seaport in N Del., on the Delaware River: pop. 72,000 (met. area 579,000): see PHILADELPHIA 2 city in SE N.C.: pop. 56,000

**Wil·son** (wil'sən), **Mount** 〖after Ben D. *Wilson*, early settler〗 mountain of the Coast Ranges, SW Calif., near Pasadena: site of an astronomical observatory: 5,710 ft. (1,987 m)

**Wilson Dam** 〖after Woodrow *Wilson* (1856-1924), U.S. president〗 dam on the Tennessee River, in NW Ala.: 137 ft. (48 m) high

**Wilt·shire** (wilt'shir, -shər) county of S England: 1,344 sq. mi. (3,481 sq. km); pop. 536,000

**Wim·ble·don** (wim'bəl dən) former municipal borough in Surrey, SE England: now part of Merton, Greater London: scene of international lawn tennis matches

**Win·ches·ter** (win'ches'tər, -chis-) county seat of Hampshire, S England: site of 11th-14th cent. cathedral: pop. 30,000

**Wind** (wind) 〖from the severe winds near its head〗 river in WC Wyo., flowing southeast into the Bighorn: *c.* 110 mi. (177 km)

**Wind Cave National Park** national park in SW S.Dak.: it contains a limestone cavern (**Wind Cave**): 43.5 sq. mi. (113 sq. km)

**Win·der·mere** (win'dər mir') lake in Cumbria, NW England: largest lake in England: 10.5 mi. (16.8 km) long

**Wind·hoek** (vint'hook) capital of Namibia, in the central part: pop. *c.* 105,000

**Wind River** 〖from the severe winds near its head〗 range of the Rocky Mountains, in WC Wyo.: highest peak, 13,787 ft. (4,202 m): in full **Wind River Range**

**Wind·sor** (win′zər) **1** city in Berkshire, SE England, on the Thames, just west of London: site of Windsor Castle: pop. 28,000: official name **New Windsor 2** ⟦after the city in England⟧ port in SE Ontario, Canada, opposite Detroit: pop. 193,000

**Windsor Castle** residence of English sovereigns since the time of William the Conqueror, located in Windsor

**Wind·ward Islands** (wind′wərd) S group of islands in the Lesser Antilles of the West Indies, extending from the Leeward Islands south to Trinidad: they do not include Barbados, Trinidad, & Tobago

**Windward Passage** strait between Cuba & Hispaniola, in the West Indies: 50 mi. (80 km) wide

**Windy City** *name for* Chicago, Ill.

**Win·ne·ba·go** (win′ə bā′gō), **Lake** ⟦after *Winnebago*, an Indian people < Fox *wiinepyeekooha*, lit., person of dirty water: with ref. to muddy waters of a nearby river⟧ lake in E Wis.: 215 sq. mi. (557 sq. km)

**Win·ni·peg** (win′ə peg′) ⟦< Cree *wiinipeek*, lit., body of muddy water, sea⟧ **1** capital of Manitoba, Canada, on the Red River: pop. 564,000 (met. area 585,000) **2** river in W Ontario & SE Manitoba, Canada, flowing from the Lake of the Woods into Lake Winnipeg: (with its principal headstream) 475 mi. (764 km) **3 Lake** large lake in SC Manitoba: 9,465 sq. mi. (24,514 sq. km)

**Win·ni·pe·go·sis** (win′ə pə gō′sis), **Lake** ⟦< Cree *wiinipeekosis*, lit., a small sea: dim. of *wiinipeek*: see prec.⟧ lake in SW Manitoba, Canada, west of Lake Winnipeg: 2,103 sq. mi. (5,446 sq. km)

**Win·ni·pe·sau·kee** (win′ə pə sô′kē) ⟦< Abenaki⟧ lake in EC N.H.: 71 sq. mi. (184 sq. km)

**Win·ston–Sa·lem** (win′stən sā′ləm) ⟦a merging of two towns, after Major Joseph *Winston* (1746-1815) & SALEM⟧ city in NC N.C.: pop. 143,000: see GREENS-BORO

**Win·ter·thur** (vin′tər toor) city in N Switzerland, near Zurich: pop. 88,000

**Wis, Wisc** *abbrev. for* Wisconsin

**Wis·con·sin** (wis kän′sən) ⟦< Fr *Ouisconsing*, name of the river < an Algonquian language, prob. Ojibwa: meaning unknown⟧ **1** Middle Western State of the NC U.S.: admitted, 1848; 56,154 sq. mi. (145,438 sq.

km); pop. 4,892,000; cap. Madison: abbrev. *WI, Wis,* or
*Wisc* **2** river in Wis., flowing into the Mississippi: 430
mi. (692 km)

**Wis·la** (vē′slä) *Pol. name of* Vistula

**Wit·ten·berg** (wit′'n bʉrg′; *Ger* vit′ən berk′) city in N
Germany, on the Elbe, in the state of Saxony-Anhalt:
the Reformation originated here in 1517: pop. 54,000

**Wit·wa·ters·rand** (wit wôt′ərz rand′) region in SW
Transvaal, South Africa, near Johannesburg, consisting of ranges of hills which contain rich gold fields

**Wol·lon·gong** (wool′ən gäŋ′) seaport in E New South
Wales, SE Australia: pop. 209,000

**Wol·ver·hamp·ton** (wool′vər hamp′tən) city in Staffordshire, WC England, near Birmingham: pop.
255,000

**Wol·ver·ine State** (wool′vər ēn′, wool′vər ēn′) *name for*
Michigan

**Won·san** (wän′sän′) seaport in North Korea, on the E
coast: pop. 215,000

**Wood·bridge** (wood′brij′) 〚after *Woodbridge,* England〛
city in EC N.J.: pop. 93,000

**Woods, Lake of the** *see* Lake of the Woods

**Woon·sock·et** (woon säk′it, woon-) 〚earlier *Wansokutt*
Hill < the name in a S New England Algonquian lan-
guage〛 city in N R.I.: pop. 44,000

**Worces·ter** (woos′tər) **1** city in E England, in Hereford
and Worcester: pop. 74,000 **2** Worcestershire **3** city
in central Mass.: pop. 170,000

**Worces·ter·shire** (woos′tər shir′, -shər) former county
of W England, now part of the county of Hereford and
Worcester

**Worms** (vôrmz; *E* wʉrmz) city in SW Germany, on the
Rhine, in the state of Hesse: scene of an assembly
(Diet of Worms), 1521, at which Martin Luther was
condemned for heresy: pop. 74,000

**Wran·gel** (raŋ′gəl; *Russ* vrän′gel′y′) 〚after Baron F. von
*Wrangel(l):* see fol.〛 island of Russia in the Chukchi
Sea: *c.* 2,000 sq. mi. (5,180 sq. km)

**Wran·gell** (raŋ′gəl) 〚after Baron F. von *Wrangel(l),*
1796-1870, Russ explorer〛 **1** mountain range in SE
Alas.: highest peak, Mount Blackburn **2 Mount** active
volcano in these mountains: 14,006 ft. (4,270 m)

**Wrangell–St. Elias National Park** national park in SC
Alas.; largest park in the world: 19,023 sq. mi. (49,269

sq. km)

**Wroc·ław** (vrôts′läf) city in Silesia, SW Poland, on the Oder River: pop. 627,000

**Wu·chang** (woo′chäŋ′) *see* WUHAN

**Wu·han** (woo′hän′) city in EC China, formed by the merger of the cities of Hankow, Hanyang, & Wuchang: capital of Hubei province: pop. 3,200,000

**Wu·hu** (woo′hoo′) city in Anhui province, E China, on the Chang River: pop. 300,000

**Wup·per·tal** (voop′ər täl′) city in the Ruhr Basin of North Rhine-Westphalia, Germany: pop. 382,000

**Würt·tem·berg** (wurt′əm burg′; *Ger* vür′təm berk′) former state in SW West Germany: see BADEN-WÜRT-TEMBERG

**Würz·burg** (wurts′bərg; *Ger* vürts′boork) city in S Germany, on the Main River, in the state of Bavaria: pop. 130,000

**Wu·xi** (wü′shē′) city in Jiangsu province, E China, on the Grand Canal: pop. 900,000: old forms **Wuh·si, Wu·sih**

**WV, WVa** *abbrev. for* West Virginia

**WY** *abbrev. for* Wyoming

**Wye** (wī) river in SE Wales & W England, flowing southeast into the Severn estuary: *c.* 130 mi. (209 km)

**Wyo** *abbrev. for* Wyoming

**Wy·o·ming** (wī ō′miŋ) ⟦ after fol. ⟧ **1** Mountain State of the W U.S.: admitted, 1890; 97,914 sq. mi. (253,596 sq. km); pop. 454,000; cap. Cheyenne: abbrev. *WY* or *Wyo* **2** city in SW Mich.: suburb of Grand Rapids: pop. 64,000

**Wyoming Valley** ⟦ < Ger *Wayomick*, etc. < Munsee (a Delaware language) *chwewamink*, lit., large river bottom ⟧ valley of the Susquehanna River, NE Pa.: site of a massacre (1778)

# X

**Xan·thus** (zan′thəs) ancient city in Lycia, SW Asia Minor

**Xi** (shē) river in S China, flowing east into the South China Sea: 1,250 mi. (2,011 km)

**Xi·a·men** (shē′ä′mun′) **1** seaport on an island in Taiwan Strait, SE China: pop. 500,000 **2** the island

**Xi′·an** (shē′än′) city in NC China, on the Wei River:

capital of Shaanxi province: pop. 2,800,000

**Xi·ang** (shē′äŋ′) river in SE China, flowing from Guangdong province north into Dongting Lake: c. 715 mi. (1,150 km)

**Xiao Hing·gan Ling** (shou′hiŋ′gän′liŋ′) mountain range in NE China running parallel to the Amur River: highest peak, 4,665 ft. (1,422 m): cf. DA HINGGAN LING

**Xin·gú** (shēŋ′gōō′) river in NC Brazil, flowing north into the Amazon: c. 1,200 mi. (1,931 km)

**Xi·ning** (shē′niŋ′) city in NW China: capital of Qinghai province: pop. 320,000

**Xin·ji·ang** (shin′jē′äŋ′) autonomous region of NW China, between Tibet & Kazakhstan: 635,830 sq. mi. (1,646,793 sq. km); pop. 13,081,000; cap. Ürümqi: also **Xin·ji·ang–Uy·gur** (-wē′gŏor′)

**Xi·zang** (shē′dzäŋ′) *Chin. name of* TIBET

**Xu·zhou** (shōō′jō′) city in NW Jiangsu province, E China: pop. 773,000

# Y

**Ya·blo·no·vyy Range** (yä′blō nō vē′yə) range of mountains in SE Asian Russia, a watershed between areas of Pacific & Arctic drainage: highest peak, c. 8,500 ft. (2,590 m): also **Ya·blo·noi** (yä′blə noi′)

**Yad·kin** (yad′kin) 〚< ? AmInd〛 river in central N.C., the upper course of the Pee Dee: 200 mi. (321 km)

**Ya·ha·ta** (yä′hä tä′) *var. of* YAWATA

**Yak·i·ma** (yak′ə mô′, -ə mə) city in SC Wash.: pop. 55,000

**Ya·kutsk** (yä kōotsk′) city in EC Asian Russia, on the Lena River: pop. 149,000

**Yal·ta** (yôl′tə) seaport in the S Crimea, Ukraine, on the Black Sea: site of a conference (Feb., 1945) of Roosevelt, Churchill, and Stalin: pop. 62,000

**Ya·lu** (yä′lōō′) river flowing from Jilin province, China, along the Manchuria-North Korea border into the Yellow Sea: c. 500 mi. (804 km)

**Ya·mous·souk·ro** (yä′mōō sōō′krô) capital of the Ivory Coast, in the central part: pop. 120,000

**Yan·gon** (yan gôn′) capital of Myanmar: seaport in the S part: pop. 2,458,000

**Yang·tze** (yaŋk′sē) *old name of* CHANG

**Ya·ni·na** (yä′nē nä′) *old name of* IOANNINA

**Yan·kee·dom** (yaŋ'kē dəm) *name for* the United States; esp., the northern States or New England

**Ya·oun·dé** (yä'o͞on dā') capital of Cameroon, in the SW part: pop. 436,000

**Yap** (yäp, yap) group of islands in the W Carolines, W Pacific: part of the Federated States of Micronesia: *c.* 80 sq. mi. (207 sq. km)

**Yard, the** SCOTLAND YARD

**Yar·kand** (yär'känd') SHACHE

**Yar·mouth** (yär'məth) GREAT YARMOUTH

**Ya·ro·slavl, Ya·ro·slavl'** (yä'rō släv'əl) city in W European Russia, on the Volga: pop. 626,000

**Ya·wa·ta** (yä'wä tä') former city in N Kyushu, Japan, now part of Kitakyushu

**Yaz·oo** (yaz'o͞o) ⟦Fr *Yasou, Yazou*, etc.: name of an AmInd people of unknown affiliation⟧ river flowing from NW Miss. southwest into the Mississippi River near Vicksburg: 188 mi. (302 km)

**Yed·o, Yed·do** (ye'dō') *old name of* TOKYO

**Ye·ka·te·rin·burg** (yi kä'tə ren bo͞org) city in Russia, in the Ural Mountains: pop. 1,300,000

**Yel·low** (yel'ō) HUANG HE

**Yel·low·knife** (yel'ō nīf') town in Fort Smith Region, Canada, on Great Slave Lake: capital of Northwest Territories: pop. 10,000

**Yellow Sea** arm of the East China Sea, between China & Korea: *c.* 400 mi. (644 km) wide

**Yel·low·stone** (yel'ō stōn') ⟦transl. of Fr *Roche Jaune,* ? transl. of native name⟧ river flowing from NW Wyo. through Mont. into the Missouri River: 671 mi. (1,079 km)

**Yellowstone Falls** two waterfalls on the Yellowstone River in Yellowstone National Park: upper falls, 109 ft. (33 m); lower falls (or *Grand Falls*), 308 ft. (94 m)

**Yellowstone Lake** lake in Yellowstone National Park, fed by the Yellowstone River: 137 sq. mi. (354 sq. km)

**Yellowstone National Park** national park mostly in NW Wyo., but including narrow strips of S Mont. & E Ida.: it contains geysers, boiling springs, etc.: 3,458 sq. mi. (8,956 sq. km)

**Yem·en** (yem'ən) country on the S tip of the Arabian Peninsula formed (1990) by the merger of the **Yemen Arab Republic**, or *North Yemen*, and a country directly east of it, the **People's Democratic Republic**

of Yemen, or *South Yemen*: 207,000 sq. mi. (536,128 sq. km); pop. 11,000,000; cap. Sana: official name **Republic of Yemen**: see ADEN (the region)

**Ye·ni·sei, Ye·ni·sey** (ye′ni sā′) river in central Siberia, flowing from the Sayan Mountains north into the Kara Sea: *c.* 2,600 mi. (4,184 km)

**Ye·re·van** (yer′ə vän′) capital of Armenia, at the foot of Mt. Ararat: pop. 1,133,000

**Ye·zo** (ye′zō) *old name of* HOKKAIDO

**Yin·chuan** (yin′chwän′) city in N China: capital of the Ningxia-Hui autonomous region: pop. 84,000

**Ying·kou** (yiŋ′kou′) seaport in Liaoning province, NE China, on an arm of the Bo Hai: pop. 160,000: old sp. **Ying′kow′** (-kou′)

**Yog·ya·kar·ta** (yŏg′yä kärt′ə) city in central Java, Indonesia: pop. 399,000

**Yo·ko·ha·ma** (yō′kə hä′mə) seaport on Tokyo Bay, Japan, south of Tokyo: pop. 2,915,000

**Yo·ko·su·ka** (yō′kə sōō′kə) seaport in Honshu, at the entrance to Tokyo Bay, Japan: pop. 428,000

**Yon·kers** (yaŋ′kərz) 〖< Du *De Jonkers* (*Land*), the young nobleman's (land)〗 city in SE N.Y., on the Hudson: suburb of New York City: pop. 188,000

**York** (yôrk) **1** city in North Yorkshire, on the Ouse River: pop. 105,000 **2** 〖after the city in England〗 city in SE Pa.: pop. 42,000 **3 Cape** *see* CAPE YORK PENINSULA

**York·shire** (yôrk′shir, -shər) former county of N England, on the North Sea: now divided into three counties: NORTH YORKSHIRE, SOUTH YORKSHIRE, & WEST YORKSHIRE

**York·town** (yôrk′toun′) 〖after the Duke of *York*, later Charles I of England〗 town in SE Va.: scene of the surrender of Cornwallis to Washington (1781)

**Yo·sem·i·te Falls** (yō sem′ət ē) 〖< Miwok (a Penutian language) *joṣ·eʔ-HmetiH*, lit., there are killers among them: ? name of an AmInd people〗 series of waterfalls in Yosemite National Park, falling into Yosemite Valley: upper falls, 1,430 ft. (435 m); middle falls, 626 ft. (190 m); lower falls, 320 ft. (97 m); total drop, with intermediate cascades, 2,565 ft. (781 m)

**Yosemite National Park** national park in EC Calif., in the Sierra Nevadas, notable for its steep-walled valley (**Yosemite Valley**), high waterfalls, etc.: 1,183 sq. mi.

(3,064 sq. km)

**Youngs·town** (yuŋz′toun′) 〖after John *Young,* an early (*c.* 1800) settler〗 city in NE Ohio: pop. 96,000 (met. area with Warren 493,000)

**Youth** (yōōth), **Isle of** Cuban isle south of W Cuba: *c.* 1,200 sq. mi. (3,107 sq. km)

**Y·pres** (ē′pr′) town in NW Belgium, near the French border: center of heavy fighting in World War I: pop. 35,000

**YT** *abbrev. for* Yukon Territory

**Yu·an** (yōō än′) **1** river in SE China flowing from Guizhou province through Hunan into Dongting Lake: *c.* 550 mi. (885 km) **2** *Chinese name of* the RED (river in Vietnam)

**Yu·ca·tán, Yu·ca·tan** (yōō′kä tän′; *E* yōō′kə tan′) **1** peninsula comprising SE Mexico, Belize, & part of W Guatemala: it separates the Gulf of Mexico from the Caribbean: *c.* 70,000 sq. mi. (181,299 sq. km) **2** state of Mexico, on this peninsula: 14,827 sq. mi. (38,402 sq. km); pop. 1,063,000; cap. Mérida

**Yucatán Channel** strait between the Yucatán Peninsula & Cuba, joining the Gulf of Mexico & the Caribbean: 135 mi. (217 km) wide

**Yu·go·slav·i·a** (yōō′gō slä′vē ə, -gə-; -släv′yə) country in the NW Balkan Peninsula, bordering on the Adriatic: established as a nation in 1918 (called *Kingdom of the Serbs, Croats, and Slovenes,* 1918-29), became a federal republic (1945): four constituent republics (Slovenia, Croatia, Bosnia and Herzegovina, & Macedonia) separated from it in 1991: 39,449 sq. mi. (102,173 sq. km); pop. 10,338,000; cap. Belgrade

**Yu·kon** (yōō′kän′) 〖prob. < Athabaskan river name < ? 〗 **1** territory of NW Canada, east of Alas.: *c.* 207,076 sq. mi. (536,324 sq. km); pop. 22,000; cap. Whitehorse: usually used with *the*: abbrev. *YT*: in full **Yukon Territory 2** river flowing through this territory & Alas. into the Bering Sea: 1,979 mi. (3,184 km)

**Yu·ma** (yōō′mə) city in SW Ariz.: pop. 55,000

**Yun·nan** (yōō′nän′) province of S China: 168,417 sq. mi. (436,200 sq. km); pop. 32,553,000; cap. Kunming

# Z

**Zaan·dam** (zän däm′) former city in W Netherlands,

now part of Zaanstad

**Zaan·stad** (zän'stät') city in W Netherlands, near Amsterdam: pop. 129,000

**Zab·rze** (zäb'zhe) city in Silesia, S Poland: pop. 200,000

**Za·ca·te·cas** (sä'kä te'käs) **1** state of NC Mexico: 28,282 sq. mi. (73,252 sq. km); pop. 1,136,000 **2** its capital: pop. 56,000

**Za·greb** (zä'greb') capital of Croatia, on the Sava River: pop. 1,174,000

**Zag·ros Mountains** (zag'rəs) mountain system in W & S Iran, extending along the borders of Turkey & Iraq & along the Persian Gulf: highest peak, over 14,000 ft. (4,270 m)

**Za·ire, Za·ïre** (zä ir') **1** country in central Africa, on the equator: the former Belgian Congo, it became independent (1960): 905,563 sq. mi. (2,345,400 sq. km); pop. 31,330,000; cap. Kinshasa **2** Congo (River)

**Zá·kin·thos** (zä'kēn thôs') one of the southernmost islands of the Ionian group, Greece: 155 sq. mi. (401 sq. km)

**Za·ma** (zä'mə, zä'mä) ancient town in N Africa, southwest of Carthage: scene of a battle (202 B.C.) in which Scipio defeated Hannibal, ending the 2d Punic War

**Zam·be·zi** (zam bē'zē) river in S Africa, flowing from NW Zambia into the Mozambique Channel: c. 1,600 mi. (2,574 km)

**Zam·bi·a** (zam'bē ə) country in S Africa: formerly the British protectorate of Northern Rhodesia, it became independent & a member of the Commonwealth (1964): 290,585 sq. mi. (752,614 sq. km); pop. 7,054,000; cap. Lusaka

**Zam·bo·an·ga** (zäm'bō äŋ'gə) seaport in the Philippines, on the SW coast of Mindanao: pop. 344,000

**Zang·bo** (zäŋ'bō) the upper course of the Brahmaputra, in Tibet: c. 900 mi. (1,448 km)

**Zan·te** (zän'tä) Zákinthos

**Zan·zi·bar** (zan'zə bär') **1** island off the E coast of Africa: 640 sq. mi. (1,657 sq. km); pop. 476,000 **2** former sultanate & British protectorate including this island, Pemba, & small nearby islands: it became independent (1963) & merged with Tanganyika (1964) to form Tanzania **3** seaport on the island of Zanzibar: pop. 110,000

**Za·po·ro·zhye** (zä'pə rô'zhə) city in SE Ukraine, on the

Dnepr: pop. 852,000

**Za·ra·go·za** (thä′rä gô′thä) city in NE Spain, on the Ebro River: pop. 590,000: Eng. name SARAGOSSA

**Zea·land** (zē′lənd) largest island of Denmark, between Jutland & Sweden: 2,702 sq. mi. (6,998 sq. km); chief city, Copenhagen: Dan. name SJAELLAND

**Zee·land** (zē′lənd; *Du* zā′länt′) province of the SW Netherlands, on the North Sea: 689 sq. mi. (1,785 sq. km); pop. 327,000

**Zeist** (zīst) city in the central Netherlands, near Utrecht: pop. 60,000

**Zet·land** (zet′lənd) *var. of* SHETLAND

**Zhang·ji·a·kou** (jäŋ′jē ä′kō′) city in Hebei province, NE China, at a gateway of the Great Wall: pop. 1,000,000

**Zhan·ji·ang** (jän′jē äŋ′) city in S China, on the Leizhou Peninsula, Guangdong province: formerly (1898-1946) in territory leased by France: pop. 220,000

**Zhda·nov** (zhdän′ôf) *name* (1948-91) *of* MARIUPOL

**Zhe·ji·ang** (je′jē äŋ′) province of E China, on the East China Sea: 39,300 sq. mi. (101,800 sq. km); pop. 38,885,000; cap. Hangzhou

**Zheng·zhou** (jen′jō′) city in EC China: capital of Henan province: pop. 1,424,000

**Zhen·ji·ang** (jen′jē äŋ′) city in Jiangsu province, E China, at the juncture of the Grand Canal & the Chang River: pop. 250,000

**Zhu** (joō) river in SE China, forming an estuary between Macao & Hong Kong: *c.* 100 mi. (160 km)

**Zhu·zhou** (joō′jō′) city in E Hunan province, in SE China: pop. 350,000

**Zi·bo** (dzē′bō′) city in Shandong province, NE China: pop. 927,000

**Zi·gong** (dzē′gôŋ′) city in Sichuan province, SC China: pop. 600,000

**Zim·ba·bwe** (zim bä′bwä′, -bwē′) ⟦after a ruined city in the SE part, probably built (*c.* 15th c.) by a Bantu people ⟧ country in S Africa, north of South Africa and west of Mozambique: a self-governing British colony, it joined with Northern Rhodesia (now ZAMBIA) and Nyasaland (now MALAWI) to form the *Federation of Rhodesia and Nyasaland* (1953-63): made unilateral declaration of independence (1965) & proclaimed republic (1970): majority rule principle accepted (1979): gained independence (1980): a member of the

Commonwealth: old names *Southern Rhodesia* (until 1964), *Rhodesia* (1964-72): 151,000 sq. mi. (391,090 sq. km); pop. 8,984,000; cap. Harare

**Zi·on** (zī'ən) ⟦ME *Syon* < OE *Sion* < LL(Ec) < Heb *tsiyon*⟧ **1** orig., a Canaanite fortress in Jerusalem captured by David and called in the Bible "City of David" **2** later, the hill in Jerusalem on which the Temple was built: Zion has historically been regarded by Jews as a symbol of the center of Jewish national life **3** Jerusalem **4** the land of Israel

**Zion National Park** ⟦after *Zion* Canyon in the park, which was named (*c.* 1850) by Mormon settlers⟧ national park in SW Utah, noted for its spectacular rock formations: 206 sq. mi. (533 sq. km)

**Zla·to·ust** (zlä'tə o͞ost') city in SW Asian Russia, in the Ural Mountains, near Chelyabinsk: pop. 204,000

**Zo·an** (zō'an') *Biblical name of* TANIS

**Zom·ba** (zäm'bə) city in S Malawi: pop. 20,000

**Zoug** (zo͞og) *Fr. name of* ZUG

**Zug** (tso͞ok) **1** canton of NC Switzerland, on the Lake of Zug: 92 sq. mi. (239 sq. km); pop. 76,000 **2** its capital, on the Lake of Zug: pop. 22,000 **3 Lake of** lake in NC Switzerland, in the cantons of Zug & Schwyz: 15 sq. mi. (38 sq. km)

**Zui·der Zee** (zī'dər zē'; *Du* zoi'dər zā') former arm of the North Sea, which extended into the Netherlands: its S section was shut off from the North Sea by dikes: see IJSSELMEER & WADDENZEE

**Zuid-Hol·land** (zoit'hôl'änt') *Du. name of* SOUTH HOLLAND

**Zu·lu·land** (zo͞o'lo͞o land') region, formerly a Zulu kingdom, in NE Natal province, South Africa, on the Indian Ocean: 10,375 sq. mi. (26,871 sq. km)

**Zur·ich** (zoor'ik) **1** canton of N Switzerland: 668 sq. mi. (1,729 sq. km); pop. 1,123,000 **2** its capital, on the Lake of Zurich: pop. 440,000: also written **Zürich 3 Lake of** lake in N Switzerland, mostly in Zurich canton: 34 sq. mi. (88 sq. km)

**Zwick·au** (tsvik'ou') city in E Germany, in the state of Saxony: pop. 120,000

**Zwol·le** (zvôl'ə) city in the NE Netherlands: pop. 88,000

# UNITED STATES AND CANADA

| State | Capital | Postal Code |
|-------|---------|-------------|
| Alabama | Montgomery | AL |
| Alaska | Juneau | AK |
| Arizona | Phoenix | AZ |
| Arkansas | Little Rock | AR |
| California | Sacramento | CA |
| Colorado | Denver | CO |
| Connecticut | Hartford | CT |
| Delaware | Dover | DE |
| [District of Columbia] | | DC |
| Florida | Tallahassee | FL |
| Georgia | Atlanta | GA |
| Hawaii | Honolulu | HI |
| Idaho | Boise | ID |
| Illinois | Springfield | IL |
| Indiana | Indianapolis | IN |
| Iowa | Des Moines | IA |
| Kansas | Topeka | KS |
| Kentucky | Frankfort | KY |
| Louisiana | Baton Rouge | LA |
| Maine | Augusta | ME |
| Maryland | Annapolis | MD |
| Massachusetts | Boston | MA |
| Michigan | Lansing | MI |
| Minnesota | St. Paul | MN |
| Mississippi | Jackson | MS |
| Missouri | Jefferson City | MO |
| Montana | Helena | MT |
| Nebraska | Lincoln | NE |
| Nevada | Carson City | NV |
| New Hampshire | Concord | NH |
| New Jersey | Trenton | NJ |
| New Mexico | Santa Fe | NM |
| New York | Albany | NY |
| North Carolina | Raleigh | NC |

| State | Capital | Postal Code |
|---|---|---|
| North Dakota | Bismarck | ND |
| Ohio | Columbus | OH |
| Oklahoma | Oklahoma City | OK |
| Oregon | Salem | OR |
| Pennsylvania | Harrisburg | PA |
| Rhode Island | Providence | RI |
| South Carolina | Columbia | SC |
| South Dakota | Pierre | SD |
| Tennessee | Nashville | TN |
| Texas | Austin | TX |
| Utah | Salt Lake City | UT |
| Vermont | Montpelier | VT |
| Virginia | Richmond | VA |
| Washington | Olympia | WA |
| West Virginia | Charleston | WV |
| Wisconsin | Madison | WI |
| Wyoming | Cheyenne | WY |

## U.S. TERRITORIES

| American Samoa | Pago Pago | AS |
|---|---|---|
| Belau | Koror | PW |
| Guam | Agana | GU |
| Northern Marianas | Saipan | MP |
| Puerto Rico | San Juan | PR |
| Virgin Islands | Charlotte Amalie | VI |

## CANADIAN PROVINCES AND TERRITORIES

| Province | Capital | Postal Code |
|---|---|---|
| Alberta | Edmonton | AB |
| British Columbia | Victoria | BC |
| Manitoba | Winnipeg | MB |
| New Brunswick | Fredericton | NB |
| Newfoundland | St. John's | NF |

| Province/Territory | Capital | Postal Code |
| --- | --- | --- |
| Nova Scotia | Halifax | NS |
| Ontario | Toronto | ON |
| Prince Edward Island | Charlottetown | PE |
| Quebec | Quebec | PQ |
| Saskatchewan | Regina | SK |
| | | |
| Northwest Territories | Yellowknife | NT |
| Yukon Territory | Whitehorse | YT |